INTRODUCTION TO BUSINESS

Allyn and Bacon

Boston   **London**   **Sydney**   **Toronto**

INTRODUCTION TO BUSINESS

A Contemporary View

SIXTH EDITION

John A.

Reinecke
University of North
Carolina at Asheville

Gary

Dessler
Florida International
University

William F.

Schoell
University of
Southern
Mississippi

Series editor: Jack Peters   **Senior editorial assistant:** Carol Alper   **Cover administrator:** Linda Dickinson
Composition buyer: Linda Cox   **Manufacturing buyer:** William Alberti   **Editorial production services:**
Barbara A. Willette   **Interior designer:** Melinda Grosser for *silk*   **Cover designer:** Lynda Fishbourne   **Editorial production administrator:** Elaine Ober

A Division of Simon & Schuster
160 Gould Street
Needham Heights, Massachusetts 02194

Library of Congress Cataloging-in-Publication Data

Reinecke, John A., 1931–
    Introduction to business   a contemporary view / John A. Reinecke,
Gary Dessler, William F. Schoell. — 6th ed.
      p.   cm.
    Includes index.
    ISBN 0-205-11832-1
    1. Business.   2. Industrial management.   I. Dessler, Gary, 1942–
    II. Schoell, William F.   III. Title.
HD31.R4417 1989
658.4—dc19   88-26066
                                               CIP

Printed in the United States of America
10 9 8 7 6 5 4 3 2 1   88 89 90 91 92 93

*The credits section for this book begins after the Glossary and is considered an
extension of the copyright page.*

BRIEF CONTENTS

CONTENTS

SECTION TWO

Management and Organization 135

Five

Management Functions and Decision Making 136

Six

Human Relations 166

Thirteen

Promotion Strategies   376

Fourteen

Distribution Strategies   402

Twenty-**O**ne

Twenty-**T**wo

Twenty-**T**hree

Appendix A

Appendix B

P R E F A C E

Only textbooks that deliver the features that you, the instructors, ask for consistently and that your students respond to are published for six editions. This sixth edition builds upon the previous ones and provides these features:

- continuous Burger King ''capsules'' applied to chapter topics
- a clear, crisp, interesting writing style
- a reading level appropriate for students who are taking their first business course
- emphasis on basic business terms with straightforward definitions
- lots of *real* examples from the business (and nonprofit) world
- global business and small business applications throughout the text
- clear, meaningful learning objectives for each chapter
- comprehensive chapter summaries
- provocative *What Do You Think?* and other controversial and up-to-date boxes

Real-World, Current Examples

In every part of the book you can find current, real examples that illustrate the ideas being presented. These are drawn from the major business news sources including *The Wall Street Journal*, *Marketing News*, *Barron's*, *The*

Insurance Review, Inc., Nation's Business, Fortune, and the daily newspapers, as well as our own teaching and business consulting experience.

Every chapter begins with a brief vignette about a business firm or non-profit organization that illustrates some of the major ideas of the chapter. This vignette is referred to at several points in the chapter. The cases at the end of the chapters—with a few exceptions in which the authors draw from a composite of their experiences as consultants—are events that occurred in actual organizations.

Other boxed features in the book will help provoke classroom discussion. They include:

What Do You Think? boxes presenting two or more perspectives on a hot business topic in the chapter subject area. In Chapter 2, for example, the topic "Today's Business and Its Challenges" is highlighted by examining two sides to the question "Is the U.S. Deindustrializing?"

The Electronic Age boxes illustrate the pervasive influence of computers and related technology on business decision making today. In Chapter 12—Product and Pricing Strategies—this feature shows how airlines use complex computer programs to set their air fares in order to maximize profit.

Business Applies boxes show how business managers apply knowledge from another field or, conversely, how a business-developed technique is applied by another field. For example, in Chapter 13 we show how Young & Rubicam, a major advertising agency employed by Breyer's Ice Cream, applies the techniques of anthropology to the challenge of understanding what ice cream means to consumers and how it fits into family life.

It's Your Business boxes show how some business concepts might affect your students' lives or maybe even your own. In Chapter 4, for example, this feature shows how a business manager turned his hobby into a full-time business. In Chapter 14 it shows how electronic selling is influencing the purchasing behavior of college students and other young people.

Business in the News boxes tell about major contemporary business-related events that have a real impact upon the subject matter of the chapter. This box in Chapter 2, for example, supplements the discussion of the economic environment of business by telling the story of the closure of the Stroh Brewery in Detroit and how that firm dealt with the impact of the closure on the jobs and lives of the Stroh employees.

Key Terms

The most important terms appearing in each chapter are shown in boldface where they first appear. The term is clearly defined at that point and, to give added emphasis, is shown in the margin. A complete list of the key terms appears at the end of each chapter. A complete glossary of important terms appears at the back of the book.

A Continuing Example

Every chapter of this text includes a capsule entitled *Application: Burger King*. This feature provides an opportunity for your students to apply the concepts and techniques in each chapter to a real-world business firm. Applying these concepts and techniques as they are being introduced will make it easier for your students to learn them. As you know, it is much easier to get interested in something you already know a lot about—and all of us know something about Burger King! On one hand, it is a big business, one that is becoming more and more global in scope. On the other hand, the many independent Burger King franchisees look upon themselves as small business owners. Like many businesses today, Burger King Corporation is ever-changing as it responds to internal and external events that offer opportunities and challenges.

Global Business and Small Business Emphasis

This edition's emphasis on the international scene is evident from the very first chapter. To give your students a special perspective on the private enterprise system, this chapter begins with a discussion of the recent movements in the Soviet Union toward some of the freedoms and incentives of the private enterprise system. We see how *perestroika* and *glasnost* in the USSR help reveal the major differences between present-day Soviet communism and U.S. capitalism. It also shows us how difficult it is to change a culture that has been so different from those of the Western democracies for so long.

In many of the other chapters, special sections are devoted to the global aspects of the chapter topic. Chapter 2, for example, discusses international trade deficits and global competition. It gives special attention to the strong competition of Japan and other successful nations of the Pacific Rim. In Chapter 4 we explain the international aspects of small business growth and the efforts being made to help small businesses get involved in exporting. In Chapter 13 we discuss the question of whether global marketing and advertising programs are really practical. Similar global applications appear throughout the book—all in addition to the coverage of international business in Chapter 23.

Small-business applications are emphasized in most chapters as well. Besides the special chapter (Chapter 4) about small business, examples of small-business problems are provided throughout the text. Many of the text examples, short cases, boxes, and chapter opening vignettes relate to small business. The Burger King Corporation capsules also have a small-business dimension when they deal with the operation of individual Burger King franchises.

Truly Current Examples

You will find that major recent events are incorporated into this text. Events like the *glasnost* movement in the USSR (Chapter 1), the stock market crash of October 1987 (Chapters 2, 18, and 21 especially), the huge flurry of mergers and acquisitions in the United States (Chapters 3 and 19), and the revolutionary new tax laws of 1986 (Chapters 3, 4, 15, and 21) are brought into focus here. We integrate these important events into our explanation of all the central topics of business administration.

Sixth Edition Changes in Text Organization and Coverage

This newest edition represents the biggest change in organization and coverage since *Introduction to Business: A Contemporary View* was first published. We have added three chapters and deleted one from the fifth edition format.

The first new chapter (Chapter 6) is entitled Human Relations. We have taken what was a small part of the fifth edition chapter on organization and expanded it to include in-depth coverage of topics like leadership, motivation, and worker-friendly programs such as flextime and quality circles. Separating human relations from Chapter 7—Organizing the Firm—has allowed more complete coverage of organization theory, including an innovative new section on fitting the organization to the situation. Chapter 7 now integrates current thinking on the contingency approach to organization.

The second new chapter has been added to the marketing section, which now includes an entire chapter devoted to promotion and one to distribution. The promotion chapter (Chapter 13) allows for much broader treatment of topics such as personal selling and sales management and greater detail regarding advertising institutions. The complete chapter devoted to distribution (Chapter 14) allows for the introduction of discussion of vertical marketing systems, channel selection criteria, and wholesale institutions, as well as much more detail on the components of the physical distribution system.

The third new chapter (Chapter 22) is entitled Business Law and Ethics. This permits much more discussion of ethics and social responsibility than was possible in the previous edition. In the light of the stock market crash, scandals in Wall Street, and influence-peddling in Washington, D.C., ethics in the business place has become a topic of major importance for students and the general public. The text incorporates this concern in many chapters. We now include customer relations, supplier relations, competitor relations, and employee relations as well as ecological considerations from an ethical viewpoint. The business law treatment adds extensive discussion of product liability issues—another business topic of rapidly rising importance.

The fifth edition chapter on career planning and job hunting has been replaced by an appendix. The treatment here has been streamlined, but a new careers supplement will be made available to instructors. This will consist of a series of practical career-guidance essays written by Gary Dessler. To provide an introduction to the many possibilities a career in business offers, each section of the text begins with a brief profile of an individual who has chosen a career in the area of business described in that section.

Another important change is the much more comprehensive treatment of risk and insurance. In this edition we examine, step by step, the process of managing risk in a business. The focus is on risk management because of the higher profile of perils like product liability in today's business world. We examine such risk strategies as combinations of risk avoidance and the use of self-insurance. We also present a much broader picture of every kind of private and public insurance available to the firm.

Acknowledgments

We are, as always, grateful to our production administrator, Elaine Ober, and to our series editor, Jack Peters, for their support and their willingness to point out our errors from time to time. We are grateful to Allen Workman for his fine development work. Very special gratitude is also due to Barbara Willette, our production coordinator, who did her duty far beyond the call, and to our product manager, Carolyn Harris, for her commitment and timeless efforts to make sure our adoptors received good service. For their help in preparing the supplements to the text we acknowledge the excellent work of Tom Pritchett, John Bowdidge, Doug Fugate, Mike Kauffman, and Caroline Fisher, as well as Carol Alper, our supplements coordinator. For typing help we want to thank Cindy Reagan.

For valuable criticisms and assistance for special topics we want to acknowledge Joe Sulock and Don Reed (insurance), Neal McKenzie (computers), Leisa Flynn (government and law), and Claudel McKenzie (accounting.)

Finally, we thank our families for soothing the pain of deadlines and for providing strong incentives to excel.

Many of the ideas and improvements in this edition are due in large measure to the many teacher-reviewers who have helped us. We owe each of these educators a great debt of gratitude for their intelligent and caring attention. In particular we wish to thank the following teachers for their formal reviews:

Dennis G. Allen, Grand Rapids Junior College
Barry Ashmen, Bucks County Community College
Jerry Boles, Western Kentucky University
John Bowdidge, Southwest Missouri State University
Bruce Burnes, St. Cloud State University
Valeriano Cantu, Angelo State University
James Carlson, Mansfield University
Bruce Charnow, Hofstra University
Monico L. Cisneros, Austin Community College
William A. Clarey, Bradley University
Helen Davis, Jefferson Community College
Fran Emory, Northern Virginia Community College
Lawrence Ettkin, University of Tennessee at Chattanooga
William E. Fulmer, Clarion University of Pennsylvania
Glenn Gelderloos, Grand Rapids Junior College
Michael Hamburger, Northern Virginia Community College
William Hamill, Gulf Coast Community College
Thomas Haynes, Illinois State University
Sanford B. Helman, Middlesex Community College
Louis Hoekstra, Grand Rapids Junior College
J. Juechter, Bronx Community College
Anthony Lucas, Community College of Allegheny

Dorothy Maass, Delaware County Community College
Michel G. Marette, Northern Virginia Community College
Charles H. Matthews, University of Cincinnati
Colene Maxwell, Central State University
Hugh McCabe, Westchester Community College
Robert J. Mullin, Orange County Community College
Mary K. Nelson, University of Minnesota
Neil A. Palombo, University of Maryland
Dennis D. Pappas, Columbus Technical Institute
Barbara Piasta, Somerset County College
Marie Pietak, Bucks County Community College
Gene Schneider, Austin Community College
Larry J. Schuetz, Linn-Benton Community College
Dennis Shannon, Belleville Area College
Sharon D. Steigman, Indiana University of Pennsylvania
Charles R. B. Stowe, Sam Houston State University
Homa Tindall, Southwestern Michigan College
Frank G. Titlow, St. Petersburg Junior College
Larry Waldorf, Boise State University
Philip A. Weatherford, Embry-Riddle Aeronautical University
Ralph Wilcox, Kirkwood Community College
Jonnie Williams, Grand Rapids Junior College

A WORD TO THE STUDENT

This book is in no small part a product of student input. Many, many students like yourself have commented to their instructors about previous editions of our book. These comments, in turn, have often been forwarded to us for consideration during the revision process. Thanks for your help in making *Introduction to Business: A Contemporary View* a better book.

As teachers, we cannot help but offer you a bit of advice. We are certain that you will benefit from making *full* use of all of the book's features. *Before* you read each chapter, take a few moments to look over the Learning Objectives and What's Ahead? at the beginning of each chapter. It is also a good idea to reread them *after* you have read the chapter—especially the learning objectives to see whether you can do what we said you would be able to do after reading the chapter.

Try to make a special effort to learn the key terms that are listed in the margins. The Review Questions and Discussion Questions at the end of each chapter can help you in reviewing each chapter and in applying what you have learned. The *Study Guide* can also be a major help—especially in preparing for exams. Your instructor can tell you more about this supplement and how you can get a copy.

We hope that you will enjoy and benefit from your first course in business. Good luck!

Jimmie Banks is full of ideas. One day, it struck him: the best business of all was right before his eyes: marketing his wife Sharon's Caribbean cooking. Sharon, 34, is from Jamaica. Jimmie, 38, was born in Manhattan of Jamaican, Cherokee, and Irish heritage.

From a one-time money-changing booth in Queens, New York, the couple sold take-out food to a predominantly poor Jamaican clientele. "You could call it a student's workshop," Jimmie said, as they learned to expand from cooking for five "to cooking for a hundred or more."

They borrowed money—from friends and relatives—to go into business. And, Banks notes, on the upward slope of the learning curve, losses are expectable. Gradually, though, they learned how to manage overhead better, and established a track record which allowed them to take advantage of wholesale prices and get credit.

Jimmie was restless in New York and wanted to move. They liked the economic, racial, ethnic, and age diversity they saw in Washington, D.C., and eventually nar-

SECTION ONE
Our Business System

rowed the focus. In December 1984, a rental agent told them they had to move fast on a property in their target locale. Jimmie hopped on a train and was able to see beyond the decrepit laundromat to envision their restaurant. The landlord put in a new roof, plumbing, and outside improvements; Jimmie supervised the interior decoration; and in May of 1985, Fish, Wings 'n' Tings opened. Washington is filled with people who work late and dine out often, and word-of-mouth fills the restaurant nightly. The food is fresh, intriguingly spiced, and brought quickly to the table. There is no coffee, bread, nor alcoholic beverages, so people do not linger—keeping table turnover high, important in a 22-seat restaurant.

Both Jimmie and Sharon, who married in 1976, went to Catholic schools. He attended the Fashion Institute of Technology in New York and she attended Queens College. But most of what they apply to their business they learned just by doing it. And many things have to be relearned or recast in a new environment, they point out. In Washington, for example, most of their employees are Spanish-speaking Salvadorans. In New York, all of their customers were black; in Washington, 70 percent are white. Such factors affect policy and public relations, Jimmie said.

They hope to tap into the downtown/Capitol Hill power breakfast-and-lunch crowd with gourmet delivery, which would not only be potentially profitable, Jimmie said, but is "a five-day business which is over at 5 o'clock." They also have plans for distinctive packaging of their products, Sharon said, including juices, salad dressings, and barbecue sauce, to sell to specialty food stores and the boutique sections of major supermarkets.

They like being their own bosses, but say it is essential "to love what you're doing," in Sharon's words. "Hard work," chimes in Jimmie, "and you have to have a goal." "If I have a goal, I don't stop until I've accomplished it," said Sharon. Do they have any advice for students based on their experience? "Sure," says Jimmie, "Do it! ... That's how this country was developed, by small ideas that became big ones."

After reading this chapter, you
will be able to:

- Explain the economic and
  social importance of business in our economic
  system.

- Demonstrate how economic
  systems help us to satisfy
  our needs with available
  resources.

- Identify the factors of production and demonstrate
  how they are inputs to the
  productive system.

- Outline and contrast the major features of capitalism,
  communism, and socialism.

- Explain and give examples
  of mixed economies.

O N E

Understanding
Private
Enterprise

In our first chapter, we will focus on four main topics: the nature of business, the role of economic systems in providing goods and services, the factors of production, and the various types of economic systems in the world today.

In our look at what business is, we will pay close attention to the relationship between business and profit. Equally important, we will discuss the relationship between business and society.

We will then discuss how economic systems respond to the fact that people's needs and wants are unlimited while the resources available for satisfying them are limited. We will examine the specialization and exchange process and the issue of measuring an economic system's performance.

Next comes an examination of the factors of production—land, labor, capital, and entrepreneurship. These resources are the inputs of the productive system. The outputs are the goods and services that satisfy our needs and wants.

In our look at the various types of economic systems in the world today, we will focus on capitalism, communism, and socialism. We will start with an overall look at the nature of each, how they operate, and their relative advantages and disadvantages. After we have a basic understanding of these aspects, we will move to a discussion of how they operate in the real world. As we will see, the distinctions among these systems are becoming more and more blurred, giving rise to more and more mixed economies. In other words, the various types of economic systems are "borrowing" from each other to create what the participants think is the "best" system.

The terms *glasnost* (public airing or public disclosure), *perestroika* (restructuring), and *demokratizatsiya* (democratization) have become familiar to us since Mikhail S. Gorbachev became General Secretary of the Soviet Communist Party in March 1985. The subsequent restructuring of the Soviet economy has brought capitalist ideas and practices to the world's first communist nation.

Mr. Gorbachev's first economic move was to apply "discipline." For example, he closed most of the hard liquor stores and slashed vodka production to deal with alcoholism and absenteeism on the job. Once common, drunkenness on the job now carries a heavy fine.

Contract brigades were also introduced to boost productivity in agriculture and industry. In agriculture a group of farmers or a single family can now manage (though not own) a tract of cropland, livestock, or some other productive asset and keep a share of the profits. Although most of a collective's production is still sold to the state at state-controlled prices, the collective can sell 30 percent of its output at unregulated farm markets.

In industry, half the nation's factories are paying salaries to teams of a dozen or more workers with different skills who sign a contract to perform certain tasks. The salaries are linked directly to goals. For example, an assembly line at an automobile plant might agree to install engines in several thousand chassis a month. If the goal is met, the factory pays a brigade council. The council, which is made up of several of the workers, then allocates salaries on the basis of attendance and individual productivity. If the goal is not met, the salaries are much lower. In the past, all workers had the same salary no matter how much or how little they worked.

An "individual labor" law that took effect in May 1987 permits individual and family businesses in twenty-nine fields, including carpentry, plumbing, dressmaking, auto repair, tutoring, and toymaking. For businesses that are too large to be run by a family, the law allows cooperative ventures. They are staffed by owners who are also permitted to hire workers.

Mr. Gorbachev's economic campaign really took off in June 1987 when the Central Committee of the Communist Party approved his four-year reform plan. The plan downgrades the central planning agency that used to run the economy. Mr. Gorbachev said, "Factories must be forced to finance their own operations and determine more of their production on the basis of commodity-money (supply and demand) relations." He also said, "It is particularly important that the actual pay of every worker be closely linked to his personal contribution to the end result, and that no limit be set."

Mr. Gorbachev followed up with programs to encourage technological innovation and modernization of aging factories. In the past, Soviet producers had little incentive to adopt new technologies, since they did not have to compete for customers. There were no foreign or domestic competitors. Industrial enterprises simply produced what the government told them to produce.

Beginning on January 1, 1988, however, things started to change at most of those enterprises. As part of "Gorbanomics," factory managers must make more of their own decisions rather than passively following the orders of government bureaucrats. Factories compete among themselves, and prices are set partly by market forces of supply and demand. Successful enterprises are rewarded. Unsuccessful ones, for the first time, risk going bankrupt.[1]

To be sure, the Soviet Union's economic system is being restructured. Mr. Gorbachev is trying to incorporate elements of our economic system in the hope of improving the performance of the Soviet Union's economic system. As a result, state-owned enterprises in the Soviet Union are being operated more and more like business firms here in the United States. In an even more dramatic departure with the past, privately owned businesses are springing up throughout the Soviet Union.

business

What Is Business?

Business consists of all profit-seeking activities that are organized and directed to provide goods and services to customers. As shown in Figure 1-1, business firms produce and market these goods and services in the hope of making a profit. The profit comes from the sales revenues firms generate by satisfying their customers' needs and wants.

Notice in the definition of business the terms *goods* and *services*. Goods like cars, furniture, shoes, and computers are *tangible*—they can be touched. Services like psychiatric counseling, lawn care, and medical exams are *intangible*—they cannot be touched.

Businesses offer their customers a combination of a tangible good and an intangible service. For example, you can touch a Domino's pizza, but you cannot touch the service that delivered it to your door. Throughout this book, we will often use the term *product* to refer to both tangible goods and intangible services.

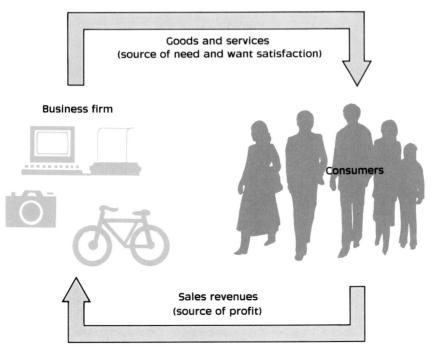

Goods and services
(source of need and want satisfaction)

Business firm

Consumers

Sales revenues
(source of profit)

FIGURE 1-1 / The nature of business activity.

BUSINESS AND PROFIT

profit

We also used the term *profit* in defining business. **Profit** is the money that remains after a firm deducts its expenses of producing and marketing goods or services (expenditures) from its revenues (receipts). The major source of revenue is from sales of the firm's good or service. To that we add any other receipts, such as the interest the firm earns on the money it has on deposit in a bank. Then we deduct the expenses incurred in operating the business. What remains is profit.

Figure 1-2 shows the basic equation that is used to compute profit or loss. Business firms can compute their profits on a daily, weekly, monthly, quarterly, or annual basis. This tells owners, managers, and tax collectors how much profit was made.

risk

Profit rewards a successful firm's current owners who have taken the risk involved in starting and running a business. **Risk** is the chance of loss. Firms reinvest some of their profit for growth, and growth creates jobs. Profit also attracts new investors, which stimulates investment, creates more jobs, and improves our economic well-being.

BUSINESS AND SOCIETY

Suppose a firm provides its customers with the goods or services they want. If it also earns an acceptable profit for its owners, the firm satisfies both groups—its customers and its owners. A profitable firm also serves society by providing jobs and paying taxes.

But does a business firm have any obligations to society beyond satisfying customers, earning a profit for the owners, providing jobs, and paying taxes? Many believe that it does. Socially responsible firms base their decisions on the *social* as well as the *economic* impact of those decisions. **Social responsibility** is the concept that business is part of the larger society in which it exists and is accountable to society for its performance. A socially responsible firm acts in a way that not only will advance the firm but also will serve society. A firm that invests in rebuilding a decaying neighborhood in its community is working toward both goals.

social responsibility

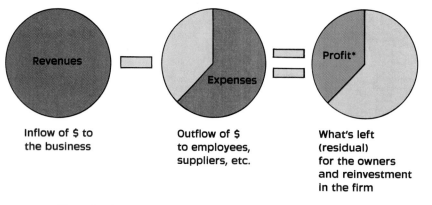

FIGURE 1-2 / The basic profit equation.

Revenues — Inflow of $ to the business

Expenses — Outflow of $ to employees, suppliers, etc.

Profit* — What's left (residual) for the owners and reinvestment in the firm

*As we will see in Chapter 15, profit can also be called *net income* or *net earnings*.

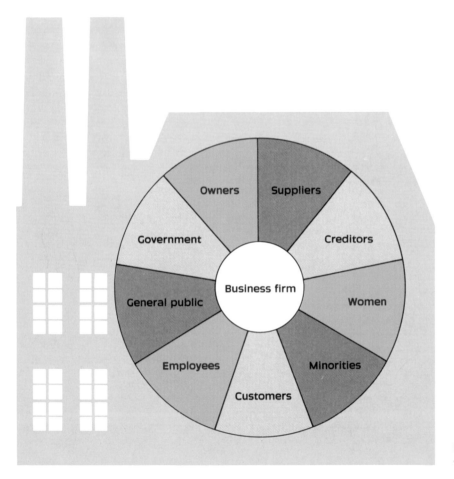

FIGURE 1-3 / The firm's stakeholders.

stakeholders

Business firms must be responsible in their dealings with their various publics, or stakeholders. **Stakeholders** are owners, customers, and all the various groups of people who are affected by a firm's actions. As shown in Figure 1-3, stakeholders include employees, suppliers, creditors, minorities, women, government, and the general public. As pointed out in the Business Applies box and indicated in the NCR ads (on pp. 8–9), the chairman and president of NCR Corporation advertises widely that his company is managed for stakeholders. We will return to this concept at several places in this book, with special emphasis in Chapter 22.

Satisfying Our Needs with Available Resources

As we have seen, business firms seek to earn a profit from satisfying customer needs and wants. As we will see in this chapter, there are different types of economic systems, and the business firm plays a

Charles E. Exley, Jr., chairman and president of NCR Corporation, advertises widely that his company is managed for "stakeholders." That means not just the shareholders (stockholders) but also the employees, the customers, the suppliers, and the communities where NCR has plants.

He makes no apology, though he voices some concern that it might sound too much like a "niceism, the kind of thing people say because it sounds nice." To the contrary, it is a practical, hardheaded thing. It is no romantic notion to say that his company depends for its vitality on the creativity and productivity of the people who are the company.

Moreover, he does not see any conflict with his duty to the shareholders. "The quality of people we have to have won't be here if their expectations are not met on a pretty consistent basis. People describe the expectations of these various groups as if a person at the top, like myself, is being tugged in all directions and I'm frantically juggling, trying to balance all these conflicts. But if you go down the list of all the points of conflict, in my judgment they are very few. They are not zero but very few. I believe that if we meet the reasonable expectations of all the other constituencies, we will do a darn good job for the shareholders."

Source: George Melloan, "NCR's Exley Manages for His 'Stakeholders,'" *The Wall Street Journal*, June 16, 1987, p. 27. Reprinted by permission of *The Wall Street Journal*, © Dow Jones & Company, Inc., 1987. All Rights Reserved.

much lesser role in some systems than it does in ours. Yet every system must face the fact that human wants are unlimited while the resources with which to satisfy them are limited. In our economic system, we rely mainly on the market forces of supply and demand to deal with this dilemma. Communist systems deal with the dilemma through central planning of their economic systems.

ECONOMIC SYSTEMS

specialization

Specialization and exchange are key tools that help us in dealing with the dilemma of unlimited wants and limited resources. **Specialization,** or division of labor, is the division of work into component tasks so that each worker can concentrate on performing a particular task instead of performing many tasks. For example, different employees at a Burger King restaurant might specialize in such tasks as broiling, taking customer orders, and clearing tables. Likewise, a farmer might specialize in growing broccoli or wine grapes, and a manufacturer might specialize in producing breakfast cereals. By specializing, a person or a firm can become more productive, producing more with a given amount of effort.

exchange

Yet no one can live on one crop or one task alone. To survive, specialists must be able to exchange. **Exchange** is trade, or giving up

To be successful, business firms must be responsive not only to shareholders, but also to customers, suppliers, employees, and the community.

one thing to get another thing. Thus each party to an exchange trades one thing for another thing. If each person in a group concentrates on producing what he or she produces best, and they all exchange for what they need, surpluses and economic growth may result through the combination of specialization and exchange.

People in a group who specialize and exchange depend on one another to satisfy wants. They become *interdependent* members of an economic system. An **economic system** is a framework of arrangements for carrying out the specialization and exchange process. The group uses scarce resources to produce and distribute the goods and services that members want. It is easy to see that our economic system relies on specialization and exchange. Think for a moment about how we all depend on each other to satisfy our wants. You get electricity from the power company, legal advice from a lawyer, food from a supermarket, and so on.

economic system

Although economic systems can be very different, they all exist to cope with the dilemma of limited resources and unlimited wants. Each economic system determines what goods and services to produce, how

This farmer specializes in the production of mushrooms. How important is it that he be able to exchange with other production specialists?

much of each to produce, how to produce them, and who will get them. But as we will see later in this chapter, *how* these decisions are made depends on the type of economic system.

MEASURING ECONOMIC WELL-BEING

standard of living

The **standard of living** is a measure of a society's economic well-being. It helps us to observe the change in a society's well-being over time and to compare one society's well-being with that of another. There are several ways to measure a society's standard of living. One such measure is Gross National Product.

Gross National Product (GNP)

Gross National Product (GNP) is an overall measure of a nation's economic output, measured as the sum of the market values of all the final goods and services that are produced during a year. We can measure a nation's progress in raising its standard of living by comparing its annual GNP per capita (total GNP divided by the number of people in the country) over a period of time. These figures can also be compared to those of other countries. Countries like the United States, Japan, and the Soviet Union measure their GNP in trillions of dollars. In fact, the United States and Japan together account for a staggering 38 percent of the world's GNP.[2] But a small country like Switzerland, which has a much smaller total GNP, still has a high standard of living. It has a high GNP per capita.

inflation

One problem with using GNP as a measure of a nation's economic output is inflation. **Inflation** is an increase in the prices of goods and services over a period of time that has the effect of reducing the purchasing power of a nation's currency. We can measure the actual growth in GNP not distorted by inflation. To do so, we express GNP in real terms. Thus *real* GNP removes the effects of inflation from the unadjusted GNP figure.

Some measures of the standard of living are crucial to businesspeople in making decisions such as whether or not to enter a particular market. China, for example, has a per capita income (China's total income divided by the number of people in the country) of about $300 a year. Nevertheless, Kentucky Fried Chicken Corporation opened its first restaurant in Beijing in late 1987. A basic meal costs $1.89—two days' wages for an average Chinese. But Kentucky Fried Chicken and other foreign marketers in China are mainly going after the 20 percent of the Chinese population who live in the more affluent cities and whose per capita income is above $300 per year.[3]

Measures likes GNP, however, do not necessarily indicate a nation's *quality of life*. For example, military spending consumes 16 percent of GNP in the Soviet Union versus 7 percent in the United States.[4] Soviet output includes a smaller percentage of consumer goods and services than ours. This is one reason why many consumer products are in short supply in the Soviet Union and why people often have to wait in long lines to buy them. Another reason for the long lines is the Soviet economic system, as we will see later in this chapter. The new laws that permit people to hold two jobs and to open their own small-scale businesses are partly intended to bring a few quick improvements to the Soviet quality of life.[5]

High production can have adverse side effects that are not measured by GNP. These include pollution, congested cities, and rapid depletion of natural resources. Such effects are more difficult to measure but do affect the quality of life. Some people question whether we are really better off simply because we produce more.

factors of production

The Factors of Production

To achieve a compromise between unlimited wants and limited resources, a society must make decisions about how to use the available factors of production, which are shown in Figure 1-4. The **factors of production** are the basic inputs of the productive system—land, labor,

FIGURE 1-4 / The productive system's inputs and outputs.

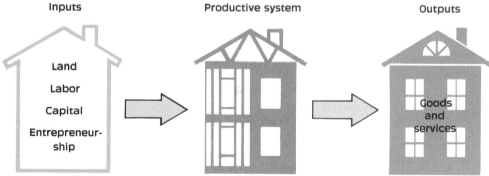

capital, and entrepreneurship. As shown in Figure 1-4, the goods and services produced to satisfy human wants are the outputs of the system.

LAND

land

Land means all natural resources. In the long run they can all run out. But with proper management, some (air, water, forests) will last for a very long time. Others (petroleum, uranium, other metals) will run out more quickly.

The United States is the greatest user of natural resources in the world. We have a large share of many of the most important resources, but we depend on other nations to help supply us with certain others. For example, we have more coal than any other country in the world, but we import huge quantities of oil.

For 300 years, Americans were in the habit of using up natural resources in one area and then moving westward to areas where resources were once again plentiful. This wasteful approach to resources has been called a "cowboy economy." During the last several decades we have begun to think of earth as a "spaceship" and our world economy as a "spaceship economy." Like the crew on a spaceship, we must conserve and recycle the scarce resources on board—they are all we have.

LABOR

labor

Labor is the human resource—the mental and physical effort available to produce goods and services. "Unskilled," "semiskilled," and "skilled" are terms that describe different types of labor. Management skill is also a type of labor.

What kind of value does labor have? How much a firm produces and the quality of what it produces are affected in part by the motivation, skills, and efforts of its labor. Motivating Soviet workers with higher wages is hard to do because of the shortages of consumer goods and services on which to spend them. Labor also probably shares some of the blame for the shoddy reputation of Soviet-made goods. This reputation was one reason Mr. Gorbachev clamped down on drunkenness on the job. In a 1986 speech, Mr. Gorbachev cited an example of a Soviet TV factory that turned out 49,000 defective sets. An article in a Moscow newspaper pointed out that 40 percent of the 28,056 fires reported in the city were caused by faulty TV sets.[6]

Mr. Gorbachev's crackdown on shoddy goods has reduced the output of consumer goods. Having less to buy with their money makes it even harder to motivate workers. Nevertheless, in late 1987, government quality control inspectors were rejecting as much as 30 percent of the output of 1,500 major plants.[7]

By contrast, Japanese workers refer to themselves as *hataraki bachi*, or worker bees. It was not until late 1987 that the Japanese Parliament reduced the 48-hour standard work week to 40 hours, and the change will be phased in gradually. Few people in Japan expect a universal five-day work week before the turn of the century. This change was part of Tokyo's drive to stimulate domestic consumption, increase imports, and reduce exports. The hope is that the more time the workers have for leisure, the more they will be inclined to spend money.[8]

CAPITAL

capital

Capital is the funds provided by investors, lenders, and retained earnings to finance a firm's activities. These funds are used to build factories, buy tools and equipment, hire workers, and so on. We often use the term *capital goods* to refer to equipment, factories, or anything made by humans that helps to produce and distribute goods and services. The Soviet Union is giving priority to modernizing its existing plants and equipment to enhance productivity.

Besides helping to make labor more productive, capital goods can sometimes replace labor. The replacement process is called *mechanization* and *automation*. The auto and steel industries, for example, have invested billions of dollars in automation to increase their productivity. Robots, once rarely seen in factories, are now commonplace. Automation is also occurring in the service industries—for example, automated teller machines for banking and automated ticket machines for airline travel. Hitachi Corporation has a plant in Japan that is almost totally automated. Four employees run the entire plant, which can put together a videocassette recorder in 1.7 minutes.[9]

But where does the money come from to buy capital goods? If a country's supply of capital goods is to grow, its people must produce more than they consume. To do this, its people must be motivated and able to postpone consumption, or save. Then the country's businesses can invest the savings in new plants and equipment.

As shown in Figure 1-5 (on p. 14), private savings are the ultimate source of new investment in our economic system. Such money provides funds that firms can borrow to acquire more efficient plants and equipment, which increases productivity. This is what creates jobs, economic growth, and rising living standards.

How much of our incomes we save depends a great deal on the outlook for the economy as a whole. Americans tended to save a greater percentage of their incomes after the big stock market crash on October 19, 1987, because of the uncertain economic outlook. The Japanese traditionally save a greater percentage of their incomes than Americans. In very recent years, however, they have stepped up spending on consumer goods and services.

ENTREPRENEURSHIP

entrepreneurship

entrepreneur

Entrepreneurship is the process of bringing land, labor, and capital together and taking the risk involved in producing a good or service in the hope of profit. An **entrepreneur** is a risk taker who starts and operates a business in hope of making a profit. There is no guarantee, however, that people who go into business will make a profit. They assume the risk of losing what they invest in their firms. Risk is always present in business activity.

Steven Jobs cofounded Apple Computer, William H. Gates III cofounded Microsoft Corporation, Mitch Kapor founded Lotus Devel-

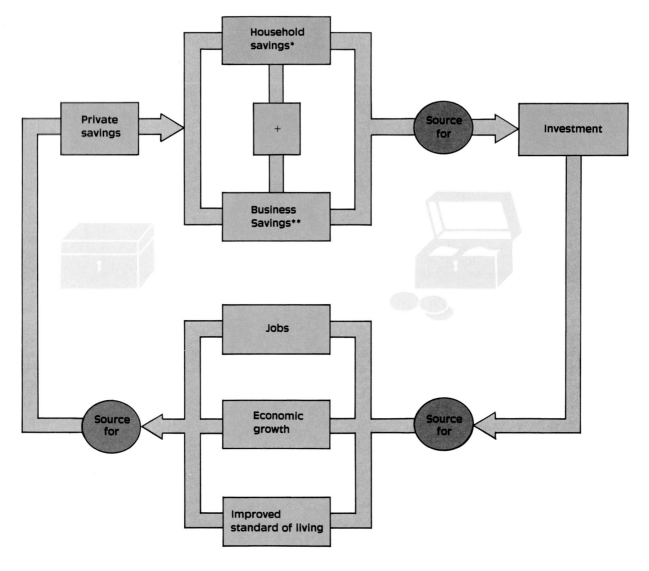

*Disposable income minus spending
**Retained earnings (reinvested profits) plus depreciation allowances

FIGURE 1-5 / The role of private savings in our economic system.

opment Company, and Frederick W. Smith started Federal Express in the 1970s. Each of these entrepreneurs went on to become multimillionaires. Gates, for example, cofounded Microsoft in 1975, while he was in his teens. At age 30, he was one of the hundred richest Americans. Other big successful entrepreneurs include Leslie Wexner (The Limited retail stores), Randi and Debbi Fields (Mrs. Fields Cookies), and Liz Claiborne (Liz Claiborne Inc. clothing).

But risk is part of doing business. Steven Jobs, Apple's cofounder, was in effect fired in 1985 by John Sculley—the man Jobs had lured

APPLICATION: BURGER KING

How Burger King Began

From their vantage point in the new Burger King World headquarters just outside Miami, President Charles Olcott and his management team had much to ponder. The surrounding palm trees and Biscayne Bay gave a tranquil atmosphere that contrasted sharply with what was happening in the fast food industry.

Since its Florida beginning in 1954, when a Burger King® hamburger cost $0.18 and a Whopper® sandwich cost $0.37, Burger King Corporation had grown to a worldwide enterprise. By 1988 there were over 5,000 Burger King® restaurants throughout Europe, the United States, Asia, the Pacific, Latin America, and the Caribbean. About 80 percent were owned by franchisees, while 20 percent were company-owned. Burger King Corporation itself employed over 43,000 people around the world, not including those who worked for franchisees. Counting franchisees' employees, total Burger King employment worldwide was over 250,000 people—not bad for a company started by two young entrepreneurs with a dream.

James W. McLamore and David Edgerton cofounded Burger King in 1954, opening their first restaurant at 3090 N.W. 36th Street in Miami. Three years later, Mr. McLamore invented the Whopper® sandwich, and by 1967 the chain had grown to 274 stores and 8,000 employees. In that year the entrepreneurs sold their company to the giant Pillsbury Corporation.

Then the pace began to quicken. The first "Have it your way®" ad campaign was launched in 1974, and the first European Burger King® restaurant was opened in Madrid in 1975. By 1977, 2,000 Burger King® restaurants had been opened, and over 3,000 more had been added by 1988. Virtually from the beginning, Burger King's managers had managed not only to survive, but to thrive where many others had failed. From a beginning with many small competitors in the 1950s, Burger King had grown to be one of the largest fast-food franchises in the world, second only to McDonald's.

The industry was changing, though, and that was what president Olcott and his management team now had to ponder. Burger King Corporation executives knew that important decisions had to be made. With more and more competition coming into the market and the market's growth slowing down, prices were under pressure and competition was severe. McDonald's, the industry giant, could afford to spend over twice as much as Buger King Corporation on advertising, and its ads could help it maintain its lead. Frozen, microwavable dinners were making inroads into the fast food industry's market. And it was getting harder and harder, especially in the United States, to find locations to put new restaurants. Good employees were also getting hard to find.

It was against this backdrop that the Burger King Corporation executives periodically met to ponder their business decisions. How—if at all—could Burger King dethrone McDonald's? What was the best way to attract the dwindling supply of new employees? How could Burger King convince the public that its flame-broiled burgers really did taste better than fried ones? What new products could Burger King Corporation introduce to capture the consumer's attention? Could profitability be improved if the restaurants were made more efficient? And how should the company raise the money to do all these things? These are examples of the many issues that people in business face. Solving such problems successfully is what makes business both challenging and satisfying.

Questions

1. Are the Burger King Corporation's executives' concerns related to profitability? What about risk?

2. What does "social responsibility" mean to a Burger King's restaurant manager?

3. Which factors of production are discussed, directly or indirectly, in this capsule? Which is the most important to Burger King Corporation at this time?

away from the presidency of Pepsi-Cola to become Apple's president and chief executive officer. Donald Burr started People Express airline in 1980, and it quickly became the fastest growing airline in history. But several years later, it was bankrupt and was bought up by Texas Air. Many, many other businesses that you will never hear about fail every year.

As we saw at the beginning of this chapter, entrepreneurs are emerging in the Soviet Union. They are finding out, however, that free enterprise offers no guarantee of success. For example, an elderly Moscow woman who had a $75 monthly pension went into the business of selling hand-embroidered nightgowns after she had registered with the local authorities. But after spending days standing out in the cold, she had not sold one nightgown. Nevertheless, the authorities cancelled her pension.[10]

Types of Economic Systems

In the discussions that follow, we will look at three major types of economic systems—capitalism, communism, and socialism. We will examine what they are, how they operate, and their pros and cons. Then we will show how many of the distinctions among them are becoming more and more blurred, giving rise to the "mixed economy."

CAPITALISM

In 1776, Adam Smith, a Scottish professor, published *The Wealth of Nations.* In his book, Smith attacked the major economic philosophy of the time, *mercantilism,* which advocated strict government control over the economy. Smith favored free enterprise. **Free enterprise** (or **private enterprise**) is an economic philosophy that advocates letting privately owned business firms operate with minimal government control.

free enterprise
private enterprise

Smith's economic philosophy advocated a laissez faire approach to the economic system. **Laissez faire** means "leave us alone": let businesspeople compete without government regulation or control. Smith believed in a free market balanced and self-regulated by the "invisible hand"—the forces of supply and demand as related to prices. That, he reasoned, would contribute far more to society's well-being than government control of the economy. Government, Smith said, should interfere only when necessary to protect society. Otherwise, people should be free to pursue their own enlightened individual self-interest. By doing so, they would advance society's economic well-being.

laissez faire

We will take a closer look at the law of supply and demand in Chapter 2. Essentially, it boils down to this: If the supply of a good were too low, its price would be high because there would not be enough to meet the demand. Suppliers, motivated by the profit motive, would produce more and more of that good. As a result, the price of the good would fall.

On the other hand, suppose the supply of a good were too great. Its price would be low because there would be too much of it to be consumed. Suppliers would stop production until the market was ready for more, as indicated by a rise in the price of the good. At some point, supply and demand would equalize and be in balance, producing stability in pricing and production.

capitalism

Adam Smith is widely regarded as the father of capitalism. **Capitalism** is an economic system in which the decisions of private individuals and privately owned business firms determine which goods and services will be produced and how they will be distributed among the people. Countries whose economies are based mainly on capitalism, such as the United States and Switzerland, are often called capitalist countries. Capitalists believe that society is best served by businesses that compete vigorously with each other to serve consumers. As stated in the Union Bank of Switzerland's ad, competition is "the incentive to do better."

As we will see throughout this book, and especially in Chapter 23, competition is becoming more and more global in nature. United States–based companies must compete for customers at home and abroad with companies based in other countries.

Competition—the incentive to do better—is becoming ever more global in nature.

PROS AND CONS OF CAPITALISM   Proponents of capitalism say that it offers people the most rights and economic freedoms. They believe that people should determine their own lives in terms of where they work, how hard they work, what products they buy, and so on.

Opponents argue that the capitalist system creates and maintains unequal distribution of income and wealth. They say it works for the "haves" and does not work for the "have nots," so "the rich get richer and the poor get poorer." Critics say that poverty and discrimination divide capitalist society. Some say that capitalism places too high a value on individualism at the expense of society. Other charges are that capitalism makes people too materialistic and often results in duplication of effort and economic waste. They wonder, for instance, whether we really need all the brands and varieties of laundry detergent that are on the market.

COMMUNISM

Communism is the economic system least like capitalism. Communist countries include the Soviet Union, Cuba, the People's Republic of China, East Germany, and Albania.

If Adam Smith is the father of capitalism, Karl Marx, a nineteenth century German social philosopher, is the father of communism. Marx based his economic theory on the idea that exploitation of poor workers by rich capitalists (entrepreneurs and managers) would divide society. This would ultimately lead to a class struggle and the collapse of capitalist society. The end result of the class struggle envisioned by Marx would be a classless society—communism. **Communism** is an economic system in which the citizens collectively own all of the country's productive capacity. Before the ultimate evolution to the stateless and classless society, however, government would own all productive resources, operate all productive enterprises on behalf of the people, and control social and economic decision making. The people would work for the government.

communism

Communist countries, as we saw at the beginning of the chapter, practice central planning. **Central planning** is the practice by which a government drafts a master plan and directly manages the economy to achieve the plan's goals. Such plans are usually developed every five years. Government determines how resources will be used and how goods and services will be divided among the people. It also sets wage rates and prices. Consumers spend fixed incomes on fixed amounts of fixed goods and services at fixed prices.

central planning

Communism allows very little freedom to its people. Individuals are less important than the system, and government determines each person's role and rewards in the system. Marx's view of communism can be summed up in the phrase "from each according to his or her abilities, to each according to his or her needs." The one-party (Communist Party) government maintains complete control and recognizes no other political parties. Communist Party bosses work in factories and make decisions, exercising political control over what in capitalist countries are business decisions.

PROS AND CONS OF COMMUNISM Advocates of communism say that their system is *egalitarian*—it offers a uniform standard of living, which means equal income and wealth in a classless society. They say that a centrally planned economy does not produce the economic duplication and waste that accompanies capitalist competition.

Critics say that communist economies have a poor track record for reaching their planning goals. For example, the Soviet Union has been unable to translate its wealth of natural resources into a standard of living comparable to that of the United States—or even that of Japan, a country that is very poor in natural resources. Critics also deny the existence of a classless society. They say that the Soviet Union is egalitarian in pay but not in privileges. For example, the children of high-ranking government officials tend to get preference in the education system. With *perestroika*, some Soviets are wondering whether pay incentives for workers will lead to the creation of "rich" and "poor" in a society that claims to be egalitarian.[11]

SOCIALISM

In between the extremes of capitalism and communism is socialism. The term *socialism* can mean different things to different people; there are many varieties of socialism.

For example, communism views socialism as an intermediary stage in the evolution from capitalism to pure communism and the stateless and classless society. Socialists do not see socialism as evolving into communism. Democratic socialists, for example, believe in democratic political processes and a welfare state. There are several political parties in social democracies, and voters vote for or against the socialist party and its policies, including the government's control over the economic system. The people enjoy many of the same freedoms that people have in capitalist systems. Government, however, plays a much greater role in economic affairs than it plays in a capitalist economy.

socialism

Socialism is an economic system in which the government practices economic planning, owns the nation's major economic resources and many of its basic industries, and imposes heavy taxes to finance a welfare state. Coal mining, banks, gas, railroads, steel, and aerospace are examples of industries that are typically owned by socialist governments. Other industries and firms, however, are privately owned.

Great Britain, France, Italy, Sweden, Norway, and Austria are examples of social democracies. Other socialist countries include India, Australia, Argentina, Peru, and such African nations as Kenya, Nigeria, and Tanzania. Sometimes, it is hard to tell whether a particular country is more accurately described as capitalist or socialist. Some of the countries along the Pacific Rim (such as Taiwan, Singapore, South Korea, and Japan) refer to their mixtures of central planning and private enterprise as "Confucian capitalism."[12]

Figure 1-6 (on p. 20) shows that an economic system provides a framework for satisfying human wants—for converting the factors of production into an output of goods and services. Notice, however, that individuals, government, consumers, and central planning play different roles in capitalist, communist, and socialist systems.

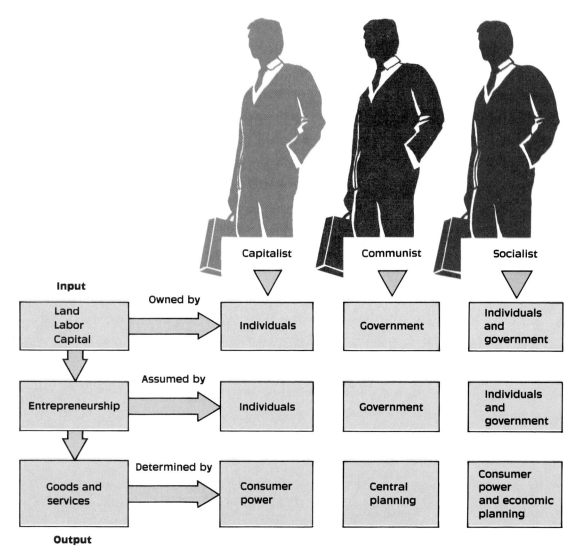

FIGURE 1-6 / A comparison of capitalism, communism, and socialism in terms of ownership, entrepreneurship, and consumer power.

PROS AND CONS OF SOCIALISM Proponents of socialism say that the system seeks to balance income and wealth among the people, doing away with extreme wealth and extreme poverty. Socialist countries impose high income and inheritance taxes and provide a "womb-to-tomb" welfare system that supplies medical and dental care, housing, transportation, and college education. Because the economy is government-controlled, it is said to be more stable than a capitalist economy—less subject to booms and busts in the level of economic activity.

Critics say that equal wealth, high taxes, and a welfare state weaken people's motivation to work, since personal effort and success do not lead to proportional personal rewards. Opponents also point out that government control does not ensure high employment.

	Communism ◄──	Socialism ───────	──► Capitalism
Private property?	None	Some	Most
Consumer power?	None	Yes	Yes
View on competition?	Wasteful	Good in some cases	Beneficial, desirable
Individual freedoms?	Very few	Yes	Yes
Central focus?	State	Individual/state	Individual
Ownership of factors of production?	State	State/private	Private
Ownership of basic industries?	State	State	Private
Ownership of nonbasic industries?	State	Private	Private
Private profit?	No	Yes	Yes
Role of government?	Maximum	Some	Least
Central planning?	Maximum	Some	None
Who ultimately controls?	The Party	Voters	Voters
Egalitarian goals?	Yes	Somewhat	No
Social and economic decision making?	State	Private/state	Private

Table 1-1 is a summary of the major differences among communism (before the evolution of the stateless and classless society), socialism (democratic), and capitalism. Next we look at how these economic systems have been modified over the years.

Real-World Economic Systems

No real-world economic system is *purely* capitalist or communist. We had a hint of that in our brief look at contemporary communism in the Soviet Union. The Business in the News box (on p. 22) provides insight into how China's adoption of some capitalist ideas and practices is attracting businesses from a capitalist country. Socialist economies are also changing in many ways.

TODAY'S CAPITALISM, COMMUNISM, AND SOCIALISM

The Great Depression of the 1930s caused widespread poverty that led many Americans to question their belief in laissez faire capitalism. As a result, the government began to play a growing role in the economy. Unemployment benefits and the Social Security program were established, and laws were passed to limit what businesses could do. For

BUSINESS IN THE NEWS

Private Enterprise Moves Upriver to a "Communist" Country

Capitalist Hong Kong's largest manufacturer of ceiling fans, Shell Electric Manufacturing Co. Ltd., does not employ a single production worker in Hong Kong. In late 1987 the company moved all of its production up the Pearl River delta into Guangdong province, in the People's Republic of China, the largest communist country in the world.

In a country where private enterprise was an unthinkable idea for about 30 years, a million factory workers have recently been churning out toys, ceiling fans, dolls, cassette players, garments, kitchenware, and many other products. Along the coast of southern China in Guangdong province, a flurry of manufacturing activity is creating a new Asian economic dynamo that has the potential to rival South Korea and Taiwan.

In the early 1980s, the People's Republic of China started using Guangdong as a laboratory for some of China's most daring experimentation with capitalism. Since then, like Shell Electric, hundreds of other manufacturing firms in nearby Hong Kong have shifted some or all of their production activities to the province. The economic alliance of Chinese neighbors links the sophistication, management skills, and marketing know-how of Hong Kong's 5.6 million population with the low-cost production base of Guangdong's 63 million citizens. Labor costs in Guangdong are 80 percent lower than in Hong Kong.

China's experimentation with capitalism came the hard way, after years of extreme and economically disastrous attempts to put all forms of production under government and political control. Communally run farms, which had never really focused on food productivity, were severely modified to provide incentives for individual farmers; these formed the nucleus of China's comeback to small-scale private enterprise. From there the principle of individual incentive was spread to the industrial and service sectors of the Chinese economy. Using government grants of property and trading rights to make machinery purchases and land leases, many Chinese learned how to form larger economic enterprises. For example, a group of peasants would buy equipment to operate a roadside market to sell their products. Others went on to form such enterprises as restaurants, selling meals to travelers and tourists, and in some cases selling stock to outside investors or borrowing money for expansion.

Building on this renewed entrepreneurial energy, the Chinese Communist Party's Central Committee decided in October 1987 to designate the country's southern coastal district as a "scout" to explore new roads to an open, market-oriented economy. In 1997, China will become the new owner of the former British Crown Colony of Hong Kong. The success of the Hong Kong–Guangdong experiment will play a large part in determining how far China will go in its experiment with capitalism. It is bound to have an impact on the future of Hong Kong's capitalism after 1997.

Source: Tom Ashbrook, "Hong Kong Sees China Gold in Cheap Labor," *The Boston Globe*, Dec. 13, 1987, pp. A1, A7. Reprinted courtesy of The Boston Globe.

example, new labor laws prohibited employers from firing or threatening to fire employees who tried to organize labor unions. Because of these and other changes over the years in our economy, the term *capitalism* is less appropriate in describing our system than it was a hun-

With the new emphasis on economic growth in China, the government is encouraging many forms of private enterprise. This entrepreneur started a bike rental shop.

dred years ago. And, as we have seen, the term *communism* is less appropriate in describing the economic system in the Soviet Union than it was before the Gorbachev era.

The same is true in China, which now has a State Commission for Restructuring the Economy.[13] Private enterprise practically ended for three decades after the Chinese Revolution of 1949. During Chairman Mao Zedong's 1966–1976 Cultural Revolution, private enterprise and personal wealth were especially condemned as "tails of capitalism" that should be cut off.[14] Private enterprise returned to China in 1979, and many changes have taken place in the economy since. Under China's Communist Party Deputy Chairman Deng Xiaoping's Second Revolution, the emphasis has switched from communist ideology to economic growth.

Some people say that the motto of communism is changing to "from each according to his hard work and ingenuity, to each according to the free market."[15] It is also true, however, that the reforms brought about in China by Deng and in the Soviet Union by Gorbachev are not supported by all members of the Communist Party in those countries. Both leaders face the dilemma of achieving prosperity through capitalist-style reforms without negating the party's power.

Beginning in late June 1988 in Moscow, the Communist Party held its first national conference in 47 years. Although there was debate over the pace of change, it appeared that the idea of perestroika was acceptable. Meanwhile, although the Communist Party in China was moving less rapidly with political reforms than in the Soviet Union, the Chinese were liberalizing their economy more rapidly.

Free-market ideas have become more popular in many Western European socialist countries, especially after Prime Minister Margaret Thatcher assumed office in Great Britain in 1979. Government ownership, which had increased in Great Britain for many years, began to decline as the government returned many state-owned enterprises like British Telecommunications, British Aerospace, and Jaguar to private ownership. Between 1979 and 1986, more than $11 billion in state assets had been sold. When Mrs. Thatcher was reelected in 1987, she had plans to sell off $30 billion more.[16]

MIXED ECONOMIES

mixed economy

One fact remains. No economic system in the world today is purely capitalist, communist, or socialist. Economic systems today are more accurately described as mixed economies. A **mixed economy** is a blend of varying degrees of private enterprise, government ownership, and government planning.

As we suggested earlier, socialism means different things in different countries. For example, when the Labour Party is in power, Great Britain's government is often called a socialist government. But it is a far less socialist government than the ones typically in power in Sweden and Denmark. Socialism in Iraq is very different from that in Western Europe and the Scandinavian countries. In Iraq and some other socialist countries, socialism is enforced by the army, which runs the government and directs the economy.

Communism also means different things in different countries. Cuba's brand of communism differs greatly from that of Yugoslavia or Hungary. Hungary refers to its type of communism as "goulash communism." Like Hungarian goulash (stew), it is a mixture. Free markets and individual initiative coexist with central planning and state-owned enterprises. There are privately owned small businesses, and farmers may sell crops on the open market. Hungarians also enjoy many personal freedoms—including the freedom to work at a second job or work for themselves and, with few exceptions, the right to travel freely to the west.[17] Hungarians are the only people in the Soviet bloc who pay an income tax.[18]

On the other hand, Fidel Castro started a "rectification" campaign in 1986. Unlike almost every other communist country, Castro is cutting back on incentive programs to reduce ineffective management and to boost labor productivity. He says that the incentive programs were subverted. He closed private farmers' markets, ditched a program that allowed citizens to buy their state-owned houses, and sharply cut back a system that paid bonuses to factory workers who exceeded their production quotas.[19]

As you would expect, there have been challenges to reform and restructuring efforts in China, the Soviet Union, and other communist countries. Early in 1987, a campaign was underway in China against Western influence. Although Deng's reforms were not abandoned, such reforms are likely to proceed more slowly in the future.

In an address to Soviet editors early in 1988, Gorbachev responded to critics of restructuring. "If we take fright and stop the processes we have begun," he said, "it would have the most serious consequences because we simply could not raise our people to such a massive task a second time. To stop now would be disastrous. We must not permit it under any circumstances."[20]

GRAFTING CAPITALISM'S FEATURES

In the discussions that follow, we will look at the major features of capitalism, which are identified in Figure 1-7. We will then show how those features have been modified over the years in our mixed economic system. We will also see how many of those capitalist features are being grafted onto the Soviet Union's and China's mixed economic systems.

INDIVIDUALISM   The core feature of the capitalist system is that the individual—not the state—is the main actor in economic life. Individual initiative and individual self-interest are the cornerstones of capitalism. There is little doubt, however, that Americans today tend to look more to government to solve economic and social problems than we did 100 years ago. For example, some people believe that our welfare system reduces individual initiative by taxing "haves" and redistributing income to "have nots."

Communism and socialism look to the state as the main actor in economic life. Deng's and Gorbachev's reforms, however, are giving greater emphasis to individual initiative. Factory workers and managers are being rewarded more and more on the basis of their individual

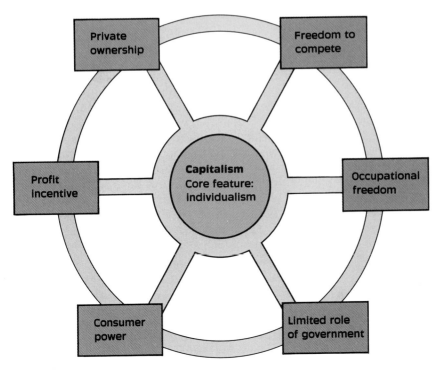

FIGURE 1-7 / Features of capitalism.

performances. Individual self-interest is being tested as an alternative to central planning on farms, in factories, and in the service industries. But some communists are concerned that providing incentives for individual productivity could conflict with the paternalistic provision of housing, food, recreation, and medical care for all workers.[21] How far can a communist economy go in the direction of individualism? That remains to be seen.

PRIVATE OWNERSHIP Related to individualism is the right of private ownership—a person's right to acquire, use, and dispose of things of value. Individual initiative would be greatly limited if a person could not own and amass property. Why work hard if the fruits of your labor will go to someone else? Zoning laws and inheritance taxes are examples of government-imposed limits on the right of private ownership in the United States. Unlike in the past, both Soviet and Chinese citizens can now own property. Many "entrepreneurs" in the Soviet Union work long hours on both state and private jobs in the hope of earning enough to buy a car or a *dacha* (a country home). Privately owned businesses are becoming more and more commonplace in both countries. But there are limits. Even with restructuring, an able-bodied Soviet of working age who tries to live exclusively on private income can be jailed for the crime of "parasitism."[22]

capital formation

PROFIT INCENTIVE Many people in capitalist countries *invest* their private property to generate more property. The incentive is the chance of making a profit. Investment, the process of putting money into business to make more money, makes possible all the new goods and services that appear on the market and creates jobs. **Capital formation**, another way to describe investment, is the process of adding to an economy's productive capacity. As we will see in Section 5, banks and other financial institutions help in this process.

Some people question whether our income tax system (which taxes higher incomes at higher rates) hurts the profit incentive. The 16th Amendment to the Constitution was ratified in 1913, giving Congress the power to collect taxes on incomes, from whatever source derived. In that same year, Congress authorized an individual income tax of 1 percent for most taxpayers, with a 7 percent maximum. During World War II the top tax rate for individuals hit a record of 94 percent.

Privately owned businesses in the Soviet Union and China are now generating profits—in countries where it used to be illegal to make a profit. The owners are investing some of their profits to expand their businesses. Since January 1, 1988, 60 percent of Soviet industry has been on a "self-financing" basis. State enterprises can decide what to produce and where to sell it. But they also must earn a profit or go out of business.[23]

CONSUMER POWER Consumer power means that consumers in capitalist countries are free to buy from anyone and firms compete for customers. As we will see in our discussion of marketing in Section Four, businesses must be guided by consumer wants in making decisions. Firms that do not provide customer-satisfying products will not have customers. These firms will then fail.

Without consumer power, consumers have to be satisfied with whatever goods and services are available. State-owned enterprises and privately owned businesses are competing in China and the Soviet Union. Consumers in those countries usually prefer to buy from the private firms because they do a better job of satisfying consumer needs. Giving consumers what they want is important if they are to work harder and become more productive.

Mr. Gorbachev's concern about quality control in factories is also evidence of more consumer power in the Soviet Union. On the other hand, some people wonder whether consumer power has declined somewhat in the United States. They point to government agencies such as the Consumer Product Safety Commission and ask whether they, and many laws, would be necessary if consumers really had so much power over producers and sellers.

FREEDOM TO COMPETE   People in capitalist countries are free to compete. Within very broad limits, a person can go into any business he or she may choose. Competition benefits both consumers and businesses. Consumers get higher-quality goods and services, greater variety, and lower prices. Competition gives firms the incentive to remain efficient and please their customers, rewarding those that do with profit. But do laws like ours that protect small, inefficient firms against competition from bigger, more efficient firms violate our freedom to compete?

Traditionally, most private enterprise in the Soviet Union has been black market (underground)—perhaps more than one-third of the total economy. The Soviet Union's "individual labor" law legalized private businesses in twenty-nine fields. Actually, this law was intended to bring the country's underground economy under control. The new law, in effect, legitimized competition in those fields.[24] Restructuring is based in large part on a recognition of the benefits of competition. As we saw earlier, Soviet firms are now being allowed to go bankrupt if they are not managed efficiently. In China, Asia Soft Drinks Factory used to sell mostly orange pop. When Coca-Cola started marketing in China, the factory's manager introduced Asia Cola, which is packaged like Coke, tastes slightly different, and sells for two-thirds the price.[25]

OCCUPATIONAL FREEDOM   Still another aspect of capitalism is freedom of choice of occupation. You are free to go into business for yourself, to work for someone else, and to choose your own career. Your choice is guided by your own best economic interests and limited only by the boundaries of your talents and education. Owners of private cars in the Soviet Union may now use their cars as taxis during time off from their regular state jobs. But they must still hold down full-time state jobs unless they are "housewives, invalids, or retired."[26] College students in China rioted in 1986 over the Communist Party's control of job allocation. The state, which runs work units, assigns all but a few college graduates to work in those units. A graduate who refuses an assignment cannot negotiate with another unit for at least three years. Meanwhile, the graduate can work only for herself or himself.[27]

LIMITED ROLE OF GOVERNMENT   Capitalists cherish their individual freedoms and do not want government to interfere with those freedoms. As we will see in this book, especially in Chapter 21, many laws have been passed to regulate business activity in the United States. Despite the deregulation movement that started in the late 1970s, government's role in our economy today is much, much greater than what Adam Smith had in mind when he wrote *The Wealth of Nations*.

Although the Communist Party is still all-powerful in China and the Soviet Union, there have been, as we have seen, a lot of changes in recent years. How limited a role government will play in these countries over the next few years is anybody's guess. Unemployment officially does not exist in a communist country. It is easy to assign six or seven people to do what could be done by two or three people. But early in 1988, Gorbachev was telling the Soviet people that restructuring could lead to unemployment of millions of people. If the economic adjustments and sacrifices far outweigh the perceived benefits, Gorbachev's opponents in the Soviet Union (and Deng's in China) may prevail.

Which System Is Best?

Clearly, this question would be answered differently by people from different types of economic systems. And, as we have seen, capitalism, socialism, and communism can mean different things to different people.

During the 1960s and 1970s, socialism made great strides in many areas of the world, including Africa, Asia, and Latin America. In

Pacific Rim countries such as Singapore are among the world's fastest-growing nations. In these countries the contrast between the old and the new can be dramatic.

Europe, "Eurocommunism" was on the move. The European communist parties were gaining strength. The lesser-developed nations tended to look to socialism to provide rapid social and economic growth.

During the 1980s, however, the tide swung in favor of capitalism. As we have seen, the two largest communist nations in the world have introduced elements of capitalism into their systems. Meanwhile, most of the Soviet satellite countries have expanded their capitalist practices. Perhaps the major action has been in the newly industrialized nations along the Pacific Rim—the world's fastest-growing region during the 1980s. Although the economic systems of countries like Japan, Singapore, Taiwan, and South Korea are not carbon copies of our type of capitalism, most of the basic features of capitalism that we have discussed in connection with capitalism in the United States are present. The one major exception is American-style individualism. What these countries have done is to modify U.S.-style capitalism to fit their cultures and requirements.

Without a doubt, the vast majority of Americans today support our capitalist economic system. It has provided us with a standard of living that makes us the envy of people around the world.

Summary

Business consists of all profit-seeking activities that are organized and directed to provide goods and services to customers. Whether the products are tangible goods or intangible services, business firms produce and market them in the hope of making a profit. Profit is a residual—what is left after a firm deducts its expenses of producing and marketing goods or services from its sales revenues. Risk is always present in business activity.

Profitable business firms serve society by providing jobs and paying taxes. Such firms also serve their customers by providing desired goods and services and serve their owners by earning profit. Social responsibility is the concept that business is accountable to society for its performance. A socially responsible business firm acts in a way that will advance the firm and at the same time serve society. It recognizes its obligations to its stakeholders.

Economic systems exist for the purpose of coping with limited resources and unlimited needs and wants. In our economic system we rely mainly on the forces of supply and demand to help us in dealing with this dilemma. The specialization and exchange process is a key to understanding the functioning of an economic system. In measuring an economic system's performance, we should not lose sight of quality-of-life considerations.

The factors of production are the productive system's inputs. The goods and services produced are the system's outputs. The factors are land, labor, capital, and entrepreneurship. Land is natural resources;

labor is the human resource; capital is the funds needed to finance a firm's activities that are provided by investors, business profits (retained earnings), and lenders; and entrepreneurship is the process of bringing land, labor, and capital together while taking the risk involved in producing a good or service in the hope of profit.

Capitalism, communism, and socialism are three major types of economic systems. Free enterprise (or private enterprise) and laissez faire are philosophies of pure capitalism. Essentially, capitalism is an economic system in which the decisions of private individuals and privately owned business firms determine which goods and services will be produced and how they will be distributed among the people.

Communism, at the opposite extreme, is a system in which the citizens collectively own all of the country's productive capacity. But until a stateless and classless society evolves, government owns and operates all productive enterprises. The people work for the government. Central planning is a key idea in communist systems.

Socialism can mean different things. Communists think of it as an intermediary stage in the evolution from capitalism to pure communism. Democratic socialists, on the other hand, look at socialism in terms of democratic political processes and a welfare state. In general, however, socialism means an economic system in which the government practices economic planning, owns the nation's major economic resources and many of its basic industries, and imposes heavy taxes to finance a welfare state.

In the real world, no economic system is purely capitalist, communist, or socialist. Economic systems today are mixed economies. Such an economy represents a blend of varying degrees of private enterprise, government ownership, and government planning. Today, communist and socialist systems have adopted some of the basic features of capitalism—individualism, private ownership, profit incentive, consumer power, freedom to compete, occupational freedom, freedom of contract, and limited role of government.

Although there is no one "best" type of economic system for everyone, the vast majority of Americans think ours is best for us. More and more, people who live in other types of systems are looking to capitalist ways to help them in coping with shortcomings of their systems.

Review Questions

1. What is the significance of profit to the business firm?

2. "A socially responsible firm is fine for society, but it ignores the economic interests of its owners." Do you agree? Explain.

3. What is an economic system?

4. "A country that increases its GNP is always better off than it was before the increase." Do you agree? Explain.

5. What are the four factors of production?

6. What did Adam Smith mean by the "invisible hand"?

7. How does government's role in the economy differ under capitalism, communism, and socialism?

8. How does democratic socialism differ from capitalism and communism?

9. Why is the term mixed economy being used more and more to describe economic systems in the world today?

Discussion Questions

1. In this chapter, we introduced the concept of the social responsibility of business. What about the social responsibility of consumers?

2. Samuel Gompers, first president of the American Federation of Labor, said many years ago, "The worst crime against working people is a company that fails to make a profit." What did he mean?

3. Does capitalism place too much emphasis on individualism?

4. Do you think that the recent changes in the economic systems in the Soviet Union and China signal the end of communism?

Key Terms

business	Gross National Product (GNP)	private enterprise
profit	inflation	laissez faire
risk	factors of production	capitalism
social responsibility	land	communism
stakeholders	labor	central planning
specialization	capital	socialism
exchange	entrepreneurship	mixed economy
economic system	entrepreneur	capital formation
standard of living	free enterprise	

Cases

RUNNING A STATE-OWNED STORE IN BEIJING

Suppose that you are the manager of a neighborhood state-owned store in Beijing, the capital city of the People's Republic of China. You cannot simply order goods because your customers want them. Instead, you have to accept what the state allocates to you. So, for example, along with Maotai liquor and Great Wall cigarettes—two top brands—you are also allocated lots of low-quality liquor and cigarettes that nobody will buy at the prices you are required to charge.

You could sell the low-quality products at a discount, lose money, and know that you will get another shipment next month that will lose more money. So you decide to let them stack up on the shelves.

Or, since the government is pressuring you to take responsibility for the store's profits and losses, you could try something more innovative. If a customer wants Maotai, sell him a bottle only if he buys a bottle of the low-quality liquor as well.

You decide on the latter course of action, and it works for a while. These "piggyback" sales mushroom. To get lean pork chops, you require your customers to buy fatback, too. You also sometimes sell beer with a pack or two of cheap cigarettes attached.

Then the government steps in. The Mayor of Beijing accuses you of abusing the consumer's right to choose and issues a ban on piggyback sales. The mayor even orders special telephones installed in some state retail shops so that managers can report any coercion from government wholesalers.

Government warehouses begin filling up with products that nobody wants but that the wholesalers have to buy. Since the government assigns the factories a production quota, its wholesalers are bound to take deliveries.

The government could get out of the wholesale and retail markets, which it promises partially to do during the next five-year plan. It could, in the meantime, refuse to accept shoddy goods from factories. But those factories employ millions of workers.[28]

Questions

1. As the manager of the store, are you an entrepreneur? Explain.
2. Why are you forced to take goods for inventory that you are certain will not sell?
3. How applicable is the concept of consumer power in this case?
4. What would happen if the state got out of the wholesale and retail markets and continued to operate the factories?

A COMEBACK FOR ARGENTINA?

Argentina, one of the world's ten richest countries in the 1920s, has long been sliding backward. Once widely viewed as having greater potential than Canada or Australia, it has pushed itself down into the category of underdeveloped nation.

President Raul Alfonsín wants to reverse this fifty-year decline and get Argentina—a country the size of India and blessed with extraordinarily fertile soil, two billion barrels of proven oil reserves, and a highly educated population—to produce rather than indulge in bitter reminiscence. To do so involves nothing less than the imposition of capitalism. For although there has been no serious communist threat here, many observers believe that capitalism, in the sense of a competitive drive for new markets and products, has never taken hold.

Nowhere has Argentina's failure been more marked than in the business class. In the place of entrepreneurs, there has emerged a group that is reluctant to invest and accept competition.

In the 1920s, Argentina already had a democratically elected government, an elaborate university system, a literacy rate close to 90 percent, and one of the best credit ratings in the world. Its economy, based on the export of grain and beef, was robust. Its per capita output of goods and services in 1929 was almost four times higher than Japan's. Observers agree on the following sources of trouble:

- A succession of military coups created a sense of instability that has discouraged major capital investment.
- The populist policies of General Juan Peron, who came to power in 1946, led, among other things, to massive welfare spending.
- General Peron's visions of economic self-sufficiency sparked a protectionist trend and the development of non-competitive industries.
- Wealthy rural estate owners, wary of industrial invest-

ment, became financiers, and much money left the country.[29]

Questions

1. Evaluate Argentina's strengths and weaknesses with respect to the factors of production.
2. Why is competition such a central part of a capitalist economic system?
3. Why is political stability in a country an important consideration to investors who are considering investing there?
4. In light of Argentina's pursuit of self-sufficiency, has the country benefited from the specialization and exchange process on a global scale?
5. What advice would you give to President Alfonsín?

LEARNING OBJECTIVES

After reading this chapter, you will be able to:

- Identify the major variables in the business environment.

- Describe the challenges to business posed by today's economic environment.

- Analyze the challenges to business posed by today's competitive environment.

- Explain the challenges to business found in the social and cultural environment.

- Identify the challenges to business posed by the political-legal environment.

- Explain the challenges to business found in the technological environment.

Today's Business and Its Challenges

W H A T ' S A H E A D

In this chapter, we will focus on the environmental challenges that confront business today. The environment within which business exists is the source of opportunity for the firm, but it is also the source of challenges. We will discuss this environment in terms of five major parts: (1) the economic environment, (2) the competitive environment, (3) the social and cultural environment, (4) the political-legal environment, and (5) the technological environment.

In our look at the economic environment, we will distinguish between macroeconomics and microeconomics, and we will explain the laws of supply and demand and the business cycle. We will also look at the challenges to business posed by federal budget deficits, international trade deficits, the decline of "smokestack America," and the energy situation.

Next comes a discussion of the competitive environment. We will distinguish among four types of market structures—pure competition, monopolistic competition, oligopoly, and monopoly. We will also contrast price and nonprice competition and examine the importance of improving the productivity of U.S. business firms to meet the challenge of global competition.

In our discussion of the social and cultural environment, we will examine our changing population, our major cultural values, and the challenges of social responsibility, consumerism, and ecology. We will also introduce the concept of business ethics.

The major focus in our discussion of the political-legal environment will be the relationship between government and business. We will also take a look at how business and politics are interrelated.

The last section of the chapter explores the major issues and challenges that exist in the technological environment. We will distinguish between technology and its application, and we will look at structural unemployment and technology transfer.

The environment presents many challenges to business. Consider, for example, how forces in the economic, competitive, social and cultural, political-legal, and technological environment

have been affecting the U.S. brewing industry.

Economic slowdowns pose a challenge in that sales of super-premium brands tend to slip as drinkers switch to lower-priced (and lower profit margin) brands. The declining number of blue-collar jobs in manufacturing and construction also hurts brewers because young, blue-collar males drink the most beer.

In the competitive environment, the industry has been undergoing massive consolidation. Hundreds of brewers used to serve highly localized markets, but five big national brewing companies now have about 90 percent of the U.S. market. This concentration poses a threat to the survival of regional brewers, many of which have already been bought up by their bigger rivals. Imports present another competitive challenge. Corona beer has been so successful that Mexico has displaced West Germany as the third-largest exporter of beer to the United States, behind the Netherlands and Canada.

Brewers today are probably facing the most challenging social and cultural environment since Prohibition. Groups like Mothers Against Drunk Driving (MADD) and Students Against Drunk Driving (SADD) are succeeding in getting stiffer penalties for drunk driving. Greater health consciousness and alcohol-free lifestyles are also posing challenges, as is the aging of America. Today, the population of beer drinkers in their early 20s (heavy beer drinkers) is much smaller than the number of people who are in their 40s (who drink much less beer). With industry sales flat to shrinking, the challenge is to stimulate brand switching among the existing beer drinkers. Another challenge lies in attracting more women to drink beer, a beverage that has traditionally not appealed to a lot of women.

The political-legal environment also poses challenges. For example, the number of bars and taverns is declining, partly because bar owners may be liable for automobile accidents caused by intoxicated patrons. The increase in the drinking age to 21 has also eliminated legal drinking by a large number of people.

The technological environment is also important. Breweries that have not automated their operations, for example, are finding it almost impossible to compete against those that have.

Of course, these environmental forces often overlap. There is some reaction against mass-produced beers that "taste the same" to many people. The major brewers are being challenged both by the imports and by domestically brewed "boutique" beers. Boutique beers are brewed by small specialty brewers like Boston Beer Company (Samuel Adams brand) and by micro-breweries like Mass. Bay Brewing Company (Harpoon Ale brand).

The brewing industry, like every other industry, is affected by the environment within which it exists. Although the variables in this environment are beyond the direct control of business managers, they must monitor the environment to keep up with developments that can affect their industries and firms. This is the only way they can be prepared to cope with the challenges that evolve from environmental developments. When it comes to meeting challenges, you can be sure it is not a case of "what you don't know won't hurt you."

The Business Environment

As Figure 2-1 shows, the business firm exists within a larger environment. This environment is the source of both opportunities and challenges. In the discussions that follow, we will look at this environment, beginning with the economic environment.

Challenges in the Economic Environment

We looked at what an economic system is in Chapter 1. *Economics* is concerned with the allocation of scarce resources (the factors of production) to satisfy unlimited human needs and wants. We can look at economics on two levels—the large-scale (macro) level and the small-scale (micro) level.

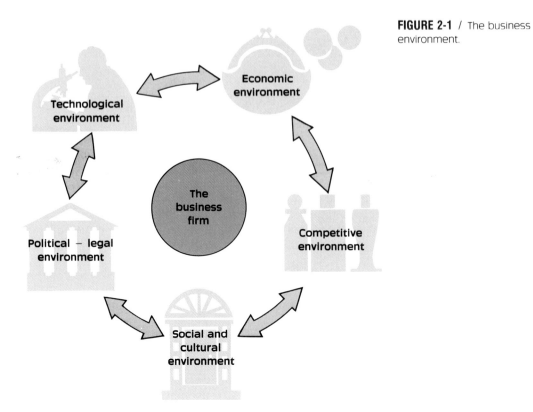

FIGURE 2-1 / The business environment.

MACROECONOMICS

The study of *macroeconomics* considers the economic system as a whole. Our government uses its monetary and fiscal policies to deal with macroeconomic problems like national unemployment and inflation.

monetary policy

Monetary policy involves the use of various tools and actions by the nation's monetary authority to regulate the growth rate of the nation's money supply. Monetary policy is based on the idea that the economy's growth rate can be influenced by regulating the money supply's growth rate. As we will see in Chapter 16, the Federal Reserve System is the monetary authority in the United States. If unemployment is high, the Federal Reserve System can increase the money supply to make it easier for firms to borrow money for expansion, thereby creating more jobs.

fiscal policy

Fiscal policy involves the government's use of tax and spending programs to cope with macroeconomic problems. For example, during a period of high unemployment the government could increase spending to create jobs. It could also cut personal taxes to leave people with more spending money.

MICROECONOMICS

The study of *microeconomics* focuses on the individual decision-making units within the economic system. In our system those units are individual households and business firms. Important economic decisions at the micro level include how many units of its product a firm should produce, how much to charge customers, and where to locate plants and warehouses. The household unit also decides how much to spend or save and what to spend its income on.

THE FORCES OF SUPPLY AND DEMAND

market economy

In Chapter 1 we said that our economic system is basically a capitalist system. We can also call it a market economy. A **market economy** is an economic system in which prices determine how the factors of production will be used and how the resulting goods and services will be distributed. The forces of supply and demand operate to determine prices at both the macro and micro levels. For example, the supply and demand for loanable funds in the overall economy influences interest rates. Likewise, supply and demand forces influence the price you pay for a room at a hotel in the host city for "Superbowl Sunday."

SUPPLY   The quantity supplied of a good or service is the number of units producers will offer for sale at a certain price. For most goods and services, more units are supplied at a higher price than at a lower price. Price and quantity offered thus vary in the same direction. This is the law of supply. The **law of supply** states that as the price of a good or service goes up, suppliers will tend to increase the quantity available.

law of supply

DEMAND   The other half of the price system is demand. Demand for a good or service exists when there are people who desire it, have the

law of demand

buying power to purchase it, and are willing to spend to acquire it. The quantity demanded is the number of units buyers will buy at a certain price. For most goods and services, more units are demanded at a lower price than at a higher price. This inverse relationship between price and quantity demanded is the law of demand. The **law of demand** states that as the price of a good or service goes up, the quantity demanded goes down.

INTERACTION OF SUPPLY AND DEMAND To understand how supply and demand forces interact to determine prices, let's develop a hypothetical example using disposable razors. Figure 2-2 shows in graphic form how the laws of supply and demand work.

The supply curve (S) shows how many razors will be demanded at a specific price at a given point in time. As the curve labeled "S" shows, manufacturers supply fewer razors at lower prices than at higher prices.

The demand curve (D) shows how many razors will be demanded at a specific price at a given point in time. As the curve labeled "D" shows, consumers demand fewer razors at higher prices than at lower prices.

The supply and demand curves in Figure 2-2 cross at a price of 50 cents per unit. Only at this price is the quantity manufacturers are willing to offer (300 units) exactly equal to the quantity consumers are willing to buy (300 units). This is the *equilibrium price* at which the quantity demanded and the quantity supplied are in balance. At higher prices, suppliers would be willing to supply more units than buyers would be willing to buy. At lower prices, buyers would be willing to buy more units than suppliers would be willing to supply.

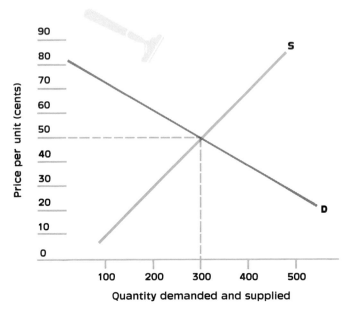

FIGURE 2-2 / Supply and demand forces interacting to form a price.

The forces of supply and demand affect the price we pay for all types of goods and services.

It does not matter what kind of price we are talking about. It could be the price we pay for a Whopper at Burger King. It could be the price we get for our labor (wages), the price we pay to borrow money (interest), or the price we pay for an apartment (rent). The forces of supply and demand are at work in every case.

THE BUSINESS CYCLE

business cycle

While some firms do prosper when the overall economy is declining, most firms' profits tend to go up and down along with the nation's overall level of economic activity. Thus a healthy economy is good for business. The **business cycle** is the fluctuations in the level of economic activity that an economy goes through over time.

The business cycle can be divided into four stages: prosperity, recession, depression, and recovery. The *expansionary* phases are recovery and prosperity. The *contractionary* stages are recession and depression. The periods of expansion and contraction can vary from several months to several years. As shown in Figure 2-3, a slowdown need not result in a depression if the recovery gets underway before the economy tumbles too far down.

The longest period of economic decline in U.S. history occurred during the Great Depression of the 1930s. The longest period of expansion occurred during the 1980s. In the post–World War II period a typical recession has lasted close to one year. A typical expansion has lasted close to four years.

The discussions that follow focus on four of the major challenges that confront us in the national economic environment:

- federal budget deficits,
- international trade deficits,
- the decline of smokestack America, and
- energy.

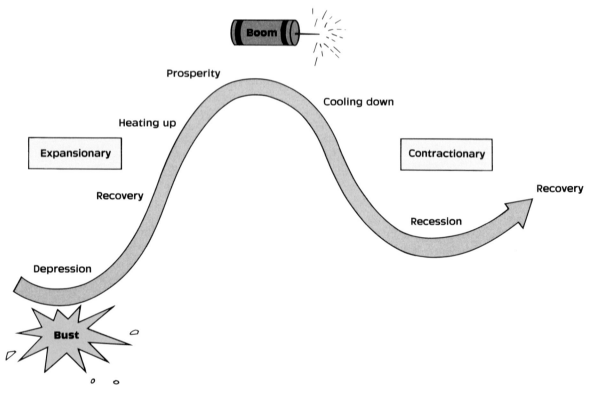

FIGURE 2-3 / The business cycle.

FEDERAL BUDGET DEFICITS

For many years our federal government's expenditures have been greater than its revenues. This pattern results in annual budget deficits. Figure 2-4 shows the budget deficits for fiscal years 1980–1987. Government spends most of its money on defense, social welfare, and inter-

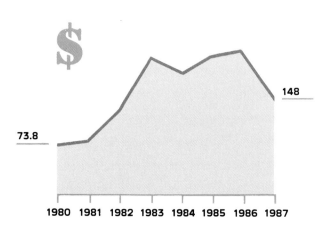

FIGURE 2-4 / The U.S. budget deficit, fiscal years 1980–1987, in billions of dollars. (*Source:* Gerald F. Seib, "Reagan's Coattails: Candidates Like the President's Ideas but Shy Away from Total Commitment," *The Wall Street Journal: A Special Report: Politics '88,* Dec. 4, 1987, p. 7D.) Reprinted by permission of *The Wall Street Journal,* © Dow Jones & Company, Inc., 1987. All Rights Reserved.

est on government debt. The money comes mostly from taxes paid by individuals and corporations. Figure 2-5 shows where the problem lies—spending outstrips tax receipts. From a base of a little over $92 billion and 18 percent of GNP in 1960, total outlays exploded eleven-fold to over a trillion dollars in fiscal 1987. Spending grew much faster than the overall economy, peaking at 24.4 percent of GNP in fiscal 1983 before dropping back a bit to 23 percent in fiscal 1987.

The long series of annual deficits has added up to a staggering federal debt. The U.S. government owes its creditors close to $3 trillion dollars. (By comparison the estimated value of all U.S. residential dwellings is about $6 trillion.)[1] These creditors include U.S. and foreign citizens and businesses that buy U.S. Treasury bonds and notes. The government must borrow more and more money each year to finance the debt along with the current year's deficit. Because the supply of money available for lending at any given time is limited, the Treasury finds itself competing with consumers, businesses, nonprofit organizations, and local and state governments for borrowed money. This huge demand in the face of limited supply tends to put upward pressure on interest rates.

If interest rates go up, the government has to borrow more to pay the interest (which adds to the debt) or raise taxes. If the Federal Reserve System increases the money supply to reduce upward pressure on interest rates, inflation could result. Fortunately, foreign individuals, organizations, and governments have been buying U.S. Treasury securities—in effect, buying part of our government's debt. Otherwise, interest rates would probably be much higher in this country.

FIGURE 2-5 / Federal spending and receipts as a percent of Gross National Product, fiscal years 1960–1987. (*Source:* Edward A. Sprague, ed., *Federal Tax Policy Memo,* Tax Foundation, Washington, D.C., 1987, p. 4.)

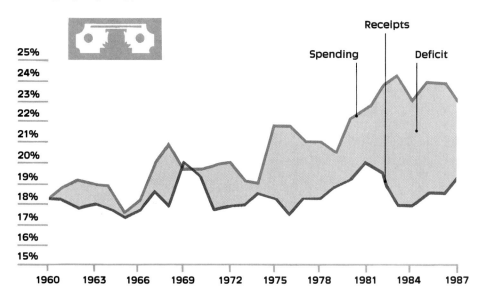

Why are foreigners willing to buy part of our government's debt? They feel it is a very safe investment because of the stability of our political and economic systems. Many foreigners can also earn a higher return on U.S. Treasury securities than they could earn on low-risk investments at home.

As indicated in Table 2-1, U.S. government debt to foreigners stood at $268.4 billion for fiscal 1987. The U.S. Treasury that year paid $23.5 billion in interest to foreigners. That $23.5 billion was nearly triple the amount requested for federal housing programs, 50 percent greater than the administration's federal education budget, more than double the request for Navy shipbuilding, and more than the total requested for cancer research, running the national parks, airline safety, trade promotion, and the Environmental Protection Agency combined.[2]

Congress passed the Gramm-Rudman Act in 1985 to help in coping with big budget deficits. The law sets target deficit limits and mandates automatic spending cuts if those limits are exceeded by more than a set amount. Under the original law, the federal budget would be balanced by 1991. A revised version pushed back the deadline for a balanced budget to 1993.

INTERNATIONAL TRADE DEFICITS

A nation has a deficit in its annual balance of trade when it imports (buys) more from other countries than it exports (sells) to them. The United States has had a deficit in its balance of trade for many years. Figure 2-6 (on p. 44) shows the trade deficits for 1980–1987.

Economists apply the terms "strong" and "weak" to currencies. For example, a "strong" U.S. dollar makes foreign-made goods cheaper in the United States and American-made goods more expensive in foreign markets. A "weak" dollar has the opposite effects. The U.S. dollar should be "weak" in relation to most other currencies because we have a big demand for foreign currencies with which to buy foreign-made

TABLE 2-1 / U.S. government debt held by foreigners, selected fiscal years, in billions of dollars

Fiscal Year	Federal Debt Held by Foreigners	Annual Interest Paid to Foreigners
1980	$121.7	$12.0
1984	175.5	19.0
1986	256.3	22.3
1987	268.4	23.5

Source: Walter S. Mossberg, "The Outlook: Cost of Paying the Foreign Piper," *The Wall Street Journal*, Jan. 18, 1988, p. 1. Reprinted by permission of *The Wall Street Journal*, © Dow Jones & Company, Inc., 1988.

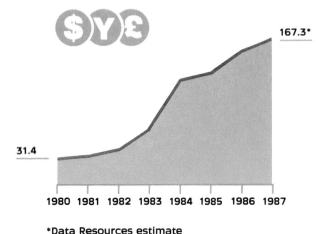

FIGURE 2-6 / The U.S. trade deficit, calendar years 1980–1987, in billions of dollars. (*Source:* Gerald F. Seib, "Reagan's Coattails: Candidates Like the President's Ideas but Shy Away from Total Commitment," *The Wall Street Journal: A Special Report: Politics '88,* Dec. 4, 1987, p. 7D.) Reprinted by permission of *The Wall Street Journal,* © Dow Jones & Company, Inc., 1987. All Rights Reserved.

products. This demand is much greater than their demand for dollars with which to buy our products.

In spite of our trade deficits, however, throughout much of the early to mid-1980s we had a strong dollar. Why? Again, the relatively high interest rates here and our stable economic and political systems combined to create a big foreign demand for dollars to invest here.

Since the strong dollar made it more expensive for foreigners to buy our products, it hurt sales for American firms, both at home and abroad. This meant reduced profits, layoffs of workers, business failures, and more trade deficits. To become competitive in world markets, many U.S. firms moved some of their plants to foreign countries where production costs were lower.

Declining competitiveness of our products at home and abroad stimulates *protectionist* sentiment. Some people want very high tariffs (taxes) on imported products. Some argue in favor of "fair trade." Unlike "free traders," "fair traders" oppose allowing free access to the U.S. market to countries that restrict imports from the United States.

The U.S. market has not been closed to imports. Such a move could easily trigger trade wars, such as those that helped to bring about the

trade war

Great Depression of the 1930s. A **trade war** is a situation in which one country imposes trade barriers against its trading partners, and they retaliate with trade barriers of their own. Instead, to help U.S. firms compete in world markets, the federal government took action in 1985 to start driving down the value of the U.S. dollar. Although this helped, it did not have a major and immediate impact on our trade deficit. Foreign firms do not want to give up market share in the United States. Many Japanese auto makers, for example, reduced their prices to hold onto their market share. (As we have seen, a falling dollar against a rising yen should mean rising prices of Japanese-made products in this country.)

A weaker dollar and a stronger yen also mean that it is not always cheaper for Japanese firms to export from Japan to the United States. This is why the Japanese are making more products in the United

States. The fact is that it is now cheaper for them to build cars in Ohio than in Osaka![3] Furthermore, when they first started making cars here, the Japanese imported most of the parts and assembled them here. Now they are making more and more of the parts here.

The weak U.S. dollar has also contributed to a big increase in foreign direct investment (foreign ownership) in the United States. At the end of 1986, foreign direct investment in the United States stood at $1.33 trillion, while U.S. direct investment abroad totaled $1.07 trillion.[4] This reversed the post–World II pattern of our firms investing more abroad than foreign-based firms invested here. Today, foreigners own such "American" companies as Carnation, Smith & Wesson, Chesebrough-Pond's, and Sohio; the RCA record label and French's mustard; and 46 percent of the commercial real estate in downtown Los Angeles.[5]

Finally, the weaker dollar has caused some of our firms to bring back to the United States some of the production that they had sent abroad earlier. In 1987, for example, General Electric decided against renewing its deal with Japan's Matsushita for 500,000 color TVs. Instead, GE decided to make the sets at a plant in Indiana that it had acquired a year earlier through a merger with RCA.[6]

Figure 2-7 (on p. 46) shows the effect of the steep drop in what the U.S. dollar would buy abroad. The haircut at the Okura Hotel barbershop ($36.40 in 1987) cost $22 a year earlier.[7]

THE DECLINE OF SMOKESTACK AMERICA

Agriculture, goods producing, and services are the three major employment sectors in our economy. The United States began changing from a mostly agricultural to a mostly goods-producing (manufacturing, mining, and construction) economy at the turn of the twentieth century. During the 1950s and 1960s, our economy began changing from an industrial to a postindustrial economy. The latter change is often referred to as "the decline of smokestack America" or *deindustrialization*. The What Do You Think? box (on p. 47) asks the question "Is the United States deindustrializing?"

The major economic activity in an agricultural economy is producing farm products, and farms are the chief source of jobs. The major economic activity in a goods-producing economy is producing tangible manufactured goods, and the chief source of jobs is the manufacturing industries. The major economic activity in a postindustrial economy is producing intangible services, and the chief source of jobs is the service industries.

The service industries—which include everything from computer software development to business consulting, from haircuts to telecommunications—now provide six out of seven new jobs. The U.S. Department of Labor projects that between 1984 and 1995, our economy will add 16 million new jobs, and almost 90 percent of them will be in services.[8] Roughly 76 million people are service industry workers. Examples of service providers are banks, consulting firms, hotel chains, restaurants, and airlines. One challenge for firms in declining industries is to find growth opportunities in the service industries.

Deluxe hotel single room (average price incl. any tax and service charges)

Paris (Georges V)	320.46
Tokyo (Okura)	316.00
London (Hilton)	295.00
New York (Vista)	231.33
Hong Kong (Hilton)	187.40
Rio (Caesar Park)	186.00
Bonn (Bristol)	151.00
Kansas City, Mo.	124.00 (Alameda Plaza)

Man's haircut in hotel barbershop

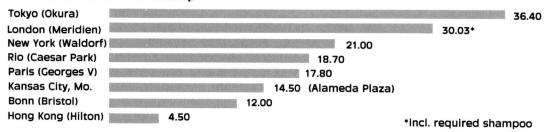

Tokyo (Okura)	36.40
London (Meridien)	30.03*
New York (Waldorf)	21.00
Rio (Caesar Park)	18.70
Paris (Georges V)	17.80
Kansas City, Mo.	14.50 (Alameda Plaza)
Bonn (Bristol)	12.00
Hong Kong (Hilton)	4.50

*incl. required shampoo

One mile metered taxi ride

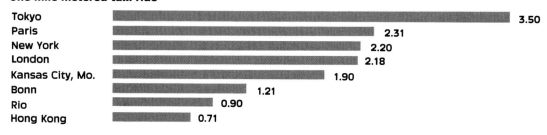

Tokyo	3.50
Paris	2.31
New York	2.20
London	2.18
Kansas City, Mo.	1.90
Bonn	1.21
Rio	0.90
Hong Kong	0.71

First-run movie

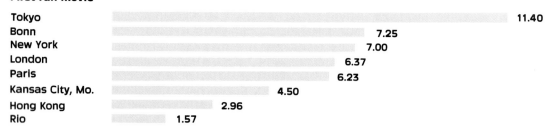

Tokyo	11.40
Bonn	7.25
New York	7.00
London	6.37
Paris	6.23
Kansas City, Mo.	4.50
Hong Kong	2.96
Rio	1.57

FIGURE 2-7 / Prices of four common items in two major U.S. cities and six cities abroad. Prices abroad were converted into dollars at exchange rates in effect in early December 1987. (*Source:* "Your Money Matters: Sticker Shock: U.S. Travelers Face Trauma of Sharply Devalued Dollar," *The Wall Street Journal,* Dec. 4, 1987, p. 37.) Reprinted by permission of *The Wall Street Journal,* © Dow Jones & Company, Inc., 1987. All Rights Reserved.

WHAT DO YOU THINK?

Is the United States Deindustrializing?

Some people say that the United States is deindustrializing—that we are becoming a nation of hamburger flippers, retail clerks, and auto mechanics. They point to high imports, plant closings, and growing employment in service industries. This is evidence, they say, that the United States is losing its industrial base and its ability to manufacture goods that can compete in the world economy. "We can't afford to become a nation of video arcades, drive-in banks and McDonald's hamburger stands," warns Chrysler Corporation chairman Lee Iacocca.

Other people argue that the United States is not deindustrializing. They recognize that steel and some other basic manufacturing industries are retrenching. But they point to statistics showing that employment rose slightly in goods-producing industries—which includes manufacturing, agriculture, mining, and construction—to 29.6 million in 1984 from 27.1 million in 1959. However, as a share of the total work force, employment in goods-producing industries fell to 27.7 percent from more than 40 percent over the same period. Employment in service industries rose to 72.3 percent from 40 percent over the same period.

Manufacturing productivity in the mid-1980s was rising at a 4.2 percent annual rate compared to a rate of 0.9 percent for nonmanufacturing businesses.

According to the Committee for Economic Development, a business-supported research group, the increases in manufacturing productivity and output show that the shift from goods to services has occurred more in employment than in output.

Is the U.S. deindustrializing? What do you think?

Source: Kenneth H. Bacon, "The Outlook: The Case Against Deindustrialization," *The Wall Street Journal,* Jan. 5, 1987, p. 1. Reprinted by permission of *The Wall Street Journal,* © Dow Jones & Company, Inc., 1987. All Rights Reserved.

Many of our smokestack industries find it hard to compete with more efficient foreign firms. Some of our older industrialized areas, especially in the Northeast, have been called "rust bowls." Many of the products these plants produced are now imported. The jobs disappeared, and the factories started rusting away.

Manufacturing still contributes about 22 percent to our GNP, roughly the same percentage it has for the past thirty years.[9] But some people worry about the "hollowing out" of our economy. Many manufacturing jobs in the United States now involve assembling a finished product from parts made abroad. In the auto industry, for example, many of the parts in U.S.-made cars are made abroad.

Some of our surviving smokestack firms depend on import protection. Most of the survivors, however, are firms that have adopted lower-cost manufacturing techniques. This includes: (1) automating their operations to enhance productivity, (2) winning concessions from labor unions to lower labor costs, (3) entering into ventures with lower-cost foreign producers, and (4) operating on a smaller scale with innovative ways of doing business.

For example, while many giant American steel mills have closed in recent years, much smaller and more efficient minimills are expected to be producing 40 percent of all the steel made in the United States by the end of the century.[10] Minimills make steel products from molten scrap metal rather than smelting the raw material from iron ore.

But automation is not a cure-all, nor is it painless for the workers who are directly affected by it. General Motors spent $60 billion from 1979 to 1986 to automate its factories. But its first attempts were embarrassing. At one plant the automated "steel-collar" workers painted each other instead of the cars.[11] Automation can also lead to layoffs. Exxon's efforts at automating its refineries enhanced its productivity but also cut employment by 48,000, or 32 percent.[12]

productivity

Productivity is the relationship between the input of resources (the factors of production) and the output of goods and services. Productivity can be increased by improving this output/input ratio—getting more output with the same or less input. Georgia-Pacific now uses blades at its sawmills that are made from a stronger metal alloy. The thinner blades take a smaller bite out of the logs. Wood that used to be turned into sawdust on the floor is now left whole to be made into 800 railcars of Georgia-Pacific products every year.[13]

ENERGY

The Arab oil embargo of 1973 caused us to search for ways to reduce our energy usage—to conserve. Throughout the rest of the 1970s and into the very early 1980s, businesses and consumers faced an "energy crisis." The Organization of Petroleum Exporting Countries (OPEC) restricted the world's supply of oil in the face of skyrocketing worldwide demand. Because of the laws of supply and demand, the price of oil also skyrocketed.

In recent years, however, energy prices have fallen owing to more efficient use of energy, conservation, non-OPEC sources, and the weakening of OPEC's ability to dictate the price of oil. The price decline has created severe economic problems for oil-producing states such as Texas, Oklahoma, Louisiana, and Alaska. It has also stimulated more usage and less conservation. We now depend more on imported oil than we did in 1973. Meanwhile, the major source of our imports, the Middle East, appears to be more unstable than it was in the 1970s. For the short term, conservation is our best hope. A long-run solution requires alternatives to natural gas and oil.

Challenges in the Competitive Environment

competition

Competition is rivalry among firms to attract customers in the hope of making a profit. Customers in the market can be households, business firms, governments, and nonprofit organizations. Each has limited money to spend on a given good or service. Sellers compete for these limited funds.

In the discussions that follow, we look at the four basic types of market structures: (1) pure competition, (2) monopolistic competition, (3) oligopoly, and (4) monopoly (see Figure 2-8). The type of market structure in which a firm operates affects the strength of competition and the number and type of competitors it faces.

TYPES OF MARKET STRUCTURES

pure competition

Pure competition means:

1. many small sellers, no one of which has much effect on total industry supply and the product's market price;
2. many small buyers, no one of which has much effect on total market demand and the product's market price;
3. a homogeneous product—all firms in a given industry offer the same product;
4. easy entry into and exit from the industry by competitors;
5. the same market conditions for all buyers and sellers; and
6. perfect information (about everyone's prices, for instance) in the hands of buyers and sellers.

This type of market structure does not exist in the real world. Buyers and sellers do not have perfect information, different brands within a product category are not homogeneous, all buyers and sellers do not operate under the same conditions, and so on. The closest real-world example would be the market for some agricultural products, such as soybeans and grain.

monopolistic competition

Monopolistic competition is a market situation in which there are many sellers and many buyers, but each seller's product is somewhat different from the others. Auto service shops and garment manufactur-

FIGURE 2-8 / The four basic types of market structures.

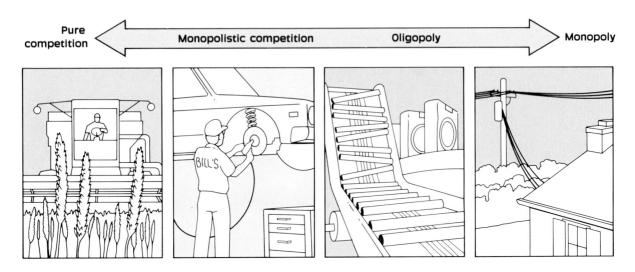

APPLICATION: BURGER KING
The Competitive Challenge

When it comes to the fast food industry, it is a real pressure-cooker out there on the streets. Over fifty big franchise chains—each with a total sales in excess of $200 million—compete for consumers' dollars. There are also thousands and thousands of small independent restaurants and diners that want the eater's dollar too.

Competition among the top franchise chains is always very keen. McDonald's is the leader, with total annual sales well over $10 billion. Burger King is second, with sales over $3 billion. Kentucky Fried Chicken, Wendy's, Hardee's, Pizza Hut, Dairy Queen, Big Boy, Taco Bell, and Arby's round out the top ten. (Other famous, smaller competitors in the same market include Long John Silver's, Dunkin Donuts, Domino's Pizza, and Roy Rogers.)

Burger King, McDonald's, and Wendy's cannot worry just about obvious competitors like Hardee's and other existing burger chains. "Substitute" products—such as pizza, fish and chips, hot dogs, Mexican food, and Chinese food—attract the consumer's dollar too. Some—like Domino's Pizza—are growing much, much faster than McDonald's and Burger King.

Even major competitors like McDonald's and Burger King have to always be on the lookout for brand new competitors. In 1987, for instance, a former Wendy's franchisee opened the first restaurant in a new hamburger chain he called "Rudy's." It sported a bright white building, an art-deco design, and huge, fresh-meat burgers, ground on the premises.

Other major food companies were not sitting still, either.

General Mills is opening dozens of new Olive Garden restaurants, for instance, serving Italian meals and pasta.

But competition is still most intense among the big three burger chains—McDonald's, Burger King, and Wendy's. These three giants continually grapple in the marketplace, seeking to improve their positions. As they fight for position, consumers benefit from new and better products, better service, and lower costs. New products like McDonald's Chicken McNuggets and Burger King's "Burger Bundles" give customer's interesting new things to eat. Service innovations such as Burger King's new double express drive-through add to buyers' convenience. And competitive pressures forced even giant McDonald's to start serving salads, which had first been introduced by Wendy's.

Competition is thus the force that makes business run, and this is nowhere more apparent than in fast foods. Direct rivals (like McDonald's), substitute products (like pizza), and new entrants in the market (like Rudy's) all keep Burger King Corporation on its toes.

Questions
1. Refer to Figure 2-1 and identify the environmental challenges to Burger King Corporation.

2. Is productivity a concern to Burger King Corporation?

3. What does the term *competition* mean to Burger King Corporation? What does it mean to a Burger King restaurant manager?

ers typically operate under conditions of monopolistic competition. There are many firms in each of these industries, and new ones can enter with relative ease. Long-run success requires an ability to make one's product different from others in ways that are more satisfying to customers.

oligopoly

Oligopoly is a market situation in which a few large firms account for the bulk of an industry's sales. Each oligopolist has a large number of the industry's customers, the actions of one firm tend to directly affect the others in the industry, and each tries to anticipate what the others will do. Ready-to-eat breakfast cereals, major home appliances, automobiles, cola drinks, automobile tires, and cigarettes are oligopolistic industries.

monopoly

Monopoly is the opposite of pure competition—one firm produces a product that has no close substitute. A firm with a patent on a process or a product for which there are no substitutes is a monopolist. Other examples are public utilities like natural gas, electricity, water, and telephone. To prevent abuse of their monopoly power, government regulates utilities' rates and services.

DEALING WITH COMPETITORS

An organization has two basic options for dealing with its competitors: (1) imitate them or (2) do things differently in the hope of becoming a unique source of customer satisfaction. A firm has a competitive advantage when its product is perceived to be more satisfying than its rivals' products.

In pursuing that satisfying difference, a firm can engage in price or

price competition

nonprice competition. **Price competition** is a competitive situation in which rivals compete mainly on the basis of price. Examples are supermarkets, discount stores, and discount car rental companies. With price competition the challenge for rivals is to become the low-cost producer or operator.

nonprice competition

Nonprice competition is a competitive situation in which rivals deemphasize the importance of price as a competitive tool. For example, price used to be the main battleground for competitors in the chilled orange juice market. In recent years, Minute Maid, Citrus Hill, and Tropicana have been competing more and more on a nonprice basis. Minute Maid introduced a "country style" product with bits of orange pulp, while Citrus Hill promotes its "delivery system" for calcium.[14] G.D. Searle & Co. created a difference in its field when it became the first pharmaceutical company to offer a money-back guarantee on its prescription drugs.[15] With nonprice competition the challenge for rivals is to create meaningful differences between their products and those of their rivals.

PRODUCTIVITY

As we have seen, U.S. firms are being challenged to increase their productivity. One response by firms in many industries is to replace their outdated plants and equipment. General Electric shut down thirty outdated plants and opened twenty new ones between 1981 and 1986.[16] Many firms are also investing more money in research and development to find new ways to design, produce, and market their products. Many are finding new applications for robots and developing new ways to motivate and manage employees by raising their job satisfaction.

Over the long run, productivity growth is the only way to raise living standards in a country. Since 1981, manufacturing productivity in the United States has grown at an annual rate of nearly 4 percent. This is a big improvement over the 1.3 percent annual rate of growth between 1973 and 1981.[17]

Businesses that become more productive help hold down inflation and improve our global competitiveness. Between November 1982 (when the 1981–1982 recession bottomed out) and November 1986 the number of manufacturing jobs in the United States increased less than 6 percent. Manufacturing output during the same period increased nearly 30 percent. However, there was a marked slowing in the growth of farm productivity and very little growth in productivity in the service industries.[18] In fact, services productivity has shown virtually no growth since the beginning of the 1980s.[19]

GLOBAL COMPETITION

This country has been importing far more than we have been exporting in recent years. (Imported goods accounted for 19 percent of all products sold in the United States in 1986, up from 13.4 percent in 1980.)[20] The U.S. share of the world export market has declined to approximately 11 percent. After World War II, firms in Japan and Western

Like Ford, U.S. firms must focus on quality to increase productivity and compete for global markets.

Europe became ever stronger in competition with U.S. firms for export sales. More recently, newly industrialized countries have become serious rivals for export sales. Examples include Brazil, Mexico, South Korea, Singapore, Hong Kong, and Taiwan.

Clearly, competition is becoming more and more global in nature. Our firms no longer have the U.S. market to themselves. Our traditional dominance in many foreign markets is also being eroded. The Boeing Company, for example, used to dominate in the manufacture of passenger jets. Now Airbus—the aircraft consortium backed by the governments of France, Britain, West Germany, and Spain—has become a major competitor.[21]

Many experts rank poor quality as the major drag on U.S. productivity and competitiveness—and the chief opportunity to trim prices and enhance profits. As many as 25 percent of U.S. factory workers do not produce anything; they simply fix other workers' mistakes.[22]

Improvements are being made. Stiffer foreign competition has paid off in stimulating many of our firms to improve their productivity and profitability. USX, the largest U.S. steelmaker, recently sold 20,000 tons of steel to a company in Osaka at a price 12 percent below what Japanese producers were offering.[23] Ford Motor Company became the world's most profitable automobile company in 1987.[24] As its ad says, "Quality is job one" at Ford today. Not too long ago, a U.S.-made car was a rarity in the parking lot at Hewlett-Packard's plant in California's Silicon Valley. Now there are hundreds of Ford Taurus sedans. Hewlett-Packard also recently bought a fleet of 8,000 Tauruses for staffers to drive.[25] General Electric will replace any major appliance or take it back for a full refund within 90 days of purchase. Whirlpool Corporation's "100 percent customer commitment" program promises to replace any major appliance free of charge within a year if the buyer is not completely satisfied.[26]

Global competition is also challenging the service industries. Dallas-based Pacific Data Services (PDS) subcontracts computer work to data centers in the People's Republic of China. Although some of the Chinese workers do not understand English, they are so careful in copying the information that PDS can guarantee a 99.95 percent accuracy rate in the electronic processing of professional journals and economic statistics. A Chinese worker earns about $4 a day. The salary and benefits for a U.S. worker doing equivalent work would be about $12 an hour.[27]

Challenges in the Social and Cultural Environment

culture

Each of us is born into and grows up in a particular society that influences our basic beliefs, values, and norms. **Culture** is a society's sum total of knowledge, beliefs, values, customs, and artifacts that people use in adapting to their environment and hand down to succeeding generations.

We will refer to certain elements of the social and cultural environment throughout this book. For example, we will see that managers must understand what is important to workers so that they can help those workers become more productive. Marketers also must understand their customers' culture if they are to offer what their customers want. The discussions that follow look briefly at (1) our changing population, (2) cultural values, (3) social responsibility, (4) consumerism and ecology, and (5) business ethics.

OUR CHANGING POPULATION

Among the major changes in our population that are important to businesspeople are the changing age composition, the changing family, the increase in nontraditional households, and geographic shifts in the population.

The average age of the population is rising because of the slowdown in the birthrate and the increase in life expectancy. Figure 2-9 shows actual and projected percentages of the U.S. population 65 years of age and over for selected years. Many firms are having to adjust to an aging population of employees and customers. Fast food restaurants like Burger King, for example, are hiring older people to work in their restaurants.

Some of the changes in the U.S. family involve unmarried mothers, later marriages, smaller families, and a higher divorce rate. Examples of nontraditional households are single adults living alone and cohabiting unmarried couples. Nearly one-fourth of all U.S. children now live with just one parent.[28] The single-adult household can be headed by a person who has never married, a separated person, a divorced person,

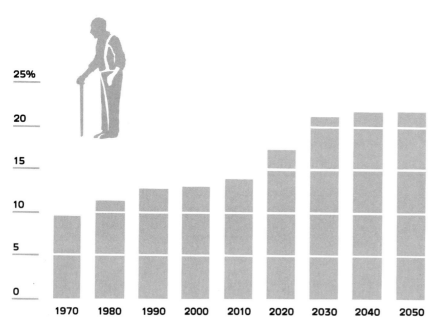

FIGURE 2-9 / Actual and projected percentages of the U.S. population 65 years of age and above. (*Source:* Kenneth H. Bacon, "The Outlook: Easing the Burdens of an Aging America," *The Wall Street Journal,* Sept. 28, 1987, p. 1. From U.S. Census Bureau projections.) Reprinted by permission of *The Wall Street Journal,* © Dow Jones & Company, Inc., 1987. All Rights Reserved.

Increasing numbers of single adults in the U.S. are living alone; they make up an important part of the market for consumer goods and services.

or a surviving spouse. Geographic shifts in the population include the movement of people to the Sunbelt and the movement of people from the central cities to the suburbs.

Some of the toughest issues business faces focus on the firm's relationship with its personnel—the firm's human resource. Business managers must deal with such sensitive and challenging job-related issues as equal opportunity, child care, comparable worth, sexual harassment, alcoholism, smoking, drugs, and a host of other issues ranging from AIDS to immigration laws.

CULTURAL VALUES

cultural values

Cultural values are a society's enduring beliefs that are shared by most of its people. Examples for most Americans include our enduring beliefs about work, leisure, equality, marriage, honesty, youthfulness, and good health. Businesspeople must understand our cultural values because they influence how we behave as employees and customers.

Consider the impact on business of the cultural value of equality. The Equal Employment Opportunity Commission (EEOC) and the U.S. Department of Labor actively enforce equal employment opportunity. Many firms have also put into effect affirmative action plans that were prepared with the EEOC's help. An **affirmative action plan** is a firm's detailed statement describing how it will actively recruit minorities and women and upgrade the jobs they currently hold. Businesses face the challenge of developing plans that are fair to both current and prospective employees.

affirmative action plan

Americans have always prized youthfulness. Think about the money we spend on health spas, weight loss programs, exercise videotapes, and cosmetics. In early 1988, for the first time, drugs started appearing on the market with solid research indicating that they really do reverse some of the minor ravages of age. Science is at the threshold of a new business—"cosmeceuticals."[29]

Although our cultural values are resistant to change, they can change gradually over time, as have our views about women in the labor force. Fuller Brush Company was started in 1906 and for many years sold exclusively through a door-to-door sales force of men. Today, more than 80 percent of Fuller's door-to-door salespeople are women. And because more and more women are working and not at home during the day, Fuller has started to sell through mail-order catalogs and its own retail stores.[30]

Think also about how our ideas on health have changed during recent years. Greater awareness of the dangers of cholesterol has changed our diets. Forty years ago, for example, our per capita consumption of pork was higher than our per capita consumption of beef. Then beef took over and stayed on top until 1987, when poultry jumped to the top.[31]

One of the most serious challenges to business today is the soaring cost of health care. The total medical bill for U.S. health care in 1987 was over $500 billion—or 11 percent of GNP. During the first nine months of 1986, General Motors (GM) spent more than $2 billion on medical care coverage for its employees and retirees and their dependents. In the same period, GM's earned profits were $2.7 billion. Whereas those profits were only marginally higher than they had been a year earlier, the company's health care bill had grown about 30 percent.[32]

SOCIAL RESPONSIBILITY

As we saw in Chapter 1, the social responsibility of business is the concept that business is accountable to various types of stakeholders, including customers, owners, employees, suppliers, and the general public. Some argue that managers must put society's needs ahead of the short-term profit objective. Others say that managers who expect to succeed in the business world must put the profit motive first. Proponents of the social responsibility concept emphasize the long-run welfare of the firm. Opponents are more likely to focus on its short-run welfare.

The traditional yardstick for measuring management's performance is short-run profit. In a large corporation, for example, stockholders (owners) receive quarterly reports on the firm's profit performance. If profits decline for several quarters, some of the firm's top-level managers might be fired.

Many managers know that socially responsible behavior enhances their company's image. This has long-run benefits for the firm. But they might also fear that short-run profit may decline in the meantime. Suppose a firm spends $500,000 to help rebuild a decaying neighborhood in its community. If each of its rivals spends the same amount to buy new cost-saving equipment instead, can the firm compete successfully against them? Although the community will be better off, what about the company, the managers, and the owners? Can we reasonably expect them to take the same long-run view taken by the community?

In general, society is demanding ever higher standards of social responsibility. It is no longer optional in many cases. It is required by laws such as the Clean Air Act and the Highway Safety Act. It is enforced by government agencies such as the Environmental Protection Agency and the National Highway Traffic Safety Administration.

Government regulation is needed when firms, in the pursuit of profit, ignore the public's growing demand for socially responsible behavior. Federal regulations require all firms in an industry to comply with the same clean air standards. This means that no firm is penalized because it tried to behave in a socially responsible manner. Clearly, the choice is between more self-regulation or more government regulation. Businesspeople must integrate the social responsibility concept into their planning and operations.

social audit
Firms that undertake social responsibility programs often conduct social audits. A **social audit** is a thorough examination and assessment of all the activities a firm undertakes to develop social goals and implement social programs. It helps management to assess the success of existing programs and to identify new areas for which programs might be developed. The audit can be conducted by the firm's personnel or by an independent, external consultant.

Socially irresponsible behavior is much more likely to occur when a firm keeps its activities secret from the public. Many firms are disclosing the results of their social audits to the general public in newspaper and magazine ads, TV commercials, and speeches by executives. By publicly disclosing their shortcomings as well as their successes, firms build credibility with the public.

CONSUMERISM AND ECOLOGY

It is important to keep in mind the fact that environmental forces interact. For example, our commitment to consumer and ecology protection is affected by developments in the economy. Consider our nation's energy needs. To reduce our dependence on imported oil, government might permit coal mining in some government-owned wilderness areas and petroleum drilling in vast stretches of undeveloped coastline. But the burning of coal creates more pollution than the burning of oil. How do we balance our desire for preserving "unspoiled areas" against our energy needs? Clearly, environmental protection yields benefits, but it also costs money. Society must decide how to balance these benefits and costs.

consumerism
CONSUMERISM **Consumerism** is the term used to describe organized efforts of consumers to demand honest and fair business practices. The beginnings of the consumer movement in the United States can be traced back to the early 1900s. Upton Sinclair's book *The Jungle* (1906) exposed the filthy conditions in meat-packing plants and helped secure passage that same year of the Pure Food and Drug Act and the Meat Inspection Act.

Firms that see consumerism as a valid reflection of consumer rights respond positively to its challenge. They have, for example, added consumer affairs departments, installed toll-free telephone numbers for consumers to call, and provided more information in their mail-order catalogs. Consumerism now includes such broad areas of concern as equal opportunity, product safety, product warranties, honest advertising, child protection, full disclosure by lenders, fair packaging and labeling, and ecology.

ECOLOGY   As we have seen, ecology is one of consumerism's concerns. **Ecology** is the relationship between living things and their environment. It includes conservation of resources, recycling of used resources, and pollution control. The Environmental Protection Agency (EPA) was established in 1969 to bring under single management the functions of fifteen federal antipollution agencies.

ecology

Pesticides, oil spills, smog, chemical dumping, solid wastes, noxious fumes, and radioactive waste all pollute our air, water, and land. **Pollution** is the contamination of the natural environment by the introduction of harmful substances that endanger our health and even our lives.

pollution

Consumers, businesses, and governments pollute the environment. Have you ever seen someone toss a candy wrapper on the ground? Do you remember the garbage from Islip, New York, that was towed from port to port for months in search of a disposal site? What about aboveground nuclear tests conducted by the government years ago, some of whose effects are just coming to light now?

In some cases we blame business for pollution that is caused by consumers. Because consumers demand convenient packaging of beverages, we have aluminum pop-top cans. But it is consumers, not businesses, who create litter through improper disposal of the used cans.

In other cases the problem lies with the way the good or service is made. For example, chlorofluorocarbons are used as coolants in refrigerators and air conditioners and for making plastic foams. When they rise from the earth, they set off chemical reactions in the stratosphere that rapidly destroy ozone. It is the ozone belt that protects us from the sun's ultraviolet radiation. Acid rain is the by-product of pollution that is emitted from tall smokestacks of coal-burning power plants in the Ohio Valley. It is blamed for damage to fish, forests, wildlife, buildings, and human health.

Regardless of who causes it, ecological damage has always cost society greatly. But it has not always been a dollars-and-cents cost to whoever caused it. Fortunately for society, pollution has become an economic cost. In some states, the law requires consumers to pay a deposit on certain kinds of beverage containers. The containers can be returned to the retail store for a refund of the deposit. The returned cans and bottles go back to the beverage manufacturer for reuse or disposal. Unrefunded deposit money can help pay for cleaning up the pollution caused by improper disposal of containers. Business firms, too, are having to pay fines and clean up costs for the pollution they cause.

Today we have laws covering air, solid waste, and water pollution. We also have laws against pollution by pesticides, noise, toxic substances, and hazardous wastes. It is becoming more and more obvious that pollution is a global problem that must be dealt with on a global scale. For example, representatives from twenty-four countries met in September 1987 to agree in principle to a treaty to limit the production of chlorofluorocarbons and similar compounds that harm the ozone.[33] The World Bank, which makes loans to countries for economic development, has established firm guidelines on how bank projects should avoid or minimize damage to tropical forests, watersheds, and wildlands.[34]

Air pollution is caused by the millions of tons of waste products that are released into the air each year by motor vehicles, power-generating plants, industrial processes, trash disposal incinerators, and municipal waste treatment plants. Illness caused or aggravated by air pollution costs us billions of dollars every year in medical treatment, lost wages, and reduced productivity. Billions more are lost in damage to buildings, personal property, forests, and crops. Indoor air pollution caused by cigarette, pipe, and cigar smoking costs us billions of dollars a year.

Water pollution is caused by obsolete sewage treatment plants, chemicals from industrial processes, runoff water and agricultural waste from farms, and offshore oil spills. Leakage from the millions of tons of buried or inadequately stored toxic wastes has created groundwater pollution in many areas. Although progress has been made in cleaning up our inland waters, we are just beginning to tackle the cleanup of our coastal waters and the seas.

recycling

Land pollution is the result of our "disposable culture," which produces billions of tons of solid waste each year. The waste includes cans, bottles, paper, and many other "throwaway" products as well as junked cars and appliances. The simplest solution is to burn much of it. Burning, however, contributes to air pollution. Another approach is recycling. **Recycling is the reprocessing of used materials for reuse.** It helps decrease land pollution by turning waste into a usable resource. The biggest land pollution problems today are toxic and radioactive wastes. They are also the costliest to deal with.

BUSINESS ETHICS

business ethics

At many points in this book, we will touch upon ethical issues in business. **Business ethics** is a collection of principles and rules of conduct based on beliefs about what is right and wrong business behavior.

In a recent survey, two-thirds of the corporate executives questioned believe that high ethical standards improve a company's competitive position. But the respondents think that "increased concentration on short-term earnings" ranks with "decay in cultural and social institutions" as the principal threats to business ethics today.[35] We will take an in-depth look at business ethics, codes of ethics, and whistle blowing in Chapter 22.

Challenges in the Political-Legal Environment

Government is one of the major institutions in our society. Business influences the way government operates, and government influences the way business operates. These two huge forces interact, as we will see in Chapter 21. The limits and duties that government places on business are major concerns of businesspeople.

COEXISTING WITH GOVERNMENT

As we saw in Chapter 1, government plays a much bigger role in our economy today than the role Adam Smith had in mind. Many people see government as a tool for prodding business and our other social institutions into working toward the goal of economic well-being for everyone. They support politicians who favor greater government regulation over self-regulation of business firms.

On the other hand, many people want government to play a lesser role. They believe that the "dead hand" of government regulation should be replaced by the "invisible hand" of the free market to spur

BUSINESS IN THE NEWS
Coping with Unemployment After a Plant Closure

When Stroh Brewery Company closed its 71-year-old Detroit plant in 1985, almost 1,200 hourly and salaried workers were laid off. By the end of the following year, all the salaried workers and all but thirteen of the hourly workers who participated in Stroh's job-search and retraining program had new jobs. The program involved $2 million in Stroh and government funds; cooperation from unions, local businesses, and communities; and a program developed by a Chicago-based outplacement firm.

The blue-collar program included individual counseling, testing to determine skills, retraining, and a job fair. Stroh spent about $100,000 to renovate a school into a job-search center with free telephones, resource materials, résumé-preparation help, and classes covering such topics as interview techniques, retirement planning, and entrepreneurship. Stroh offered counseling for emotional problems.

Workers were encouraged to sign up for the program during orientation sessions before the plant closed, and they could enter at any time. The program, originally scheduled to close in December 1985, was extended through July 1986.

The outplacement firm developed a computerized skills inventory for each worker in the program, then called 4,000 local companies and said, "Give us names of positions you need to fill, and we'll match them up with our people." Meanwhile, Stroh ran ads in local newspapers encouraging employers to hire its "educated, productive employees" and offering "interviewing facilities and the assistance of job-development specialists eager to work with you."

competition, enhance productivity, and reduce prices.[36] They support politicians who oppose laws and government agencies that they consider to be overly restrictive.

The United States has gone through periods of regulation, deregulation, and reregulation. The challenge to businesspeople is to adapt company actions and policies to the existing political situation. For example, a huge corporation that wants to buy up a major competitor cannot afford to ignore the political environment. Although the laws that pertain to such acquisitions may have been passed years ago, their current interpretation and enforcement are affected by politics.

The traditional adversarial relationship between government and business in the United States is giving way to more cooperation in confronting and solving social problems. For example, government tried to reduce unemployment and poverty with its job training efforts in The Great Society programs of the 1960s. Now the government gives firms subsidies to run training programs to upgrade the skills of the unemployed. Government also gives tax breaks to firms that set up plants in poor neighborhoods. The Business in the News box discusses a program that was put together by government, business, labor, and a local community to deal with a plant closure.

public-private partnership

When government relies more on incentives and less on regulation to get business involved in solving social problems, the number of public-private partnerships increases. **Public-private partnerships** are programs that involve business and government working together to solve social problems. For example, thousands of teenagers looking for summer work in big cities have been hired by such partnerships in recent years.

BUSINESS AND POLITICS

Because the political-legal environment affects business, businesspeople try to influence it. But how deeply involved in politics should business be?

lobbying

One of the oldest approaches to business involvement in politics is lobbying. **Lobbying** is efforts by a group of people who have the same special interest to influence the passage, administration, or enforcement of laws. The American Bankers Association, for example, is an industry association that engages in lobbying. The individual bank members compete with one another, but they do have some common interests.

political action committee (PAC)

The 1974 amendments to the Federal Election Campaign Act permit corporations to form PACs. A **political action committee (PAC)** is a group of people or organizations that is formed to raise campaign contributions for candidates for public office. PACs give corporate employees and others a stronger voice in the election process. Corporations may not contribute to them, though their employees may, and there are limits on what PACs may contribute or expend during campaigns for elective federal offices. PACs must report how much they raised from employees and for whose campaigns the money was spent. Many companies also work through their trade association PACs.

Challenges in the Technological Environment

technology

Technology is the application of science that enables people to do entirely new things or perform established tasks in new and better ways. Technology affects what a society can do and how it goes about doing it, including what goods and services it can produce and how they will be made and distributed.

Business firms, colleges and universities, research foundations, and government contribute to our growing fund of technological knowledge, which doubles at least every ten years. Competition among business firms is often based mainly on technology. The United States is also involved in various "technological races" with other nations. For example, we are in a technological race with the Japanese in artificial intelligence and with the Soviets in conducting complex scientific missions in space.

Basic, or scientific, research focuses on acquiring new knowledge. *Applied* research, or engineering, is concerned with the application of knowledge—how the knowledge can be used. It is through research in the physical sciences (physics, chemistry, geology, etc.), the social sciences (psychology, sociology, anthropology, etc.), the biological sciences (botany, microbiology, zoology, etc.), and mathematics that knowledge is acquired and applied.

Business firms spend billions of dollars every year in their research and development (R&D) departments. They conduct both pure and ap-

This scientist is engaging in applied biomedical research. The goal is to produce artificial blood.

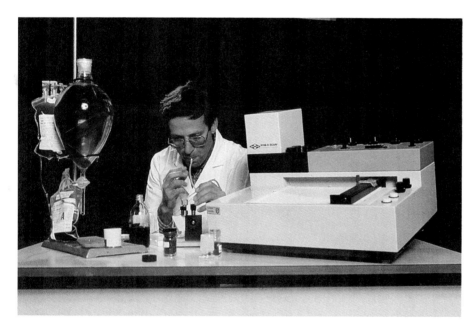

plied research with the ultimate objective of developing new products. U.S. firms devoted 3.4 percent of their sales revenues to R&D in 1987. Some firms, of course, invested a much higher percentage. For example, Digital Equipment Corporation and Eastman Kodak devoted 10.8 percent and 7.5 percent, respectively, of their sales revenues to R&D in that same year.[37]

APPLYING TECHNOLOGY

The application of technology has raised our standard of living. It has given us a great variety of new products, increased our productivity, and contributed to healthier and longer lives. It has also given us more leisure time, helped us cope with problems like dwindling energy supplies, and reduced the need for humans to perform dangerous and unhealthy jobs. On the other hand, the application of technology has added to social problems like unemployment, pollution, crime, and stress on the job. However, other technology might reduce or overcome some of these negative effects. While one type of technology might create pollution, another type might clean it up.

A major challenge to businesses is to keep informed of relevant scientific and engineering advances. Managers can monitor the technological environment by scanning scientific journals, observing new products at trade shows, and attending technological conferences. Firms in high-technology industries engage in technology forecasting. **Technology forecasting** is the process of gathering and interpreting evidence of scientific advances in a field and forecasting the direction of technological change and its impact on the firm.

Firms conduct cost-benefit studies to determine whether they can use new technology in their operations. This *technological assessment* requires that a firm consider the impact of adopting the new technology. Even after a firm has adopted new technology, it may decide to drop it. For example, Federal Express Corporation introduced ZapMail, an electronic document transmission service in 1984. The company scrapped the service in 1986 because of technical bugs and customer resistance to its relatively high price.

STRUCTURAL UNEMPLOYMENT

Technological change creates *structural unemployment*. The structurally unemployed are people who lack the skills needed for available jobs. Unemployed steel workers, for example, could lack the skills for available high-technology jobs in the microelectronics industry.

The challenge for business is to assist in retraining and relocating these people for jobs that are opening up. Some people believe the solution lies in "high tech." High-technology firms spend heavily on R&D and have a high percentage of technical workers on their payrolls. But productivity is rising so fast in high-tech industries that they cannot absorb many additional workers. Some high-tech firms are also moving their manufacturing operations to lower-wage countries. Many high-tech jobs can be filled by unskilled, low-cost workers overseas.

technology forecasting

Many of the structurally unemployed are finding work in the service industries, but they often earn less money. And, as we saw earlier in this chapter, service jobs can also be moved overseas.

TECHNOLOGY TRANSFER

The patent process in the United States serves to protect new ideas or products from being copied here for a period of seventeen years. International agreements also protect ideas and inventions from being copied in some other nations. However, such protections are ignored in some countries, and many new products and processes are brought into the world marketplace illegally. Coping with the growing volume of *counterfeit products* is a major challenge for firms ranging from manufacturers of airplane parts to manufacturers of blue jeans. Counterfeit airplane parts have been suspected of causing several major plane crashes.

Lack of a basic educational structure and a skilled labor force limits the spread of new technology to the less-developed countries. For example, there would be little chance to develop and apply nuclear medical technology or robotics in Somalia or Haiti. Far more likely is the opportunity to spread the use of simpler technologies, sometimes called *appropriate technologies.*

Because much of the technology developed in the United States today has military application, our government limits or prohibits its flow to other nations. The Department of Defense and the Department of Commerce exercise control over what can be exported from the United States and to whom it can be exported. It has been estimated that U.S. restrictions on high-tech exports cost U.S. businesses more than $11 billion a year in lost business.[38] That lost business could have helped to offset our balance of trade deficit. But there has been a string of scandals involving the transfer of technology to the Soviet bloc. The most publicized case in recent years involved a subsidiary of Japanese-based Toshiba. In 1987 the United States learned that the subsidiary had slipped to the Soviet Union machines that enabled the Soviets to build submarines quiet enough to escape U.S. naval detection.[39]

Summary

The business environment is made up of forces in the economic, competitive, social and cultural, political-legal, and technological environment. This environment is the source of opportunities and challenges for the business firm.

Macroeconomics is concerned with the economic system as a whole. We use monetary policy and fiscal policy in dealing with macroeconomic problems. Microeconomics, on the other hand, focuses on the individual decision-making units within the economic system. The forces of supply and demand determine how the factors of production will be used and how the output will be distributed in a market economy. These forces interact to determine prices. A healthy economy is good for business. The vast majority of firms are more profitable during expansionary phases of the business cycle than during contractionary phases. Among the major economic challenges facing business today are federal budget deficits, international trade deficits, the decline of "smokestack America," and energy supplies.

The nature of the competitive environment within which a firm exists depends a lot on the type of market structure: pure competition, monopolistic competition, oligopoly, or monopoly. Nonprice competition deemphasizes the importance of price as a competitive tool. Among the major challenges in the competitive environment are enhancing our productivity and meeting the challenge of increasingly global competition.

The culture within which business is conducted is a major source of challenges. Changing ages, lifestyles, and locations of customers affect business. Changes in our cultural values can also pose serious challenges to business. In general, society is demanding more and more that business meet its social responsibility. Major challenges here include responding to consumerism and ecological concerns. Society also expects firms to behave ethically in dealings with their stakeholders.

The political-legal environment is a major source of challenges. The traditional adversarial relationship between business and government is giving way to more cooperation in solving social problems. The activities of lobbyists and political action committees often raise the issue of business's involvement in politics.

Our technological knowledge is increasing at an explosive rate. There is little doubt that the application of technology has benefited us. But it can also add to social problems. Structural unemployment and the issue of technology transfer are among the challenges that business confronts in this area.

Review Questions

1. How does macroeconomics differ from microeconomics?

2. Explain the interaction of supply and demand forces to determine an equilibrium price.

3. What is meant by a "weak" U.S. dollar?

4. Why is productivity so important to business firms?

5. What are the four basic types of market structures?

6. What is meant by global competition?

7. What is the traditional yardstick for measuring management's performance? How does this affect the issue of business's social responsibility?

8. What is the nature of consumerism in the consumer movement's current era?

9. What is a public-private partnership?

10. What is the relationship between technological change and structural unemployment?

Discussion Questions

1. What types of business firms might sell more and be more profitable during the contractionary stages of the business cycle?

2. Why should businesspeople be concerned about huge federal budget deficits and international trade deficits?

3. Is free trade good for the United States?

4. Some countries have tougher pollution laws than other countries. Firms in all of these countries often compete with each other in the global marketplace. What are the implications regarding their relative productivity?

5. Should the U.S. government give tax breaks and other types of help to save our declining "smokestack" industries?

Key Terms

monetary policy
fiscal policy
market economy
law of supply
law of demand
business cycle
trade war
productivity
competition
pure competition

monopolistic competition
oligopoly
monopoly
price competition
nonprice competition
culture
cultural values
affirmative action plan
social audit
consumerism

ecology
pollution
recycling
business ethics
public-private partnership
lobbying
political action committee (PAC)
technology
technology forecasting

Cases

SONY MAKES A BIG DECISION

Sony Corporation started the home video revolution in the United States when it introduced its first Betamax model in 1975. But it failed to persuade some rivals to adopt the same technical standards. They brought out the incompatible VHS machines, which ran away with the market, partly because they initially allowed for longer taping. Moreover, while some people said Beta provided a superior picture, more prerecorded material was available in the VHS format.

In 1983, Sony of America executives concluded that Sony had lost the format battle. But the parent company continued to fight. On principle, Sony preferred the superior technology, and it feared alienating the big base of Beta devotees.

In 1987, Sony said that it saw no point in entering a market that had turned fiercely competitive with manufacturers proliferating, sales growth lagging, and prices tumbling. "We don't like to just chase sales volume—we like to do the more profitable items," the chairman of Sony of America said in October 1987. In the United States alone, manufacturers' sales of VCRs totaled $5.25 billion in 1987. But sales of the hottest growth product in consumer electronics in the 1980s were stagnating, largely because 52 percent of U.S. households—up from 3 percent six years earlier—already had VCRs.

Early in 1988, Sony announced plans to sell VHS machines in Europe, starting in the spring. Sony Corporation of America announced that it would introduce the VHS machines later that fall. Sony said that some consumers prefer to buy systems of a single brand, so the existence of Sony VHS recorders might help sell Sony TV sets. Also, dealers had pressured Sony to sell VHS machines, thinking its name would make for an especially salable item.

But Sony of America saw little chance of making a profit on VHS machines at the low end of the market, where many companies churn out essentially similar commodities. Sony of America planned to develop new features and special designs.[40]

Questions

1. Why have prices of VCRs come down over the years?
2. How do marketers that "churn out essentially similar commodities" make money in the VCR market?
3. How important is technology in the market for consumer electronics?

CASTING A VOTE ON CORPORATE SOCIAL RESPONSIBILITY

The Council on Economic Priorities, which was founded in 1969, gets most of its funding from individuals and foundations. Its goal is to enhance corporate performance as it affects society in critically important areas such as military spending, political influence, and fair-employment practices.

Recently, the Council issued its first comprehensive shopping guide for the socially conscious consumer: *Rating America's Corporate Conscience*. The book rates food products, health-care products, automobiles, hotels, appliances, and dozens of other consumer products according to various categories of social performance. The authors said, "This book will help you cast an economic vote on corporate social responsibility when you shop— whether you're buying toothpaste, a typewriter, or an airline ticket."

The book is filled with charts that list various products by brand name, tell what company produces each product, and then rank the company on key social concerns. The principal criteria include: (1) Does the company invest in South Africa, and if so, has it complied with the Sullivan principles on fair labor practices? (2) How much of its annual earnings does the company contribute to charity? (3) Does the company have women or minorities on its board of directors or among its officers? (4) Does the company have contracts related to conventional or nuclear weapons? (5) Is the company willing to provide facts and figures on its social programs?[41]

Questions

1. Is the Council on Economic Priorities conducting social audits?
2. Describe what you think would be the characteristics of a typical purchaser of the book *Rating America's Corporate Conscience*.
3. What is meant by "This book will help you cast an economic vote on corporate social responsibility when you shop—whether you're buying toothpaste, a typewriter, or an airline ticket"?

THREE

LEARNING OBJECTIVES

After reading this chapter, you will be able to:

- Compare the advantages and disadvantages of sole proprietorships, partnerships, and corporations.
- Explain the procedure for forming a corporation.
- Distinguish between close and open corporations.
- Contrast common stockholders and preferred stockholders.
- Explain the tasks of a corporation's board of directors.
- State the advantages and disadvantages of large-scale business operations.
- Describe changing patterns of corporate ownership.
- Identify and explain forms of ownership other than sole proprietorships, partnerships, and corporations.

Forms of Business Ownership

W H A T ' S
A H E A D

n this chapter we will look at the three major forms of business ownership in the United States: the *sole proprietorship*, the *partnership*, and the *corporation*. Most U.S. firms are sole proprietorships, but corporations account for a disproportionate share of the sales revenues and profits of U.S. firms.

We will look at the advantages and disadvantages of each form of ownership. As will become clear, no one form is "best" in all situations; the one that is best for a one-outlet auto repair shop is not likely to be the best for a company that manufactures automobiles.

Because the corporation is the most complex form of ownership, we will examine it in considerable detail. We will discuss how a corporation is formed, common and preferred stockholders, the board of directors, and corporate officers. We will also look at the advantages and disadvantages of large-scale operations and the changing patterns of corporate ownership in recent years. These days the ownership and control of big corporations are very much in the news.

In the last part of the chapter we will focus attention on other forms of business ownership that have evolved from the three major forms. These are the limited partnership, the joint venture, the cooperative association, and the mutual company. These forms have evolved to overcome some of the disadvantages of the sole proprietorship, the partnership, and the corporation.

James Koch gave up a $250,000 job with the Boston Consulting Group to start his own brewery. He is now the Chief Executive Officer of The Boston Beer Company, which produces Samuel Adams Boston

Lager. Samuel Adams has been chosen the best beer in America for the past three years. Mr. Koch says that his family recipe for the beer is what has fueled the success of his business venture. He wanted to structure his business to ensure a strong personal tie between Jim Koch and the company and between Jim Koch and the beer. To protect the integrity of the beer, Mr. Koch is the sole keeper of the recipe.

When starting the business, Mr. Koch discovered that he needed more capital than he was able to personally invest. Although a sole proprietorship was out of the question for him, Mr. Koch also rejected the option of incorporating, since his control over the operation would be diluted by the control of the stockholders. He did not want to consider a partnership, in which he would have to share the management of the business with a partner.

To attract investment money, Mr. Koch decided to form a limited partnership of about 25 partners with himself as the single general partner. The limited partners receive a financial return on their investment, while the general partner has complete management control of the business. When Mr. Koch needed additional money to open a new brewery, he was able to attract an additional $4 million through this arrangement and still retain absolute control of The Boston Beer Company.

Before he started in business, Mr. Koch had to decide the form of ownership that would best meet his particular needs. As it turned out, none of the three major forms—the corporation, the general partnership, and the corporation—was ideal. Instead, Mr. Koch settled on the limited partnership as the best form of ownership in his specific situation. Let's begin the chapter with a closer look at the forms of ownership of a business firm.

The Sole Proprietorship

sole proprietorship

Figure 3-1 shows the three major forms of private business ownership. The sole proprietorship is the oldest and most common form of private ownership in the United States. A **sole proprietorship** is a business owned by one person. The sole proprietor is the classic example of the entrepreneur.

ADVANTAGES OF THE SOLE PROPRIETORSHIP

Suppose John Brady wants to go into the automobile detailing business. Detailers perform an extremely thorough job of cleaning cars. John might find that the sole proprietorship is the easiest way to go into

Sole Proprietorship	Partnership	Corporation
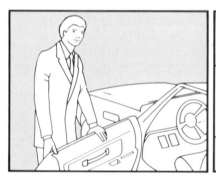		
John Brady, sole proprietor	John Brady and Marcy Feinberg, partners doing business as Squeeky Kleen Kar Kompanie	John Brady and Marcy Feinberg, among the stockholders in Squeeky Kleen Kar Kompanie, Inc.

FIGURE 3-1 / The three major forms of business ownership.

business. There are no laws on setting up a sole proprietorship. Of course, the business must be legal, and local and state laws require licenses and permits. Usually, the sole proprietor must register the firm's name at the county courthouse. This way two firms cannot operate under the same name. Otherwise, John can go into business any time he pleases. Starting the business is simple in a sole proprietorship.

As sole owner, John owns the firm and its profits (or losses) outright. John will enjoy the freedom of being his own boss—he will work for himself. He will also get a lot of satisfaction out of watching the firm grow under his guidance. Sole proprietors are very much involved in their businesses.

Auto detailing can provide a business opportunity for sole proprietorships, partnerships, and corporations.

The sole proprietorship has another advantage. The owner can make management decisions without approval from anyone else. John can decide for himself what hours to work and whether to expand his business. He also does not have to reveal his business plans to outsiders. He need not disclose financial data to anyone except tax collectors.

John is the firm, so he pays only personal income taxes on its profits. There is no income tax on the firm as a separate entity.

If John wants to discontinue his business, he simply sells his inventory and equipment. He does not need permission from anyone to dissolve the business. To sum up, sole proprietors:

- find it simple to start the business and easy to dissolve it;
- own all profits;
- derive personal satisfaction from being one's own boss;
- can make management decisions without approval from anyone else;
- pay no tax on profits of the business as a separate entity, only on personal income.

DISADVANTAGES OF THE SOLE PROPRIETORSHIP

unlimited liability

Because John is the firm, he is legally liable for all its debts. He has unlimited liability. **Unlimited liability** means that the business owner is responsible for claims against the firm that go beyond the value of the owner's ownership in the firm. Liability could extend to John's personal property (furniture, car, and personal savings) and, in some states, his real property (home and other real estate). Suppose John goes out of business. He sells his inventory, equipment, and other business property but still owes his creditors $25,000. Those creditors can legally lay claim to John's nonbusiness property.

Business creditors can force John to withdraw money from his personal savings account. He might also have to sell his car and other personal property. In some states he would have to sell his home. This unlimited liability exists because there is no legal distinction between John and his business. He risks losing everything he owns.

The amount of money John can invest in the firm is limited. All he can invest is what he has and what he can borrow. In many cases it is difficult to raise more money. Such limitations discourage this type of ownership.

The firm's success often depends on one person's talents and management skills. John might find that, as the firm grows, he is spreading himself too thin. Making one's own management decisions might no longer be an advantage. If John's talents and skills are not enough, problems will crop up. At this point, John must be willing to share some of the management tasks with others.

If John were to die, go to prison, or go insane, the business would legally end. It could be passed on to a son or daughter, but then a new proprietorship would be formed. A sole proprietorship is not permanent. This makes it hard for the firm to grow and attract employees who want permanent jobs with opportunities for career advancement. To sum up, sole proprietors:

- have unlimited financial liability;
- have difficulty raising funds for expansion;
- often have no one to share the management burden;
- suffer from impermanence of the firm.

The Partnership

partnership

Most states have adopted the Uniform Partnership Act. It defines a **partnership** as "an association of two or more persons to carry on as co-owners of a business for profit." Partnerships came about to overcome some of the more serious drawbacks of sole proprietorships. Both date back to ancient times.

ADVANTAGES OF THE PARTNERSHIP

partnership agreement

Suppose that instead of going into business as a sole proprietor, John Brady and Marcy Feinberg form a partnership. John and Marcy have to enter into a partnership agreement, called the *Articles of Partnership* or *Articles of Copartnership*. A **partnership agreement** is an oral or written contract between the owners of a partnership that identifies the business and states the partners' respective rights and obligations. The agreement states the name, location, and business of the firm. It also specifies the mutual understanding of each owner's duties, obligations, and rights in running the business, sharing in the profits or losses, withdrawing from the business, and dissolving the partnership.

Although the agreement can be oral or written, putting it in writing is wise to help avoid future conflict between the partners. Other than setting up this agreement, getting started is as simple as for the sole proprietorship.

Because John and Marcy are in business together, they can pool their funds, talents, and borrowing power. They can invest more than either one could invest alone, and they are more able to borrow money. By pooling their talents they can divide the tasks and enjoy the benefits of specialization.

Like a sole proprietorship, a partnership is not taxed as a business separate from its owners. The owners, not the firm, are taxed. To sum up, partners:

- can start a business with little difficulty;
- can pool their funds, talents, and borrowing power;
- have more chance to specialize than sole proprietors;
- also enjoy personal satisfaction in running the business;
- also pay no tax on profits of the business as a separate entity, only on their own personal incomes.

DISADVANTAGES OF THE PARTNERSHIP

In a *general partnership*, all partners, like sole proprietors, have unlimited financial liability for the partnership's debts. It is a *joint liabil-*

FIGURE 3-2 / A partnership agreement.

PARTNERSHIP AGREEMENT

THIS PARTNERSHIP AGREEMENT made and entered into this first day of January 1989 by and between John Brady of Los Angeles, California and Marcy Feinberg of Los Angeles, California.

WITNESSETH:

1. The parties hereby agree to form a partnership.

2. The name of the partnership shall be Squeeky Kleen Kar Kompanie.

3. The business to be conducted shall be an automobile detailing business.

4. The principal place of business of the partnership shall be at 807 East Main Avenue, Los Angeles, California.

5. The capital of the partnership is to consist of the sum of $80,000. John Brady is to contribute $40,000 in cash, and Marcy Feinberg is to contribute $40,000 in cash. No interest shall be paid to the partners on any contributions to capital.

6. Whenever required, additional capital shall be contributed by the partners in proportion of the initial capital contribution.

7. The net profits of the partnership shall be divided equally, and the partners shall equally bear the net losses.

8. Each partner shall be entitled to a drawing account as may be mutually agreed upon.

9. Neither partner shall receive a salary.

10. Each partner shall have an equal right in the management of the partnership.

11. John Brady shall devote his entire time and attention to the business. Marcy Feinberg shall devote her entire time and attention to the business.

12. Either partner may retire from the partnership after giving the other partner at least 90 days written notice of his or her intention so to do. The remaining partner shall have the option of purchasing the retiring partner's interest or to terminate and liquidate the business. The purchase price shall be the balance in the retiring partner's capital account based upon an audit by an independent public accountant to the date of retirement. The purchase price shall be payable 50 percent in cash and the balance in 36 equal monthly installments and shall not bear interest.

13. Upon the death of a partner, the surviving partner shall have the option to either purchase the interest of the decedent or to terminate and liquidate the business. The purchase price and payment shall be the same as above set forth.

14. The partnership shall begin the tenth day of January 1989 and shall continue until dissolved by retirement or death of a partner or by mutual agreement of the partners.

IN WITNESS WHEREOF, the parties have signed this agreement.

Witnesses:

Mason Durio _John Brady_ (SEAL)

Laurence Dauser _Marcy Feinberg_ (SEAL)

ity. This means that John is responsible for business debts incurred by Marcy and vice versa. Their combined personal and (in most states) real property are available to their business creditors.

A *limited partnership* is another type of partnership permitted under the law. It limits the liability of one or more, but not all, of the partners. We discuss the limited partnership more fully later in the chapter.

Suppose John and Marcy's business fails. They still owe creditors $50,000 after selling the partnership's property to pay off the creditors. Look at the partnership agreement in Figure 3-2. John and Marcy each contributed $40,000 in cash (see #5) to start the business. They agreed to bear equally any losses (see #7). But suppose Marcy can pay off only $20,000 of her $25,000 share of the unpaid debt. She has already sold off all her personal and real property. John will be liable for paying his $25,000 plus the $5,000 Marcy is unable to pay.

In forming a partnership, one must choose one's partner(s) with great care. Personal conflicts cause many business failures. Typical disagreements are over how long the partners intend to be in business, the amount of money each is to invest, what their salaries will be, how profits or losses will be shared, the duties of each, procedures for ad-

Disability coverage is one of many details that should be considered in forming a partnership.

mitting new partners, and procedures for dissolving the partnership. This is why the partnership agreement should be in writing.

A partnership is legally ended upon the death, withdrawal, or insanity of a partner. The heir of a deceased partner is not a partner. If the surviving partner and the heir agree, however, they can form a new partnership. In some cases, partners buy partnership insurance and enter into a buy-and-sell agreement. This ensures that money will be available upon the death of one partner. Then the other(s) can buy out the deceased partner's share from the estate. The buy-and-sell agreement spells out the value of the partnership shares. It also preserves the business for surviving partners. As suggested in the New York Life ad (on p. 75), partners should also consider disability insurance protection.

A partner cannot simply withdraw his or her investment in the business. He or she must find someone who is willing to buy in. That person can be an outsider or a present partner. In either case that person must be acceptable to the remaining partner(s). In a sense, each partner's investment is frozen in the business. To sum up, partnerships suffer from:

- unlimited and joint financial liability;
- the potential for personal disagreement;
- impermanence of the firm;
- the freezing of each partner's investment in the business.

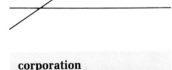

The Corporation

corporation

The corporate form of ownership overcomes some of the disadvantages of sole proprietorships and partnerships. A **corporation** is a legally chartered organization that is a separate and legal entity apart from its owners. It has most of the rights that a person has. For example, it can

The corporate form of organization is not restricted to business firms.

buy, hold, and sell property in its own name. A corporation is created when the incorporators (founders) apply for and are granted a charter by the state in which the organization is being formed.

Besides being a form of business ownership, the corporate form is also suitable for nonprofit organizations such as municipalities, charities, churches, political parties, colleges, and museums. Nonprofit organizations incorporate to qualify as nontaxable entities and to provide legal protection for their members.

ADVANTAGES OF THE CORPORATION

stockholders

A corporation issues stock certificates to its stockholders as evidence of ownership in the corporation. **Stockholders,** or shareholders, are the owners of a corporation. Each stockholder becomes a part-owner of the corporation by buying shares of its stock. A stockholder owns part interest in the entire corporation. The value of that part varies as the value of the shares of stock changes. This is determined by the supply of and demand for the shares on the market.

Because a corporation is a separate and legal entity, a corporation's stockholders are not the corporation. The stockholders therefore have limited financial liability. This is the corporation's major advantage over sole proprietorships and partnerships. If you buy stock in a corporation, the most you can lose is what you pay for your shares. This is true regardless of how much the firm owes its creditors. The corporation itself, however, has unlimited liability. For example, suppose a corporation owns another firm (a subsidiary) and is unable to pay off its debts. The corporation can be forced to sell its subsidiary to get money to pay the debts.

Let's return to John and Marcy's business. Suppose the partnership is successful and the owners want to expand by opening three new shops. However, John and Marcy have little money to put into expansion, and they have borrowed up to their credit limit.

A logical step would be to incorporate. Suppose John and Marcy need $500,000 to expand. It would be hard to borrow a lump sum of $500,000. It would be just as hard to find another partner willing to put up the entire amount. They might find it easier to get 1,000 people to invest $500 each. Corporations usually find it easier to get money for expansion than sole proprietorships and partnerships do.

A corporation can exist forever because it is separate from its owners. The death, insanity, or imprisonment of a stockholder does not end the corporation. This permanence helps to attract personnel who value long-term career advancement potential with one firm.

A proprietor might have trouble selling his or her business. Selling one's interest in a partnership requires the approval of the other partners. But transfer of ownership is simple in a corporation. Stockholders just sell their shares of stock. They do not need permission from anyone else. All they need is a buyer.

Organized stock exchanges such as the New York Stock Exchange make it easy for buyers and sellers to deal with each other. Every day, millions of shares in hundreds of corporations are traded. Very seldom do the buyer and seller see each other. They buy and sell through

APPLICATION: BURGER KING
Acquisition by Pillsbury

The headlines in the trade paper *Nation's Restaurant News* said it all: "Pillsbury's restaurant sales depress corporate profits." Apparently, slumping sales at several of Pillsbury's restaurant chains were keeping Pillsbury's profits down. Analysts knew that something would have to be done about it. The question was what.

The destinies of Burger King and Pillsbury became intertwined in 1967, when Burger King's founders, James W. McLamore and Edgerton, sold their company to Pillsbury. By 1967 the Burger King chain had grown to 274 restaurants. However, McDonald's was growing quickly by then. McLamore and Edgerton knew that to maintain market share would take a lot more money than even their very successful firm could muster.

Therefore in 1967 they sold Burger King to Pillsbury for $18 million. Joining the diversified food giant provided several big advantages for Burger King. Pillsbury could provide financial clout to expand more quickly and to finance the opening of many new stores. And the giant food firm's depth of planning and management experience could help the small but growing Burger King to compete in the big leagues.

For Pillsbury the acquisition also seemed to be a good idea. When a firm is as large as Pillsbury, it cannot always continue to grow as quickly as firms do when they are small. Burger King, said Pillsbury's president at the time, was thus "an opportunity to participate in the rising trend toward more away from home meals. Burger King has demonstrated the ability of a franchise to grow in the most rapidly expanding segment of the food business, where quality, convenience, and economy are important."

On the whole, the arrangement has worked out about as planned for both Burger King and Pillsbury. Burger King opened 274 restaurants in the first thirteen years of its existence. In the next ten years under Pillsbury, Burger King opened about 1,700 new restaurants; the 2,000th restaurant opened in 1977 in Hawaii, putting locations in all 50 states.

What then is the drawback to being acquired by a large-scale corporation? For one thing the acquired firm's destiny is no longer just in its own hands. Now a board of directors and top executives at the parent firm must assess and approve big decisions. Being owned by a big corporation can provide the funds and clout a company needs to grow. But it can also mean being governed by an outside force that could cut off all those funds. This can even mean being sold off, against the smaller firm's will. John Stafford, a former Pillsbury president, had an elegant silver-framed motto on his desk saying, "Bad numbers will get you every time."

Questions
1. Why do you think Burger King's founders sold the company to Pillsbury?

2. Did Pillsbury's purchase of Burger King constitute a hostile takeover?

3. Does Burger King face competition from any sole proprietorships?

Sources: "Pillsbury Co. Says It Agreed 'in Principle' to Buy Burger King," *The Wall Street Journal*, Jan. 20, 1967, p. 12; "Too Many Cooks in Pillsbury's Kitchen?" *Business Week*, Jan. 25, 1988, pp. 56–58; "Pillsbury's Restaurant Sales Depress Corporate Profits," *Nations Restaurants News*, March 9, 1987, p. 168.

stockbrokers. We will discuss the operation of stock exchanges in Chapter 18. To sum up, a corporation:

- exists as a separate legal entity;
- provides limited liability for its owners;
- enjoys long life;
- transfers ownership easily;
- has more financial capability.

DISADVANTAGES OF THE CORPORATION

One of the biggest drawbacks to the corporate form of ownership is that corporations are subject to special taxation. Sole proprietorships and partnerships do not pay income taxes as business firms. The owners pay the income taxes. As an entity separate from its owners, however, a corporation pays federal and state taxes on its profits. If the corporation pays cash dividends to stockholders from its after-tax profits, the stockholders pay personal income taxes on the dividends. From the stockholder's perspective, corporate profits are taxed twice. Furthermore, corporations pay franchise taxes to states in which they do business.

S corporation

There is a way for corporations to avoid double taxation. An **S corporation** is a corporation with no more than 35 stockholders that has the option of being taxed somewhat like a partnership. An S corporation pays no income tax as a firm. This means that there is more profit left for the owners to divide. The owners pay taxes on the dividends they receive from the corporation. They enjoy the advantages of incorporation while avoiding double taxation.

To be granted a charter, incorporators must conform to state laws. Each state has its own incorporation laws, and some of them are complex. Often a lawyer is hired to set up a corporation. Lawyers' fees and state incorporation fees must be paid.

Clearly, corporations are more difficult and costly to form than sole proprietorships and partnerships. They are also more difficult and costly to dissolve.

Corporations are subject to more state and federal laws and public disclosure requirements. If a corporation wants to sell its shares of stock nationwide, it must get approval from the Securities and Exchange Commission (SEC). A new corporation might want to sell its shares only in the state where it is incorporated. Then it must get approval from a state agency, usually the secretary of state. Corporations also are required to file reports and publish information about their operations and finances. Complying with public disclosure requirements is costly, and the information can often be used by competitors. It can also put managers under so much pressure to achieve short-term earnings targets that they neglect long-term strategic planning. To sum up, corporations suffer from:

- special and double taxation;
- complex and costly formation and dissolution;
- considerable government regulation and public disclosure requirements.

Form of Ownership	Advantages	Disadvantages
Sole proprietorship 	• Simple to start • Proprietor owns all profits • Personal satisfaction • Sole decision maker • No tax on business as distinct from owner • Easy to dissolve	• Unlimited financial liability • Hard to raise funds for expansion • Often have no one to share management burden
Partnership 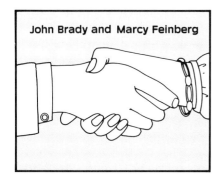	• Few restrictions on starting • Pooling of funds, talents, and borrowing power • More chance to specialize than sole proprietorship • Personal satisfaction • No tax on business as distinct from owners	• Unlimited and joint financial liability • Potential for personal disagreements • Relative impermanence • Frozen investment
Corporation 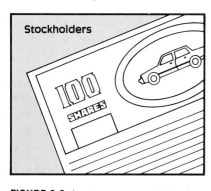	• Separate legal entity • Limited financial liability of owners • Long life • Easy transfer of ownership • Greater financial capability	• Special and double taxation • Complex and costly to form • Government regulation and public disclosure requirements

FIGURE 3-3 / Advantages and disadvantages of the major forms of ownership.

Figure 3-3 summarizes the advantages and disadvantages of the three forms of business ownership. Figure 3-4 indicates that of the almost 17.5 million business firms in the United States, 70 percent are sole proprietorships, 20 percent are corporations, and 10 percent are partnerships.

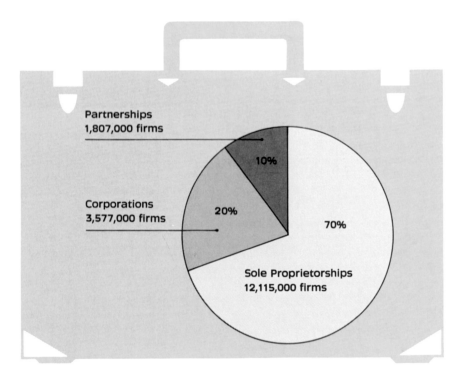

Partnerships
1,807,000 firms

Corporations
3,577,000 firms

10%

20%

70%

Sole Proprietorships
12,115,000 firms

FIGURE 3-4 / U.S. business firms by form of ownership. (*Source: The State of Small Business: A Report of the President,* U.S. Government Printing Office, Washington, D.C., 1987, p. 15.)

FORMING A CORPORATION

Although it is not necessary, people who plan to form a corporation should consult a lawyer to help ensure that they do not overlook any important legal requirements. Choosing a state in which to incorporate is a major decision because legal requirements and incorporation fees vary from state to state. Delaware is the most popular state in which to incorporate—40 percent of the companies listed on the New York Stock Exchange and about half of the Fortune 500 companies are incorporated there.[1] Corporate fees and taxes are Delaware's second-highest source of revenue, after personal income taxes.[2]

Corporations can be classified as domestic, foreign, or alien. A corporation is considered to be a *domestic* corporation in the state in which it is incorporated. In other states where it plans to do business, it must register as a *foreign* corporation. If it plans to do business in other nations, it must register in each of them as an *alien* corporation (see Figure 3-5 on p. 82).

Each state has a state official or agency that provides incorporators with an application for a corporate charter. Usually, it is the secretary of state. After the form has been properly filled in and returned along with the required fees, the secretary of state checks to make sure the corporate name has not already been taken by another firm, and then **corporate charter** issues the corporate charter. A **corporate charter** is a contract between the incorporators and the state that authorizes the formation of the corporation. In most cases the secretary of state also sends a copy of the charter to the clerk of the county in which the new corporation's head-

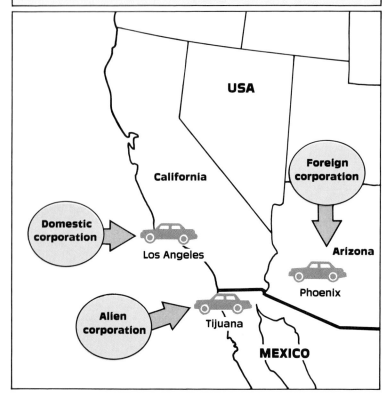

John Brady and Marcy Feinberg incorporated Squeeky Kleen Kar Kompanie in Los Angeles, California, and the corporation is doing business in Phoenix, Arizona, and Tijuana, Mexico:

FIGURE 3-5 / Classification of a corporation based on where it is doing business.

quarters is located. The charter is notarized (certified, or made legally effective) by the county clerk and recorded.

THE STOCKHOLDERS

As we saw earlier, the owners of a corporation are called stockholders, or shareholders. *Close corporations* are owned by a few stockholders. Stock (shares of ownership) in such corporations is not actively or widely traded on stock exchanges. Family businesses are often close corporations. Sometimes, even large corporations are owned by only a few stockholders. Their stock is not actively or widely traded either. Examples of close corporations include E&J Gallo Winery, Inc. and Mars, Inc. (the manufacturer of Milky Way candy bars and Kal Kan pet food). Such corporations can also be described as *privately held, closely held,* or *private corporations*. In many cases, most shares of a close corporation are owned by one family. For example, the O'Malley family has owned the Los Angeles Dodgers for well over three decades. This is the last team that is controlled by a family with no other major source of income.[3]

Open corporations are owned by a large number of stockholders. Stock may be actively or widely traded. Thus the investment is highly *liquid*—it can be converted into cash quickly. IBM, GM, and AT&T are examples of open corporations. They are often called *publicly held corporations* or simply *public corporations*. This means that many members of the general public own their stock.

Sometimes a small, closely held corporation offers shares of stock for sale to the public. This is referred to as *going public*. Apple Computer and Home Shopping Network were once closely held but are now publicly held.

Taking a corporation private is the opposite of going public (see Figure 3-6). In this case, one or a few stockholders and/or corporate officers buy the stock owned by many other stockholders, and a formerly open corporation becomes a close corporation. Recent examples are Mary Kay Cosmetics and Levi Strauss. Some firms are taken private to enable management to focus more on long-term performance. (Stockholders tend to be very interested in a stock's short-term profits, dividends, and stock price performance.) As a spokesperson for Mary Kay Cosmetics said, "Going private gives us the opportunity to get out of the fishbowl and to make marketing decisions in a longer time frame than a public company has. Sometimes you need to invest in the future, and sometimes the future is more than 90 days away."[4]

FIGURE 3-6 / Going public versus going private.

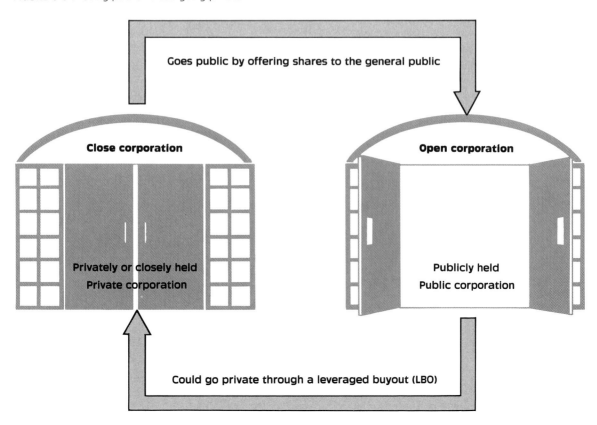

Goes public by offering shares to the general public

Close corporation

Privately or closely held
Private corporation

Open corporation

Publicly held
Public corporation

Could go private through a leveraged buyout (LBO)

leveraged buyout (LBO)

Many firms are taken private through a leveraged buyout. A **leveraged buyout (LBO)** is the acquisition of a company by a group of investors that is financed largely with borrowed funds secured by the firm's own assets. The LBO transaction is often based on the involvement of the acquired company's own management in the acquiring group.

LBOs are sometimes used by employees who face the prospect of being laid off. The employees buy out the employer's company or a division of that company. They become stockholders as well as employees. More than 1,000 U.S. companies have sizable employee ownership.[5] Examples include Hallmark Cards and Weirton Steel Corporation.

common stock

COMMON STOCKHOLDERS   There are two basic types of stock: common stock and preferred stock. **Common stock** is shares of ownership in a corporation that confer voting rights and rights to residual earnings to common stockholders. Figure 3-7 shows a common stock certificate.

If a corporation goes bankrupt, the common stockholders are the last to receive any proceeds from the sale of the corporation's property. Common stockholders are the residual owners of a corporation. Residual earnings are earnings that remain after the corporation has met the prior claims of creditors, including bondholders and preferred stockholders. Dividends to common stockholders are paid from a corporation's residual earnings. Actual payment of such dividends does not occur until the board of directors declares a common stock dividend.

FIGURE 3-7 / A common stock certificate.

Corporations issue annual reports and hold annual meetings for their stockholders. During a stockholders' meeting, management reports on corporate performance. Stockholders vote in elections of board members, the choice of an independent certified public accountant, and other proposals that require stockholder approval.

The number of votes a stockholder has depends on the number of shares he or she owns. Each share of common stock carries one vote. Thus a person with twenty shares has twenty votes. *Cumulative voting* gives small stockholders more power in electing the board of directors. With cumulative voting the number of votes a stockholder has is the number of his or her shares times the number of directors to be elected. If five directors are to be elected, a person with twenty shares would have one hundred votes (20 shares × 5 directors). These votes may be cast all for one person or in any way the stockholder chooses.

Stockholders must be notified of the date, time, and place of meetings. Many of them do not attend, so a proxy form is included with the meeting notice. A **proxy** is a person who is appointed to represent another person and to vote as directed at a stockholder's meeting. By signing a proxy form a stockholder transfers his or her right to vote at a stockholders' meeting. A **proxy fight** is a contest between a corporation's management and one or more outsiders to solicit enough votes to keep or take away control of a corporation's board of directors.

In addition to directors' elections, stockholders regularly vote on other business as well. For example, they might vote on a proposal to change the corporation's name or the state of incorporation. In recent years, many corporations have voted to change their names. International Harvester changed its name to Navistar, and Consolidated Foods changed to Sara Lee Corporation. Quite a number of firms such as Genentech have reincorporated in Delaware. Stockholders are also asking more questions about corporate social responsibility. These have included hiring and promotion policies for women and minorities, conservation, pollution, and doing business in countries that stockholders believe violate the human rights of their citizens.

PREFERRED STOCKHOLDERS **Preferred stock** is shares of ownership in a corporation that usually do not confer voting rights but do give preference with respect to dividends and assets. As we have seen, preferred stockholders have a right to receive the dividend indicated on their stock certificates before common stockholders receive any dividends. Usually, these dividends are at a fixed rate and, unlike common stock dividends, are not subject to change. Such dividends are not owed until declared by the corporation's board of directors. If the corporation goes out of business and pays off its debts, preferred stockholders have the right to receive their share of any remaining assets before the common stockholders receive anything. We will discuss the various types of preferred stock in Chapter 18.

THE BOARD OF DIRECTORS AND CORPORATE OFFICERS

The **board of directors** is a group elected by the stockholders to govern a corporation's affairs and to develop general corporate policy (see

Figure 3-8). In small corporations the major stockholders often manage the business. But in larger corporations, with thousands of stockholders, the directors guide the affairs of the business. It is easy for a board to keep itself in power as long as it does a good job in the opinion of voting stockholders. Unseating a board member can be difficult.

The board of directors elects its own officers. The *board officers* ordinarily include a chairperson of the board, a vice-chairperson, and a secretary. The board also holds periodic meetings, typically once a month.

corporation bylaws

The stockholders have the authority to draw up the corporation's bylaws. However, they usually leave it up to the board. **Corporation bylaws** are the rules by which a corporation will operate. They include

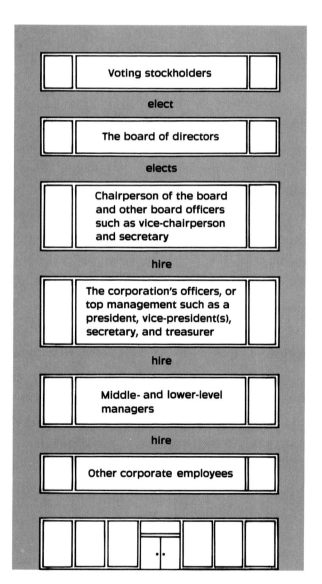

FIGURE 3-8 / The corporate structure.

the place and time of meetings, the procedure for calling meetings, directors' pay, duties of the corporate officers, regulations for new stock issues, and the procedure for changing the bylaws.

Another task of the board is selecting the *corporation's officers*. These are the president, vice-president(s), secretary, and treasurer. The corporate officers are employees of the board. They are also the corporation's top management. They hire other, lower-level managers to help run the firm. Boards sometimes select only the president or chief executive officer (CEO). He or she then selects the other corporate officers.

The board must account to the stockholders for the actions of the corporate officers. As "watchdog," it can accept or reject the officers' actions in managing the corporation.

In some corporations the board meets frequently and participates in the firm's day-to-day management. This is especially true in small, closely held corporations. On the other hand, some boards are content just to select the company president. The president then chooses other corporate officers. The president runs the corporation subject to "rubber stamp" approval by the board.

Thus distinctions between the board and the corporate officers are often blurred. In some corporations the chairperson of the board is also the company's CEO. He or she is called "chairperson and CEO." The other corporation officers may also be on the board. They are then called *inside* directors. Board members who are not corporate officers are called *outside* directors.

Board members have certain legal obligations. They must act in the best interest of the stockholders, be reasonable and prudent in doing their jobs, and manage the corporation's affairs as carefully as they do their own. They are liable for illegal acts and fraud and in some cases for using poor judgment.

It has become much more common in recent years for irate stockholders to sue board members. One result is that there is less willingness to serve on boards. Thus some states permit stockholders to approve amendments to corporate charters that limit directors' liability in certain circumstances. The overall trend, however, is toward smaller boards, fewer meetings, and more inside directors on boards.[6] The Business in the News box (on p. 89) discusses the difficulty of recruiting outside directors in recent years.

So far we have discussed the relative advantages and disadvantages of the three forms of ownership. There are also advantages and disadvantages to any large-scale operations, no matter what the form of ownership.

ADVANTAGES OF LARGE-SCALE OPERATION

Table 3-1 (on p. 88) identifies the ten largest industrial corporations in the United States in 1987. The larger a firm, the more likely that it can afford specialized departments and personnel. Examples include research and development, product testing, marketing research, and advertising departments. Specialized personnel include engineers, chemists, market researchers, and advertising copyrighters. Very often,

TABLE 3-1 / The ten largest industrial corporations in the United States (ranked by sales), 1987

Rank	Company	Sales ($ millions)	Profits ($ millions)	Assets ($ millions)	Profit as Percent of Sales
1	General Motors	101,781.9	3,550.9	87,421.9	3.5
2	Exxon	76,416.0	4,840.0	74,042.0	6.3
3	Ford Motor	71,643.4	4,625.2	44,955.7	6.5
4	Intnl Bus. Machines	54,217.0	5,258.0	63,688.0	9.7
5	Mobil	51,223.0	1,258.0	41,140.0	2.5
6	General Electric	39,315.0	2,915.0	38,920.0	7.4
7	Texaco	34,372.0	(4,407.0)	33,962.0	—
8	American Tel. & Tel.	33,598.0	2,044.0	38,426.0	6.1
9	E.I. du Pont de Nemours	30,468.0	1,786.0	28,209.0	5.9
10	Chrysler	26,257.7	1,289.7	19,944.6	4.9

Source: Fortune Directory, April 25, 1988, pp. D11–D12. FORTUNE 500, © 1988 Time Inc. All rights reserved.

the greater the number of units of a product that are produced, the less it costs to produce each additional unit. Large firms are thus said to have *economies of scale*.

Large firms can borrow more money and get favorable interest rates. They also have access to more investment money than small firms. For example, pension fund managers use some of the money to buy stock in big corporations. Employees in the pension plan thus become indirect owners of these corporations.

professional managers

Large firms also tend to be more permanent. This helps them to hire personnel who value permanent employment. **Professional managers** are employees whose career is management and who manage firms in which they are not major owners. Sole proprietors, partners, and the owners of small corporations are usually *owner-managers*. Only larger firms can afford to hire professional managers. Successful partnerships, however, can attract high-quality personnel. These people might expect an offer to buy into the firm. This practice is common in law and accounting firms.

DISADVANTAGES OF LARGE-SCALE OPERATION

Some people believe that firms can be too big—that they can lead to reduced competition and too much concentrated economic power. Such power can be abused. Other people view the concentrated power of large businesses as being offset by similar power in the hands of labor unions and government. If these *countervailing powers* are roughly equal, they are likely to prevent any one from becoming too dominant.

BUSINESS IN THE NEWS
Outside Directors Are Harder to Find

The earliest boards of directors in the United States were made up almost entirely of the corporations' major stockholders. Outsiders did not sit on boards until about 100 years later.

During the 1960s, however, corporations started to push the election of outsiders. By the next decade, outsiders constituted the majority on many boards. Meetings were pleasant and low-key affairs, and the outsiders provided the independent, objective perspective that is so important.

But during the 1980s, many of the "outside" directors have actually been tied closely to the corporations on whose boards they sit—as close friends of the chief executive officer, the head of the company's consulting firm, or the head of the company's bank. Furthermore, a growing number of people are declining invitations by nominating committees to run for election as outside directors, many current outside directors are not seeking reelection, and some are leaving before their terms expire. These people are convinced that the annual fees an outside director receives are not enough compensation for the increasing legal hassles from government regulators and dissident stockholders and the time demands involved in serving. Increasingly, companies are turning to professional recruiters, who themselves are finding it harder to find qualified candidates. As a result, there is a trend toward smaller boards, fewer meetings, and fewer outside directors.

Sources: David B. Hilder, "Risky Business: Liability Insurance Is Difficult to Find Now for Directors, Officers," The Wall Street Journal, July 10, 1985, pp. 1, 14; "On the Boards: Directors Face Tougher Scrutiny," Time, Feb. 11, 1985, p. 69; Amanda Bennett, "Hot Seats: Board Members Draw Fire, and Some Think Twice About Serving," The Wall Street Journal, Feb. 5, 1986, pp. 1, 10; "The Job Nobody Wants," Business Week, Sept. 8, 1986, pp. 56–61; "Getting Ahead: The Art of Landing a Boardroom Seat," Business Week, Dec. 22, 1986, p. 71; David J. Dunn, "Directors Aren't Doing Their Jobs," Fortune, March 16, 1987, pp. 117–119.

Large-sized businesses are also accused of being too impersonal. Lack of contact between workers and managers makes workers feel uninvolved. Smaller firms, the argument goes, provide much more personal, human contact.

Very large firms can also suffer from reduced management effectiveness and efficiency. Unlike smaller firms run by owner-managers, huge firms are run by many levels of hired managers. Bureaucracy and red tape can slow down decision making and reduce the firm's ability to adjust to change quickly. Hired managers sometimes avoid taking risks in order to protect their jobs. They might also lack the intense drive of the owner-manager.

CHANGING PATTERNS OF CORPORATE OWNERSHIP

In recent years the news media have focused on the many types of "deals" that are taking place in corporate America—for example, mergers, acquisitions, and divestitures. From descriptions of the activities involved in pulling off these deals, many new terms have crept into the vocabulary of business: *poison pill*, *greenmail*, *golden parachute*, and *white knight*, to mention only a few.

The result of these various types of deals is an ongoing restructuring of corporate America. Companies are transforming themselves as never before. In the discussions that follow, we focus on some of the more important trends in corporate ownership. We will elaborate on many of these later in this text.

merger

In a **merger,** two firms combine to create a new firm. The new firm is usually created under friendly terms, and the stockholders of each merger partner usually receive newly issued stock of the new firm.

acquisition

In an **acquisition,** one firm purchases another firm or a controlling interest in another firm. To make an acquisition, one firm bids for part or all of another firm's stock. The acquiring firm might offer cash for the targeted firm's stock, or it might offer to exchange part of its own stock for the desired shares of the targeted firm.

These various combinations of companies can be classified generally as vertical mergers, horizontal mergers, or conglomerate mergers. In a *vertical* merger the combining (or integrating) firms exist at different levels in the process of producing and marketing the product. For example, Hartmarx, the largest manufacturer of men's suits in the United States, engaged in *forward* vertical integration when it bought retail chains like Wallachs and F.R. Tripler. Southland Corporation

Through vertical integration, Southland Corporation can supply its 7-Eleven stores with gasoline from its own refinery.

engaged in *backward* vertical integration when it bought an oil refinery to supply its 7-Eleven stores with gasoline.

In a *horizontal* merger the integrating firms exist on the same level in the process of producing and marketing the product. Reebok's merger with Avia, a rival aerobic shoe manufacturer, is an example.

In a *conglomerate* merger the integrating firms exist in different industries. A firm that wants to diversify into a new line of business might be a merger partner in a conglomerate merger. USX (formerly U.S. Steel) diversified into the oil business when it bought Marathon Oil Company.

golden parachute

Golden parachutes are often involved in a merger or acquisition. A **golden parachute** is a package of benefits that is offered to inside directors and other top-level managers who lose their jobs as a result of merger or acquisition.

hostile takeover

Not all acquisitions are friendly. In a **hostile takeover** the target

WHAT DO YOU THINK?
Should Hostile Takeovers Be Outlawed?

Hostile takeovers have always been controversial. Nevertheless, raiders have been very busy during recent years chopping up and reassembling a long list of U.S. firms.

People who don't want to outlaw hostile takeovers say:

1. Raiders are assisting in the process of restructuring corporate America so that U.S.-based firms can be more competitive in global markets as a result of cutting costs and increasing productivity.

2. Raiders help to ensure that professional managers work to maximize the value of the firm and thereby maximize the return to stockholders.

3. Raiders help to keep the entrepreneurial spirit alive and, as outsiders, can often recognize profit opportunities that corporate insiders do not see.

People who want to outlaw hostile takeovers say:

1. Raiders cause corporate directors and officers to devote so much time and effort to fighting off hostile takeover bids that they neglect strategic long-range planning. They focus instead on day-to-day survival.

2. Raiders cause targeted companies to take on big debt loads in their efforts to fend off a hostile bid. If interest rates go up or the economy slips into recession, the debt burden could wreck the companies.

3. Raiders take the short-term view and are too quick to sell off plants and divisions to make a quick profit without consider-

ing the impact on communities and employees.

Should hostile takeovers be outlawed? What do you think?

Sources: "Do All These Deals Help or Hurt the U.S. Economy?" *Business Week*, Nov. 24, 1986, pp. 86–88; Michael W. Miller and Laurie P. Cohen, "Corporate Raiders Predict Harder Times," *The Wall Street Journal*, April 23, 1987, p. 6; Laurie P. Cohen, "Institutions Assail Top Court's Decision on Takeovers as Costly for Shareholders," *The Wall Street Journal*, April 24, 1987, p. 4; "Takeover Artists Take a Direct Hit," *Business Week*, May 4, 1987, p. 35; "Takeover Hurdle," *Time*, May 4, 1987; "The Brethren Battle Takeovers," *Fortune*, May 25, 1987, p. 9.

firm's board of directors opposes the acquisition, but the acquiring firm buys enough shares in the corporation to take control. As the What Do You Think? box (on p. 91) asks, "Should hostile takeovers be outlawed?"

tender offer

A hostile takeover bid typically starts with a tender offer. A **tender offer** is an offer by one party (a raider) to buy all or a portion of another firm's stock at a higher price than its current market price. Carl Icahn and T. Boone Pickens are raiders who have received a lot of media attention in recent years.

The targeted company's board of directors typically responds to a tender offer with defensive actions—for example, trying to convince stockholders not to sell their shares to the raider or challenging the tender offer in court. Other antitakeover measures (shark repellents) seek to make the firm a less attractive target.

poison pill

A **poison pill** is a defense that management adopts to make the firm less attractive to a current or potential hostile suitor in a takeover attempt. The objective is to make the pill so distasteful that a potential acquirer will not want to swallow it. For example, a pill adopted by Household International Inc. several years ago entitles its stockholders to buy $200 of an acquirer's stock for $100 upon acquisition. It is triggered when a hostile suitor acquires a stake of at least 20 percent in Household.[7] Some stockholders, however, say that boards that use the poison pill defense may be acting against their stockholders' best interests. By reducing the attractiveness of their firms as a potential takeover target, the board could be depressing the value of their shares.

white knight

Firms that are targeted for an unfriendly takeover can also defend themselves with another strategy. The board of directors can pursue a friendly takeover by a white knight. A **white knight** is a firm that takes over another firm but allows the acquired firm to retain its existing board and corporate officers. In many cases the acquired firm continues operating as an autonomous unit of the acquiring firm.

Still another hostile takeover defense is the stock buyback. In a *stock buyback* the targeted firm repurchases some of its outstanding stock in an attempt to boost its price on the market and thereby make it more expensive for raiders to buy. Some corporations divest themselves of subsidiaries or divisions and use the proceeds for a stock buyback. Figure 3-9 illustrates the defenses against a hostile takeover.

greenmail

Raiders often engage in greenmail. **Greenmail** occurs when (1) a raider buys a large portion of a cash-rich corporation's stock, (2) the raider informs its board of the takeover attempt, and (3) the board buys back the greenmailer's stock at a premium price in return for the greenmailer's promise not to go after the corporation for a stated period of time. Stockholders typically oppose greenmail because they do not have the option to sell their shares back to the corporation at the premium price. Furthermore, the market price of their shares often drops after a greenmail arrangement has been made. Some corporations have added antigreenmail provisions to their corporate charters.[8]

divestiture

In a **divestiture** a firm sells off one or more of its divisions or units. A corporation that owns all or most of the stock of another corporation is a *parent* corporation; the owned corporation is a *subsidiary*. Recently, RJR Nabisco, Inc., the parent, divested itself of its Kentucky Fried Chicken subsidiary.

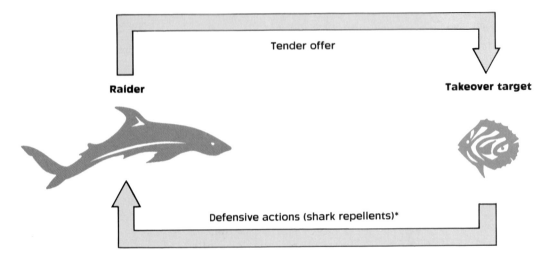

Tender offer

Raider   **Takeover target**

Defensive actions (shark repellents)*

* Convince takeover target's stockholders not to sell shares to the raider
  Challenge the tender offer in court
  Adopt a poison pill defense
  Pursue a friendly takeover by a white knight
  Engage in a stock buyout

FIGURE 3-9 / Defenses against hostile takeovers.

Other Forms of Business Ownership

The sole proprietorship, partnership, and corporation are the three major forms of ownership. Over the years, some of these have been modified to overcome some of their disadvantages. Examples are limited partnerships, joint ventures, cooperative associations, and mutual companies.

LIMITED PARTNERSHIPS

Earlier, we focused on the general partnership in which all partners are co-owners. Each partner has unlimited and joint liability for the firm's debts.

limited partnership

A **limited partnership** is a business in which one or more, but not all, of the partners are liable for the firm's debts only to the extent of their financial investment in the firm. This helps general partners attract investment dollars from people who do not want unlimited liability or who do not want to participate in managing the firm. Under the law, partners are assumed to be general partners unless it is made known they are limited partners. If a limited partner participates in managing the firm, his or her limited liability must be disclosed to the firm's creditors.

Limited partnerships are especially popular in real estate, energy, and movie production. The Cincinnati Reds baseball team is owned by a limited partnership. Mrs. Marge Schott is the general, or managing, partner. She owns controlling interest in the team and makes the business decisions. The limited partners are investors.[9]

The *master limited partnership* came into existence in the early 1980s. It combines the tax advantages of a partnership with the liquidity of a publicly traded stock. In other words, these partnerships are similar to stock offerings in that they are publicly traded on stock exchanges such as the New York Stock Exchange. Thus they are more liquid than general or limited partnerships.

JOINT VENTURES

joint venture

A **joint venture** is a special type of partnership set up by individuals or firms to accomplish a specific task or project. In some cases, one general partner manages the venture and the other partners are limited partners.

The task or project often is short-term. Once it has been accomplished, the joint venture ends. For example, several people might pool their funds and talents to buy an older home, remodel it, and sell it. They divide the profit, and the joint venture ends. Another example is an underwriting syndicate, in which a group of brokerage firms get together to sell a new stock issue for a corporate client.

Joint ventures can also be formed for an undefined period of time. This form of ownership is especially important in international business. For example, General Motors and Toyota's joint venture, New United Motors Manufacturing, Inc., produces the Nova subcompact car in California.

COOPERATIVE ASSOCIATIONS

cooperative association (co-op)

A **cooperative association (co-op)** is an incorporated organization whose user-members (owners) get back any revenue left after expenses are paid. The association's board of directors is elected by the members, each of whom has one vote. Examples include the following:

- **Employee credit unions** accept savings deposits from members who own shares in the co-op. Members can borrow from the co-op. Savers receive interest, and borrowers pay interest to the credit union.
- **Agricultural co-ops** help member farmers market their products. The Florida Orange Growers Association is an example.
- **Buying co-ops** help members buy their products at lower prices. Farmers may get together and set up a co-op to buy items such as seed and fertilizer.
- **Consumer co-ops** operate customer-owned retail facilities. Consumers get together and form a buying pool to get quantity discounts and to replace wholesalers and retailers. Owner-members in rural areas also set up consumer co-ops to sell electricity.

MUTUAL COMPANIES

Prudential, Metropolitan, and John Hancock are among the biggest life insurance companies. They are mutual companies. Many savings and

mutual company

loan associations and savings banks are also mutual companies. A **mutual company** is a corporation that issues no stock and is owned by its policyholders or depositors and whose surplus revenue, if any, is distributed among the owners in the form of dividends.

If you buy an insurance policy from Prudential, you become an owner. You receive a dividend on your policy. Unlike a dividend from a corporation, it is not taxable. When you deposit savings in a mutual savings and loan association or savings bank, you also become an owner. You receive dividends on your savings. But the dividends are considered to be interest. You pay income taxes on them.

Summary

The three major forms of private ownership of business firms are the sole proprietorship, the partnership, and the corporation. Each form has advantages and disadvantages.

The sole proprietorship is easy to start and dissolve. The owner owns all profits, derives a great deal of personal satisfaction from running the business, is the sole decision maker, and pays no tax on the business as distinct from himself or herself. The disadvantages include unlimited financial liability, difficulty in raising funds for expansion, and often an absence of others with whom to share the management job.

The partnership encounters few restrictions on starting and permits a pooling of funds, talents, and borrowing power. It also provides more opportunity to specialize than the sole proprietorship. Like the sole proprietor, partners can derive a great deal of satisfaction from their businesses, and they pay no tax on the business as distinct from themselves. The disadvantages include unlimited and joint financial liability, potential for personal disagreement, relative impermanence, and a frozen investment.

The corporation's advantages include the fact that it is a separate legal entity. The owners have limited financial liability and can transfer their ownership easily. Long life and greater financial capability are other advantages. The disadvantages are special and double taxation, complex and costly formation, and typically more government regulation and public disclosure requirements.

In most states the secretary of state receives applications for and issues corporate charters to incorporators. Close corporations are owned by a few stockholders. Open corporations are owned by many, and the stock is actively traded. Common stockholders own common stock. These are shares of ownership in the corporation.

A corporation's board of directors is elected by the stockholders to govern its affairs. The board elects its own officers and typically also draws up the corporation bylaws. It also selects the corporate officers.

The advantages of large-scale business operations include the ability to maintain specialized departments and personnel, ability to borrow more money and get favorable interest rates, and access to more investment money and professional managers. The disadvantages include impersonality, perhaps reduced management effectiveness and efficiency, a tendency to avoid risks, and perhaps less intensive drive than owner-managers have.

U.S. firms are transforming themselves as never before. Among the many types of "deals" are mergers, acquisitions, and divestitures. Hostile takeovers have been especially common in recent years.

Forms of ownership other than the three major types include limited partnerships, joint ventures, cooperative associations, and mutual companies.

Review Questions

1. Is a sole proprietor's business separate and apart from the sole proprietor as a person? Explain.

2. Partners have unlimited and joint financial liability. What does this mean?

3. What is the difference between an alien corporation and a foreign corporation?

4. How does a close corporation differ from an open corporation?

5. What do "going public" and "taking a corporation private" mean?

6. Who are the residual owners of a corporation? Explain.

7. Explain how a raider might go about staging a hostile takeover.

8. What is the major difference between a limited partnership and a general partnership?

Discussion Questions

1. "An effective partnership is one in which the partners always agree on all matters related to the business." Do you agree?

2. A corporation's board of directors is supposed to represent the interests of the stockholders. The chief executive officer (CEO) is often a member of the board, perhaps its chairperson. Furthermore, members of the CEO's top management team are often inside directors. Is there a conflict of interest here?

3. Some states permit a corporation's stockholders to limit the liability of outside directors. The stockholders can vote to forfeit the right to sue them for some forms of negligence. Is this good for the stockholders, the corporation, and society?

4. Is the offering of golden parachutes fair to small stockholders in large corporations?

Key Terms

sole proprietorship	S corporation	preferred stock
unlimited liability	corporate charter	board of directors
partnership	leveraged buyout (LBO)	corporation bylaws
partnership agreement	common stock	professional managers
corporation	proxy	merger
stockholders	proxy fight	acquisition

golden parachute	white knight	joint venture
hostile takeover	greenmail	cooperative association (co-op)
tender offer	divestiture	mutual company
poison pill	limited partnership	

Cases

KEEPING IT IN THE FAMILY

A recent survey of 200 owners of family-owned businesses found that maintaining family ownership of their business is a goal for most owners of such firms. The study also found that many family-owned firms face special problems that could jeopardize continued ownership for the next generation. Other major findings regarding family business owners include the following:

1. 42 percent said they would rather sell their business outright if no family member could succeed them.
2. 2 percent would consider going public.
3. 57 percent would not allow employees to acquire stock in the company.
4. 45 percent already had selected a successor.
5. 22 percent said they had planned to appoint and train a successor.
6. 19 percent would appoint a professional manager as successor.
7. 16 percent would appoint an employee as successor.

According to a spokesperson for one of the survey's sponsors, "The survey points to the need for owners of family enterprises to face up to these issues and not live in a dream world. It is important to take steps to run the business as a business and not as an extension of the family."[10]

Questions

1. Which form of ownership is most common among small business firms?
2. Why would such a small percentage of respondents consider going public?
3. How would you explain the reluctance of the majority of respondents to appoint a professional manager as a successor?

SHOULD THE DENVER NUGGETS GO PUBLIC?

In the spring of 1987 the owners of the National Basketball Association's Denver Nuggets were planning a stock offering. The previous December, the Boston Celtics had gone public by selling limited partnership units on the New York Stock Exchange. Don F. Gaston, Alan N. Cohen, and Paul R. Dupee, who had bought the Celtics for $15 million in 1982, sold 40 percent of the team to the public. The controlling partners grossed $46.8 million from the sale.

But there are some potential drawbacks associated with public offerings by sports organizations. For example, owners often do not wish to share control of their franchises. Norman Braman, owner of the National Football League's Philadelphia Eagles puts it this way, "It's tough enough to have a zillion fans, but to have them as shareholders, that's beyond comprehension."

Some owners are fearful of the reporting requirements associated with going public. Other considerations include league rules and interests. For example, although it is reviewing the issue, the National Football League flatly prohibits public offerings. An executive of Major League Baseball fears that publicly held teams might be more likely to relocate. Their first responsibility would be to stockholders, not to baseball.

In the spring of 1987, one of the National Basketball Association's more immediate concerns was that possible windfall revenues from public offerings would stiffen the players union's resolve to eliminate the salary cap in labor talks. Owners at the time were crediting the cap—a ceiling on each team's total player payroll—for much of the league's resurgence in recent years.[11]

Questions

1. What factors might affect the success with which a sports organization goes public?
2. What are the advantages and disadvantages to a sports organization of having fans as part-owners?
3. Would you advise the owners of the Denver Nuggets to go public?

FOUR

Small Business and Franchising

LEARNING OBJECTIVES

After reading this chapter, you will be able to:

- Explain what a small business firm is.

- Evaluate the economic and social contributions of small businesses in the United States.

- Identify the major factors that contribute to success and failure in small business.

- Assess your potential for entrepreneurship.

- Name and explain the six steps in starting a small business.

- Describe how a franchising system works.

- Identify the benefits of franchising to franchisees and the franchisor.

- Explain how the Small Business Administration helps small business.

In this chapter we will look at a key component of our business system—small business. We hear and see a lot about giant corporations in the news, TV entertainment programs, and casual conversations with friends. It surprises many people when they are told that approximately 98 percent of the nonfarm businesses in the United States are *small* proprietorships, partnerships, and corporations. The names of these small firms are not household words, but U.S. consumers deal with millions of them daily. As we will see, small firms are not simply smaller versions of big firms. There are many important differences between small and large firms.

Small businesses employ about 60 percent of our private sector labor force and generate almost half of the Gross National Product. Small firms provide many entry-level jobs for teenagers, women, minorities, and immigrants. They also introduce many new products each year. We will also look at other indicators of small business's economic and social contributions to our business system. Although small businesses exist in every type of industry, they are most important in retail trade and services.

We will take a close look at the factors that contribute to small business success and failure. Because of the great interest in entrepreneurship in recent years, we devote a large part of the chapter to a discussion of small business and entrepreneurship. We will examine the question "should you go into business for yourself?" along with a brief look at the benefits and burdens of entrepreneurship. We also explain three approaches to becoming a small business owner: taking over the family's business, buying out an existing firm, and starting a new firm.

Next we develop a six-step approach to starting a small business. We begin with a situation assessment and end up opening the doors to serve customers.

Franchising is a major topic in the chapter. We will explain how a franchising system works. This includes a close look at the benefits of franchising to the two parties to a franchising agreement: the franchisor and the franchisee. We will also encourage you to think about franchising as a way for you to go into business.

The chapter ends with a brief look at the operations of the Small Business Administration (SBA). As we will see, the SBA provides financial, management, and procurement assistance to small businesses.

There is a growing appetite for unusual foods in the United States. It is creating opportunities for people who had never thought of going into business for themselves, especially women eager to profit from their cooking skills. In 1987, almost 30 percent of makers of specialty foods were women, compared with 10 percent in 1982. Specialty foods are an $8 billion-a-year business and growing about 12 percent annually.

The business often takes little more than a good recipe to enter, and stories of some big successes from modest beginnings—such as Mrs. Fields, Inc., the Park City, Utah, cookie maker—are convincing others that they can do as well. But while growth and profitability can be considerable, the risks in specialty foods are also great. The faddish nature of specialty foods and the lack of any business experience by many getting into the field limit the scope of many ventures. The initial idea may be fine, but without constantly developing new products and capturing broader markets, these companies may be hard pressed to survive.

"It doesn't take much to start; it does take money to keep the product on the shelf," says Annice Jacoby, a New Yorker who traces the start of her business to a batch of 6,000 fortune cookies she baked for a 1984 Christmas party. The cookies' success led her to team up with Deborah Kauf-man to form Divines, Inc. The company's first product, called Divine Poetry in Chocolate, is a hand-folded, chocolate-dipped fortune cookie containing lines from a poem.

After launching the product the two women had to scramble for money from friends and private investors to keep going. Although the cookies are relatively cheap to make, the chocolate and the packaging are expensive. And traveling to gourmet food shows—a necessity in the business—can cost more than $5,000 a trip. Still, Divines, Inc. appears to be making it; sales of its fortune cookies approached $600,000 in 1987. Further growth for the firm, however, will require additional capital.

Getting such capital can be difficult. Many new companies complain that lenders and investors do not understand innovative food businesses. For example, most of these businesses are too small to appeal to venture capital investors. And corporations that once sought to acquire specialty food businesses are now staying away because they have had trouble integrating their small acquisitions into their other operations.[1]

Ms. Jacoby and Ms. Kaufman have done what thousands of other entrepreneurs do every year in the United States. They recognized a market opportunity and put together the effort and resources they needed to exploit that opportunity and make a profit. They are realizing "the American dream" of being in business for themselves. But like nearly every other new firm, the owners must find the capital with which to finance their business's growth. Let's begin the chapter with a look at the nature of a small business. As we will see, a small business is not simply a scaled-down version of a large business.

What Is a Small Business?

To most people a "small business" is something like an auto repair shop, a beauty salon, a flower shop, or a hardware store. Such businesses are usually owned and managed by one person with little or no outside help. When they are operated as family businesses, they are often called "mom-and-pop" businesses.

Smallness, however, is relative. A neighborhood mom-and-pop grocery store is small in comparison to a giant supermarket chain like Kroger. Kroger sells more than $17 billion of merchandise a year and employs about 180,000 people. Kroger, on the other hand, is "small" in comparison to General Motors, which sells more than $100 billion a year of cars and other products and employs almost 900,000 people. Besides annual sales revenues and number of employees, other measures of size include assets, net worth, and market share.

In this chapter we will rely basically on the Committee on Economic Development's (CED) concept of what constitutes a small business. A **small business** is a firm that meets two or more of the following criteria (see Figure 4-1 on p. 102):

small business

1. The owners manage the business.
2. One person or a small group of people provides the financing.
3. The owners and employees live near the firm.
4. The firm is small in comparison to others in the same industry (size may be measured in assets, number of employees, or sales revenues).

ECONOMIC AND SOCIAL CONTRIBUTIONS OF SMALL BUSINESS

Roughly 98 percent of the nonfarm businesses in the United States are small. Altogether these small firms employ about 60 percent of the nation's private sector labor force and generate almost half of the Gross National Product. They furnish two out of three workers with their first jobs and provide many entry-level jobs for teenagers, women, minorities, and immigrants.

Small firms generate jobs that are more likely to be filled by younger, older, and female workers. Such workers often prefer, or are only able, to work part time. Small firms are often more willing than larger firms to adjust to their needs. Small firms train first-time jobholders

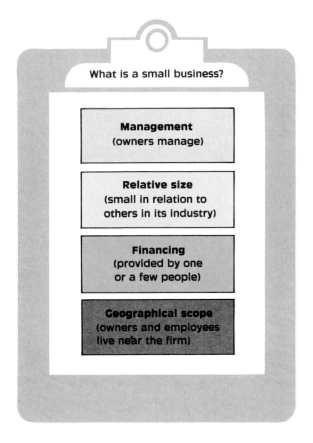

What is a small business?

Management
(owners manage)

Relative size
(small in relation to
others in its industry)

Financing
(provided by one
or a few people)

Geographical scope
(owners and employees
live near the firm)

FIGURE 4-1 / Criteria for deciding whether a business firm is small. A firm must meet at least two of these to be considered small.

in basic job skills. They also train many workers who reenter the job market. Thus students, homemakers, and retirees are most likely to be hired by small firms.

Each year, thousands of women like Annice Jacoby and Deborah Kaufman of Divines, Inc. and members of minorities enter the business world by opening up small businesses. In recent years, women have started new businesses at three times the rate men have. Approximately one-third of all full-time small businesses are owned by women.[2] Nonwhite self-employed workers account for most of the minority firms in the United States.

Small firms also introduce many new products. New industries such as semiconductor manufacturing, robotics, and gene splicing have been founded on technologies developed by small firms. In general, small firms are more flexible and willing to take the risks of experimenting with new technologies than many of our larger firms. In fact, many big corporations today are seeking to stimulate the entrepreneurial spirit in their firms—a process called "intrapreneurship."

Small firms are also important suppliers to large firms. In the automobile industry, for example, thousands of small firms supply component parts to the auto manufacturers. Increasingly, large firms are also buying services that are provided by small firms.

business incubator

Perhaps the most important contribution small business makes to our economic system is in helping to keep "the American dream" alive. A person can, with hard work and determination, become his or her own boss.

Some indication of the importance government, universities, private investors, and others attach to small business is apparent in the establishment and operation of business incubators. A **business incubator** is a facility that is operated by a government unit, a university, or a private investment group to provide low rent, shared office services, and management advice to new business ventures. A typical business incubator consists of one or more large buildings, such as an abandoned plant and warehouse. The earliest of the more than 200 incubators in the United States were general-purpose incubators. Many of the newer ones, however, are specialized. For example, the city of Miami and Florida International University set up the Biomedical Research and Innovation Center in downtown Miami, within minutes of a dozen hospitals and medical research institutes. The center's first three tenants are developing products for artificial hearing, biotechnology, and medical-imaging diagnostics.[3]

POPULAR TYPES OF SMALL BUSINESS

Small businesses exist in every type of industry—agriculture, forestry, and fishing; mining; construction; manufacturing; transportation, communication, and utilities; wholesale trade; retail trade; finance, insurance, and real estate; and services. However, in order of importance, they are most important in retail trade, services, construction, wholesale trade, and manufacturing.

Retail businesses sell their products directly to consumers. A few giant retailers like Sears, Kmart, and Safeway account for a huge share of total retail sales. But there are tens of thousands of small retail enterprises such as bakery, greeting card, record, apparel, jewelry, and numerous other types of shops and stores.

The services industry, unlike the retailing industry, is not dominated by giant firms. Service providers such as restaurants, movie theaters, dry cleaners, auto repair specialists, dentists, and funeral homes tend to be small, local businesses. Except for insurance, and to a lesser extent banking, most service providers offer their services in rather limited areas. Many sectors of the services industry are dominated by labor-intensive, small-scale operations that require only limited amounts of capital in fields that are relatively easy to enter.[4] As we will see later in this chapter, franchised operations like Burger King and Midas Muffler are national or international in scope. But the local franchised outlets are owned mostly by small businesspeople.

Small businesses in the construction industry are local enterprises that build homes, apartment complexes, swimming pools, roads, and so on. Wholesale trade is dominated by local wholesalers—small firms that buy in large quantities from producers and resell in smaller quantities to retailers and other types of businesses. Manufacturing is also a concentrated industry in which most of the sales revenues are generated by a relatively few big national and international corporations. But there are thousands of small manufacturing firms that create products from raw materials and operate in local areas. Typical examples include steel fabricators and sawmills.

Success and Failure in Small Business

Small businesses and large corporations tend to differ in terms of their resources, capabilities, and missions. For example, some people start their own firms hoping to achieve a comfortable living while doing what they want "on the job" instead of having to work for someone else. These people care more about how their businesses fit their desired lifestyles than about growth of their firms. Thousands of neighborhood shops and stores, for example, are owned by people who derive more satisfaction and self-esteem from personal relationships with their customers than they could derive from an aggressive pursuit of growth.

Not all small firms want to remain small. Firms that want to grow need to plan ahead.

On the other hand, there are many small businesses like Divines Inc. whose owners are primarily interested in growth. As suggested in the Price Waterhouse ad, such firms are not content to remain "small" businesses. Instead, they want to take the fast track to growth. As we will see later in this chapter, these small business owners often turn to outside venture capitalists to provide them with the financial resources they need to grow rapidly.

Some people say that small businesses that do not seek growth are not entrepreneurial firms. According to the director of the Center for Entrepreneurship at Baylor University, "An entrepreneurial firm is one that is growing and plans to continue to grow."[5] He does not equate business startups with entrepreneurship.

FACTORS IN SMALL BUSINESS SUCCESS

Figure 4-2 identifies the major strengths of small business firms.

GREATER FLEXIBILITY Small firms are typically more flexible than large firms. For example, they can adapt their plans very quickly in response

FIGURE 4-2 / Major strengths of small business firms.

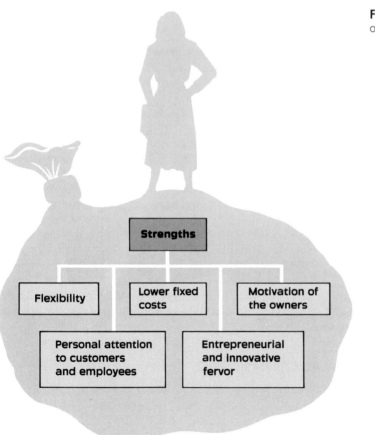

to environmental changes. Large firms, with many layers of management, cannot respond as quickly.

MORE PERSONAL ATTENTION TO CUSTOMERS AND EMPLOYEES   Small business owners have more direct contact with their customers and have a better feel for what they want than very large businesses. They can respond quickly to changes in those wants and offer customers more personal service. As we will see in Chapter 11, large firms spend heavily on marketing research to keep tabs on changing customer wants.

The relationship between the owners of small business and their employees is more direct and personal than in large businesses. Labor and management in large corporations tend to communicate through labor and management representatives. In small businesses the owner and workers communicate more directly and personally.

LOWER FIXED COSTS   Small companies often have lower fixed costs than large firms. Fixed costs are costs that do not vary in total as the volume of business varies. Thus the small firm might be able to sell its product at a lower price than a larger competitor with higher fixed costs. Small firms typically do not have full-time lawyers and certified public accountants on the payroll as do larger firms. Small firms hire these specialists on a temporary basis only when needed. Thus the cost is much less. Lower fixed costs often enable small firms to underprice large firms.

The brewing and steel industries are dominated by a few giant firms. Yet the rate of growth of microbreweries and minimills has been much greater in recent years than the rate of growth of the high-fixed-cost giants.

GREATER ENTREPRENEURIAL AND INNOVATIVE FERVOR   As we saw in Chapter 1 an entrepreneur is a risk taker who starts and operates a business in hope of making a profit. The hired managers who run big corporations seldom hold any significant ownership in them. They have less to gain by taking the risk, for example, of developing new products. As a result, they might tend to be overly conservative in running the corporations. To simulate the entrepreneurial environment in small firms, some large firms are applying entrepreneurial techniques. As we saw earlier, they refer to it as "intrapreneurship."

GREATER MOTIVATION OF THE OWNERS   As we have suggested, hired managers generally do not have a significant ownership stake in their corporations. Small business owners do, and this in itself can motivate them to work harder. In addition, the desire to be independent and one's own boss is a powerful motivator.

FACTORS IN SMALL BUSINESS FAILURE

Of the roughly five million small businesses that are started each year, only about half will still be in business five years later. The failure rate is high, but the longer a firm is in business, the greater the chances that it will survive. In other words, the chances of making it through the fifth year are much greater than the chances of surviving the critical first year. The major causes of failure are poor management and inadequate financing.

POOR MANAGEMENT Researchers who study small business failures agree that the number one cause is poor management. As Figure 4-3 shows, this includes inadequate preparation to run a business, failure to learn from experience, and unbridled optimism.

Thousands of people who have little or no education and training in small business management go into business every year. Most of them fail. They start out with what they think is a good business idea and rush to put it into practice without adequate research or preparation.

Many new entrepreneurs believe that they will acquire the management skills they need to be successful as they survive the critical first few months in business. But many do not last long enough to acquire through experience the skills they need. One of the main reasons is poor recordkeeping—for example, inadequate monitoring of expenses and cash. This hinders planning, implementation, and control.

Pessimists are very unlikely to go into business for themselves. It takes a certain amount of optimism to get yourself charged up for the challenges of entrepreneurship. But it is easy for many people to let

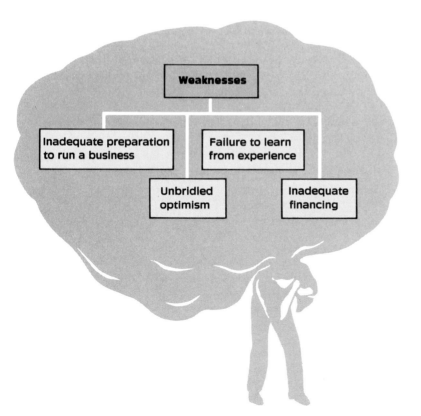

FIGURE 4-3 / Major weaknesses of small business firms.

their optimism transform itself into unrealistic dreaming. The "this product *can't* fail" syndrome is a major reason why people start businesses—but also a major cause of business failures.

INADEQUATE FINANCING Attention to financing needs must begin before the startup stage of a new business. The entrepreneur must forecast expenses and have available the cash needed to establish the business on a sound footing. Like Divines, Inc., however, many businesses start out with inadequate capital and limited sources of funds. The major source for new businesses is the owner's personal resources. The second major source is financial institutions. But owners who start off with insufficient funds of their own often have their loan requests turned down because the owners do not have enough of their own money invested in the business.

Financial problems do not end after the business has had a successful start. Every year, thousands of firms fail because they cannot pay bills as they become due. The shortage of funds is due in large part to poor forecasting of expenses. Many business owners must therefore close or sell their businesses just when they were on the brink of succeeding.

Small Business and Entrepreneurship

The entrepreneurial drive to start one's own business is what the private enterprise system is all about. Chances are good that you have experienced it. Perhaps as a child you set up a lemonade stand. As a teenager you might have been a member of Junior Achievement or DECA (Distributive Education Clubs of America).

In the late 1800s the U.S. economy was shifting from agriculture to industry, and a handful of entrepreneurs built the steel, oil, automobile, and chemical industries. This was the "golden age" of entrepreneurship in the United States. Between World War I and World War II, however, entrepreneurial activities shifted away from individuals to big corporations. More recently, entrepreneurship has resurfaced, and the new entrepreneurs are young and self-reliant.

Everyday in the United States, about 3,000 people start businesses.[6] What about you? Have you ever thought about going into business for yourself?

SHOULD YOU GO INTO BUSINESS FOR YOURSELF?

Assume for a minute that you want to go into business for yourself. You have a rich relative who will lend you the money to get started. You also have a product or service that will definitely lead to a good profit if you succeed as manager. Should you go into business for yourself?

Given these assumptions (and they might not be realistic), you still must consider a third vital input—you, the entrepreneur. You must assess your willingness and ability to make it in business for yourself. Figure 4-4 contains several very basic questions you should ask yourself.

YES	NO	
☐	☑	**1. Are you afraid of risk?**
☐	☐	**2. Do you feel you should enjoy the good life today because you might not be here tomorrow?**
☐	☐	**3. Do you have trouble getting along with people?**
☐	☐	**4. Do you lose interest in things that don't work out as quickly or as well as you think they should?**
☐	☐	**5. Are you easily frustrated?**
☐	☐	**6. Do you have trouble coping in situations that require quick judgments?**
☐	☐	**7. Do you cave in under stress?**
☐	☐	**8. Are you unable to learn from your mistakes?**
☐	☐	**9. Are you too good to do manual labor?**

FIGURE 4-4 / Assessing your potential for entrepreneurship.

If you answered yes to most of the questions in Figure 4-4, you are not ready to start your own business. You probably lack the traits needed to succeed.

If you answered *no* to most of the questions, you probably have the traits needed to succeed. Entrepreneurs have a strong need to achieve. They:

- take reasonable risks,
- press onward in spite of setbacks,
- set goals and commit themselves to meeting them,
- communicate with others,
- work well with others,
- tolerate rejection, frustration, and stress,
- make decisions and carry them out,
- learn from mistakes,
- think creatively and analytically.

Do you measure up? If so, you should start to weigh the benefits and burdens of starting your own firm.

THE BENEFITS OF ENTREPRENEURSHIP

Perhaps the best thing about being your own boss is your sense of freedom. You make all the decisions and get a lot of satisfaction from

IT'S YOUR BUSINESS
Turn Your Hobby into a Business

As personnel director for a division of New York Hospital several years ago, Michael Soetbeer wore a three-piece suit and sat behind a desk piled with paperwork. Today he's wearing a chef's hat, a warm coat, and a gold chain with a charm of a hotdog on a bun. He is selling gourmet hotdogs on the main street of his hometown, Ridgefield, Connecticut.

guiding your firm's growth. Fulfilling the American dream is good for your ego. You take pride in having made it on your own.

People who work for others tend to get less satisfaction from their work. Entrepreneurs seldom complain that running their own business is routine and boring. It is also possible to make a lot of money. In addition to a salary, the value of your firm might increase manyfold over the years. The It's Your Business box discusses an entrepreneur who profited from turning his hobby into a business.

THE BURDENS OF ENTREPRENEURSHIP

Small business owners must accept the burdens of entrepreneurship. Being in business for yourself requires your full attention. You seldom leave the office or shop at 5 P.M. as you might when you work for someone else. Nor do you leave job problems at work. They follow you home, often to prey on your mind over dinner or even while you try to sleep.

The independence that you sought can elude you. You do not report to a boss, but you do have to bend over backward for your customers. They are your "boss." You also have to contend with creditors, employees, suppliers, and tax collectors. In other words, as an entrepreneur you are never really free.

When you own a small business such as an inn, your work day may extend to being available to greet late arrivals.

As we saw in Chapter 3, small firms can seldom afford to hire enough employees so that each can specialize. You might have to prepare ads, keep records, make sales calls, and collect bad debts. You must be able to "wear many hats." All these tasks take up lots of time, but you cannot neglect long-range planning. You have to set goals and develop plans to meet them, or else your business will fail.

Even if your firm succeeds, you still might have little money to spend. You might work hard for months and not take a penny out except for the salary you pay yourself. Instead, you might have to reinvest your profits in the firm for long-term growth. Or you might need to meet short-term demands for cash. You might not even be able to draw a salary until the firm becomes a truly going concern. Going into business for yourself therefore requires that you carefully weigh all the pros and cons.

HOW TO BECOME A SMALL BUSINESS OWNER

A person becomes a small business owner in any one of three ways. Each has its own set of problems and opportunities.

TAKING OVER THE FAMILY'S BUSINESS   Every year many firms are taken over by relatives. In many such cases the people taking over were "brought up" in the business. Thus they know the business from the ground up and are well prepared to step in and take over when the former owners of the firms have died or are no longer able or willing to run the business.

But sometimes the person taking over has not worked in the firm. Furthermore, such a takeover is often on short notice. The result is that there is seldom time for new owners to decide whether being in business for themselves is what they really want. A person who feels obligated to the former owner or the family to take over the business, but is not prepared for entrepreneurship, is likely to fail.

BUYING AN EXISTING FIRM   Many people go into business by buying an existing firm. Naturally, you should first find out why the owner wants to sell. If the owner wants to retire, check out the firm's profit over the past few years. If it is acceptable, you might be able to reach an agreement whereby the seller helps you learn the business from the ground up.

On the other hand, the owner might be trying to unload a business that has not made money. Your job is to find out why the firm made no profit. Is the good or service the problem? Is the cause poor management? What would it take to turn the business around?

Some owners will sell a profitable firm in hopes of "making a killing." Buyers often pay a premium price for such firms because it is easier and perhaps less risky than starting from scratch. Caution is in order, however. The seller might have a history of selling out and then opening a competing firm nearby. This is especially true of firms that sell services. For example, the owner of a profitable auto repair shop sells out. Then, within a matter of weeks, he opens up a new shop a few blocks away. His customers will most likely follow him to his new shop. That is why it is essential to get a "no compete" clause in the contract when you buy a firm. The seller agrees not to set up a competing firm in the area for a specified time, such as two years.

STARTING A NEW FIRM   Starting a new firm is better in certain ways than buying an existing firm. The new entrepreneur can build the firm from the ground up. There are no unhappy customers, no obsolete plant or inconvenient store location, and no bad debts, and you are not paying a premium to the owner for the privilege of buying an existing firm. On the other hand, there is no customer base to begin with.

THE INTERNATIONAL DIMENSION

Small firms typically cannot get export financing from banks. Big banks generally are not interested in making small loans. Small banks, lacking experience in export financing, are wary of the risks. Some states are setting up financial aid programs for small exporters. Most of these programs seek to make small banks more comfortable with export financing by guaranteeing repayment of the loans. For example, the Illinois Export Development Authority will lend banks 90 percent of the funds they use to make an export-related loan.

State and local development agencies are in the business of stimulating entrepreneurship. They have been courting small business owners for many years. More recently, international development authorities overseas have been making a pitch to attract small U.S. firms. Some small firms set up operations overseas to supply nearby subsidiaries of U.S.-based firms. Others do it in response to incentives offered by various development agencies. Still others do it because of lower costs, especially labor cost, and to avail themselves of technology that is being developed overseas.

Starting a Small Business

Starting your own firm from scratch takes a lot of planning. Running it takes a lot of know-how. You cannot do it all without any outside help. At the very least, you should get the advice of an accountant, an insurance agent, a lawyer, and a banker. You should also practice entrepreneurial networking. **Entrepreneurial networking** is a person's concerted effort to meet and share problems and experiences with other people in similar businesses, including those who have also just started out in business for themselves.

Figure 4-5 shows a six-step approach to starting a new business. The discussions that follow briefly explain what is involved in each

entrepreneurial networking

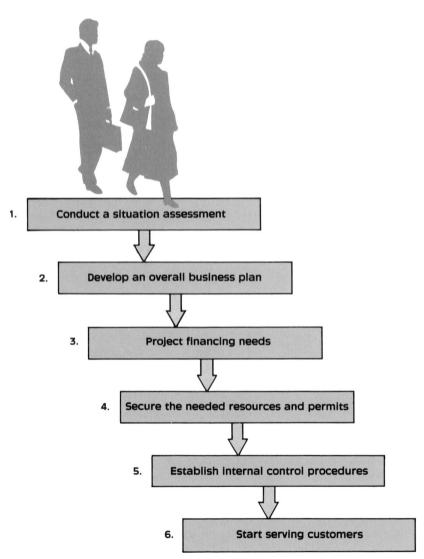

FIGURE 4-5 / Six steps in starting a business.

1. Conduct a situation assessment
2. Develop an overall business plan
3. Project financing needs
4. Secure the needed resources and permits
5. Establish internal control procedures
6. Start serving customers

step. A fuller explanation of many of these steps is provided throughout the rest of this book.

CONDUCT A SITUATION ASSESSMENT

The *situation assessment* involves taking an in-depth look at yourself and the environment in which you hope to do business. Why do you want to go into business for yourself? Are you tired of working for somebody else? Do you simply want a chance to make it on your own? How much time and effort can you put into your business? What rate of return do you want to make on the money you put into the firm? Be honest and realistic in answering these questions. The basic objectives you set for your business provide the benchmarks for comparing your firm's performance.

After you have answered these questions, you should analyze your resources. How much cash and other assets do you have to invest in the business? Can you afford to quit your present job? Try to identify and analyze any weaknesses and distinctive competencies you might have in relation to your competitors. What you are doing is making a careful assessment of your capacity for entrepreneurship.

Next you should take an in-depth look at the environmental variables that we discussed in Chapter 2. The goal is to match your overall objectives and resources with market opportunity. What wants do potential customers have that you can satisfy better than existing firms?

Close monitoring of the environment can help you spot opportunity. For example, an auto mechanic opened his own shop in January 1982. He noticed that people were keeping their cars longer before trading them in. The United States was in a recession, and people were afraid of being laid off. The price of new cars was high, and interest rates on new car loans were high as well. This convinced him that the time was right to start his own car repair business. The logic was simple. The older the car, the more likely that it will require maintenance and repair services.

The What Do You Think? box (on page 116) gives a few examples of major failures to recognize business opportunity. But once you identify an opportunity, devote some time and effort to developing estimates of market potential and sales potential. **Market potential** is the maximum possible sales of a given type of product in a specific market over a stated period of time for all sellers of that product. It sets an upper limit for industry sales.

Your firm's sales potential is also important. **Sales potential** is the share of market potential that a firm might realize if it made a maximal commitment of its resources to the effort.

Some people say that opportunity no longer exists for small firms. But as we saw earlier, bigger might not mean better as far as business is concerned. A small firm is usually more adaptable than a large firm. It can often react to change a lot more quickly. Figure 4-6 identifies several situations that tend to favor small firms.

Besides helping you get a sharper focus on market opportunity, the

market potential

sales potenial

When a product does not lend itself to large-scale mass production

When customer convenience is more important than price and selection

When demand and/or supply fluctuate with the seasons

When potential sales in a market are not large enough to attract a large firm

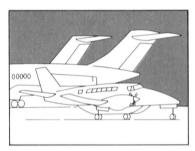

When large firms compete with each other for the big market segment and ignore one or more smaller segments

When the good or service being offered requires a lot of personal attention to the customer by the seller

FIGURE 4-6 / Examples of situations that tend to favor small firms.

environmental analysis also helps you identify threats to the proposed business and develop strategies for coping with them.

DEVELOP AN OVERALL BUSINESS PLAN

business plan

The overall **business plan** is a document that spells out in detail the firm's mission, its objectives, and the actions (strategies and tactics) needed to achieve the firm's objectives. It also specifies the firm's form of ownership.

mission statement

The firm's **mission statement** is a document in which top management establishes the specific nature and scope of its market and operations by answering the questions "What business are we in?" and "What do we want the business to become?" The answers to these strategic questions establish (1) the firm's reason for being, (2) broad guidelines regarding what customer wants will be served with what goods and services, (3) the firm's social responsibilities and its noncustomer stakeholders, and (4) the owner's expectations about the firm's performance.

After preparing the mission statement you must establish a set of broad objectives that state the level of measurable performance you

In the 1940s a young inventor, Chester Carlson, took his idea to twenty corporations, including some of the biggest in the country. They all turned him down. In 1947 he finally got a tiny Rochester, New York, outfit named Haloid Co. to purchase the commercial rights to his electrostatic paper-copying process. Haloid became Xerox Corporation, and both it and Mr. Carlson got very rich. What did Haloid see that the others didn't?

On New Year's Day 1962, four nervous young musicians played their first record audition for executives of Decca Recording Co. The executives were not impressed. "We don't like their sound," one explained later, adding that guitar groups were on their way out. The foursome's manager begged Decca to reconsider and promised that he would personally buy 3,000 copies of any single his group recorded. Decca refused. Over the next few months, four other record companies turned the group down. If there were a Failure Hall of Fame, it would have to have a wing for those whose mistake was not recognizing multimillion-dollar opportunities when they looked them in the face. In that wing there would have to be a niche for Decca, which many years ago blew a chance to sign the Beatles.

Hewlett-Packard Company dropped the ball in 1975, when one of its young, low-level engineers, working on his own time, jerry-built a gadget that few people envisioned at the time: a personal computer. He offered it to his employer, which decided to pass. The engineer, Steve Wozniak, went off with his device to cofound one of recent history's biggest success stories, Apple Computer, Inc.

What does it take to recognize business opportunity? What do you think?

Source: Michael M. Miller, "Sometimes the Biggest Mistake Is Saying No to a Future Success," *The Wall Street Journal*, Dec. 15, 1986, p. 30. Reprinted by permission of *The Wall Street Journal*, © Dow Jones & Company, Inc., 1986. All Rights Reserved.

hope to reach at specified future dates. Given the mission and the objectives, you can then proceed to develop strategies and tactics for accomplishing them. Figure 4-7 outlines the contents of a good business plan.

For a manufacturer the overall business plan would specify objectives and plans for production, marketing, and personnel. It would state the quantity and type of equipment needed to produce the product. It would say how the product is to be sold and how many employees are needed to get started.

To make such decisions, you will need to estimate the number of units or dollar volume the firm expects to sell in a specific market during a given period of time, given its intended commitment of resources to the business. If you are a manufacturer, for example, the sales forecast will guide decisions about the amount of raw materials to order, how much finished product to keep in inventory, and the number of production workers you will need. We will discuss sales forecasting in greater detail in Chapter 15.

An **executive summary** with:

* a description of the company and its future plans
* the current stage of development the company is in
* whether the management team is complete; if not, when and how it will be completed

A **product section** with:

* a description of the product, where it is in its life cycle (i.e., a new product or a mature product)
* future product research and development efforts
* the status of patent or copyright applications

A **manufacturing and distribution section** with:

* a description of the complexity and logistics of the manufacturing process
* the company's production capacity and current percentage of capacity use
* a description of the company's distribution system

A **marketing section** with:

* information on the industry that the company is competing in; focus on industry trends and profit potential
* a marketing plan, especially a customer profile, an analysis of market needs, and a geographic analysis of markets
* an analysis of why the company's marketing efforts are different from competitors' efforts

A **financial information section** with:

* financial statements for the current year and the 3 previous years if applicable
* financial projections for the next 3 to 5 years and assumptions for sales, cost of sales, cash flow, pro forma balance sheets and key statistics, such as the current ratio, debt/equity ratio, and inventory turnovers
* a listing of pending lawsuits filed by or against the company

FIGURE 4-7 / Contents of a good business plan.

PROJECT FINANCING NEEDS

Many new business owners fail to adequately project their financing needs. The four major tasks here are to (1) set up a capital budget, (2) prepare month-by-month projected income statements, (3) prepare month-by-month projected cash flow statements, and (4) prepare a projected balance sheet. We provide a brief overview of each task below. Further explanation will come in the chapters on accounting and finance.

SET UP A CAPITAL BUDGET   The business plan is the basis for setting up a *capital budget.* This is a projection of your capital needs over a stated period of time. The capital budget tells you how much money you will need for acquiring buildings and equipment. The more your equipment is subject to obsolescence, the more important the capital budgeting process is because new equipment will have to be purchased more often.

PREPARE MONTH-BY-MONTH PROJECTED INCOME STATEMENTS   In this step you forecast sales revenues and operating expenses. You do this month by month during the startup phase of your business. This gives you a good idea of how much money you will make during each of the early months you are in business. If these projections are way below your profit objectives, start looking for ways to increase sales, cut expenses, or both.

PREPARE MONTH-BY-MONTH PROJECTED CASH FLOW STATEMENTS   Money flows into and out of your firm as you carry on your business activities. Cash inflow comes mainly from sales. Cash outflows are necessary to pay for supplies, salaries, telephone, and so on. Some of these expenses are one-time expenses. For example, you may have to pay a deposit to the telephone company when you open for business. Other expenses, such as wages and supplies, are recurring.

The main element in estimating cash inflows and cash outflows is timing. You must meet your bills as they come due. Perhaps you can buy equipment on credit and pay in monthly installments with cash inflows from sales. This could have a big effect on the amount of money you need to get started.

PREPARE A PROJECTED BALANCE SHEET   A projected *balance sheet* shows the estimated net worth of your firm at the end of the first year. This tells you what your firm owns and what it owes. Projections of your financing needs provide an estimate of how much money you need to get started and survive the critical early months in business.

SECURE THE NEEDED RESOURCES AND PERMITS

A new firm secures capital through equity and/or debt financing. Equity capital is funds provided by the owner. Debt capital is borrowed funds.

venture capitalists

Venture capitalists are individuals and businesses willing to provide equity capital to entrepreneurs who have new products or new product ideas that are as yet unproven on the market but have a good chance of becoming successful. Apple, Genentech, Nike, and Häagen-Dazs were all venture capital startups.

Some venture capitalists will help finance the startup of a new firm. Others are interested only in firms that have been set up and need more financing for rapid growth. Venture capitalists often acquire a controlling interest in the firms they help to finance.

Good venture capitalists, however, are more than passive investors. They might start by investing $10,000 into an entrepreneur's idea for a new product while the entrepreneur develops a business plan. Later, they might also supply management expertise, marketing and operations advice, and other financial contacts as the startup company grows. In some cases, venture capitalists have replaced company founders when the companies started to outgrow the founders' ability to manage them.[7]

Kleiner Perkins Caufield & Byers is the San Francisco–based venture capital firm that invested $200,000 in a startup biotechnology firm named Genentech. In 1981, Genentech went public, selling shares of stock in the company to the general public. Its initial stock offering opened on Wall Street at $35 a share and shot up within minutes to $88. Suddenly, the venture capital firm's investment was returned 800-fold.[8]

Debt financing might be available from banks, savings and loan associations, and consumer finance companies. These and other types of financial institutions will be discussed in Chapter 16. We discuss Small Business Administration loans later in this chapter.

Besides money you will need other resources. As we will see in Chapter 8, attracting qualified and motivated employees (the human resource) is crucial. Insurance protection against risk is another important resource. Insurance agents can advise you on the types of coverage you will need in your line of business. We will take an in-depth look at insurance in Chapter 19.

One of the most important resource decisions you will make is the location for your business. Manufacturers need access to workers with the needed skills and access to raw materials and transportation. For wholesalers, nearness to retailers and institutional buyers such as schools and hospitals is important. The location decision is most important to retailers. If you sell products that consumers like to compare, locate near other retailers who sell similar items. Location in a shopping mall will help you attract walk-in customers.

Before you start operations you must have the required licenses and permits. Which ones you need will depend on state and local laws. The best advice is to check with the local municipal or county zoning department, the local chamber of commerce, the local sheriff's office, or the state and local departments of revenue.

ESTABLISH INTERNAL CONTROL PROCEDURES

Before opening for business, make sure the proper internal controls are in place. This includes an accounting system to keep track of revenues, expenses, and any cash that comes in. A security system must protect against employee theft and customer shoplifting. There must be cash controls to prevent sales clerks from pocketing money, and so on. How effective these controls are affects whether you make a profit or incur a loss.

START SERVING CUSTOMERS

Your primary objective for going into business is to make a profit. You must serve your customers, since without them your business will fail. Your firm will not be profitable if its costs are greater than its sales revenues. Therefore keep a close check on sales revenues and your costs of doing business.

In other words, the firm's performance after you start serving customers must be matched against the objectives you set for the business. We will discuss this matching process—*controlling*—in greater detail in Chapter 5.

After you start operations your focus will shift from starting the business to ensuring its survival and growth. In the discussions that follow we take a look at franchising. This is a very popular way for small businesspeople to go into business.

Franchising

As we mentioned earlier, about half of all independent small businesses fail within their first five years. People who go into business by buying into an established and reputable franchise have a much better chance of success. Only about one-tenth of all franchises fail within their first five years.[9]

Roughly half a million franchised businesses account for one-third of total retail sales in the United States. Furthermore, franchised companies employ more than seven million people. By the year 2005, franchising will have become a $1-trillion-a-year industry, about double the current level. Franchising will also account for half of all retail sales.[10]

Examples of franchise operations include Holiday Inn, Pizza Hut, Burger King, H&R Block, Jiffy Lube, and Midas Muffler. In each case a firm developed an idea and procedures for doing business that could be duplicated in many outlets. This firm, called a franchisor, licenses others (franchisees) to use the idea, name, and procedures.

franchisor

The **franchisor** is a firm that licenses other firms to use its business idea and procedures and to sell its products or services in return for royalty and other types of payments. For example, the Burger King Corporation is the franchisor that licenses the many thousands of small businesspeople (franchisees) who make and sell Burger King products at Burger King restaurants (franchised units) in local market areas.

franchisee

The **franchisee** is the firm that is licensed to use the franchisor's business idea and procedures and is often granted an exclusive right to sell the franchisor's products or services in a specified territory. Each franchisee owns his or her franchised unit(s).

Burger King, for example, licenses independent franchisees to make and sell Burger King hamburgers. Each franchisee pays an initial franchise or license fee and yearly payments to Burger King Corporation. The payments are for the right to use the Burger King trade name, for financial and managerial assistance, and for the other benefits that we will discuss shortly. The Burger King capsule discusses how Ramon Moral became a very successful franchisee.

franchising agreement

The franchisor and the franchisees are related to each other through the franchising agreement. A **franchising agreement** is a contract between a franchisor and a franchisee that spells out the rights and obligations of each party. The agreement creates a franchise, a franchising system, a franchisor, and a franchisee.

Many franchisors are owned by parent firms. For example, Pillsbury Company owns Burger King, and PepsiCo owns Pizza Hut. On the other hand, McDonald's Corporation and Domino's Pizza Inc. are independently owned. They have no parent firms.

Franchise operations vary in the proportion of company-owned outlets to franchisee-owned outlets. In general, the trend is toward

APPLICATION: BURGER KING

A Business of His Own

Like many of his compatriots, Ramon Moral came to this country over 20 years ago to escape from Fidel Castro's Cuba. With little more than his wits and a dedication to hard work he began his career at Burger King, doing cleaning and maintenance work at the company's Miami headquarters.

Because of Mr. Moral's commitment and skills, promotions came quickly in the expanding Burger King organization. After moving up the ladder from worker to manager to director he was promoted to vice-president for operations for the Burger King Corporation. In this major position, Mr. Moral was responsible for overseeing all matters pertaining to the operations of the Burger King stores. For example, he had to ensure that they were designed and managed most efficiently.

For many people a vice-president's position is the capstone of their careers. But there were still greater challenges ahead for Ramon Moral. After several years he decided that he wanted to take on the challenge of starting and expanding his own business. He turned (as you might have guessed) to the Burger King franchise program. Mr. Moral left a secure job at corporate headquarters to open his first Burger King just outside Miami, Florida. His new career as an entrepreneur was on its way.

Going into business for yourself, says Ramon Moral, is a big step, one you should not take lightly. You have to carefully consider whether you want to work for someone else or be your own boss. That is not always an easy choice. Being in business for yourself means not having to take orders from someone else or worry about whether you will get fired. It also gives you a chance for great success, since your firm's growth is mostly limited by your own hard work, skills, and potential.

But there is another side to the coin. Being your own boss also means leaving the security of your employer and having to assume the responsibilities that your employer used to handle for you. Your employer was the one who had to worry about boosting sales, keeping expenses down, and paying suppliers, for instance. Now you will be the one on the firing line, and not everyone can take the pressure, no matter what they think.

Burger King wants to know a lot about you before selling you a franchise (as do most other legitimate franchisors). Name, business experience, education, and personal financial statement are just a few of the items you must provide. You will also be asked to write an essay describing factors that you think might be relevant in considering your application, such as your lifestyle, family background, and intellectual pursuits. To make doubly sure that the franchise is good for you and you are good for the franchise, you will be required to work at least 50 hours under the guidance of a store manager in a store near you before your franchise application is approved. It will also mean a big commitment of time and money. Burger King will want you to devote your full time and attention to the franchise. Furthermore, you (and perhaps your partner) will need a minimum of $150,000 to invest.

But how successful it can be! Ramon Moral now owns three Burger Kings, and he is considering several other sites. The average Burger King franchise sells over a $1 million a year. Since the profit margin on an average Burger King is about 10 percent (profit margin is the profit divided by the sales), the typical franchisee with three stores would have a net income of over $300,000 per year. And the sky is the limit.

Questions

1. Why do you think Mr. Moral left his vice-president's position to become a Burger King franchisee?

2. Is Mr. Moral an entrepreneur?

3. Refer to Figure 4-5 and explain how the franchisor (Burger King) could assist Mr. Moral in performing these six steps.

more company-owned outlets. This gives the franchisor greater control over operations. Many franchisors also own the rights to the land on which the franchisee's business sits. That gives the franchisor a lot of control over the franchisee's business.

FRANCHISEE BENEFITS

As we mentioned earlier, franchising has enabled many people to go into business for themselves. Franchisees own and operate their own businesses while at the same time enjoying the benefits of being part of a type of chain organization. Figure 4-8 highlights some of the benefits of franchising to franchisees.

FRANCHISEE RECOGNITION Some franchise operations reach into many different countries. Some operate only in one city. Regardless, the franchised outlets (shops, stores, restaurants, etc.) enjoy widespread consumer recognition because all units are basically alike. The franchisor usually provides the franchisee with a blueprint for construction. The franchisor also usually insists on standardized operation of all outlets. These standard policies are spelled out in the franchisor's operations manual and franchise agreement and are backed up with standardized forms and control procedures. The name "Burger King" can draw in customers who might not stop at an unknown burger stand.

MANAGEMENT TRAINING AND ASSISTANCE Many franchisors operate training schools for franchisees. Burger King operates "Burger King University," with its own dean, faculty, and programs of study. Franchisees learn business skills like recordkeeping, purchasing, marketing, and building good customer relations. Ongoing training is also important. Franchisors' representatives visit franchisees at their place of business to give them advice and assistance. Franchisees with special problems

FIGURE 4-8 / Franchising's benefits to franchisees.

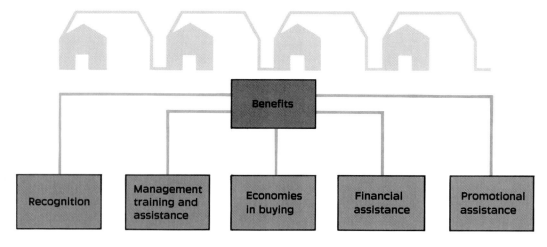

can turn to the franchisor for special assistance. The Sylvan Learning Corporation ad discusses the various types of assistance the franchisor offers its franchisees.

ECONOMIES IN BUYING   A franchisor can make or buy ingredients, supplies, parts, and so on in large volume. These are resold to franchisees. The prices are lower than the franchisees would pay if they made or bought them on their own because of the economies of large-scale production and buying. Burger King has a special division called "Distron" that buys large quantities of produce, cups, plates, and so on for resale to franchisees.

FINANCIAL ASSISTANCE   Usually, a franchisee puts up a certain percentage of initial costs. These costs include the cost of land, buildings, equipment, and promotion. The franchisor helps with the rest. For example, the franchisor might make a direct loan to the franchisee, in which case the franchisee pays back the loan with revenues earned by the franchisee. Another approach is for the franchisor to help the franchisee to secure a loan from various types of lenders. The franchisor also sells supplies to franchisees on credit. In some cases the two parties agree on a joint venture. The franchisee does not pay back the money put up by the franchisor. Instead, the franchisor becomes a part-owner of the franchisee's business.

The assistance offered by franchisors enables many people to go into business for themselves as franchisees.

PROMOTIONAL ASSISTANCE Franchisors usually supply their franchisees with various types of promotional aids. These include in-store displays, radio scripts, and publicity releases. Franchisors also can help them develop promotional programs.

FRANCHISOR BENEFITS

Franchising also offers many benefits to franchisors, as shown in Figure 4-9.

FRANCHISOR RECOGNITION A franchisee benefits from being able to use the franchisor's name and products. The franchisor benefits by expanding the area over which the trade name is known. A franchisor can achieve national and perhaps international recognition much more quickly by franchising than by any other form of expansion. One reason why McDonald's today has more restaurants than Burger King is that McDonald's stressed franchising earlier than Burger King did. Burger King's founders emphasized company-owned stores at first. This slowed down Burger King's expansion.

PROMOTIONAL ASSISTANCE A local franchisee pays a lower rate for a newspaper ad than a national franchisor. By sharing the cost the franchisor and the franchisee both benefit. This is called *cooperative advertising*. Also, franchisors can team with franchisees to use local radio and TV advertising rather than blanket network coverage. This avoids wasting coverage in areas that do not have a franchisee. Localized promotion can suit customer tastes in a given area and tie in with local events.

FRANCHISEE PAYMENTS The franchising agreement sets out the amount and type of payments the franchisee will make to the franchisor. Most franchisors charge an initial franchise fee to buy into the franchise. This fee is often determined by market size in the franchisee's territory.

FIGURE 4-9 / Franchising's benefits to franchisors.

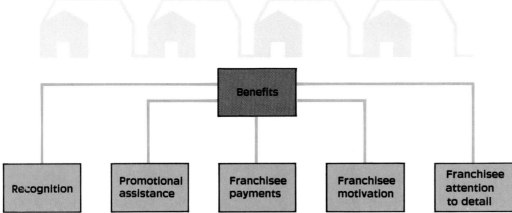

Franchising has enabled many franchisors to achieve international recognition very quickly.

In addition, most franchisors receive a periodic royalty, which is a set percentage of monthly or annual sales or profits, usually from 2 percent to 30 percent. Another typical type of franchisee payment is the advertising fee, which goes toward helping to cover the franchisor's cost of advertising the business throughout the franchise's market area. For example, total startup costs (real estate, equipment, and inventory) for a Burger King franchise run from about $700,000 to over $1 million. The royalty fee is 3.5 percent, and the advertising fee is 4 percent.

FRANCHISEE MOTIVATION As business owners, franchisees are their own bosses: Their profits belong to them. A franchisee is therefore more likely than a hired manager to accept long hours and hard work. Corporations that operate chain stores often have trouble recruiting and developing well-motivated store managers. Unlike franchisees, these people are employees.

FRANCHISEE ATTENTION TO DETAIL The headquarters of a chain store operation must keep payroll, tax, and other records on all of its units. It must be concerned with local laws regarding sales taxes, licenses, permits, and so on. Franchisees handle these details in franchise operations.

FRANCHISING AND YOU

Do you have a future in franchising? The answer depends on your willingness to work, your ability to find a good franchise opportunity, and your ability to buy into the operation. One franchise consultant tells prospective franchisees that they must plan to cover six areas of costs associated with a startup franchise: (1) the franchise sale price, (2) pre-opening expenses, (3) training expenses, (4) business operational needs for the first six months, (5) personal operational needs for the first six months, and (6) emergency dollars.[11]

Many independent business owners have been very successful as franchisees. Keep in mind, however, that there are some drawbacks to franchising:

- Unscrupulous franchise promotors might be selling franchises that have little merit.
- Monthly payments must be made to the franchisor even if profits are low.
- There is little room to be creative because product and operations are uniform.
- There is less independence than you might expect, since the franchise might specify the products you sell, your business hours, and your recordkeeping procedures.
- Other franchisees might start in nearby areas (saturate the market).
- The franchisor might be unable to live up to commitments in the franchising agreement.
- Poor performance by some of the franchisor's other franchisees might harm your business's image.
- Franchisors often make policy decisions without consulting their franchisees.

FIGURE 4-10 / How a franchising system works.

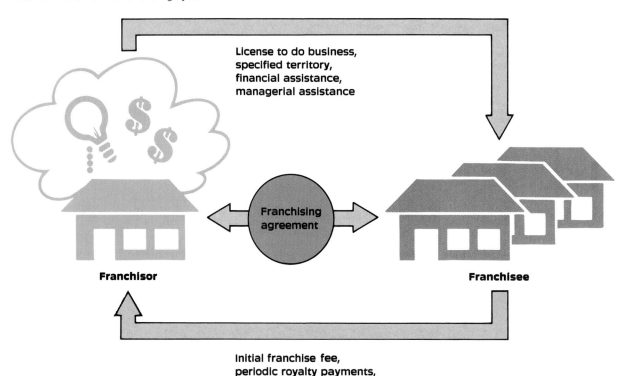

License to do business, specified territory, financial assistance, managerial assistance

Franchising agreement

Franchisor

Franchisee

Initial franchise fee, periodic royalty payments, advertising fee

The Federal Trade Commission (FTC) requires franchisors to give prospective franchisees a *disclosure document* and then ten business days to decide whether to sign a franchising agreement. The disclosure document contains detailed information about the franchisor's business experience, initial franchise fees, and other initial payments needed to obtain the franchise. It also contains information about the continuing payments that franchisees must pay after the franchise opens, as well as other information. You should always do extensive research and consult a lawyer before signing any franchising agreement.

Your success as a franchisee probably depends as much or more on the franchisor's corporate management than on your own efforts. The strength of franchising is the inflexible, time-tested "business format." Because of standard operating policies, you might feel less independent and more limited in how creative you can be. In a sense you are not your own boss, and this makes franchising unattractive to many entrepreneurs. The franchisor usually exercises some degree of continuing control over your operations. If you are not performing up to the terms in the franchising agreement, the franchisor may cancel the agreement and substitute a company-owned outlet in its place. Figure 4-10 summarizes how a franchising system works.

Small Business Administration (SBA)

The Small Business Administration

The **Small Business Administration (SBA)** is an independent agency of the U.S. government that was created in 1953 to promote and protect the interests of small business firms. It helps ensure that competition will not lead to survival of only large firms. The SBA's three major functions on behalf of small businesses are: (1) providing financial assistance, (2) providing management assistance, and (3) providing procurement assistance.

FINANCIAL ASSISTANCE

The SBA makes or participates in making term loans to qualified small firms for almost any purpose, such as buying inventory or building a plant. Two basic types of SBA loans are direct loans and guaranteed loans.

Direct loans are made with the SBA's own funds. Usually, these are made only for high-risk businesses, and the interest rate is several percentage points lower than comparable bank rates. The SBA is prohibited by law from making a direct loan if the applicant can get a loan from a private souce. The SBA's direct loan program is being phased out.

Guaranteed loans are actually made by private lenders to small business owners, but the SBA guarantees 90 percent of the loan. This SBA guarantee enables many entrepreneurs, who might otherwise be turned down, to get loans.

Small Business Investment Company (SBIC)

The SBA also licenses Small Business Investment Companies to aid small firms by making it easier for them to get long-term capital. A **Small Business Investment Company (SBIC)** is a privately owned, privately operated, SBA-licensed venture capital company that helps finance small firms that want to expand and modernize.

An SBIC finances small firms by straight loans and by equity-type investments. In a straight loan the SBIC takes collateral that banks will not accept. Although an SBIC's transactions with small firms are private, they must abide by SBA rules.

An SBIC often prefers to act as a venture capitalist. There are several ways to do this. One approach is for the small firm to give the SBIC common stock in return for funds it needs to expand.

In effect, SBICs give the small business owner access to equity capital without the need to make a public stock offering. SBICs range from very small to very large. Stock in some of them is publicly traded. Minority Enterprise Small Business Investment Companies (MESBICs) serve socially and economically disadvantaged American entrepreneurs.

MANAGEMENT ASSISTANCE

The SBA gives management help to small firms through its Office of Management Assistance. SBA loan approvals often require applicants to take positive steps to improve their management skills.

The SBA cosponsors management training courses with schools and colleges to instruct small business owners in the functions of management. It also sponsors management conferences and problem clin-

SCORE volunteers have helped many small businesses to survive and prosper.

ics. SBA field offices have professionals on their staffs to counsel small business owners.

The SBA also provides management counseling. The Service Corps of Retired Executives (SCORE) is staffed by volunteers who are retired executives and management consultants. The Active Corps of Executives (ACE) is staffed by volunteers who are currently employed executives and practicing management consultants. Both counsel small business owners at no charge except for the volunteers' out-of-pocket expenses. The **Small Business Institute (SBI)** is an SBA-sponsored program in which faculty members from collegiate business schools with whom the SBA has contracts supervise senior and graduate students who serve as consultants to small business owners free of charge.

Small Business Institute (SBI)

The SBA also operates Small Business Development Centers. A **Small Business Development Center (SBDC)** is an SBA-sponsored operation in which faculty members from collegiate business schools and experienced businesspeople conduct research and provide consulting services to small business owners on a fee basis.

Small Business Development Center (SBDC)

PROCUREMENT ASSISTANCE

Because Congress has mandated that small businesses receive a share of government contracts, the SBA helps small firms secure them. For example, SBA Procurement Center Representatives are stationed at selected military and civilian procurement centers to help small business owners get government contracts.

small business set-asides

Small business set-asides are government contracts that are restricted to competition among small firms. Minority set-asides are government contracts that are awarded to minority-owned firms without competitive bidding. Federal agencies remove certain contracts from competitive bidding and give them to the SBA to be awarded to minority-owned firms.

S ummary

A small business firm meets two or more of the following criteria: (a) the owners manage the business, (b) one person or a small group of people provides the financing, (c) the owners and employees live near the firm, and (d) the firm is small in comparison to others in the same industry.

Approximately 98 percent of the nonfarm businesses in the United States are small. Altogether, they employ about 60 percent of the nation's private sector labor force and generate almost half of the Gross National Product. They furnish two out of three workers with their first jobs and provide entry-level jobs for teenagers, women, minorities, and immigrants. Small firms also introduce many new products, are important suppliers to large firms, and help to keep the American dream alive.

The factors that contribute to success in small business include greater flexibility, more personal attention to customers and employees, lower fixed costs, greater entrepreneurial and innovative fervor, and greater motivation of the owners. The factors that contribute to failure include inadequate preparation to run a business, failure to learn from experience, unbridled optimism, and inadequate financing.

In assessing your potential for entrepreneurship the questions to ask focus on your feelings about and capacity for dealing with risk, putting off the "good life," getting along with others, losing interest quickly, coping with frustration, making quick judgments, coping with stress, learning from mistakes, and performing manual labor. Are you willing to take reasonable risks? Are you able to press onward in spite of setbacks; set goals and commit yourself to meeting them; communicate; work well with others; tolerate rejection, frustration, and stress; make decisions and carry them out; learn from mistakes; and think creatively and analytically?

The six steps in starting a small business are as follows: (a) Conduct a situation assessment—taking an in-depth look at yourself and the environment. (b) Develop an overall business plan—spelling out in detail the firm's mission and objectives and the actions necessary to achieve them. (c) Project financing needs—setting up a capital budget, preparing month-by-month projected income statements, preparing month-by-month projected cash flow statements, and preparing a projected balance sheet. (d) Secure the needed resources and permits—obtaining the human, financial, and other resources and the required permits and licenses to do business. (e) Establish internal control procedures—setting up an accounting system, a security system, cash controls, and so on. (f) Start serving customers.

In a franchising system the franchisor develops an idea and procedures for doing business that can be duplicated in many outlets. The franchisor licenses franchisees to use the idea and procedures. In return, the franchisees make royalty and other types of payments to the franchisor. The franchising agreement spells out the rights and obligations of each party.

The Small Business Administration is an independent agency of the U.S. government that was created in 1953 to promote and protect the interests of small business firms. Its three major functions on behalf of small businesses are providing financial assistance, providing management assistance, and providing procurement assistance.

Review Questions

1. What is a small business?

2. How do small businesses contribute to our economic and social well-being?

3. What are the major strengths and weaknesses of small businesses?

4. What is the entrepreneurial drive? Assess its presence in the United States today.

5. What are the benefits and burdens of entrepreneurship?

6. Identify the six steps in starting a new business and explain what is involved in each step.

7. How does a franchising system work?

8. What are the advantages to the franchisor of franchising? What are the advantages to the franchisee?

9. How does the Small Business Administration help small businesses?

Discussion Questions

1. Startup firms typically suffer from chronic cash shortages. What is your reaction to a proposal to exempt from income taxes for five years the profits that small business owners reinvest in their firms?

2. What are the implications for small business in the United States of the shift from an industrial economy to a service economy?

3. Is a franchisee an independent businessperson?

4. Should the U.S. government finance the operations of the Small Business Administration?

Key Terms

small business
business incubator
entrepreneurial networking
market potential
sales potential
business plan
mission statement

venture capitalists
franchisor
franchisee
franchising agreement
Small Business Administration (SBA)

Small Business Investment Company (SBIC)
Small Business Institute (SBI)
Small Business Development Center (SBDC)
small business set-asides

Cases

ENTREPRENEURSHIP THRIVES IN THE RUST BELT

Short on cash and business experience but long on blue-collar skills and enthusiasm, new groups of entrepreneurs are springing up in one of our most devastated industrial areas—the rust belt. Many of these people are striking out on their own rather than choosing low-paying service employment or no work at all.

One of the hottest spots is Ohio. One evening in Youngstown, in the heart of depressed steelmaking country, a dozen men and women are taking an entrepreneurial class at Youngstown State University. The group, nearly all blue-collar workers who lost jobs during the slump, listens intently as a local businessman, George McClay, explains how to fill out an application for a Small Business Administration loan.

Mr. McClay is not very encouraging. "You're putting your neck on the line out there," he says. "You may not make money in the first three months. In fact, you may not make anything for six months."

But the warnings do not seem to faze the class. Enthusiasm runs high as members of the group discuss plans for ventures ranging from rib restaurants to home-repair outfits. One student, 46-year-old Eugene Caleris, has already opened a van-customizing shop in nearby Warren, Ohio, since his steel mill job went sour. "After the last layoff," Mr. Caleris says, "I told my wife I've been a foreman and I know how to get a job done. I'm not going to work for anyone anymore."[12]

Questions

1. What role does the environment play in entrepreneurship?
2. Should Mr. McClay have been more optimistic in talking to the would-be entrepreneurs?
3. Mr. Caleris apparently thinks that being a foreman is somewhat like being an entrepreneur. Are they the same?

THE AMERICAN WOMAN'S ECONOMIC DEVELOPMENT CORPORATION

Turning women into successful entrepreneurs is Bea Fitzpatrick's mission. As founder of the American Woman's Economic Development Corporation (AWED) in New York City, she has reached more than 35,000 women from all fifty states and Canada with business training, counseling, conferences, and seminars. AWED operates through a staff of thirteen and more than 400 experienced businesspeople who volunteer their time.

AWED conducted its first management training and technical assistance program with a group of eighteen women in 1977. The pilot program was funded with a grant of $124,000 from the Economic Development Administration of the U.S. Department of Commerce. Now AWED operates on a $1.26 million budget of mostly private funds supplied by companies and individuals.

Ms. Fitzpatrick is an outspoken foe of the loan programs and special treatment offered by some government agencies. She believes that government-backed loans are often not repaid because the recipients do not know how to run a business, and their businesses fail. The government, she says, "is giving the wrong kind of help and giving it in the wrong way."

"We don't give anyone money. We just give them good information and training. Then we find banks are anxious to give them loans." Some of the programs AWED offers include:

- "Managing Your Own Business," an eighteen-month training series for women who have been in business a year or more. In once-a-month seminars it covers such areas as business practices, accounting, marketing, selling, and finance.

- "Chief Executive Roundtables," a two-year series of monthly programs for women whose businesses gross more than $1 million annually.

- "Starting Your Own Business" and "Building Your Own Business," eighteen-week programs for women who have just launched companies or who are thinking of starting new ones. An alternative to the eighteen-week course is an intensive 2½-day seminar on starting a business.

- Counseling. In addition to counseling at its offices, AWED has devised a system of counseling by telephone to serve women outside New York City. Telephone sessions typically run 90 minutes, and the client pays $35. For $10 a woman may place a "hotline" call for a quick answer to an urgent business question. The calls are toll-free.

• Conferences and seminars. Topics include the mechanics of starting a business, how-to's for a service business, financing your venture, and how to have both a baby and a business.[13]

Questions

1. In what ways are AWED and the SBA alike? How do they differ?

2. Do you agree with Ms. Fitzpatrick's opposition to government loan programs?

3. What do you think motivates business firms to contribute money to AWED?

obert L. Loughhead was a key player as the people of Weirton, West Virginia, where 25,000 area residents work for the steel company, saved their jobs and the town's economy. Life was grim in Weirton in the early 1980s when National Steel Corp. sought to close the town's steel plant. The only hope appeared to be an employee buyout. Some workers wanted to accept the pension offers and let the plant close. Other workers advocated the "givebacks," but all of them worried about the 20% cut in hourly wages, the no-strike clause, and the no-cost-of-living-raise provisions required to keep the plant viable.

Today, Weirton Steel is thriving, one of the largest of the 8,000 employee-owned businesses in the U.S. Many factors played a role in the turnaround, but Loughhead believes that the changes in attitude engendered by employee ownership were a vital component.

The attitudes did not change overnight, however. When Loughhead came in as CEO, "I concluded that we would have to stop trying to get even and start finding ways to get along ... We had the same

SECTION TWO
Management and Organization

goals—to help the business succeed and grow ... Everyone had to learn to listen." Loughhead had always advocated employee involvement and was enthusiastic about managing the transition to employee ownership. He had also been a hands-on, "walking around" style of manager, long before those became fashionable terms. Loughhead said that implementing a strong, democratic plan was toughest on middle managers who are still held accountable for bottom line results from the top brass, but now have to take advice as well from those they supervise. They feel caught and sometimes threatened.

Good communication, Loughhead said, is the key to making it work. At Weirton, video technology helped accomplish this. A weekly video "newsletter" was produced. Employees could pop the tape into one of the VCRs around the plant and find out the latest developments: how the company was doing financially, news about orders or problems, or what the board of directors was up to. The openness made everyone feel involved and eased the rumor mill atmosphere that can undermine morale.

Now 58 and semi-retired, Loughhead says the Weirton experience was the capstone of a career that began as an accountant. In 1959 he joined Jessop Steel as controller, and then moved into general management, eventually rising to Chief Executive Officer. In 1977, he joined Copperweld Steel Co. as president and was recruited from there to join Weirton in 1983, before the vote on the employee buyout, a deal which closed on January 11, 1984.

Loughhead has a bachelor's degree in business administration from Geneva College in Western Pennsylvania. He believes a solid grounding in economics is important for tomorrow's business leaders, and advocates more emphasis in all business curricula on employee involvement and how this relates to "competitiveness." Democratization of the workplace is no fad, Loughhead said, but is "absolutely essential." "Boards of Directors and management must recognize that the real world is not in the board room, but rather, on the plant floor, in the customers' plants, in the suppliers' plants, and in the purchasing agent's office where a salesman is trying to get an order .... Strategic plans put together in the board room without that input do not have as great a chance of success."

FIVE

After reading this chapter, you
will be able to:

- Explain what a manager is.
- Explain the differences and
  similarities between top
  management, middle man-
  agement, and first-line
  management.
- List and describe each of
  the functions in the management process.
- Explain the basic steps in
  planning.
- Describe the management-
  by-objectives technique.
- Describe the control
  process.
- Describe the basic managerial skills.
- Explain the decision-making
  process.

Management Functions and Decision Making

Businesspeople like cookie-maker Debbie Fields and builder Donald Trump are not the only ones that have to be good managers. Of course, Mrs. Fields could never have started (let alone continued to run) all those stores unless she was a top-notch manager. And Mr. Trump never could have accumulated and controlled his network of hotels if he could not manage his operations. But the fact is that a remarkable array of other occupations depend on managing, too. Hospital administrator, symphony conductor, football coach, and school principal, are just the tip of the iceberg when it comes to jobs that require effective management.

Moving up from worker to manager is one of the most exciting steps in any person's career. As we will see in this chapter, managers are people who get things done through others. A manager therefore needs a whole new set of skills for getting the job done. Instead of actually doing the work, managers have to depend on people skills, technical skills, and many other skills to organize their subordinates and ensure that they get the job done.

In this chapter we discuss what managers do and the skills all managers need. We will discuss such matters as the basic functions all managers perform (planning, organizing, staffing, directing, and controlling). And we will describe in some detail the kinds of skills successful managers need. Finally, we will discuss the topic of decision making and in particular the stages in the decision-making process.

If you check the lanes the next time you go bowling, you will probably find that the equipment is brought to you by the Brunswick Corporation, one of the world's largest manufacturers of bowling and other recreational equipment. What will not be so obvious, though, is that just a few years ago, Brunswick was on the ropes. There was considerable doubt that they could survive without selling off their bowling division.

At that point, Brunswick's chief executive Jack Reichert began the kind of restructuring that has characterized countless other U.S. companies over the past several years. His actions paint a vivid picture of what a competent manager can do to turn a company around.

Mr. Reichert started cutting costs by moving to a decentralized form of management. He eliminated the chief operating officer's job (his own previous title) and four group vice-president positions. He reorganized, consolidating eleven divisions into eight. He sold two of the firm's three corporate airplanes and closed the executive dining room. He saved about $2 million a year in real estate costs by renting out two-thirds of the firm's sprawling headquarters. As part of the move to decentralized management, a move that is increasingly familiar in the United States today, Mr. Reichert reduced Brunswick's corporate staff—the people at corporate headquarters—from about 550 to 185 people. Overall, these actions resulted in annual savings of about $20 million. There are now only six layers of management (rather than eight) between Mr. Reichert and the lowest ranking employee.

In Mr. Reichert's new organization the presidents of each division now report directly to him. Decisions that once took weeks or months now take just hours or days. For instance, the president of Brunswick's chain of 130 bowling centers needed a next-day answer on whether he could spend $400,000 to install automatic scorers to ward off a regional competitor. He called Mr. Reichert. "We discussed it, and he said, fine, go ahead," the president said. That would not have happened in the earlier environment.

While he was cutting costs and reorganizing, Mr. Reichert was also revamping the company's strategic plan. The company's highly profitable medical business had been sold as part of a strategy to defeat a hostile takeover attempt in 1982. Mr. Reichert took over shortly thereafter and resisted advice to sell the company's recreation and leisure businesses and concentrate on its defense and industrial businesses. He decided to focus more on marine power products such as outboard motors and stern drives, fishing tackle, and bowling equipment, as well as defense. While he was doing all this, he was also striving to improve morale throughout the firm. For example, he expanded the corporate incentive program fourfold to include the top 500 managers. In one year he spent almost $1 million after taxes to double the 3½ shares awarded each employee under their employee stock ownership plan. In response to these changes, sales and profits have soared while Reichert has kept costs low at the new "lean, mean Brunswick."[1]

Like Brunswick's Mr. Reichert, managers are usually in the middle of all the action. Whether developing a new plan, organizing employees, or setting up incentive plans, managers are the people who "make things happen." In this chapter we take a close look at what managers actually do and the skills they must have to do it.

What Is Management?

management

Management is the process of achieving the organization's aims through the activities of planning, organizing, staffing, directing, and controlling.[2]

Although our focus in this book is on managing business firms, you should understand that managers are needed in any situation that calls for coordinated effort. For example, Professor Leonard Sayles has compared the manager's job to being like a symphony orchestra conductor

> endeavoring to maintain a melodious performance in which the contributions of the various instruments are coordinated and sequenced, patterned and paced, while the orchestra members are having various personal difficulties, stage hands are moving music stands, alternating excessive heat and cold are creating audience and instrument problems, and the sponsor of the concert is insisting on irrational changes in the program.[3]

Armies, scout troops, hospitals, football teams, and all other organized endeavors also depend on managers to plan and organize the work to be done and to ensure unified effort. In a battle the general has to formulate a strategic plan that lays out how his or her armies will do battle. The general also has to choose subordinates and ensure that each is assigned orders that, if carried out, will contribute to the army's victory.

It is simply not possible to have organized effort on any scale without a manager who can coordinate the enterprise's efforts effectively toward achieving its goals. Thus management has been with us since antiquity. Cave-dwelling tribes needed managers to lead them in their search for food. Even the ancient Egyptians depended heavily on some sophisticated management concepts. Have you ever seen the old movie extravaganza "The Ten Commandments" starring Charlton Heston? Watching him organize the thousands of activities involved in designing and building the great pyramids of Egypt, you can appreciate the magnitude of the management jobs these early "executives" faced.

THE MANAGEMENT PYRAMID

Most businesses have "pyramids" of their own. It is customary to classify managers by level according to whether they are top management, middle management, or first-line management. This is illustrated in Figure 5-1 (on p. 140). In most firms the distribution of upper-, middle-,

Top management

Board of directors
President
Executive vice-president
Vice-presidents

3 %

Middle management

Department heads
Plant manager
Plant superintendent

12 %

Lower management

Supervisors
Foremen

85 %

FIGURE 5-1 / The management pyramid.

and lower-level managers is shaped much like a pyramid. There are fewer people in top-level than in middle-level management. Likewise, there are fewer middle-level managers than lower-level managers. Of course, in very small firms the owner might be the only manager. Very large firms will undoubtedly have many more than three levels of manage-

Middle-level managers have managers for subordinates. First-line managers have nonmanagers as subordinates.

management pyramid

ment. For example, there might be six or seven layers of managers between the president and the nonmanagement production employees at a giant corporation. The **management pyramid** illustrates the levels of management in an organization (upper, middle, and lower) and reflects the fact that there are fewer managers at each successively higher level in an organization.

Different levels of managers have much in common. They all get work done through subordinates. They all get involved in planning for others, organizing the work of others, recruiting, motivating, and controlling. And they all usually spend about two-thirds of their time with people—talking, listening, attending meetings, and so forth.[4]

But there are some very important differences. First, executives and middle managers *both have managers for subordinates*—they are in charge of other managers. Supervisors (first-line management), on the other hand, have workers (nonmanagers) as subordinates. The emphasis of their jobs is also different, as is illustrated in Figure 5-2. Managers who are higher in the organization spend more time planning, organizing, and staffing. Lower-level managers spend more time directing and controlling the work.

Top managers spend more time than other managers planning and setting objectives. Middle managers then take these objectives (for example, "double sales in the next two years") and translate them into specific projects (such as "hire three new salespeople and introduce two new products"). First-line supervisors then spend most of their time actually directing and controlling the employees who work on these projects. First-line supervisors are thus always "on the firing line." Their job is getting the work done on time. They have standards to meet and must press their people to keep quality up and costs down. Let's look more closely at each management level.

TOP MANAGEMENT

Do you know how much Lee Iacocca, Chairman of Chrysler Corporation, earned in 1987? In that year his total pay (including salary, bonus, and stock options) amounted to $17,896,000. Paul Fireman, Chairman of Footwear Company Reebok International, earned $15,424,000. Lawrence G. Rawl, Chairman of Exxon, earned $5,464,000.[5]

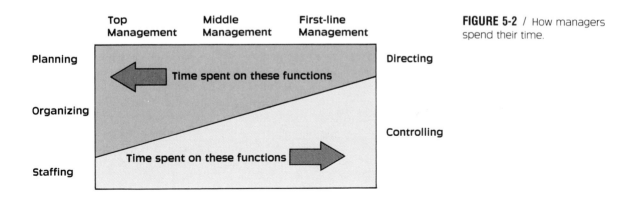

FIGURE 5-2 / How managers spend their time.

In other words, top executives are generally very well paid, especially if they are associated with major business corporations. What do chief executives and other top managers do to warrant such handsome pay? Many critics charge that these top managers are overpaid. Commenting on Mr. Iacocca's income, for instance, Owen F. Bieber, President of the United Auto Workers, said, "No one individual can possibly be worth that much money to a corporation."[6]

That may be true, but just consider what Mr. Iacocca accomplished during his first six years as Chairman and CEO of Chrysler.

When Lee Iacocca was elected Chairman of the Board and Chief Executive Officer of Chrysler on September 20, 1979, he took over a company that had its back to the wall. Chrysler had lost over $200 million in 1978. When the Shah of Iran was overthrown in January 1979, fears of another oil crisis caused consumers to drastically curtail their purchases of large cars, which were Chrysler's bread and butter. Unable to produce enough small cars to meet the demand and faced with an oversupply of new large cars, the company approached the federal government for a loan. It was rebuffed.

Mr. Iacocca came on board in September of that year and took command at once. He shepherded through $1.5 billion dollars in federal loan guarantees. He arranged for almost the same amount of assistance by banks that held a stake in Chrysler's continued existence. He convinced the United Auto Workers to grant Chrysler major contract concessions. These allowed him to lay off thousands of workers, cut salaries, and delay pay increases. Mr. Iacocca accepted a starting salary of $1 per year until Chrysler was back in shape. He closed numerous plants, built new ones, and lopped off layers of management. He revised the firm's strategy, focusing more on smaller, high-quality cars. He encouraged a commitment to quality throughout the firm. He sold off non-car businesses. He became the firm's personal representative in its new ads.

By early 1988, Chrysler Corporation was flying high. The loan guarantees had long been paid off, and its stock had risen from a low of $3 per share to $39 or more. In 1987, Chrysler bought auto makers Lamborghini and American Motors Corporation and an interest in Maserati. In less than seven years, Mr. Iacocca took a giant corporation teetering on the brink of bankruptcy and turned it into a vibrant, competitive firm. The average number of cars built per employee at Chrysler jumped from about ten in 1980 to almost twenty in 1984. By early 1988 the firm had moved from number ten to number five in the world market for cars. It had done this largely through the managerial capabilities of Lee Iacocca. He was able to take an enormously complex set of challenges and formulate the changes that the company had to make. Through the force of his managerial skills he was then able to implement the required changes in a relatively short span of years. Do you think that Owen Beiber was right when he said that "no one individual can possibly be worth that much money to a corporation"?

What exactly do we know about top managers' work? For one thing, we know that top managers spend more of their time than do lower-level managers in developing plans for the enterprise. It is usually top management that decides what products the firm will sell and what strengths it will use to compete in the marketplace, for instance. To make these plans, top management needs information about competitors, the economy, and the firm's customers. In fact, Professor Henry Mintzberg has found that the processing of information is a key part of the top manager's job.[7] The chief executives that Professor Mintzberg focused on in his study spent 40% of the time they spent with other people at work on activities devoted exclusively to the transmission of information.

Professor Mintzberg also found that, to get the kinds of information they needed, the five chief executives he studied were in contact with an incredibly wide range of people. Figure 5-3 gives an idea of the kinds of contacts chief executives have.

These chief executives spent about 48 percent of the time that they spent with other people with their subordinates. They spent the rest of their time with other people such as clients, suppliers, company directors, and "independents" like government agency heads.

MIDDLE MANAGERS

The term "middle management" covers a wide range of managerial jobs. These fall roughly between the vice-presidents on the top management level and the front-line supervisors on the bottom level of the management pyramid. Production managers, sales managers, purchasing managers, personnel managers, marketing research managers, advertising managers, and quality control managers are just some of the titles of people in "middle management."

As we mentioned above, middle managers spend much of their time translating the goals and plans of top managers into specific proj-

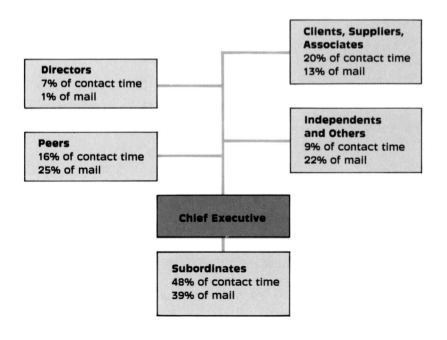

Directors
7% of contact time
1% of mail

Peers
16% of contact time
25% of mail

Clients, Suppliers, Associates
20% of contact time
13% of mail

Independents and Others
9% of contact time
22% of mail

Chief Executive

Subordinates
48% of contact time
39% of mail

FIGURE 5-3 / The chief executive's contacts. (*Source:* Reprinted by permission of the *Harvard Business Review*. An exhibit from "The Manager's Job: Folklore and Fact" by Henry Mintzberg (July/August 1975). Copyright © 1975 by the President and Fellows of Harvard College; all rights reserved.)

APPLICATION: BURGER KING
Moving Up in Management

How do you go about becoming a Burger King® restaurant manager? What is it like to be one? What is the career potential of the job?

In most cases you will not start off as a restaurant manager but as a crew member or perhaps an assistant store manager. There is a "crew development ladder" in each restaurant, says an executive at Burger King University, Burger King Corporation's Miami training facility. A person might start as a crew member before graduating from high school. These are the people who take care of food preparation, customer service, and restaurant sanitation. On that job a crew member must learn all about the different stations in the restaurant. Some of these are the broiler/steamer, the drink station, and the Whopper®

sandwich/burger board where the burgers are prepared.

The next step up could be to production leader (PL). A PL is the working supervisor for the food production operation in the back of the restaurant. The PL is responsible for jobs like reviewing the number and positioning of employees, ensuring uniform dress and hygiene, and ensuring that all stations are stocked to appropriate levels (since running out of burgers could be disastrous).

Training coordinator is the next higher position. The store's training coordinator trains new employees in correct station operating procedures. This is a very important job. New crew members are always being hired or switched from job to job, and it is obviously crucial that each crew member be able to do his or her job quickly and effectively.

The next step up the ladder could be to shift supervisor. The shift supervisor is still an hourly paid employee, not a manager. A shift supervisor

thus cannot hire, fire, or discipline employees, although he or she can make recommendations to his or her restaurant management. But a shift supervisor is trained to supervise both food preparation and customer service personnel as a working supervisor. A shift supervisor is right on the front line, controlling, directing, and maintaining restaurant operational standards at all times. A shift supervisor must also be thoroughly knowledgeable about cash-handling techniques—for example, how to void an erroneous order.

A shift supervisor could be promoted to assistant manager. The major function of an assistant manager is to manage a restaurant shift, supervising approximately thirty-five crew members in a restaurant with average sales of about $1 million per year. The immediate supervisor is the restaurant manager, who of course cannot be there for every shift, seven days a week. The assistant manager is therefore in charge of the restaurant in the manager's ab-

ects. First-line supervisors and their subordinates then have to implement these projects.

Over the years, the middle management section of the management pyramid has swelled. Many people today consider it to be too bloated. For example, the middle managers of Apex Company's Sales Division might include a director of sales, several regional sales managers, and numerous market research and advertising managers, perhaps all reporting to a vice-president.

The mergers, consolidations, and stress on boosting corporate performance that swept the United States in the 1980s caused a squeezing

sence. The assistant manager hires crew members, sees that they are trained, supervises their work, evaluates crew member performance, and completes various reports such as daily inventory and cash control records and purchase transmittal forms (to make sure the restaurant has the supplies it needs). This job probably requires a high school diploma and two years of college or equivalent supervisory experience.

When a restaurant manager position opens, a decision has to be made about which assistant manager to promote. This decision is usually made by the owner of the restaurant, perhaps with input from the regional Burger King Corporation personnel and district management experts. A manager works five shifts per week, including four day shifts and one swing (evening) shift on the busiest day of the week. He or she must also put in an occasional night shift.

This is a big and busy job. Typically, a manager has two assistant managers reporting to him or her and has the overall responsibility "to operate a Burger King restaurant in a manner which ensures maximum profit-

ability, sales, and compliance with Burger King operating standards." The manager is in charge of the whole ball game, so to speak. If you become a manager, you will have to make sure to hire enough employees, schedule their work, supervise the crew to make sure customers are treated promptly and courteously, and make sure employees are provided with on-the-job training in all aspects of restaurant operations. You will be in charge of maintaining financial controls in the store to make sure all cash is accounted for, and (with the assistant manager) will have to handle customer complaints. You will also participate in a variety of community relation activities in order to generate good will toward the restaurant and maintain the company's image as a good corporate citizen.

Where can you go after that? As one regional vice-president, who has had most of the jobs just described, said:

> Being a regional vice-president is similar to being a restaurant manager in many ways. Now my customer is the franchisee because he pays us for the right to own one of our restaurants.

The support and service we provide to a franchisee have to be timely and efficient, with the same high standards we strive for in each restaurant.

I've gained something valuable from every job opportunity I've had with Burger King, and as regional vice-president I use it all. I don't regret taking any extra steps along the way. I've always come out ahead.

Questions

1. What benefits do Burger King Corporation and Burger King employees derive from the "crew development ladder" concept? Are there any drawbacks?

2. What are the major similarities and differences between a shift supervisor's job and a restaurant manager's job?

3. If you were the head of Burger King University, which of the managerial skills would you consider to be most important to a restaurant manager? How would you help trainees to develop these skills?

out of such middle managers. For example, between 1982 and 1987, U.S. corporations eliminated the jobs of almost half a million middle- and upper-level managers. By 1990, another 400,000 might well have been laid off.[8] Many of these people were earning $50,000 or more. It has been estimated that finding a new job takes someone about one month per $10 thousand of previous income. It is therefore not unusual for many middle managers to be out of work seven months or more. Even IBM, a champion of lifetime employment, had found ways to lop off 12,000 of its U.S. work force by the end of 1987. IBM did this through attrition, a freeze on hiring, and a new voluntary retirement plan. Many of the middle managers who remained with the firm are being "redeployed" to other jobs. For instance, an assistant sales manager in New York might be redeployed as a field sales person in Fort Lauderdale, Florida.

FIRST-LINE SUPERVISORS (DAY-DAY OPERATIONS)

The jobs of many first-line supervisors have changed dramatically in recent years for two reasons. First, middle managers are being squeezed out of the management pyramid. Therefore the planning and decision making formerly done by middle managers is increasingly the responsibility of first-line supervisors. Second, the nature of the work force is changing, requiring new management styles. Companies must deal with an increasingly educated, sophisticated, and (on the average) older work force. These workers demand a less authoritarian supervisory approach than did workers in the past. So-called "Japanese management techniques" also require a more participative approach to first-line management. In the Japanese method, for instance, cars are built by small teams of cooperating employees rather than on long assembly lines.

The Ford Motor Company has set up a new program called "employee involvement" at most of its plants. Problem-solving groups of employees and supervisors meet every two weeks to analyze and solve production and quality problems. At some Ford plants, assembly line workers also have "stop buttons." These enable them to stop the entire assembly line if they see a defect in a car. Changes like these are aimed at boosting productivity and quality.

But doing so requires a different breed of first-line supervisor. A foreman who used to describe himself as being a "hard-nosed, loud-mouthed disciplinarian" now spends more time chatting with employees. He also spends more time drawing better plans for the flow of material and making minor engineering changes without calling the plant engineers. He cannot spend his time marching up and down the assembly line barking at workers to get their jobs done. The new type of first-line supervisor has to depend much more on logic, technical expertise, intelligence, and leadership to work with teams of increasingly sophisticated workers. This new supervisor will have to spend more time planning and organizing the work to be done. Less time will be spent directly supervising his or her employees.[9]

The Management Process

the management process

From the discussion of Jack Reichert of the Brunswick Corporation at the beginning of this chapter, we can see that all managers perform certain basic functions. **The management process** consists of the basic functions of planning, organizing, staffing, directing, and controlling. All managers—whether they are supervisors at IBM, city managers, school principals, or bank managers—carry out these five basic functions. Of course, a manager usually cannot neatly pigeonhole specific hours as being for "planning" rather than "controlling," for example. A manager might find that in developing plans for her team (planning), she must simultaneously motivate the members to make suggestions (leadership). However, classifying management work into these five functions gives us an organized way to describe many of the important activities in which most managers engage. (For an expanded view of the sorts of roles managers play, see the Business in the News box.)

PLANNING

planning

Planning is the process of setting goals and deciding on the methods of achieving them. As summarized in Figure 5-4, there are four main steps in the planning process:

Step 1. Develop forecasts and basic planning assumptions. For example, do you foresee big increases in competitor's efforts next year which will require that you increase your advertising budget?

Step 2. Define specific objectives. Here, for instance, you might decide your goal is to "increase our market share by 8 percent." Note that unless you know what goals you are shooting for (in this case increasing market

FIGURE 5-4 / Steps in the planning process. (*Source:* Gary Dessler, *Management Fundamentals: Modern Principles and Practices,* 4th edition, 1988. Reprinted by permission of Prentice Hall, Inc., Englewood Cliffs, New Jersey.)

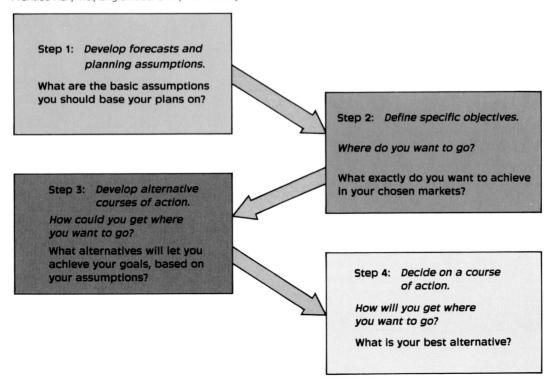

share by 8 percent) you really cannot do much serious planning. For instance, increasing market share might mean increased advertising and hiring more salespeople. If you had a different goal—such as boosting your profitability—your plans would probably look entirely different. For example, instead of spending more on advertising and salespeople, you might want to install more modern machines.

Step 3. Develop alternative courses of action. Here you decide how to get where you want to go. After making forecasts and assessing your strengths and weaknesses,

BUSINESS IN THE NEWS
The Renewal Factor

In his new book, *The Renewal Factor*, Robert H. Waterman, Jr. (coauthor with Tom Peters of *In Search of Excellence*) makes the point that managers should do more than just manage their firms. He says they must actively try to change and renew their firms to make sure they can survive in a changing world. Here are the eight major things Mr. Waterman says this renewal is based on:

1. Informed optimism. Renewing companies treat information as their main competitive advantage and flexibility as their main strategic weapon. Mr. Waterman says, "Their ability is to sense opportunities where others can't, see it where others can't, act while others hesitate,

and demur when others plunge. They behave as informed opportunists, equal emphasis on both words."

2. Direction and empowerment. Mr. Waterman says that renewing companies treat everyone as a source of creative input. All the renewing companies he studied are busy taking out layers of management, cutting staff, and pushing decisions down. The result of all this is not just better operations and lower administration costs. "It is also more autonomy for each person. Because of delayering, reduction in corporate staffs, and radical decentralization, people at almost every level are finding they have more freedom and more flexibility. Leaner organizations set the stage for renewal. They make each one of us more important. They empower the individual."

3. Friendly facts, congenial controls. Firms that are good at

renewing themselves, says Mr. Waterman, treat facts as friends and financial controls as liberating. First, they have an enormous hunger for facts and "see information where others see only data." They love comparisons, rankings, and anything that combines the data in ways that help to make it more useful. Controls are not seen as keeping workers under managers' thumbs. They are viewed more as "benign checks and balances that allow them to be creative and free" because the controls will let everyone know when things are heading off track.

4. A different mirror. Top managers in companies that are good at renewing themselves are not isolated from their employees and the world around them. Instead they listen—to their customers, competitors, first-line employees, suppliers, consultants, outside directors, politicians, and just about everyone else. In other words, you might find that there are several courses of action you *could* follow to accomplish your goals.

Step 4. Decide on a course of action. Finally, you will want to evaluate your alternatives and make a choice.

Planning is important because it provides direction and a sense of unity for a firm. It helps to ensure that the firm's efforts are all aimed at achieving the same objective, rather than being haphazard and uncoordinated.

It is not difficult to see what happens without a well-conceived plan. For example, imagine that you are getting ready to declare your major at school. You must decide not only what major you will empha-

---

they seek a different mirror, something to tell them what they and their companies really look like and how they are coming across. On the basis of that information these firm's top managers can keep their companies renewed and changed.

5. Teamwork, trust, politics, and power. Renewers, says Mr. Waterman, "constantly use words such as teamwork and trust. They are relentless in fighting office politics and power contests and in breaking down the barriers that paralyze action." Most of the renewing companies "had a calm at the centers: there was quiet intensity and determination without the helter-skelter behavior, slamming doors, shouting voices, frenetic movement, and general bedlam that poses for productive activity at stagnating companies."

6. Stability in motion. The renewing companies also know how to keep things moving. In many of the renewing companies he studied, Mr. Waterman found all sorts of devices to keep the organization fluid. As

he says, "people move more often and with greater degrees of freedom across functions, divisions, from line to staff and vice versa. They move laterally. Promotion from within is the rule, but key skills are brought in when needed from the outside." Renewal requires a constant interplay between stability and change. Renewing organizations find and manage a delicate balance: enough security so that people will take risks, enough uncertainty so that people will strive.

7. Attitudes and attention. What a manager does, says Mr. Waterman, is a lot more influential than what he or she says. "Attention makes a difference, and so do attitudes and expectations. If I expect you to do well, you probably will do well, and if I expect the reverse, you probably won't do as well. Psychologists call it the Pygmalion Effect. Managers who renew companies understand this." If you want someone to act like a winner, you have to show that person that you think of him or her as a winner.

8. Causes and commitment. Finally, renewing companies and their managers "seem to be able to pick causes and communicate them in a way that conveys an element of risk—of challenge—but not foolishly so." In fact, "renewing organizations seem to run on causes. Quality is the most prevalent cause, even for longtime champs like Maytag and Hewlett-Packard. At Ford, it's employee involvement, quality, and the customer. At Club Med, Inc. the cause is to make each person's vacation an escape, "an antidote to civilization." The cause that energized the San Francisco Symphony was its aspiration to be among the world's great orchestras. Causes and a commitment to those causes are thus cornerstones on which renewing companies build their renewal.

Source: Robert H. Waterman, Jr., *The Renewal Factor: How the Best Get and Keep a Competitive Edge,* Bantam Books, New York, 1987. Reprinted by permission of Bantam Books, a division of Random, Doubleday, Dell Publishing Group, Inc.

---

size but also, within that major, which specific required and elective courses you will take. At the same time you might have to make a decision about what job or jobs to take while you are in college. You hope to develop the work experience you will need to get a good job in your chosen field after you graduate.

Without a career plan that identifies your target occupation after graduation you will find it difficult to specify which major is best for you, which courses you should take, and which extracurricular activities would be best. Planning serves a similar purpose in business firms. It provides a unifying direction. The firm's managers can then use this in evaluating which decisions are best for their firm.

Plans do not always work out as you would like them to. Several years ago, Deere and Company, the country's largest maker of farm equipment (such as tractors) decided to build a highly automated production plant in Waterloo, Iowa. Management's plans were formulated on several assumptions. One was that demand for tractors would continue to grow. Instead, a depression in the farm belt drastically cut the demand for farm equipment in the early 1980s. Deere's billion-dollar plant stood virtually idle until 1987, when domestic and foreign demand picked up. Planning, in other words, is certainly important. But plans are no better than the assumptions they are built on and the way in which they are carried out.

Most managers distinguish between strategic planning and operational (or "tactical") planning. **Strategic planning** is the process of developing a broad plan for how a business is going to compete in its industry, what its goals should be, and what policies will be needed to achieve these goals.[10] Strategic planning usually focuses on questions like "How diversified should our firm be?" and "How should we distinguish ourselves from our competitors?" The Consolidated Frieghtways ad shows how the firm plans for the future.

Here are some examples of strategic planning with which you may be familiar:

> Coca-Cola Company's decision to reduce its dependency on the soft drink market by purchasing part of Columbia Pictures and by establishing a licensing arm to license its name on a new line of clothing.
> Pepsi Cola Company's decision to diversify by purchasing such businesses as Frito-Lay and Pizza Hut.
> United Airline's decision to purchase Hertz Rent-a-Car and Hilton Hotels in order to become a "fully integrated" travel company. If all had gone according to plan (which it did not), travelers could have made one call to United, whose reservation clerks could then book their flight, arrange for their rental car, and make their hotel reservations all at the same time.

Operational planning is the process of formulating shorter-term plans for implementing the firm's overall strategic plan. For example, top management at Burger King Corporation made the strategic decision to expand geographically and open stores outside of the United States. It then fell to others to formulate operational plans for how exactly this would be done. In England a Burger King subsidiary then

Strategic planning is long-range
planning.

had to formulate operational plans for identifying and purchasing locations in and around London and for acquiring suppliers and staff.

Different levels of managers usually emphasize different types of
planning. As illustrated in Figure 5.5 (on p. 152), top-level managers
devote most of their planning time to strategic planning. Lower-level
managers (such as supervisors) are usually not very involved in strategic planning. Their main planning effort is devoted to operational or

Upper-level
managers

Strategic
planning

Middle-level
managers

Operational
planning

Lower-level
managers

FIGURE 5-5 / The relative importance of strategic and operational planning at the various levels of management.

tactical planning. This often involves little more than planning the day's production run for the plant. Middle-level managers devote some planning time to both strategic and operational planning. For example, sales and production managers are an important source of the information about competitive changes on which top management will base its strategic plans. At the same time these middle managers are responsible for taking top management's plans and developing shorter-term operational plans to implement them.[11]

objective

Setting goals or objectives is the heart of the planning process. This is because a manager first has to identify what he or she wants to achieve before courses of action can be formulated. An **objective** is a specific achievement to be attained at some future date. For example,

Middle- and lower-level managers formulate operational plans to implement top management's strategic plans.

"achieving a 40 percent share of the fast food market in London by 1992" might be a goal for Burger King Corporation.

Firms usually set goals in different areas. For example, as summarized in Figure 5-6, the General Electric Company sets goals in eight key performance areas, including profitability, market position, and productivity. Goals should always be specific and measurable so that a firm knows when it has achieved them (or has fallen short). These specific, measurable goals not only enable a firm to formulate plans. They also become the standards against which employees' performance is measured.

management by objectives (MBO)

Management by objectives (MBO) is a technique in which a superior and subordinates jointly set the subordinates' goals and periodically assess progress toward these goals. The term MBO almost always refers to a comprehensive organizationwide program for setting goals. The use of MBO is based on the assumption that when employees participate in setting their own goals, they are more apt to be committed to accomplishing them.

The MBO process itself consists of five steps, as follows:

1. **Set the firm's overall goals.** First, the company's overall strategic plan and objectives are formulated.
2. **Set departmental goals.** Next, department heads and superiors jointly set goals for their departments.
3. **Discuss departmental goals.** Next, department heads discuss de-

---

1. *Profitability:* How much profit a manager earns relative to the size of his or her investment.
2. *Market position:* The market share of the manager's product.
3. *Productivity:* For example, in terms of payroll costs relative to products produced.
4. *Product leadership:* In terms of GE's ability to lead an industry in the development and marketing of new and existing products.
5. *Personnel development:* For example, in terms of how effectively a manager trains and promotes his or her subordinates.
6. *Employee attitudes:* At GE employees take attitude surveys which allow managers to pinpoint potential morale problems.
7. *Public responsibility:* The company also believes that its responsibility to employees, suppliers, local communities, and the business community should be measurable. For example, responsibility to suppliers could be measured by administering surveys to those suppliers.
8. *Balance between short- and long-range goals:* Finally, GE also tries to ensure that managers do not overemphasize short-range goals (such as for increased productivity) at the expense of long-range profitability (by, for example, reducing machine maintenance expenditures).

FIGURE 5-6 / Goals for General Electric. (Based on discussion in William Travers Jerome III, *Executive Control—The Catalyst,* John Wiley & Sons 1961, pp. 219–237.)

partment goals with all subordinates and ask them to develop their own individual goals.

4. **Set individual goals.** Each manager and subordinate in each department then jointly set the subordinate's goals and assign a timetable for accomplishing them.

5. **Feedback.** Periodic performance review meetings between superior and subordinates help them to monitor and analyze progress toward the subordinate's goals.[12]

Ideally, the result of this process is a hierarchy of goals like that presented in Figure 5-7. Notice how the goals at each level are formulated in such a way as to contribute to the goals of the higher level. For example, the Topeka plant's inventory control manager has a goal of reducing inventory costs by 10 percent. This contributes to the Topeka plant manager's goal of reducing overall production costs by 16 percent. In turn, the plant manager's goal of reducing production costs contributes to the goal of the production vice-president. This is to reduce total corporate production costs by 15 percent. Similarly, the vice-president's goal of reducing production costs contributes to the president's goal of increasing the company's profitability by 10 percent.

ORGANIZING

organizing

Once the firm's plans have been made, the work that needs to be done to carry out these plans must be *organized*. **Organizing** is the process of arranging the resources of the firm in such a way that its activities systematically contribute to the firm's goals. The purposes of organizing are to give each person a distinct task and to ensure that these tasks are coordinated in such a way that the firm accomplishes its goals. Thus an organization consists of people who carry out tasks that are coordinated to contribute to overall goals. Organizing is discussed in Chapter 7.

STAFFING

staffing

Staffing is the process of recruiting, selecting, training, appraising, and developing employees. It is a crucial management function. Firms certainly need resources like cash and equipment. However, it is the firm's human resource—its employees—that determines success or failure. Staffing is explained in Chapters 8 and 9.

DIRECTING

directing

Once the firm's plans, organization, and staff are all in place, the manager must direct the firm's activity so its various goals are achieved. **Directing** is the process of providing the motivation and leadership that is necessary for ensuring that the firm's employees do their jobs and accomplish their goals. In the Brunswick example at the beginning of this chapter, top managers knew that they had to provide the necessary leadership and motivation if their subordinates were to perform well. New salary and incentive programs were instituted, providing greater rewards for top performers. Leadership and motivation are discussed in Chapter 6.

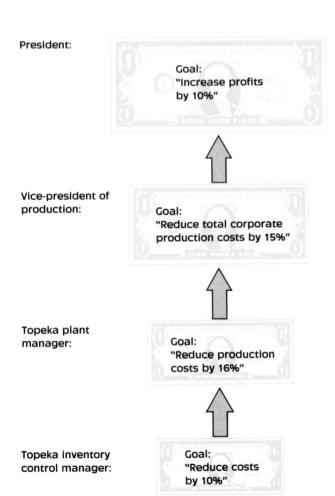

President:

Goal: "Increase profits by 10%"

Vice-president of production:

Goal: "Reduce total corporate production costs by 15%"

Topeka plant manager:

Goal: "Reduce production costs by 16%"

Topeka inventory control manager:

Goal: "Reduce costs by 10%"

Note: Each lower level goal contributes to the achieving of the next higher level goal. Other managers—like the vice-president of sales, the Topeka plant manager, and the production manager at the Topeka plant—would also have specific goals assigned to them. There is thus a hierarchy of goals.

FIGURE 5-7 / A hierarchy of goals.

CONTROLLING

controlling

Every manager must ensure that his or her workers are performing as expected. **Controlling** is the task of ensuring that activities are providing the planned results. As summarized in Figure 5-8 (on p. 156), the function of controlling involves setting a control standard or target, measuring performance, identifying deviations, and taking corrective action if necessary. All control systems collect, store, and transmit information on profits, sales, or some other factor. All control systems are aimed at influencing employee behavior (such as by "getting costs back down to where they should be"). This is one reason why the phrase "controlling someone" often has negative overtones. Controlling also requires that targets, standards, or goals be set. This is why the word "planning" is always used along with the word "control."

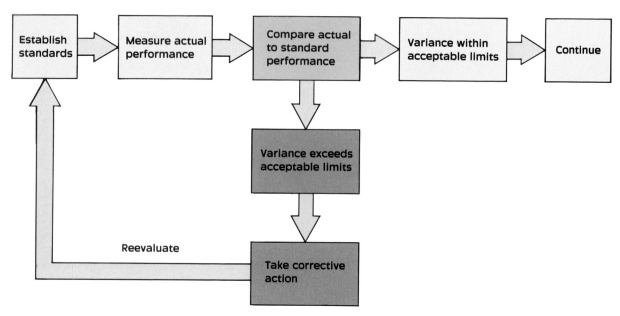

FIGURE 5-8 / The control process.

Examples of what happens when activities go out of control are all around us. For example, on the cover of its September 15, 1986 issue *Fortune* magazine presented a picture of a smiling President Reagan. The caption was "what managers can learn from manager Reagan." The article explained how President Reagan set broad goals for his subordinates and then let them have enough freedom to achieve these goals on their own. But while President Reagan was upstairs in the White House, Lieutenant Colonel Oliver North was negotiating with heads of state and secretly sending arms shipments around the world. It seems that on this matter, at least, President Reagan and his White House staff might have lost control over a major area of responsibility. The results have been agonizing for all concerned.

As mentioned above, planning and controlling are inseparable. For example, when a person prepares a budget, he or she is planning *and* setting up a control device. Suppose the budget plan is to save $100 a month for twelve months. If the savings account shows a balance of only $200 halfway through the year, the goal is not being met. Awareness of this should lead to corrective action. The earlier the deviation is discovered, the more quickly corrective action can be achieved.

management by exception

The principle of **management by exception** holds that only significant deviations or exceptions from standards should be brought to the manager's attention. For example, a firm establishes a quality control standard that allows three defects per hundred units. Under the management by exception rule, only significant deviations from the standard (four or more defects per hundred units in this case) should be brought to the manager's attention. The principle of management by exception is aimed at conserving the manager's time. It also ensures that he or she need address only important matters. The manager need not be too bothered with control reports as long as performance is in line with planned standards.

Basic Managerial Skills

In every occupation, certain skills are needed for success. A surgeon must be decisive and have the technical skills to perform intricate operations. A champion athlete must have the combination of reflexes and skills that enable him or her to run, play, or jump better than almost anyone else.

It should come as no surprise that managers also need certain skills. The more successful managers seem to have more of these skills than do others. Not every manager needs the same amount of each skill. This is because some skills are more important for some types of jobs or industries than are others. Generally speaking, though, every manager should have each of these skills to some degree. The basic **managerial skills** are:

managerial skills

- Conceptual skills
- Interpersonal or "people" skills
- Technical skills
- Emotional skills
- Analytical skills
- Motivation to manage.[13]

■ Decision Making
■ Negotiating Skills

Figure 5-9 shows the degrees of each skill needed at the different management levels.

FIGURE 5-9 / Skills that all managers need at every level.

	Conceptual	Analytical	Emotional	People	Technical	Motivation to manage
Top management	High	High	High	High	Low	High
Middle management	Medium	Medium	Medium	Medium	Medium	Medium
First-line management	Low	Low	Medium	Medium	High	Medium

IT'S YOUR BUSINESS
Do It Now!

It's midnight, and the report that has been sitting on your desk for three weeks is due tomorrow. You've had a hard day, but you know that if the report isn't in on time you could lose your job. You drag yourself to your desk and vaguely wonder why you put off the report in the first place. You knew it had to be done, and you feel guilty about having procrastinated.

What is procrastination? How can you reduce your tendency to put things off? Recent work by psychologists at the counseling center of the University of California at Berkeley provides some answers, as reported in *Psychology Today*.

Procrastination means needlessly and irrationally postponing something you know you have to do. If you put it off because you are sure you can get out of doing it or because you haven't got all the data you need, you are probably not procrastinating.

Why do people procrastinate? There are several common causes, most of which boil down to protecting a vulnerable sense of self-esteem. People who procrastinate tend to fall into one of several categories:

Test-avoiders: These people are afraid of failing to meet their own high standards, standards that demand outstanding performance every time. By waiting until it is too late to do a "great" job, they can explain away a mediocre performance by telling themselves they "didn't have enough time."

Rebels: For these people, adhering to someone else's timetable means being controlled or dominated. Procrastination becomes a means of retaining a sense of power and control.

Myopics: Some procrastinate because they consider certain tasks onerous or unpleasant. They feel they should put their efforts into other, more satisfying or necessary pursuits. They opt for immediate gratification over what is often in their long-run best interests.

Revengers: Procrastination can be a way of getting back at a person—such as a boss—or a job the person doesn't like.

Masochists: These people have low self-esteem and get a perverse kick out of being caught producing the job late. The masochist's reward comes from being yelled at or abused.

Self-defeaters: Some actually fear doing well; procrastination guarantees that they don't excel.

How do you reduce your own tendency to procrastinate? There are several approaches.

First, draw up a list of the excuses you use, such as: "I've been working so hard I deserve a break." Then monitor your thoughts and try to analyze your excuses as they occur. Experts say that few people can give up procrastinating until they understand the function it serves in their lives.

Dispute your irrational assumptions. When most people procrastinate, they make irrational assumptions such as: "I'll be able to get that project done the night before it's due." Level with yourself about the actual consequences of delay.

Break the task into parts. Many procrastinators believe that unless they have a large block of time available, there is no point in getting started. With the project divided into pieces, even a half-hour of work a day becomes an accomplishment.

Reward yourself with something you really enjoy everytime you complete a part. Or make some big reward—such as a new camera or a trip—contingent on completing the whole project. This is most important when the task is unpleasant. Keep a checklist to mark off as you complete each part.

Combine rewards with punishment. Force yourself to eat an unappetizing meal whenever you fail to complete that day's part of the project, for example.

Expect setbacks from time to time. Bounce back from an "off day" and get to work on the task the next day.

Source: "Mind Games Procrastinators Play," *Psychology Today*, Jan. 1982, pp. 32–37, 44.

CONCEPTUAL SKILLS

A manager with conceptual skills can see the organization as a whole—as a complex of parts that interact with and depend on one another. The manager also sees how the organization relates to its environment, including customers and competitors.

As you can imagine, managing a company—even a fairly small one—can be complicated. Giving one employee a raise might lead other employees to demand more money too. Raising prices might mean that customers buy less and your production machines stand idle. A competitor's new advertising campaign might need a quick response that could also require hiring two new salespeople.

A company is a system in which all parts are interrelated, like the gears in a machine. The company must also interact with elements outside the firm, such as customers and competitors. Few decisions that a manager makes affect only one area without somehow causing changes in other areas. For example, raising prices might reduce sales, which would mean less production needed, so some employees would have to be laid off. Successful managers therefore must have *conceptual skills*. They must have the ability to see the relationships among all these factors and to see the company as a whole. They can therefore anticipate how a move on their part will affect and be affected by the other parts of the system.

INTERPERSONAL OR PEOPLE SKILLS

Managers get their work done *through other people*. Therefore the ability to influence, supervise, lead, and control people at all levels is a skill all managers must have.

People skills are human relations skills. They allow the manager to get along and work with people, both superiors and subordinates. To build team effort, managers have to work effectively with group members. People skills include communication, motivation, and leadership. They are perhaps the most important managerial skills and are discussed in more detail in Chapter 6.

TECHNICAL SKILLS

Technical skills involve a manager's ability to understand and use techniques, methods, equipment, and procedures—to understand how things operate. These skills are most important at the lower management level. First-line supervisors, for example, must know how to operate the machinery their subordinates use. As a manager moves up the management hierarchy, technical skills become less important than conceptual and interpersonal skills.

EMOTIONAL SKILLS

Imagine for a moment that you have just gotten a good job as the assistant manager of a large store. Someone else who has worked at the store for years really wanted your job. Every time you come in late or stay away a bit too long for lunch, she calls your boss, who happens to be

An important people skill is being able to disagree in a courteous, friendly manner.

her cousin. She is also thoughtful enough to send you copies of letters that she sends your boss explaining why she thinks you are buying all the wrong merchandise for the store.

Managing is often filled with situations like these, ones that can turn a person's stomach into knots. Managers therefore need emotional skills. This is the ability to be stimulated by emotional and interpersonal crises rather than exhausted or wrung out by them. Since there is often a lot riding on a manager's shoulders, he or she must have the capacity to bear high levels of responsibility without losing the ability to act. These are the emotional skills a manager needs.

ANALYTICAL SKILLS

Should Chrysler buy American Motors or not? Should Joan hire Sam or take a chance on Bill? Should Apex Company buy that machine or not? Almost everything a manager does involves analyzing situations and making decisions. That is why analytical skills—the ability to identify, analyze, and solve problems under conditions of incomplete information and uncertainty—are also crucial management skills. We will discuss these later in this chapter.

THE MOTIVATION TO MANAGE

Part of the reason some people are successful managers is that they are highly motivated to be managers. They have a strong desire to be assertive and to tell others what to do. They also have positive relationships with their own bosses. People who are motivated to manage enjoy competition and like standing out from the crowd by taking unique highly visible positions. And they exhibit a willingness to accomplish even those routine day-to-day administrative chores that are a part of managerial work.

Decision Making

Everything a firm does is the result of decisions made by its employees. They decide on goals, what products to make, and what equipment to buy. They also decide what advertising to use, where to get funds, and where to sell products. It is true that the basic functions of management are planning, organizing, staffing, directing, and controlling. But each function involves decisions—for instance, decisions about what goals to set, what people to hire, and how to motivate one's employees.

routine decision

nonroutine decision

There are two basic types of decisions: routine decisions and nonroutine decisions. A **routine decision** is a decision that must be faced over and over. For example, deciding how much withholding tax to subtract from an employee's paycheck is a routine decision. A **nonroutine decision** is one that is nonrecurring and so cannot be completely planned for in advance. Sudden illness, a competitor starting an advertising campaign, or someone opening a competing store across from yours requires nonroutine decision making.

Each type of decision demands a different approach to decision making. Managers often set up policies to handle routine decisions. An office manager might set up a policy of "no smoking in the office." This does away with the need to make a decision each time a worker asks whether he or she may smoke. Nonroutine decisions, on the other hand, call for a lot more creativity and analysis.

decision-making process

The **decision-making process** is the seven basic steps that one goes through to make a decision:

1. Recognizing a problem or opportunity.
2. Gathering information.
3. Developing alternatives.
4. Analyzing alternatives.
5. Choosing the best alternative.
6. Implementing the decision.
7. Evaluating the decision.

First, *a business opportunity must be recognized* before it can be explored. Similarly, a problem must be recognized before it can be attacked. Here, it is important to define the problem clearly and decide whether or not anything will be done about it. For example, Coca-Cola Company was concerned that Pepsi was increasing its share of the market. The company decided to do something about it. It decided to introduce a "new" Coca-Cola.

After recognizing the problem or opportunity, the decision maker's next step is to *gather information*. This might involve talks with company personnel and outsiders who might provide greater insight. Company records and secondary sources of information such as libraries also might be used. Coca-Cola conducted market research to gather information about how consumers liked the taste of its new Coke.

Because computers can store huge amounts of data, many firms now have management information systems. These are made up of people and machines. People feed in the data needed for decision-making purposes. These data are processed, summarized and reported to decision makers who need them.

The information gathered should provide a good feel for the opportunity or problem. Next the decision maker begins to *look for alternative courses of action*. The help of others might be sought in brainstorming sessions. In such sessions, people are encouraged to suggest alternatives freely as they come to mind. Creativity is important, so no evaluation is made of the suggestions at this stage. The aim is to come up with new ways of looking at the opportunity or problem. Then alternative ways of dealing with it are developed. For example, Coca-Cola could have introduced its new Coke alongside of the old formula instead of replacing the old formula. Of course, if there is only one alternative, there is no decision to make.

After making a list of alternatives, the decision maker begins to *analyze them critically*. Alternatives that are not likely to pay off are eliminated. So are those that involve high risk compared to expected payoff. Those that remain are often ranked in terms of their expected payoff or benefits to the firm. The payoff could be stated in terms such as least cost, maximum profit, or maximum service.

This process might involve analyzing the projected consequences of each of the remaining alternatives. For example, "if we don't introduce a new Coke, what will our profits be compared to those if we do introduce it?" Projecting consequences like this is always tough because it involves forecasting the future. Nevertheless, the necessary thought process helps to ensure that decision makers consider the future effects of present decisions.

Ideally, the decision maker should be able to *choose the best alternative* that meets his or her criteria. Suppose Coca-Cola Company's goal is to win back a 40 percent share of the soft drink market. Each alternative (such as changing Coke's formula) must then be evaluated in terms of whether it will accomplish this. On the other hand, if Coca-Cola's goal had been to boost profits, a different alternative might have been chosen, such as cutting costs.

Once the decision has been made, the manager must make sure that *the decision is implemented*. Doing so will require all the managerial skills the person can muster. For the new Coke, new syrups had to be produced, a new ad campaign developed, and new cans and bottles designed.

Finally, as the decision is being implemented, the decision maker will want to *evaluate the results* of the decision. Operations are monitored to see whether the decision is being implemented properly. Monitoring also provides feedback to the manager. This helped Coca-Cola's managers to assess whether or not the "right decision" was made and whether corrective action was needed. Because of feedback, Coca-Cola decided to reintroduce "Classic Coke."

Summary

Managers are people who get things done through others. Management is the process of achieving the organization's aims through the activities of planning, organizing, staffing, directing, and controlling.

Different levels of managers have much in common. They all get work done through subordinates. They all get involved in planning for others, organizing the work of others, recruiting, motivating, and controlling. And they all usually spend about two-thirds of their time with people. On the other hand, executives and middle managers both have managers for subordinates. Supervisors have workers—nonmanagers—as subordinates. Also, as they move up the management pyramid, managers usually spend more of their time planning and organizing. At the lower levels, more time is spent on directing and motivating workers.

The basic functions of management are planning, organizing, staffing, directing, and controlling. Plans are methods, formulated beforehand, for doing or making something. Organizing means arranging the resources of the firm in such a way that its activities systematically contribute to the firm's goals. Staffing involves recruiting, selecting, training, appraising, and developing employees. Directing means providing the motivation and leadership that is necessary for ensuring that the company's employees do their jobs and accomplish their goals. Control is the task of ensuring that activities are providing the planned results.

The four main steps in planning include developing a forecast and basic planning premises, defining specific objectives, developing alternative courses of action, and deciding on a specific course of action.

Strategic planning involves developing a broad plan for how a firm is going to compete in its industry, what its goal should be, and what policies will be needed to achieve these goals. Operational planning, on the other hand, involves formulating short-term plans that are aimed at implementing the firm's overall strategic plan.

Management by objectives (MBO) is a technique in which a superior and subordinates jointly set the subordinates' goals and periodically assess progress toward these goals.

Ideally, the result of this process is a hierarchy of goals. The goals at each level are formulated in such a way as to contribute to the goals of the higher levels.

The function of controlling involves setting a control standard or target, measuring performance, identifying deviations, and taking corrective action if necessary.

Managers all need certain skills. Conceptual skills refer to the manager's ability to see the organization as a whole—as a complex of parts that interact with and depend on one another. Interpersonal or people skills refer to a manager's ability to influence, supervise, lead, and control people at all levels. Technical skills involve a manager's ability to understand and use techniques, methods, equipment, and procedures—to understand how things operate. Emotional skills refer to the person's ability to be stimulated by emotional and interpersonal crises rather than wrung out by them. The manager also needs emotional skills to bear high levels of responsibility without losing the ability to act. Analytical skills—the ability to identify, analyze, and solve problems under conditions of incomplete information and uncertainty—are also crucial management skills. Motivation to manage refers to the successful manager's high desire to be assertive and to tell others what to do. Motivated managers enjoy competition and standing out from the crowd.

The stages in the decision-making process are as follows: recognizing a problem or opportunity, gathering information, developing alternatives, analyzing alternatives, choosing the best alternative, implementing the decision, and evaluating the decision.

Review Questions

1. What types of managerial skills are needed at each level of management? Explain.

2. List and describe the five major functions of management.

3. Describe the similarities and differences between operational and strategic planning. Which one is more important? Why?

4. What is meant by management by objectives (MBO)? What are its advantages? What are some potential problems in implementing the MBO approach?

5. List and describe the stages in the decision-making process.

6. What is meant by a hierarchy of goals?

Discussion Questions

1. Some experts say that middle-level managers have a tougher job than top- or lower-level managers. This is because the work of a middle-level manager is more varied in managerial and nonmanagerial duties. Discuss.

2. Do you think the management techniques that work successfully in Japanese firms could work equally well in U.S. firms?

3. "The major difference between workers and managers is that workers work and managers think." Do you agree?

Key Terms

management
management pyramid
the management process
planning
strategic planning
operational planning

objectives
management by objectives
(MBO)
organizing
staffing
directing

controlling
management by exception
managerial skills
routine decision
nonroutine decision
decision-making process

Cases

MANAGEMENT ERRORS ON THE USS STARK

The "total collapse of the USS Stark's fighting capabilities" triggered a "cascade of failures" that turned the frigate into a sitting duck the night it was attacked by an Iraqi war plane, according to the U.S. Navy's formal investigative report.

"Stark never fired a weapon nor employed a countermeasure either in self-defense or in retaliation," said the report. The report went on to detail numerous errors in judgment and outright mistakes by the Stark's officers and crew in the minutes before the apparently accidental attack.

The report itemized seven weaknesses in the training that Stark's Captain Glenn Brindel gave his crew. It concludes that he had "failed fundamentally to prepare them for their mission." These cumulative failures led to the total collapse of his ship's defensive readiness posture, the inquiry said. "The commanding officer failed to provide combat oriented leadership by allowing Stark's anti-air warfare readiness to disintegrate to the point that his combat information center team was unable to defend the ship."

A number of examples of the Stark's unpreparedness at the time of the attack were detailed in the report. For example, when the Iraqi aircraft began its attack run, "the position of the weapons control officer was vacant." That officer was responsible for ensuring that weapons were ready to fire. Even if the weapons control officer had been present, no one was manning the key weapons he would have used to track and fire on any incoming missiles. The technician assigned to this job had "left the combat information center on personal business." Similarly, the machine guns "were not loaded and the gunners assigned to them were lying down."

According to the report, all of these things occurred in spite of the fact that the USS Stark and its officers should have been better prepared. About a day before the attack they had received another report that "highlighted the possibility of an indiscriminate attack." Furthermore, the rules of engagement at the time of the attack (that governed what the Stark should do if it was attacked) were sufficiently clear to allow the Stark to defend itself. The investigative report recommended that the ship's captain and the tactical action officer face court marshal under military rules. However, the two men left the Navy before such action was taken.[14]

Questions

1. Which of the five management functions did the ship's captain seem to have executed poorly in this case?
2. Why do you think these errors could have been made despite the fact that the Stark had been warned and should have been better prepared?
3. What does this case illustrate about the need for and inadequacies of managerial planning?

GREMLINS AT AMES DEPARTMENT STORES

When he became president of Ames Department Stores, Inc. in 1986, Peter B. Hollis got a lot more than he bargained for. The company had a reputation for being one of the best managed retailers. Ames, centered in Connecticut, had recently nearly doubled in size by acquiring a Pennsylvania chain. The sky looked like the limit.

But that was before the store's inventory started disappearing. Retail stores take periodic inventories to compare the merchandise that was bought for the store with what is now left in the stores. The difference should be what was sold, and it should show up on the books as sales for the period. In the case of Ames, though, the auditors found enormous discrepancies between what should have been in the stores and what was actually there. In the retail trade this difference is known as "shrinkage." This is an innocent-sounding term that actually refers to missing inventory that cannot be explained by what was sold. Some of the usual reasons for shrinkage are customer theft and employee theft.

But in the case of Ames the auditors and consultants do not think that theft explains the shrinkage. It looks more like the culprit was sloppy management and sloppy management controls. For example, store managers were not allowed to take big markdowns when they held occasional clearance sales. So to move out the merchandise, they might have sold it at a lower price than they reported and wrote the difference in as "shrinkage." Part of the problem is that store managers had apparently been left with lots of merchandise from the previous year that should have been cleared out of the store long ago. Facing a difficult time getting rid of these items, they might have been more willing than usual to hide the lower sales prices under the catchall phrase "shrinkage."[15]

Questions

1. In terms of conceptual skills, what are some of the different activities in a chain of stores like Ames that Peter Hollis has to consider?
2. Ames tried to control its managers in part by prohibiting them from taking too large a markdown on sales items. What does the store managers' behavior tell you about the problems managers can run into with control systems?
3. If you took over today as president of Ames, what are some of the managerial steps you would take to clear up this problem?

S I X

After reading this chapter, you will be able to:

- Describe how the human relations movement evolved.
- Compare and contrast Theory X and Theory Y.
- Explain the factors that make leaders effective.
- Describe Maslow's hierarchy of needs.
- Explain two techniques for boosting motivation.
- Distinguish among three "worker-friendly" programs.

Human Relations

In the previous chapter we listed five basic management functions: planning, organizing, staffing, directing, and controlling. In this chapter we turn to one of these functions, the directing function. We have seen that all managers must plan, organize, hire, staff, and control. But a manager who cannot also lead and motivate employees and form effective teams will not succeed. We therefore focus on these topics in this chapter.

We first discuss the nature of the human relations approach to managing. This approach emphasizes the importance of the human element at work. Some important human relations topics are work groups and leadership. Next we explain the nature of motivation and discuss new "worker-friendly" programs, including quality circles and flexible work hours.

It was a great experiment, but it was an experiment that failed. Donald Burr, President of People Express airline, wanted to start an airline like no other. Even today, when most people think of

People Express, they think of cheap fares. But it was also Mr. Burr's human approach to managing people that set his airline apart from the rest.

Burr believed that "people are the enterprise." He thought that without each employee's full commitment, his company would fail. He did all he could to help ensure that when it came to its employees, People Express was truly people oriented. First, he decided to be very selective in recruiting and to select only highly motivated workers. Recruiters first spent about five hours with a recruit. Selected recruits then had to attend a training session. Only those who survived this step were hired.

Furthermore, every employee was called a "manager." There were only three job classifications: flight managers (pilots and schedulers), maintenance managers (who supervised maintenance operations), and customer service managers (who did everything else—serve drinks, hand out boarding passes, and so on). Everyone was asked to help out when things got busy. If they needed more reservations clerks or baggage handlers to help out during a peak, everyone—including pilots—would pitch in.

To be hired, all employees had to buy at least 100 shares of the company's common stock (at up to 60 percent below the market price). Even top salaries were set at modest levels. Mr. Burr himself received $48,000 in 1981, probably one-sixth of what comparable managers in the industry were

making. Pilots made $30,000, about half of what other pilots earned. The organization structure itself was "flat." It had only three levels: managing officers, general managers, and employees. Thus employees got less close supervision, since each of their managers had many employees to supervise.

How did all this work out? As the saying goes, "the operation was a success but the patient died." Burr got the motivation and commitment that he sought, and morale was very high. (The Air Line Pilots Association failed twice to unionize pilots, for instance.) If high morale, teamwork, motivation, and inspiring leadership were enough to save a company, People Express would have survived.

Unfortunately, in this case they were not enough. Overexpansion and competition finally did People Express in, and in 1987 it was bought by Frank Lorenzo's Texas International Airlines, Inc.

While it lasted, though, the experiment at People Express showed how powerful a human relations approach could be. In two short years, People Express had the highest load factors in the industry (a main measure of productivity). All told, employees owned an average of about 2500 shares of stock each. For a while, in 1986, it seemed that after only five years, People Express was on the verge of becoming a major contender. Human relations techniques like motivation, leadership, and groups almost—but not quite—carried the day.[1]

Donald Burr's efforts to make People Express a people-oriented airline for its employees shows how managers can boost morale and motivation. Mr. Burr's belief that "people are the enterprise" sums up the essence of the human relations approach to management.

human relations

The Human Relations Approach

Human relations is an approach to managing that emphasizes the importance of the human or "people" element at work. It might seem obvious today that "people matter" and that how workers think and feel affects how they perform. However, this obvious fact was not always so clear.

For example, the scientific management approach to managing prevailed in the early 1900s. The basic theme of this approach was that work could be studied scientifically. The goal was always to find the one best way to do a job. To accomplish this, scientific management experts used stopwatches, cameras, and special charts to measure everything a worker did. Then, when they found the "one best way" to perform a job, they used financial incentives to try to make sure the worker would do the job right.

The problem with this approach is that it often led to highly routinized, "dehumanized" jobs and working conditions. For example, the experts found that the most efficient way to build a car was to have each worker do only one specialized job (such as attaching the right bottom bolt to the right front fender). But after weeks (or months or years) of doing such a tedious job, workers could hardly be blamed for wanting to rebel. Poor product quality, absenteeism, and tardiness were just some of the symptoms of workers' dissatisfaction. (In fact, the word "sabotage" is popularly thought to have come from this. The legend is that when French workers rebelled, they sometimes threw shoes— *sabots* in French—into their machines to damage them.)

Frederick Winslow Taylor is considered the father of scientific management. As an engineer at the Midvale Steel Company at the turn of the century, he was intrigued by the fact that some workers had the energy to hurry home and work on their cabins, even after a hard twelve-hour day. He knew that if he could find a way to harness this energy during the workday, huge productivity gains would be possible. His solution was to analyze each job scientifically. He looked for the one best way to do it. Then he rewarded hard work with incentives. Other experts of this era included the husband-and-wife team of Frank and Lillian Gilbreth, who developed a way to describe and standardize each small motion a worker made on the job. (By the way, the Gilbreths' enthusiasm for efficiency carried into their home as well. They had twelve children and then wrote a book about raising them called *Cheaper by the Dozen*.) Another expert was Henry Gantt, who invented a chart for scheduling work that is still in use. We will discuss Gantt charts in Chapter 10.

THE HAWTHORNE STUDIES

In 1927 a series of studies was begun at the Hawthorne, Illinois, plant of the Western Electric Company, just outside Chicago. These Hawthorne studies paved the way for the new human relations approach to management.

The first of these studies was actually aimed at testing an important scientific management assumption: that worker output would rise if the level of light in the plant was turned up.

To test this, the researchers isolated a few female workers in a separate room of the plant. Here they could watch the workers' reaction to changes in the level of light. But to the researchers' surprise, output did not fall as illumination was reduced. In fact, it actually increased, at least until it was too dark to see.

The researchers were astonished. What could possibly account for this surprising result? They eventually explained their findings as resulting from the changed social situation of the workers. By showing personal interest in them and their problems, the observer in this room had inadvertently made the workers feel that they were special. He had granted them many privileges, such as special birthday celebrations. Furthermore,

> No longer were the girls isolated individuals, working together only in the sense of an actual physical proximity. They had become participating members of a working group with all the psychological and social implications peculiar to such a group.[2]

Hawthorne effect

Experts would later coin a phrase to describe what happened at the Hawthorne plant: the Hawthorne effect. The **Hawthorne effect** is what happens when it is the researchers' interest in the people they are studying, not the experimental variables, that causes the workers to be more productive.

Later studies at Hawthorne involving interviews with thousands of workers confirmed the earlier conclusions. They found that workers were motivated not just by pay and working conditions but by needs and desires. They discovered that workers who felt adrift and degraded by oversimplified jobs sought companionship and security in their work group. And they found that employee performance depended on the supervisor's leadership style and on the employees' belief that the company was treating them as valued, unique individuals. The Hawthorne studies were thus a turning point in the way managers look at human behavior at work. From this time on the human element in the workplace would be seen as crucial to success. Future managers like Donald Burr of People Express would help put such ideas into practice.

THEORY X AND THEORY Y

Theory X

The work of Douglas McGregor is a good example of the sort of thinking that is typical of the human relations movement. According to Dr. McGregor, the highly specialized jobs and dehumanizing atmosphere of scientific management reflected a certain set of assumptions about human nature. He called these assumptions "Theory X." **Theory X** is an approach to management that assumes that:

- Most people dislike work and responsibility and prefer to be directed.
- People are motivated not by the desire to do a good job, but by financial incentives.
- Most people must be closely supervised, controlled, and coerced into achieving organizational objectives.

Dr. McGregor also said that supervisors' behavior would always reflect their basic attitudes and assumptions about their workers. In other words, if you have Theory X attitudes, you will probably assume that workers dislike their jobs and thus require your close supervision.

Theory Y

McGregor questioned the wisdom of the Theory X approach. He proposed that managers adopt a healthier set of assumptions about human nature. He called this set "Theory Y." **Theory Y** is an approach to management that assumes that:

- People can enjoy work and will exercise substantial control over their own performance if given the chance.
- Workers are motivated by the desire to do a good job and by the chance to associate with their peers, not just by financial rewards.
- People might actually do better work if control is kept to a minimum and they are not threatened with punishment.

McGregor therefore focused each manager's attention on his or her assumptions about workers. "Expect the best from them," said McGregor, "and they'll react in kind." But assume that they are worthless, and the result will be poor performance.

WORK GROUPS

One of the main findings of the Hawthorne studies was that work groups are important. Most employees do not just work as individuals. They work as members of groups, and these groups influence their members' behavior. Some of the groups are *formal* in that they are formally established by the organization. A small four- or five-person department is an example of this. An *informal* group might consist of workers who are friendly and have lunch together. Whether formal or

Work groups can influence their members' behavior on the job.

informal, groups develop common sentiments, attitudes, and norms—acceptable rules of conduct.

We know that these sentiments, attitudes, and norms affect the behavior of individual group members. A group influences its members by substituting its own standards or norms for the standards set by managers—for instance, by saying in effect "don't produce more than three units per hour no matter what the boss says." A person's work group can also affect his or her ability to perform the job well by providing or withholding help. Groups are also a big source of rewards and punishment. A person's work group can be a source of tremendous satisfaction as well as a buffer against job-related tensions. If the worker violates the group's norms (for instance, by producing too much), the group can punish him or her by withholding friendship, or worse. Groups therefore have a big effect on their members' performance.

LEADERSHIP

leadership

Leadership is another topic that attracted new interest after the Hawthorne Studies. **Leadership** occurs whenever one person influences another to work toward some predetermined goal. Leadership is thus an important part of managing. Managers who cannot lead will be ineffective at best; planning, organizing, staffing, and controlling alone are not enough. Two main theories have evolved on what makes leaders effective: the trait approach and the style approach to leadership.

The idea that some leaders have personality traits that make them great leaders was initially inspired by a "great man" theory of leadership. Basically, this theory holds that great leaders like Margaret Thatcher and Lee Iacocca are great because they were born with certain personality traits such as intelligence, dominance, and self-assurance. Followers of this theory believe that if they study the personalities and backgrounds of great leaders, they will sooner or later find the combination of traits that made these people outstanding leaders.

Effective leaders do seem to have certain traits in common that they are born with or develop when they are young. For example, one expert found that effective leaders were intelligent, self-assured, and decisive. They also tended to be high achievers and to have a high need to "self-actualize," which means to utilize their capabilities to the fullest.[3] Personality traits thus help to explain why some people are good leaders.

You probably realize that it is not just a person's traits that are important but the person's style as well. One intelligent boss might be considerate and fun to work for, while another boss (equally smart) is autocratic and difficult to be around.

leadership style

A person's **leadership style** is the pattern of behavior that the person exhibits over time in leadership situations (situations in which he or she must influence other people). Research at Ohio State University and the University of Michigan has isolated two basic types of leadership styles. A leader with a *task-oriented style* will tend to emphasize work results and rigid standards. This type of leader will generally try to closely monitor everything subordinates do. The work itself is obviously this person's main concern. On the other hand, a leader with an employee-oriented style has a strong concern for employees. This person's main emphasis is on boosting morale and coaxing employees to work together so as to get the job done.

In practice, most leaders are not exclusively task- or employee-centered. They are a little bit of each.

This idea is illustrated by the managerial grid. The **managerial grid** is a graphic way of showing various leadership styles that was developed by Robert Blake and Jane Mouton to show how leaders can balance their concerns for the task and for their employees. As shown in Figure 6-1, the grid has two dimensions: concern for people and con-

managerial grid

FIGURE 6-1 / The managerial grid. (*Source:* Reprinted by permission of the *Harvard Business Review.* An exhibit from "Breakthrough in Organizational Development" by Robert R. Blake, Jane S. Mouton, Louis B. Barnes, and Larry E. Greiner (November–December 1964), p. 136. Copyright © 1964 by the President and Fellows of Harvard College; all rights reserved.)

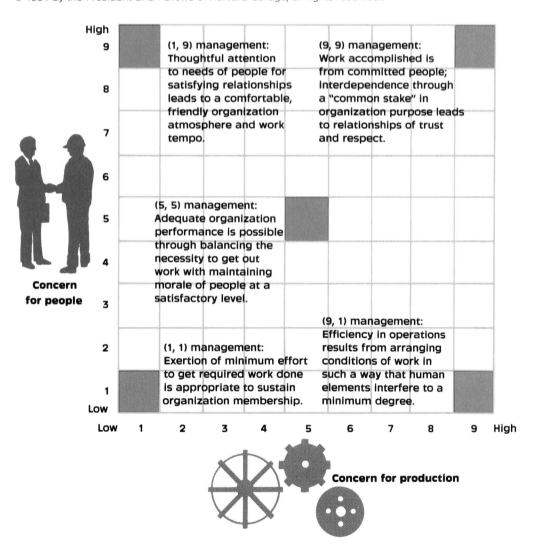

cern for production. Leaders who are high in their concern for production but low in their concern for people are "9, 1" leaders. For them, efficiency in operations is best achieved by organizing the job so that the workers cannot interfere in how it is done. This might seem like a good idea, but we have already seen how ignoring the human element at work can backfire. At the other extreme, a "1, 9" style—low concern for production, high concern for people—is probably not ideal either. It can lead to "country club management." Here everyone is happy and friendly, but the work itself may not get done.

Blake and Mouton say that "9, 9" management (high concern for people and high concern for production) is best. There is an atmosphere of trust and commitment combined with an emphasis on getting the job done.

PARTICIPATIVE LEADERSHIP

participative leadership

As summarized in Figure 6-2, employee-centered leaders also tend to be participative leaders. In **participative leadership,** leaders present problems or tentative solutions to their employees and let the employees take part in deciding how to solve the problem. Task-oriented leaders are different—they tend to make the decisions themselves, announce the decisions to their employees, and expect the employees to follow through.

Japanese managers have practiced participative management for many years. They base decisions on worker input, and they practice

FIGURE 6-2 / Participative versus autocratic leadership. (*Source:* Reprinted by permission of the *Harvard Business Review.* Based on an exhibit from "How to Choose a Leadership Pattern" by Robert Tannenbaum and Warren H. Schmidt (March–April, 1958), pp. 95–101. Copyright © 1958 by the President and Fellows of Harvard College; all rights reserved.)

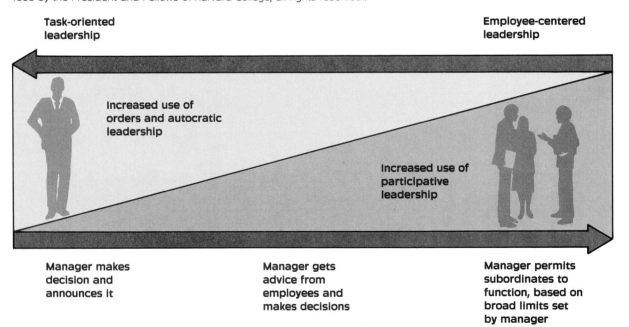

Task-oriented leadership

Employee-centered leadership

Increased use of orders and autocratic leadership

Increased use of participative leadership

Manager makes decision and announces it

Manager gets advice from employees and makes decisions

Manager permits subordinates to function, based on broad limits set by manager

Employee-centered

Performance: Poor	Performance: Good	Performance: Poor
High control	Moderate control	Low control

Task-oriented

Performance: Good	Performance: Poor	Performance: Relatively good

FIGURE 6-3 / Fitting the style of leadership to the situation. (*Source:* Fred Fiedler, Martin Chemers, and Linda Mahar, *Improving Leadership Effectiveness: The Leader Match Concept,* Wiley, New York, 1977. Copyright © 1977 by John Wiley and Sons, Inc. Reprinted by permission of John Wiley and Sons, Inc.)

consensus management. Theory Z is the term used to describe their participative philosophy. Because of its success in Japan, more U.S. managers are using it. Whether Theory Z can work as well here as in Japan remains to be seen. It might not be the best style for us, since we have a different culture and different values.

Participative management will not work if leaders cannot inspire subordinates to participate. Nor will it work if subordinates do not want to participate. In addition, situations that call for quick decisions limit the time available for true participation.

CONTINGENCY LEADERSHIP

contingency leadership theory

Contingency leadership theory holds that the style of leadership that is best for a situation depends on (is contingent on) the needs of the situation. You have probably read about or experienced this need to fit the leadership style to the situation. For example, if a fire broke out in a crowded hall, would you want an employee-centered leader to ask everyone's opinion on the best way to get them all out? Probably not. You would want a real autocrat who would quickly assign exits and lead everyone out.

One famous contingency approach to leadership was developed by Professor Fred Fiedler. Stripped to its essentials, Professor Fiedler's contingency theory holds that task-oriented leaders excel when the situation gives them either very high control or very low control. In situations that are not so clear-cut, an employee-oriented leader is best. This is summarized in Figure 6-3.

Fiedler explains his theory as follows. He says that in very *high* control situations the group is *ready to be directed.* In such situations (as when a fire breaks out in a hall) the subordinates expect to be told what to do. Therefore the leader should be mostly task-oriented. On the other hand, in a situation in which the leader has very *low* control, the work group could fall apart if the leader does not make everyone focus on the task. For example, suppose the leader took over a situation in which workers do not know what their jobs are and question the leader's ability to direct them. Here again, says Fiedler, a task-oriented

IT'S YOUR BUSINESS
Your Leadership Style

Professor Fred Fiedler uses the "least preferred co-worker"

(LPC) scale shown below to identify leadership styles.

As you can see, the instructions for the scale require that you think of the one person now or at any time in the past with whom you could work least well. Then you have to describe that person. Indicate, for in-

stance, whether you would describe the person as pleasant or unpleasant, friendly or unfriendly, rejecting or accepting.

Before you read any further, fill in the LPC scale, using the instructions provided. Make sure you answer all questions. Then, to determine your pre-

Think of the person *with whom you can work least well.* He or she may be someone you work with now or someone you knew in the past. He or she does not have to be the person you like least well, but should be the person *with whom you had the most difficulty in getting a job done.* Describe this person as he or she appears to you.

										Scoring
Pleasant	8	7	6	5	4	3	2	1	Unpleasant	___
Friendly	8	7	6	5	4	3	2	1	Unfriendly	___
Rejecting	1	2	3	4	5	6	7	8	Accepting	___
Tense	1	2	3	4	5	6	7	8	Relaxed	___
Distant	1	2	3	4	5	6	7	8	Close	___
Cold	1	2	3	4	5	6	7	8	Warm	___
Supportive	8	7	6	5	4	3	2	1	Hostile	___
Boring	1	2	3	4	5	6	7	8	Interesting	___

leader might be best. (Teachers know this. They are typically "tough" the first few times they meet their new classes until they have established their authority.)

In the middle are those situations in which it is not as clear whether the leader has much control. For example, suppose you take over a new department staffed with engineers. They seem to under-

dominant style, look back at the scale. Under each line that you marked is a number from 1 to 8. For each row, write the number of the one you choose in the scoring column at the right of the scale. Then add up your scores and enter the total at the bottom of the page. Please be sure to recheck your addition.

- If your score is 64 or above, you are a "high LPC" *employee-*centered leader, says Fiedler. High LPC leaders tend to describe even their least preferred co-worker in favorable terms.

- If your score is 57 or below, you are a "low LPC" *task-oriented* leader. Low LPC leaders tend to describe their least preferred co-worker in unfavorable terms.

- If your score falls between 58 and 63, you do not have a pre-dominant style; you are a little of both.

Source: Fred Fiedler, Martin Chemers, and Linda Mahar, *Improving Leadership Effectiveness: The Leader Match Concept*, Wiley, New York, 1977. Copyright © 1977 by John Wiley and Sons, Inc. Reprinted by permission of John Wiley and Sons, Inc.

Quarrelsome	1	2	3	4	5	6	7	8	Harmonious	___
Gloomy	1	2	3	4	5	6	7	8	Cheerful	___
Open	8	7	6	5	4	3	2	1	Guarded	___
Backbiting	1	2	3	4	5	6	7	8	Loyal	___
Untrustworthy	1	2	3	4	5	6	7	8	Trustworthy	___
Considerate	8	7	6	5	4	3	2	1	Inconsiderate	___
Nasty	1	2	3	4	5	6	7	8	Nice	___
Agreeable	8	7	6	5	4	3	2	1	Disagreeable	___
Insincere	1	2	3	4	5	6	7	8	Sincere	___
Kind	8	7	6	5	4	3	2	1	Unkind	___
									Total	___

stand what their jobs are. And they accept your authority but, as professionals, do not want to be bossed around. Here you could rely on a more employee-oriented style. Your main concern would be maintaining high morale and a close-knit work group so that the workers felt motivated to do their jobs.

In summary, a leader's effectiveness depends on the person's traits and style and on the situation. In terms of traits, effective leaders tend to be self-assured and able to make good decisions. But the person's style is important too. Most leaders exhibit some degree of both task- and employee-oriented styles. The style that is best depends largely on the nature of the situation. To test your own leadership style, see the It's Your Business box (on pp. 176–177).

Basics of Motivation

motivation

Motivation represents a person's desire to satisfy an unfulfilled need. For example, everyone has a need to eat. But after you finish a big meal, this need is generally satisfied. Someone could not motivate you by offering you a steak dinner. But if you did not eat for several hours, the need to eat would again be aroused. At that point, if someone were to offer you a steak dinner (an "incentive"), you might be motivated to take it.

Much of what we know about motivation therefore revolves around what we know about people's needs. Needs are important because it is an unsatisfied need (such as the need for food) that creates motivation. A person who is hungry is motivated to find food; one who needs security is motivated to find it; and a person with a need to accomplish challenging tasks might try to climb a mountain. Let's look more closely at what some experts have said about human needs and motivation.

MASLOW AND THE NEEDS HIERARCHY

Psychologist Abraham Maslow says that humans have five basic categories of needs. Maslow calls these categories physiological, safety, social, ego, and self-actualization needs. He says they form a *needs hierarchy* or a ladder (as in Figure 6-4). Each need becomes active or aroused *only when the next lower need is reasonably satisfied.*

PHYSIOLOGICAL NEEDS   The lowest level in Maslow's hierarchy contains the physiological needs. These are the most basic needs we all have— for example, the need for food, drink, shelter, and rest. If a person is very hungry, thirsty, or tired or without shelter from the elements, he or she will be highly motivated to satisfy these needs. This person might not be very interested in pursuing higher-level needs. On the other hand, once these physiological needs are reasonably satisfied, the next higher level needs become the ones that motivate the person's behavior.

SAFETY NEEDS   When the physiological needs are reasonably satisfied—when a person is no longer thirsty, has enough to eat, has a roof overhead, and so forth—then safety needs become activated. They become the needs which the person tries to satisfy, the needs that motivate. These are the needs for protection against danger or deprivation—the need for security.

SOCIAL NEEDS   Once physiological and safety needs are satisfied, according to Maslow, they no longer motivate behavior. Now the social needs become the active motivators of behavior—needs for things like affiliation, giving and receiving affection, and friendship.

EGO NEEDS   Next in the hierarchy are the ego needs. These are needs that people have for self-confidence, independence, achievement, and things like recognition and appreciation.

SELF-ACTUALIZATION   Finally, there is an ultimate need. This need begins to motivate a person's behavior only after all lower-level needs are reasonably satisfied. This is the need for self-actualization or fulfillment, the need we all have to become the person we feel we have the

FIGURE 6-4 / Maslow's needs hierarchy. (*Source:* Based on Abraham Maslow, *Motivation and Personality,* Second Edition, Harper & Row, New York, 1970, pp. 35–58.)

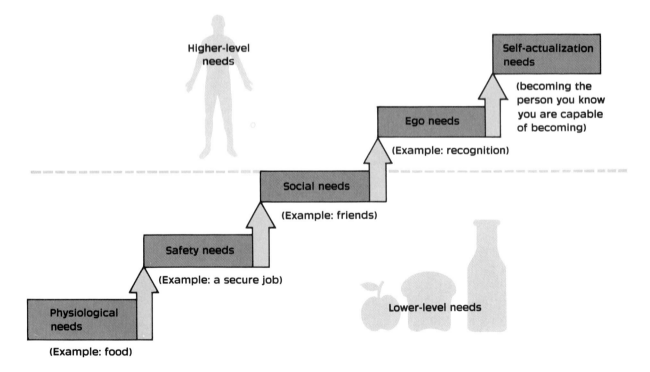

Note: Each higher-order need becomes active only when lower-level needs are fairly well satisfied.

potential for becoming. This is the need that drives an artist to express herself on canvas, the need that motivates a student to work all day and then take a college degree in night school. One of the big things to keep in mind, says Maslow, is that unlike lower-level needs (physiological, safety, and social needs), the ego and the self-actualization needs are rarely if ever completely satisfied.

This is an important point. It is possible, says Maslow, to adequately satisfy a person's basic needs for things like food, shelter, security, and even friendships. But higher-level needs (like those for recognition or becoming the person you believe you are capable of becoming) can never really be fully satisfied, he says.

HERZBERG AND MOTIVATOR-HYGIENE THEORY

Psychologist Frederick Herzberg has taken Maslow's theory one step further. Herzberg divides Maslow's hierarchy into a lower-level set of

FIGURE 6-5 / Hygienes and motivators. (*Source:* Reprinted by permission of the *Harvard Business Review.* Adapted from an exhibit from "One More Time: How Do You Motivate Employees" by Frederick Herzberg (January/February 1968). Copyright © 1968 by the President and Fellows of Harvard College; all rights reserved.)

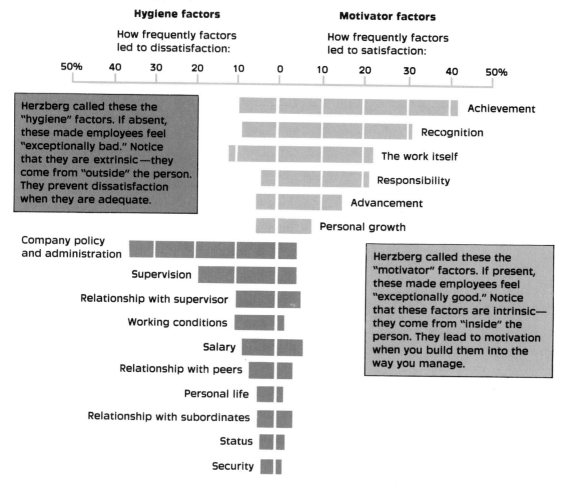

needs (physiological, safety, and social) and a higher-level set (ego, and self-actualization). Herzberg says that the best way to motivate someone is to offer to satisfy that person's higher-level needs.

Here's why. Offering a person a raise or better working conditions, says Herzberg, is no way to motivate someone, since physiological and safety needs are quickly satisfied. The right way to motivate someone, says Herzberg, is to arrange the job so that *the person gets a sense of achievement out of doing it.* Then, by performing the job, the person is motivated to keep trying to satisfy his or her limitless craving for achievement, recognition, and self-actualization.

Herzberg believes that there are two kinds of incentives that bosses can use to motivate workers. **Hygienes** are incentives that satisfy lower-level needs. **Motivators** are incentives that satisfy higher-level needs. As shown in Figure 6-5, Herzberg says that if "hygienes" (such as good working conditions, good salary, and good supervision) are missing or inadequate, employees will become dissatisfied.

On the other hand, says Herzberg, motivators (such as opportunities for achievement, recognition, responsibility, and more challenging jobs) do not just prevent dissatisfaction; they also motivate employees. (See Figure 6-5.) They can motivate employees because they appeal to employee's higher-level needs for achievement, self-esteem, and self-actualization. Remember that these are needs that are never completely satisfied. Thus, according to Herzberg, the best way to motivate employees is to build challenge and opportunities for achievement into their jobs. That way, they have what amounts to a built-in incentive to work harder, since they are getting such a kick out of doing their challenging jobs. In summary, says Herzberg, make sure your workers don't become dissatisfied. First, give them satisfactory salaries, working conditions, and supervision. Then really "turn them on" to their jobs by making their jobs so challenging that they get a sense of achievement doing them.

hygienes
motivators

Motivation in Action

Motivation theories like those of Maslow and Herzberg would not be very useful if they couldn't be implemented in practice. On the next few pages we discuss some techniques that managers actually use to motivate employees.

JOB ENRICHMENT

job enrichment

The method that Herzberg recommends for applying his theory is called job enrichment. **Job enrichment** involves building motivators like opportunities for achievement into the job by making it more interesting and challenging.

In practice, there are five things you can do to enrich a subordinate's job.

1. **Form natural work groups.** Change the job in such a way that each person is responsible for—"owns"—an identifiable body of work. For example, instead of having all typists in a typing pool

do work for all departments, give each typist responsibility for just one or two departments' work.

2. **Combine tasks.** For example, let one person assemble a product from start to finish instead of having it go through several separate operations performed by different people.

3. **Establish client relationships.** Let the worker have contact as often as possible with the client. For example, let your secretary research and respond to customer requests instead of automatically referring all such problems to you.

4. **Practice vertical loading.** Let the worker plan and control his or her own job instead of having it controlled by outsiders. For example, let the worker set his or her own schedule, do his or her own trouble-shooting, and decide when to stop and start working.

5. **Open feedback channels.** Finally, find more and better ways for the worker to get feedback on his or her performance.

As you can see, all these methods involve enriching the worker's job. For instance, let them deal directly with the firm's customers. Or combine tasks so that a worker not only does the work but does his or her own inspection as well.

GOAL SETTING

Sometimes just having a specific goal to shoot for can improve motivation. For example, truck drivers in one study were found to be loading too few items in their trucks. This meant a lot of wasted space.[4]

What was the problem? The consultants believed it was largely because the drivers were usually just urged to "do your best" when it came to loading the truck to its maximum weight. The consultants decided to try an experiment. They arranged for a specific goal (94 percent of the truck's net weight) to be given to each driver.

Sometimes the best way to improve job performance is to set high but clear goals that subordinates can achieve.

The results of this study were impressive. Performance (in terms of weight loaded on each truck) rose dramatically as soon as the truckers were assigned specific hard goals. And performance remained at this much higher level. Here is how the consultants explained their findings:

> The setting of a goal that is both specific and challenging leads to an increase in performance because it makes it clearer to the individual what he or she is supposed to do. This in turn may provide the worker with a sense of achievement, recognition, and commitment, in that he or she can compare how well he is doing versus how well he has done in the past.[5]

The moral to this story is that sometimes the easiest solution to a problem is the best one. In many cases when employees do not seem to be "motivated," complicated human relations programs are not required. Sometimes, all it takes is setting specific, challenging goals for the employees and praising them when they reach their goals. Sometimes, in fact, when performance is down, it is not because workers do not want to do a good job. Instead, it is because they don't know what their standards are or don't understand that they are not working up to par. Specific, challenging goals can clear up such "motivation" problems overnight.

BEHAVIOR MODIFICATION

behavior modification

Behavior modification involves changing (modifying) behavior through the use of rewards or punishment. It is based on this central principle: *Behavior that leads to a reward tends to be repeated, while behavior that leads to punishment tends not to be repeated.*[6]

Providing the right rewards or punishments is the essence of behavior modification. To see how this would work in practice, consider this example. You are a supervisor in a warehouse, and almost every morning a certain worker is late for work. When you confront him, you get upset. Your face turns red, you start yelling that he "shouldn't come in late again," and your hair stands on end while your eyes bulge. You then walk away to your office in a huff, leaving your grinning worker surrounded by his colleagues. They are now making comments like "Wow, that was great, I've never seen Lee's eyes bulge like that before," while they slap their pal on the back and roar with laughter.

What is the problem here? Why do you think he comes in late each day? Why does punishment—disciplining him in front of his coworkers—seem to have no effect on him?

A big part of the problem is that instead of punishing this fellow for coming in late, you are actually (inadvertently) rewarding him. The adoration that he gets from his colleagues once you leave is terrific reinforcement for him to continue coming in late. Besides, there is not much risk if the worst discipline he can expect from you is a screaming fit. What does he have to lose?

You could use behavior modification to straighten out this mess. First, remove the positive reinforcement that he gets. Express your displeasure in the privacy of your office (and preferably a bit more calmly). Next, make it clear that there is some real punishment attached

APPLICATION: BURGER KING
Service with a Smile

What do you think is one of the most pressing problems facing fast food restaurants like Burger King? If you answered competition from other fast food chains, you would be only partially right. Time and again, people at Burger King and other chains will tell you that one of the biggest challenges facing them is getting crew members to staff their restaurants.

One Burger King Corporation executive points out that "the equivalent of the U.S. population passes through a Burger King every five and a half to six weeks." Burger King serves almost nine million people a day. You know from your own experience that customers don't like to wait. At the same time the number of teenagers in the labor force is shrinking, so getting good help is even more of a challenge today than it was just a few years ago.

What do you do to attract and keep good people? What do you do to keep them working hard and courteously? A human resource executive at Burger King Corporation says that there is a lot a firm like Burger King can do to motivate its employees.

The motivation programs range from programs that owners implement themselves in each of their restaurants to systemwide programs. For example, one restaurant manager in Beaufort, South Carolina, found an inexpensive way to get his customer service people to be more courteous. He told his crew members that it was very important that they serve their customers with a smile and that he would buy each crew member his or her first hairdo after starting to work for the store. He found that this almost forced them to smile because they felt so proud of how they looked. This was a simple yet effective motivational program.

But Burger King doesn't stop there. In the past few years, Burger King Corporation has set up a program whereby workers employed more than three consecutive months can earn up to $2,000 over a two-year period toward their post-secondary education. This has gone a long way toward reducing employee turnover. The Burger King Crew Educational Assistance Program lets employees build up bonus credits as long as they keep working in the restaurant. They are paid after they graduate.

But it is not just bonus programs but the environment of the restaurant that keeps employees happy. That is why it is important to put in good people-oriented managers and concentrate on building morale by treating crew members fairly and the way you'd want to be treated yourself. That is really the crux of human relations management.

Questions

1. Why is staffing so important to Burger King restaurants? Why is the shrinking number of teenagers in the labor force a challenge for Burger King? What would you do about it?

2. Suppose you are a Burger King restaurant manager. Do you think your leadership style at noon would be identical to your leadership style at 3:00 P.M.? Why or why not?

3. As director of human resources for Burger King Corporation, how would you incorporate the concept of worker-friendly programs into Burger King Corporation's operations?

to coming in late. For example, tell him that after three mornings late he will be suspended without pay for one whole day. To really clinch it, add the possibility of a reward if he is on time every day for a month.

Worker-Friendly Programs

A working mother can arrange her hours so that she begins work at 10 A.M. and leaves at 4 P.M. This lets her drop off and pick up her school-age children. Two college students arrange to share one full-time job. In this way they can ensure that the job is performed properly, while they still have the flexibility to attend their classes and do their projects. A group of ten employees meets once a week to analyze and solve quality problems on the job. Or an employee works at home and "telecommutes," as described in the Business in the News box.

worker-friendly programs

Programs like these represent the sorts of worker-friendly programs that increasingly represent human relations management today. **Worker-friendly programs** are ones that make it easier for employees to adapt their work lives to the needs of their home lives and careers. In today's economy, many families are either single-parent families or ones in which both parents work. Therefore being able to adapt work life to what is going on at home is more important than ever before.

QUALITY CIRCLES

quality circle

A **quality circle** is a group of five to ten specially trained employees who meet for an hour once a week to spot and solve problems in their work area. There are two main advantages to using quality circles at work. One is that the workers themselves usually like the opportunity to analyze and solve job-related problems and implement solutions. (This is especially important in an era in which employees are increasingly sophisticated and better educated.)

Quality circles can also be a boon to a firm's quality and productivity. No one understands the problems on the shop floor like the workers who do the job. It therefore makes a lot of sense to have these people analyze and solve problems on the job and carry out solutions to improve performance.

When quality circles were first introduced, membership was usually voluntary. Groups generally came up with their own lists of problems to address. Experience with such groups showed that this was not an efficient use of quality circles.

Today, to make sure that they are useful, circles usually address problems that are assigned to them by management (rather than identifying problems themselves). For example, at Northrop Corporation the groups are responsible for setting improvement targets and keeping reports on their progress. They also compete with other groups to achieve their goals. Honeywell Corporation has replaced about 100 of its traditional quality circles with about 1,000 "work groups." As is usually the case with this new type of quality circles, the Honeywell groups are generally not voluntary. They usually involve all or most

How would you like a job in which you could live and work at the beach even though your office was 500 miles away? How would you like to keep working even though you were skiing for five hours a day at Aspen? Sound good? Then telecommuting might be for you.

Telecommuting means that a worker can work at home on his or her computer, entering data, writing memos, or analyzing reports, and then "commute" to work by telephoning the data in via a modem.

But not many people can actually telecommute, right? Wrong. *Business Week* estimates that as of 1986, 7 million Americans were telecommuting to work in their offices via computer and telephones. The numbers should climb dramatically during the next ten years or so. One expert estimates that by 1995 about 18 percent of the work force (about 18 million people) will be telecommuting. And over the next 20 years, she says, "Most people in most levels of business will work at home at least two or three days a week."

What sorts of people can work at home? They range from high-priced lawyers to modestly paid data-entry personnel. Blue Cross and Blue Shield of South Carolina found that its home-based clerical employees were 50 percent more productive than office workers in keying insurance claims into the computer and coding material. Best Western Hotels in Phoenix is using the residents of the Arizona Center for Women, a minimum security prison, as an office staff. Telecommuting can also be a boon to handicapped workers. Through telecommuting they can hold responsible jobs even if they cannot come to the workplace.

Telecommuting is not for everyone, of course. Lots of companies find that transporting documents back and forth from office to home is too troublesome. Many workers find they miss the interaction and gossip that can be had only by being there in the office with the co-workers. But there seems little doubt that telecommuting is here to stay and that more and more firms will use it for more and more of their jobs.

Sources: "These Top Executives Work Where They Play," *Business Week*, Oct. 27, 1986, p. 132; "It's Rush Hour for Telecommuting," *Business Week*, Jan. 23, 1984, p. 99; Bureau of National Affairs, "Bulletin to Management," Jan. 9, 1986, p. 16.

shop-floor employees, rather than just a few. Management also usually assigns problems to them, rather than waiting for them to generate their own problems. Circles like these seem a lot more successful at solving problems and boosting quality and profits than the old type.

FLEXIBLE WORK ARRANGEMENTS

Employers are also instituting new flexible work arrangements. This often involves giving workers more freedom to choose the hours that they work.

flextime

Flextime is a plan whereby employees' flexible work day is built around a core of midday hours such as 11:00 A.M. to 2:00 P.M. and workers determine their own starting and stopping hours. For example, workers may opt to work from 7:00 A.M. to 3:00 P.M. or 11:00 A.M. to 7:00 P.M. Well over 10 percent of the U.S. work force is on a flextime schedule. This does not count professionals, managers, salespeople, or self-employed persons who customarily set their work hours anyway.[7]

Some employers have switched to a four-day work week. Employees in these firms work four ten-hour days instead of the more usual five eight-hour days. Compressed work week plans like these have several advantages. For the employer they often mean less absenteeism and tardiness. Workers also gain. Working four days a week instead of five means 20 percent fewer trips to and from work. Child-care expenses might also be reduced for parents who work only four days.

job sharing

work sharing

flexiplace

Job sharing is a concept that allows two or more people to share a single full time job. For example, two college students may share a forty-hour-a-week job, one student working mornings and the other working afternoons. **Work sharing** refers to a temporary reduction in work hours by a group of employees during economic hard times in order to avoid layoffs. Thus 400 employees might all agree to work (and get paid for) only 35 hours per week in order to avoid the layoff of thirty workers. **Flexiplace** means that employees are allowed or encouraged to work at home or in satellite offices closer to home. Today flexiplace is easier than ever because of telecommuting.

OTHER WORKER-FRIENDLY PROGRAMS

Helping to guarantee that employees will not get laid off in economic hard times is the ultimate worker-friendly program. Today progressive companies are trying to do just that.

For example, Japanese companies have experimented with three approaches. One is to subcontract a lot of work out to very small businesses, which then bear the burdens of downturns in the economy. The second Japanese device (which some U.S. firms are now imitating) is to

One benefit of flexible work arrangements is an easier commute to work during off-peak hours.

pay nearly half of salaries in bonuses. These bonuses disappear in a recession when profits shrink. Because the firm's basic salary costs are relatively low, employees should be able to keep their jobs. This should work out for the workers if they are careful to keep their expenses down to what could be covered mostly by their nonbonus salaries.

The third approach is the employment of more part-time workers. This approach is spreading quickly throughout the United States. At Delta Airlines and Federal Express, for instance, part-timers or "temporaries" are laid off in recessions. In the future a firm's core workers (along with managers and other professionals) will probably be offered stock incentives and greater job security. In return the workers will offer flexibility and be willing to move within the company from one job to another as the company's need changes. In a recession it will be the part-timers or temporaries who are let go. Ideally, these workers will understand that they were only temporary to begin with, and they will have planned for their layoff.

Summary

The human relations approach to managing emphasizes the importance of the human element at work. We contrasted it with scientific management, an approach that emphasized developing highly efficient and routinized jobs in which workers were often treated like parts of their machines. Important scientific management experts included Frederick Winslow Taylor, Frank and Lillian Gilbreth, and Henry Gantt.

The Hawthorne studies were begun in 1927 to test the effect of lighting on employee performance. The researchers found that the attention that was lavished on the employees made them feel more important. The employees therefore worked much harder and with a higher level of morale than they would have otherwise. This was the beginning of the human relations approach to managing.

Several concepts are closely associated with this human relations movement. For example, Douglas McGregor's Theory X held that some managers expect the worst from their employees, assuming that people dislike work and are not motivated by the desire to do a good job. In its place, McGregor suggested Theory Y, which holds that people can enjoy work and are motivated by the desire to do a good job.

The importance of work groups was another concept triggered by the human relations movement. For example, the Hawthorne studies help to illustrate how important a person's work group is in determining how the person behaves at work.

Leadership is an important part of managing. Leadership occurs whenever one person influences another to work toward some predetermined goal. One approach to leadership holds that some leaders have personality traits (such as decisiveness, intelligence, and dominance) that make them great leaders. However, the leader's style is important, too. There are two basic styles of leadership: task-oriented and employee-oriented. The managerial grid helps to illustrate different combinations of task-oriented and employee-oriented styles of leadership.

Leadership experts like Fred Fiedler point out that it is important to fit the leadership style to the situation. For example, task-oriented leaders might be best in situations in which the leader has either very high or very low control of the situation. In middle-of-the-road situations a more employee-oriented style is best.

Motivation represents a person's desire to satisfy an unfulfilled need. Needs are therefore at the center of motivation theory. We discussed several ways of looking at people's needs. Abraham Maslow arranged needs in a hierarchy, moving from physiological to safety to social to ego and finally up to self-actualization needs. Each need becomes active in motivating behavior only when the lower-level needs have been satisfied. Herzberg takes Maslow's theory one step further by dividing needs into a lower-level set and a higher-level set. The best way to motivate someone, says Herzberg, is to appeal to higher-level needs (ego and self-actualization). Hygiene factors (such as pay and better working conditions) appeal to lower-level needs and must be adequate or the employee will become dissatisfied. But to motivate the person over the long term, says Herzberg, the job itself must be interesting and challenging.

We discussed several techniques for actually motivating employees at work. Job enrichment involves building motivators such as opportunities for achievement into the job by making it more interesting and challenging. Goal setting involves setting specific, challenging goals for the employees and then praising workers when they reach their goals. Behavior modification involves changing behavior through the use of rewards or punishment. It is based on the idea that behavior that is rewarded tends to be repeated while behavior that leads to punishment tends not to be repeated.

Worker-friendly programs are increasingly popular today. For example, quality circles—groups of five to ten specialized trained employees who meet for an hour once a week to spot and solve problems in their work area—are widely used. Such groups get employees involved in their jobs, make them feel more important, and allow them to have valuable input into how their jobs are carried out. The use of flexible work arrangements such as flextime and shortened work weeks is also spreading.

Review Questions

1. What was the main problem with scientific management?

2. What is the significance of the Hawthorne Studies?

3. Distinguish between Theory X and Theory Y.

4. What is meant by "leadership"?

5. Name the factors that determine a leader's effectiveness.

6. Explain the mechanics of Maslow's motivation theory.

7. Compare and contrast goal setting, job enrichment, and behavior modification.

8. What is meant by "worker-friendly" programs?

Discussion Questions

1. Explain why an understanding of human relations concepts and techniques is important for all supervisors.

2. Do you think scientific managers held Theory X or Theory Y assumptions? Why?

3. Describe a practical example to illustrate Maslow's needs hierarchy.

4. Present two actual examples of how groups influence their members' behavior.

5. Describe two examples of how you would use behavior modification in practice.

Key Terms

human relations
Hawthorne effect
Theory X
Theory Y
leadership
leadership style
managerial grid

participative leadership
contingency leadership theory
motivation
hygienes
motivators
job enrichment

behavior modification
worker-friendly programs
quality circle
flextime
job sharing
work sharing
flexiplace

Cases

WHAT MAKES AN EFFECTIVE LEADER?

When it came to leadership traits, William Kagler seemed to have them all. He was decisive, demanding, and achievement-oriented. He was well on the way toward being chairman and chief executive officer of Kroger Co., the largest supermarket chain in the United States. In March 1987, Mr. Kagler was fired as president of the firm, not because he didn't do his job well but because in some respects he might have done it too well. As president of the firm, Mr. Kagler carried out a major restructuring at Kroger, one that involved widespread staff cuts and store closings. He had earned his promotion to president by winning a reputation in the supermarket industry as a tough negotiator with unions, among other things. He was a high-visibility leader, traveling widely to get new ideas to improve Kroger's stores (such as sushi bars). He routinely distributed videotapes of himself making speeches, which he circulated to Kroger employees. His was a no-nonsense, task-oriented style. Under his leadership the company trimmed down and got back in shape.

Then why did the chairmen fire him? Mr. Kagler told a *Wall Street Journal* reporter, "My behavior over time was an experience he didn't want to endure any longer." Mr. Kagler's boss at the time, Chairman Lyle Everingham was a quiet, private man who had begun his career at Kroger as a produce clerk. Mr. Kagler, on the other hand, was driven. Rightly or wrongly, he was seen by his critics as heavy-handed and arrogant. Diplomacy, it seems, was not one of his strengths. When anyone—including Lyle Everingham—did something that Mr. Kagler thought was wrong, he wasn't shy about expressing his views. "Maybe I could have been more diplomatic," he said, "but, no, I wouldn't have." In fact, he wasn't above bursting out of his office on occasion, making sarcastic comments to secretaries about how colleagues (including his boss) were too slow-moving when it came to making changes Mr. Kagler thought necessary.

For a while at least, Mr. Kagler's impatient, hard-driving style was quite effective. Sales and profits both increased. At the end, though, it wasn't so much the substance of his accomplishments that determined his fate. It was his ability (or lack of ability) to work amicably with his boss and exhibit the kind of style that the company felt was needed for the next few years.[8]

Questions

1. What do you think Mr. Kagler's story illustrates about effective leadership?
2. From the little you know about Mr. Kagler, would you say that his attitudes are those of a Theory X or a Theory Y manager? On what do you base your conclusion?
3. Do you think it is possible for a leader to fit his or her style to the situation? Or do you think most people's basic personalities limit them to a specific leadership style?

SWEATSHOPS ARE BACK

We hear so much about quality circles, job enrichment, and participative leadership today that it is sometimes hard to believe that the sweatshops of an earlier era are alive and well in many towns around the country. The "sweatshops" are exactly that—crowded, often poorly ventilated places where workers do very routine jobs. Most of them are recent immigrants, usually earning no more than the minimum wage—and often less.

Sweatshops have always been most closely associated with the garment industry. In the past, tens of thousands of immigrants from Europe toiled under brutal conditions in garment factories in New York City. For a while these sweatshops were all but wiped out. Even the lowest wages paid in the United States became high in relation to those paid in places like Hong Kong. This meant that prices of U.S.-made garments were too high to compete.

Today, though, sweatshops seem to be back. When the value of the dollar dropped, U.S. garment manufacturers became more competitive with those overseas, so there is more demand here again for super-low-priced garment manufacturing. Owners who run sweatshops do not just keep their wages rock-bottom low. They rarely pay any fringe benefits, and their factories often operate just this side of the law, with dark and dangerous working conditions. One report, for instance, described workers at a forty-employee shop doing their jobs in a dirt-floored basement underneath a barber shop. Most of these employers do not have time clocks or other formalities for carefully keeping track of how long workers work. Signs are rarely found outside of the factories, since many sweatshop owners prefer to keep the existence of their shops a secret—at least from the government. Many pay all wages "off the books," so that Social Security and withholding taxes do not have to be deducted or declared. This is all quite illegal, of course. But as hundreds of thousands of illegal immigrants continue to try to make a life for themselves in the United States, it is a problem that is bound to grow, no matter how hard federal and state governments try to eliminate it.[9]

Questions

1. Since job enrichment is supposed to boost employee morale and productivity, do you think sweatshop owners would consider installing job enrichment plans? Why or why not?
2. Can you apply Maslow's theory of needs to this case? In other words, how do you think that Maslow's theory explains how sweatshop employers are able to get away with treating their employees the way they do?
3. Of the techniques we discussed, which technique do you think would be most effective for boosting motivation in a sweatshop? Why?

SEVEN

Organizational Strategies

LEARNING OBJECTIVES

After reading this chapter, you will be able to:

- Explain the principles of organization.

- Explain the factors that affect a manager's optimum span of control.

- Briefly describe each of the sources of authority in organizations.

- Compare and contrast delegation and decentralization.

- Compare and contrast line authority and staff authority in an organization.

- Give examples of line organizations and line-staff organizations.

- Give an example of each of the different bases for departmentalization.

- Explain how the informal organization can affect how a company operates.

W H A T ' S
A H E A D The concept of organizing is as old as antiquity. The ancient Egyptians had to organize to build their pyramids and control the Nile. The Romans had to organize to control the residents of their lands. Even the Bible discusses how to organize, when Moses' father-in-law Aaron explains to Moses how to organize his followers for the trek out of Egypt.

Today, of course, examples of organizing are all around us. The U.S. government is organized into different departments like Labor, Treasury, and State. Burger King has different departments for functions such as sales, development, and franchising. In fact, knowing how to organize is one of the most important skills a manager can have, since if the employees' efforts are not organized, chaos and wasted motion will result.

Therefore we turn in this chapter to the subject of organizing. Organizing involves dividing the work of the organization into departments, delegating authority, and establishing coordination and control systems to ensure that everyone is working in unison to fulfill the organization's goals. We will discuss these activities in this chapter.

By now the creation of the special project team that created IBM's original PC computer is practically a legend at IBM. The company is known for white button-down shirts, dark suits,

and a highly coordinated, disciplined organization structure. In this instance, IBM realized that it needed to develop a small desktop computer product that could meet the growing personal and business needs of its customers. And it had to do it fast.

The solution? IBM created a special, autonomous project team located in a nondescript little building not too far from a major IBM development and manufacturing site in Boca Raton, Florida. It was one of several entrepreneurial "Independent Business Units" that IBM was creating at the time to encourage faster product development in response to customer needs.

The PC team was given an unusual amount of freedom. The team's boss, Philip Estridge, got the authority to design the PC pretty much as his group saw fit, with minimal review required from Armonk. Unlike traditional IBM design teams, the Boca Raton group was allowed to build their computer around standard off-the-shelf parts, even if that meant going outside IBM. The idea, said Mr. Estridge, was to have a small group with a single mission and the organizational freedom to attain it. The PC was produced exceptionally quickly and proved an instant success.

That is not the end of the story. Once the PC products shifted into full-scale worldwide production, marketing and distribution, the small team structure became inadequate. IBM's answer was to expand the team into a full-fledged IBM division—still headed by Mr. Estridge—with more than 10,000 employees handling IBM's most publicized product.[1]

organizing

The incident at IBM illustrates several important aspects of organizing. **Organizing** means arranging the firm's resources in such a way that its activities contribute to the firm's goals.[2] As at IBM, different goals—such as developing a new product or manufacturing it—may require different types of organizing. Organizing also involves delegating authority to managers like Philip Estridge so that they have the means to get their jobs done. How to organize and how to fit the organization to the situation are the subjects of this chapter.

organization chart

Organization Charts

The usual way to depict an organization is with an organization chart, as shown in Figure 7-1. An **organization chart** shows the title of each manager's position and, by means of connecting lines, shows who is accountable to whom and who is in charge of what department.

The organization chart also shows the chain of command (sometimes called the scalar chain or line of authority) from the president to

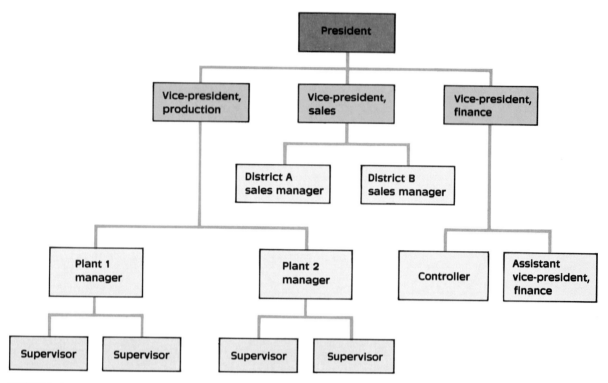

FIGURE 7-1 / An organization chart.

the lowest supervisory positions in the firm. The chain of command shows the path an order should take in going from the president to employees at the bottom of the chart. Responses travel along the same chain of command back up to the top. In Figure 7-1 the chain of command from the president to the supervisors is from the president to the vice-president of production to either of the plant managers and then to the supervisors. The chain of command from the president to the district sales managers is from the president to the vice-president of sales and then to each sales manager.

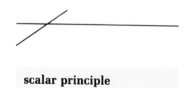

scalar principle

Principles of Organization

Early management experts such as Henri Fayol formulated principles of good organizing. The **scalar principle** states that there should be a clear chain of command from the highest to the lowest position in an organization. In a typical corporation this chain of command runs from the board of directors to the president, to the vice-presidents, to middle managers, to supervisors, and finally to the workers. Fayol believed that in sending orders down the scalar chain (or in sending requests up) it was best to stick to the chain of command rather than trying to go around it. But he understood that in some cases, to get the work done quickly, it might be best to violate the chain of command. For instance, in an emergency a supervisor might call the president directly. This would eliminate the delay that would normally occur if the supervisor had to send word through the chain of command.

unity of command principle

The **unity of command principle** states that each person in an organization should report to only one supervisor. This ensures that orders are understood and that one person does not get conflicting orders from two or more supervisors. Consider what would happen if an employee had more than one supervisor. What if the orders conflict? Which order should be followed?

span of control

Span of Control

A manager's **span of control** (or span of management) is the number of subordinates reporting directly to that manager. In Figure 7-2 the span of control of the president is seven and the span of control of the vice-president of sales is six.

There is no such thing as an ideal or "best" span of control. Early writers like Henri Fayol recommended a very narrow span of control of only five or six subordinates. The assumption was that the boss could then keep a close eye on each subordinate. But studies of spans in actual companies show that spans are often much wider than five or six. In fact they are sometimes ten or more. There is now a trend toward encouraging wider spans of control. The feeling is that with a wider span a manager cannot get overly involved in the details of each subordinate's job. In that way, each subordinate should get a chance to exercise more discretion and self-control, which should lead to higher morale.

In practice, the ideal span of control for someone depends on the situation. For example, if subordinates perform very similar or routine

FIGURE 7-2 / Span of control.

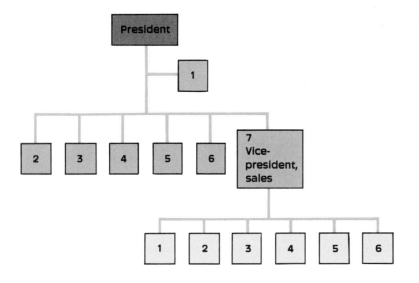

Managers of workers who perform routine tasks, as in hospital food preparation, have a wide span of control.

tasks (as in an office-cleaning squad), the manager's span of control is likely to be wide. First-line supervisors, particularly on assembly lines, tend to have wide spans of control.

On the other hand, top-level managers tend to have narrow spans because they spend considerable time supervising vice-presidents, each of whom has a complex job. Even if the vice-presidents have a great deal of autonomy, it is more difficult and time-consuming to supervise employees who have complex jobs than to supervise those with simple, routine jobs.

Several other factors can also affect the span of control. For example, the number of people a manager can supervise depends to some extent on the manager's personal traits. Some people are better than others at juggling demands from several subordinates. Others happen to put a high value on keeping close tabs on each subordinate. The employees' motives are important, too. Employees who are highly motivated to do their jobs require less monitoring and thus permit wider spans of control.

Technology and computerization can also affect the span of control. For example, big retail chains like K mart and Sears use computers to record sales of various products in each outlet. The computers simplify store managers' decisions about what to buy. They also enable district managers to keep tabs on and supervise a greater number of store managers.

There is a close relation between the average span of control in a company and the number of management levels in the firm. For example, suppose a company with sixty-four workers to be supervised contained an average span of control of eight. There would be eight supervisors directing the workers and one manager directing the supervisors. This would be a *flat organization.* If, on the other hand, the span of control were four, the same number of workers would require sixteen supervisors. They would in turn be directed by four managers. These four managers would be directed by one manager. This would be a *tall organization.* Figure 7-3 shows organization charts for these two examples.

Years ago the prevailing wisdom was that tall organizations improved performance by requiring small spans and closer supervision. Today there is definitely a trend toward flatter organizations and wider spans of control. There are two main reasons for this. First, flatter hierarchies mean that decisions are made more quickly because the information does not have to pass through as many levels. As we explained in Chapter 5, it also means that several layers of middle managers can be eliminated. This can save a firm millions of dollars.

More and more companies today are going from tall to flat. Executives at General Motors were horrified to find that while there were only five or six management layers between the president and the

FIGURE 7-3 / Flat versus tall organizations.

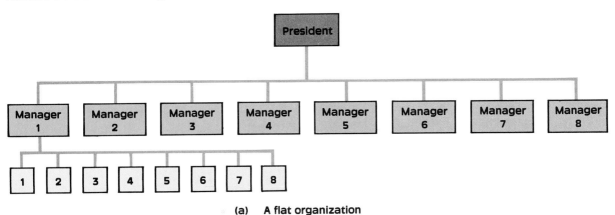

(a)   A flat organization

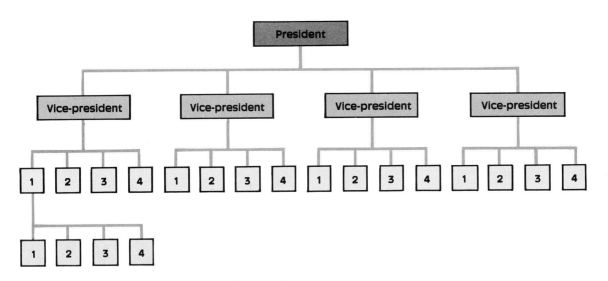

(b)   A tall organization

SEVEN / ORGANIZATIONAL STRATEGIES

workers at Toyota, there were twice that many at General Motors. The firm is now working hard to cut out many layers. Crown Zellerbach Corporation, the giant lumber and paper products firm, lopped off three layers of management in their container division. The firm's sixteen plant managers have now become more powerful. Without those extra layers of managers to report to, the plant managers now make a lot more decisions themselves and do more of their own planning. They are also personally responsible now for their plants' failure or success. Such responsibility can have a very motivating effect on a manager.

Authority in Organizations: Who's the Boss?

authority

Authority is the right to take action, the right to make decisions, the right to direct the work of others, and the right to give orders. It is a crucial factor in organizing, since managers and employees must be *authorized* to carry out the jobs assigned to them.

DELEGATION

delegation

responsibility

Organizing departments and jobs would be impossible without delegation. **Delegation** is the process of assigning responsibility, granting authority, and establishing accountability.

Responsibility is the obligation of a subordinate to perform an assigned task. In delegating a task the superior assigns a responsibility to the subordinate, and the subordinate accepts that responsibility.

The assignment of responsibility for some department or job must go hand in hand with the delegation of enough authority to get the job done. For example, it would be inappropriate to assign a subordinate the responsibility for designing a new product and then tell her she does not have the authority to hire designers or choose the best design.

But while *authority* can be delegated, *responsibility* cannot. You can assign responsibility to a subordinate. However, most managers and management experts would agree that you are still ultimately responsible for ensuring that the job gets done properly. Since you retain the ultimate responsibility, delegation of authority always entails the creation of accountability. **Accountability** is the act of holding subordinates liable. When they have been delegated adequate authority to fulfill their responsibilities, they are accountable for performing their tasks and reporting their results to their superiors. Thus your subordinates become accountable to you for the performance of the tasks you assigned to them.

accountability

DECENTRALIZATION VERSUS CENTRALIZATION

decentralization

Decentralization means delegating authority to subordinates for most decisions while maintaining control over companywide matters. At General Motors (GM) the executives in charge of each car line (Buick, Chevrolet, and so on) were traditionally able to make a wide range of production, sales, and design decisions regarding their cars. The president of GM retained tight centralized control over matters like allocating money for new plants and managing the cash that came from sales of GM cars. Broad delegation plus selective controls equals decentralization.

centralization

Many writers compare *centralized* and *decentralized* organizations. **Centralization** means that decision-making authority is concentrated in the hands of a few people at the top of a firm. On the other hand, decision making in decentralized organizations is spread throughout the firm. Here, middle- and lower-level managers have more decision-making authority than in more centralized firms. This should free top-level managers to devote more time and effort to long-range planning. The AIG ad discusses a decentralized approach to decision making.

When an organization is highly *centralized*, most decisions must be channeled up the chain of command to the president. When an organization is highly *decentralized*, most decisions can be made lower in the organization. The president need only be contacted regarding certain major decisions.

Decision-making authority is dispersed throughout the decentralized organization.

Our approach to structuring
an organization is a little bit different.

In business, the pyramid principle can lead to a type of management in which those at the top keep those at the lower levels from exercising initiative. At AIG, we've built a new kind of insurance group.

One that gives people at every level decision-making responsibility. This makes AIG far more sensitive to changes in the marketplace anywhere in the world. And far more responsive to your insurance needs.

This approach explains why AIG companies are the largest underwriters of commercial and industrial risks in the U.S., and a leading global provider of life, accident and health insurance. To learn more, contact

AIG, Dept. A, 70 Pine Street, New York, NY 10270. Then watch us turn things around for you.

Insurance Companies That Don't Think Like Insurance Companies **AIG**

LINE AND STAFF AUTHORITY IN ORGANIZATIONS

line authority

There are two basic types of authority in organizations, line authority and staff authority. **Line authority** is the authority to issue orders to subordinates down the chain of command. Managers in charge of crucial activities like sales and production usually have line authority.

staff authority

On the other hand, managers with staff authority generally cannot issue orders. **Staff authority** is the authority only to assist and advise line managers.

There are two basic types of staff positions. *Personal or general staff* reports to the executive it serves. One familiar example is the assistant to the president. His or her job is to absorb, analyze, and synthesize information and advise the president.

Specialist staff is a second type of staff position. Specialist staff managers—for personnel, industrial engineering, or quality control, for instance—assist and advise the line managers in a firm by providing expert advice in their specialized areas. For example, the personnel manager helps all managers recruit, screen, and train employees.

There are three exceptions to the rule that only line managers can issue orders. First, a staff person—say, a personnel manager—often has his or her own subordinates. Within the personnel department the personnel manager exerts line authority and issues orders to his or her own subordinates. Second, a chief executive sometimes authorizes a staff manager to issue orders to other managers in a specific area. For example, a personnel manager might be authorized to issue orders to production and sales managers regarding the tests they may use for selecting employees. In such a case the personnel manager is said to have *functional authority*—in this case, with respect to personnel testing. **Functional authority** means that a staff manager can exercise authority over line people in a specific, narrow area. Finally, a staff person might get "line" authority through the power of his or her per-

functional authority

As specialist staff who are responsible for recruiting, hiring, and training employees, personnel managers have an important influence on hospital operations.

sonality or because he or she has easy access to the president. In such a case a staff person could issue orders to other managers.

LINE AND STAFF ORGANIZATIONS

line organization

A line organization, as depicted in Figure 7-4, is the simplest type of organization. A **line organization** is an organizational structure in which each manager is directly responsible for a crucial activity required to accomplish the organization's goals. For a manufacturing company these would include production, sales, and finance, for example.

Line organizations are typical of very small companies. Suppose four or five friends get together to manufacture and sell lawn furniture. They are probably not going to set up a company that includes staff managers for things like personnel or quality control (at least at the beginning). One friend will probably become president, while each of the others will take on responsibility for other major activities the company has to perform such as production, sales, and finance. If there is any staff work to be done (such as hiring subordinates), the friends will do these tasks themselves.

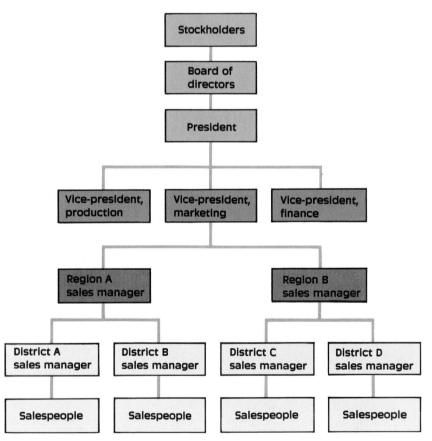

FIGURE 7-4 / A simplified line organization.

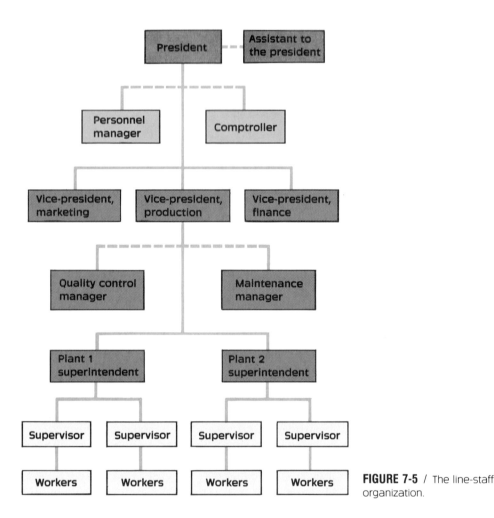

FIGURE 7-5 / The line-staff organization.

line-staff organization

Among medium and large firms particularly, *line-staff* structures like the one in Figure 7-5 predominate. A **line-staff organization** is an organizational structure that has both line and staff departments. As a firm grows, it usually makes more sense to appoint staff managers for matters like personnel than to make line managers do these jobs themselves. This gives the line managers more time to devote to the essential activities they are really responsible for such as manufacturing the product and getting it sold.

One problem with appointing separate staff managers for jobs like personnel is that conflicts can arise between the line and staff managers. For example, the plant manager might be in a hurry to hire workers to run the plant. She could become annoyed when the personnel manager wants to make all the candidates go through tests and background checks. Or the marketing research department might recommend against selling a product that the sales manager really wants the firm to sell. Setting up a line-staff structure to help line managers can therefore cause conflict and problems.

Departmentalization

Every firm has to carry out certain activities to accomplish its goals. For a manufacturer these might include manufacturing, selling, and accounting. For a city they might include fire, police, and health protection. For a hospital they include nursing, medical services, and radiology. For a bank they include lending, bookkeeping, and security. **Departmentalization** is the process through which a firm's activities are grouped together and assigned to managers.

departmentalization

ORGANIZING DEPARTMENTS

There are five main ways to organize departments. They include organizing departments around:

- Functions
- Products
- Customers
- Territories
- A matrix

FUNCTIONAL DEPARTMENTALIZATION Departmentalizing a company by function involves grouping activities around essential functions such as production, marketing, and finance or basic processes like plating and welding. In other words, the departments are organized according to the basic activities in which the firm must engage. This is the most familiar form of departmentalization and is depicted in Figure 7-6.

Functional departmentalization is the most widely used approach to organizing departments. It is a simple, straightforward, and logical way to organize. It makes sense in most instances to build departments around the firm's basic functions or processes. On the other hand, the great simplicity of this approach can backfire if the firm gets too large or has a great many products to manufacture and sell. For example, using the same production department to manufacture ten different products can be more confusing than using the department to produce just one or two products. For this reason, other ways to organize departments have evolved.

PRODUCT DEPARTMENTALIZATION In product departmentalization the departments are built around products or product lines. For example, you may know that for years the General Motors Corporation was organized

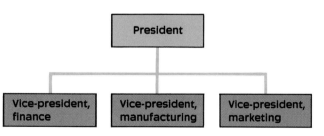

FIGURE 7-6 / Departmentalization by function.

APPLICATION: BURGER KING
Getting Organized

The organization of a typical Burger King® restaurant is a very straightforward matter. As we saw in Chapter 6, a restaurant manager oversees two assistant managers, who in turn supervise several shift supervisors and about thirty-five employees in all, each of whom is assigned a specific job like flame-broiling burgers.

But, as you can imagine, the organizational structure of the giant Burger King Corporation itself is much more complicated. There are several levels in the chain of command. At the top is Charles S. Olcott, president and chief operating officer of Burger King Corporation. Reporting to him is the president of Burger King International and a chain of executives and senior vice-presidents.

Below these senior vice-presidents is a chain of vice-presidents, directors, managers, and supervisors. The Burger King Corporation headquarters staff handles functions like marketing, research and development, and finance. There are then eleven vice-presidents in charge of each of Burger King Corporation's eleven North American regional offices (see the accompanying map). Those regional vice-presidents in turn report to one of four executive vice-presidents.

Questions

1. As a Burger King franchisee, would you prepare an organization chart for each of your restaurants? Explain.

2. "The one best approach to departmentalization for Burger King Corporation is product departmentalization." Comment.

3. Is Burger King Corporation more like a bureaucracy or an adhocracy? Explain.

1	Atlanta Region	8	Mid Atlantic Region
2	Northeast Region	9	San Francisco Region
3	Dallas Region	10	New Orleans Region
4	Detroit Region	11	Chicago Region
5	Los Angeles Region	12	Canada Region
6	Florida Region	★	Corporate Headquarters
7	Minneapolis Region		

Burger King Corporation
Region Offices

around its five basic car lines—Chevrolet, Pontiac, Buick, Oldsmobile, and Cadillac. As another example, product departmentalization in a dairy company is illustrated in Figure 7-7.

CUSTOMER DEPARTMENTALIZATION Customer departmentalization involves organizing departments to serve the needs of particular customers. At the General Electric Company, departments are built to serve particular customer groups such as aerospace customers, consumers, industrial customers, and construction industry customers.

TERRITORIAL DEPARTMENTALIZATION In territorial departmentalization, separate departments are organized for the geographic areas in which the enterprise does business. For example, the U.S. Federal Reserve System (which oversees much of the country's banking system) is divided into twelve geographic areas centered in cities such as Boston, New York, and San Francisco.

MATRIX DEPARTMENTALIZATION Managers sometimes want the advantages of a simple functional set of departments but also want specialists from each department to work together as a team on a specific project. For example, Chase Manhattan Bank is organized geographically with separate offices set up in various countries. At the same time, Chase's top management wants to be able to pull together specialists from each country into project teams. Each team is aimed at assisting a particular big customer such as IBM, Ford, or ITT.

Matrix departmentalization is aimed at handling problems like that. For example, as illustrated in Figure 7-8, a company's aerospace business could be divided into functional departments for production, engineering, and personnel. But superimposed over this functional organization are two project groups for the Satellite project and the Mars project. Each of these project groups has its own project leader. One or more representatives from each functional department are temporarily assigned to each project. For the life of the project the project members act as a team.

One potential drawback to the matrix approach is that the functional specialists end up with two bosses. (Remember the unity of command principle.) Thus a production department employee has to report not only to the production manager, but also to the project leader to whom he or she is assigned. Conflicting orders can be a problem.

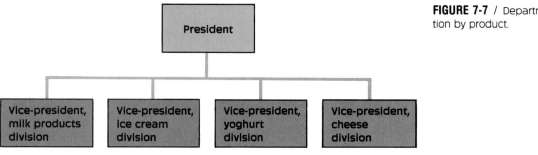

FIGURE 7-7 / Departmentalization by product.

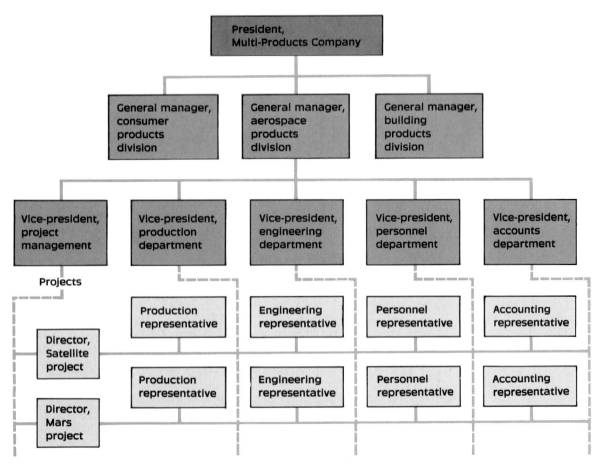

FIGURE 7-8 / Matrix departmentalization. (*Source:* Adapted from John Mee, "Matrix Organizations," *Business Horizons*, vol. 7, 1964, pp. 70–72. Copyright © 1964 by the Foundation for the School of Business at Indiana University. Used with permission.)

DEPARTMENTALIZATION IN PRACTICE: A HYBRID

In practice, you are not likely to find a company that is organized only around functions, products, customers, or territories. The organization charts for most large firms are hybrids. Top management is more likely to decide to establish, say, functional departments at the vice-president's level. Then the sales department itself might be departmentalized territorially, with separate sales managers for the north, east, south, and west regions. Meanwhile, the production department might be divided by product with separate plant managers for each of the firm's products.

Fitting the Organization to the Situation

What determines how a company should be organized? How do you know whether you should use departmentalization by product or function? A wide or narrow span of control? Centralized or decentralized decision making?

Organization theory is aimed at answering questions like these. **Organization theory** is concerned with understanding, explaining, and predicting how best to structure an organization to fulfill its goals. Today, much of the work in organization theory is aimed at explaining how to fit the organization structure to the nature of the firm's task. IBM's use of "Independent Business Units" is an example of how firms work to adapt their organizations to the nature of the task.

organization theory

WHAT DETERMINES HOW YOU ORGANIZE?

When Steven Jobs first started Apple Computer Company it was a pretty "wild and crazy" place to work. There was no formal organization chart, and there were no real departments. People were hired to work on teams, and work together they did, often through the night. All relationships were very informal. If a researcher wanted to buy, say, a new part for a project, the person could just drop by Jobs's office and get approval.

This informal approach to organizing enabled Apple to create many new products in record time in the early days of the personal computer industry. But soon competition became more keen. Other, more efficient producers (such as IBM) were able to make and distribute their computers more quickly and less expensively, partly because of their large, efficient production and sales organizations. This is part of the reason that John Scully created a more formal organization structure at Apple almost as soon as he took over as president. Small, innovative teams still work on developing new products at Apple. But in areas like production and sales, Scully eliminated duplicate departments and instituted functional departmentalization. Apple is now able to produce and sell computers much more efficiently.

Just as at Apple, management experts know that different organization structures are appropriate for different tasks. For example, quickly designing creative new products requires a lot of interaction among employees. Here you want to avoid a lot of bureaucratic red tape, so a fairly informal structure (like that in the early Apple Company) seems most appropriate. On the other hand, organizing to accomplish routine jobs (such as processing payroll checks) in which there are few unexpected problems and the same routine decisions every day requires a more structured approach to organizing. Here (as at the newly redesigned Apple Company) formal departments are set up, employees are given specialized jobs to do, and everyone is encouraged to adhere to the chain of command. Two types of organizations that illustrate these different approaches to organizing are the bureaucracy and the "adhocracy."

THE BUREAUCRACY

When most people hear the word "bureaucracy," they think of uncooperative bureaucrats and mountains of red tape. Bureaucracy today often means a slow-moving organization in which even simple decisions can take a year to make. But that is not what bureaucracy originally meant.

The idea of a bureaucracy was first proposed by a German philosopher, Max Weber, in the early 1900s. During this period, most managers were not very sophisticated. There were virtually no theories or textbooks that explained how to organize and manage companies. Weber thus proposed "bureaucracy" as a solution to the almost total lack of sensible organizing that prevailed at the time. From that point of view, Weber's suggestions represented a leap forward in the area of management expertise. **Bureaucracy** is an approach to organizing that is characterized by

- A well-defined chain of command,
- A division of work between departments,
- A system of rules covering the rights and duties of all employees,
- A system of procedures for dealing with routine decisions,
- A selection process for employment and promotion based on technical competence, and
- An impersonality of relationships in which everyone is rewarded and punished on the basis of the same set of rules.

Weber's bureaucracy was basically a set of good principles of organizing. He thought managers could apply these to bring order to their disorganized firms.

Bureaucratic organizations are still in wide use. Bureaucracies are seen in post offices, for instance, and in the production divisions of most large auto manufacturers. Most of the work to be done is routine and repetitive. Therefore the methods for accomplishing that work can be standardized. The result is a company in which there are many rules and regulations, functional departmentalization, centralized decision making, and extensive use of both line managers and staff experts.

THE ADHOCRACY

If you drive around the area known as Silicon Valley in California, you will find hundreds of companies that seem downright disorganized. Most of them are electronics firms. These firms experience very high rates of technical and product change. As a result, they are forced to come up with new products continually.

These firms are organized much differently from firms that are geared to exist under routine, stable conditions. Experts have termed these new organizations "adhocracies." An **adhocracy** is an approach to organizing in which there is a deliberate attempt to avoid pigeonholing employees into specialized jobs and to forbid blind adherence to the chain of command. Employees' roles are continually redefined as they move from project to project. Organization charts are usually avoided. Decision making is decentralized. This might prove unsettling for employees. However, in these firms there is usually a set of common beliefs and a sense of common purpose (a "company culture"). This helps to hold the employees together and ensure that the work of the firm is done effectively.[3]

bureaucracy

adhocracy

TABLE 7-1 / **Differences between bureaucracies and adhocracies**

	Bureaucracy	**Adhocracy**
Type of tasks to be done	Routine	Innovative
Departmentalization	Functional	Project teams, products
Span of control	Narrow	Wide
Degree of centralization	Decisions centralized	Decisions decentralized
Adherence to chain of command	Close adherence	Little adherence
Communications	Tend to follow organization chart	More informal, more interdepartmental communications
Tall versus flat organization	Tall	Flat

A CONTINGENCY APPROACH TO ORGANIZING

Different organizational structures are appropriate for different tasks. At one extreme are organizations for performing predictable, routine tasks such as assembling autos or bookkeeping. Efficiency is emphasized, and successful organizations are bureaucratic. They stress adherence to the rules and to the chain of command. They are characterized by highly specialized jobs, functional departmentalization, and centralized decision making.

At the other extreme, companies such as research labs and high-tech electronics firms generally face unpredictable environments and rapid technological change. In these firms, creativity and entrepreneurial activities must be emphasized. To facilitate such activities, these companies are generally organized more like adhocracies. They do not force employees to play by the rules or to adhere closely to the chain of command. An employee's job can change daily, and departments are built more around projects or teams than functional specialties. Decision making is decentralized. These differences between bureaucracies and adhocracies are summarized in Table 7-1.

The Informal Organization

informal organization

The **informal organization** represents the informal contacts, communications, and ways of doing things that employees always develop. Thus a salesperson might develop the habit of calling a production supervisor in the plant to check on the status of an order. This is quicker than going through the chain of command (by having his or her sales manager check with the plant manager, who in turn checks with the supervisor).

Every firm has such informal organizations, and no firm could function without one. This is because most organizations are confronted by many problems and unexpected events. It would be impossible to specify in advance what each employee should do when confronted by all unexpected problems. Furthermore, sticking to the chain of command is often too time consuming. Communication, the grapevine, and corporate culture are three important aspects of this informal organization. (A fourth—informal groups—was discussed in Chapter 6.)

COMMUNICATIONS IN ORGANIZATIONS

communication

Communication means the transfer of information from a sender to a receiver. All organizations are networks of communications in which written memos, reports, procedures, and oral communications flow throughout the firm. In bureaucratic organizations, communications tend to be written and highly formalized. In adhocracies there is more emphasis on oral, free-flowing, informal communications.

In theory the company's organization chart is supposed to restrict most communication to certain formal channels. This works well enough when quick responses are not needed. But imagine how badly it works when a snap decision must be made. It could take several days for the message to make its way through the chain of command and for the response to be returned. This is one reason why there is always some informal communication in organizations. It is "informal" in that it does not formally follow the organization chart.

These kinds of informal communication links are especially important in adhocracies and whenever a firm has to make a fast decision. In their study of innovative companies, Thomas Peters and Robert Waterman found that these companies use several techniques to encourage free-flowing communications. Such techniques include name tags for all employees and open offices (without tall walls). They are summarized in the Business in the News box.

Attitude surveys and an open door policy are two ways in which companies encourage upward communication from employees to top management. Attitude surveys are aimed at getting information from employees about things like their attitudes toward hours of work, supervisor's style, and the fairness and honesty of management. An open door policy means that the boss has "an open door" and employees can feel free to drop by and talk to him or her. Often it is the head of the company that establishes such a policy. The policy lets subordinates transmit concerns through a channel outside the formal chain of command. For example, production employees can bypass the production manager and go directly to the owner of the firm. This not only helps top management get a better feel for what employees are thinking, it can also act as a safety valve. The employees get a chance to express their discontent rather than letting the problem smolder.

Through informal communication, employees develop ways to get things done outside the chain of command.

RUMORS AND THE GRAPEVINE

Rumors and the grapevine are good examples of how the informal organization operates. In one study the researchers found that when management made an important change in the organization, most employees would hear the news first by the grapevine. A supervisor and an official memorandum ran a poor second and third, respectively.[4]

In their book *In Search of Excellence*, Thomas Peters and Robert Waterman found that the intensity and sheer volume of communication in excellent companies was unmistakable. Specifically, they identified several techniques that encouraged informal communication.

At Walt Disney Productions, for instance, everyone from the president down wears a name tag with just his or her first name on it. At 3M there are numerous meetings, few of which are scheduled; most are characterized by the casual getting together of people from different departments. They discuss problems in a casual, campuslike atmosphere.

At the successful companies, meetings and presentations are held in which "the questions are unabashed; the flow is free; everyone is involved." Nobody hesitates to cut off the chairperson, the president, or board members. What is encouraged, in other words, is an open exchange of ideas. People go after issues bluntly and straightforwardly.

The more effective companies also provide physical support such as blackboards and open offices to encourage frequent informal interaction. In one high-tech firm, for instance, all employees from president down work in six-foot-high doorless cubicles. These encourage openness and interaction among employees. Corning Glass installed escalators (rather than elevators) in its new engineering building to increase the chance of face-to-face contact. Similarly, another company got rid of the small, round tables in its dining room. It substituted long, rectangular tables that encouraged strangers to come in contact, often across departmental lines. Managers are encouraged to get out of their offices, walk around, and strike up conversations with those in and outside their own departments.

What all this adds up to, says Peters and Waterman, is "lots of communication." In most excellent companies you cannot wander around long without "seeing lots of people sitting together in rooms with blackboards working casually on problems."

Source: Based on Thomas J. Peters and Robert H. Waterman, Jr., *In Search of Excellence,* Harper & Row, New York, 1982. Reprinted by permission.

---

the grapevine

The grapevine is the entire network of informal contacts in a firm. Rumors are spread by the organizational grapevine, often with alarming speed:

> With the rapidity of a burning powder trail, information flows like magic out of the woodwork, past the water fountain, past the manager's door and the janitor's mop closet. As elusive as a summer zephyr, it filters through steel walls, bulkheads, or glass partitions, from office boy to executives.[5]

There are at least three reasons why rumors get started: lack of information, insecurity, and emotional conflicts.[6]

Lack of information is important. For example, employees who see an unscheduled disassembling of a machine might speculate that machines are being transferred to another plant and that workers will be laid off. *Insecurity* is a second cause of rumors. Anxious employees are more likely to perceive events negatively and to share their worries with others. *Emotional conflict* also fosters rumors. For example, there are often emotional conflicts between union and management or between two strong-willed executives. Rumors tend to develop as each side tries to interpret or distort the situation in the way most favorable to them.

The best way to refute a rumor is to release the truth as quickly as possible. This is because the more rumor is repeated, the more it will be believed and distorted. On the other hand, rumors often do turn out to be reasonably accurate, if somewhat distorted. Most rumors are usually built around a kernel of truth. It is this kernel that gives the rumor its believability.

COMPANY CULTURE

company culture

Company culture is the system of shared values and beliefs employees have about the standards and criteria used in the firm to judge achievement, individual contributions, and expertise. Shared values and beliefs in a firm reflect a sort of code of conduct. This code guides employees in how they should do their jobs, treat each other, and treat the customers.[7]

Examples of company culture abound. Take Apple Computer under Steven Jobs. It was able to attract a band of highly motivated young professionals who wore T-shirts with mottos like "Working 90 hours a week and loving every minute of it." Steve Jobs established a culture at Apple that emphasized informality and doing interesting jobs over sticking to the rules and just working for a paycheck. Competitiveness is a big part of the culture encouraged at Pepsico, Inc., the company that supplies Pepsi Cola and Frito-Lay Potato Chips. Pepsico constantly moves managers to new jobs, pressuring them to show continual improvement in market share. It expects them to be physically fit and to join company athletic teams. This all screens out less competitive managers. The ones that remain have adopted the competitive values that top management believes are required for the company to become number one.

At companies like IBM and 3M, stories and myths are always circulating among employees. These provide examples of how company heroes took actions that exemplify the company's basic values. At IBM the story is retold about how a salesman walked at great risk through the snow in order to get a needed part delivered to a customer. At Johnson & Johnson there are numerous stories about how far individual employees were willing to go to ensure that Johnson & Johnson products were of the highest quality possible.

In well-managed, innovative firms, company culture plays a very important role. The informal, free-flowing communications and the decentralized decision making in such firms could send them out of control if employees went their own ways instead of working together.

WHAT DO YOU THINK?
How Should the World Bank Have Been Reorganized?

The World Bank is based in Washington, D.C. It is funded by industrialized countries for the purpose of channeling loans to developing, third-world countries.

Mr. Barber Conable took over as president of the World Bank in 1986. His first year in office was generally regarded as a disaster. The main problem was an attempt to reorganize the bank's staff. The reorganization cost more than $100 million and threw the entire bank into disarray.

Why would Mr. Conable reorganize the bank in the first place? In fact, the reorganization was long overdue. During the preceding years the bank had been changing the kinds of loans it made to developing countries, and the bank's bureaucracy had been very slow to react to the new demands being placed on it. The World Bank,

in fact, was widely viewed as a typically overstaffed, underemployed international bureaucracy whose staff was living high on large, tax-free salaries. Mr. Conable wanted to streamline the bank and make it more responsive to its third-world customers.

Mr. Conable, decided to appoint the top executives in his new organization structure himself. Those executives then appointed the staff they wanted in the next tier, and so on down to the bank's most junior levels. Mr. Conable felt that this so-called cascade approach was the best way to cut out years of accumulated deadwood so that the bank could keep only its most effective managers in the organization structure.

Problems occurred almost at once. First, there was pressure from the bank's patrons (industrialized countries like France, Germany, and Japan) to appoint their own citizens regardless of who was best for the jobs. Furthermore, the process took many weeks, during which the lowest tiers of staff worried

about being dismissed. Mr. Conable tried to let staff express preferences about where they wanted to work. That information then had to be reconciled with what the bosses wanted and with the pressures from different countries to have their own people in important positions. The bottom line is that the World Bank is leaner now and structured more logically for its new roles. However, the reorganization almost brought the bank's operation to a halt for a year, and morale was still very low in early 1988.

Was Mr. Conable's participative, cascade approach a good idea or was there a better way to restructure the World Bank? What do you think?

Source: Reprinted by permission from "The World Economy" Survey, *The Economist*, Sept. 26, 1987.

In the best of firms this usually does not happen because of the values and beliefs that all employees share. In these firms, in other words, nothing gets very far out of line because each employee is a committed employee, and each knows what the firm expects. In the best of firms there is considerable self-control based on commitment to a set of shared values. This enables innovative firms to operate without a rigid system of close supervision and rules and procedures.

Organizing means arranging the resources of the enterprise in such a way that its activities systematically contribute to the enterprise's goals.

Several factors influence how many subordinates a manager can supervise. For example, if all subordinates perform very similar or routine tasks, the manager's span is likely to be wide. Furthermore, some people are simply better than others at juggling demands from several subordinates.

The employees' motives are important too. Highly motivated employees require less monitoring and thus permit wider spans of control. Technology and computerization can also affect the span of control. Computers can simplify store managers' decisions and enable district managers to supervise more store managers, for instance.

Authority comes from several sources, one of which is the person's position or rank. Other sources of authority are personal attributes, such as charisma, and knowledge and expertise.

Delegation simply means assigning authority to a subordinate. The delegation process itself involves assigning responsibility, granting authority to carry out that responsibility, and establishing accountability on the part of the subordinate. Decentralization means delegating most decisions to subordinates while maintaining control over essential companywide matters at higher levels. Broad delegation plus selective control equals decentralization.

Managers with line authority are authorized to issue orders to their subordinates, and all manage essential activities such as production and sales. Staff managers, on the other hand, generally cannot issue orders. They can only assist and advise line managers in areas such as quality control, market research, and personnel.

In a line organization there are typically no positions devoted to nonline activities such as personnel, market research, and quality control. These activities would be carried out by the line managers themselves. In line-staff organizations, staff positions are generally placed on the organization chart but in outlying boxes, outside the regular line chain of command.

There are five main ways to organize departments: around functions, products, customers, or territories and by matrix.

The organization structure should fit the task. At one extreme are bureaucracies, which are useful for firms that perform predictable, routine tasks. Here efficiency is emphasized. Bureaucratic organizations stress adherence to rules and to the chain of command, functional departmentalization, highly specialized jobs, and centralized decision making. At the other extreme, companies such as research labs face rapid technological change. They are organized as "adhocracies." They do not force employees to play by the rules, and they tend to be organized around temporary project teams. Decision making is decentralized.

The informal organization represents the informal contacts, communications, and ways of doing things that employees always develop.

There is always some informal communication in organizations—for example, between the sales and production managers. Rumors and the grapevine are good examples of how the informal organization operates. Rumors are often triggered by a lack of information, insecurity, or emotional conflict. A company's culture can be defined as the system of shared values and beliefs that employees have about the standards and criteria used in the company to judge achievement, individual contribution, and expertise. It reflects a sort of code of conduct and therefore constitutes part of the informal organization in any enterprise.

Review Questions

1. List the bases upon which an organization can be departmentalized. Give an example of each.

2. Why is the span of management for top-level managers usually much narrower than the span of management for lower-level managers?

3. Explain how responsibility, authority, and accountability are related to delegation.

4. What is the difference between line authority and functional authority?

5. What is the role of a staff person in an organization?

6. Explain the use of a matrix organization structure.

7. Contrast the formal organization and the informal organization.

Discussion Questions

1. Is it possible for a vice-president in a company to have more authority than the president? Discuss how this might occur.

2. Why do you think the term "bureaucracy" has come to have negative overtones?

3. What sorts of organizations come to mind when the term "centralized" is mentioned? How about when "decentralized" is mentioned? Why are some companies centralized?

4. Describe the culture of a company (or class) that you have especially enjoyed being in. Why was it so enjoyable?

Key Terms

organizing	accountability	departmentalization
organization chart	decentralization	organization theory
scalar principle	centralization	bureaucracy
unity of command principle	line authority	adhocracy
span of control	staff authority	informal organization
authority	functional authority	communication
delegation	line organization	the grapevine
responsibility	line-staff organization	company culture

Cases

DECENTRALIZATION AT KEMPER CORPORATION

If you want to see how decentralization works in practice, look at Kemper Corporation. Originally primarily an insurance firm, in 1987 the company controlled nineteen separate firms selling financial services ranging from stocks to mutual funds to life insurance.

The interesting thing about Kemper Corporation is the way in which chairman Joseph Luecke has organized this far-flung financial services company. Basically, each of the nineteen divisions is run as a completely separate entity with little or no control from Kemper's top management. There are several reasons for running the company this way. First, separate businesses are run by strong-willed individuals who do not like taking orders and might pack up and leave if they had to take orders—taking their customers with them. Furthermore, each business can concentrate on its own individual markets and customers and respond with new products when required.

But sometimes this hands-off approach can cause problems. For example, one division drifted completely out of control and lost millions for itself and Kemper. Management still believes that the advantages of decentralization outweighed the disadvantages, though.[8]

Questions

1. Do you believe that, in this case at least, the advantages of decentralization outweighed the disadvantages?
2. What does this case illustrate about the relationship between decentralization and control?
3. What sorts of things could Kemper's top management have done to avoid problems like the huge loss in that division?

A DRY-CLEANER ORGANIZATION

Jack Trumble opened his first dry-cleaning store right after college, but by January 1988 he had a serious problem. Ironically, his problem was caused by his success.

Mr. Trumble had opened his first store three years earlier after getting a degree in business. He and his wife worked long, hard hours, and because of their good quality service, their store became widely known. Soon they could barely handle the traffic at their single location, so they decided to open satellite stores. No cleaning or pressing was done in these satellite or "drop" stores. The garments were picked up and dropped off at these stores by a fleet of the company's trucks and brought to the central plant for cleaning and pressing.

As the company's service became known, its success increased. The Trumbles were able to open up several more cleaning plants and satellite drop stores. When the company had grown to five plants and over twenty drop stores, the owners knew that it was time for them to set up an organization. They knew that they were simply burning themselves out. From 5:00 in the morning until 10:00 at night they were on the go, trying to handle all the details of coordinating the pick-up trucks, employment problems, and bookkeeping, not to mention overseeing the cleaning and pressing.

The question, though, was how to organize their enterprise. Each plant had to have at least a manager (who usually also did the cleaning and spotting) as well as one or more pressers and several people to bag the clothes and handle the counter. The drop stores just had counter people to take care of clients. And, of course, there were the truck drivers (four of them).

Questions

1. What suggestions would you make to the Trumbles on how to departmentalize their enterprise?
2. Is there any need for staff employees? If so, what should their position be?
3. Draw an organization chart showing what you think the organization should look like.

Cam Starrett, Senior Vice President of Human Resources for Avon Products, Inc., graduated from the University of Cincinnati in 1971 with a degree in political science. Many "poly sci" majors went on to law school. Starrett knew that wasn't the path for her, but wasn't quite sure what was. She landed a job at a college bookstore as a "sales specialist" in charge of all nonbook items and discovered she loved retailing. "We did a land office business," she recalled in a telephone interview from her Avon office, telling how she greatly expanded the product line: "I was in charge of all the fun stuff."

She moved to Boston and parlayed her experience into a job with one of that city's major retailers, Filene's. She started as an assistant branch manager and quickly moved into buying. Two years of travel, product development, and putting together "a very interesting home and table linens department" followed before she was promoted to merchandiser. In 1979, she was named manager of Filene's Cape Cod store which was not meeting its objectives. Under

SECTION THREE

Human Resources and Production Management

Starrett's direction, however, the store performed noticeably well. She accomplished the same feat at a major mall store and was then brought into corporate management as director of personnel. Soon, she was named Vice President of Human Resources, and, in two more years, Senior Vice President with additional operating responsibility for the entire customer service division.

"Filene's is one of the few retail stores in the United States which is completely unionized, except for the very new stores, so obviously I ended up doing union negotiations .... I learned all the benefits and compensation issues and all the training and development issues. It was a great experience and made me commit to human resources as a career."

In 1985 she was recruited by Avon, which had sales of $2.76 billion in 1987. She is the only woman on Avon's nine-person corporate management committee, although she says the company is "terrific" for working women. "For decades, the company has offered women the opportunity to have significant earnings on a flex-time basis," she elaborated.

Starrett uses a variety of tools to enhance her management talents. She has hired experts—to help "push my learning curve in an area where I didn't feel so confident." She loves to read and says biographies and histories have given her many insights. "I have to be pro-active, I have to be value-added to my boss and to my team, I have to strive to work smart versus working harder ... I believe that you have to be warm and empathic, you have to be enthusiastic. Those are ideals I hold for myself, and I like to work with people who share those ideals. Underpinning it all is a lot of hard work."

Starrett supervises human relations at the corporate level, which entails multinational management, compensation, and benefits issues. "From a human resource perspective, we have to look at each country's laws ... in Europe, a lot of countries have national vacations .... Most have retirement or pension laws. Some have health insurance laws ...." Equally important, she said, is to make sure that the values, visions, and objectives of the company are carried out worldwide—"quite a challenge when you're trying to communicate with people who are living 10,000 miles away."

EIGHT

Human Resource Strategies

LEARNING OBJECTIVES

After reading this chapter, you will be able to:

- Explain the purpose of job analysis.

- List the popular sources of job applicants.

- Describe several important employee selection tools.

- List some important employee training techniques.

- List some important employee benefits and services.

WHAT'S AHEAD

Employees form the heart of any business. Employees, the firm's human resource, include—among others—maintenance workers, salespeople, assembly line workers, typists, and managers at all levels. They are important because a firm is more than its machines and physical plant. It takes people to make a firm's other resources useful—by running its machines, for example, or selling its products, servicing its customers, or managing its operations. Without good personnel, even the best-equipped firm will not function well. Indeed, it will probably fail.

Managing people is part of every manager's job. As we will see, however, as firms grow, they usually create special staff departments to help their managers manage people. This human resource (or personnel) department administers the organization's human resource activities.

We will take an in-depth look at the role the human resource department plays in a firm. As we will see, this role depends on the authority granted to the human resource department by top management. In some firms the human resource manager does have functional authority over certain personnel activities. For example, he or she might decide which test job applicants must pass or the top salary a particular job can pay.

As will become clear in this chapter, human resource management involves much more than hiring employees. It also includes training employees, assessing their job performance, paying them fairly, and helping them reach career goals.

For over fifty years, IBM has boasted that "we haven't laid off anybody." Indeed, for all that time, IBM has been in the vanguard of U.S. firms offering full, secure employment. IBM was determined to continue that practice even when business turned down and profits began dropping in 1985 and 1986.

In 1986, IBM announced one of its most important personnel actions. It was a strictly voluntary early retirement incentive. The plan's attractive features and a meticulous effort to communicate the facts to eligible employees led to a reduction of more than 12,000 people in IBM's U.S. work force by the end of 1987. In addition, hiring was reduced. Overtime was slashed from about 5 percent of total hours worked to only 1 percent or so. The use of outside contractors and supplemental workers was cut. Furthermore, employees were asked—again voluntarily—to take all their vacation time instead of saving it for use in future years. This made it easier to spread available work among all employees.

Why did IBM do this? IBM has always believed that by providing job security it would ensure the high degree of loyalty that would make the firm great. In fact, the story of IBM's growth since the mid-1950s has been phenomenal. To a large extent the firm's success is reflected in the deep commitment it has had to its personnel—its human resource.

IBM is not the only firm to understand that its success is ultimately tied to how it manages its human resource, but IBM was one of the first. Its human resource management system—including recruiting, hiring, training, appraising, rewarding, and promoting from within—has always been aimed at getting the best from each of its employees by offering the best in return.[1]

Like IBM, other modern firms recognize the importance of their human resource—the personnel who staff the firm. The aim of good human resource management is to treat employees as human beings and to satisfy their needs for successful careers and rewarding jobs.

The Human Resource

human resource

human resource management

A firm's **human resource** is its employees, including both workers and managers. The human resource may be the most important resource a firm has. Along with planning, organizing, directing, and controlling, human resource management (or "staffing") is one of the basic functions all managers perform. **Human resource management** (or personnel management) consists of activities like recruiting, selecting, training, appraising, and compensating employees.

The best way to understand human resource management is to break it down into a sequence of separate but related activities. In the rest of this chapter we will discuss each of the following steps in the human resource management chain:

- Determining human resource needs: personnel planning
- Recruiting applicants to fill those needs
- Selecting applicants for employment
- Training and developing employees
- Appraising employee performance

- Compensating employees
- Managing careers: promotions and terminations

Determining Human Resource Needs: Personnel Planning

All companies have to plan for the job openings that inevitably develop in their organizations. Employees quit, are fired, or are promoted. Openings develop as the company expands. Thus for most firms, determining personnel needs is an ongoing process.

FORECASTING HUMAN RESOURCE NEEDS

The smartest method for determining personnel needs is to predict needs before they become urgent. This involves forecasting the number and types of jobs that will be opening up. It might also involve deciding which current employees could be trained and promoted to fill those jobs. If not enough inside candidates are available, the firm must plan on recruiting new employees to fill those jobs.

personnel replacement chart

Some employers use personnel replacement charts like the one in Figure 8-1 (on p. 224) to keep track of inside candidates for their most important positions. A **personnel replacement chart** shows the current performance and ability of each employee who could be a potential replacement for the firm's important positions. Many firms today use computerized information systems to compile information on each employee's experience and educational background. This information can then be used to help management decide what inside employees (if any) are available to fill planned job openings.

Temporary help agencies that specialize in nursing professionals help hospitals to plan for stable employment.

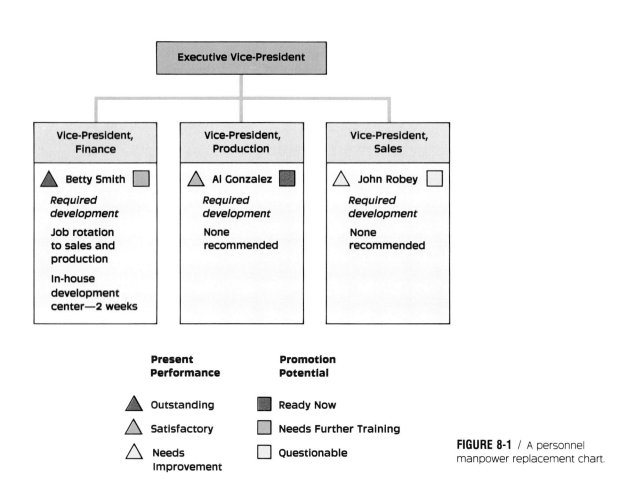

FIGURE 8-1 / A personnel manpower replacement chart.

In forecasting human resource needs, the demand for your product or service is of the greatest importance. If you believe that business will improve next year, you might have to plan for new openings. But it is not just the number of open positions that is important; the *supply* of job candidates is important too. The supply of available inside candidates will thus need to be known. The employer will also gauge local market conditions to try to predict how hard it will be to recruit new employees once business picks up. If a tight market is predicted, the employer will probably begin recruiting new applicants earlier and perhaps from farther away.

JOB ANALYSIS: SPECIFYING HUMAN RESOURCE NEEDS

job analysis

Job analysis is the next step in determining a firm's human resource needs. **Job analysis** is the procedure through which a firm determines the duties and nature of the jobs to be filled and the skills and experience needed by the people who are to fill them.

Human resource managers use several tools to do this. One is a job analysis questionnaire, which asks questions such as "What are the major duties of your job?" and "What machines or equipment do you use on your job?" Another way to conduct a job analysis is to have each employee keep a diary or log of what he or she does on a typical day. Direct observation—actually watching what the employee does—is another useful technique for determining the nature of the job.

In any case the job analysis usually produces two documents, a job description and a job specification.

job description

A **job description** is a written statement of what the jobholder actually does, the specific duties involved, and any tools, machinery, and supplies needed. (See Figure 8-2.) The job description includes several types of information. First is identifying information. This specifies things like the title of the job and the department in which it is found. Next is a summary of the job. This describes in two or three lines the general nature of the job. Next specific duties are listed. A properly written job description should tell a new employee what the job entails and the duties the person is expected to perform.

job specification

The **job specification** takes the job description and states the qualifications needed for that job in terms of things like education, skills, and experience. It shows the employer what kind of person to recruit for.

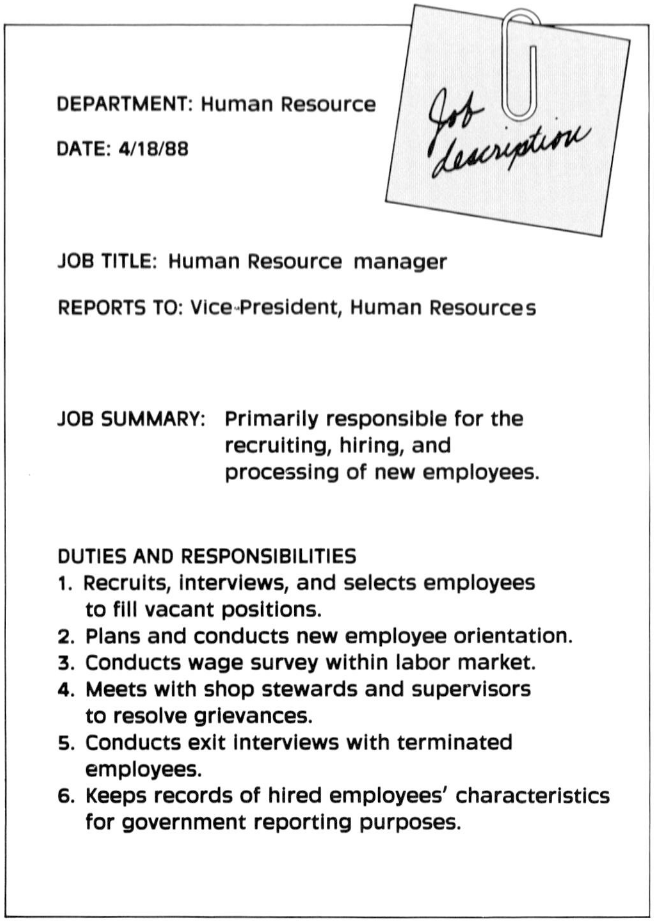

FIGURE 8-2 / An example of a job description.

DEPARTMENT: Human Resource

DATE: 4/18/88

Job Description

JOB TITLE: Human Resource manager

REPORTS TO: Vice-President, Human Resources

JOB SUMMARY: Primarily responsible for the recruiting, hiring, and processing of new employees.

DUTIES AND RESPONSIBILITIES
1. Recruits, interviews, and selects employees to fill vacant positions.
2. Plans and conducts new employee orientation.
3. Conducts wage survey within labor market.
4. Meets with shop stewards and supervisors to resolve grievances.
5. Conducts exit interviews with terminated employees.
6. Keeps records of hired employees' characteristics for government reporting purposes.

Recruiting Job Applicants

Once a firm has decided to fill a position, the next step is to develop a pool of applicants. **Recruiting** is the process of attracting job applicants (potential employees) with the use of such tools as advertisements, employment agencies, and word of mouth.

How a company does its recruiting depends on the job that is being filled and on job market conditions. The more skills that are needed, the more complex is the search process. The supply of and demand for people of certain skills can also complicate the search.

There are many ways to recruit employees. *Internal sources of candidates* are often a firm's biggest source of candidates. Some firms, like Delta Airlines, have a policy of promoting from within. In these firms, employees usually work their way up from job to job, and executives are chosen from inside candidates. Promotion from within can boost employee loyalty. It might also be safer to promote employees from within, since the employer is more likely to know the person's skills. Promotion from within does have some drawbacks. For example, it can result in fewer new points of view being brought to bear on an issue.

Advertising is another good way to attract candidates. As illustrated in Figure 8-3, local newspaper ads are usually the best source of blue-collar help, clerical employees, and lower-level administrative employees. Employers also advertise in trade and professional journals like *Chemical Engineering* for specialists. Ads in newspapers like *The Wall Street Journal* are often used to attract high-level management applicants.

Employment agencies are also widely used. The U.S. Employment Service, for example, is funded by the Department of Labor to assist states in placing unemployed workers. Public agencies are an important source of hourly blue-collar and clerical workers. The private employment agencies that you often see advertising are important sources of clerical, white-collar, and managerial personnel. Private agencies charge fees for each applicant they place. These are usually set by state law and are posted in the agencies' offices. Today, these fees are usually paid by the employer ("fee-paid"). *Temporary help agencies* are increasingly popular. They help employers to fill temporary vacancies for manual, clerical, or even professional employees. This may occur during especially busy periods or when regular employees are ill or on vacation.

Executive recruiters (also known as "headhunters") are hired by employers to seek out top management candidates for their clients, as indicated in the Manpower Recruiters ad. They fill jobs in the $30,000-and-up salary range, although $50,000 is often the lower limit. Job switching between competitors is often involved when firms are trying to hire top managers. For example, Liz Claiborne, Inc. hired former officials at Macy's Department Store as division heads. Leslie Fay Company hired as division heads managers from Lord and Taylor's and Gimbels Department Stores. Hiring managers away from their employers is often called *pirating or raiding.*

Other recruiting techniques are used as well. *Word-of-mouth recruiting* involves having current employees tell their friends and rela-

FIGURE 8-3 / A help-wanted ad.

Executive recruiting firms take on the task of finding and screening candidates for their clients' top management positions.

tives that a job is available. As a college student, you also know that many firms recruit on college campuses.[2] (In Appendix A we will discuss how to prepare for an employment interview with a campus interviewer.)

Selecting Applicants for Employment

Once you have a pool of applicants, the next step involves screening and selecting the best person for the job. For this, employers use tools like job application forms, employment interviews, and selection tests.

EQUAL OPPORTUNITY AT WORK

For many years, discrimination at work was widespread. Women were routinely limited to clerical and secretarial jobs. Blacks were often barred from moving up to skilled technical jobs or management positions. Older workers were often fired or forced to retire so that they could be replaced by younger, lower-paid workers.

Beginning in the 1960s, several major federal laws were passed that were aimed at ending these kinds of discrimination. Table 8-1 lists some of the most important actions the three branches of government have taken toward equal employment opportunity. For example, the Civil Rights Act of 1964 outlawed job discrimination based on race, color, religion, sex, or national origin. The Equal Pay Act of 1963 outlawed pay differentials based on sex. The Age Discrimination in Employment Act of 1967 prohibits discriminating against people between ages 40 and 65. A 1978 amendment extended the age to 70, and in 1987 the cap was removed entirely.

To pursue a discrimination case, a person must show that the employer's actions had an adverse impact on the person's minority group. Basically, *adverse impact* means that a significantly higher percentage of that person's minority group is being rejected for employment or promotion. For example, suppose your employer has a policy stating that "no one under 5'10" tall will be considered for this job." Since women are shorter on the average than men, this policy would probably have an adverse impact on women. A woman who is 5'9" and rejected for this job might sue the employer, claiming discrimination.

Of course, the firm could defend itself. One way to do so is to show that the requirement (in this case, being 5'10" tall) is a bona fide occupational qualification. A **bona fide occupational qualification (BFOQ)** is a selection requirement based on sex, age, religion, or national origin that is justified and legal as a basis for selecting job applicants. For example, most airlines used to hire only female flight attendants, claiming that travelers preferred being served by women. A male applicant who was rejected on the basis of sex filed a lawsuit against Southwest Airlines. He claimed that sex was not a BFOQ. He won the suit. Southwest and other airlines then began hiring both male and female flight attendants. However, national origin might be a BFOQ for waiters and waitresses in an ethnic restaurant.

bona fide occupational qualification (BFOQ)

TABLE 8-1 / Summary of important government action aimed at equal employment

Legislation	What It Does
Title VII of 1964 Civil Rights Act, as amended	Bars discrimination because of race, color, religion, sex, or national origin; and instituted EEOC.
Executive orders	Prohibit employment discrimination by employers with federal contracts of more than $10,000 (and their subcontractors); establish office of federal compliance; require affirmative action programs.
Federal agency guidelines	Guidelines covering discrimination based on sex, national origin, and religion, as well as employee selection procedures; for example, require validation of tests.
Court decisions: *Griggs v. Duke Power Co.*, *Albemarle v. Moody*	The court ruled that job requirements must be related to job success; discrimination need not be overt; the burden of proof is on the *defendant* to prove that the qualification is valid.
Equal Pay Act of 1963	Equal pay for men and women must be provided for performing similar work.
Age Discrimination in Employment Act of 1967	Prohibits discriminating against a person in any area of employment because of age.
Vocational Rehabilitation Act of 1973	Requires affirmative action to employ and promote qualified handicapped persons and prohibits discrimination.
Vietnam Era Veterans Readjustment Assistance Act of 1978	Requires affirmative action in employment for veterans of the Vietnam War era.
Pregnancy Discrimination Act of 1978	Prohibits discrimination in employment against women who are pregnant or have related conditions.
State and local laws	Often cover organizations too small to be covered by federal laws.

The Equal Employment Opportunity Commission (EEOC) is the arm of the U.S. Department of Labor that enforces equal employment opportunity laws. In addition the Federal Office of Personnel Management reviews the policies of all federal agencies to ensure that they comply with equal employment opportunity laws. It also consults with state and local governments. Another important agency is the Civil Rights Division of the U.S. Justice Department. It can bring suits against private employers or labor unions that engage in a "pattern or practice of discrimination."

Most states and cities have their own fair employment practices acts. These often cover employers who are not covered by the federal laws. For example, such laws might extend protection to employees of very small companies that would not normally be covered by federal legislation.

Sometimes when an employer has had a history of discrimination, it might have to go beyond just equal employment. *Affirmative action* requires the employer to make an extra effort to hire and promote those in the group that the employer used to discriminate against. An **affirmative action plan** shows what remedial steps the firm plans to take to encourage hiring and/or promoting members of classes of people who were previously discriminated against.

affirmative action plan

EQUAL OPPORTUNITY FOR WOMEN   Partly because of these equal opportunity laws (and partly because of changing values and the need for more families to supplement their incomes), women are active in the workplace as never before. Nearly half of all workers today are women, up from 33 percent 20 years ago. Between now and 1995, roughly two-thirds of the 15 million new entrants into the job market will be women.

But companies are finding that it takes more than equal employment opportunity laws to ensure equal employment opportunities for women. For example, without day-care centers and maternity leave, many women would find it impossible to pursue their careers. Across the country, firms are changing their rules to accommodate female employees.

For example, firms like AT&T and BankAmerica are instituting new or extended maternity and parental leave policies. These make it easier for women to pick up their careers when they return to work. Similarly, new promotion systems in many firms make it easier for women to take time off to have children and then return to continue their careers. Many firms (such as 3-M and Merck) have helped to open child-care centers near their headquarters. Many other firms now let employees start work at any point between, say, 7:00 and 10:00 A.M. This gives parents more flexibility to take care of family matters while not jeopardizing their jobs.

sexual harassment

DEALING WITH SEXUAL HARASSMENT AT WORK   **Sexual harassment** is defined by the Equal Employment Opportunity Commission as "unwelcomed sexual advances, requests for sexual favors, and other verbal or physical conduct of a sexual nature that takes place under any of the following conditions:

1. Submission is made a condition of the person's employment.
2. Submission to or rejection of such conduct is used as a basis for employment decisions affecting the person, or
3. It unreasonably interferes with the person's work performance or creates an intimidating, hostile, or offensive work environment."

The U.S. Supreme Court's first decision on sexual harassment came in June 1986 in the *Meritor Savings Bank, FSB* v. *Vinson* case. In this case a bank manager was accused of sexually harassing a female employee by repeatedly forcing her into sexual relations. The court ruled that the victim was sexually harassed even though (1) she may not have suffered any economic injury and (2) she voluntarily participated in the relationship. It was enough that the harassment had created a hostile work environment for the victim. Because of the seriousness of this matter, most companies today are instituting policies against sexual harassment.[3] (See the It's Your Business box for some guidelines on what you can do if you are sexually harassed at work.)

THE JOB APPLICATION FORM

With a pool of applicants the firm's human resource department can begin selecting the person the firm will hire. For most employers the

In today's business world, no one should have to be a victim of sexual harassment. Any employee—male or female—who believes that he or she has been sexually harassed can and should take steps to eliminate the problem.

Start with a verbal request to the harasser and his or her boss that the unwanted overtures cease. The next step should be for you to write a letter to the accused. This should be a polite, low-key letter written in three parts. The first part should present the detailed facts as you see them: "This is what I think happened. . . ." Include all facts and relevant dates. In the second part of the letter, describe your feelings and what damage you think has been done (for example, "Your action made me feel terrible" or "I'm deeply embarrassed"). Mention here any perceived or actual cost and damages along with feelings of dismay, distrust, and so on. Finally, state what you would like to have happen next—for example, "I ask that our relationship from now on be on a purely professional basis." You should deliver the letter in person if possible, to ensure that it arrives. If necessary, take a witness to accompany you when you deliver the letter.

If the letter and appeals to the employer do not suffice, you should turn to the local office of the EEOC to file the necessary claim.

Sources: Frederick Sullivan, "Sexual Harassment: The Supreme Court Ruling," *Personnel*, Vol. 65, No. 12 (Dec. 1986), pp. 42–44; Mary Rowe, "Dealing with Sexual Harassment," *Harvard Business Review*, Vol. 61 (May–June 1981), pp. 42–46; Jonathon Monat and Angel Gomez, "Decisional Standards Used by Arbitrators in Sexual Harassment Cases," *Labor Law Journal*, Vol. 37, No. 10 (Oct. 1986), pp. 712–718.

---

job application form

application blank or form is the first step in the selection process. A **job application form** is a document that collects job-related information on matters like name, address, previous employers, and education. It helps the employer to determine whether the applicant has the required education, experience, training, and other skills and background for the job. Figure 8-4 (on p. 232) shows a typical application form.

Most employers today make sure their applications conform to equal employment laws. You should rarely see questions regarding race, religion, sex, or nationality on an application. Similarly, many firms that once required applicants to attach a photo to the job application have dropped this practice. This helps to ensure that race will not be considered in the selection process. Other, more subtle indicators of a person's background are also best avoided. These include questions regarding maiden name, height and weight, national origin, or high school graduation date.

TESTING

selection test

A **selection test** is a set of questions, problems, or exercises for determining a person's knowledge, abilities, aptitudes, or qualifications for a

FIGURE 8-4 / A job application form.

BURGER KING

CREW MEMBER

APPLICATION FOR EMPLOYMENT

Burger King Corporation
AN EQUAL OPPORTUNITY EMPLOYER — M/F/H

Discrimination in employment because of race, creed, color, national origin, ancestry, age, sex, physical or mental handicaps, or liability for service in the armed forces of the U.S. is prohibited by federal legislation and/or by laws against discrimination in some states.

PERSONAL

LAST NAME	FIRST	MIDDLE INITIAL	PHONE

STREET ADDRESS	CITY	STATE	ZIP CODE

SOCIAL SECURITY NUMBER

NAME AND PHONE OF PERSON TO BE NOTIFIED FOR EMERGENCY
(Do not answer in New York State)

KNOWN PHYSICAL DEFECTS WHICH COULD AFFECT YOUR ABILITY TO PERFORM POSITION BEING APPLIED FOR

IS YOUR CITIZENSHIP OR IMMIGRATION STATUS SUCH THAT YOU CAN LAWFULLY WORK IN THE U.S.? ☐ YES ☐ NO
IF HIRED, CONTINUED EMPLOYMENT MAY BE DEPENDENT UPON PRESENTATION OF PROOF OF CITIZENSHIP OR PRESENTATION OF AN ALIEN REGISTRATION NUMBER

ARE YOU ☐ 14-15 ☐ 16-17 ☐ 18 OR OLDER   IF UNDER 18, PROOF OF AGE MUST BE PROVIDED PRIOR TO HIRING

EDUCATION

NAME OF SCHOOL AND ADDRESS	DATES FROM (Mo./Yr.)	TO (Mo./Yr.)	GRADUATED YES	NO	NUMBER OF COLLEGE CREDIT HOURS	MAJOR	AVERAGE
JUNIOR HIGH							
HIGH SCHOOL							
COLLEGE							
OTHER							

EXTRACURRICULAR ACTIVITIES

CURRENTLY ENROLLED IN HIGH SCHOOL/WORK/STUDY PROGRAM ☐ YES ☐ NO

GENERAL/ACTIVITIES

DATE AVAILABLE TO START

DAYS AND HOURS AVAILABLE TO WORK	DAY	SUNDAY	MONDAY	TUESDAY	WEDNESDAY	THURSDAY	FRIDAY	SATURDAY
	FROM							
	TO							

WHAT INTERESTED YOU IN BURGER KING?

WHAT ARE YOUR HOBBIES, SPECIAL INTERESTS, AND ACTIVITIES?
(Do not include those indicating race, creed, nationality or religion)

DO NOT ANSWER THE FOLLOWING QUESTION IN NEW YORK STATE OR — IF CONVICTION OCCURRED MORE THAN SEVEN (7) YEARS AGO — IN WASHINGTON STATE. A RECORD OR CONVICTION DOES NOT DISQUALIFY YOU FROM EMPLOYMENT CONSIDERATION.

HAVE YOU EVER BEEN CONVICTED OF A FELONY OR MISDEMEANOR OTHER THAN A TRAFFIC VIOLATION? ☐ NO ☐ YES
IF YES, STATE CHARGE, COURT, DATE AND DISPOSITION OF CASE.

EMPLOYMENT/WORK EXPERIENCE

COMPANY NO. 1 (Present or most recent employer)		ADDRESS/PHONE NUMBER	
EMPLOYED (Month & Year) FROM TO	RATE OF PAY START ENDING	AVERAGE NUMBER OF HOURS WORKED PER WEEK	
POSITION(S) HELD		SUPERVISOR'S NAME/POSITION	

DESCRIBE YOUR DUTIES

MAY WE CONTACT THIS EMPLOYER? ☐ YES ☐ NO
DAYS LOST FROM WORK (Do not answer in New York State)

REASON FOR LEAVING

COMPANY NO. 2		ADDRESS/PHONE NUMBER	
EMPLOYED (Month & Year) FROM TO	RATE OF PAY START ENDING	AVERAGE NUMBER OF HOURS WORKED PER WEEK	
POSITION(S) HELD		SUPERVISOR'S NAME/POSITION	

DESCRIBE YOUR DUTIES

MAY WE CONTACT THIS EMPLOYER? ☐ YES ☐ NO
DAYS LOST FROM WORK (Do not answer in New York State)

REASON FOR LEAVING

THE INFORMATION I AM PRESENTING IN THIS APPLICATION IS TRUE AND CORRECT TO THE BEST OF MY KNOWLEDGE, AND I UNDERSTAND THAT ANY FALSIFICATION OR MISREPRESENTATION HEREIN COULD RESULT IN MY DISCHARGE IN THE EVENT I AM EMPLOYED BY THE BURGER KING CORPORATION. I AUTHORIZE BURGER KING CORPORATION OR ITS REPRESENTATIVES TO CONTACT ALL FORMER EMPLOYERS AND TO FURTHER INQUIRE AS TO ANY INFORMATION GIVEN BY ME ON THIS APPLICATION.

APPLICANT'S SIGNATURE   DATE

DO NOT WRITE BELOW THIS LINE — FOR BURGER KING RESTAURANT USE ONLY

COMPANY NO. 1 REFERENCE CHECK		GOOD	AVERAGE	POOR
APPLICANT ELIGIBLE FOR REHIRE: ☐ YES ☐ NO	ATTENDANCE:	☐	☐	☐
DATES OF EMPLOYMENT VERIFIED: ☐ YES ☐ NO	PERFORMANCE	☐	☐	☐
CHECKED BY CONTACTED?	DATE:			

COMPANY NO. 2 REFERENCE CHECK		GOOD	AVERAGE	POOR
APPLICANT ELIGIBLE FOR REHIRE: ☐ YES ☐ NO	ATTENDANCE:	☐	☐	☐
DATES OF EMPLOYMENT VERIFIED: ☐ YES ☐ NO	PERFORMANCE	☐	☐	☐
CHECKED BY CONTACTED?	DATE:			

MANAGERS/INTERVIEWER'S NOTES:

job. The size of the firm and the type of job will influence what selection tests are used, if any.

Intelligence tests (often called "IQ" tests) test basic thinking abilities such as memory, numerical ability, verbal fluency, and reasoning ability. Aptitude tests measure the applicant's aptitude for the job in question. For example, a mechanical comprehension test (see Figure 8-5) tests the applicant's understanding of basic mechanical principles. It therefore reflects the person's aptitudes for jobs such as machinist or engineer. Performance tests are the tests with which you are probably most familiar. They measure skill in a given area, such as typing or Spanish.

Interest inventories compare your interests with those of people in various occupations. Suppose you take the Strong-Campbell Interest Inventory. You would receive a report showing your interests (for things like the outdoors, reading, or travel). The report would include a graph comparing your interests to those of people already in various occupations.

Personality tests measure basic aspects of an applicant's personality, such as introversion, stability, and motivation. Personality tests like the California Psychological Inventory are designed to predict whether a person will be able to accept a lot of stress on a job and whether a person will work well with other people, for example.

Look at Sample X on this page. It shows two men carrying a weighted object on a plank, and it asks, "Which man carries more weight?" Because the object is closer to man "B" than to man "A," man "B" is shouldering more weight; so blacken the circle under "B" on your answer sheet. Now look at Sample Y and answer it yourself. Fill in the circle under the correct answer on your answer sheet.

FIGURE 8-5 / Two problems from the test of mechanical comprehension. (*Source:* Bennett Mechanical Comprehension Test. Copyright © 1967–70, 1980 by The Psychological Corporation. Reproduced by permission. All rights reserved.)

X

Which man carries more weight? (If equal, mark C.)

A   B

EXAMPLES

	A	B	C
X	○	●	○
Y	○	○	○

A   B   C

Y

Which letter shows the seat where a passenger will get the smoothest ride?

Although polygraph (lie detector) tests may be effective in screening out dishonest job applicants, the tests are not reliable enough to be useful to most employers.

THE SELECTION INTERVIEW

Just about everyone gets interviewed before being hired. This lets employers personally size up candidates and make judgments about things like their enthusiasm and intelligence. Interviews also help employers decide how each candidate will get along with other people.

Interviews actually take place at several points in the selection process. There is usually a brief *preliminary interview*. Here the interviewer (perhaps the firm's human resource manager) interviews the candidate and explains the job. The applicant has an opportunity to ask questions and briefly discuss his or her skills and job interests. Then, after the candidate has taken any selection tests, there might be an *in-depth interview*. Here selected company employees get a chance to speak with the applicant for an hour or so. Of course, the candidate will also be interviewed by the manager for whom he or she will be working. The manager is the person who usually makes the final decision on whether or not to hire.

Interviewers have to be careful to avoid discrimination in conducting interviews. For example, questions like "Do you plan to have children?" or "What does your husband think of your going to work?" are problems. This is because they might lead to discrimination against women. (In the past, employers often turned women down for jobs. They were afraid that after training, the woman would quit her job to raise children or to follow her husband to his new job.) Questions like these should therefore be avoided. If not, the firm could be subject to a lawsuit or other government action.

THE BACKGROUND INVESTIGATION

background investigation

At about this point the applicant's references are checked. A **background investigation** checks the applicant's history by contacting former employers (if any), neighbors, teachers, and others who might be familiar with his or her past.

The value of reference checking is a matter of debate. It certainly seems smart to check a person's references before hiring. On the other hand, what the references say often becomes a matter of public record. Courts have held that candidates can sue people (like former employers) who cannot prove the uncomplimentary things they say about them. Therefore many employers now say only complimentary things, particularly in writing. Others have policies that prohibit providing any information except the candidate's years of service, salary range, and job title.

PHYSICAL EXAMINATIONS

A medical examination is often the final step in the selection process. Employers use physical exams to make sure the applicant meets the physical requirements of the job. Remember that physical qualifications (like "must be at least 5'11" tall) that are not really required to do the job are illegal. It is also illegal to deny a physically or mentally handicapped person a job if that person can perform the job. The same is true for people with a hidden handicap such as epilepsy. Recently, as we will see, courts have also ruled that people with the AIDS virus cannot be denied employment or fired from most jobs.

Training and Developing Employees

Once new employees have been recruited and selected, the next step is to orient and train them. At this stage the employer provides them with the information and skills they need to perform their new jobs.

EMPLOYEE ORIENTATION

employee orientation

Employee orientation is the process of providing new employees with basic information about the firm. This basic information includes facts like how to get on the payroll, how to obtain identification cards, and what the working hours are.

A good orientation program helps to reduce a new employee's first-day jitters. The person gets detailed information about the firm's history, its products, and its operation. He or she then has a chance to ask questions. Usually, new employees are given a tour of the facility and are introduced to co-workers. Company policies and rules are explained, as are company-sponsored employee services. These are often spelled out in a personnel manual or an employee handbook.

The orientation program might include introducing the new employee to the values and "culture" of the company and the kind of behavior that is expected of its personnel. At AT&T, for example, newly hired people are told about employees who made sacrifices on the job to help provide uninterrupted phone service during emergencies such as storms. Telling new employees what the firm expects of them helps to reinforce their commitment and dedication to the firm. It also helps to ensure that all employees are indoctrinated with the values the employer believes are important.

APPLICATION: BURGER KING
Training to Be a Manager

Training is a crucial job in any well-run company. People cannot do their jobs well if they are not well trained, so in a sense all good performance starts with effective training.

Training is also a basic step in a company's human resource management process. Remember that employees must be recruited, hired, and then trained before their work can be evaluated and a reward system developed for them.

While you might enter Burger King management as a crew member, the most likely starting point according to Al Jesness is as an assistant manager of operations (AMO) for a restaurant. This job generally requires a high school degree and some college or some equivalent experience. What kind of training can you expect as a new AMO?

You will start with Phase 1, which involves seven weeks of in-restaurant training. The purpose here is to turn you into an AMO trainee who is familiar with, and who can execute with some proficiency, all the crew-level production, service, and cleanliness-related duties in the restaurant. To do this, you will need a basic working knowledge of restaurant equipment. Once you have learned those jobs "from the bottom up," you will need to learn the basic duties of the shift supervisor (who is an hourly employee with some supervisory responsibility during his or her shift). During this first phase you will also complete training that enables you to do the daily opening and closing paperwork.

Here is a run down of each of the next nine phases, which are usually conducted over about a two-year period:

Phase 2: This is a one-week classroom training program in which you will learn things like crew training, time management, handling employees, and safety and security.

Phase 3: Here you will return for two weeks of in-restaurant training. The purpose is for your boss to rate your execution of actual shift management duties and certify you as a "shift-ready" manager. In other words, the restaurant manager will have to decide whether you have what it takes to run a restaurant.

Phase 4: This part of the program usually takes six months and is conducted in a Burger King® restaurant. This is where you will practice and perfect everything that you have learned so far. You will be given

ON-THE-JOB TRAINING

on-the-job training

On-the-job training means having a person learn a job by actually performing it on the job. Virtually every employee, from mailroom clerk to company president, gets some on-the-job training when he or she starts a job.

The basic method of on-the-job training is simple. The trainee works under the guidance of an experienced worker who advises and trains the new worker. This is often called the *coaching* or *understudy* method. Sometimes this just involves having trainees observe the supervisor to develop the skills for running a machine, for example. This method may be used even for higher-level jobs. For example, the position of "assistant to" is often used to train and develop the company's future top managers. Job rotation, in which the employee moves

specific things to achieve in crew training, administrative control, safety/security, equipment maintenance, and restaurant operations. You will be expected to manage them all effectively. At the end of six months you will be rated by your supervisor.

Phase 5: During three days of classroom training you will begin moving into more "managerial" training. You will learn more about employee interviewing, crew motivation, and scheduling employees.

Phase 6: During another six months of in-restaurant training your responsibilities will be expanded a bit. You will be expected to apply the interviewing, motivation, and scheduling techniques you learned in Phase 5 to accomplish specific performance objectives (such as effectively interviewing a certain number of crew applicants) back in the restaurant. Notice that you are gradually taking on more and more managerial responsibilities.

Phase 7: The purpose of Phase 7, which takes two and a half days in the classroom, is to train you in areas such as local store marketing, conducting performance reviews, and restaurant finance. Again, this is a broadening of your responsibilities.

Phase 8: Back in the restaurant for another six months of training, you will be given specific jobs applying matters you learned in Phase 7, involving local store marketing programs, conducting performance reviews and managing restaurant finance, for instance. You will be evaluated again at the end of your six-month period.

Phase 9: In two more days in the classroom you will improve your skills in delegation, problem solving, goal setting, and personal planning.

Phase 10: This is the last of the required assistant management training phases. During another six months in a restaurant you will be expected to accomplish specific performance objectives in delegation, problem solving, and personal planning under the guidance of your restaurant manager. If you have done a good job, you might well be on your way to a promotion to restaurant manager.

Questions
1. What advice would you give to Burger King Corporation regarding the recruitment of people for the position of assistant manager of operations?

2. Advise Burger King Corporation's top management on the relative importance of on-the-job training and off-the-job training in preparing people for the position of assistant manager of operations.

3. Why do the early stages of the training program for the position of assistant manager of operations include learning so many different in-restaurant jobs from the bottom up?

from job to job at planned intervals, is another on-the-job training technique.

OFF-THE-JOB TRAINING

There are several reasons to train employees off the job rather than on it. For complex jobs like that of salesperson, some classroom training might be in order. Here the employer can explain to groups of salespeople the advantages of new products and how to sell them. Off-the-job training is also useful when it would be dangerous to train the person on the job or when doing so would interrupt the work flow. *Vestibule training* involves training employees on machines just like those they would use on the job but in a special facility off the job. This is the

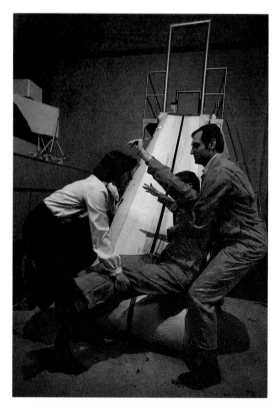

Off-the-job training in emergency evacuation procedures teaches new airline employees and updates the skills of those with longer service.

method used to train airline pilots. Pilot trainees learn about the new planes on a flight simulator. As you can imagine, this is much safer than having them learn how to fly the plane when it is filled with people three miles above the ground.

Training is an ongoing process. New employees must be trained, of course, but those with longer service must also be updated. Today, computers, closed circuit TVs, programmed text materials, videotapes, and other technical aids are widely used in training and retraining employees.

MANAGEMENT DEVELOPMENT PROGRAMS

management development programs

Management development programs are training programs that prepare employees for management positions and improve the managerial skills of present managers. Management development programs include in-house programs like on-the-job coaching and job rotation. They also include attendance at professional programs such as American Management Association seminars and courses given by colleges and universities.[4]

Management development programs are built around a variety of techniques. The *lecture method* is good for presenting facts. It is therefore a good way to inform managers about things like the meaning of new laws that regulate business activity. In the *case method*, participants are given a problem situation to analyze and solve. *Simulation techniques* force trainees to act out realistic business situations to give them practice in decision making. In a *management game,* for example, several teams compete against each other. Each team is a separate "company." In *role playing,* each trainee is given a specific role to read and act out. The aim here is to create a realistic situation and then have the trainees assume the roles of specific persons in that situation.

ORGANIZATION DEVELOPMENT

organization development

Organization development is a process for improving the company as a whole by letting the employees themselves analyze problems and suggest the solutions. *Team building* is one organization development technique. As in most organization development efforts, participants are first trained to work together as a team. Data is then gathered about their company using instruments such as *attitude surveys.* On the basis of this information, participants in the organization development program then identify the department's problems. Solutions to these problems are planned by the team.

One big advantage of organization development is that the employees themselves identify the problems and recommend the solutions. This can lead to sensible solutions that the people involved will be willing to implement.

Sensitivity training (also known as T-group or laboratory training) is another organization development technique. It aims to increase a participant's insights into his or her own behavior and the behavior of others. It does this by encouraging an open expression of feelings in the consultant-guided T-group "laboratory." (The T is for training). The assumption is that newly sensitized employees will then find it easier to work together amicably as a team. This close-knit team should then be able to go on and solve the company's organizational problems more effectively.

ASSESSMENT CENTERS

An assessment center is a series of exercises in which management candidates perform realistic management tasks under the watchful eyes of expert appraisers. Each candidate's potential for management is thereby assessed or appraised.

Assessment centers are used both for identifying future managers and for developing current managers. An assessment center is based on the idea that the best way to evaluate how a person will do on a job is to observe that person's behavior on the same or similar jobs.

A typical assessment center might be set up in a large conference room and go on for two or three days. During this time, managers and potential managers might take selection tests, engage in management games, make individual presentations, and conduct group discussions. One thing the assessors look for in a program like this is how each participant reacts to stress or to being criticized by colleagues. They also watch to see which candidates emerge as leaders of the group discussions.

Appraising Employee Performance

Once employees have been working for some time, their performance should be appraised. **Performance appraisal** is the process of evaluating an employee's actual performance in relation to the standard or desired performance.

Performance appraisal is used for three things. First, it provides

FIGURE 8-6 / An example of a graphic rating scale. (*Source:* Dale Yoder/Paul D. Staudohar, *Personnel Management & Industrial Relations,* 7th edition, © 1982, p. 213. Reprinted by permission of Prentice-Hall, Inc., Englewood Cliffs, N.J.)

Employee: _____ Job title: _____ Date: _____

Department: _____ Job number: _____ Rater: _____

SCORE-RATING

FACTOR	UNSATISFACTORY So definitely inadequate that it justifies release	FAIR Minimal; barely adequate to justify retention	GOOD Meets basic requirement for retention	SUPERIOR Definitely above norm and basic requirements	EXCEPTIONAL Distinctly and consistently outstanding
QUALITY Accuracy, thoroughness, appearance and acceptance of output					
QUANTITY Volume of output and contribution					
REQUIRED SUPERVISION Need for advice, direction or correction					
ATTENDANCE Regularity, dependability and promptness					
CONSERVATION Prevention of waste, spoilage; protection of equipment					

Reviewed by: _____ (Reviewer comments on reverse)

Employee comment: _____

Date: _____ Signature or initial: _____

information for making promotion and salary decisions (the most frequent uses of performance appraisals). The appraisal also gives an employee feedback about how he or she is doing. This can motivate the person to continue the right behavior or correct what is wrong. Finally, the appraisal gives each employee and his or her supervisor a chance to plan any required changes.

Many techniques are used to appraise employee performance. As we discussed in Chapter 5, many firms use *management by objectives* programs. In such programs, employees are given tasks to complete and are appraised based on how well they achieve them. Many firms use *graphic rating scales* like the one shown in Figure 8-6. It lists factors like quality of work, quantity of work, and attendance that are to be appraised. The employee's performance on each factor can range from unsatisfactory to exceptional.

To be useful, appraisals must be viewed as fair by the employee. For this reason it is very important that employees (and students) know ahead of time the standards by which they will be measured. It is also important to clear up job-related problems with the employee and to set measurable performance targets and a schedule for achieving them.

Compensating Employees

employee compensation

Employee compensation is all forms of pay or rewards going to employees and arising from their employment. It includes *direct financial payments* like wages, salaries, and bonuses. It includes *indirect payments* like fringe benefits (such as insurance and vacations). And it includes *nonfinancial rewards* like more challenging jobs and flexible working hours (discussed in Chapter 6).

HOW EMPLOYEES ARE PAID

Workers are paid on the basis of either the *output* they produce or the *time* they spend on the job (or a combination of the two).

wage

Most workers are paid on the basis of the time they spend on their jobs. A **wage** is an employee compensation that is based on the number of hours the employee has worked. Thus a person who earns $8 per hour and works 40 hours a week gets $320 in wages for that week. A

salary

salary is an employee compensation that is fixed on a weekly, biweekly, monthly, or annual basis. Salaried workers usually work for a fixed amount of pay per year. Most white-collar and managerial jobs are salaried jobs.

piece rate

Many workers are paid on the basis of the output they produce. Perhaps the oldest example of this is a piece rate. A **piece rate** is a certain amount of pay a worker receives for each acceptable unit of output he or she produces. Many salespeople are paid on the basis of the amount they sell. Specifically, they are paid a *commission* based on the number of items they sell.

incentive pay

To encourage greater productivity, more and more firms today are offering some type of incentive pay. **Incentive pay** is pay a worker receives for producing above the normal output or *quota*. For example, suppose an employee is paid an hourly wage of $8.00 for producing a quota of fifty pieces per hour. But for any acceptable pieces that are produced above that quota the worker might also receive incentive pay amounting to, say, 20 cents per piece. This encourages workers to be more productive. They work harder at producing more items without the supervisor having to badger them into doing so.

DECIDING HOW MUCH TO PAY

Deciding exactly how much to pay for each of the jobs in a firm usually depends on five main things: wage and salary surveys, job evaluations, performance ratings, equity, and compensation laws.

WAGE AND SALARY SURVEYS When it comes to what salaries to pay, most employers rely heavily on surveys of what other employers are doing. These surveys may be formal and based on multipage questionnaires. Or they may be informal and conducted over the phone from employer to employer.

A firm can pay above, at, or below the prevailing pay levels. If there are many unemployed people who have the skills the firm needs, the firm might decide to pay at or below the prevailing wage rates. On the other hand, suppose the firm has a policy of hiring only top-notch employees. Then they might elect to pay more than prevailing wage rates to make sure they can attract and keep the best workers.

JOB EVALUATION Job evaluation is the activity aimed at determining the relative worth of each of the company's jobs. The basic procedure of job evaluation is to compare the content of jobs in relation to one another. To do this, experts from the human resource department might study all the jobs in the firm. They then rate each in terms of the factors (like effort, responsibility, and skills) required to do each job. The jobs can then be compared to one another on the basis of how they rank in terms of these factors.

On the basis of this evaluation a pay range can be set for each job. New employees usually start at the lowest rate for the job and advance to higher rates as they gain experience, skill, and seniority. *Performance ratings* can have a big effect on what a particular employee is paid, of course. Someone who is appraised very highly might jump to the top of the pay range for a job, for instance.

EQUITY How would you like to get a $10 raise, only to find out that the man at the next desk is already earning $90 more than you are? Wouldn't you be pretty upset? That raises the issue of equity, one of the most important factors in determining pay rates.

equity theory of pay

The **equity theory of pay** basically states that a worker compares his or her inputs (or effort) and his or her outputs with those of other workers doing the same or similar jobs and a person tries to maintain a balance between what he or she puts into a job and what he or she gets out of it. An inequity results when an imbalance is perceived between these inputs and outputs. Then a person who thinks he or she is underpaid might react by working more slowly or by producing lower-quality work.

Part of the reason for job evaluation is to make sure that such perceived inequities do not occur. But in practice they often do. For example, some people are better at negotiating raises for themselves than are others. Reducing such perceived inequities is a very important but also a very delicate job.

COMPENSATION LAWS   There are also many legal guidelines in compensation. Perhaps the most familiar is the Fair Labor Standards Act. This act was originally passed in 1938 and has been amended many times. It contains minimum wage, maximum hours, overtime pay, equal pay, recordkeeping, and child labor provisions covering the majority of U.S. workers.

One important provision of the Fair Labor Standards Act governs overtime pay. It states that for covered employees, overtime must be paid at the rate of at least one and one half times normal pay for any hours worked over 40 in a work week. Another provision covers minimum hourly wages. In 1988 this was $3.35 per hour for the majority of those covered by the act.

Many other federal and state laws also govern what employers can or cannot pay. For example, the 1963 Equal Pay Act states that employees of one sex may not be paid wages at a rate lower than that paid to employees of the opposite sex for doing the same or similar work.

COMPARABLE WORTH

comparable worth

In spite of advances, women still tend to earn less than men. In part, this is because there are not nearly as many women in the higher-paying male-dominated jobs. Most women are concentrated in lower-paying jobs. **Comparable worth** is a legal concept that aims at paying equal wages for jobs that are of comparable value to the employer. This might mean comparing dissimilar jobs, such as those of nurses and truck mechanics or secretaries and electricians. Proponents of comparable worth say that all the jobs in a company must be evaluated and then rated in terms of basic dimensions such as the level of skill they require. All jobs could then be compared on the basis of a common index. People in different jobs that rate the same on this index should then be paid the same.[5] Experts hope that this will help to reduce the gap between men's and women's pay.

Employee Benefits and Services

In addition to wages and salaries, almost all firms provide their employees with some benefits and services. These range from unemployment compensation (for employees who are laid off from work) to more unusual benefits like personal financial counseling. Employee benefits represent a big chunk of most firms' total payroll bills—about $4.00 out of every $10.00 that employers spend on compensating employees. The New England ad (on p. 244) explains how its Employee Benefits Group can help client firms in developing their employee benefit plans.

TYPES OF BENEFITS

Benefits can be classified as supplemental benefits, insurance benefits, retirement benefits, or services. You are probably most familiar with supplemental pay benefits. These are benefits that employees receive when they cannot or do not work. They include unemployment compensation (if the person is laid off), vacation and holiday pay, sick pay, and severance pay (if the person is discharged). Unemployment compensation is required by law. Employers must pay an unemployment tax to the government. The size of this tax depends on the number of employees the firm has had to lay off. These taxes are then used to support unemployment compensation when a laid-off employee applies for benefits at the state unemployment compensation office.

Most firms also provide *insurance benefits*. For example, workers' compensation benefits are required by law. They provide income or medical services in the event of a worker's death or disablement. Many employers also provide a group life insurance plan for their employees, as well as hospitalization, medical, and disability insurance.

Retirement benefits provide employees with an income after they retire. As you know, you begin accumulating Social Security retirement benefits when you start working. Many firms also have *pension*

Many firms turn to specialists for help in developing their employee benefits plans.

plans. These might be paid for by the employer or the employee (or both). In either case they are aimed at providing income for retired employees.

Today, many employers also offer a wide variety of *employee services* benefits. These range from familiar ones like company cafeterias and credit unions to more exotic benefits like exercise programs, company country clubs, and even lakefront vacations. Another popular benefit is called an *employee assistance* program. These programs help employees cope with problems arising from drug and alcohol abuse, marital and family problems, and financial problems, among others.[6] With the increasing number of dual-worker families today, company-assisted *day-care centers* are another ever more popular benefit.

Particularly for managers, perquisites or "perks" are popular benefits. Examples of perks are free use of a company car or plane, first-class travel, and a reserved parking space. Payment for membership in a country club or a spa is another. Perks are still very popular today. However, firms are becoming more cost conscious. More and more of them are phasing our perks like first-class air travel and company airplanes.

EMPLOYEE BENEFITS AND THE LAW

Employers provide benefits partly to attract and keep good employees and partly because some benefits are required by law. For example, worker's compensation and unemployment compensation are both required.

One important law governing employee benefits is the Pregnancy Discrimination Act. With respect to benefits like sick leave, it requires employers to treat women affected by pregnancy, childbirth, or related medical conditions the same as any other employee who is unable to work. The Employment Retirement Income Security Act of 1974 (ERISA) protects company pension plans. Before enactment of ERISA, pension plans often failed to provide expected pension benefits to employees (for instance, if the company went out of business). Now pension benefits are basically insured by the government. The worker's right to his or her pension benefits is guaranteed if he or she stays with the firm for a specified number of years. The ominously titled COBRA—the Consolidated Omnibus Budget Reconciliation Act of 1985—is another important law. Among other things, it requires most private employers to make available to terminated or retired employees and their families continued health benefits for a period of time.

FLEXIBLE BENEFITS

Not all employees want or need the same benefits or services. For example, younger employees might want more time off or dental benefits for their families. Older employees might want to supplement their pension benefits.

As a result, many firms have set up flexible, cafeteria benefit plans.

cafeteria benefit plans

Cafeteria benefit plans are flexible benefit plans that enable employees to pick and choose from available options and develop individualized benefit plans. For example, at one Minneapolis-based American Express subsidiary the 2,500 employees automatically get core benefits. These include things like a minimal level of life insurance. But beyond the core benefits they can also choose from a list of options. These include bigger pension benefits, more medical coverage, even cash.

REDUCING HEALTH CARE BENEFIT COSTS

Employers obviously do not have an unlimited amount of money to spend on benefits. Therefore one of human resource departments' biggest jobs is reducing the firm's expenditures on health care benefit costs. Giant firms like General Motors can spend several hundred million dollars per year on such benefits.

In the increasingly cost-conscious economy of the 1980s and 1990s these costs must be reduced, and firms have done this in several ways. Many plans now reimburse hospital costs at less than the 100 percent that was often the norm several years ago. Other firms have raised the deductibles on their health insurance plans. For example, the employees themselves might have to pay the first $200 of doctor bills before the insurance kicks in. Still other plans are urging employees to get a second opinion from another doctor before agreeing to some costly medical procedure. Contracting with a health maintenance organization (HMO) to care for employees' medical problems for a set fee is another way in which firms try to control their health benefits costs.

EMPLOYEE SAFETY AND HEALTH

Another benefit all employers should provide is a healthy, safe work environment. In a recent year there were over 14,000 deaths and almost 2½ million reported injuries resulting from accidents at work. This probably grossly understates the real numbers.

Because of concerns about worker safety, the Occupational Safety and Health Act was passed by Congress in 1970. Its purpose was "to assure so far as possible every working man and woman in the nation safe and healthful working conditions and to preserve our human resources."

Under the provisions of the act the Occupational Safety and Health Administration was created within the Department of Labor. The **Occupational Safety and Health Administration (OSHA)** is a federal agency that sets safety and health standards for U.S. workers. The basic standard is that "each employer must furnish to each employee employment and a place of employment which are free from recognized hazards that are causing or are likely to cause death or serious physical harm to employees."

OSHA's standards are enforced through inspections and (if necessary) citations. Every employer covered by the act is subject to inspection by OSHA compliance officers. Compliance officers are authorized to "enter without delay and at reasonable times any factory, plant, establishment . . . where work is performed" and inspect it. However, unless they get the employer's permission, the inspectors must have a warrant to enter the premises.

Human resource departments must be alert to possible hazards in the workplace such as video display terminals, which seem to be linked with a variety of health problems.

Occupational Safety and Health Administration (OSHA)

ALCOHOLISM AND AIDS

burnout

Today, reducing workplace hazards is not limited to cleaning up oil spills and making sure that moving parts of machinery are guarded. For example, alcoholism is often a health problem at work. Progressive employers no longer react to this problem by simply disciplining or discharging errant employees. Instead, in-house counseling or referral to outside agencies such as Alcoholics Anonymous is often the preferred response. Burnout is another health problem, especially among aspiring managers.[7] **Burnout** is the total depletion of one's physical and mental resources caused by excessive striving and stress to reach some unrealistic work-related goal. Here again, human resource departments not only try to identify and monitor such problems. They also set up counseling programs to try to reduce them. Video display terminals (VDT's) present a newer health problem. Many employees who have to work closely monitoring such displays are complaining of a wide range of ills, from backaches to impaired vision and miscarriages. Human resource departments can help the situation—for instance, by providing more flexible work spaces and by ensuring that employees get rest breaks. Acquired immune deficiency syndrome (AIDS) is another health problem that employers are faced with, as explained in the What Do You Think? box (on p. 248).

Career Management

career management

Today, it is not enough to use the human resource department to satisfy the firm's staffing needs. Progressive firms also try to ensure that their employees get an opportunity to fully develop their potential. Today there is more of a *career management* perspective in what human resource departments do. **Career management** means giving employees the assistance and job opportunities that will enable them to form realistic career goals and realize them.

Employers can do many things to help their workers have more meaningful careers. One is seeing to it that job applicants get realistic previews of what to expect on their new jobs. Another is ensuring that they get interesting jobs that challenge their abilities. Providing periodic job rotation and improved, career-oriented performance appraisals (that appraise employees in light of their career goals) and good training and development are others. Beyond that, promotions, dismissals, and retirement are three big issues in any worker's career.

PROMOTING EMPLOYEES

promotion

Promotion means moving up to a higher position in the firm, usually one that provides more pay and more challenge. It is a way of rewarding people for performing well in their jobs.

Good promotion programs must address several issues. One is the question of seniority versus competency. In many firms, employees are promoted on the basis of *seniority*, in other words on the basis of how long they have been with the firm. Other firms base promotion deci-

WHAT DO YOU THINK?
Should a Person with AIDS Be Discharged?

Should a person who tests positive for AIDS be allowed to continue to work on his or her job? Or should the person be discharged so as to quell co-workers' real or imagined fears about working with this person?

John W. (not his real name) works for a county government in Florida. Like many people with AIDS, John has a horrible choice to make. He knows that if he tells his employer about his disease, he might be dismissed or subject to harassment by fearful co-workers. But if he chooses to suffer in silence, he will find it increasingly difficult to explain the many absences required by his doctor's appointments. And he might find it impossible to get the firm to process the insurance forms he will need to cover his doctor's expenses unless he reveals the nature of his illness.

Like many employers, the county that John works for has no explicit policy on AIDS. Although the problem is a critical one—there might be an estimated 1½ million AIDS carriers in the United States by 1990,

and productivity lost to AIDS illness and deaths will cost U.S. industry more than $50 *billion* by then—relatively few firms have decided what to do about it.

At one extreme, some employers (like Bank of America) have a progressive policy in place. Employees with AIDS are encouraged to inform the company, and the company promises to keep their condition personal and confidential. The human resource department then works with the sick person—for instance, by permitting more flexible work hours. Co-workers who are aware of the person's disease can request and receive a transfer. However, the AIDS victim is allowed to stay on his or her job.

At the other extreme, some employers react to AIDS by immediately discharging the infected worker.

What is the legal position of such employers? It is in doubt. Several years ago, the U.S. Justice Department published guidelines suggesting that employers were within their rights to discharge AIDS victims as long as co-workers expressed a fear about working with them. But more AIDS victims are now fighting for their rights, and they are winning. In a 1987 case (*School Board of Nassau*

County, FLA v. *Arline*) the court held that employees who are physically impaired by contagious diseases are "handicapped" within the meaning of the 1973 Rehabilitation Act. Many legal experts believe that employers should therefore now assume that the Rehabilitation Act (which protects handicapped people from discrimination) also protects people with AIDS. Today, over twenty states and several cities have, in fact, passed legislation or had court rulings that make AIDS legally a handicap. Employers in these locales may not unfairly discriminate against people with AIDS.

Should AIDS sufferers simply be discharged? Should they be isolated? Should co-workers be permitted to transfer? How would you handle this problem? What do you think?

Sources: Lorraine Lutgen, "AIDS in the Workplace: Fighting Fear with Facts and Policy," *Personnel*, Nov. 1987, pp. 53–60; Joan O'Hamilton, Julie Flynn, Patrick Houston, and Reginald Rhein, "The AIDS Epidemic and Business," *Business Week*, March 23, 1987, pp. 122–126; Bureau of National Affairs, "AIDS Discrimination: State and Local Development," *Fair Employment Practices*, Jan. 8, 1987, p. 4.

sions on *competence*, in other words on how well the person performed previous jobs. Another issue is whether promotion choices should be formal or informal. In some firms, formal programs are set up: job openings are publicized and employees are encouraged to apply. In other firms the process is informal. It might not be what you know but who you know that is especially important in getting promoted in such firms.

DISMISSALS

dismissal

Dismissal is an involuntary temporary or permanent separation of the employee from the firm. Some workers are laid off temporarily when business is slack. Of course, a layoff can become permanent if business never picks up and laid off workers are not called back. Other dismissals are permanent. They can be caused by unsatisfactory performance, misconduct, lack of qualifications for the job, or changed requirements for the job. In reality, dismissals at work are not always caused by objective deficiencies on the job. They can also be caused by personality conflicts between an employee and his or her supervisor or coworkers. In all cases of dismissals (but particularly in these) the human resource department should be responsible for ensuring that the employee is treated fairly and that the dismissal is justified. **Discharge** is the term normally used to describe the permanent dismissal of an employee against his or her will.

discharge

Many companies now provide outplacement counseling for employees who are dismissed. *Outplacement counseling* basically means hiring outside experts to counsel discharged employees regarding how to choose the sorts of jobs to look for next. They also explain how to go about getting a new job that is appropriate to their needs and talents.

resignation

Resignation occurs when employees voluntarily leave their employer's service. Employees resign for many reasons. Some leave for a job with another employer. Some quit to dramatize a point of difference with a firm or their supervisor.

Wise employers know that poor morale is a detriment to the firm. To uncover such problems, many human resource departments conduct exit interviews. An **exit interview** is a meeting between a manager and an employee who is leaving the firm for the purpose of determining why the employee is leaving. In this way, conditions might be changed so as to discourage others from leaving.

exit interview

One reason human resource departments have to be careful that dismissals are fair is that employees today are suing employers for unfair dismissals, and they are winning. This is a recent phenomenon. For many years the rule in the United States was that without an employment contract an employee could be terminated "at will" by the employer. In other words, the employer could dismiss an employee for any reason, whenever the employer chose to do so. An employee could resign for any reason at any time. Today, discharged employees are taking their cases to court. In many states, employers are finding—to their surprise—that they no longer have a blanket right to fire. For example, in thirteen states, courts have said that company manuals or handbooks (or even employment interviews) may constitute "implied contracts" that legally bind employers. If your handbook says that employees will not be laid off without "due process," a person who is fired without a chance to appeal might successfully sue your firm. Obviously, human resource departments now have to monitor dismissals and company policies very closely.

RETIREMENT

We saw earlier in this chapter that many firms have a retirement plan as one employee benefit. Employees with continuous service with such firms for a number of years get pensions (ongoing income) from the firms during their retirement years. **Deferred compensation** is benefits that are received from an employer after retirement rather than while the recipient is working for that employer.

deferred compensation

Most retirement plans are based on the employee's age. Today, the Age Discrimination in Employment Act (ADEA) makes it unlawful for most employers to discriminate against employees or applicants who are over 40 years of age. This means that in most cases there is no longer any age at which there is mandatory or forced retirement. As a practical matter most employers permit employees to retire at age 65 and to begin receiving their pensions at that point. Today, to cut costs, many firms are also encouraging employees to retire early. As an encouragement for early retirement, some companies like Kodak and IBM add incentives. For example, they might, during a two-month "window," permit employees to retire at age 60 (instead of 65) and still gain full pension benefits as if they had worked until 65. This can be a great incentive for early retirement. It lets employees retire early (and perhaps go on to new jobs at other firms). At the same time it lets firms like IBM dramatically reduce their payroll costs without having to take the drastic step of discharging long-term employees. This can in turn increase IBM employees' loyalty to the firm.

Many personnel departments also provide *preretirement counseling*. Special educational programs inform people who are about to retire about important retirement-related matters like Social Security benefits, investments, and second careers inside or outside the firm. In a sense, such preretirement counseling is the final step in the human resource department's overall employee career management program.

Summary

Human resource management (also called "staffing" or "personnel management") is one of the basic functions all managers perform. It consists of activities that include personnel planning, recruiting, selecting, training and developing, appraising, compensating, and career management.

Job analysis is the procedure through which a firm determines the duties and nature of the jobs to be filled and the skills and experience that are needed to fill them. It results in a job description (a written statement of what the job holder actually does) and a job specification (which states the personal qualifications needed for that job).

Once a job has been defined, applicants must be recruited to fill it. Sources of job applicants include internal sources, advertising, employment agencies, executive recruiters, and word-of-mouth recruiting.

Government efforts aimed at eliminating discrimination at work include the Civil Rights Act of 1964, the Equal Pay Act of 1963, the Age Discrimination in Employment Act of 1967, and various court rulings. Basically, these all come down to making it illegal to discriminate against a person for purposes of employment because of that person's age, race, sex, religion, or country of national origin.

Important selection tools include the job application form, selection tests, and interviews. Personnel tests measure things like applicants' aptitudes, performance, interests, and personality. A background investigation and physical examinations are also frequent parts of the selection process.

Employee training techniques include on-the-job training, job rotation, classroom training, and vestibule training.

Management development programs prepare employees for management positions and improve the managerial skills of present managers. They include in-house programs like on-the-job coaching and job rotation. They also include attendance at professional programs like American Management Association seminars and college courses. Popular techniques here include the case method, simulation techniques, management games, role playing, outside seminars, and organization development. Assessment centers, another popular management development technique, can be used for evaluating which management candidates should be promoted.

Deciding exactly how much to pay for each of the jobs in a firm usually depends on five main things: wage and salary surveys, job evaluations, performance ratings, equity, and compensation laws. Job evaluation is aimed at determining the relative worth of each of the company's jobs. Wage and salary surveys provide a picture of what other firms are paying for comparable jobs. Performance ratings reflect the quantity and quality of a person's work. Equity is important because it is usually desirable for people doing the jobs with the same level of effort and competence to be paid about the same. Compensation laws like the Fair Labor Standards Act provide legal guidelines that companies must use in compensating employees.

Important benefits and services include supplemental pay benefits—for example, for vacation and holidays; time and benefits; employee service benefits (like company cafeterias); insurance benefits; and employee assistance programs.

Promotion and dismissal are also important matters. Good promotion programs must address several issues. One is the question of seniority versus competency. Another is whether a promotion should be formal or informal. Dismissal—an involuntary temporary or permanent separation of the employee—is sometimes necessary. Dismissal can take the form of a layoff or a discharge.

Review Questions

1. Explain how a job analysis, a job description, and a job specification are related to each other.

2. Identify and explain the types of selection tests that can be used in making employment decisions.

3. Explain the conditions under which on-the-job and off-the-job training are best used.

4. Identify and discuss five techniques of management development.

5. Why is it important to have a good performance appraisal system?

6. What is involved in wage and salary administration?

7. Explain the difference between (a) retirement and voluntary resignation and (b) dismissal and discharge.

Discussion Questions

1. Why do you think it is difficult for firms to find temporary workers with special skills? Do you think this situation will improve in the future?

2. How effective do you think corporate affirmative action plans are in eliminating discrimination against women and minorities?

3. Applicants to managerial positions are usually given more "subjective" tests than are applicants for nonmanagerial jobs. Why is this?

4. Should a firm retrain employees whose skills have become obsolete if it can hire people who already possess the needed skills?

5. Do you think pay raises for employees should be based on performance or on seniority?

Key Terms

human resource

human resource management

job analysis

job description

job specification

personnel replacement chart

recruiting

bona fide occupational qualification (BFOQ)

affirmative action plan

sexual harassment

job application form

selection test

background investigation

employee orientation

on-the-job training

management development programs

organization development

performance appraisal

employee compensation

wage

salary

piece rate

incentive pay

equity theory of pay

comparable worth

cafeteria benefit plans

Occupational Safety and Health Administration (OSHA)

burnout

career management

promotion

dismissal

discharge

resignation

exit interview

deferred compensation

FROM MAILROOM CLERK TO DIRECTOR TO UNEMPLOYED

When it comes to making management changes, subtlety is not the strongest point of Mr. John Gutfreund, chairman and chief executive of Salomon Brothers, the biggest U.S. investment bank. On July 14, 1987, he announced that a vice-chairman, Mr. Lewis Ranieri, had resigned, although it was apparent to almost everyone that Mr. Ranieri had resigned under pressure.

The rise of Mr. Ranieri at Salomon Brothers was the stuff that legends are made of. For Mr. Ranieri, loyalty to the firm, which he liked to call "the family," was paramount. He joined Salomon Brothers at the age of 19 in the mailroom and worked his way to the top. He always liked to tell the story of how, at the age of 20, Salomon Brothers lent him the money to pay $10,000 of medical bills. At the time of his resignation he still lived frugally, in the same house he had lived in for 20 years, and he was widely respected on Wall Street.

Why was Mr. Ranieri "encouraged" to leave? Salomon said quietly that his style was just too abrasive for the firm's new formalized management style and that there was a personality conflict with Mr. Gutfreund. Yet the two had worked together for 20 years and certainly should have known each other long before Mr. Ranieri moved up to the third highest position at Salomon Brothers.

The unexpected exit of Mr. Ranieri had Wall Street worried about Salomon Brothers, and that was not the only worrying thing.

At the beginning of 1987, nearly half of Salomon Brothers' employees had been at the firm for less than a year, a result of the investment bank's recent global expansion. There was also an exodus of midlevel talent from the firm.[8]

Questions

1. Do you think that Salomon Brothers treated Mr. Ranieri fairly in apparently asking him to leave after all those years?
2. Was his dismissal handled the way you would have handled the same situation? Why or why not?
3. If you were head of Salomon Brothers, would you be concerned about the fact that nearly half of the employees had been at the firm for less than a year? What would you do about it?

DRUGS ON THE JOB

After several years of problems with drug abuse on the job, the Second National Bank thought it was time to take action. Therefore in March 1987 the bank instituted a new drug rule that prohibited employees from reporting to work under the influence of drugs or using any controlled substances on or around the bank's premises. Bank officials informed all employees of this new rule and received from them, in writing, acknowledgement that they had received and understood the new antidrug rule.

However, within two months, a bank guard noticed Betty, one of the bank's tellers, bobbing and weaving as if (as the guard said) she was "drugged out" when she reported to work in the morning.

The guard mentioned his suspicions to the bank's senior vice-president, who walked over to Betty's teller window just in time to see her give a customer two ten dollar bills in change instead of two ones. The officer called Betty aside and, noticing the bleary look in her eyes and the way she was weaving, sent her immediately to the bank's medical office. The doctor there asked Betty what medication she was taking. She said she had taken several medicines. She was then asked to take both blood and urine tests, to which she agreed. The results of the tests indicated that Betty had enough drugs in her system to seriously impair her functioning. She was therefore terminated immediately under the bank's new rule.

"But that's not fair," said Betty. "First of all, I've been a good employee for five years, and have never had any problems like this or any other. And anyway the drugs I was taking are all prescription medicines. It's not as if I was a cocaine addict or anything."[10]

Questions

1. Do you think Betty should have been fired?
2. Is it important that she was taking prescription medicines instead of illegal controlled substances?
3. What would you now advise the bank to do about Betty?

NINE

Labor Relations

LEARNING OBJECTIVES

After reading this chapter, you will be able to:

- Outline the history of unionism in the United States.

- List the federal labor laws and explain the major provisions of each.

- Tell why workers join unions and explain how unions are organized.

- Give examples of union objectives.

- Explain how unions recruit and organize new members.

- Describe the steps in the collective bargaining process.

- Explain what is meant by grievance handling.

- Briefly discuss the weapons that labor and management can use during contract negotiation and grievance handling.

W H A T ' S
A H E A D

In this chapter we will take a close look at labor relations. Our major focus will be the union movement in the United States—its past, its present, and its future.

The chapter opens with a brief history of unionism in the United States. As we will see, U.S. workers first attempted to organize for collective action at the time of the American Revolution. But it was not until the 1930s that employers were required to bargain collectively with employees. We will survey the major labor laws that were passed during and after the Great Depression.

Next comes an inquiry into the reasons why workers join unions and the reasons why employers usually resist unionization of their workers. Then we take a look at how unions are organized.

In our discussion of union objectives, we will look at the issue of union security and its relationship to right-to-work laws. This will lead us to an examination of the ways unions go about getting new members and the nature of the collective bargaining process. As we will see, both labor and management often use weapons to pressure each other throughout contract negotiation and grievance-handling procedures.

The chapter ends with a look at the future of unionism and the prospects for union-management cooperation.

February 8, 1987, was not a good day for Frank Borman. Borman had risen to colonel in the U.S. Air Force before joining the astronaut corps and piloting a spaceship to the moon. But now he was engaged in a bitter fight in what turned out to be his last meeting as chairman of Eastern Airlines.

The problem had begun some years earlier. Airline deregulation made it hard for Eastern to compete. Weighed down by huge finance payments on new planes, Borman found it almost impossible to get a profitable year out of Eastern. Every year, the airline seemed to fall deeper in debt, with losses mounting into the hundreds of millions of dollars.

To keep the company going, Colonel Borman tried several dramatic moves. Perhaps the most controversial was his decision to demand givebacks and concessions from his unions. "Givebacks" are just that: the unions agree to give back all or part of wage or benefit increases they had won earlier. But in return for the givebacks, union members demanded shares of stock and four seats on Eastern's board. Borman had little choice but to go along with the unions' demands.

Throughout most of 1985 and 1986 the airline fought to survive. Finally, at the climactic February 1987 meeting, Colonel Borman told his directors that Eastern's banks would extend their loans,

but only if the unions made further concessions. Representatives of all Eastern's unions agreed, except for Larry Bryan, the president of the machinists union. He said he would agree to the concessions on one condition—the board must fire chairman Frank Borman. The board refused.

That set in motion a series of late-hour meetings with Frank Lorenzo, chairman of Texas Air Corporation. Mr. Lorenzo had previously shown interest in buying Eastern, but only on his own terms. Now as midnight approached, negotiators for Eastern and Lorenzo worked feverishly to hammer out an agreement before Eastern's loans went technically into default. Mr. Lorenzo and Texas Air prevailed, finally buying Eastern Airlines at very favorable terms.

The purchase was ironic, from the point of view of Mr. Bryan's machinists. After a decade of bitter labor relations, Mr. Bryan had finally overthrown his management adversary, Colonel Frank Borman. But in his place, Mr. Bryan now had to deal with Frank Lorenzo, a man viewed by some as a champion union-buster.[1]

The relationship between Eastern and its employees' unions has hardly been ideal during recent years. Union leaders and the rank-and-file members look unfavorably upon givebacks—such as an agreement to give back a wage increase that was negotiated earlier during the collective bargaining process. We begin the chapter with a look at the stormy history of the union movement in the United States.

A Brief History of Unionism in the United States

U.S. workers' earliest attempts to organize for collective action occurred at the time of the American Revolution. Workers formed small local groups called "benevolent societies." If a member became ill and could not work, the others helped to care for the family. The nearest thing to a modern labor union was formed by shoemakers in Philadelphia in 1792.

Soon the pace began to quicken. The Industrial Revolution of the 1800s brought great changes to the way in which goods were manufactured. Many workers saw the growth of big factories and mechanization (substituting machines for human labor) as a threat. Small-scale production was increasingly replaced by large-scale production. To deal with these and other threats to their security, workers turned more and more to unionization. And unions began to focus more on higher wages and better working conditions than on just benevolent activities.

As we saw earlier in this book, however, the laissez faire philosophy was at the heart of our economic system until the 1930s. Most Americans rejected government interference in business and economic affairs. Nor did unions have widespread public support. In spite of that, many attempts were made to form unions. In 1869 a group of tailors met and joined the Knights of Labor. They were interested mostly in political goals, including setting up consumer cooperatives and land reform. In 1886, Samuel Gompers formed the American Federation of Labor. It focused mainly on "bread-and-butter" issues (such as better wages for its members).

In many cases, efforts to organize workers were violent. For example, the Haymarket Riot in Chicago in 1886 resulted in the deaths of seven police officers and four workers. Sixty-six people were injured protesting the use of police to break up employee efforts to strike. Employers cited the rights of private property and freedom of individual contract to justify antiunion moves. Courts often held that unions were criminal conspiracies against trade and property. The employment contract was between the individual workers and the employer, they said, not between the employer and employees as a group.

blacklists

For many years, employers battled with workers who favored unions. **Blacklists** contained the names of workers who were known to favor unions. Employers circulated these blacklists, and the blacklisted workers were refused employment.

Union leaders Robert Kanter, Walter Reuther, Richard Frankensteen, and J.J. Kennedy watch the approach of Ford Service Department just before "The Battle of the Overpass" on May 26, 1937.

yellow-dog contract

unfair lists

Often, an employer would require workers to sign a yellow-dog contract before hiring them. A **yellow-dog contract** required an employee to agree, as a condition of employment, not to join a union.

Labor unions circulated lists also, called "unfair lists." **Unfair lists** contained the names of employers whom unions considered unfair to workers because these employers would not hire union members. Violent strikes and riots were fairly common during the nineteenth and early twentieth centuries.

During the early 1930s, things began to change. As much as 25 percent of the U.S. labor force was out of work during the Great Depression. Laissez faire economics began to lose public support, and government turned its attention to getting workers back to work. Still, union-management clashes sometimes turned bloody.

Labor Legislation

Until about 1930 there were no special labor laws. About then, Congress began to pass laws to guarantee workers the right to form and join unions.

labor union

A **labor union** is an organization of employees that is formed to

collective bargaining

collective bargaining
agreement

deal collectively with the employer so as to advance the employees' interests. **Collective bargaining** is the process of negotiating a labor agreement between union and employer representatives and the process of administering an existing agreement. A **collective bargaining agreement** sets forth the terms and conditions under which union members will offer their services to an employer.

THE NORRIS-LAGUARDIA ACT OF 1932

The Norris-LaGuardia Act marked the shift in labor law from repression to government protection of union activity.[2] It was passed during the Depression. Unemployment was rampant, and many people felt that only through unions could employees influence their work situations.

The Norris-LaGuardia Act did several things for unions. It guaranteed to each employee the right to bargain collectively "free from interference, restraint, or coercion." It declared yellow-dog contracts unenforceable. And it limited the court's ability to issue injunctions for activities like peaceful picketing and payment of strike benefits. *Injunctions* are court orders that were used routinely to force employees to refrain from certain acts, such as picketing.

THE WAGNER ACT OF 1935

The Norris-LaGuardia Act did not have enough power to restrain employers from fighting labor organizations by whatever means they could muster. Therefore three years later, the Wagner Act (also called the National Labor Relations Act, or NLRA) was passed. The Wagner Act:

- banned certain types of employer unfair labor practices,
- provided for secret ballot elections and majority rule for determining whether a firm's employees were to unionize, and
- created the National Labor Relations Board (NLRB) for enforcing these two provisions.

Because of the enormous new rights it gave employees, the Wagner Act is often called labor's "Magna Carta."

The Wagner Act labeled five employer unfair labor practices "statutory wrongs" (but not criminal offenses):

1. interfering with, restraining, or coercing employees in exercising their right to organize.
2. dominating or interfering with either the formation or the administration of labor unions.
3. discriminating in any way against employees for their legal union activities.
4. discharging or discriminating against employees simply because the latter had filed "unfair practice" charges against the company.
5. refusing to bargain collectively with their employees' duly chosen representatives.

An unfair labor practice charge is filed on a form like that in Figure 9-1. The charge is filed with the National Labor Relations Board. The Board then investigates the charge and determines if formal action should be taken.

THE TAFT-HARTLEY ACT OF 1947

Union membership increased rapidly after passage of the Wagner Act in 1935. But by the late 1940s a series of massive postwar strikes, an improving economy, and other factors began to change people's minds about unions. The public became more concerned about what they viewed as "union excesses."

The Taft-Hartley Act (or Labor-Management Relations Act) reflected the public's less enthusiastic attitude toward unions. Its provisions were aimed at limiting unions in four ways:

1. by prohibiting union unfair labor practices,
2. by enumerating the rights of employees as union members,
3. by enumerating the rights of employers, and
4. by allowing the President of the United States to temporarily bar strikes in situations in which a strike might "imperil the national health and safety."

The Taft-Hartley Act listed several practices that unions were prohibited from engaging in.

First, unions were banned from stopping employees from exercising their bargaining rights. For example, it was now illegal for a union to tell an anti-union employee that he or she would lose his or her job once the union gained recognition. Similarly, the union cannot force an employer to discriminate in any way against an anti-union employee, as often occurred before the passage of this act.

The act also made it an unfair labor practice for a union to refuse to bargain "in good faith" with the employer about wages, hours, and employment conditions.

featherbedding

Finally, the Act outlawed featherbedding. **Featherbedding** is an activity by which unions require employers to pay employees for services they neither perform nor offer to perform.

THE LANDRUM-GRIFFIN ACT OF 1959

The Labor-Management Reporting and Disclosure Act is also known as the Landrum-Griffin Act. It is an amendment to the Taft-Hartley Act. It is intended to ensure the democratic operation of unions and to give employers added protection from unscrupulous union practices and leaders.

Passage of this law was aided by the McClellan Senate committee's investigation of labor racketeering. Committee members had uncovered cases in which some union leaders were engaged in blackmail, arson, and other unsavory practices. Such practices included embezzling union funds for personal use and accepting bribes and payoffs from employers.

FORM NLRB 501
(2 81)

UNITED STATES OF AMERICA
NATIONAL LABOR RELATIONS BOARD
CHARGE AGAINST EMPLOYER

INSTRUCTIONS: File an original and 4 copies of this charge with NLRB Regional Director for the region in which the alleged unfair labor practice occurred or is occurring.	DO NOT WRITE IN THIS SPACE	
	CASE NO.	DATE FILED

1. EMPLOYER AGAINST WHOM CHARGE IS BROUGHT

a. NAME OF EMPLOYER	b. NUMBER OF WORKERS EMPLOYED

c. ADDRESS OF ESTABLISHMENT (street and number, city, State, and ZIP code)	d. EMPLOYER REPRESENTATIVE TO CONTACT	e. PHONE NO.

f. TYPE OF ESTABLISHMENT (factory, mine, wholesaler, etc.)	g. IDENTIFY PRINCIPAL PRODUCT OR SERVICE

h. THE ABOVE-NAMED EMPLOYER HAS ENGAGED IN AND IS ENGAGING IN UNFAIR LABOR PRACTICES WITHIN THE MEANING OF SECTION 8(a), SUBSECTIONS (1) AND _____ OF THE NATIONAL LABOR RELATIONS ACT,
(list subsections)
AND THESE UNFAIR LABOR PRACTICES ARE UNFAIR LABOR PRACTICES AFFECTING COMMERCE WITHIN THE MEANING OF THE ACT.

2. BASIS OF THE CHARGE (be specific as to facts, names, addresses, plants involved, dates, places, etc.)

BY THE ABOVE AND OTHER ACTS, THE ABOVE-NAMED EMPLOYER HAS INTERFERED WITH, RESTRAINED, AND COERCED EMPLOYEES IN THE EXERCISE OF THE RIGHTS GUARANTEED IN SECTION 7 OF THE ACT.

3. FULL NAME OF PARTY FILING CHARGE (if labor organization, give full name, including local name and number)

4a. ADDRESS (street and number, city, State, and ZIP code)	4b. TELEPHONE NO.

5. FULL NAME OF NATIONAL OR INTERNATIONAL LABOR ORGANIZATION OF WHICH IT IS AN AFFILIATE OR CONSTITUENT UNIT (to be filled in when charge is filed by a labor organization)

6. DECLARATION

I declare that I have read the above charge and that the statements therein are true to the best of my knowledge and belief.

By _____   _____
(signature of representative or person filing charge)   (title, if any)

Address _____   _____
(telephone number)   (date)

WILLFULLY FALSE STATEMENTS ON THIS CHARGE CAN BE PUNISHED BY FINE AND IMPRISONMENT
(U.S. CODE, TITLE 18, SECTION 1001)

FIGURE 9-1 / NLRB form 501: Filing an unfair labor practice charge.

The Wagner, Taft-Hartley, and Landrum-Griffin Acts are the pillars of U.S. labor law. See Table 9-1 for a summary of the important features of the major federal labor laws.

Why Do Workers Join Unions?

Workers join unions for many reasons. First, there is strength in numbers. A strike by one worker would not have much effect. A collective strike, however, can cripple a firm's work flow.

Second, union members are represented in collective bargaining by professional negotiators. The outcome is likely to be better for each worker than if each negotiated alone.

A third reason is the feeling of power that workers get from union membership. Although the employer-employee negotiations are handled by professionals, the workers at least have a chance to vote for union officers. They also have veto power over any settlement that is reached regarding wages, fringe benefits, and working conditions.

Finally, many workers believe that union membership keeps employers interested in and concerned with their well-being.

But it would be a mistake to assume that employees just unionize to get more pay or better working conditions. Certainly these are important factors. More often, the urge to unionize boils down to a belief that only in that way can workers protect themselves against the arbitrary actions of managers.[3] In practice, this usually means that low morale is a sure signal that a union could be formed.

Why Do Employers Resist Unions?

For its part, the employer usually resists being unionized. There are several reasons for this. Perhaps the most obvious is that the union can and will restrict management's freedom of action. Decisions such as who gets laid off when business is slow, who gets to work overtime, and who gets a raise will be subject to challenge by the union. Some employers also believe that the presence of a union reduces employees' loyalty to the firm. When collective bargaining results in a pay raise, for instance, workers might think that the union "won" the raise, not that the employers "granted" it. As a result, employers fear that workers' loyalty will shift from the firm to the union.

The need to gain more productivity from workers is another issue that causes employers to resist unions' demands. Management often blames productivity problems on restrictive work rules (such as a union rule that a baggage handler may not help at an airline reservations desk even if he or she has nothing to do). For their part, unions argue that management too often will not invest in training programs to upgrade labor skills. They also blame low productivity on poor worker-manager communications, bureaucratic red tape in big firms, and inadequate research and development expenditures.

TABLE 9-1 / Major federal labor laws

Norris-LaGuardia Act (1932)
1. Greatly limits the use of the injunction by employers engaged in a labor dispute
2. Outlaws the yellow-dog contract

National Labor Relations Act (NLRA), or Wagner Act (1935)
1. Makes it illegal for employers to
   a. interfere with the rights given workers under the act
   b. interfere in the organization or operation of a union
   c. discriminate against workers who file charges or testify under the act
   d. discriminate in hiring and firing because of union affiliation
   e. refuse to bargain collectively with unions
2. Created the National Labor Relations Board (NLRB)

Labor-Management Relations Act, or Taft-Hartley Act (1947)
1. Makes it illegal for unions to
   a. coerce workers to join unions
   b. coerce employers to discriminate against workers who do not join unions
   c. refuse to bargain collectively with employers
   d. set excessive or discriminatory union dues
   e. force an employer to pay for services that were not performed or offered to be performed
2. Outlaws the closed shop
3. Permits states to pass right-to-work laws
4. Provides for injunctive processes in national emergency strikes and in certain types of illegal strikes

Labor-Management Reporting and Disclosure Act, or Landrum-Griffin Act (1959)
1. Requires unions and employers to file reports with the Secretary of Labor
2. Sets up rules for election of union officers
3. Guarantees each union member the right to
   a. attend and vote in union meetings and elections
   b. vote on proposals to increase union dues
   c. testify and bring suit against the union for violations of the act and for discriminatory treatment
   d. receive a hearing before the union can take disciplinary action against the member

When productivity does go up, management and labor often disagree over who should get the rewards. Management will take the position that at least part of the increase is the result of new and better systems and machines. The workers will argue that their hard work should be rewarded. The unions will pressure management to open its books for review and to pay some of the increased profit to workers. Disputes like this simply add to the general feeling on the part of many employers that they are better off without unions.

How Are Unions Organized?

It is useful to understand how unions are organized and how the local union that workers join is related to a national federation like the AFL-CIO.

TYPES OF UNIONS

The two basic types of unions are craft and industrial unions.

craft unions

Craft unions are labor unions that are organized by crafts or trades such as plumbers, printers, and airline pilots. They restrict membership to workers with specific skills. Members of craft unions might work for several different employers during the course of a year. For example, many construction workers are hired by their employers at union hiring halls. When the job for which they have been hired is finished, they return to the hall to be hired by another employer.

industrial unions

Industrial unions are labor unions that are organized according to industries such as steelmaking, automaking, and clothing manufacturing. They include both semiskilled and unskilled workers. Examples include the United Auto Workers Union, the United Mineworkers, and the Amalgamated Clothing Workers of America.

LOCAL, NATIONAL, AND INTERNATIONAL UNIONS

local union

The **local union** (or "local"), the basic unit of union organization, is made up of members in a single, relatively small geographical area. It may be a local of a craft union or an industrial union. For example, plumbers in Chicago might be members of the local plumbers' (craft) union. Truck drivers and warehouse workers in that same area might be members of a Teamsters' local (an industrial union). It is the local union that a worker joins and that collects his or her union dues. It is usually the local union that signs the collective bargaining agreement for its employees.

national union

Many local unions are affiliated with a national union. A **national union** is the organization set up to bring all the member local unions together for bargaining purposes. Each local union sends delegates to its national union meetings. There are close to 200 national unions in the United States. Those that have members in other countries are called *international unions*. The United Auto Workers (UAW) is international. It is made up of local unions in the United States and Canada.

THE AFL-CIO

union federation

A **union federation** represents the unions that comprise it in presenting labor's views on political and social issues. It also helps to resolve conflicts among its affiliated unions. The AFL-CIO is a national federation of 13.7 million members in approximately ninety-four affiliated unions. Before 1955 the American Federation of Labor (AFL) housed craft unions. The Congress of Industrial Organizations (CIO) contained industrial unions. In 1955 the two merged to become the AFL-CIO. The AFL-CIO is made up of many, but not all, national unions. The Teamsters Union is a large national union that rejoined the AFL-CIO in 1987 after years of nonmembership.

Union Objectives

Generally speaking, unions have two aims: (1) to improve the wages, security, and standards of living of their members and (2) to strengthen union security.

IMPROVING MEMBERS' WORKING CONDITIONS AND STANDARDS OF LIVING

Unions concerned about hazardous working conditions fought for and won the use of protective outer garments for employees.

Unions seek to improve their members' standard of living. Pay and the benefits package—working conditions, pensions, and paid vacations— are bargainable issues. The employer must be willing to negotiate these issues in good faith.

Working conditions today are much better than they were during the "sweatshop" days of the Industrial Revolution. However, dirty and dangerous jobs still exist. Brown lung, black lung, lead poisoning, and asbestosis are examples of dangerous industrial diseases. The Occupational Safety and Health Act was passed, with major support from unions, to help improve the situation. Today, robots are performing some of the dullest and most dangerous jobs in many plants.

Job security is another important aim, especially today, when there are so many plant closings and mergers. The seniority provision in most contracts spells out the workers' rights when layoffs, transfers, and promotions occur. Employees are ranked in terms of length of service. Those with longer service are supposed to get better treatment.

The problem is that this is often more easily said than done. For example, when Texas Air Corporation bought People Express, it thereby gained 295 new captains. This dramatically slowed the career progress of younger pilots from Continental Airlines, which Texas Air had bought earlier. When Continental's unions refused to renegotiate their labor contracts, what did chairman Frank Lorenzo do? He took the company bankrupt. This is a legal term meaning, among other things, that all of Continental's union contracts were void. The pilots (and other employees) then had to agree to work for the new, lower salaries or leave the firm.

IMPROVING UNION SECURITY

union security

Unions also fight hard for union security. **Union security** is the right the union has to represent a firm's workers. Ideally (from the union's point of view), the union is the exclusive bargaining agent for all employees in the firm. In practice, there are five types of union security (see Figure 9-2 on p. 266):

- The closed shop
- The union shop

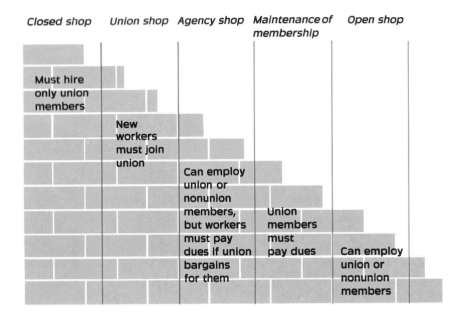

Maximum protection for union			Minimum protection for union	
Closed shop	Union shop	Agency shop	Maintenance of membership	Open shop
Must hire only union members	New workers must join union	Can employ union or nonunion members, but workers must pay dues if union bargains for them	Union members must pay dues	Can employ union or nonunion members

FIGURE 9-2 / Five types of union security.

- The agency shop
- The open shop
- The maintenance of membership arrangement

closed shop

The strongest type of union security is the closed shop. A **closed shop** is a type of union security in which an employer can hire only union members. The Taft-Hartley Act outlaws the closed shop. However, some states do allow it. In these states a closed shop is permissible only if the employer is not engaged in interstate commerce.

union shop

The Taft-Hartley Act permits the union shop. A **union shop** is a type of union security in which an employer may hire nonunion workers even if the employer's present employees are unionized. But new workers must join the union within 30 days of being hired or else be fired. Roughly 90 percent of all unionized blue-collar workers work under a union shop agreement.

agency shop

Some states permit an agency shop. An **agency shop** is a type of union security in which all employees for whom the union bargains must pay dues, but they need not join the union. This is a compromise between the union shop and the open shop.

open shop

An **open shop** is a type of union security in which an employer may hire union and/or nonunion labor. Employees need not join or pay dues to a union in an open shop. Both members and nonmembers are covered by the union contracts regarding pay and benefits. Union people believe that the open shop is at best a weak type of union security. It gives the same benefits to employees who are not union members (and who do not pay dues) as it does to those who are dues-paying members.

Union members are not even required to maintain membership in the union.

maintenance of membership agreement

Finally, there is a maintenance of membership arrangement. A **maintenance of membership arrangement** is a type of union security that does not require workers to join the union, but union members who are employed by the firm must "maintain membership" by paying dues to the union while the labor contract between the union and employer is in effect.

RIGHT-TO-WORK LAWS

right-to-work laws

The Taft-Hartley Act also lets states pass right-to-work laws. **Right-to-work laws** outlaw the union shop. They weaken union bargaining strength and make it harder to organize workers. A firm's unionized and nonunionized employees are paid the same wage for the same work. Union members believe that nonunion workers take advantage of union-won benefits without paying union dues. Unions want to repeal that section of the Taft-Hartley Act that allows states to pass right-to-work laws. Figure 9-3 shows which states have right-to-work laws.

doublebreasted firm

There is an added complication today. There has been a trend in the construction industry toward going *doublebreasted*.[4] A **doublebreasted firm** is a unionized employer that sets up a nonunion subsidiary to do some of its work. Many unionized contractors who lost business to nonunion ones have set up nonunion subsidiaries. This type of setup has also become more common in the airline and trucking industries. In 1987, Eastern Airlines tried to set up such a separate nonunionized subsidiary to do its ground maintenance. The courts said

FIGURE 9-3 / The states that have right-to-work laws.

WHAT DO YOU THINK?
Is Union-Management Cooperation a Good Thing?

Unionized companies that want to develop a program for improving productivity face an additional problem: What role should the union play in this process? Unions often resist productivity improvement efforts for the same reasons that employees in general sometimes resist them. They might not fully appreciate the greater long-term threat to job security posed by low productivity, and they might fear that any program to boost output per worker could jeopardize some workers' jobs. The net result is often that if management pursues improvement without involving the union, the union may well resist those efforts. In fact, some experts believe that the very fact that management does not seek union input and support is itself a red flag, one that suggests that the firm does not have the employees' best interests at heart.

The evidence suggests that labor and management can work together to boost productivity. For example, the U.S. Department of Labor has reported the results of over 200 successful labor-management efforts in a wide variety of industries. Here are some examples:

- A possible plant closing was averted through a cooperative effort between Aluminum Company of America (ALCOA) and the United Steel workers.
- A Beech Aircraft Corporation suggestion program administered by a labor-management productivity counsel has been credited with saving several million dollars over a period of years.
- The Chicago, Milwaukee, St. Paul, and Pacific Railroads saved over $3 million through a cooperative process involving a number of unions.
- A joint labor-management pro-

gram involving Malden Mills Industries, Inc. and the International Ladies Garment Workers Union resulted in $1.5 million in savings in a single year.

This small sampling of labor-management success stories demonstrates that cooperative efforts between union and management can work. If handled correctly, they offer significant opportunities for performance improvement.

On the other hand, it is apparent from explosive situations like that at Eastern Airlines that union-management cooperation can be difficult or impossible to achieve. Some people believe that firms that say they want to cooperate are just wolves in sheep's clothing, trying to lull unsuspecting workers into giving up their union rights. Is union-management cooperation a good thing? What do you think?

Source: John G. Belcher, Jr., "The Role of Unions in Productivity Management," *Personnel*, Jan. 1988, pp. 54–59.

---

that Eastern, which already had a mechanics union, could not do this. Unions view the growth of doublebreasted arrangements with alarm.

LOBBYING

Unions (and business) both engage in lobbying to attain their aims. Lobbying is efforts to influence the passage of laws or to influence their administration or enforcement. It is carried out by lobbyists.

The labor lobby is powerful and well organized. The AFL-CIO Committee on Political Education (COPE) lobbies for passage of prolabor laws. It also helps prolabor candidates get elected. Among recent legislative goals of unions have been restricting imports of foreign-made products; raising the federal minimum wage; creating a $980 million worker-retraining fund for displaced workers; and requiring companies to give advance notice of plant closings.

How Do Unions Get New Members?

How a union goes about getting new members depends first on the type of union it is. Skilled craft workers like carpenters in a geographic area often seek membership in their local unions. The union then helps them find work that pays union wages and benefits. People who wish to learn a craft might seek to join a union as apprentices.

Industrial unions usually devote a lot more effort to recruiting and organizing new members than do craft unions. Suppose an industrial union (or craft union, for that matter) wants to organize workers at a local plant. This process involves five steps: (1) initial contact, (2) obtain authorization cards, (3) hold a hearing, (4) have a campaign, and (5) hold the election.

STEP 1: INITIAL CONTACT

During the initial contact stage the union determines the employees' interest in organizing. Sometimes the initiative comes from the employees. Or the first contact might come from a union representative. He or she might seek out a few employees to try to interest them in helping organize the company's workers.[5]

STEP 2: OBTAINING AUTHORIZATION CARDS

Next, the union must show that a sizable number of employees might be interested in joining the union. The next step is thus for union organizers to try to get the employees to sign authorization cards. Thirty percent of the employees must sign such cards before an election can be petitioned.

STEP 3: HOLDING A HEARING

National Labor Relations Board (NLRB)

At this point the union petitions the National Labor Relations Board to hold an election. The **National Labor Relations Board (NLRB)** is the federal agency created by the Wagner Act to supervise union elections and prohibit unfair labor practices committed by employers and unions. However, firms often claim that most of their employees do not really want the union. Then the NLRB gets involved. Among other things the NLRB examiner will hold a hearing to determine whether 30 percent or more of the employees actually signed the authorization cards.

STEP 4: THE CAMPAIGN

Next the union and the employer campaign for their points of view. The union will claim that it will help prevent unfairness, improve unsatisfactory wages, and set up a grievance system. The employer will emphasize the high cost of union dues and the fact that unions might cause strikes. However, neither side can threaten, bribe, or coerce employees (see Figure 9-4).

FIGURE 9-4 / NLRB form 66: Notice to employees.

Form NLRB 666
(7–72)

★ NOTICE TO EMPLOYEES

FROM THE

National Labor Relations Board

A PETITION has been filed with this Federal agency seeking an election to determine whether certain employees want to be represented by a union.

The case is being investigated and NO DETERMINATION HAS BEEN MADE AT THIS TIME by the National Labor Relations Board.   IF an election is held Notices of Election will be posted giving complete details for voting.

It was suggested that your employer post this notice so the National Labor Relations Board could inform you of your basic rights under the National Labor Relations Act.

YOU HAVE THE RIGHT under Federal Law

- To self-organization
- To form, join, or assist labor organizations
- To bargain collectively through representatives of your own choosing
- To act together for the purposes of collective bargaining or other mutual aid or protection
- To refuse to do any or all of these things unless the union and employer, in a state where such agreements are permitted, enter into a lawful union security clause requiring employees to join the union.

It is possible that some of you will be voting in an employee representation election as a result of the request for an election having been filed.   While NO DETERMINATION HAS BEEN MADE AT THIS TIME, in the event an election is held, the NATIONAL LABOR RELATIONS BOARD wants all eligible voters to be familiar with their rights under the law IF it holds an election.

The Board applies rules which are intended to keep its elections fair and honest and which result in a free choice. If agents of either Unions or Employers act in such a way as to interfere with your right to a free election, the election can be set aside by the Board.   Where appropriate the Board provides other remedies, such as reinstatement for employees fired for exercising their rights, including backpay from the party responsible for their discharge.

STEP 5: THE ELECTION

Finally, the election is held. The purpose of the election is to see whether a majority of employees want the union. (By the way, to win the election, the union must win only a majority of the votes cast, not a majority of the employees in the firm.) If the union wins the election, it is certified by the NLRB as the employee's bargaining agent. If a rival union is trying to organize the workers, the NLRB will conduct an election to see which one will be certified. The union and company can then begin negotiating a collective bargaining agreement or contract.

The Collective Bargaining Process

As we mentioned earlier in the chapter, collective bargaining is the process of negotiating a labor contract between union and employer representatives. The contract covers matters such as wages, hours of work, and seniority rights. A typical contract, which spans a two- or three-year period, is the result of days or weeks of discussion, persuasion, compromise, and haggling. The stages in contract negotiation are (1) preparing to bargain, (2) bargaining, (3) dealing with disputes, and (4) signing a contract.

PREPARING TO BARGAIN

In preparing to bargain on a new contract the union sets up a negotiating team, usually long before the current contract is due to expire. This team develops a list of demands that will satisfy the union membership. Often union members vote a strike authorization to take effect if the current contract expires before a new one has been negotiated.

The management negotiating team tries to anticipate and prepare for the union's demands. For example, management might expect the union to bargain for a big wage hike. Management negotiators then enter the bargaining sessions armed with forecasts. These show how higher wages would hurt the firm's ability to compete.

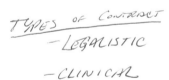

TYPES OF CONTRACT
—LEGALISTIC
—CLINICAL

BARGAINING IN GOOD FAITH

During the early bargaining sessions the union presents its demands first. Then management proposes changes in the old contract that it would like to see. Any issues brought up for discussion can be objected to by either party. As we have seen, however, the law requires both parties to bargain in good faith on bargainable issues. **Bargainable issues** are those that employer and union are permitted by law to discuss. Under the law, there is a long list of mandatory bargaining items. These are items about which both union and management must be willing to bargain. They include wages, hours, paid vacations, overtime pay, sick leave, and rest periods. **Bargaining in good faith** means that proposals are matched with counterproposals and that labor and management make every reasonable effort to arrive at an agreement. Suppose management believes that one of the union's demands infringes on manage-

bargainable issues

bargaining in good faith

ment's rights. If management refuses to bargain on this point, the union might file a complaint with the NLRB. The NLRB will decide whether the issue is bargainable.

By now, both sides have their demands on the table, and it might look as if there is little chance of agreement. The bargaining process then focuses on concessions. Each team is authorized to make concessions in order to narrow the gap between labor's demands and management's offers. The closer the bargainers get to the expiration date of the current contract, the harder they usually work to hammer out a tentative agreement.

DEALING WITH UNION-MANAGEMENT DISPUTES

Sometimes the talks bog down, and it looks as though the negotiators will be unable to reach an agreement. Each side has weapons that it can use to pressure the other to break the impasse. These weapons, which include strikes, will be discussed later in this chapter.

Before using these weapons the negotiators are likely to turn to outsiders for help—to conciliators, mediators, and, if the existing contract permits, arbitrators. These outsiders are neutral third parties.

conciliation   In **conciliation** the conciliator is a neutral third party whose task is to prevent labor-management negotiations from breaking down. He or she has no authority to force a settlement, however. If negotiations do break off, the conciliator tries to get the two parties back to the bargaining table. The aim is to find a solution to the problem that bogged down negotiations.

mediation   Mediation goes a step further. In **mediation** the mediator is a neutral third party whose task is to suggest a compromise that will get the labor-management negotiations moving ahead and to persuade the parties to accept this compromise. Like the conciliator, the mediator has no authority over either party.

arbitration   Arbitration goes a step further than mediation. In **arbitration** the arbitrator is a neutral third party whose task is to develop a solution to a problem that has labor-management negotiations bogged down. The arbitrator's decision may be legally binding on both parties and enforceable if the parties previously agreed to such binding arbitration. In certain unusual circumstances, binding arbitration can be imposed by the courts.

Some states have conciliation and mediation services. However most conciliators and mediators are provided by the Federal Mediation and Conciliation Service. This agency was set up by the Taft-Hartley Act. When arbitration is involved, the parties can ask the American Arbitration Association to supply them with one or more arbitrators. These arbitrators must be mutually acceptable to labor and management.

SIGNING A CONTRACT

The goal of the bargaining phase is a tentative agreement. The union negotiators can then recommend the tentative agreement to the union membership, but rank-and-file union members must vote on it. If the membership ratifies (accepts) the agreement, a formal, binding contract is prepared and signed by both labor and management. However, if the rank-and-file membership rejects the tentative agreement, the negotiators return to the bargaining table. They continue to bargain until a tentative agreement is ratified and becomes the labor contract.

A national contract covers major issues like wage rates and fringe benefits. Local unions and plant managements work out local provisions on rest periods, sanitary facilities, wash-up periods, and so on. These can vary from plant to plant. However, local negotiations are, in general, consistent with the national contract. If an agreement cannot be worked out on an issue at the local level, the plant might be struck by the local union.

GRIEVANCE PROCEDURES

grievance procedures

Labor contracts usually include grievance procedures. **Grievance procedures** provide an orderly system whereby the employer and the union determine whether or not the labor contract has been violated.

grievance

A **grievance** is a complaint that is filed against a condition thought to be unjust or wrong. Of course, not all complaints are grievances. Only complaints that relate to alleged violations of the labor contract (or the law) are grievances. Handling these grievances is often called *administering the contract.*

In most cases the grievance procedure is a sequence of steps the employee should follow to correct the cause of the grievance. It also includes time limits for each step. It usually specifies rules like "all charges of contract violation must be reduced to writing."

Grievance procedures differ from firm to firm. Let us suppose that a supervisor tells an employee to do a task the worker does not think is part of his job. The worker decides to file a grievance. The first step might be for the grievant and shop steward (a union representative in the plant) to meet informally with the grievant's supervisor and try to find a solution. If one is not found, a written grievance is filed. A meeting is then scheduled among the employee, shop steward, and the supervisor's boss. If there is no agreement here, the grievance may be presented in writing to the union grievance committee and the plant manager. If the issue is still unresolved, it may be presented in writing to still higher union and company officials. Ultimately, the issue may be submitted to binding arbitration. All parties agree to abide by the decision of an impartial arbitrator.

HANDLING GRIEVANCES IN NONUNION COMPANIES

Employees of unionized firms are not the only ones who need grievance procedures; workers in nonunionized firms need them too. In nonunionized firms this usually means that grievants have a formal right to take their grievances to higher and higher levels in the company. For example, the Burger King capsule (on p. 274) describes the grievance procedure in a typical Burger King® restaurant.

APPLICATION: BURGER KING
Handling Grievances

Good labor relations at Burger King Corporation—or at any other well-run company—means a lot. Particularly in the fast-food industry, where turnover rates of 200 percent per year are not uncommon, employers must do all they can to keep their employees happy.

In fact, firms like Burger King and McDonald's are under particular pressure to attract and keep good employees. Finding, recruiting, and keeping good employees is a bigger problem today than it has ever been before. That is because there are fewer teenagers available and there are many more service firms recruiting them.

One way to handle this problem is to maintain the best possible labor relations so that problems do not come up that make workers want to leave. As a Burger King Corporation human resources executive put it, "The job really hinges on the local restaurant environment. Some people, in fact, will only work for Burger King, and will turn down more money at a competitor. Putting in a good, people-oriented manager and then making sure that employees have pride in their work and enjoy what they're doing is the best way to maintain good labor relations. You have to remember that for many of these employees, it's the first job that they'll have, and the way they're treated, and the self-esteem that they develop will flavor their attitudes toward work for years to come."

Because of such supportive attitudes, Burger King has taken pains to develop a grievance procedure that works well. Grievances that do arise may involve technical questions such as "Why were these taxes deducted from my paycheck?" Or they may involve disagreements over job assignments or vacation schedules.

At Burger King Corporation, grievances are handled through a "communications and problem solving procedure." The emphasis on communications and problem solving says much about the procedure's aims. It is supposed to keep the lines of communication open. Employees need to know that they will always have a chance to express their concerns and that someone will always listen. Employees also know that it is not likely that anyone in the store can treat them unfairly, since there is always that open avenue of appeal.

Burger King Corporation's grievance procedure, taught to crew members during their training, is a four-step process. Here is what it says:

1. Your restaurant manager is the first one you should talk with if you have a problem at work. Your manager cares about your problem, and you should feel free to bring any problem to him/her.

2. If your manager's solution of the problem does not satisfy you, state the reason why in writing, and submit it to your district manager.

3. If your district manager does not resolve your problem to your satisfaction, contact your area manager.

4. If the problem is not resolved by your area manager, the final step is to ask for a review of your problem by an unbiased review board chosen with guidance from your regional human-resource manager. The review board will review your appeal on an individual basis and respond promptly. The decision of the review board is final and binding.

Questions

1. Why are service workers less unionized than factory workers?

2. How does the grievance procedure in Burger King® restaurants help to maintain good labor relations?

3. Why are good labor relations so important to Burger King Corporation?

WEAPONS OF LABOR AND MANAGEMENT

Throughout contract negotiation and grievance-handling procedures, both labor and management use weapons to pressure each other. These weapons are used when the parties are unable to agree on a new contract. They are also used when employee discontent is widespread, or when there is a dispute over the interpretation of contract terms.

LABOR'S WEAPONS Labor's main weapons are

- The strike
- The picket
- The boycott
- The corporate campaign

strike

A strike is most often called when a contract has expired but a new one has not been ratified. A **strike** is a temporary withdrawal of all or some employees from the company's service. The presumption is that the employees will return when their demands are met or a compromise is worked out. The strike is the union's ultimate weapon. Ordinarily, it is not used unless the union has the financial resources (strike fund) to support the strikers and ride out the strike.

picketing

In **picketing,** employees (pickets) form a picket line and walk around a plant or office building carrying placards (signs) that inform other workers and the public that the employer is considered (by the union) to be unfair to labor. Strikes are usually accompanied by picketing. However, picketing may take place without a strike.

In general, picketing is protected under the right of free speech as long as it does not include any fraud, violence, or intimidation. An effective picket line might keep other employees who belong to different unions from entering a plant. Thus if a picket line around a plant is honored by truck drivers, the picketed firm might find itself without deliveries.

boycott

A **boycott** is a concentrated effort by which a union tries to get the public to refuse to deal with the boycotted firm. For example, when the

Prohibited from going out on strike in many areas, teachers may work to rule, performing only tasks specified in their contracts and working only the contracted number of hours.

farm workers' union went on strike, it tried to get consumers around the country to stop buying California fruits and vegetables.

The Taft-Hartley Act allows the NLRB to secure a federal injunction against unions that engage in illegal strike, picket, or boycott activities. (By the way, these three tools are also used by nonunionized employees and other social action groups to win their aims.)

corporate campaign

The corporate campaign is a newer approach to organizing those firms which strongly resist unionization. The **corporate campaign** involves picketing to inform the employer's customers and others that the firm is nonunionized, a boycott to induce the employer's workers and customers to stop buying the firm's products, and a broader strategy aimed at the outside directors on the target firm's board of directors. As you know from Chapter 3, outside board members are not officers of the corporation. However, they are often executives of other firms that buy from the target firm or executives of banks that lend money to it. The union's goal is to get the directors to pressure the target firm's management to stop interfering with the organizing effort. Otherwise, the outside directors' firms could also be targeted for picketing and/or boycotting. For example, directors of the union-resisting Stevens Textile Company, some of whom were bankers, were told by the union that funds might be withdrawn from their banks because of their support of Stevens's policies.

MANAGEMENT'S WEAPONS   Management's main weapons are

- The lockout
- The injunction
- Strikebreakers
- Contracting out work
- The employers' association

lockout

For many years, management used the lockout to counter labor's threat to strike or to organize. In a **lockout,** employees are denied access to the plant until they accept the employer's terms of employment. The employees are (sometimes literally) locked out and prohibited from doing their jobs.

Today, the lockout is mainly a defensive weapon. For example, if the firm's product is perishable, then a lockout might be legal to neutralize a union's picket line. If the pickets prevent delivery trucks from leaving the plant, the firm's products could be ruined. The firm might then resort to a lockout.

Lockouts are not used often, but they can be effective. In July 1987 the television directors' union threatened networks with a strike. The networks, working together, told the union that if a strike were called, all directors working for all networks would be locked out. Two days later the directors lifted their strike threat.

injunction

In some cases, firms obtain injunctions to halt strikes. An **injunction** is a court order that prohibits a specified activity. For example, a wildcat strike (while a contract is in effect) might be stopped with an injunction.

strikebreakers

Some firms turn to hiring strikebreakers, often as a last resort. **Strikebreakers** are nonunion employees hired to take the place of the striking employees. When TWA cabin attendants went on strike in

1986, scores of new attendants were hired to replace them. The strike was thus broken. However, the airline was later forced to hire back the striking attendants it had fired. The courts held that the strike was legal and that an employer cannot penalize employees for participating in a legal strike.

More and more firms are *contracting out work* as a way to blunt their unions' effects. Contracting out work is one of the issues that worries the United Auto Workers Union. Instead of doing all the assembly work they used to do themselves, many auto manufacturing firms are now contracting out work to nonunion contractors. This lessens the impact that the unions can have and results in fewer jobs—and thus fewer union workers.

Employers' associations are especially important in industries that have many small firms and one large union that represents all workers. Member firms sometimes contribute to a strike insurance fund. Such a fund could be used to help members whose workers have struck. They are similar in purpose to the strike funds built up by unions.

The television networks have an employers' association. It was by working through their association that networks threatened the lockouts that helped end the 1987 strike threat by the directors' union.

DECERTIFICATION

decertification

The same law that grants employees the right to unionize also allows decertification. **Decertification** is the process by which employees legally terminate their union's right to represent them.

Decertification campaigns do not differ much from certification campaigns (those leading up to the initial election).[6] For its part the union organizes membership meetings, house-to-house visits, and other tactics to win the election. For its part the employer uses meetings, letters, and improved working conditions in trying to obtain a decertification vote.

Employers are also increasingly using what unions refer to as "union-busting" consultants. On the whole, these consultants stress assisting management in improving their communications with the shop floor. They help management identify and eliminate the basic pressures that led to the prounion vote in the first place. Ideally, this is not a last-minute effort. Instead, a promanagement vote on either a certification or decertification election tends to be the result of long-term sensible actions on the part of management.

The Future of Unionism

Union membership has dropped from about 29 percent of the U.S. work force in 1975 to about 19 percent in 1988. Several things account for this decline. By the 1970s and 1980s, most of the new jobs being created in our economy were in the service sector (see Figure 9-5 on p. 278). Service workers have never been highly unionized. Many work part time, and the typical firm is small. This makes it harder and more costly for unions to organize them, since the union would have to deal with many more employers.[7]

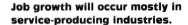

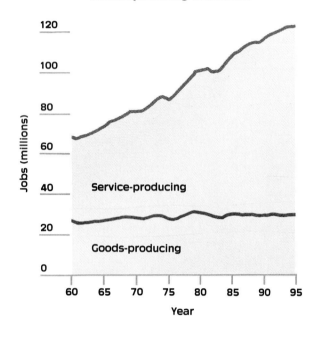

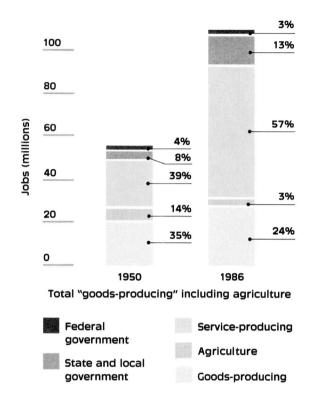

FIGURE 9-5 / Job growth in the service sector. (*Source:* Reprinted by permission from *Bulletin to Management,* vol. 38, no. 30, p. 236 (7/23/87). Copyright 1987 by The Bureau of National Affairs, Inc., Washington, D.C.)

While service sector jobs are gradually taking over former factory strongholds like Pittsburgh, factory jobs are leaving for the Sunbelt and overseas. Sunbelt states in the South and Southwest are likely to have right-to-work laws and to lack a strong tradition of unionism.

The last ten years have also been an era of restructuring for U.S. industry. Faced with intense international competition, deregulation, outdated equipment, and corporate raiders, hundreds of thousands of union members have been laid off.

Today, however, unions are acting to reassert their dominance as employee representatives. For example, the AFL-CIO has embarked on new activities. One is a program to train 1,000 union activists in the fundamentals of how to react to the television camera. They want to better explain themselves and the union movement to the general public.[8] During the last ten years or so, unions have also made a major effort to organize white-collar workers. More than 10 percent of white-collar workers have already been unionized.

BUSINESS IN THE NEWS
Unions Push for New Laws

Ideas that are proposed and pushed by organized labor have a way of becoming the law of the land. That was true with the minimum wage law many years ago, for instance, and it is still true today. For example, a 1988 federal law that makes most uses of the polygraph, or "lie detector," illegal for employment purposes was passed at the instigation of the AFL-CIO. Also in 1988, a law requiring advance notice to employees of contemplated plant closings and mass layoffs was made part of the trade bill.

These days, other laws are being promoted by organized labor. For example, perhaps the most important new law could be one that both ends the historic at-will relationship and takes regulation of that area away from the fifty states. The law that the AFL-CIO has in mind would replace the at-will rule with a federal ban on terminating any employee against his or her will unless the termination is "for cause."

A second law would require health-care benefits for virtually all employees. For example, in its 1987 executive council statements, the AFL-CIO "call upon Congress to require employers, as a condition of doing business, to assure a minimum package of specified health care benefits to all workers and their dependents, including part-time and laid-off workers."

Sources: Statements adopted by the AFL-CIO Executive Council, Bal Harbour, Florida, Feb. 16–20, 1987; AFL-CIO, 815 Sixteenth Street, N.W., Washington, D.C. 20006; Commerce Clearing House, *Human Resources Management: Ideas and Trends*, May 1, 1987, pp. 65–69.

WORKER OWNERSHIP AND CONTROL

Furthermore, unions are increasingly going after ownership and control. As Lynn R. Williams, president of the United Steelworkers Union, puts it, "We're not going to sit around and allow management to louse things up like they did in the past."[9] Today, for instance, some 8 million workers belong to employee stock ownership plans. These "ESOP's" are basically pension plans through which a company's employees accumulate shares of the company's stock. Nonmanagement employees now sit on boards of directors at more than 300 firms in their role as representatives of the firms' employee stock ownership plans. As another example, in 1987, United Airline's pilots union came close to raising the money it needed to buy the firm and install its choice as president of the company.

UNION-MANAGEMENT COOPERATION

There is also a trend toward closer union-management cooperation. When GM decided to build its all-new Saturn car, its planning included the United Auto Workers Union. To reach a consensus between management and labor, "agreement teams" were formed. Six people—three union members and three from management—along with an advisor met to rough out an outline for a bargaining contract. Each team listed about sixteen items that were necessary for an agreement, and the teams then broke up to hammer out more detailed agreements.

Many union leaders remain skeptical of the new cooperation. Many feel that it smacks of collaboration with an enemy. Other union officials fear that the new harmony could undermine the union's attraction for its members. It would do this by making management seem less of an adversary. But on the whole, labor-management cooperation seems to be off to a good start.

Summary

Milestones in the history of labor in the United States include the formation of the American Federation of Labor in 1886, and the passage, starting in the early 1930s, of major labor laws that made it easier for unions to organize and demand collective bargaining with employers.

The major federal laws regarding unions are the Norris-LaGuardia Act (which guaranteed the right to collective bargaining); the Wagner Act (which barred unfair labor practices on the part of employers; the Taft-Hartley act (which prohibited union unfair labor practices); and the Landrum-Griffin Act of 1959 (which protected union members from illegal acts on the part of union leaders).

Workers join unions for many reasons: to protect themselves from arbitrary actions by managers; for better pay; and for better working conditions, for instance. Many unions consist of a hierarchy that includes a local union, which belongs to a national union, which in turn might belong to an international federation like the AFL-CIO.

Generally speaking, unions have two aims: to improve the wages, security, and standards of living of their members and to strengthen union security.

The process of recruiting new members involves five basic steps: establishing initial contact, obtaining authorization cards, holding a hearing, having a campaign, and holding the election.

The steps in collective bargaining are preparing to bargain, bargaining, dealing with disputes, and signing a contract. Preparing to bargain involves setting up a negotiating team and developing a list of demands. Bargaining in good faith means that proposals are matched with counterproposals and that both parties make every reasonable effort to arrive at agreement. Disputes can be settled through conciliation, mediation, or arbitration. Signing the contract involves first arriving at a tentative agreement. Then the union negotiators must obtain the approval of the union membership for the agreement.

No contract could cover every situation in which problems might arise. Grievances may therefore be filed. A grievance is a complaint that is filed against a condition thought to be unjust or wrong. Most grievance procedures consist of a hierarchy of steps. The grievance might first be discussed between the grievant, the shop steward, and the grievant's supervisor. The next step might be to the supervisor's boss and finally to the area manager.

Labor's main weapons are the strike, picket, boycott, and corporate campaign. Management's main weapons are the lockout, the injunction, strikebreakers, contracting out work, and the employer's association.

Union membership declined steeply in the early 1980s. Several factors contributed to this, including more service jobs and fewer smokestack jobs. Unions are fighting back, though. They are instituting new public relations programs and fighting for ownership control of more and more firms.

Review Questions

1. List the major federal labor laws and explain their main provisions.

2. Distinguish between a craft union and an industrial union.

3. Compare the closed shop, the union shop, the open shop, and the agency shop.

4. Why would a local union negotiate concessions to a national contract?

5. How does arbitration differ from conciliation?

6. How are employee grievances handled in a unionized plant?

7. Identify and explain the weapons of labor and management.

8. What is a corporate campaign?

9. Why do some employers want "givebacks" from unions?

Discussion Questions

1. How is the decline of smokestack industries related to the future of unionism in the United States?

2. What do you think the fight between Eastern Airlines and its unions says about the prospects for labor-management cooperation?

3. The "corporate campaign" can seriously undermine a firm's performance. Is that a good reason to ban such campaigns?

4. Do you think it is fair for employers to expect "givebacks" from their employees? Why or why not?

5. Discuss why you would or would not join a union.

Key Terms

blacklists
yellow-dog contract
unfair lists

labor union
collective bargaining
collective bargaining agreement

featherbedding
craft unions
industrial unions

local union	right-to-work laws	grievance
national union	doublebreasted firm	strike
union federation	National Labor Relations Board (NLRB)	picketing
union security		boycott
closed shop	bargainable issues	corporate campaign
union shop	bargaining in good faith	lockout
agency shop	conciliation	injunction
open shop	mediation	strikebreakers
maintenance of membership arrangement	arbitration	decertification
	grievance procedures	

Cases

BRYAN GOES AFTER EASTERN— AGAIN

By the end of 1987, if Charles Bryan, the head of Eastern Airlines' mechanics union, was worried about dealing with Frank Lorenzo, the new head of Eastern, you would never know it. Mr. Bryan had just slammed down a demand for a 20 percent pay increase for his people. Instead of backing down, he appeared to be charging straight ahead. The question was whether he was being realistic or whether it was just a grandstand play for the sake of his union members.

In fact, things had not turned out as badly for Eastern's unions as many people expected when Frank Borman left the airline and Mr. Lorenzo took over. Eastern Airlines began by insisting upon 40 percent salary cutbacks and hinted several times that it would simply transfer Eastern planes to Continental Airlines if the airline didn't get what it wanted from its union members. By mid-1988, though, Eastern had not made any drastic moves, for several reasons. First, Eastern was doing well and turned a substantial profit in 1987 (com-

pared to a substantial series of losses in the preceding years). At the same time, Continental Airlines was not doing well and really could not absorb many of Eastern's planes.

Yet the tension at Eastern between the airline and its unions remained explosive. The mechanics and pilots unions were in newspapers and on the air almost every day in late 1987 with claims of how Eastern management was forcing unsafe planes to fly. The airline's management insisted that its planes were safe. The airline threatened to have more of the maintenance carried out by separate nonunion subsidiaries. Increasing numbers of pilots were leaving Eastern for greener pastures at other airlines.[10]

Questions

1. If it was up to you, what would you do to help alleviate the explosive management-labor situation at Eastern Airlines?
2. Do you think it is possible that Eastern's workers would actually be better off without a union? Why or why not?

3. Do you think management and labor would agree to a binding arbitration to settle their contractual differences? Why or why not?

THE NFL STRIKE

When the football players began their 1987 strike, their hopes were high, and they marched out to the picket lines with confidence. Under the guidance of their union head, Gene Upshaw, the National Football League Players Association hoped to win a series of important concessions from the NFL owners. Besides pay raises and better benefits, the players said that by far the most important issue was the right to free agency. In other words, the players wanted the right, after their contracts were up, to negotiate with any team they chose to try to get themselves better deals. As the rules stood, a player had no real choice but to sign a new contract with his current team or not play at all. (The brief life of the USFL briefly provided NFL players with an alternative that in fact raised many of their salaries.) The players felt that only through competition between owners for their services would they be able to obtain the rapid pay increases that they thought they deserved.

They therefore went out on strike and immediately tried to solidify their position. Other unions agreed to join them on the picket lines, and the players worked hard to convince the public that their cause was a just one.

What they apparently had not figured on, however, was the power and cunning of the NFL owners. These owners are among the richest people in the country, with several billionaires among them. Their money gave them staying power that far exceeded that of the players. The players also had not foreseen that the owners would put together replacement teams of nonunion players. These teams played the already scheduled games. While the games were not heavily attended in the stadiums, the television networks still showed the games (and paid the owners). It turned out that the owners actually made a substantial profit on these games, since the revenues kept coming in while their labor bills were drastically reduced (since they did not have to pay their regular football players). The public also did not cooperate with the players. It is likely that most people could not identify with the financial problems of men who were averaging over $200,000 a year in income. To make matters worse, more and more union players began crossing the picket lines and returning to work. Finally, on October 15, 1987, the Players Association threw in the towel and came back to work without an agreement.[11]

Questions

1. What weapons did the Player's Association use in this case? Which did the owners use?
2. Do you think the union was smart to go out on strike? Why or why not?
3. What do you think of the way the owners handled the strike? Do you see any problems it could cause for them down the road?

After reading this chapter, you will be able to:

- Give examples of the inputs, processes, and outputs of production.

- Explain the differences between intermittent and continuous production processes and the basic nature of mass production.

- List the six basic steps in a typical production planning and control system.

- Explain what is meant by the "factory of the future."

- Distinguish between quality control and inventory control.

- Explain why the purchasing task is important.

Production and Operations Management

WHAT'S AHEAD

Every firm—be it a bank, a fast food restaurant, or the Ford Motor Company—must have a production system. In this chapter we begin by defining what a production system is and then discussing the three main components of production systems, inputs, production processes, and outputs.

We will see that one of the first steps in production management involves designing the production system itself. We therefore discuss important matters such as where to locate the plant, what type of production process to use, and how to lay out the physical facilities. We also discuss the nature of mass production and explain the importance of assembly lines.

Whether it is producing cars or a new city hall, a firm must have some system for planning and controlling production. In this chapter we therefore explain the basic elements of production planning and control including matters like production schedules and expediting.

We next describe the "factory of the future," perhaps the most exciting concept in manufacturing today. With its computer-directed automated production systems, robotics, "just-in-time production," and computer-aided design, this new approach to manufacturing represents a virtual revolution in production planning and design.

Controlling the quality and controlling the inventory levels of the company's inputs and outputs are the next important production management tasks that we discuss. Finally, we explain materials management—in particular, important production matters such as purchasing and warehousing.

It is so eerie that it seems like science fiction. As the car body moves down the assembly line, a robot arm reaches in through the front door window and welds a part on the car's dashboard.

Automated spray machines cover car after car with precisely the right amount of paint.

Hundreds of computers are linked in a network so that computer-controlled production machines can be monitored continuously. Parts arrive at the work stations just in time, ready to be attached before the car body moves along. The car itself was designed on a computer. Information on each part's correct dimensions is contained in the plant's computer systems. Computer commands for machining are produced and electronically sent to automated milling machines, which automatically machine the parts to the right size. They then check the parts against the data on the original design. Only uniform parts are sent on to the final assembly.

But it is not science fiction. Ford Motor Company's new Aerostar plant is actually set up this way.

Ford's assembly plant in St. Louis was enlarged and completely re-equipped with new facilities and tooling to accommodate the Aerostar. Typical of this new technology are more than 550 computers linked in a network so that computer-controlled machinery can be monitored continuously. These computers, plus accurate robot welders and manufacturing innovations such as the use of one-piece body-side panels, make it possible to build vehicles of very consistent quality.

Aerostar's underbody assembly line uses forty welding robots, including twenty-four gantry models—Ford's first overhead-mounted robots in the United States. Gantry robots can carry up to 200 pounds of tooling and require less floor space than side-mounted models. Robots also are key elements in Aerostar's welding and painting processes. Ninety-seven percent of Aerostar's 4000 spot welds are done by robots or other automated equipment. Robots apply enamel to Aerostar's interior surfaces. The robots and automatic spray machines that apply paint to the exterior not only eliminate operations that are tedious and unpleasant for workers, but also produce a consistent finish that is virtually defect free.

A key element in the successful integration of these new manufacturing techniques was the involvement of plant employees in the design of the new systems. Early in the development phase, proposed methods were reviewed with the people who would be directly responsible for certain operations. Employees made 434 suggestions, about 60 percent of which were adopted.

Increasingly, other such factories are being designed and built. They are the vanguard of the "factory of the future," a factory that is characterized by automation, robotics, and computer-aided design and manufacturing.[1]

Plants like Ford's Aerostar plant in St. Louis are based on state-of-the-art technology. Such plants are helping U.S. firms to become more productive and more competitive in the global marketplace.

The Inputs to Production

All companies must produce a good or a service (or both) to stay in business. As we saw in Chapter 1, goods are tangible items like cars and steel. Services are intangible items like dry-cleaning and medical checkups. In this book we often use the term *product* to refer to both goods and services. Efficient management of the production of products is crucial to the success of any firm.

In other words, every firm—no matter what its size or its product—must have a production system. A **production system** is one that converts inputs (such as raw materials, labor, or capital) into outputs (goods or services).[2] Any production system thus consists of three main parts: inputs, conversion processes, and outputs. A university contains a production system that consists of things like professors, classes, and students. The successful university converts entering freshmen (inputs) into educated graduates (outputs). A bank takes savings and converts them into investments and loans. A fast food restaurant takes inputs such as people, burger patties, and potatoes. It converts these to meals and services for satisfied customers. And, of course, an auto-manufacturing plant takes labor, steel, and glass and uses its machinery to produce cars for you and me. Table 10-1 (on p. 288) gives some more examples of inputs and outputs.

Production management is the set of activities aimed at planning, designing, staffing, and controlling a firm's production system. Actually, to be perfectly accurate, we will talk in terms of production *and operations* management. The reason is that managing production is no longer just a task for companies with production plants. Of course, manufacturing—producing tangible goods that we can see and feel—is still an important sector of our economy. But the service industries are becoming just as important, if not more so. And to stay competitive, it is as important for service firms to manage their operations efficiently as it is for the Ford Motor Company.

Before proceeding, let's take a brief look at the inputs, processes, and outputs of a production system.

As Figure 10-1 (on p. 289) shows, to produce something, the following resources are usually needed as inputs:

- Capital
- Material
- Human
- Financial
- Information

Capital resources include the plant investment (which can range from a huge refinery to a barber shop) and equipment such as lathes or typewriters.

production system

production management

TABLE 10-1 / Examples of inputs and outputs

Organization	Input	Output
Jewelry store	Merchandise Store building Sales clerks Registers Jeweler Customer	Customer sales
Post office	Sorting machines Trucks Postal clerks and carriers Postmaster Mail	Delivered mail
Hospital	Doctors and nurses Staff Buildings Beds and equipment Power Supplies Patients	Recovered patient
Manufacturing plant	Machines Plant Raw materials Workers Managers	Consumer goods Materials for purchase by other firms
University	Faculty and staff Classrooms Library Supplies Students	Graduates Research Public service

Source: Lee Krajewski and Larry P. Ritzman, *Operations Management: Strategy and Analysis,* © 1987 Addison-Wesley, Publishing Co., Inc., Reading, Massachusetts. Table 1.1 on page 4. Reprinted with permission.

Material resources include raw materials (such as raw cotton), semimanufactured products (such as sheet steel), and manufactured parts (such as spark plugs).

Human resources include skilled labor, unskilled labor, and managers. Skilled labor differs from unskilled labor in that skilled workers can perform special tasks that cannot be performed by all employees. Examples include carpenters, pipefitters, and dental technicians. Managers, of course, are responsible for directing the activities of others.

Financial resources include money that comes from the owners' own funds or from borrowing. Corporations often sell shares of stock to obtain additional financial resources. The various sources of financing are discussed in the chapters on finance.

"Knowledge is power," a philosopher once said, and that is certainly true today. Companies are making increasing use of information resources. Many service firms, including law firms, accounting firms,

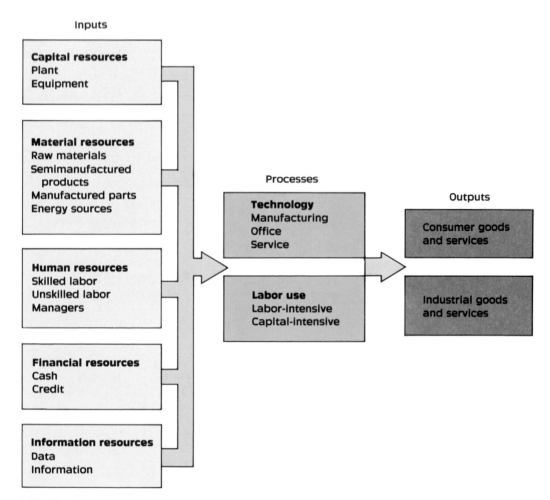

Inputs

Capital resources
Plant
Equipment

Material resources
Raw materials
Semimanufactured
 products
Manufactured parts
Energy sources

Human resources
Skilled labor
Unskilled labor
Managers

Financial resources
Cash
Credit

Information resources
Data
Information

Processes

Technology
Manufacturing
Office
Service

Labor use
Labor-intensive
Capital-intensive

Outputs

Consumer goods
and services

Industrial goods
and services

FIGURE 10-1 / The production system.

and market research firms, are basically in the business of absorbing, processing, and producing information. In the vignette we saw that even manufacturing firms like Ford recognize how important information is today for running their firms. For example, several years ago, General Motors bought Electronic Data Systems (EDS) for several billion dollars. It did this in part because EDS is an expert in designing computer systems that enable GM managers to produce their cars much more efficiently. We will discuss these types of innovations further when we discuss the "factory of the future."

Production Processes

TECHNOLOGY

All production and operations systems use a production process or technology to convert inputs into outputs. Technology is the method a

Computer technology is important for service firms like Federal Express, whose on-line tracking system has helped it to become the leader in the overnight package delivery business.

company uses to transform inputs into outputs like goods and services. *Manufacturing technology* includes things like the arrangement of the machinery in a factory as well as the machinery itself.

Factories are not the only places where we find technology. Today, new *office technologies* are reshaping offices.[3] For example, word processors help to create, store, retrieve, and print documents electronically. Telecommuting lets employees do their work even while thousands of miles away from their offices.

Service firms also use technology. For example, Mrs. Fields Cookies stores use a computer system that helps managers to run their stores more efficiently. Each morning when they open the store, the system tells them how many of which cookies they sold on that day last year. That helps them know how much of each type of cookie to bake and how many cookies they should sell that day. At Burger King, operations management experts have redesigned facilities and systems to make serving their meals more efficient. In many stores, for instance, customers now serve drinks to themselves, and new double-window drive-throughs reduce waiting time for customers.

LABOR-INTENSIVE VERSUS CAPITAL-INTENSIVE PROCESSES

labor-intensive processes

All production processes differ in the amount of human input they need. **Labor-intensive processes** are production processes that depend more on people than on machines. Labor-intensive processes are most likely to be used when labor is cheap or when there is an artistic element in the work. There are also some kinds of jobs in which it is hard to use machines because the process varies a lot. For example, you probably would not want to have your hair cut by a robot, would you? Many kinds of farming are still highly labor-intensive. Producing oranges, lettuce, and numerous other crops is much more labor-intensive than producing cotton and wheat.

capital-intensive processes

The opposite situation exists when machines can do the job better than people. **Capital-intensive processes** are production processes that depend more on machines than on people. The huge petroleum refinery is a classic example of a capital-intensive process. A refinery that might cost hundreds of millions of dollars to build might operate with fewer than 100 employees. Service providers are also becoming more capital-intensive. Many banks have installed automated teller machines, and car rental firms such as Hertz have introduced automatic car return systems.

The Outputs of Production

The outputs of production can be divided into two broad classes. *Consumer products* are goods and services that individuals and households buy. *Industrial products* are purchased by businesses and institutions. Consumer goods include all those tangible things like cornflakes, cars, clothes, and Coke that people buy for their own consumption. Consumer services include personal services like haircuts, drycleaning, and bowling as well as services like legal work and tax preparation.

Industrial products are bought mostly by businesses or by institutions like the federal government or the United Way. They include tangible goods like steel for cars, bricks for building, and wood for pencils. (Notice that one firm's outputs are often another firm's inputs.) Industrial services include things like market research reports, legal advice, and security systems.

The output—the good or service—has to be designed carefully. Of course, it must meet the customers' needs. But the firm must also be able to produce it in such a way that it is profitable and does not detract from the firm's other products. Product planning really involves both production and marketing and is discussed more fully in our chapters on marketing. At this point we will describe just a few features of the product-planning process.

Product (or service) planning amounts to answering the following questions:

- What kind of product can be sold at a profit?
- How much can be sold?
- What styles and sizes should be produced?
- What special features should the product have?

The answers to these questions require study, often in the laboratory, to determine the best inputs of raw materials and component parts. In many firms, this kind of thinking is done on a continuous basis by a product development department. The basic questions are always "will it sell?" and "can it be produced at a satisfactory profit?"

The product development department's research could lead to new products. It could also lead to improvements in existing products that would enable the firm to remain competitive in the market. Procter & Gamble, a leader in the personal and home-care products industry, invests millions of dollars in research and development each year to maintain that leadership.

Designing Conventional Production Systems

A first step in production management involves designing the production system itself. This means deciding three things: (1) where to locate the plant, (2) what type of production process to use, and (3) how to lay out the physical facilities.

PLANT LOCATION

Several important questions relate to planning the plant itself. These include deciding where to locate the plant and how to design the building.

Plant location decisions are important. They affect overall costs, employee morale, and many other elements of a firm's operation. The first question is "Where do we want to locate?" In a recent survey the three most important factors were:

1. Favorable labor climate,
2. Proximity to markets, and
3. Quality of life.[4]

A favorable labor climate is usually essential. Factors to consider here include availability of labor, low labor costs, and possible unionization.

Proximity to markets can be important too. For items that are relatively inexpensive to produce but heavy, bulky, or expensive to ship, the firm will try to place its plant as close to its customers as possible. Processed foods, cans, and paper products are examples.

Quality of life is usually rated much lower as a factor by executives, but it is important nevertheless. In some high-tech industries, available resources like theaters, universities, and libraries can be big factors in choosing a site, since such firms often use quality of life to attract their work force.

Other factors must be considered as well. For example, input transportation costs depend mainly on how far suppliers of raw materials and parts are from the plant site. They also depend on the kind and cost of transportation facilities that connect them. The What Do You Think? box explains another factor in site selection.

Governments often compete to attract new businesses. Some firms have relocated to Phoenix, Arizona, because it has no corporate franchise tax and low corporate income taxes.

Water and power supplies can also be crucial. Chemical plants that use a lot of water are concentrated along the Mississippi River. Energy-intensive firms are being attracted to the Albuquerque, New Mexico, area because it is rich in energy reserves.

Plant location decisions are becoming harder to make. Labor in and

WHAT DO YOU THINK?

Should There Be Japanese Factories in the United States?

It has been called the "rust belt" of the United States—and for good reason. Tens of thousands of jobs in states like Michigan, Illinois, Ohio, and Indiana were lost as manufacturers in the auto and steel industries closed down plants to boost their profit margins. As the great factories closed, towns went with them. The markets, restaurants, cleaners, and dozens of other businesses that were there to serve the factory workers closed down too. In the U.S. Congress, pressure increased to pass trade bills that would put quotas or tariffs on foreign-made goods such as cars and steel and thus help rejuvenate the rust belt states.

The problem is that tariffs and quotas might not be good for the country as a whole. In the short run they do save jobs. But the millions of consumers who buy cars and other items have to pay higher prices for domestic goods. They partially foot the bill for the jobs that are saved.

But as the pressures mounted in Congress, an extraordinary thing began to occur. One after another the great auto builders of Japan—Nissan,

Honda, Mazda, and Toyota—began pumping billions of dollars into building new plants in the rust belt states. Today, Hondas are produced in Ohio, Nissans in Tennessee, Toyotas in Kentucky, and Mazdas in Michigan, for instance. And each of these plants has succeeded, not because of state-of-the-art technology but to a large extent because of what has become known as Japanese management methods.

There is, for example, a pervasive cooperativeness between management and workers in these plants. Workers often start the day with calisthenics, and small problem-solving groups meet periodically to analyze problems and find solutions. Just-in-time supply systems are used in which parts for a day's production appear literally just in time, thus cutting down on inventory costs. And throughout the plants there is a culture or set of shared values that stresses quality production.

Japanese executives who are often in charge of these plants try hard to ensure that the transition from Japan to the small rust belt towns has been a smooth one. They encourage

and attend company picnics, join local Chambers of Commerce, and do their part to become good citizens of their communities (while of course remaining Japanese).

Yet some people in the United States have mixed feelings about these Japanese plants. They are grateful for the jobs and the economic base that these jobs provide. But at the same time they might not like the idea of having to work for foreigners in their own hometowns. Some people just feel uneasy about selling bits of America to foreigners. Others resent seeing profits flow overseas. Are Japanese factories in the United States a good thing or not? What do you think?

Sources: William Holstein, "Japan Is Winning Friends in the Rust Belt," *Business Week*, Oct. 19, 1987, p. 54; Carey English, "How Japanese Work Out As Bosses in U.S.," *U.S. News & World Report*, May 8, 1985, p. 75; Joel Dreyfus and Dylan O'Reilly, "Japan's Uneasy U.S. Managers," *Fortune*, Apr. 25, 1986.

near major population centers is becoming more scarce. Traffic congestion, crime, pollution control requirements, and plant obsolescence are forcing many plants to leave urban centers. These moves often involve heavy losses from moving or abandoning heavy equipment.

In deciding between two possible locations a firm might estimate the profitability of each. To do so, it would take into account the expected effects of each location on sales and costs.

Once a general area has been selected, the next thing to do is to choose a specific site. The firm surveys available parcels of land. These must be suitable in terms of size, zoning restrictions, drainage, and access to transportation. If several sites are satisfactory, the decision might depend on cost. Or a firm might find a suitable existing plant for sale or lease, which could mean an earlier date for plant opening. For example, Bridgestone Tire Company of Japan started making tires in the United States after it bought a steel radial truck tire plant in Tennessee from Firestone.

TYPES OF PRODUCTION PROCESSES

intermittent production

There are two main types of production processes: intermittent and continuous production. An **intermittent production** process starts and stops and starts again, maybe several times per hour. Production might be triggered only when stocks fall below a critical level. It might also be used to build up stocks when machines and workers would otherwise be idle.

unit production

There are three types of intermittent production systems: unit, batch, and mass production. A **unit production** system (sometimes called "job shop" or "jobbing") basically produces small quantities of product, often one at a time. Ships, aircraft, and homes are usually built this way. Craftsmen such as fine cabinetmakers, tailors, and piano makers usually work this way. They produce their items one at a time.

batch production

Batch production involves producing products in small batches—say, two or three at a time or twenty gallons at a time. For example, a restaurant might produce twenty pounds of mashed potatoes for Friday evening. A specialty ice cream maker might produce forty gallons of "chocolate rocky road" to sell on Saturday night. Similarly, homebuilders often build several very similar homes at once, and a machine shop might produce ten special radio parts for a customer's order.

mass production

Mass production is another intermittent production process. **Mass production** involves producing a large number of standardized items (like cars, ready-to-wear pants, toys, or hamburgers), in a standardized manner. Mass production is an intermittent production process, since it does shut down periodically. However, a Ford plant might be kept running for days producing large numbers of Broncos, for example.

The mass production process rests on four "legs": standardization, mechanization, specialization, and the assembly line. For a product to be mass produced efficiently it must be more or less *standardized*. In other words, it must conform to standard specifications and consist of components that are interchangeable. For example, the Ford Taurus is standardized. All Tauruses look more or less the same. Parts (like doors) from one will fit just as well into any other. Mass production also depends on *mechanization*, a heavy reliance on machines for producing the work. In general, the machines that do each job (and the people that run them) are *specialized*. They are set up to do one specific job (such as inserting a right front headlight) over and over and over again.

Mass production usually depends on an assembly line. An **assembly line** consists of a fixed sequence of specialized machines and work stations for producing a product. The product to be produced (such as a car) moves from station to station getting doors, fenders, and headlights put on. As you can see in the Burger King capsule, hamburgers at Burger King are made this way too. The raw burger patties start at point A and move to broiling, wrapping, and storing.

assembly line

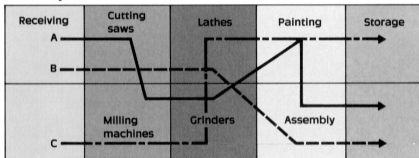

Process layout

FIGURE 10-2 / Process, product, and fixed layouts. (*Source*: Reprinted by permission from Kae H. Chung, *Management*, Allyn and Bacon, Boston, 1987, p. 508.)

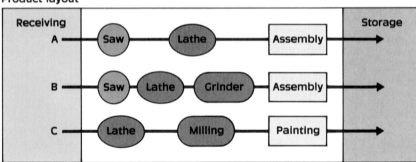

Product layout

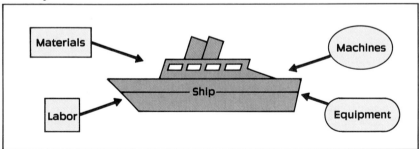

Fixed layout

continuous production

A **continuous production** process is a production process that operates more or less continuously. A Coca-Cola bottling plant repeats the same process countless thousands of times without pause. The demand for Coke products is large and easy to predict. The process, as in the case of most continuous processes, is highly automated. This means that little human supervision is needed because computers and machines can deal with nearly everything that could happen to interrupt operation.

Most continuous production processes produce products for stock. This means that output is kept in inventory in anticipation of demand. Firms would lose money doing this if they did not have good reason to expect a fairly steady demand.

Philip Morris and Exxon use a continuous production process. They can usually predict the demand for their product (cigarettes, oil) and produce it in the amount needed for the expected demand. Their operations go on around the clock.

PLANT LAYOUT

The third main aspect of production system design is how to lay out the facility. There are three main choices: process, product, and fixed layouts. Figure 10-2 (on p. 295) shows an example of each type of layout.

process layout

Process layout is a type of plant arrangement in which the machinery, materials, and labor are laid out on the basis of the functions they perform. For example, in a small machine shop (see Figure 10-2), item A might go from receiving to cutting, to milling, to lathing, to painting, to storage. Each process (such as milling) stays where it is on the shop floor. Item A is carried from process to process. Different products may follow different routes. For instance, product B goes straight from receiving to lathes. It bypasses the cutting and milling machines.

product layout

Product layout is a type of plant arrangement in which the machines, material, and labor needed to produce one particular product are laid out in an established sequence. This is common in automobile plants. Each station is designed to do its specialized job in helping to build that particular product.

fixed layout

Fixed layout is a type of plant layout in which the product stays in one place and the machinery, materials, and labor are brought to that one location. That is the way large ships are built, for instance. The ship stays in a drydock. The necessary labor, material, and machines are brought to it.

Finally, a *mixed layout* combines process, product, and/or fixed layouts. That is the case with the Burger King® restaurant shown in Figure 10-3, for instance. The kitchen is set up on a process basis, with freezers, grills, and food arranged into separate functions or "departments." But the salad bar is set up on a product basis; the salad is made one step at a time as you move along the line. Similarly, the burgers themselves, once they hit the broiler, are produced in a product-type assembly line.

Suppose Burger King added regular restaurant service so that customers would be served by waiters. What type of layout would that require?

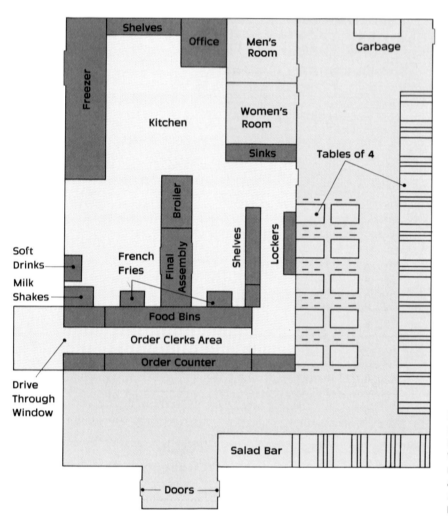

FIGURE 10-3 / Layout of a Burger King restaurant. (*Source:* Larry D. Alexander and Thomas W. Ripp, "Burger King," reproduced in Samuel Certo and J. Paul Peter, *Strategic Management,* Random House, New York, 1988, p. 843.)

Production Planning and Control

Production planning is aimed at determining what products to produce and where, when, and how to produce them. Production control is aimed at ensuring that production plans or schedules are being met. All firms—whether General Motors, McDonald's, or Allstate Insurance—need a system for production planning and control.

The most common type of production planning and control is called order control. It is used when custom products or small lots of products are to be made, and it helps to illustrate the basic production planning and control process. It involves six steps:

1. Receive the orders from customers.
2. Develop a list of required materials.
3. Develop a route sheet.
4. Develop production schedules.

APPLICATION: BURGER KING
This Restaurant Is a Factory

It might not look like a production facility, but that is exactly what it is. As you can see from the typical floor plan in Figure 10-3, the typical Burger King® restaurant is set up much like a production facility, with separate production stations for activities like flame broiling, sandwich preparation, french fry manufacturing, and shelf and office space. If you watched what went on in the back of a Burger King® restaurant, you would know how important production management can be in this industry.

As a crowd of hungry lunch hour customers line up at the counter, the pace begins to pick up for the production team at the restaurant. One crew member is stationed at the broiler and is already transferring burger patties from the freezer to a revolving broiler rack. This machine automatically grabs the patties at the crew member's end and automatically carries them under and through the broiler in about 35 seconds at a heating temperature of 800° Fahrenheit.

As the patties are run through the broiler, another crew member down by final assembly places burger buns on a revolving warming rack. He or she then assembles the burgers with the buns and places the two in a steamer. In this steamer/holding tray the "burger board" crew members find what they need to fill their orders (which are punched on a computer screen above where they are working).

By this time things are very busy, and both the manager and assistant manager are pitching in wherever they can. They might help out one crew member who is falling behind on the french fries and help to pack the burgers back at final assembly. Suddenly, the manager yells out "Level 5," and everyone starts to work at double time. In many restaurants like these, everyone's speed is determined by the level that the manager or assistant manager thinks is warranted by the number of customers waiting at the counter. At Level 2 the kitchen crew can slow down, and only two Whopper® sandwiches are required to be in the holding chute, as well as one item of each of the other burgers. At Level 5, things are very busy. At Level 6, employees know that the restaurant is filled to capacity.

Things are kept efficient at the drive-through window too. Did you know that when a car approaches the drive-through board to order a meal, a "transaction timer" at the drive-through window is set off? The timer stops when the car pulls away, but it starts ringing loud and long after 40 seconds. The idea is to make sure that no car has to wait more than 40 seconds once it reaches the board.

There are lots of other things Burger King Corporation does to make its restaurants more efficient. Computerized french fry machines sound a warning when the fries are done. Computer terminals with television displays are linked to the cash registers and placed in the kitchen. This lets the cooks see immediately the incoming orders on a screen rather than relying on verbal orders that are sometimes misunderstood. Soft drink dispensers fill up cups to the right amount with just one push of a button. And top management continually encourages individual franchisees and restaurant managers to make productivity suggestions (for which they may receive cash rewards).

Questions
1. Is the Burger King production process labor-intensive or capital-intensive? Is it intermittent or continuous? Explain.

2. Standardization, mechanization, specialization, and the assembly line are the four "legs" of the mass production process. Explain their applicability to the production process at Burger King® restaurants.

3. Explain the importance of quality control to Burger King Corporation.

5. Dispatch notices to operators to begin work.

6. Follow up/expedite to see that the schedule is being met.

STEP 1: RECEIVE ORDERS

The process begins with the receipt of the customer's order. The sales order contains information such as product and model to be produced, requested delivery date, and required quantities. When products are manufactured for stock or inventory rather than immediate sale, an order form is issued by the person in charge of maintaining inventories.

STEP 2: DEVELOP THE BILL OF MATERIALS

Next the company compiles a list of the raw materials and parts required to fill the order. Many companies maintain forms that list the materials needed to make a product. The list is called a *bill of materials* list. Without such a list it might be necessary to have a specialist analyze the customer's order and develop a list of required inputs. Figure 10-4 shows a bill of materials for a school desk.

This step usually culminates in a job cost sheet listing the materials, labor, and overhead costs involved in filling the order. Among other things this can be used for estimating how profitable (or unprofitable) it will be for the company to fill this particular order.

STEP 3: DEVELOP THE ROUTE SHEET

Routing determines the sequence of operations to be performed and the path (or route) to be taken by the order. The route sheet lists the types of machines required to get each part of the job done and the time required for each step in the operations.

Part Identification	Description	Units of Raw Material Required
frame	premium steel rods 1 inch in diameter	10
seat	commercial grade vinyl 20" x 15"	1
backrest	commercial grade vinyl 8" x 12"	1
bolts/ screws	standard	1 package (1 dozen each)

FIGURE 10-4 / A bill of materials for a school desk.

STEP 4: DEVELOP THE PRODUCTION PLAN OR SCHEDULE

The production schedule is often presented on a chart that shows in detail what manufacturing operations are to be carried out and when. A PERT chart, such as that in Figure 10-5, is often used for scheduling products. (PERT stands for Program Evaluation Review Technique.) A PERT chart (or PERT network) shows all activities that must be completed, each in its proper sequence.

The two major components of a PERT network are events and activities. Events are depicted by circles and represent specific accomplishments, such as "foundation laid." Activities are represented by arrows. They are the time-consuming aspects of the project (such as "lay foundation"). By carefully studying the PERT chart the scheduler can determine the critical path. This is the sequence of events that, in total, requires the most time to complete.

Many versions of PERT have been developed since PERT was first introduced by the U.S. Navy. The critical path method (CPM) is similar to PERT. However, CPM includes cost estimates for each activity, while PERT usually does not.

STEP 5: DISPATCHING

Dispatching means issuing the orders for performing the work. These orders are usually contained on written forms. These are often called shop orders, job tickets, or manufacturing orders. They specify the

FIGURE 10-5 / A PERT chart for building a stadium.

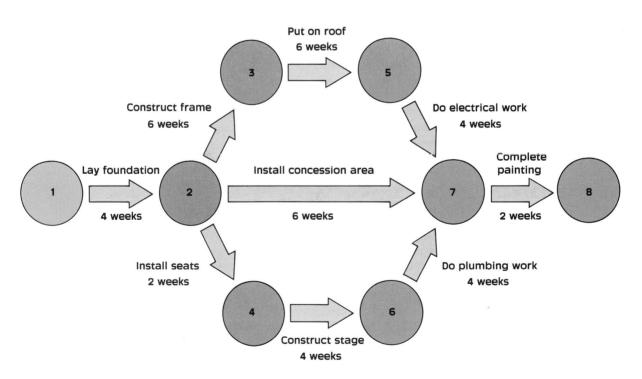

work to be performed and authorize release of the necessary materials, labor, and tools. The shop order provides a space where operators and inspectors can sign after each operation has been completed; then it goes with the work to the next operation. Requisitions for materials, parts, and tools are used to authorize the production shop to obtain necessary materials.

STEP 6: FOLLOW UP/EXPEDITE

In production management jargon, production control is often called follow-up or expediting. It is the "control" aspect of production planning and control. Its aim is to ensure that the production schedule is being adhered to.

FIGURE 10-6 / A Gantt chart showing scheduled and actual performance. The Gantt chart shows, for each order, when the operation was to start and stop and where each order actually stands as of January 20. Orders 027, 035, and 087 are behind schedule; order 079 is ahead of schedule. (*Source:* Gary Dessler, *Management Fundamentals: Modern Principles and Practices,* 4th edition, © 1985, p. 374. Reprinted by permission of Prentice Hall, Inc., Englewood Cliffs, New Jersey.)

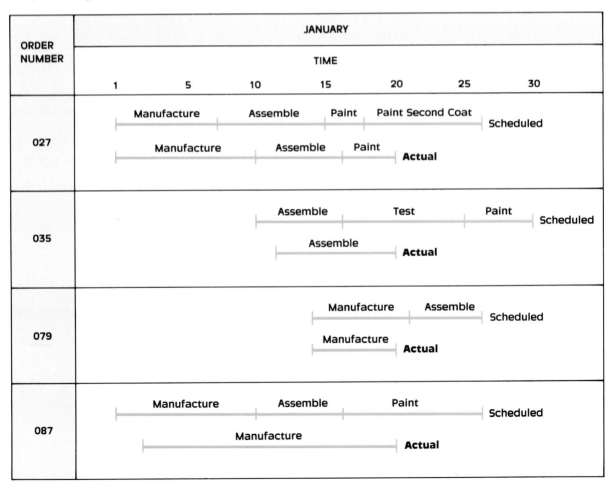

There are many different techniques for controlling production. One is for the production supervisor to prepare a report at the end of each day. This report lists orders received, orders processed, and orders remaining. In many companies this reporting process has been computerized. The information is fed into computer terminals at the job site. Then it is summarized in daily computerized production control reports.

Still other companies make use of Gantt scheduling charts for controlling production. The Gantt chart (named after Henry Gantt, who developed the charting technique in the early 1900s) shows the scheduled start and stop dates of each production step. As you can see in Figure 10-6 (on p. 301), a Gantt chart shows both scheduled and actual progress for each order. These charts show quickly whether the production department is meeting its planned schedules.

After comparing actual and planned progress, you might find that some orders are well behind schedule. This might not only affect the required shipping date, but could also have a domino effect by slowing down other scheduled orders. Because of this, many companies retain special expediters. Their specialty is solving production problems and breaking up production bottlenecks. Corrective action might entail hiring extra labor, working overtime, or subcontracting out some of the work.

Factory of the Future

As was explained in the example at the beginning of the chapter, the factory of the future is actually here today. For example, Ford Motor Company's new Aerostar plant is actually set up like this.

factory of the future

A **factory of the future** is one composed of five basic elements: automation, robotics, just-in-time inventory, a flexible manufacturing system, and computer-aided design and manufacturing. We will discuss just-in-time inventory systems in the following section and flexible manufacturing, automation, robotics, and computer-aided design and manufacturing in this section.[5]

FLEXIBLE MANUFACTURING

Production experts have long dreamed of inventing a production system that would let them produce small batches of similar products as efficiently as they can produce single products on a mass production line. The new flexible manufacturing system can do just that—it can produce a variety of products on a single production line. (Normally, a production line consists of specialized machines that can produce only a single, standardized product).

The typical flexible manufacturing system (FMS) has three components:

1. Several work stations and a computer that controls their operations;
2. A computer-controlled transport system for moving materials

BUSINESS IN THE NEWS
Operations Management at the Supermarket

To see that it is not just factories that are automating today, all you have to do is visit your neighborhood supermarket. In fact, with increased competition and the need to keep costs down, experts say that the most important trend in the grocery industry is the changing technology of electronic support tools.

The use of technology goes beyond the common scanning systems that you are probably familiar with at the checkout counter. For example, drivers delivering snacks, soft drinks, and other products often use hand-held computers to keep track of deliveries and prices. The grocery store clerks who receive the goods are similarly equipped. They use computers that read the universal price codes of merchandise to enter delivery information into central computers. This kind of technology has certainly tightened inventory controls, but it has also lengthened the process of delivering goods, since the drivers and store clerks do their computer checking separately.

However, the management consulting firm of Arthur D. Little, Inc. of Cambridge, Massachusetts, is working with a group of grocery stores and suppliers nationwide to test a new system. This will allow deliverers to enter information directly into the hand-held computers of the receiving clerks. The consulting firm says that the new system could save the grocery store industry at least $500 million a year. These new computerized delivery systems do a lot more than let store owners know how much inventory is on hand. For example, they can inform management about whether merchandise is authorized to be received, whether it is delivered at the correct wholesale price, and whether it is marked at the right retail price.

Operations management, which began on the factory floor, is thus at the center of the drive to make service companies like supermarkets competitive in the future.

Sources: Susan Sandler, "Computerized Plans Grow in Food Field," *Supermarket News,* June 16, 1986, pp. 1, 23; "Skillful Usage of Modern Technology," *Progressive Grocer,* March 1985, p. 50; Janet Guyon, "How Grocers May Save on Their Own Shopping," *The Wall Street Journal,* May 10, 1988, p. 41.

and parts from one machine to another and in and out of a system; and

3. Loading and unloading stations.

A simplified example of a flexible manufacturing system is shown in Figure 10-7 (on p. 304). In this system there are computer-controlled machines (CNCs) capable of bending, forming, and sanding products. There are also automated guided vehicles (AGVs). These travel around a long oval track in the center of the layout, moving materials to and from the computer-controlled machines. Of course, the automated guided vehicles are controlled by the main computer and told when and where to deliver parts and products or pick them up.

There are tool changers behind each computer controlled machine. Each holds an assortment of tools. The proper tool is selected automatically for the next machining step by the computer. Changing from one

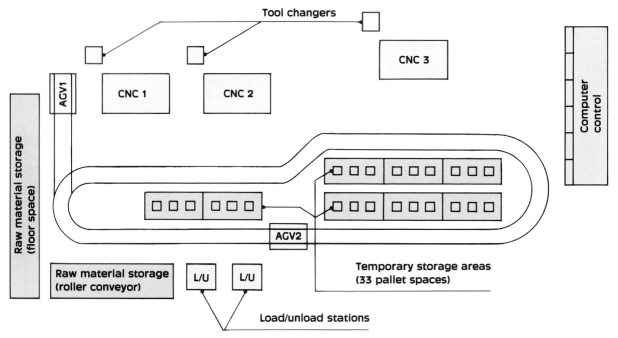

FIGURE 10-7 / A flexible manufacturing system at Mazak Corporation. (*Source:* Lee Krajewski and Larry P. Ritzman, *Operations Management: Strategy and Analysis*, Addison-Wesley, Reading, Mass., 1987, p. 199. Courtesy of Vincent Mabert and Mazak Corporation. Reprinted by permission.)

tool to another takes only two minutes. This is one reason why it is possible to produce a variety of products on this one production line. At the bottom are two load and unload stations. Here workers load and unload parts for the automated guided vehicles.

During the day shift this particular production line is staffed by workers. However, during the evening and night shifts the flexible manufacturing system operates automatically, without workers at the load/unload stations. Parts that need to be repositioned or unloaded are moved by the automated guided vehicles to a temporary storage space next to the track and are left there. They are retrieved by workers during the next day shift.[6]

AUTOMATION

automation

Automation is a second feature of the factory of the future. **Automation** means a system, process, or machine that operates automatically, a self-regulating system in which mechanical or electronic devices replace much of the monitoring and adjusting performed by workers.

Automation has actually been with us since the late 1940s, when it was first used in the automobile industry. For example, books like the one you are now holding have long been bound on automated machines. These automatically reach out, take the pages and cover, fold them together properly, and bind the book together at the spine. It is not just the factory of the future that uses automated machines.

However, you cannot have a factory of the future without automation. For example, a flexible manufacturing system obviously relies on automated machines. The computerized machines that actually do the work are automated. They do their work automatically, guided each step of the way by the computers. The Foxboro Company ad shows prospective customers how its Intelligent Automation System can enhance their productivity.

ROBOTICS

When most people think of a "factory of the future," the first thing that comes to mind is the use of industrial robots. However, in factories, robots are not as cute or intelligent as R2D2 of Star Wars fame, at least not yet. A robot is simply an automated machine, one that can be programmed to perform an operation over and over and over again.

Robots are often used to perform jobs like welding, spray painting, and materials handling (getting a part from point A to point B). Welding robots, for example, can perform their welding jobs over and over again without human direction. They are guided to the proper point with electronic sensors.

Automation is not just for the factory of the future; small and large firms can use automated systems to become more competitive today.

With computer-aided design, parts can be designed, tested, and redesigned without the use of expensive prototypes.

COMPUTER-AIDED DESIGN AND MANUFACTURING (CAD/CAM)

computer-aided design (CAD)

Computer-aided design and computer-aided manufacturing are other features of the "factory of the future." **Computer-aided design (CAD)** is a process that enables designers of machinery parts and other items to sketch their design on a computer screen with an electronic pencil. The computer determines the precise measurements.

With a CAD system, old designs can be quickly modified, and new designs can be considered and revised without taking the time to draw them out on paper. CAD can also be used to subject the computerized design to tests of strength and stress and wind resistance without having to build expensive prototypes or models. Then, when the design is accepted, the computer will already "know" the specifications of its components. This can make it easier for the firm to use the computer to control the steps in the parts' manufacture. Most firms use computer-aided design and computer-aided manufacturing together.

computer-aided manufacturing (CAM)

We have already touched on computer-aided manufacturing. For example, in the "factory of the future's" flexible manufacturing system the machines themselves are computer-controlled. **Computer-aided manufacturing (CAM)** is a process that guides via computer the steps involved in producing a product.

Controlling Quality and Inventory

Controlling the quality and inventory levels of the firm's inputs (raw materials) and outputs (products) are also important production management tasks.

QUALITY CONTROL

quality control system

A **quality control system** is a production system that sets a standard for an input or output, and it makes comparisons against this standard to prevent nonstandard items from going into or coming out of the production process.

This does not mean that quality must always be high. It means only that the level of quality must be known and checked so that it is kept within an acceptable range. Low quality might be acceptable for certain products when high quality would be too costly.

What constitutes a range of acceptable quality varies from firm to firm. The range is very narrow for firms in the aircraft and nuclear energy industries. It is much broader for firms that make nails, garbage cans, and household furniture.

Some firms always insist on the highest-quality products and tell us about it in their ads. Owen sausage, for example, advertises that it could reduce its costs by using cheaper ingredients but that would hurt its reputation for quality. Quality standards may also vary within a firm. For example, KitchenAid sets higher standards for its top-of-the-line dishwasher than for its bottom-of-the-line model.

It is almost impossible to check each and every input or product output to ensure that its quality is acceptable. Ordinarily, this would be too costly. Most manufacturers use sampling in quality control inspection. Thus a bicycle manufacturer's purchasing department might require that a sample of fifty 20-foot sections be examined whenever a shipment of steel tubing arrives. Instructions might require that a shipment be accepted if no more than one defective section is found in the sample. This is called *acceptance sampling*. In certain types of production, of course, 100 percent inspection is required. The sale of even one faulty heart pacemaker could have very serious results.

In addition to enforcing production standards, inspections are sometimes done as a preventive measure. Regular inspections might reveal defective parts or poor workmanship that can be corrected while the product is still on the production line. Service-oriented firms also stress the need for inspections and quality control. Airlines, for example, are regularly inspected. Serious discrepancies in their equipment or procedures are reported to the Federal Aviation Administration.

Companies today increasingly rely on a dedicated work force to monitor a product's quality as it moves through the manufacturing process. In many auto plants, workers on an assembly line can press "panic" buttons that shut down the line temporarily if they see a car moving through that should be repaired. Previously, a product like this might have simply moved to the end of the line and been finished. A hidden defect (such as an improper weld under a seat or floorboard) might not have been noticed until the customer had bought and driven the car. To stay competitive today with their foreign rivals, many U.S. firms are thus following Ford's lead in making "Quality job one."

fishbone diagram

The quality circle problem-solving groups discussed in Chapter 6 are often used to analyze and solve quality problems. Sometimes they use fishbone diagrams like that in Figure 10-8 (on p. 308) to analyze and solve problems. A **fishbone diagram** summarizes the four main

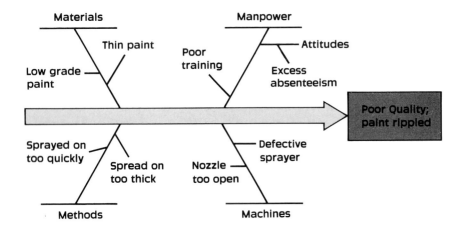

FIGURE 10-8 / A fishbone diagram. (*Source:* Gary Dessler, *Improving Productivity at Work,* © 1983, p. 111. Reprinted by permission of Prentice Hall, Inc., Englewood Cliffs, New Jersey.)

possible sources of a quality problem—materials, manpower, methods, and machines. For example, if car bodies are being produced with rippled paint, the problem might be thin paint (materials), poor training (manpower), a defective sprayer (machines), or too thick a layer of paint (methods). The quality circle members can use the fishbone diagram to identify the causes of the quality problem. They can then suggest solutions.

Many companies use quality control charts such as that in Figure 10-9 to control the quality of their products. There are many different types of charts but the basic idea is always the same. A **control chart** is

control chart

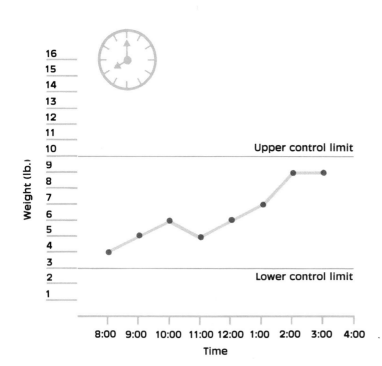

FIGURE 10-9 / An example of a quality control chart. (*Source:* Gary Dessler, *Management Fundamentals: Modern Principles and Practices,* 4th edition, © 1985, p. 381. Reprinted by permission of Prentice Hall, Inc., Englewood Cliffs, New Jersey.)

a production device on which upper and lower limits are drawn and some measurable aspect of a sample of the product (length, weight, etc.) is measured after inspection of the product. If the measurements begin to show a trend toward the upper or lower control limit, then quality might be going out of control. The reason for the trend (such as a worn-out production machine) must then be determined.

CONTROL OF INVENTORY LEVELS

Inventories include raw materials, parts, and finished and partly finished goods. Controlling inventory levels requires balancing the need to keep enough inventory in stock with the expense of holding too much inventory in stock.

There are some good reasons for keeping high levels of inventory. A firm using assembly line production is less likely to run out of parts and partly finished components. Running out of inventory can mean expensive down-time. Big orders (and possibly big customers) can be lost if deliveries are not made as promised.

There are some equally good reasons for keeping inventories low, however. First, inventories require an investment of funds. A factory with a lower inventory operates more efficiently. In other words, it produces products with a smaller investment than does a factory with a large inventory. Second, inventories take up scarce space. Third, prod-

Effective inventory control is especially important for perishable products like flowers.

ucts in inventory may decrease in value. That is, they may deteriorate or be stolen or damaged. Inventory items may also be subject to obsolescence. That is, they may become out of date or less efficient than newer products. In fact, new inputs or new finished products may even be invented or discovered that will make existing inventories obsolete.

Huffy Corporation, a manufacturer of bicycles, used to keep a large quantity of ready-to-sell bicycles in its warehouse. It did not want to be caught short of inventory and lose sales. But the demand for bicycles did not increase as much as expected. The firm lost money because of the high costs of its excess inventory. Today, Huffy keeps about half as many bicycles in inventory. It has not lost any sales, however, because computerized inventory controls and better relationships with suppliers and sellers helped to improve the inventory management system.

Some firms use mathematical formulas to determine the best inventory levels to maintain. These formulas include such things as the cost of losing an order, storage costs, interest, and expected delivery time. They help managers determine how much input to order and the time intervals between orders.

The Toyota Motor Company pioneered an approach to inventory management that permits managers to keep inventory levels and related costs low. **Just-in-time (JIT) inventory management** is an inventory control system that is designed to tie inventory levels more closely to short-run production needs in order to reduce inventory requirements at production facilities.

Here is how it works. In the JIT system, production at any work station is triggered by the demand for its output from the next work station. For example, suppose a production line is just about finished assembling a car. A signal goes out to the subcomponent work stations to make components such as doors and send them to the assembly line for placement in the next car to be produced. The purpose of JIT is to produce (or deliver) the right items in the quantities needed by subsequent production processes (or customers) at the time needed. That way, the company eliminates the need to keep work-in-process inventory on hand. That saves the company money because keeping parts and components lying around in stock ties up money that could be used elsewhere—for installing better machines, for example.

In Japan, requests for producing parts are often done by the *kanban system*. This specifies how many and what items should be produced and shipped. The word "kanban" means card or visible record in Japanese. In a JIT system it is usually a 4″ × 8″ plastic card. In factory of the future installations, JIT requests are often triggered electronically. Computers at one station "tell" the other stations what and when to ship.

In many auto plants today, even the suppliers are tied in to the JIT system. That way the car company does not have the expense of keeping lots of the supplier's parts (such as tires) lying around in inventory. Instead, they are produced and shipped just in time for the day's production run.

JIT inventory management is also spreading to the service sector. For example, the bar codes on a pair of Levis jeans are read at the cash register to ring up the sale. This information might also go directly to

just-in-time (JIT) inventory management

Levi Strauss and Company to let them know that the store now needs another pair of jeans in that size.

Materials Management

The variety of materials purchased by a firm—raw materials, partly finished products, finished products, and supplies—requires special management. These products must be purchased, physically handled, and stored. The most vital activity in managing materials, one that often requires a special department, is purchasing.

THE PURCHASING TASK

The purchasing task can have a great effect on profits for manufacturers, retailers, and wholesalers. In manufacturing this is especially true when materials and parts are a major part of total manufacturing cost. Many firms establish a separate purchasing department with its own manager.

In addition, large firms are likely to use centralized purchasing instead of allowing individual departments to make their own purchases. This can result in cost savings from large-volume buying, coordinated purchasing and receiving functions, and standardized purchase specifications.

Finance, purchasing, production, and engineering people often work together as a team to develop a list of specifications for equipment and to plan for its procurement. The objective is to get the level of quality needed by the user department at the best price. This requires a systems approach to decision making in which the net welfare of the firm is the guiding principle. For example, buying high-quality materials from a particular supplier might be more expensive from the point of view of one department but cheaper from the point of view of the firm as a whole if it reduces waste.

PURCHASING POLICIES   Over time, firms usually develop standard purchasing policies. For example, some follow a policy of building up inventories when prices are right. The purchasing agent, a "professional purchaser," generally has a very good idea of when prices are right.

Some purchasing agents concentrate all purchases for a specific good or service with one supplier, often because that supplier's past performance has been excellent. Other purchasing agents do not follow that policy. They fear being taken for granted or "putting all their eggs in one basket." A strike at a supplier's plant, for example, could place the buyer firm in a bad position.

Other purchasing policies involve such matters as taking discounts offered by suppliers. Discount practices are discussed in Chapter 12.

Some firms follow a policy of leasing equipment whenever possible, rather than purchasing it. Leasing offers a tax advantage because lease payments are a deductible business expense. It also shifts part of the risk of equipment obsolescence to the lessor and ties up less of the lessee's capital.

A common purchasing policy involves reciprocity. **Reciprocity** is a purchasing policy under which a customer buys from a supplier if that supplier also buys from its customer—"you buy from me and I'll buy from you." Reciprocity is widely practiced by industrial sellers and buyers. It makes buyer and seller interdependent, and it guarantees the seller a customer for its own products. For example, a manufacturer of uniforms might agree to buy its materials from a textile company that in turn agrees to buy uniforms for its workers from the apparel manufacturer.

Today the purchasing function is usually handled by professionals. Two tools that they use are value analysis and vendor analysis.

VALUE ANALYSIS   **Value analysis** involves reviewing existing product specifications as set by user departments (those units for which purchasing is done) and identifying and eliminating nonessential requirements. The review might involve a committee of engineers, cost accountants, production representatives, and others. They review the specification set by the user department. Wherever a specification (spec) (such as "steel will be at least 98 percent pure") is thought to add unnecessary cost, the function of that spec is examined. Perhaps it can be eliminated, or perhaps there is a cheaper way of doing it. Such a review requires close contact with potential suppliers to verify costs.

Value analysis has played an important role in the auto industry, especially after the federal government imposed mandatory miles-per-gallon requirements. One thing that value analysis showed was that parts made from fiberglass-reinforced plastic can be substituted for steel parts in many cases. This helps to reduce a car's weight and fuel consumption. Careful investigation of the costs of alternative inputs can thus lead to significant savings.

VENDOR ANALYSIS   **Vendor analysis** evaluates and rates the technical, financial, and managerial abilities of potential suppliers in terms of their past performance. It is a method of substituting facts for feelings in the selection of suppliers.

A purchasing department might analyze possible suppliers, make a decision, and then send a purchase order to the supplier. Some purchasing departments invite sellers to submit bids. In some cases the buyer elects to award the purchase contract to the lowest bidder. This competitive bidding requires that the buyer specify in detail what it is that he or she wants to purchase. In other cases, specifications are not so exact, and bids received are subject to further negotiation over price and quality.

WAREHOUSING

Finished products coming off the assembly line must be moved to a storage facility so that orders can be processed and the products can be packed and shipped. **Warehousing** refers to the selection and use of buildings or facilities to store finished goods. We discuss warehousing in Chapter 14.

Summary

A production system is one that converts inputs like raw materials, labor, or capital into outputs like goods or services. Any production system thus consists of three main parts: inputs, conversion processes, and outputs.

All production and operation systems use a production process or technology to convert inputs into outputs. All businesses including factories, offices, and service businesses like Mrs. Fields Cookies utilize technologies.

A first step in production management involves designing the production system itself. To do this, managers have to decide where to locate the plant, what type of production process to use, and how to lay out the physical facilities. Important factors in plant location include a favorable labor climate, proximity to markets, and quality of life.

Designing the production system is only one step in the overall production process. In addition, production planning is aimed at determining what products to produce and where, when, and how to produce them. Production control is aimed at ensuring that the established production plans or schedules are being met. Production planning and control often involves six steps: receive the orders, develop lists of required materials, develop a route sheet, develop production schedules, dispatch notices to operators to begin work, and follow up/ expedite.

There are two main types of production processes: intermittent and continuous. An intermittent production process starts and stops and starts again, perhaps several times per hour. We explained unit, batch, and mass intermittent processes. A continuous production process operates more or less continuously, hardly ever being shut down except for maintenance or repairs.

There are three main ways to lay out a production facility. In a process layout the machinery, materials, and labor are laid out on the basis of the functions they perform, as in a machine shop. In a product layout, things are laid out as on an assembly line. Finally, in a fixed layout the product stays in one place, and the labor, materials, and machinery are brought to it, as when a large ship is being built.

Five features combine to make a factory a "factory of the future": automation, robotics, just-in-time inventory, flexible manufacturing systems, and computer-aided design and manufacturing. In these factories, automated guided vehicles (AGVs) follow computer-generated orders in guiding material from work station to work station. At each work station the exact jobs to be done are also determined by computers.

Controlling the quality and controlling the inventory levels of the firm's inputs and outputs are also important production management tasks. Quality control involves setting a standard for an input or output and then making comparisons against the standard to prevent nonstandard items from going into or coming out of the production process. Similarly, inventory control systems are established to balance the need to keep enough inventory in stock with the expense of holding too much inventory in stock. Just-in-time inventory management is a new technique for controlling inventory. In the JIT system, production at any work station is triggered by the demand for its output from the next work station.

Inputs or materials must also be purchased. Purchasing has evolved into a science in itself. Centralized purchasing departments develop purchasing policies and procedures to help ensure that the firm gets goods and services of the required quality and minimum price.

Review Questions

1. Distinguish between production planning and production control.

2. How does the use of CAD/CAM affect product design?

3. Suppose a plant is located near suppliers but far away from customers. What does that imply about the nature of inputs and outputs and their transportation costs?

4. Give examples of the inputs, processes, and outputs of production.

5. How can a Gantt chart be helpful to managers in service-oriented firms?

6. What is the essential idea in value analysis?

7. Explain the meaning of the term "warehousing."

8. What constitutes a "factory of the future"?

9. Compare and contrast continuous and intermittent production.

Discussion Questions

1. Which do you think is more important for efficient factory production—"factory of the future" technology or a motivated work force? Why?

2. Is your college an example of process, product, or fixed layout? Why?

3. What factors do you think help to explain the relatively high quality of Japanese cars?

4. One of the biggest problems fast food restaurants face is the diminishing supply of teenage employees. Do you think that automation could help owners overcome this problem? Name two jobs in a fast-food restaurant that you think could be automated.

Key Terms

production system	batch production	fixed layout
production management	mass production	factory of the future
labor-intensive processes	assembly line	automation
capital-intensive processes	continuous production	computer-aided design (CAD)
intermittent production	process layout	computer-aided manufacturing (CAM)
unit production	product layout	

quality control system	just-in-time (JIT) inventory management	value analysis
fishbone diagram		vendor analysis
control chart	reciprocity	warehousing

Cases

THE COLUMBUS MUSEUM OF NATURAL HISTORY GIFT SHOP

The Columbus Museum of Natural History opened a gift shop two years ago and named Lois Henry as the shop manager. Lois' product plan calls for ten general groups of merchandise: containers, art works, Eskimo crafts, Indian goods, geological items, paper goods, books, regular jewelry, scientific instruments (such as binoculars and barometers), and seasonal goods.

Ms. Henry is pleased with many aspects of the gift shop. She likes the merchandise offered, the store layout, and the work force (sales clerks). Annual sales exceed $230,000 and are still climbing. However, inventory-related problems have proved to be a thorn in her side.

Inventory turnover is much too low, which squeezes profit margins and causes cash flow problems. Inventory turnover refers to how many times per year a store's inventory is sold—in other words, how long an item stays on the shelf before it is sold. High inventories are caused by over-estimating future sales for some items and by the current strategy of reviewing most items only every five months. At the present time, Ms. Henry has no way to spot slow-moving or obsolete items.

Despite the high overall inventory, many items are sold out before replenishment orders arrive. Ms. Henry gets several stockout notices from the sales clerks each week. She suspects that lost sales are becoming a serious problem.

In reflecting on these problems, Ms. Henry believes that it is time to improve her inventory policies and introduce a more systematic inventory control system.[7]

Questions
1. What new inventory policies or rules should Ms. Henry institute? Why?
2. If running out of an item is such a serious problem, why not overstock it?
3. Do you think a just-in-time inventory management system would work in this store? Why or why not?

MAINTENANCE PROBLEMS AT EASTERN AIRLINES

During the first half of 1988, Eastern Airlines was hit by a series of serious maintenance problems. Planes had to be grounded because of engine malfunctions, emergency doors that did not work, and other minor and major problems. The problems finally culminated in orders from the Federal Aviation Administration that all of Eastern's planes and maintenance procedures were to be inspected by the FAA during May 1988.

During this period, the public was bombarded by news releases from both Eastern and its unions. The unions (including the machinists that were responsible for most of Eastern's maintenance) kept emphasizing that Eastern's maintenance was not up to par and that many of the airline's planes were unsafe to fly. The company said that these charges were false and even brought back former chairman (and astronaut) Frank Borman to attest to the airline's safety.

The problems at Eastern underline the importance of maintenance, particularly where complex machinery is involved, and also the role played by employee morale in keeping maintenance quality up.

Questions
1. What can a company like Eastern do to help ensure that reluctant employees still do their jobs when it comes to maintenance?
2. Do you think it is actually possible that some or all maintenance workers did not do their jobs properly, even though they knew that passenger safety was involved?
3. What would you do to make sure that maintenance on your aircraft was being carried out properly?

Wearing gloves, kerchiefs, and running shoes, the plump clear bottles with the bright labels march across the Brooklyn Bridge, the towers of Manhattan and the Statue of Liberty in the background. They are the engaging animated containers of Original New York Seltzer (ONYS), a product that has catapulted 24-year-old Randy Miller into international success.

In the Depression, Randy's great-grandfather Jake peddled seltzer and fruit syrups in New York. After Randy graduated from high school in 1982, he and his father Alan, an aerospace engineer who also has a doctorate in psychology, decided to revive the family business, bottling the water in the original plant in Brooklyn but marketing it in Southern California where they lived.

Alan kept his day job to maintain cash flow, while his teenaged son "lined up and worked with the distributors, expanded the route by obtaining new accounts, and made all the deliveries" from the back of a 1968 Mustang convertible. In the third year the product took off, when Randy's persistence

SECTION FOUR

Marketing Management

and the sodas' taste appeal lead to their widespread distribution through beer wholesalers. The times were right for a healthy nonalcoholic beverage with pizzazz, but many credit Randy's marketing instincts for giving ONYS its considerable and growing market niche.

Despite putting in 13-hour days at the company, Randy maintains his avocations of drag racing, exotic animal raising, and stunt work. In 1987, in the company's first major promotion, Randy leapt off a ten-story hotel roof clutching a bottle of black cherry seltzer. He hit an airbag below, rolled off, and triumphantly swilled the soda. The video of that stunt became a 30-second ad on MTV and garnered international media attention.

"Over the years I've worked in every aspect of my business from the ground up," Miller said. "When I first started, I learned to deal with the accounting, the money, inventory, production, distribution, sales ... I didn't give up. If I didn't know how to handle something, I'd figure it out." Randy and Alan Miller had a sure sense of what was right for their business and did not use outside consultants or experts. "Every move we made was conservative and well thought out." His early marketing strategy, he said, "was simple: get it on the shelf. We wanted people to try it. The product would sell itself...."

"Our product is more expensive because we're using very expensive extracts," Miller said, noting that if market research had been done to see if the idea would fly, the results "probably would have come back negative .... But the Miller's faith in their product was rewarded. "The Japanese people are going bananas over it," Miller said, having recently completed a big distribution deal there. "We're in Canada, France, Italy, most of Europe. Next year, we'll probably roll out to South America ... We'll be in most of the world."

The Millers stress cleaniless, clarity, and quality control. According to Randy, his responsibility is "to insure that ONYS continues to manufacture and distribute the best tasting, highest quality soft drink in the world."

Marketing Strategies **11**

Product and Pricing Strategies **12**

Promotion Strategies **13**

Distribution Strategies **14**

ELEVEN

Marketing
Strategies

After reading this chapter, you will be able to:

- Describe the marketing functions.

- Show how marketing creates utility.

- Explain the marketing concept.

- Describe the four parts of the marketing mix.

- Distinguish between consumer and industrial/organizational target markets.

- Describe the marketing research process and the major types of data sources for such research.

- Explain the roles of motivation research and consumer purchase decision models in marketing.

- Outline briefly the history of the consumer movement.

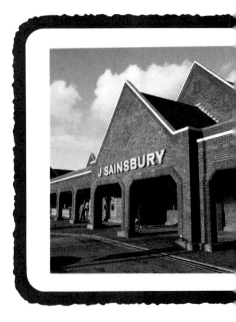

WHAT'S AHEAD

We have seen how business firms produce goods and services. We turn now to marketing and the strategies it employs. Marketing activities are focused on the exchange process by which something of value, usually a good or service, is traded for something of similar value, usually cash or credit. Marketing functions such as buying, selling, storing, and transporting contribute to the usefulness of goods and services beyond that created by production. Performing such functions adds time, place, and ownership utility to products.

Most modern firms practice the marketing concept when they concentrate on the goal of customer satisfaction. They aim to please a specific target market, which may be made up of other firms or of consumers. How a firm satisfies its customers depends on its marketing mix. This mix includes the product, price, promotion, and distribution strategies that it uses.

We will examine the basic types of target markets—industrial/organizational and consumer—and how marketers use research techniques to understand them better. Market data sources and research designs are also explored.

We will also look at some basic concepts of consumer behavior, including motivation research and some of the consumer purchase decision models used by marketers. This leads into an analysis of market segmentation methods and strategies as well as a look at the consumer movement and how it has affected marketing decisions. We close with a brief advance look at the marketing of services.

Britain's audio industry was founded by skilled engineers who designed some of the world's best loudspeakers. But while the British engineers were adding refinements that impressed serious

listeners, the Japanese ran away with the mass market.

In Britain, many industry leaders feel that the loss of such markets was caused by a lack of "commercial" (marketing) leadership. The British automobile industry, too, has suffered from lack of marketing skills. Britain's auto industry has lost more than 80 percent of its home market to foreigners. Brands such as MG, Austin, Morris, and Triumph—despite leaps in productivity and quality in recent years—have continued to lose market share. Marketing in the modern sense has been lacking in Britain.

However, modern marketing is beginning to show itself in areas such as Britain's soft drink industry. Cadbury Schweppes, a giant in the candy and soft drink business, has formed a joint venture with the Coca-Cola Company. Together, Cadbury and Coca-Cola will try to make Britain's fragmented soft drink business follow the American model with its emphasis on brand identity, big ad spending, and distribution strength. "This is a market which deserves better marketing," says Donald R. Keough, the president of Coca-Cola.

The leading food retailer in Britain is J Sainsbury PLC. The Sainsbury Group has doubled its sales over the past five years. In March 1988 it became the first U.K.-based company with retail sales exceeding 5 billion pounds ($9,468 million). In the 1950s, Sainsbury began to develop self-service stores. In 1955 it opened what was then the largest supermarket in Europe. It now operates 279 supermarkets with a total sales area of 5,463,000 square feet. In ten years its sales have grown sixfold. Slowly but surely, modern marketing is coming to Britain.[1]

The emergence of modern marketing techniques in Britain despite strong traditional resistance to "commercialism" among top management proves that marketing has come of age. It shows that the ability to compete in world markets requires more than good production skills. The role of marketing in modern business as well as in other institutions is outlined in this and the next three chapters.

Marketing and Its Functions

marketing

Marketing is the process of planning and executing the conception, pricing, promotion, and distribution of ideas, goods, and services to create exchanges.[2] Logically, this includes nonbusiness exchanges like those that occur in politics or religion (election campaigns promising reform in exchange for votes or churches offering spiritual benefits for people who become members). We will, however, focus mostly on the exchanges (sales) sought by profit-making firms.

THE EVOLUTION OF MARKETING

Marketing has evolved rapidly in this century. It had to evolve to keep up with the advances in production that we read about in the previous

TABLE 11-1 / The marketing functions

Function	Nature
Buying	Identifying and selecting sources of supply, evaluating sources of supply, negotiating terms of purchase.
Selling	Identifying, locating, and communicating with targeted customers, stimulating demand and negotiating terms of sale.
Storing and transporting	Warehousing, storing, inventory management, transporting, customer service, order processing, materials handling.
Standardization and grading	Setting quantity and quality standards for products, labeling.
Gathering and providing marketing information	Identifying and analyzing market opportunity, doing surveys and experiments, and gathering data from internal and external sources.
Risk taking	Assuming, transferring, and controlling the risk inherent in marketing.
Financing	Granting credit.

chapter. In the early 1900s, businesses equated marketing with "selling what we can produce." Today, marketing means something much more aggressive and customer-oriented. People have more money to spend, and competition is stiffer. Business firms must be much more alert to the changing market than they were in the past. Most leading firms in this country have responded by adopting the marketing concept, which we will examine later in this chapter.

THE MARKETING FUNCTIONS

marketing functions

Marketing, as shown in Table 11-1, includes the performance of seven functions that are needed to bring products from the producer to the user. The **marketing functions** are (1) buying, (2) selling, (3) storing and transporting, (4) standardization and grading, (5) gathering marketing information, (6) risk taking, and (7) financing. These functions may be performed by one firm, or they may be shared by groups of firms. In Chapter 14 we will show that the firms that perform these marketing functions most efficiently will survive. As such functions are performed, they add four kinds of utility to the products.

form utility

Marketing and Utility

Production processes such as those we discussed in Chapter 10 often make materials more useful by changing their form. **Form utility** is the usefulness of a product that results from a change in form. Pert Plus shampoo, for example, becomes useful for washing hair only after various ingredients have been combined to add color, scent, and other features and after these ingredients have been processed and bottled. The Procter & Gamble plant in Cincinnati creates form utility when it makes Pert Plus and bottles it.

Unfortunately, form utility is not enough to satisfy the millions of consumers who want to buy Pert Plus and have it handy in their homes when they need it. It must have three additional types of utility before it is fully useful. These are *place utility*, *time utility*, and *ownership utility*. **Place utility** is the usefulness of a product that results from a favorable change in its location. Shampoo on a loading dock in Cincinnati must be moved to Denver, for example, before its usefulness to a Denver household can be realized. The railroad or trucking company that transports the cases of Pert Plus creates place utility for people in Denver.

place utility

Time utility is the usefulness of a product that results from having it available *when* the consumer wants it. Perhaps the Parker family in Denver has nearly run out of shampoo. The family-size container of Pert Plus on the supermarket shelf is not yet fully useful to Bill and Suzanne Parker for several reasons. One is that it needs more place utility. Being on the supermarket shelf is better than being at the factory in Cincinnati, but the shampoo still must be moved to the Parkers' house. Another reason is that more time must pass before the last bit of shampoo at home is used up and they experience an immediate "need" for the next bottle. That bottle of Pert Plus on the Safeway shelf is gaining time utility as the supply at home is being used up. Safeway has collaborated in the utility-making process by keeping the shampoo until the Parkers are ready for it. Safeway has helped to create time utility.

time utility

While on the drugstore shelves, over-the-counter drugs like aspirin gain time utility for their future users.

ownership utility

Finally, the bottle of Pert Plus on the Safeway shelf is not fully useful, as far as the Parkers are concerned, until they own it. Because of the concept of private property, they must buy the shampoo. **Ownership utility** is the usefulness of a product that comes about through the passage of legal title to the final user. When Bill Parker goes to the Safeway store and pays for the shampoo, it becomes his to use. When the new bottle arrives in the Parkers' bathroom, it becomes fully useful.

Marketing activities are involved directly in creating the product's place, time, and ownership utility and indirectly in creating form utility. Marketing research, for example, may have helped Procter & Gamble decide which scent to add to Pert Plus.

The Marketing Concept

marketing concept

The **marketing concept** is the belief that a whole firm must be coordinated to serve the needs of its present and potential customers and to do so at a profit. When a firm adopts the marketing concept, it focuses its entire operation on customer satisfaction. This means first finding out what customers really want and then seeing to it that all elements in the firm's organization cooperate to give it to them. When Al Copeland founded Popeye's Famous Fried Chicken and Biscuits, he understood the marketing concept from the start. He knew how important quick service and consistent quality were to young people and people with moderate income. He also knew that spicy, Cajun-style chicken and side dishes were favorites in Louisiana and the Gulf Coast region where he got started. Copeland studied the tastes of his customers and built an effective franchise organization specifically to give this group of customers what they want.

Adopting the marketing concept means that the financial, production, and marketing functions of the firm must all be guided so as to pursue the common goal. The need for a marketing orientation throughout the firm has led many businesses to select their leaders from their marketing departments.

The Marketing Mix

marketing mix

Marketing decision makers must design a set of strategies appropriate for the chosen target market. The **marketing mix** is the set of marketing strategies (promotion strategies, product strategies, price strategies, and distribution strategies) chosen to reach and influence a certain market. These strategies must be coordinated such that the target market is satisfied and the firm makes a profit. (See Figure 11-1 on p. 324.)

VARIATIONS IN THE MIX

The relative emphasis firms place on these four parts of the marketing mix depends on the target market (which we will examine more closely

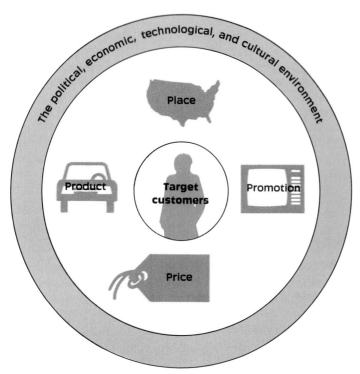

FIGURE 11-1 / The marketing mix.

in this chapter), the product type, and many other factors that we will learn about in the next three chapters. The product is the key element in the marketing mix, for example, in selling cards and many relatively new products. Hubotics, Inc. of Carlsbad, California, markets Hubot, a 100-pound, 44-inch-tall robotic "member of the family." RB Robot Corporation of Golden, Colorado, markets an RB5X robot. It is safe to say that the product is the dominant part of the mix for these companies. The novelty and uniqueness of robots make product a more important marketing element than promotion, distribution, or price.

On the other hand, place (distribution) is probably more important in marketing a convenience product like a soft drink than is the drink itself. The same is true for snack foods and laundry detergents. When Anheuser-Busch started marketing Eagle snacks, it used the same wholesalers for the snacks as for its line of beers. For other firms, price or promotion might be the most important element in the marketing mix.

THE ENVIRONMENT AND THE MIX

As we saw in Figure 11-1, environmental factors such as politics, technology, economics, and culture cannot be ignored in making decisions about the marketing mix. For example, interest in national defense in the early 1980s contributed to the growth of firms like Raytheon and General Dynamics. The growing number of one-person households influenced the product planning for Campbell's Soup Company by increasing the demand for single-serving portions. Also, more efficiency apartments were built during the boom in residential construction in 1983–1984. Technological advances in microelectronics gave rise to hundreds of new types of digital watches, games, and small appliances in the early 1980s. Such environmental changes create opportunities as well as problems for marketing managers.

Product and pricing strategies are presented in Chapter 12. The promotion strategies, including advertising and personal selling are discussed in Chapter 13, and distribution strategies are treated in Chapter 14. Before we can design such strategies, we must define the target market toward which they will be directed.

The Target Market

target market

The **target market** is the group of present and potential customers that a firm aims to satisfy with its goods and services. Defining such a target is the first step in successful marketing. Usually, the process of definition of the target market starts with deciding whether the firm intends to serve (1) business organizations and/or other institutions or (2) consumers such as individuals or households. We will also take a brief look at a special kind of market known as the intermediary market.

Industrial/Organizational Markets

industrial/organizational markets

Industrial/organizational markets are markets for goods or services that will be used to produce other goods or services. For example, when Caterpillar Tractor buys tractor tires or a doctor buys an examining table, these buyers are industrial/organizational buyers. Such buyers purchase goods and services for reasons that are different from those of ordinary consumers. These purchases do not give direct satisfaction but help the buyer to produce something else. The demand for industrial products is a *derived demand*. It is derived from the demand for the good or service the buyer produces.

FEATURES OF THE INDUSTRIAL MARKET

Besides the derived nature of the demand, industrial/organizational markets have several other special characteristics. First, the target market has a relatively smaller number of customers than consumer markets. The Boeing Company and McDonnell Douglas build airplanes for sale to airlines and the military. They have a much smaller number of potential customers than does a single Burger King restaurant in a large city.

Industrial/organizational markets are often more concentrated geographically than are consumer markets. Many industries that are the sole users of certain products are centered in one or a few areas. The aircraft industry on the West Coast, the auto industry in Detroit, and the

Industrial products like commercial airliners are targeted to a small number of buyers.

steel industry in the Great Lakes area are only a few examples. A firm that sells electronic parts for aircraft is likely to locate in California, where many of its customers are.

Industrial markets are also different from household consumers because they have more formal systems for buying. They set up purchasing departments to handle procurement. For example, DuPont's energy and materials department buys raw materials, supplies, and equipment for all of the firm's domestic and foreign branches and subsidiaries. DuPont's purchasing department also plans for long-range energy buying. Large firms such as DuPont buy thousands of different products from hundreds of different sellers.

Industrial/organizational buyers tend to be influenced by cost and/or profit considerations to a greater extent than most consumers. Rapid technological change is also important to them. Machines and processes become obsolete. If the purchasing department is not careful, the firm can find itself with large inventories of parts or supplies that have little or no value.

GOVERNMENT MARKETS

Government agencies make up a large part of the industrial/organizational market. They often purchase the same products that are sold to businesses. Federal, state, and local governments are like industrial firms in many ways. For example, they often use a formal purchasing system—that is, they draw up product specifications and request bids from several suppliers.

Marketing to the federal government is a special case because of its complex purchasing system. There are firms that sell only to the government. Large defense purchases can involve years of lobbying and debate in Congress. Furthermore, it might be long after a contract is awarded that the government receives the finished product. There are about 80,000 local government units in the country. Roughly 20 percent of our Gross National Product is bought by government agencies at the local, state, or national level. The products range from spacecraft to paperclips.

There are two types of federal government buying—civilian and military. Each government agency buys some products on its own. However, the General Services Administration does a lot of centralized buying of standard products for the civilian sector of the U.S. government. The Department of Defense handles military buying. The Defense Supply Agency buys products that the various branches of the military use in common. Many state and local governments have agencies that are similar to the General Services Administration. Independent agencies such as state highway departments are often large buyers, too.

The Consumer Market

consumer market

The **consumer market** is the market for all goods and services that will be bought and used for their own sake (not to produce other goods and services). Firms that sell products (meaning services as well as tangible) to consumers face a huge, tricky market. It is huge because in the United States alone there are more than 240 million consumers. It is tricky because the household buyer is not as professional as the industrial firm and is therefore less predictable. Furthermore, most U.S. consumers have a high level of income and buy a fantastic number of different products. With this high standard of living come frequent changes of taste in products. Let's examine the impact of these consumer market characteristics.

CONSUMER MARKETS AND DISCRETIONARY INCOME

In a rich nation like the United States or Canada, many choices are available to consumers. The more income a family or individual has, the smaller the proportion of income required for absolute necessities. Wealthy buyers can shift their spending patterns around. What a buyer has available to spend on things other than necessities is called *discretionary income*. Figure 11-2 shows that one family, the Collinses, has 33 percent more after-tax income ($40,000 versus $30,000) than another family, the Browns. It also shows that the discretionary part of the Collinses' income is 200 percent greater than that of the Browns ($6,000 versus $2,000). Rising income, then, means that businesses find it harder to predict what will be bought. This complicates the marketing task and makes it even more important to watch the consumer closely. The consumer's tastes can change quickly.

In recent years there has been a big increase in the number of *multiearner families*—families with more than one earner. The rise in job opportunities for women together with the rising number of working wives means a big jump in discretionary income for many families. These multiearner families spend more on household help and dining out and less on child-related products. They often represent a market for luxury products. The rising number of affluent dieters has led to a

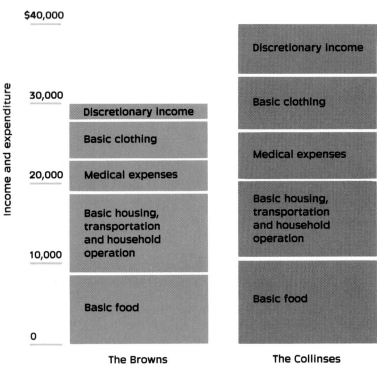

$40,000

30,000

20,000

10,000

0

Income and expenditure

Discretionary income

Basic clothing

Medical expenses

Basic housing, transportation and household operation

Basic food

Discretionary income

Basic clothing

Medical expenses

Basic housing, transportation and household operation

Basic food

The Browns

The Collinses

The Browns and the Collinses are each four-member families of two adults and two children. The Browns' income after taxes is $30,000. After spending $28,000 on necessities, they have only $2,000 to spend or save as they like. The Collinses, with $40,000 income, spend $34,000 on necessities and have $6,000 (three times as much as the Browns) left over. As income increases, discretionary income increases at a greater rate.

FIGURE 11-2 / Discretionary income of two families.

boom in sales of Lean Cuisine and other gourmet-health frozen dinners. The impressive number and buying power of "yuppies" (young urban professionals) and "dinks" (families with double income and no kids) account for the rise of luxury-oriented stores and products.

The success of the marketing process in coping with income and taste changes also depends on technological changes within the firm and in competing firms. A firm never really knows when a rival will devise a new product that outdates the firm's present product. Or the new product might make the firm's own present product unnecessary. The rise of the compact disk and its impact on sales of cassette tapes and ordinary record albums is a dramatic new example of this.

Consider the switch during the 1970s from traditional full-size cars to smaller, more fuel-efficient ones. Prompted by the strong competition from Japan and West Germany, U.S. auto makers adapted to changes in taste and technology. As gas prices fell, the trend reversed. Gas economy began to decline as a purchase motive, and "performance" and luxury rose in importance.

Competition for the consumer dollar is tougher than ever before. It is the main challenge in marketing consumer products. A number of different marketing strategies are used to meet the challenge, as we will see in the chapters that follow.

Intermediary Markets

Besides industrial/organizational and ultimate consumers markets, marketers also must often contemplate the needs and the role of a third kind of "market." This is the intermediary market, the firms that buy products for resale. As we will see in much greater detail in Chapter 14, such intermediaries, also known as middlemen, usually hold products briefly during the process of bringing them from the producer to the user. Retailers and wholesalers are examples of middlemen. We turn now to the process by which marketers get to know their markets better.

Marketing Research

marketing research

Marketing research is the application of the scientific method (fact finding, analysis, and experiments) to marketing problems and opportunities. If a firm believes in the marketing concept, then it makes sense to use marketing research to help select appropriate target markets and to design a marketing mix that works best for the selected target market. It also often helps the marketer to understand consumer behavior and motivation.

Intelligent decisions about marketing strategies (broad plans of action) require a clear understanding of the people who are or might become customers (the target market). Marketing research can provide this kind of understanding. Using a variety of methods such as surveys, questionnaires, and statistical tools, market researchers uncover the facts, opinions, and attitudes of people in the target market and report these to marketing decision makers. Figure 11-3 illustrates the growth and continued reliance of business firms on marketing research throughout the 1980s. Market Facts, Inc., a large Chicago-based market research firm has been polling U.S. firms about their expected spending on marketing research. In each year from 1980 to 1983 and again in 1987 the majority of firms predicted increased spending on this vital marketing tool.

GENERATING DATA

primary data

Marketing data is generally classified as primary or secondary. **Primary data** is data originated and collected to solve a particular problem or to evaluate the effects of new marketing strategies. Belk's Department

Percent who said current year spending would be:

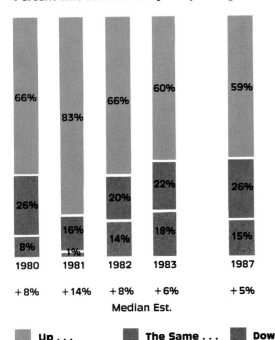

1980	1981	1982	1983	1987
66%	83%	66%	60%	59%
26%	16%	20%	22%	26%
8%	1%	14%	18%	15%
+8%	+14%	+8%	+6%	+5%

Median Est.

■ Up . . .   ■ The Same . . .   ■ Down . . .

FIGURE 11-3 / Comparison of marketing research spending expectations, 1980–1987. (*Source:* "Future Is Bright for Research Spending," *Marketing News,* vol. 21, May 22, 1987, pp. 1, 22. Reprinted from *Marketing News,* published by the American Marketing Association.)

Store, for example, surveyed its customers to evaluate the effects of the new department layout in one of its North Carolina stores.

Market surveys get primary data from both existing customers and prospective customers. The surveys are conducted by telephone, by mailed questionnaire, or by personal interview (often in shopping malls).

secondary data

Secondary data is data previously collected either by the user or by someone else for some purpose other than dealing with the current problem or decision. For example, before opening a new supermarket, Winn-Dixie, Inc. always examines the latest population census data for the neighborhoods under consideration. This data helps firms to estimate market potential and sales potential, as we saw in Chapter 4.

Census data is an example of secondary data. The Bureau of the Census reports income, age, and other important market data for each state and city in the United States. The census provides especially detailed market information for major population centers. Figure 11-4 shows the Consolidated Metropolitan Statistical Areas (CMSAs) and the Metropolitan Statistical Areas (MSAs), which hold more than three-fourths of the nation's people. Each of the twenty-three CMSAs contains one or more metropolitan complexes with at least a million people. Each of the 257 MSAs (with a few exceptions) consists of a county with a city of 50,000 population in it, together with adjacent counties that have close economic ties with the city. Many marketers concentrate their efforts in such population centers because it is easy to reach customers there. Census publications provide market researchers with the population data they need.

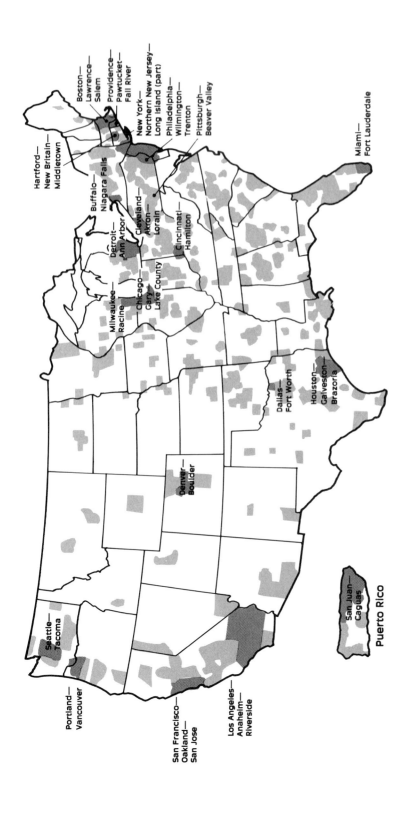

FIGURE 11-4 / Consolidated Metropolitan Statistical Areas and Metropolitan Statistical Areas.
(*Source*: Bureau of the Census.)

■ Consolidated Metropolitan Statistical Area   ▨ Metropolitan Statistical Area

APPLICATION: BURGER KING
Staying in Touch

When you are in the fast food restaurant business, there is nothing—absolutely nothing—more important than following the marketing concept: in other words, listening to your customers. Here is a small example of how Burger King Corporation did just that several years ago.

While Burger King Corporation has always been a very market-oriented firm, several years ago it was not specifically targeting any promotional campaigns to the Hispanic market. Even though Burger King was based in Miami, which has a large Hispanic population, some fast food competitors were preferred 7 to 1 by Spanish-speaking people over Burger King. Competitors were just working very hard to focus their marketing campaigns on their many Hispanic customers.

For example, one competitor advertised aggressively on Spanish-language radio stations, participated in events like the Miss Colombia pageant and Puerto Rican Day parade, and donated $100,000 for victims of the Mexican earthquake that occurred several years ago.

Burger King, on the other hand, was not specifically targeting Hispanic customers, reaching them only with its regular, general advertisements.

The point was really brought home to Burger King several years ago. WLTV, Miami's leading Spanish-language TV station, rented a billboard near the company's Kendall-area headquarters with the message "Burger King, you're missing a whopper of an audience." The company listened and now runs Spanish ads targeted to Hispanics.

Today, in fact, Burger King devotes a lot of time and money to very carefully researching its markets. Their vice-president of marketing research says that Burger King Corporation is constantly engaged in taking telephone surveys of 350 to 400 people per day, using names generated by a special computerized list. The firm wants to know what restaurants these people are aware of, which they have tried, and whether they are familiar with the company's (or the competitor's) advertising programs. A lot more of the company's market research is aimed at trying to assess the market potential of new Burger King products.

Questions

1. Explain to crew members at a Burger King® restaurant how the restaurant creates utility.

2. What lessons did Burger King Corporation's management learn from its experience with the Hispanic market in Miami?

3. Why is marketing research so important to Burger King Corporation?

RESEARCH DESIGN

research design

Research design is the overall plan for conducting marketing research and obtaining data. Sometimes it is an exploratory design. This means that the problem is not yet well-defined. Researchers might talk to employees or to experts in their industry to get a better feel for the problem. Sometimes, exploratory research relies on the conduct of focus group interviews.

focus group interviews

Focus group interviews consist of an unstructured exploratory discussion on a given topic by eight to twelve people led by a moderator.

These interviews are usually tape-recorded and watched through one-way mirrors. These are especially helpful for generating ideas and for clarifying research needs. The Buick Division of General Motors used focus groups to help develop the Regal coupe and to refine its advertising program. The medical profession has also used focus groups extensively, as discussed in the Business Applies box. However, because the groups are small and not randomly selected, the findings cannot be used to reach final conclusions about markets.

Much marketing research is descriptive in nature. Descriptive marketing research may begin where exploratory research leaves off. It emphasizes fact-gathering to describe the characteristics of a market or the behavior of customers. When a sponsor of the Bill Cosby Show

BUSINESS APPLIES

Focus Group Techniques Help Health Care Professionals

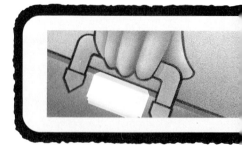

Doing marketing research with doctors is far more difficult than with children—and not nearly as entertaining," according to an experienced market researcher in the health care field. Marketing has been accepted as an important part of health care development in recent years, but the techniques of marketing research have to be adapted to the field.

The growth of new medical goods and services has been explosive. Pressures are mounting in medicine—cost containment, alternate delivery systems, malpractice, professional advertising, a surplus of providers, a shortage of clients, etc. This leads to an increased reliance on new methods to get health-care professionals and patients to provide marketing-related information. The medical industry needs feedback about the quality of patient care, the at-

titudes of doctors and nurses, and their reactions to new technology.

Focus groups are proving to be an especially valuable tool in meeting the marketing needs of medicine. However, getting doctors and other health care professionals to participate in such focus groups presents some special problems. One is recruiting itself. Successful recruiters must have actual experience with medical specialists because doctors are often sheltered by their staffs. A second special problem is how or whether to offer compensation to participants. Emphasizing the opportunity to influence the thinking of medical or dental decision makers generally works better than emphasizing a gift for participating. However, gifts such as an American Express gift certificate or a sports watch are sometimes offered.

Successful focus groups for doctors should also be conducted at a facility that is convenient to the participants. Having healthy food and drink available and an authoritative, well-prepared moderator are viewed as essential to focus group success. The moderator must be especially sensitive to the fact that the term "marketing" is still something of a dirty word to some physicians, despite its widespread application in the profession.

Source: Murray Simon, DDS, D.R.S., "Physician Focus Groups Require Special Techniques," *Marketing News,* Jan. 30, 1987, pp. 22–23. Reprinted from *Marketing News,* published by the American Marketing Association.

purchases ratings and audience data from A. C. Nielsen Co., the sponsor is getting descriptive research data that will help it develop a more effective advertising program. As another example, Konica cameras come packaged with a registration card. The card requests the buyer to fill in facts about herself or himself and mail it in to the company. These cards tell the firm about the people who buy their cameras.

A third type of marketing research seeks to establish cause-and-effect relationships between marketing efforts and results. This causative or predictive research depends on the scientific method of experimentation. When Time, Inc. first thought about launching *Picture Week*, a splashy, fast-paced photo newsweekly, it ran extensive market tests in thirteen markets. On the basis of this experiment and subsequent market tests costing more than $15 million in total, Time decided against publishing the new magazine.

probability sampling

These tests are scientific in that they use principles of probability sampling. **Probability sampling** is the selection of items from a large group so that each member of the group has a known (and often an equal) chance of being selected. This sampling procedure permits the user to make conclusions about the larger group from the findings in the sampled group. Having used probability sampling in its market tests, Time, Inc. felt safe in deciding that the national market would not accept the new magazine.

MOTIVATION RESEARCH

Instead of finding out such facts as who the customers are, what they buy, when they buy, and the like, motivation research asks the question "why do they buy?" This approach assumes that what people buy often depends on complex motives that can be understood only by psychological probing. Experts in human motivation test a sample of people to find out the basis for their product choice. The researcher might try to find, for example, what a given brand name "means" to certain people. These researchers often use techniques borrowed from psychology to discover and understand consumer motives and/or attitudes. The idea is to design the "right" marketing mix for large groups of potential buyers—the mix that correctly interprets consumer behavior.

The big role of psychologists in marketing research is evident in The Vanderveer Group, Inc. ad. This firm specializes in the application of psychology to marketing and marketing research. Knowledge and skills from the field of psychology have helped marketers understand consumer behavior, attitudes, and motivation.

Consumer Behavior

consumer purchase decision models

In the effort to make correct marketing decisions, marketers have developed models of consumer decision making. **Consumer purchase decision models** are representations of the processes by which consumers arrive at a purchase. Well-conceived models include components that represent the consumer's environment, past experiences, and values

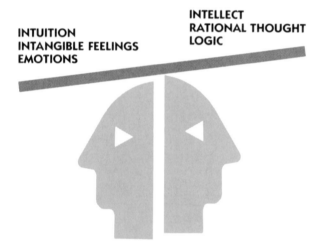

Knowledge of psychology can help marketers understand the consumers they are trying to reach.

and components that represent the search process, the purchase decision, and postpurchase behavior. Such models are generally of two kinds: programmed (habitual) and complex decision models. (See Figure 11-5.) The programmed or habitual purchase model is simple. It shows how the buyer first becomes aware of a need of some kind. In this case the buyer has learned from past experience that buying Product X satisfies this need. He or she (with little or no search or conscious analysis of the problem) then buys Product X.

When a consumer is confronted with a new need situation or a high-priced or otherwise very special purchase, the decision to buy is more complex. (See the right-hand side of Figure 11-5.) The buyer cannot resort to simple habitual buying. When the need appears, the buyer calls on his or her past experience, values, attitudes, and social and economic environment. The buyer then makes a search for products that might best fulfill the need and reaches an informed, rational decision to buy. Although it is not shown in the figure, the buyer might feel postpurchase uncertainty or alter some attitudes or values as a result of the purchase experience. Most buyer decisions tend to be in the programmed category. Otherwise, we would have to spend too

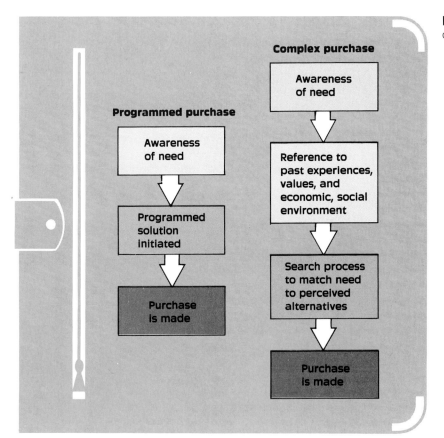

FIGURE 11-5 / Consumer decision models.

much of our time in buying decisions. It would take a week to get out of the supermarket!

Consumer models, which are often much more complex than the two we saw in Figure 11-5, help marketers by (1) forcing them to give more thought to their customers' buying processes, (2) identifying areas in which marketers need more information, and (3) providing a basis for segmenting markets. We turn now to the strategy of market segmentation.

Market Segmentation

mass market strategy

Some firms pursue a mass market strategy. A **mass market strategy** defines the target market as all potential buyers of brands in a product category. This strategy aims a common marketing strategy at an entire broad market. Mass market strategy is no longer common among large, well-known firms. Henry Ford used to practice it in the "Model T" days. Morton Salt practices it (more or less) today.

market segmentation

As the firm begins to understand the market better, it usually practices some form of market segmentation. **Market segmentation** is the strategy of breaking down the market into parts and applying a special marketing mix to each part that the firm wishes to serve. Profitable segmentation is based on an effective marketing research program. The idea is that within the general (mass) market for a product there is usually more than one set of needs to be satisfied. To improve its market position, a firm might aim several different marketing mixes at

The market share for Victoria's Secret lingerie shops is defined demographically along lines of sex, income, and age.

different market segments. Procter & Gamble designed Crest and Gleem toothpastes to appeal to different groups of customers.

In some cases, market planners focus on just one segment of a market. Holtzman's Little Folk specializes in children's apparel. Sometimes, a very specialized magazine is the ideal way to reach a particular segment. In Britain the magazine *Marxism Today* reaches "yummies" (young, upwardly-mobile Marxists) and advertises Karl and Groucho Marx T-shirts, boxer shorts bearing the logo of the Soviet airline Aeroflot, and other Communist Party novelty items.

To decide which means of segmentation to use, marketers must research the market and compute the cost of segmenting. Markets are often segmented on the basis of:

- Age
- Sex
- Race
- Income level
- Personality traits
- Geography
- Educational level
- Lifestyle

Facts about age, sex, income, and education are called the demographics of the target market. Many firms segment the market on the basis of a combination of demographics and personality and lifestyle differences among buyers. In Figure 11-6 a clothing manufacturer examined the demographic characteristics of age, sex, race, and urban or rural resi-

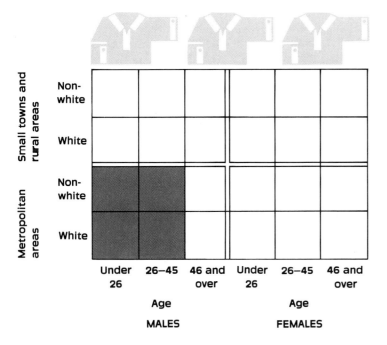

FIGURE 11-6 / Selecting market segments for sportswear.

dence to arrive at well-defined market segments. After studying past purchase behavior the marketing manager selected the segment made up of males under 46 years of age in all racial groups in metropolitan areas. Profitable segmentation requires knowledge of potential customer wants and behavior, changes in the makeup of the market, and what competitors are doing.

Consumerism

Questions about how well the marketing system creates or helps to create utilities and whether the marketing concept is really working are continually being raised. This brings us into the realm of consumerism.

As we saw in Chapter 2, U.S. consumerism is a movement started in the early 1900s to strengthen the power of individual buyers in the marketplace. It grew during the 1930s and helped to pass the Wheeler-Lea Act of 1938. This gave the federal government the power to prosecute firms for fraud in advertising and for other deception of consumers.

Throughout the 1960s and 1970s the consumer movement grew stronger and its list of objectives grew longer. Leadership in the movement has been provided primarily by Ralph Nader. Nader became well known in 1966 when he wrote *Unsafe at Any Speed*, a book criticizing General Motors and its Corvair automobile. By pointing out dangerous design defects in the Corvair, Nader succeeded in gathering public support throughout the country. With a broad base of support in Congress and good press coverage, the consumer movement got several important laws passed. The new laws gave consumers more protection in the areas of packaging, product safety, and information on consumer financing plans. Much of the "grass roots" support came from young people. Many young lawyers on the local and national levels worked to draw up and pass consumer laws. They, along with many ordinary consumers, have continued to put public pressure on businesses to become more consumer conscious.

Although the intensity of the consumer movement has diminished, its spirit is still alive in the form of improved safety and information. Marketing today is still influenced by the consumer movement.

A quick check of JC Penney's catalog will reveal several pages of consumer information. Among the subjects covered are credit and financing plans, product warranties, and how to save money on shipping costs. Information about product service and how to return merchandise as well as facts about the care and use of products are also included. Many manufacturers and retailers have a consumer affairs department to help improve communication between marketers and consumers. Quite often, the head of the department reports directly to the president of the company. To help consumers communicate quickly, Whirlpool Corporation has a toll-free "Cool-Line" that anyone can call for information or to register complaints about Whirlpool products.

Is the Marketing of Services Different?

As we saw in Chapter 2, ours is rapidly becoming a service economy. The consumer and industrial/organizational markets both demand increasing amounts of services. The work force is turning more and more to providing such services to earn a living. (See the What Do You Think? box.) The growth in services has called for a parallel growth in services marketing.

The basic concept of marketing is the same for services as it is for goods. However, as we will see in Chapters 12–14, the marketing of services usually demands a different kind of effort than does the marketing of goods. Marketing legal services, for example, is quite different from marketing breakfast cereals or computers. The reasons for this will become apparent in the following chapter when you have learned a bit more about the marketing mix.

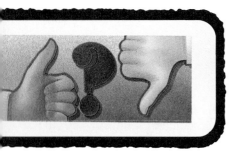

WHAT DO YOU THINK?

Will Manufacturers Turn to Services for Future Growth?

Two generations of marketers, executives, and business students have studied Theodore Levitt's article "Marketing Myopia" (*Harvard Business Review*, July–August 1960). Levitt showed how firms like the petroleum companies did not understand the business they were in—they focused on petroleum instead of energy needs. Railroads focused on railroads instead of transportation. These firms were myopic (shortsighted).

In the 1980s, marketing myopia still exists, according to Irving D. Canton. Some manu-facturers mistakenly try to develop product sales growth where little potential exists. Mr. Canton says that today's service-dominated economy offers a "way out" for firms facing low-growth markets for their manufactured products.

Some major firms have caught on. Digital Equipment Corp. gets about one-third of its revenues from computer maintenance services. Gerber Products, which dominates the no-growth baby foods market, is also building its future around its customers rather than its food technology. It has built upon its reputation by adding nonfood products and by developing a chain of Gerber Day Care Centers. General Motors Acceptance Corporation is providing an increasing share of GM's revenues—partly by moving into home mortage financing.

By buying RCA, General Electric invested in the growth of telecommunication services, selling what its technology does rather than just selling the technology itself. Owning RCA's NBC television network puts GE squarely into a growing service industry.

Will many more manufacturing firms overcome their present-day marketing myopia by finding an appropriate niche in today's service-hungry markets? What do you think?

Irving D. Canton, "Marketing Myopia Revisited," *Marketing News*, vol. 21, March 13, 1987, p. 1. Reprinted from *Marketing News*, published by the American Marketing Association.

Summary

The marketing functions are buying, selling, transporting, storing, standardization and grading, providing marketing information, risk taking, and financing. These functions may be performed by one firm or shared by groups of firms. Place utility, time utility, and ownership utility are added to products by the marketing process. Together with the form utility provided by production processes, these make products fully useful.

The marketing concept is the belief that a whole firm must be coordinated to serve the needs of its present and potential customers and to do so at a profit. When a firm adopts the marketing concept, it focuses its entire operation on customer satisfaction.

The marketing mix is the set of marketing strategies (promotion strategies, product strategies, price strategies, and distribution or place strategies) selected to implement the marketing concept—to reach and influence the target market. There are two major classes of target markets. Industrial/organizational markets are markets for goods or services that a firm or institution uses to produce another good or service. Consumer markets are markets for goods or services that people buy for their own use.

Marketing research is the application of the scientific method to marketing problems and opportunities. Two classes of data are collected by market researchers. Primary data is data originated and collected to solve a particular problem. Secondary data is data that was previously collected for other purposes but now used to solve a current marketing problem. Motivation research asks the question "why do they buy?" It studies complex motives for buying. Models of programmed and complex consumer purchasing processes help marketers understand and deal with the consumer's "reasons for" and ways of making purchases.

Marketers have generally approached markets either as a mass market or as different segments. The mass market is treated uniformly. When market segmentation is practiced, one or more of the parts (segments) of the mass market are approached in a special way, each with a different marketing mix. The basis for defining the segment or segments may be demographic (age, sex, income, etc.), by personality, by lifestyle, or according to other market characteristics.

Consumerism, a movement to declare and defend the rights of consumers, was especially strong in the 1960s. Its existence challenges marketers to apply the marketing concept within the constraints of consumer protection laws. Many firms have seen the benefits of building better consumer relations and better communication with their customers.

Review Questions

1. What is marketing and how has it changed in the twentieth century?

2. If a product has only form utility, is it useful to a customer? Why or why not?

3. Describe some of the features that distinguish the industrial/ organizational market from the market for consumer products.

4. Distinguish between primary and secondary sources of marketing data.

5. Distinguish among the exploratory, descriptive, and causative research designs.

6. Contrast the models of programmed and complex consumer purchase decisions.

7. Market segmentation can be accomplished on several bases. Name three of these and give an example of each.

Discussion Questions

1. Which marketing functions are related to the creation of place utility? Which are related to ownership utility? Explain your answers.

2. If a firm adopts and implements the marketing concept, all of its actions are oriented to the satisfaction of its target market. Is that desirable? Why or why not?

3. Why is marketing research necessary?

4. Two divergent views of the proper relationship between buyer and seller are "let the buyer beware" and "let the seller beware." Which is the more accurate view? Why?

Key Terms

marketing
marketing functions
form utility
place utility
time utility
ownership utility
marketing concept
marketing mix

target market
industrial/organizational markets
consumer market
marketing research
primary data
secondary data
research design

focus group interviews
probability sampling
consumer purchase decision models
mass market strategy
market segmentation

Cases

HOW DO YOU MARKET CABLE TV?

In the late 1970s and early 1980s, pay cable TV ventures like Home Box Office and Showtime/The Movie Channel were growing fast. But in early 1985, as movies became available on videocassette months before they appeared on pay networks, thousands of subscribers began to drop out every month. In early 1986 the number of customers of the major pay networks fell sharply.

Things turned around later in 1986 as HBO and the Disney Channel began strong promotional campaigns and registered a net growth for that year of 1.2 million subscribers (4.2 percent). Price cutting was also part of the marketing mix. This meant a drop in revenue per subscriber, according to industry analysts. New product offerings are also part of the marketing mix. This includes a "pay-per-view" service that allows a subscriber to buy a single movie or special sports event. The industry leaders have signed exclusive movie contracts with major studios and have added made-for-TV movies, series, and exclusive events such as boxing matches.

Another factor in the competitive situation is evidence of declining movie rentals among long-time VCR owners. Viewers are beginning to look at pay TV as a way of getting a lot of programming at relatively low rates rather than as a way to see the best movies right away.[3]

Questions
1. Have the major pay-TV firms fully embraced the marketing concept? Discuss.
2. Which marketing function or functions are most directly involved in the new marketing effort?
3. What is being exchanged when a subscriber signs with HBO?

KEEPING SMALL BANK CUSTOMERS HAPPY

The Foremost Bank & Trust Co. knows that keeping its customers happy is more important than ever before. Faced with growing competition from savings and loans and credit unions in the area, not to mention the opening of a new branch of the largest bank in the state, Foremost has started to think about marketing.

Among the strategies under consideration by Jack Barwinkel, Foremost's vice-president for marketing, are the following:

1. free checking for six months to all new customers,

2. an account warranty program in which the bank would pay $20 to any customer in whose checking account an error is made,

3. locating special drive-in only branches at the east and west ends of town, and

4. running a weekly "employee spotlight" ad on the local TV station featuring the bank employees who had received customer service awards during the past year.

Mr. Barwinkel was also considering the use of undercover "shoppers" to evaluate customer service and a new customer service survey to detect areas of client dissatisfaction.

Questions
1. Which of the four marketing strategies would you recommend and why?
2. How do each of the four mentioned strategies fit in with the marketing mix?
3. Should the marketing research under consideration be done before the strategy choice is made? Why or why not?
4. Is the research under consideration primary or secondary research?

TWELVE

Product and Pricing Strategies

LEARNING OBJECTIVES

After reading this chapter, you will be able to:

- Identify the "bundle of satisfactions" that a product offers to its user.

- Describe the life cycle of a product.

- List the advantages of broad and narrow product mixes.

- Describe the stages of new product development.

- Explain the difference between a brand and a trademark and how they are protected from imitation.

- Distinguish between demand and cost approaches to setting basic price.

- Explain the use of break-even analysis.

- Describe two possible pricing strategies for introducing a new product.

In this chapter we examine the roles of product and price in the marketing mix. We will start with a description of the types of consumer and industrial products. We will introduce the concept of the product life cycle and show how product strategies change during the product's life. We will also examine in detail the seven stages through which a firm goes in developing new products. This process includes designing products to appeal to specific market segments. We also will review the roles of packaging and branding and how trademarks and patents protect products.

The price element in the marketing mix is also given careful review. We will examine the cost approach and the demand approach to pricing as well as combinations of these approaches. We will see how breakeven analysis can be applied to pricing and will examine several kinds of discounts that may be applied to basic price.

The chapter closes with a discussion of the skimming and market penetration approaches to new product pricing strategy. We will also describe special retailing pricing devices, including markups and price lining.

It's a tough audience for a little kid. Forty business people are staring, pens poised. They are about to decide whether she is worth the $2 million her backers invested. She is Crystal Starr, a

5-1/2 inch doll that Hasbro, Inc. is introducing to analysts and toy store executives. It is the Christmas season, but she is being considered for introduction the following Christmas.

Crystal Starr is the central character in a line of dolls called "Moondreamers," which Hasbro spent two years developing. Creating a new toy isn't easy. Hasbro sifts through 4,000 ideas each year. It is a lengthy and expensive process to refine the best ideas, shave pennies off production costs, and cater to the interests of retailers.

The idea has to be exciting enough to catch the fancy of children. The idea for Moondreamers came from a Vermont illustrator. Hasbro liked the story line—a cast of characters called "Moon Beamers" who live in "Starry Up" and send dreams to children on earth. The theme also lent itself to another selling point: TV cartoons. "The trade now measures a product by its ability to have a cartoon show," says Stephen Schwartz, Hasbro's senior vice-president for marketing.

Going from sketches to models proved difficult. Little girls demand long hair on dolls, but the face had to be different from competitors. At first the models looked chubby, so they were slimmed down. They took four months to complete. The costumes took eight months to complete in bulk. Finally, confident that it had a winner after nearly a year of development, Hasbro gave a sneak preview of the five-doll line to four top toy retailers. The retailers were unimpressed.

Before giving up, Hasbro researchers visited two shopping malls in New York and New Jersey and interviewed 100 little girls and their mothers: 96 percent of the children said they would ask their mothers to buy Moondreamers, and 75 percent of their mothers said they would either definitely or probably buy them.

Hasbro then did more redesign work. It enlarged the line to nine dolls for more variety and, to give the product some real distinction, added glow-in-the-dark hair. This took seven months of work by staff chemists. A second preview drew a favorable response from retailers. The dolls went on sale at $7.99 each, somewhat less than the price on the new Mattel, Inc. line of minidolls.[1]

In the pages that follow, we will review the product strategies such as those pursued by Hasbro. We will see how products like Moondreamers evolve through the development process and how their life cycles are tracked. We will also examine pricing strategies such as Hasbro might have pursued.

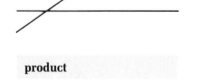

product

Product Strategies

The relationship between a firm and its customers focuses mainly on the product. The **product** component of the marketing mix is viewed as a "bundle of satisfactions," which might include a variety of things such as the warranty, the brand, the package, and the services that go with it. What a firm puts into its product to build buyer-perceived value depends in part on the changing values of the nation. The trend toward convenience and "instant gratification" in the United States, for example, leads producers to emphasize time-saving in their products' "bundle of satisfactions." Fast food restaurants, microwave ovens, and Domino's home-delivered pizza are only a few examples.

In 1987 the major U.S. auto manufacturers upgraded their warranties significantly. To help its sagging sales, General Motors upgraded its powertrain warranty from 3 years and 36,000 miles to 6 years and 60,000 miles. Ford and Chrysler soon followed suit. This made a significant improvement in the "bundle of services" perceived by buyers or potential buyers of U.S. cars.

A "product" can be a physical thing or good like the Hasbro Moondreamer dolls. Or it can be a service such as a reservation made by a travel agent or the excitement of Disney's "imagineering" as built into its Star Tours show. Or it can be, like the fast food restaurants, a combination of goods and services. Sometimes a product, like Sebastian's Thick Ends hair conditioner in the advertisement on page 348, consists of a very personal, glamour-oriented "bundle of services." It is the promise of glamour and sophistication that is being portrayed, not the chemical content of the conditioner.

Even in the case of a tangible appliance, such as a General Electric trash compactor, what is the buyer really buying? He or she is buying a physical object that consists of a motor, a steel casing, and other parts. This object will perform the function of compacting trash, but the total product is much more than the item itself. What about the benefits the buyer is getting? The product will reduce the number of trips the buyer must make to take out the trash. This provides the buyer with convenience and more time to spend at leisure. The retailer who sells the compactor is also a critical factor. The retailer offers a convenient location, parking, credit, a selection of products, its salespeople's expertise,

In the case of fashion goods, the bundle of satisfactions received depends on the buyer's personal taste and color preference.

The "bundle of services" offered by this ad is more than the tangible product.

a returned merchandise policy, and all the other things that attract customers. The enjoyment of shopping itself is for many customers an important part of the "bundle of satisfactions."

Classes of Products

In the previous chapter we noted that, for purposes of analysis, markets can be conveniently divided into two major classes: industrial/organizational and consumer markets. We will use the same scheme to classify products made for these two markets. In each of these markets we will further divide products into different classes and show how each subclass is marketed.

INDUSTRIAL/ORGANIZATIONAL PRODUCTS

Industrial/organizational products include:

- Installations—such as plants, office buildings, and land—and very expensive assets like cranes or mainframe computers
- Raw materials, such as cotton, iron ore, and lumber
- Accessory equipment, such as typewriters, accounting machines, and small forklift trucks
- Supplies, such as maintenance items (brooms and light bulbs), repair items (nuts and bolts to repair equipment), and operating supplies (lubricating oil and typewriter ribbons)
- Component parts and materials, such as tires, batteries, and steel beams
- Business services, such as uniform rental, security services, and cargo transportation

These goods have either narrow or broad target markets. The target depends on how widely the goods are used in industry. Many types of supplies (stationery and fuel), accessory equipment (typewriters), and services (legal assistance) are used by nearly all firms. On the other hand, most types of major equipment or installations, raw materials, and parts have a much narrower market. It is common practice in marketing some installations, for example, to build the product to the buyer's exact specifications. The Steelcase ad illustrates the marketing

Office furniture and equipment are industrial/organizational products with a broad target market.

of major equipment and accessory equipment to industrial/organizational markets.

CONSUMER PRODUCTS

Although many products are hard to classify, we can distinguish among four kinds of consumer products:

- Convenience goods
- Shopping goods
- Specialty goods
- Consumer services

A good, as we have seen, is tangible, while a service is not. Whether a specific good is a convenience good, a shopping good, or a specialty good depends on how often it is purchased, its significance to the buyer, and the buyer's preference for a specific brand. In other words, the classification depends on buyer behavior.

convenience goods

Convenience goods are items bought frequently, demanded on short notice, and often purchased by habit. Cigarettes and many foods and drugs are examples. These are usually low-priced products that people do not think much about when buying. Buyers do not make very careful price and quality comparisons.

shopping goods

Shopping goods are items that are taken seriously enough to require comparison and study. Most clothing, appliances, and cars fall into this category. Gifts are almost always shopping products. Stores that sell shopping goods are frequently grouped together, often in planned shopping centers, to help customers make price and quality comparisons.

specialty goods

Specialty goods are products for which strong conviction as to brand, style, or type already exists in the buyer's mind and that the buyer will make a great effort to locate and purchase. Usually, such products are high in value and are not purchased frequently. Examples are Leica cameras and Steinway pianos. For some customers, however, a can of soup could be a specialty product. It depends on the individual consumer's buying behavior. A certain item (a shirt, for example) could be classed in three different ways by three different people. However, this classification system works because many consumers behave alike when buying a given good. Marketers can classify most products in the way that most consumers classify them and act accordingly.

How a firm classifies a product influences the way in which it is marketed. A manufacturer that classifies its product as a convenience good will want it sold in as many places as possible. Coke, Wrigley's gum, and Marlboro cigarettes are available in countless supermarkets, drugstores, and vending machines. If the product is viewed as a shopping good, it is likely to be placed in stores that are near other stores that sell similar items. A typical consumer shopping for a new TV wants to be able to compare Zenith, Sony, RCA, and so on. A specialty good's manufacturer worries less about retail location. For example, there are relatively few Rolls-Royce dealerships. A consumer who wants to buy a Rolls-Royce is generally willing to make a special effort to find a dealer, even if the dealer is several hundred miles away. Since

TABLE 12-1 / **Classes of consumer goods**

	Convenience	**Shopping**	**Specialty**
How far will a buyer travel?	Short distance	Reasonable distance	Long distance
How much does it cost?	Usually low-priced	Usually middle- to high-priced	Usually high-priced
How often purchased?	Frequently	Occasionally	Infrequently
Emphasis on comparison?	No	Yes	No
Purchased habitually?	Often	Not usually	Not usually
Which advertising media?	Television, newspapers, and general magazines	Television, newspapers, and general magazines	Special-interest magazines and catalogs

specialty buyers will go out of their way to locate the product, the firm's distribution is simplified. Table 12-1 summarizes the features of the classes of consumer goods.

In summary, consumer goods producers try to put themselves in the mind of the buyer to figure out how most buyers classify a product. This is an application of the marketing concept. It makes it more likely that the marketing effort will be truly matched to what consumers want.

Consumer services, because they are intangible, cannot be stored. They are directly dependent on the skills of the service giver. These two facts affect the way in which most services are marketed. The intangibility means that they are often marketed directly rather than through retailers or wholesalers. Because services are based on personal skills, much of the product quality depends on training. Evidence of such training is important to customers. Mr. Goodwrench is perceived as a well-trained specialist in car repair. A Chartered Life Underwriter (CLU) is perceived as a well-trained specialist in life insurance matters. Services may also be seen as convenience products (such as a laundromat), shopping products (such as a microcomputer repair shop) or specialty products (such as an exclusive resort).

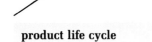

product life cycle

The Product Life Cycle

The life history of a product is called the **product life cycle.** The cycle has four phases: introduction, growth, maturity, and decline. Figure 12-1 (on p. 352) shows a typical life cycle for a product. The microwave

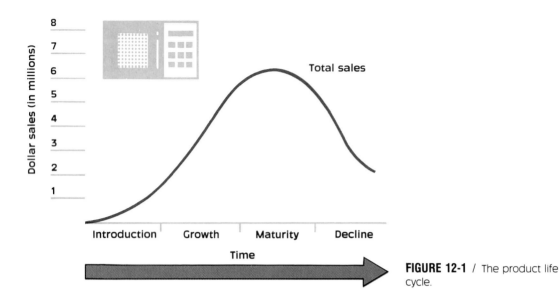

FIGURE 12-1 / The product life cycle.

oven has not yet reached the decline stage, but it has probably entered the maturity stage. Both product classes and individual brands of products have life cycles. The brand's lifetime is shorter than that of the product class. People still drive cars (product class), but they can no longer buy Edsels, DeSotos, and Packards (brands). Let us examine the four phases of the cycle.

INTRODUCTION

The first phase of the product life cycle is the most critical. The marketer's basic goal is to gain initial market acceptance of the new product. This requires a strong promotion effort to create awareness and interest in the target market. It also requires careful initial pricing and strong distribution in the right places. It is essential to use marketing research to monitor customer reaction. On the average, only about one of twenty new products is successful. During a product's introductory stage, sales volume is relatively low.

GROWTH

If a new product has been introduced with success, sales will increase rapidly during the growth stage. Customers who first bought the product in the introduction stage may be making repeat purchases, and additional customers begin buying as well. Notice in Figure 12-1 the steep increase in the sales curve that occurs in the growth stage of the cycle. On the negative side, competitors and prospective competitors are now really taking notice of the product's success and might already (depending on patent protection, complexity of production facilities needed to compete, and financial and distribution strength) have begun to produce and sell a competing product.

MATURITY

Sales volume begins to level off and decline in the maturity stage, which is usually the longest part of the cycle. By now, many rival brands are on the market. Rivals often copy features of successful brands, so the various brands tend to become very similar. Once the market is saturated (nearly everyone in the target market has bought a similar product), the profit potential for all competing brands begins to fall. Tagamet, an anti-ulcer drug produced by SmithKline Beckman Corp., once had 100 percent of the market. In 1983 a competing brand, Zantac, was introduced by London-based Glaxo Holdings, PLC, and Tagamet's market share dropped to 70 percent.[2]

Many marketers try to extend the lives of their profitable brands. Procter & Gamble added calcium to their Citrus Hill juice as a feature that would extend the popularity of the brand. Coca-Cola Company responded with its own calcium-added Minute Maid product.

DECLINE

Marketers usually cut back on promoting a product near the end of its maturity stage. This is the time when a better product appears or a need disappears and the old product begins to decline. Owing to constantly changing technology, many products enter their decline stage quickly. One video game may be replaced by another in a matter of months. Products that have entered the decline stage of their life cycles include home movie cameras, which have been replaced by videocameras. Many pager or "beeper" systems are being replaced by cellular telephone devices.

Sometimes, even after a product or brand is discontinued, it makes a comeback. Everyone knows about the return of the original Coca-Cola formula under the name "Coca-Cola Classic." There are many other examples. General Motors found enough public attachment to and interest in the Nova (discontinued in 1980) that it revived the brand as the first auto to be made by a GM-Toyota joint venture. Warner-Lambert has brought back three chewing gum brands that had disappeared in the mid-1970s. Blackjack, Clove, and Beemans gums were returned to production because of emotional letters from many former customers.[3]

technological obsolescence

fashion obsolescence

planned obsolescence

An existing product or service suffers obsolescence when it is no longer as desirable or as useful as it once was. **Technological obsolescence** is what happens when someone invents something that works better than the existing product. The compact disc, for example, is replacing other audio recording forms. **Fashion obsolescence** occurs when a firm designs something that people feel is prettier or "more stylish" than an existing product. The rug colors and designs in the Couristan ad (on p. 354) are subject to fashion obsolescence. All of these product improvements are planned by someone else. However, a firm practices **planned obsolescence** when it produces something new that replaces its own existing product, making it obsolete. A manufacturer's research and development (R&D) efforts often have the side

Reflections

Every choice you make in your home's design is a reflection of you. Choose from Couristan's wide selection of traditional and textured contemporary area rugs for the right touch in every room. Timeless Treasures for your home from Couristan.

The contemporary Seville "Jewel-Tone Design," in the foreground, complements the Oriental design Kashimar "Antique Sun Design," in the rear.

CREATIVE ELEGANCE IN AREA RUGS AND FINE BROADLOOM
A TRUSTED NAME SINCE 1926

PURE WOOL PILE

See our wide selection of area rugs at your authorized Couristan dealer or send $4 for our Kashimar catalog and Seville brochure to:
Couristan, Inc., Dept. CH 9-86, 919 Third Ave., New York, NY 10022

Changing fashions in home design lead to the marketing of new styles and colors of items like area rugs.

effect of contributing to the obsolescence of the firm's own existing product or the product of a competitor.

Regardless of the type of obsolescence—technological or fashion—a product that is no longer purchased is obsolete. As we have seen, a firm spends money on R&D to improve its product so that it will not become obsolete. Sometimes R&D leads to an entirely new product that makes the old one obsolete. In 1987, Compaq Computer Corporation introduced three new models of its Deskpro 286 that it claimed were 50 percent faster than most competitors in its class. Compaq was the first major computer supplier to incorporate the new, faster, 80286 Intel Corp. microchip. Existing Compaq models and those of competitors were made relatively obsolete by this dramatic upgrade in computer speed.[4]

The Product Mix—Broad or Narrow?

product mix

A manufacturer's or a retailer's **product mix** is the array of products it produces or sells. General Mills produces hundreds of different types of products, while Coca-Cola produces a much smaller number. The breadth of the product mix affects how a firm does its marketing.

First of all, there is safety in numbers. A firm with a broad product mix has a kind of insurance against the dangers of obsolescence. Also, economies of scale (lower costs per unit as volume rises) often make the difference between success and failure. A firm with many products can spread its overhead cost over the entire product mix. This means savings in production costs if the products are manufactured in the same factory, especially when the products share much of the same machinery in their manufacture.

Eastman Kodak Co. has broadened its product mix considerably in recent years. In 1986 alone it added 100 new products, including new automatic 35 mm cameras, new films, batteries, blood-analysis tests, electronic publishing systems, and many others. Campbell Soup Co. has also broadened its product mix greatly with the addition of Prego spaghetti sauce, Le Menu frozen dinners, the Fresh Chef line of refrigerated soups, Great Starts frozen breakfasts, L'Orient oriental dinners, and Fresh Express packaged snacks, among others.

A broader product mix can also cut unit distribution cost. A firm can save on distribution costs by using the same salespeople or transportation system for many of the products in its mix. Thus Kodak's or

A shoe store like this has a narrow product mix but great depth in its variety of styles, colors, and sizes available.

Broad mix

Spreads the
overhead cost

Good chance of
other product
exposure and sale

Narrow mix

Creates image
of a specialist

Campbell's salespeople can represent many products when they call on customers. The company can ship in larger, more economical quantities, especially when larger numbers of products are sold through similar distribution networks. More of this will be explained in Chapter 14.

At the retail level and, to some extent, at the wholesale level, firms with many products (a broad product mix) have an advantage in the form of product exposure. A shopper who goes to Montgomery Ward to buy a computer game might see children's clothing and household products as well. He or she might purchase some of these other products. In a more specialized store such as Radio Shack this is less likely to happen. A store with a narrow mix can enjoy some advantages, however. Such a store tends to have great depth in its product mix. A shopper can buy only electronics and related products at Radio Shack, but there is a much greater variety of electronics at Radio Shack than at Montgomery Ward. Radio Shack projects an image as an electronics specialist. On the other hand, the wider product mix of a department store like Montgomery Ward or Macy's also allows the store to spread rent, insurance, and utilities costs over many, many types of products. Figure 12-2 summarizes the advantages of broad and narrow product mixes.

New Product Development

The way in which a firm conceives of and introduces its new products has a great influence on its marketing. We have looked in some detail at the way Hasbro developed the Moondreamer dolls. Other firms, particularly those whose products are not so fashion-oriented, might not be quite so cautious. The product type, the size of the firm, and the number of products it already has can alter the pattern of the development process. As the Burger King capsule (on p. 358) shows, successful firms devote much analysis to new product development.

What follows, however, is a general outline of the process that firms go through with new products. Figure 12-3 shows one view of the stages of product development. After each stage, either a "go" or a "no-go" decision is made. The firm must decide at each point whether it is profitable to continue with the product development process.

IDEA GENERATION

New product development starts with generating new product ideas. Hasbro got the Moondreamer doll idea from a professional illustrator outside of the firm. Some firms benefit by forming committees whose job it is to generate ideas. The committee might use brainstorming techniques. Sometimes an idea is a spin-off from the firm's ongoing research activities. Sometimes an alert marketing staffer comes across someone else's new invention and discovers that the rights to it are available for purchase. Sometimes an idea comes from a salesperson or from a customer.

SCREENING

The next stage is screening. Often, outside consultants appraise the new idea. They look carefully at the cultural, economic, and technological environments. They also look at the firm's special capabilities to see which ideas seem to match them. They might also rely on consumer

FIGURE 12-3 / The new product development process.

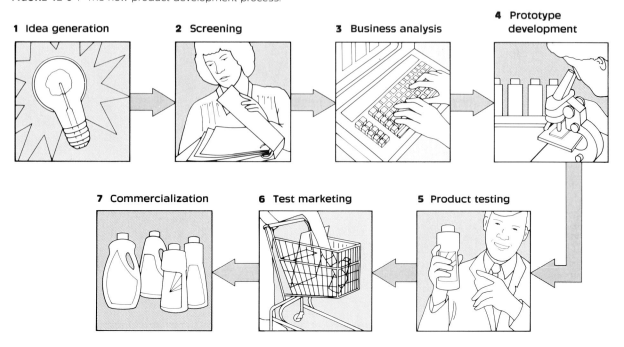

New products are the life blood of a company like Burger King. But if you think creating new products is mostly a creative task, you are wrong, according to an executive who has been involved with new products and consumer promotions for Burger King Corporation. "Companies like Burger King have no problem generating dozens of new product ideas every week," he says. "Everyone suggests them, from the people in new product development to those in marketing and marketing research, the managers and assistant managers, and sometimes even crew members in the restaurants. Everyone, in other words, always has some idea for a new product.

"The trick to effective new product development is to analyze a potential product to determine whether it is practical and whether it will be successful. You want a practical product, one that your crew members can serve without upsetting the smooth functioning of the restaurant. Of course, you also want a product that will be welcomed by consumers."

A great deal of analysis therefore goes into each new product and product move. For example, before Burger King Corporation switched from Coke to Pepsi several years ago, it analyzed how much time would be wasted telling customers who asked for Coke that only Pepsi was now served. Burger King even uses a computer to predict how much labor any new product will require and to consider matters such as supplier availability and price stability for any new ingredients.

Burger King's introduction of french toast sticks is a good example of how the company tries to fill a need with a new product. Lots of people like french toast for breakfast, but convenience and speed are very important for breakfast foods. Since most of the breakfast trade at a Burger King® restaurant comes through the drive-through window, a person who orders the french toast has to be able to eat it "on the run." How to do that? By producing french toast sticks, of course, instead of square pieces of french toast that have to be cut with a fork or knife.

Lots of testing goes into a new Burger King product before it is finally introduced nationwide. First, the concept is tested with a small focus group of consumers, often using just a picture. Then the concept is refined, and an actual product is tested at various prices. This helps Burger King Corporation assess the marketability of the product as well as whether it is practical to produce it in the restaurants. At the same time, various marketing and advertising strategies are being tested for the product to determine the best way to market it. Only after it has been fully tested is the product introduced.

Does this careful analysis always work? Most often it does, but sometimes problems do pop up. For example, several years ago, when Burger King introduced its new bagel breakfast, it had to add additional suppliers when the product's popularity made it impossible for one supplier to keep up with the demand. However, by and large, this careful process of screening and analyzing potential products helps to ensure not only that products are practical, but also that all Burger King restaurants have a stream of the right products to attract new customers.

Questions

1. What should the staff in charge of new products and consumer promotions do to maximize the usefulness to Burger King Corporation of all the new product ideas that are being generated?

2. Develop some useful criteria or guidelines for screening new product ideas at Burger King Corporation.

3. How might breakeven analysis be useful to Burger King Corporation?

opinion. Prospective customers might help to screen a new idea. Customers might be surveyed or interviewed in focus groups—small groups in informal settings—to get their honest reactions to the product idea. Often, a product concept test is used. The product is described in detail to potential users, who give their reaction to it.

BUSINESS ANALYSIS

Next is business analysis of the idea. This is the job of the cost accountants, the engineers, and the computer model builders. They help forecast profitability. Forecasting models might consider the effects of the new idea on the existing product line, the sales force, middlemen, and other parts of the marketing mix.

PROTOTYPE DEVELOPMENT

The next stage is the production of a working model of the product—a *prototype*. The prototype can be used in subsequent stages of development and can help determine the best method of production in volume as well as estimates of large-scale production costs. The Hasbro Moondreamer doll prototypes, as discussed at the beginning of the chapter, served several useful development functions.

PRODUCT TESTING

Once the prototype has been made, the product can be subjected to product testing. Typical prospective buyers are given the product to use under normal conditions and asked to comment. Their ideas are examined to see whether they should be incorporated into the final version for test marketing.

TEST MARKETING

With many of the "bugs worked out," the product can be produced in limited quantities for test marketing. Test marketing brings the product into selected stores in test markets under normal conditions. Sales results serve as the measure of success for the new product. By this stage, many of the pricing, promotion, and distribution ideas must also have been developed. Although many large firms use test marketing regularly, there are cases in which, to save time as well as the heavy cost, this stage is skipped. Sara Lee Corporation introduced a new line of fruit muffins in 1986 without test marketing for fear that any delay would lose them market share to the established Pepperidge Farm brand and a new toaster muffin introduced by Pillsbury Company. How long that type of muffin would remain popular was of some concern to Sara Lee.[5]

COMMERCIALIZATION

At each of the preceding stages the firm has made a go/no-go decision. If all of this works, then the final stage of commercialization is reached.

This means that the product is produced and marketed on a full commercial scale.

Packaging

All the elements that make up the broad concept of "product" must be considered in developing the product mix. Among these is the package. In recent years, packaging has become a more important part of the product. Packaging does several things:

- Protects the product
- Divides the product into convenient units
- Becomes part of the product
- Facilitates storage and transportation
- Helps with promotion

Think of how polyethylene packaging protects thousands of food and clothing items sold in self-service stores! The egg carton and the plastic six-pack holder allow convenient unitizing. Despite ecologists'

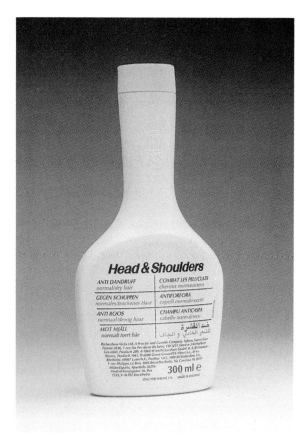

The "Eurobottle" containing Head & Shoulders shampoo helps to promote the product by conveying a sales message in several languages.

concern for its impact on the quality of life (see the What Do You Think? box), plastic packaging has come to play a major role in modern marketing.

Another packaging development is the aseptic package. Made of layers of polyethylene, foil, and paper, it keeps milk and other liquids fresh without refrigeration for months. With the development of a range of shapes and sizes, the aseptic package has been used for baby food, milk, soup, and applesauce as well as juice drinks. It eliminates refrigeration costs, takes little shelf space, and is easy to handle. The general public, however, has not fully accepted this packaging breakthrough because they do not see or understand its benefits compared to the more traditional cans and bottles.[6]

WHAT DO YOU THINK?
Is Modern Plastic Packaging Worth the Ecological Risk?

It is convenient, versatile, shatterproof, lightweight, and extremely cost-effective. Plastic packaging has revolutionized the way in which many products are sold. It fits in beautifully with self-service, reduces in-transit breakage, and lets the buyer see the product when that is important. It can be produced in any shape and color, and it is very durable.

Its durability, unfortunately, is also one of its most negative features from the ecological point of view. Plastic packaging has become a nightmare for ocean life, and evidence has shown that some forms could have harmful effects on humans and other land animals. The federal Office of Technology Assessment (OTA) has concluded that tens of thousands of sea birds and about 100,000 marine mammals die each year because of plastic debris. The plastic is eaten and often induces suffocation in sea turtles and birds. Other forms of foam packaging (which is plastic-based) have proven harmful to the earth's ozone layer. Many forms of plastic packaging also present significant litter control problems for urban areas. Most forms are not biodegradable, and only a little more than 1 percent is ever recycled.

To combat the problems with plastic packaging, eight bills had been introduced in Congress by the end of 1987. These included a bill that was intended to control the discharge of plastic wastes by ships at sea. The State of New York and other northeastern and western states have enforced laws against nonbiodegradable packaging.

Some progress has been made by packaging firms. Eco-Plastics of Toronto has produced Ecolyte, which turns to dust after 60 days of exposure to sunlight. A Swedish firm has produced a plastic-aluminum can called LETPAK, which can be easily incinerated.

The importance of plastic packing to many forms of marketing is obvious. It seems to be growing in importance. And yet the dangers that it poses for society, especially in the ecology, are very serious ones. Is modern plastic packaging worth the ecological risk? What do you think?

Source: Diane Schneidman, "Plastic: Progress and Peril," *Marketing News*, vol. 21, Dec. 18, 1987, pp. 1, 6–7. Reprinted from *Marketing News*, published by the American Marketing Association.

A similar improvement in food preservation, but one that is less obvious to the customer, is "modified atmosphere" packaging, which involves regulating the air flow around fruits and vegetables to slow or speed their ripening in transit. This and genetic improvements in fresh vegetables and other technology have reduced the need for refrigeration.

The way that a product is packaged for consumer use influences the larger, case-size unit for shipping. The Container Corporation of America has developed two new concepts. One is STACCA, a vertical, displayable tray concept with a reinforced cornerpost for vertical load-bearing strength twice that of regular slotted containers. These trays can be stacked higher and straighter on the pallet, with little danger of bursting, warping, or falling over. The other concept is called SECCA-PRINT. It provides a sharper printed image and better color on the corrugated box. Both make for excellent store displays.[7]

When products are shown on TV, the package is shown up close, and the product's brand is featured prominently on the package. This helps the shopper to remember the ad and to focus on the specific packaged product in the supermarket or other self-service store. Brands are an important part of marketing all by themselves.

Branding

brand

A **brand** is "a name, term, symbol, or design, or combination of them which is intended to identify the goods or services of one seller or group of sellers and to differentiate them from those of competitors."[8]

A successful brand makes a lasting impression in customers' minds. A brand name should be distinctive and easy to remember. What lends a brand name good "memory value" are simplicity, familiarity, a pleasant sound, and some association with the product's function. Memory value makes the brand name work better as a kind of "mental bridge" between advertising and the self-service store. It also aids word-of-mouth product endorsement.

Brand names like Coke, Jell-O, Jeep, Scotch Tape, Styrofoam, Vaseline, Formica, and Xerox are so widely known that many people think they are generic words that describe a product category. Actually, they are brand names, and their owners go to great lengths to protect them as such. Federal Express does not want "Let's Federal Express it!" to become the same in people's minds as "Let's ship it!"—even though that would indicate a high degree of consumer acceptance. The reason is that once the brand name becomes generally accepted as representing the product type, the protection of the name from imitation might be endangered.

manufacturer brands

Brands that are owned by manufacturers are called **manufacturer brands** or national brands. All of the preceding examples are manufacturer brands. Brands also play a role in the marketing strategy of wholesalers and retailers. Brands developed by middlemen are called **distributor brands** or *private brands*. Sears's Kenmore appliances and Craftsman tools are examples. They are produced by other firms for

distributor brands

Sears. Large grocery chains also have private brands. Firms generally make a larger profit per unit on private brands. To improve their image, stores like Montgomery Ward & Co. and Kmart are now offering more well-known manufacturer brands. Names like Michelin and Maytag are found in Montgomery Ward stores, for example.

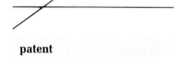

Patents and Trademarks

patent

Legal protection is available for products and brands. A **patent** protects from imitation an invention, a chemical formula, or a new way of doing something. A patent makes it very hard for a competitor to copy the new product or new idea for a period of seventeen years. The United States Patent Office accepts applications for patents. If an idea is "patentable," it is registered and protected. The STACCA packaging concept by the Container Corporation of America is a good example.

trademark

The patent office also protects trademarks. A **trademark** is a characteristic symbol or a style of lettering of a brand name that is registered with the U.S. Patent Office. Once the trademark is accepted by the patent office, it is protected for a period of twenty years and can be extended for like periods indefinitely. The name Toys "Я" Us has been imitated by many firms. The firm has fought off infringement of its name each time and has always won the legal battle under the federal trademark law. Pools Я Us, Skates Я Us, Films Я Us, and many others have tried and failed to cash in on the recognition value of the established brand.[9]

Pricing Strategies

price

Although advertising gets the most attention of all the marketer's competitive tools, price still plays a large role. However well-designed a product might be, it will not sell unless it is priced effectively. The **price** element in the marketing mix means the dollar cost per unit that buyers must pay, as well as the terms or conditions of sale that accompany price. The pricing strategy of a firm starts with setting basic price. The strategy might be quite different from firm to firm.

Setting Basic Price

Many firms establish specific pricing objectives, such as maximizing profit or achieving a given market share. Guided by such objectives, firms set a basic price for each product. We will examine two major approaches to the problem of setting basic price: the cost approach and the demand approach (see Figure 12-4 on p. 364). Then we will see how some firms combine these two approaches.

Cost approach

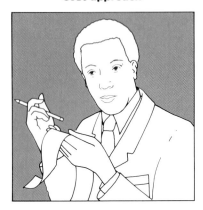

This seller is cost conscious. He builds up a price for what he is selling. He adds all the costs—manufacturing, transporting, dealer margins, etc., and a profit.

Demand approach

This seller wants to sell! She examines the market and estimates the quantity demanded for the product at various prices—with an eye on her competitors.

FIGURE 12-4 / Two approaches to price.

THE COST APPROACH

markup

The cost approach to setting basic price involves building unit selling prices on the basis of cost. This approach is simple when the cost of one unit is easy to identify. A **markup** is an addition or add-on to cost to reach a selling price. It is usually expressed as a percentage. The manager of a small discount clothing store uses a percentage markup applied to unit costs for an item or group of items. Thus the store might buy 100 suits at $80 each and apply a 50 percent markup on cost, resulting in prices of $120 per item for the customers (150 percent of $80). This same percentage markup might be applied to all items in the store. If so, the basic price policy is a very simple one with a cost basis. Demand factors in this case influence markups only in an indirect way.

Manufacturers who sell to governments often use cost-based pricing, sometimes called cost-plus pricing, because the law requires it. This approach allows the contracting firm to cover its cost of production and to make a certain profit. Some small defense contractors deal exclusively with the federal government. In such cases the firm's pricing could be entirely dictated by government contract pricing specifications.

BREAKEVEN ANALYSIS

breakeven analysis

Breakeven analysis is the computation of a price-quantity combination at which a firm covers its fixed and variable costs. It can be demonstrated in mathematical or graphical (chart) form. Figure 12-5 illustrates the breakeven chart for a firm that sells its product at $100 per unit. The total sales revenue line shows the price per unit times the number of units sold. Each time sales increase by ten units, total reve-

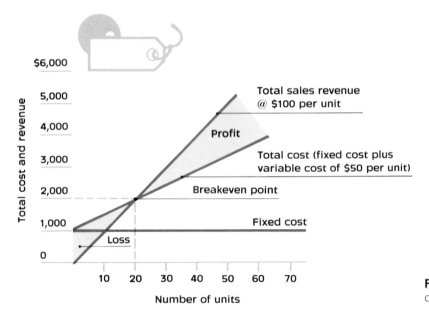

FIGURE 12-5 / A breakeven chart.

nue increases by $1,000. On the same chart there are two cost lines: one for fixed costs and one for total (fixed plus variable) costs. *Fixed costs*, often called overhead, are expenses that remain the same regardless of the number of items produced. Overhead expenses often include rent and fire insurance premiums. In the example, these fixed costs amount to $1,000. *Variable costs* are expenses that change as the number of units produced and sold changes. Raw materials and labor costs, for example, rise as the volume of units produced rises. In the example, each additional unit produced and sold costs $50 above and beyond the fixed cost. The total cost line therefore begins at the left side of the chart at $1,000 (zero production) and slopes up to the right at a rate of $50 per unit of added production. At twenty units, total costs equal $2,000; at sixty units, total costs equal $4,000.

At the level of twenty units of production the cost and revenue lines cross. This is the breakeven point, the production level beyond which the firm begins to make a profit. For each unit produced and sold beyond this breakeven point the firm realizes an increase of $50 in profits. This is so because unit revenue minus unit variable cost ($100 − $50) equals $50.

A breakeven chart can help a manager decide several things. It can help a manager decide whether to install expensive new machines that would change the production cost structure. It can help to set prices or to decide whether to buy or to lease a plant. A retailer could also use such a chart to make similar decisions. Without the use of a breakeven chart you can compute the breakeven point (*BP*) by dividing total fixed cost (*TFC*) by the difference between unit revenue, or price (*P*), and unit variable cost (*VC*):

$$BP = \frac{TFC}{(P - VC)}$$

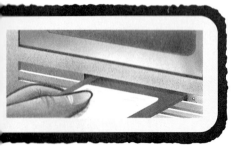

THE ELECTRONIC AGE
The Airlines Can Fine Tune Their Ticket Prices

Airline fare wars used to send executives and securities analysts diving for the trenches—and travelers grabbing for their suitcases. But it is not so simple anymore. Using high-tech planning, airlines can now manage fare cuts to selectively broaden the market for empty seats.

The new computer pricing approach is called "yield management." It requires sophisticated software and sophisticated humans to handle it. TWA's computer-system subsidiary, PARS, monitors the fares of competitors and creates pricing scenarios on a flight-by-flight basis that predict the ef-

fect of fare adjustments on TWA's bottom line.

Similarly, at any moment, Continental's computer is monitoring the status of reservations on 495,000 future flights. The computers measure bookings against expectations and call attention to any flight that is off the normal pace, depending on the season, flight time, cities being served, day of the week, and whether a predominantly leisure or business market is being served. Fares and advertising can then be revised.

The more scientific system for setting prices should result in less erratic profits for airlines. It will also mean bargain fares that are temporary and harder for travelers to predict, depending on passenger loads on specific routes, days of the week, and times of the day.

The Friday afternoon flight from New York to Boston, for

instance, might have only a dozen reservations a week before departure, but a computer-generated history predicts that most reservations on the route will be made on the day of departure. Therefore few discount seats are made available. On the other hand, the off-season midweek flight from Houston to London could be filled almost entirely with discounted seats to draw leisure travelers who might not otherwise travel.

For the airlines this revolutionary new use of computers could mean more predictable—and higher—profits.

Source: Paulette Thomas, "Computers Permit Airlines to Use Scalpel to Cut Fares," *The Wall Street Journal*, Feb. 2, 1987, p. 27. Reprinted by permission. © Dow Jones & Company, Inc., 1987. All rights reserved.

THE DEMAND APPROACH

The demand approach to pricing requires the seller to think like the buyer. It focuses on the buyer and his or her possible reaction to price changes. More precisely, it estimates the demand curve, which, as we noted in Chapter 2, consists of the various amounts that buyers will buy at each of a range of prices. The demand approach to pricing involves estimating the true demand curve and focusing on the buyer psychology that underlies the curve.

The DeBeers ad suggests that this diamond-seller employs the demand approach to pricing. The ad headline says "two months' salary may seem like a lot at first. Until you divide it by forever." This eliminates the shock of the high dollar-and-cents price of an engagement ring by putting it in the context of the lifetime significance of the purchase.

An understanding of what the product means to the buyer is crucial to the demand approach to pricing.

Elasticity of demand is computed by dividing the percentage change in quantity demanded that occurs when price is changed by the percentage change in price itself. If, when a price is raised by 10 percent, the quantity demanded changes by more than 10 percent, the demand is said to be *elastic*. If the quantity demanded changes less than 10 percent, the demand is said to be *inelastic*. If a selling firm estimates that demand for the product is elastic, it might set the price very low. If, on the other hand, the firm presumes demand to be inelastic, it might set the price higher. In recent years, major law firms' fees have been rising rapidly, partly because many firms found that their clients were not very sensitive to higher fees when major legal problems arose. The demand for legal services (at least among upper-income consumers) is relatively inelastic.[10]

The concept of a customary price is important in understanding the demand approach to pricing. The classic example of a customary price was the nickel candy bar. Candy makers resisted raising this price for many years despite increases in their production costs. Of course, the cost increases eventually became too great, and the price had to be increased. There is also a customary difference between branded items and their unbranded (generic) equals. Ingles Supermarkets, for example, carry soups, canned milk, and many other food products in unbranded (generic) containers as well as these same products with national brands such as Campbell's and Borden's. Buyers expect the prices of the generics to be lower than the prices of the branded items.

COMBINED APPROACHES

Many firms set prices by using elements of both the cost and demand approaches. They examine the net profit effect of various prices—the effects on revenue as well as unit profit. Breakeven charts at different prices may be used to help in such analysis. Some firms use a technique borrowed from economic theory called *marginal analysis*. This technique helps a firm to estimate the most profitable combination of price and quantity to employ. It is a relatively simple version of a complex pricing tool called a pricing model. A **pricing model** is a mathematical equation or set of equations that takes into account all of the important factors in a pricing situation to help decide on the "best possible" price. Past experience in pricing and knowledge of market conditions help to determine the equation that best predicts pricing results. Experience and knowledge are essential for the successful use of pricing models. Still, no matter how carefully pricing is done, firms can make major errors in judging buyers' reactions to price changes. The airlines have made some headway in using such models to price tickets in recent years.

pricing model

Discounts

The specific prices a manufacturing firm actually charges often vary from the basic or "list" price. Such variations generally result from an established discount policy. Discounts from "list" prices are granted for a number of reasons. For instance, a **cash discount** is a reduction in price as a reward for prompt payment in full. A **trade position discount** allows special pricing for customers based on their position in the

cash discount
trade position discount

When airlines give frequent flyer discounts, they are giving cumulative quantity discounts to passengers.

functional discount

quantity discount

channel of distribution. A wholesaler would pay less than a retailer, and a retailer would pay less than a household consumer.

A **functional discount** is a discount that is granted to a customer in return for services rendered. A retail grocer, for example, may receive a discount or allowance from a manufacturer if the grocer features the firm's brand in local newspaper ads. Some people feel that this practice is not really a discount but rather a simple purchase of a service. Such a discount could also be called a *promotional allowance*.

Still another common discount is the **quantity discount,** which means granting lower prices to those who buy larger quantities. Some quantity discounts are *cumulative*. This means that the quantity used for figuring the discount is accumulated over time. The frequent flyer programs offered by many airlines are a kind of cumulative quantity discount. The Acme supermarkets in Philadelphia are mimicking this strategy by giving "frequent buyer" credits toward the purchase of luxury products. Customers may save their cash register receipts and use them to obtain a set of quality china, for example, at a bargain price. When a discount depends on the amount of one single purchase, it is called a *noncumulative quantity discount*. A firm's discount policy makes its pricing more flexible in special competitive situations. Table 12-2 (on p. 370) shows how some of these discounts are computed.

TABLE 12-2 / **Examples of discounts**

Cash discount	The Smith Insurance Agency receives a bill for $1,000 from Walter Stationery Supplies, Inc. with payment terms of 2/10, net /30. A cash discount of 2/10, net /30 means that the full price is due within 30 days of the invoice date. But Smith Insurance is entitled to a 2 percent discount if payment is received within 10 days, which is 20 days earlier than the due date. If Smith pays the bill in 30 days, it is like paying 36 percent interest per year, because there are 18 twenty-day periods in a year (18 × 2 percent = 36 percent). Even if Smith has to borrow money at 20 percent, it will pay them to take the cash discount.
Quantity discount	A quantity discount is based on the quantity of merchandise a buyer buys from a seller. There are two types: noncumulative and cumulative.
Noncumulative quantity discount	Suppose a wine bottler offers the following discounts on cases of wine:

Cases purchased on individual order	Discount percentage
1–10	0.0
11–25	2.0
26–50	3.5
Over 50	5.0

If Johnny's Liquor Store ordered 12 cases at a base price of $50 a case, the store would pay the bottler $600 less 2 percent, or $588.

Cumulative quantity discount	When purchases are totaled during a year and the discount percentage depends on the total volume of purchases made during that year, this is a cumulative quantity discount. If Johnny purchases 210 cases during the year and the bottler's discount schedule is as shown below, Johnny will get a check for $315 from the bottler at the end of the year. (210 × $50) × 3 percent = $315.

Total cases purchased in 1989	Discount percentage
1–100	2.0
101–500	3.0
Over 500	4.0

Trade position discount	A manufacturer receives two orders for small appliances. One comes from a wholesaler and the other from a retailer. The wholesaler gets a discount of 50 percent off the suggested price to ultimate consumers. The retailer gets a discount of 30 percent from the same suggested price to ultimate consumers.
Functional discount	A processor of frozen turkeys grants a special discount of 2 percent to a supermarket chain in return for featuring the product in the chain's weekly ad in Chicago newspapers the week before Thanksgiving.

Pricing New Products

There are two approaches to pricing a new product: market penetration pricing and market skimming pricing. Featuring a low price when introducing a new product is called **market penetration pricing.** The goal is to build a large initial market share and build brand loyalty before competitors can enter the market. The initial low price discourages some competitors who foresee a small profit at such a low price.

In the past, Texas Instruments, Inc. used market penetration pricing in introducing its various models of pocket calculators. It intended

market penetration pricing

to build a large market share and discourage rivals, especially Japanese producers, from entering the market. By capturing a large market share a firm can produce in large volume and, it is hoped, reduce per-unit costs by gaining economies of scale.

market skimming pricing

Featuring a high price when introducing a new product is called **market skimming pricing.** The goal is to get the greatest possible early revenue from sales to cover product development costs before competitors enter the market. This approach is often used by small firms and firms with large development costs. It might also be used by firms that are not well protected by patents and a good reputation. This policy lets the firm "get it while the getting's good." For example, SmithKline Beckman Corporation invested millions of dollars to develop the ulcer treatment drug, Tagamet. The firm practiced skimming pricing to recoup its development costs as quickly as possible.

Retail Pricing

Most retail stores use a markup system of pricing. Maxine Flynn is owner-manager of Maxine's, a dress shop in Mobile, Alabama. She knows that, on the average, her cost of doing business—including salaries, rent, and desired profit—is about half her sales revenue. She also knows that the cost of her fashion goods inventories represents the other half. Usually, she plans prices so that, allowing for sales on slow movers, she realizes a 50 percent gross margin. This means that the average initial retail price that she puts on an item must be somewhat more than double what she paid for the item. A shipment of better dresses from her Dallas supplier costs an average of $100 a dress. Dresses must be marked up to $250 each so that the final selling price will, with luck, average $200 or more. This is just enough to provide a gross margin of 50 percent of sales.

Maxine's initial markup can be stated as a percentage of her retail selling price ($150/$250, or 60 percent). The markup can also be stated as a percentage of her cost for a dress ($150/$100, or 150 percent). It is a good idea always to say whether markup is expressed in terms of the intended selling price or in terms of the cost. Of course, Maxine will use different markups on different items. Markups will depend on the competition and on the expected inventory turnover rate of each item.

inventory turnover rate

The **inventory turnover rate** (ratio) is equal to the cost of goods sold in a period divided by average inventory value. If Maxine's inventory is worth $50,000 on January 1 and $70,000 on December 31, the average inventory is $60,000. If the cost of goods sold during the year is $600,000, the turnover is $600,000/$60,000, or ten "turns" per year.

The greater the turnover Maxine expects on an item, the lower the markup she is likely to add to its cost price. Slow turnover items are likely to have high markups. Fast turnover merchandise absorbs less overhead (rent, etc.) per unit sold. There are economies of scale here. Higher markups on expected slow-moving items allow for significant markdowns of such items later if they are not moving even at the expected rate of turnover. Markdowns are common in fashion goods retailing.

If Maxine uses different markups on different items, she will try to average them out to provide her desired profit. Sometimes retailers use a very low markup on a certain item to attract customers. This is known as a *leader item*. The goal is to increase sales of items carrying a higher margin. Such a practice can be illegal if the leader item is sold below cost. Some firms use illegal "bait and switch" schemes to attract customers. This means advertising an inexpensive item that is really not available, then convincing the customer to buy a more expensive substitute. Such schemes are illegal in interstate commerce, and many states outlaw them in intrastate commerce (within their own borders).

price lining

Partly to simplify choices for customers and partly to simplify the salespeople's job, the retailer could use price lining. **Price lining** means grouping products with many different unit costs from many manufacturers at three or four sales price levels. For example, suppose a retail store purchases ten types of men's sport coats in a season. Marking up each of these by the same percentage could result in ten different prices for sport coats. The store might purchase coats in a cost range from $71.00 to $108.00 per unit. Using price lining, the firm would then present them to customers for sale at only three prices: $99.95, $149.95, and $199.95.

Price lining makes it easier for the customer to find the type of coat he needs. It also makes it easier for the salesperson to get the customer to "trade up." The customer comes into the store expecting to buy the $99.95 sport coat he saw in the newspaper ad. In the end he might buy the $149.95 coat after comparing quality.

The prices this store selected are "odd" amounts close to the next "$10 break." Partly out of tradition and partly because of a slight psychological effect, retailers tend to set a price at, say, $99.95 rather than $100.00. A price that begins with "ninety" sounds like more of a bargain than one that begins with "one hundred." Other stores, like Neiman-Marcus, might, on the other hand, use even prices such as $100 as a sign of their upscale status. In food stores, special promotions such as "one-cent sales" and "two-for-one sales" are also part of the art of retail pricing.

Summary

Product and price are two key elements in the marketing mix. Products are classified for marketing purposes as industrial/organizational products and consumer products, depending upon who uses them. Consumer products (including services) are further classified as shopping, convenience, or specialty products, depending on how consumers approach their purchase. Consumer services often require special marketing treatment.

Products go through a life cycle, including the stages of introduction, growth, maturity, and decline, and product strategies change from stage to stage. Before new products are even introduced, there are seven stages through which they must pass—from idea generation to commercialization.

Packaging serves to protect, to divide, to aid in storage and transportation, and to promote the product. Packaging even becomes part of the product itself. Branding is used to create differentiation in products and to help customers remember them. Patent and trademark protection are essential parts of product strategy.

Marketers, starting from a stated pricing objective, may take either a cost- or a demand-oriented approach to setting basic price. Breakeven analysis helps to develop the cost approach. Examination of the expected demand curve and its elasticity are part of the demand approach. Pricing models make use of both approaches, as does marginal analysis. Several kinds of discounts might be applied to the established basic price, including cash, quantity, and trade position discounts.

New product pricing can be characterized by skimming or by market penetration approaches. The former sets prices high for a quick return of revenue. The latter seeks to gain a large, permanent market share. Retail pricing is centered on markups, price lining, and psychological pricing.

Review Questions

1. List the major subclasses of industrial/organizational and consumer products.

2. Explain what is meant by conceiving of a product as a "bundle of satisfactions."

3. Explain the introduction and growth phases of the product life cycle.

4. Describe the stages of idea screening and business analysis in the new product development process.

5. What are the various roles of packaging?

6. Is breakeven analysis more likely to be used in the cost approach to pricing or in the demand approach?

7. What is the difference between a cash discount and a trade position discount?

8. What motives might lead a firm to pursue a market skimming pricing strategy?

Discussion Questions

1. How could the manufacturer lengthen the life cycle of your favorite brand of toothpaste?

2. What packaging functions does a six-pack of Coke perform?

3. List six brand names that you think have good "memory value." Name six that you think have poor value. What makes the difference?

4. Why is a retailer likely to take the cost approach to pricing?

Key Terms

product
convenience goods
shopping goods
specialty goods
product life cycle
technological obsolescence
fashion obsolescence
planned obsolescence
product mix

brand
manufacturer brands
distributor brands
patent
trademark
price
markup
breakeven analysis
pricing model

cash discount
trade position discount
functional discount
quantity discount
market penetration pricing
market skimming pricing
inventory turnover rate
price lining

Cases

POSITIONING STEUBEN GLASS

In the evolution of a brand's life cycle it is often necessary for the firm to alter the customers' perception of the brand compared to competitors. Steuben Glass, which for years relied on an image of very expensive, exclusive, "top-of-the-line" crystal and glassware, has been reassessing this image in recent years. Management asked the questions: "Just how elitist and exclusive can we afford to be?" "Can we afford to let huge numbers of potential buyers perceive themselves as undeserving of our product?"

Steuben began to reposition its product line by featuring $400 bowls and vases in its ads and pointing out that Steuben is not only for kings and emperors. This is a far cry from the "snob appeal" of an earlier ad for a limited-edition crystal bowl selling at $35,000. Like many manufacturers and retailers of luxury products, Steuben has been attempting to

broaden its market without alienating its existing customers. The new target is the huge number of professional, two-earner households.

One of the newer ads noted, for example, that a Steuben bowl was given by "Dr. Kent Nye Johnson of Middlebrook, Va. to his wife, Julie, to commemorate the birth of their first son." Steuben's vice-president for advertising expressed the firm's reasoning for such an ad: "We want to strike a balance between accessibility and prestige."[11]

Questions

1. In what class of product does Steuben glass traditionally fall? Does the recent repositioning affect this classification?
2. How is the product mix of Steuben broadened by this shift?
3. Review the stages of new product development discussed in the chapter and describe how Steuben's decision to offer lower-priced products might have been reached.

HEWLETT-PACKARD PRICES THE MODEL 840 COMPUTER

Hewlett-Packard, the California-based maker of computers and scientific instruments, reduced the price of its new Model 840 minicomputer by 28 percent soon after its introduction. Hewlett-Packard saw the move as a positive one because it enabled the firm to "fine tune" the 840's manufacturing operations more quickly than originally expected. The low price led to increased sales, allowing the firm to move to volume production and create cost savings from certain advantages inherent in its internal architecture. The new internal architecture, code-named Spectrum, was under design for six years and is said to have required an investment of some $250 million. It is called a "reduced-instruction-set" computing design, which is supposed to sharply reduce the complexity—and hence the cost—of the microchips used in the 840 and other Spectrum-based H-P computers.

Industry analysts felt that the 840 was intentionally overpriced at first so that, with low demand, H-P would have time to "iron out the kinks" with a selected group of initial users. The new price put the 840 about 10 percent below Digital Equipment Corporation's comparable equipment.[12]

Questions

1. How did both the cost and demand approaches to pricing enter into H-P's introduction of the 840?
2. Was the first price an example of "skimming"?
3. How does the expected life cycle of computer models affect the pricing and product development policies of computer manufacturers?

THIRTEEN

Promotion Strategies

After reading this chapter, you will be able to:

- Explain the role of promotion.

- Describe the activities of an advertising agency.

- Show how advertising media are selected.

- Demonstrate the use of the AIDA process in advertising.

- Describe the steps in the personal selling process.

- Outline the major responsibilities of a sales manager.

- Show how publicity, public relations, and sales promotion differ.

WHAT'S AHEAD

In this chapter we explore the role of promotion in marketing. We will start by defining promotion. We will contrast the roles of two major promotional strategies: advertising and personal selling. We also describe sales promotion, public relations, and publicity. We will see how advertising agencies operate, and the criteria they employ to select from the major media of television, newspapers, radio, magazines, direct mail, and specialty media. We will also examine the composition of a printed advertisement and show how it works.

The various forms of personal selling are also described, as is the AIDA (attention, interest, desire, action) process as applied to selling and advertising. This is followed by an explanation of the various functions of sales management, including selecting, training, motivating, and monitoring of the sales staff. We close with an examination of trade- and consumer-oriented sales promotion and a brief look at public relations and publicity.

In 1987, Schlott Realtors, one of the largest home marketers in New York City, began using advertisements on major local channels as a key element in its marketing mix. Dick Schlott, the president, presents his "Sunday Showcase of Homes" on a local TV channel at 9:00 A.M. Sundays. Each half-hour show features videotaped "showings" of various Schlott-represented properties in all price ranges. Every home advertised in this way is available for open house inspection on Sunday afternoon. The program is also supported by a toll-free number so that operators can direct would-be homebuyers to the right Schlott office to take a closer look at homes that interest them. Mr. Schlott is enthusiastic about the results. The large number of eager buyers arriving at the realty offices keep sales associates busy. This reinforces the image of Schlott Realtors as a firm that a home buyer or seller would feel confident in working with.

The TV part of Schlott's multi-media campaign is supported by newspaper advertising, banners, desk cards, a direct mail campaign, and special signs for featured houses. Mr. Schlott also uses the services of public relations experts.[1]

Mr. Schlott has a coordinated promotional mix to help market homes. In this chapter we will see just how comprehensive the realtor's promotional mix is. We will also learn about the informational, persuasive, and reminding functions performed by Mr. Schlott's set of promotional strategies. We start with a definition of promotion.

What Is Promotion?

promotion

promotional mix

advertising

personal selling

sales promotion

public relations

Promotion is any communication used for the purpose of increasing sales directly or indirectly. It is the most dynamic and aggressive element of the marketing mix. The promotion component of the marketing mix may consist of several major promotional activities. The **promotional mix** is the particular combination of advertising, personal selling, sales promotion, public relations, and publicity used by a firm. Schlott Realtors made a significant change in its promotional mix when the firm added its TV "Showcase of Homes."

Advertising is defined as any nonpersonal promotional activity for which a fee is paid by an identified sponsor. It is complementary to the other major promotional activity—personal selling. **Personal selling** is any direct personal communication for the purpose of increasing a firm's sales.

A good promotional mix also usually includes three additional activities. **Sales promotion** is a special set of activities that seek to induce or motivate desired responses in target customers, company salespeople, and middlemen and their salespeople. Sales promotion might include contests ("Win a Million Dollars By Entering the Reader's Digest Sweepstakes!") or sending out free samples of goods such as Zest soap.

Public relations includes any communication to correct erroneous impressions, to counter the impact of events that might harm the firm's reputation, or to explain the firm's purposes. It is often directed to people other than the usual target market, such as the government, stockholders, or citizens of the community in which one of the firm's manufacturing plants is located. **Publicity** is communication that is transmitted through the news media as a legitimate part of the news.

THE PURPOSES OF PROMOTION

Whether it takes the form of advertising, personal selling, sales promotion, or some other form, promotion is communication that has one of the following five aims:

- To gain attention
- To teach
- To remind
- To persuade
- To reassure

Promotion can do any of these things at any point in a product's life cycle. For example, G.D. Searle used a massive ad campaign to promote its sweetener, NutraSweet. Since the sweetener was entirely new, it was important to gain the public's attention and to establish the brand with heavy promotion.

Seagram's series of ads featuring Bruce Willis was intended primarily to gain attention and to persuade the TV audience to try the new wine cooler line. Canon's ad campaign featuring Jack Klugman succeeded in teaching present and potential customers the benefits and features of their line of copiers by demonstrating some of its capabilities. This kind of promotion is common during the growth phase of a product's life cycle. In many cases this type of promotion eases the personal selling efforts of salespeople calling on prospective customers.

The Coca-Cola Company spends tens of millions of dollars every year to promote its products. For years the primary function of its ads has been to remind us that Coca-Cola is available nearly everywhere. The change in Coke's product formula in 1985 led the firm to change the focus of its advertising for the first time in years. Coke switched to persuading us that the product change was an improvement. Meanwhile, before Coca-Cola Classic was introduced, Pepsi tried to persuade us that Coke's change was made to imitate Pepsi. Persuasion is the most common function of advertising today. The persuasion is usually to try something new or to switch brands.

Finally, a lot of promotion is aimed at reassuring customers that they made the right decision in buying the firm's product. Auto makers and dealers, for example, often send letters to new car buyers congratulating them on their purchase decision. The purpose is to reassure the buyers that they bought the "right" car. This can help to reduce uncertainty.

PUSH VERSUS PULL STRATEGY

In formulating its promotional mix the firm can use

- A push strategy
- A pull strategy
- A gravity strategy

Enlarge it. Reduce it. Or create any size in between. Canon's new PC-7 personal zoom copier makes it easy to get the copy you need. In seconds.

With a zoom ratio of 70% to 122%, you can make almost any size copy up to legal size from originals as large as 10 x 14.

And like all Canon personal copiers, the PC-7 uses Canon's exclusive PC Mini-Cartridges that let you copy in five great colors (black, brown, blue, red or green). And it's the only cartridge system to put everything that can wear out or run out in one compact unit. To make your personal copying virtually maintenance free.

What's more, it's the first personal copier designed with a copy board that doesn't move when you make copies. To help you save on valuable work space.

Personal zoom copying. A big idea that belongs in any size business. It's what makes the PC-7 the newest star in the Canon PC family.

Canon
《《PC》》
PERSONAL COPIERS

"Canon's personal zoom copier is the newest star in my family."

Promotion of copiers, which are in the growth phase, emphasizes the products' special features.

A *push strategy* "pushes" the product toward its final user. For a consumer product a manufacturer might rely heavily on its own sales force and the efforts of wholesalers and/or distributors. It might advertise in trade publications such as *Food Broker* and might engage in heavy trade-oriented sales promotion.

A *pull strategy* focuses directly on ultimate consumers or industrial users through advertising. This builds up demand at the user level and "pulls" the product through the channel, forcing the cooperation of middlemen who want to participate in the profitable volume of sales.

A *gravity strategy* places very little burden on the promotional program. It concentrates on producing a superior product—"building a better mousetrap"—and depending on word of mouth to sell it.

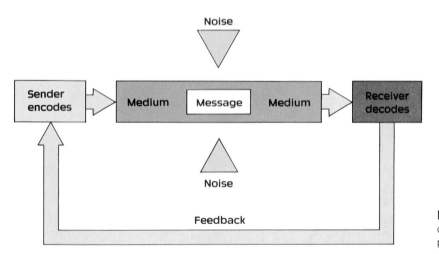

FIGURE 13-1 / The communication process in promotion.

COMMUNICATION IN PROMOTION

communication process

Because of the dynamic nature of competition, promotion must be viewed as a continuous process of communication. The **communication process** is that process by which information (including facts and feelings) is transmitted from one person or group to another. Figure 13-1 is a model of this process. It shows that a message must be encoded (expressed in a certain way) by the sender (often an ad agency). Then it is sent through a certain medium (such as a salesperson or television, magazine, or billboard) and decoded (interpreted by the target market). This must occur despite any noise (distractions) that might interfere with the communication. Noise might be competing ads, interference with TV reception, or poor color reproduction in printed ads. The existence of noise leads advertisers to rely on frequent showings of ads and to raise the volume on broadcast messages.

A complete model of communication must also allow for feedback. Feedback means that when a message is sent out, a response of some kind is usually communicated back to the original sender. In most cases the desired response to an ad is purchase of the product by target customers.

The choice of a medium can influence the way in which the message is received. For example, it would probably be a mistake to promote burial insurance during a TV comedy program. All promotional methods can be analyzed in the context of this model of communication. Advertising is no exception.

Advertising

Modern Americans are very familiar with advertising. They are subjected to it during a large part of each day of their lives, much of it through TV and radio. Advertising volume in the United States was expected to grow to more than $122 billion in 1989. This is roughly 3 percent of the Gross National Product.[2]

Part of the reason for this growth is advertising's unique ability to reach large numbers of people at the same time and at a moderate cost per contact. Sometimes, as in broadcasts of the Olympic Games, an advertising program can be directed at one time to people all over the world.

CLASSES OF ADVERTISING

brand advertising

primary demand advertising

institutional advertising

Individual firms spend most of their ad budgets on brand advertising, also known as selective demand advertising. **Brand advertising** is advertising to promote the particular brand of product sold by the advertiser. Ads for Delta Airlines and Isotoner gloves are examples. **Primary demand advertising** takes place when a firm or the members of a trade association advertise a general class of product without mentioning brands. You have probably seen magazine ads urging you to drink more milk, for example.

Sometimes firms also engage in institutional advertising. **Institutional advertising** is promotion of the firm's good name rather than any of its products. By publicizing its success with an experimental solar-powered car, General Motors used institutional advertising to counter its loss of prestige in the 1980s.

ADVERTISING INSTITUTIONS

The principal institutions involved in making advertising decisions are

- Advertising departments of firms
- Advertising agencies
- Advertising media such as newspapers, television stations, or magazines

Most large and medium-sized firms have a separate department to oversee advertising activities. If a firm adheres to the marketing concept, its advertising department comes under the authority of the top marketing executive. In this way, advertising is coordinated with other promotional activities and with the rest of the marketing mix.

The advertising department serves as a link between the firm and the advertising agency. The departments of major firms spend large sums of money for advertising. Procter & Gamble spends more than $600 million in a year on TV ads alone and much more when the other ad media are included.

Small firms, on the other hand, do not often have advertising departments. One or two people usually handle the firm's advertising. When they have an idea for an ad campaign, they present it to the local newspaper, radio, or TV station. If the small firm buys a certain amount of newspaper space or radio or TV time, the newspaper or TV station itself will handle the production of the ad. Small food stores and fashion boutiques often take this approach to advertising.

advertising agency

An **advertising agency** is a firm that specializes in planning, producing, and placing advertisements in the media for clients. The agency is the principal creative center for most medium-sized and large firms that need to advertise. It serves its clients by planning advertising

WHAT DO YOU THINK?

Is a Global Promotional Program Practical?

For several years, controversy has raged over the idea that multinational firms should develop "global" promotion and marketing programs.

Theodore Levitt of Harvard has supported this idea, noting that mass communication and high technology are turning the world into a common marketplace in which people want the same lifestyles and products. The "globalization" theory claims that this creates similar patterns of consumption in diverse cultures and lets firms standardize manufacturing of products as diverse as Revlon cosmetics and Sony TVs. Black & Decker has adopted such a strategy for power tools and Colgate-Palmolive for its dentifrice and liquid cleaners.

Philip Kotler of Northwestern University takes a different view. He believes that diversity of tastes, culture, and economic development requires different promotional strategies in different countries. Surveys by two New York advertising agencies—Vitt Media International and Bygraves Bushnell Valladares Sheldon—lend some support to Kotler's position. They found only a small minority of international firms actually using global promotional strategies. Vitt Media's survey found that 79 percent of respondents reported developing distinctly different media plans in each country to reflect cultural and linguistic differences. Forty percent said that universal advertising that rises above cultural differences can be created only on rare occasions. The Bygraves survey generally supported these findings. It found that European marketers agreed that differences in economic development, language, media, and government regulations are major impediments to successful global marketing.

Are global promotion and marketing practical? What do you think?

Sources: "Differences, Confusion Slow Global Marketing Bandwagon," *Marketing News* Jan. 16, 1987, p. 1; Bill Saporito, "Black and Decker's Gamble on 'Globalization,'" *Fortune,* May 14, 1984, pp. 40–45. Also Dennis Chase, "Global Marketing: The New Wave," and Mitchell Lynch, "Harvard's Levitt Called Global Marketing 'Guru,'" *Advertising Age,* June 25, 1984.

---

campaigns and creating specific ads. It also buys time and space in the broadcast (radio and TV) and print (newspapers and magazines) media and checks to see that ads appear as agreed. Sometimes ad agencies perform marketing functions such as marketing research and public relations. Agencies are normally paid a 15 percent commission based on the dollar amount of advertising placed in the media. They also charge an additional fee for marketing research or other special services.

account executive

A key role in the advertising agency is played by the account executive. An **account executive** is in charge of the entire relationship between the agency and a particular client (account) and coordinates the work of the group of professionals involved in the client's ad program, including copywriters, artists, TV directors, and media buyers.

advertising media

The **advertising media**—newspapers, magazines, television, radio, billboard, and others—carry the messages designed by firms and their

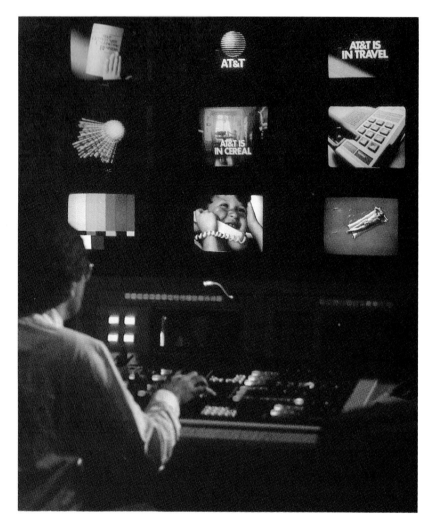

Advertising agencies use their creative resources to produce effective TV commercials.

agencies to many receivers (customers or potential customers). The most important media are newspapers, television, and direct mail, in that order. The volume of advertising in each of the major media is shown in Figure 13-2.

The amount of current dollars spent on media has doubled since 1980. The relative share of print media is down somewhat, as is that of radio. Television is holding its share, although some of this is now cable. Direct mail has made the major gains.

Motion pictures have become an advertising medium of sorts. More than thirty advertising firms now specialize in placing branded product appearances in full-length motion pictures. Pan American Airways, Jim Beam whiskey, Coleman lanterns, and Igloo containers all paid for appearances in *Volunteers*, starring Tom Hanks and John Candy. Pepsi, Bank of America, Cadbury candy, and Toyota trucks all appeared in *Back to the Future*. Many movies reach more than 100 million customers, counting international distribution, video rentals and pay TV.[3]

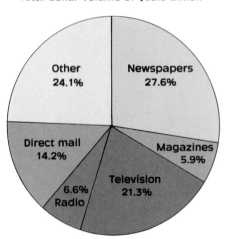

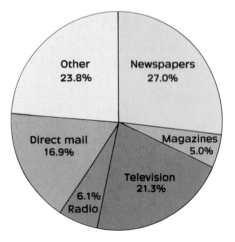

FIGURE 13-2 / Share of total advertising volume by media, 1968 and 1987. (*Source:* McCann-Erickson, Inc. 1980 data from *Statistical Abstract of the United States, 1988.* 1987 data estimated by authors from various sources.)

Advertising Management

Advertising management includes six major activities,[4] some of which may be performed by the advertising department and some by the ad agency hired by the firm. They are as follows:

- Defining the advertising target
- Defining advertising objectives
- Setting the ad budget
- Measuring ad effectiveness
- Developing the creative strategy
- Selecting ad media

The advertising target is the audience to whom advertising is directed. It is the same as or a special part of the target market (which we discussed in Chapter 11). Advertising objectives can be expressed in terms of an expected amount of sales or of "making a certain number of people aware of our new product." Awareness is a big step in the direction of sales. The Expressions boutique, for example, planned an ad campaign with the objective of being known by 30 percent of professional women in the city of Charlotte, North Carolina, by the end of the year. The boutique assumes that the sales will follow.

Firms set ad budgets in many ways. Some are simple and rather arbitrary, such as spending all the money that is available, or spending a percent of sales, or matching what competitors spend. A more sensible method is to start with one or more of the ad objectives and then cost out what it will take to accomplish these. The sum of these costs becomes the advertising budget if top management approves.

APPLICATION: BURGER KING
Hiring a New Advertising Agency

"O ne of the biggest reasons you want to be big in this industry," says Burger King Corporation's vice-president for franchise affairs "is that it is the big guy who has the advertising clout." That's one reason why McDonald's—with over twice the overall marketing budget of Burger King Corporation—can advertise so much more.

When you haven't got the money of your bigger competitor, your advertising strategy has to stress something really unique, and be super-hard-hitting. That's why Burger King Corporation kicked off the "battle of the burgers" in October 1982 with surveys claiming that customers preferred Burger King's flame broiled burgers to those of McDonald's or third-place Wendy's.

Unfortunately, some of the company's subsequent advertising campaigns were not as successful. Do you remember Burger King's "Herb" campaign in 1986? Herb was a nerdy-looking character who was billed as the only person in the country who had never been in a Burger King restaurant. Dissatisfied with this advertising, Burger King Corporation soon sought a new agency to handle its $200 million domestic advertising account.

How does a company like Burger King go about choosing a new advertising agency? Here is how Burger King Corporation did it.

First, Burger King reviewed the top thirty agencies and eliminated more than half of them because Burger King didn't think that a small agency would have the resources to service it properly. Burger King then contacted ten of the remaining agencies and narrowed the choice to six who gave "credentials presentations." Burger King said to them, "Tell us about your agency, resources, analogous campaigns, and so on."

On the basis of their answers, Burger King asked three of the agencies to come back, this time with detailed presentations. Each was given a specific assignment such as "present creative solutions to a promotion aimed at children for a new breakfast product." They were also asked to make suggestions on creating or changing a new national identity for Burger King. Each agency was given four hours to present, in their own office, their ideas for a campaign to a Burger King team comprised of Burger King Corporation marketing executives as well as other executives, including the president, franchisees, and a Pillsbury representative.

The new agency chosen was N. W. Ayer. The new campaign, introduced in March 1988, was "We do it like you'd do it.®" It remains to be seen how effective this new campaign will be.

Questions

1. How important is sales promotion in Burger King Corporation's overall promotional effort? What about public relations and publicity? Give examples.

2. Do you think Burger King Corporation made the right decision when it eliminated smaller advertising agencies from further consideration during the process of selecting a new agency?

3. Why is the relationship between the advertising agency and the client so important? How would you describe an ideal relationship?

Measuring ad effectiveness is a major reason for marketing research. The idea is to find out the degree to which sales success is tied to the total amount a firm spent or to the amount spent for specific ads or ad campaigns. In other cases, ad effectiveness can be measured by "audience share" or "awareness" or "attitude-related" scores. A.C.

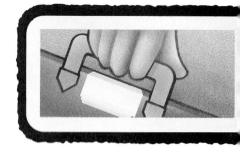

For its Breyers ice cream account, the Young & Rubicam advertising agency wanted to get a taste of what ice cream really means to American consumers. First came traditional focus group interviews. Then market researchers decided to try something novel: They visited six families at home to observe ice cream indulgence first-hand. They photographed people lounging in their favorite chairs and taking that first scrumptious lick. They snooped in freezers, inspected bowls and utensils, watched people spoon on toppings, and listened to one woman describe how she dims the lights and flips on her stereo before digging in.

"We learned about people's emotional response to ice cream and found that it's a very sensual, inner-directed experience," says Robert Baker, marketing director for Breyers at Kraft, Inc. "Hopefully, this extra research will guide the agency in developing more effective advertising."

Young & Rubicam is peering more deeply into people's lives these days for a number of its clients, both to create ads that ring true and to come up with new product ideas. Although they spend less than a day with a family, the agency's researchers observe such things as how parents and kids interact, which brands are in the refrigerator, and how a home is decorated.

Because Young & Rubicam believes it becomes absorbed in people's lives, it calls its research "ethnography," an an-

thropological term for the study of cultures. "Ethnography eliminates some of the distance between us and consumers and brings them alive for our creative staff," says Susan Gianinno, research director. "The biggest mistake ad agencies make is to presume they know people just because they have a lot of quantitative data."

Source: Ronald Alsop, " 'People Watchers' Seek Clues to Consumers' True Behavior," *The Wall Street Journal* Sept. 4, 1986, p. 29. Reprinted by permission. © Dow Jones & Company, Inc., 1986. All Rights Reserved.

Nielsen, the best-known TV rating service, provides advertisers with data on the number and types of viewers for specific programs.

A general evaluation of reactions to TV advertising campaigns is provided by Video Storyboard Tests, Inc. This firm polls 30,000 viewers each year to measure which of the major TV advertising efforts are best-liked. In one such survey, Coke (featuring Max Headroom) rated best, followed by McDonald's and the California Raisin Advisory Board's "Heard it through the grapevine" series.

DEVELOPING THE CREATIVE STRATEGY

AIDA process

The **AIDA process** is a way of analyzing an ad in terms of bringing the reader or listener through stages of attention, interest, desire, and action. Let's look at some actual ads to see what creative strategy is all about.

The four main parts of a print media ad are the headline, the illustration, the copy, and the signature. Headlines are attention getters and interest builders or "teasers." Look at the Johnson & Johnson Sundown Sunscreen ad. Sometimes headlines go a long way toward building desire for the product. The illustration often does the biggest part of the AIDA process. With good photography, color, and imagination the illustration can almost "do it all." Doesn't the Duncan Hines ad make

She's 20. He's 24.

Sundown has more protection than ever before. Waterproof protection. So even the fairest child can spend more time outside, having fun in the sun. SPF 20 is available in lotion and stick. SPF 24 in cream.

SUNDOWN® SUNSCREEN
All the protection you need.

© J&J CPI, 1988.

Johnson & Johnson

An attention-getting headline is a way to get the reader to look more closely at the ad.

your mouth water? Illustrations are especially good at gaining attention, often by direct eye contact with the reader and by conveying a sense of identification or familiarity with the product.

Ad copy, the written or spoken part, is the desire builder. It gives facts and anticipates objections by the reader. The dependence on copy

An appetizing illustration is especially important in advertising food.

Ad copy can engage a reader's interest by providing information on the product's distinctive features.

varies greatly with the kind of message to be conveyed. Illustrations "carry the ball" in most food ads, so copy becomes secondary. Copy is very important, however, in business-directed ads, especially when technical details are crucial. This is true of the Texas Instruments ad. In this example the copy is also used to induce action by means of the coupon. Ads often include a call to action such as "Call 1-800-(phone number) for the dealer nearest you."

The signature is usually the familiar company trademark or brand name. It shows who is sending the message. This is illustrated in all of the accompanying ads.

The ads shown in this chapter display many appeals or themes used to reach customers. The advertiser may use an appeal to an appetite—for food, sex, or prestige, for instance—to develop the interest of a targeted customer.

The arrangement of parts in a print ad—headline, illustration,

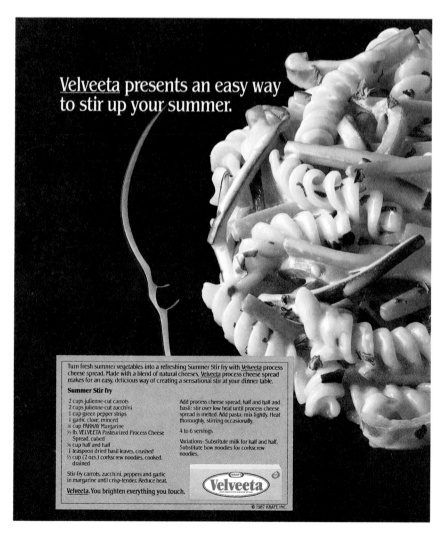

A good layout combining headline, illustration, copy, and signature carries the reader easily through the AIDA process.

copy, and signature—is called the layout. Ideally, the layout makes it easy to carry the reader through the phases of attention, interest, desire, and action. The Velveeta ad is a good example of this. A similar AIDA-based "game plan" can also be used in personal selling or in TV commercials. Watch for the AIDA process in action when you see commercials on TV.

CRITERIA FOR SELECTING AD MEDIA

An advertiser selects media (often with an agency's help) with a number of questions in mind. The advertiser first asks, "Which medium will *reach the people I want to reach*?" If Maybelline wants to advertise a new cosmetic to teenagers, it might select *Seventeen* magazine. Noxzema skin cream and Heineken beer have used radio stations broadcasting to thirsty, sunburned beach crowds in New Jersey. To promote Chevy trucks, General Motors runs ads on an all-night radio network that reaches 650,000 long-haul truckers.

Sometimes media reach very special markets. The term "narrowcasting," as opposed to "broadcasting," refers to special-audience cable media such as MTV and the Playboy channel. There are even special forms of direct mail. For example, Digital Learning Systems, Inc. produces diskette-based ads and sends them directly to personal computer users. They even designed an interactive, full-color diskette for Smith, Kline & French Laboratories that was used to promote prescription drugs at a pharmaceutical trade show.[5] Printed mailers and personalized cover letters are often used to reach specialized audiences. Mailing list firms can provide a marketer with lists of doctors, rock music fans, or turkey breeders among many, many others.

A second important criterion for media choice is "Can the medium *deliver the message effectively*?" Some messages need visual communication, some specifically need color, and still others need sound or movement. Foods especially benefit from color in print or broadcast communication. Selling an electric organ requires a sound-oriented medium. Some messages need color, sound, and motion. This combination is available only on color TV, the medium with the greatest set of "communicating tools."

Another vital question is "*How much will it cost per contact?*" This is called the CPM (cost per thousand persons reached by the ad). This cost will vary greatly, but the one-dimensional media such as radio and newspapers usually have a low CPM. TV costs more. The cost of a one-minute commercial during a recent Super Bowl was $1,050,000, or $17,500 per second. However, the CPM was only about $10 because over 100 million people saw the game on TV. By contrast, the CPM of one-minute commercials shown at movie houses by Screenvision Cinema network is $18.

There are other special factors in media selection. For example, print media provide *more permanence*. They can reach people several times or be taken to the store as a shopping aid. Some media (local radio and television stations and daily newspaper) provide *frequent contact* and a relatively *short lag time* between creation of an ad and its appearance.

Personal Selling

There is often no substitute for one-to-one human persuasion. We see it nearly every day. One person can do a lot to convince another of a point of view, whether it's to try a new brand of beer or to change an attitude toward a politician.

The special quality of personal selling is the one-to-one relationship between the seller and the buyer. The seller can give very special attention to the buyer's needs. The tone of personal selling can vary from that of a sideshow barker to that of a skilled computer salesperson. The style is different, but the goal is the same: to sell. Both hope to guide the receiver through the familiar AIDA process.

A PERSONAL SELLING PROCESS

Figure 13-3 shows a typical example of how a salesperson might follow the AIDA process. First, the fact that the salesperson has made an appointment to see the prospect means that he or she has already gained the prospect's attention. The salesperson reinforces this by showing awareness of the prospect's needs. He or she generates interest by showing the product's benefits and explaining how they can solve the prospect's specific problem. The salesperson might answer several objections raised by the prospect, beginning to build genuine desire for the product. These answers might involve explaining the "easy credit plan" or the service and warranty details. By asking for the sale the salesperson goes directly after the goal of inducing action. Getting the buyer to act is a lot easier in personal selling than in advertising and other promotion. The salesperson has the advantage of being able to observe the customer and to know just when to close the sale.

Advertising and personal selling work well together. Advertising "pulls," while personal selling "pushes" products toward the buyer. Avon, for example, advertises on TV to stimulate interest in its products. It also has a huge door-to-door sales force to make personal calls on target customers. Many advertisers, especially for kitchen gadgets and record albums and tapes, tie TV ads directly to a telephone sales opportunity by giving toll-free 1-800 numbers for interested prospects to call.

FORMS OF SELLING

need satisfaction selling

The modern view of personal selling is that salespeople are expected to engage in need satisfaction selling. **Need satisfaction selling** is personal selling that helps prospects identify and solve problems. A Mary Kay Cosmetics salesperson, for example, might show a woman how a certain type of makeup could help her deal with her very sensitive skin. Most industrial salespeople have to be problem solvers for their customers. They might need training in engineering, chemistry, data processing, and other technical areas to be effective. Different groups within major computer firms' sales forces are trained to solve the special computer problems of banks, educational institutions, or hospitals.

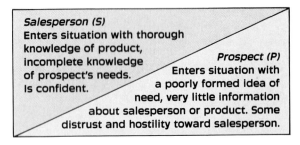

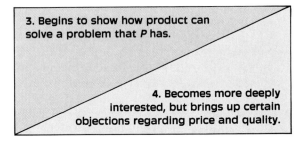

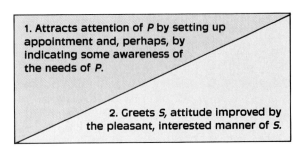

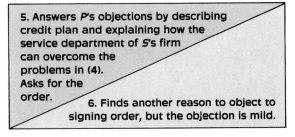

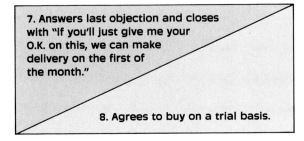

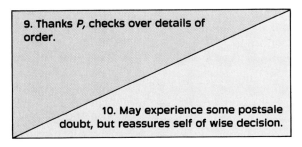

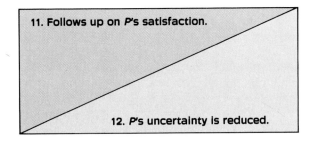

FIGURE 13-3 / A typical personal selling sequence.

Need satisfaction selling is not the only approach to sales. Other forms of sales approaches include stimulus-response selling and barrier selling, neither of which is a true application of the marketing concept. The former is a standard, predesigned ("canned") sales pitch. It is employed mostly by poorly trained salespeople. Barrier selling is

Personal selling focuses on identifying and solving customers' problems.

also called successive commitment selling. It is a high-pressure technique that uses repeated requests for agreement from the prospect. It has the goal of "forcing" the prospect to decide immediately.

The nature of the product, competitive conditions, the stage of the product's life cycle, and other factors determine which sales skills are needed. Most department store selling requires quite a different kind of preparation and ability than does selling a computer system to a giant corporation. The job of a retail sales clerk is mostly simple order taking. **Order taking** is receiving and filling requests from customers—often repeat business. **Order getting** is active, aggressive pursuit of sales and conversion of prospects to customers. **Missionary selling** is a specialized selling effort aimed at making the jobs of the manufacturer's regular sales force and those of retailers and wholesalers easier without actually writing orders for the product. For example, a highly trained computer salesperson might spend much of his or her time cultivating a good relationship with customers and laying the groundwork for long-term sales.

order taking
order getting
missionary selling

STEPS IN SUCCESSFUL SELLING

While different salespeople operate in many different ways, most successful ones do the following:

prospecting
qualifying

- They do some prospecting and qualifying. **Prospecting** means getting sales leads. **Qualifying** means screening sales leads for likelihood of purchase and profitability as customers.
- They get to know their products in every way possible, including the strong points and weak points.
- They formulate sales approaches that best suit their product and their customer as well as their own personal talents.

- They learn to answer customers' objections.
- They learn to be persistent, positive, and confident enough to close the sale.
- They follow up to ensure customer satisfaction.

When Del Monte decided to introduce a new line of Mexican foods in U.S. grocery stores, its salespeople did not have to do prospecting or qualifying. They did have to convince Del Monte's established wholesalers and retailers to stock the new products and perform other sales activities listed above. Salespeople had to learn about the new line of products. They had to develop some sales strategies to encourage the wholesalers to stock the products and to encourage the wholesalers' salespeople to push their sale to retailers. Meanwhile, other Del Monte representatives were calling on retailers. Their job was to inform retail grocers about such details as package sizes, merchandise return policy, and introductory pricing deals. When grocers objected to allocating scarce shelf space to the new products, Del Monte sales reps countered by offering cooperative advertising. **Cooperative advertising** is advertising for which the cost is shared by the manufacturer and retailer.

cooperative advertising

Sales Management

Managing the sales effort requires a variety of skills. A sales manager must deal with a special set of problems. Sometimes it is hard for sales managers to maintain good sales staff morale because managers lack continuous personal contact with salespeople. They must find effective ways of keeping in touch.

Sometimes motivation is weakened by periods of low sales volume or by loss of large accounts. Pay plans or territories might need changing. Sometimes the sales objectives themselves—greater sales volume, a better sales-to-call ratio, reduced sales expense standards—need to be reconsidered if they are frustrating your hard-working salespeople.

The sales manager's responsibilities include

- Building an effective sales force
- Directing and motivating the sales force
- Monitoring the sales effort

BUILDING A SALES FORCE

To build a sales force, the sales manager must first decide how large a force is needed to reach customers of all types in all potentially profitable areas. The manager must then decide whether to structure the force according to *geographic* territories, *product* specialization, *customer-type* specialization, or *task* specialization. Task specialization means letting some salespeople deal only with developing new customers and others to serve established customers in their territories.

The manager must develop sources of good recruits and use effective methods of recruitment and selection to maintain a fully staffed sales force. He or she must also maintain an effective sales training program to keep the sales force up to date and prepared to meet the competition. The training might include role playing, lectures, simulation exercises, demonstrations, and manuals and textbooks for study.

DIRECTING AND MOTIVATING THE SALES FORCE

Directing and motivating the sales force includes developing workable pay plans, which might include salaries, commissions, bonuses, or combinations of any of these. Some sales experts recommend strong manager-incentive programs with bonuses to keep sales managers' motivation up.

Incentives directed toward higher-order motivations, such as those discussed in Chapter 6, can also be developed. These might involve awarding special privileges, honors, or titles. Some firms rely heavily on the use of motivational speakers such as Will Jordan, Zig Ziegler, or football coach Lou Holtz of Notre Dame. However, the trend is away from these, since their effect seems to be very short-lived. Firms are shifting more to a delicate balance of careful training and financial reward.[6]

MONITORING THE SALES EFFORT

The third task, that of monitoring the sales effort, is a special form of the management function of control. The sales manager must first set up standards. These might include both sales quotas and sales expense budgets for sales territories, products, and individual salespeople. The sales manager must also compare actual sales results to standards and then, if necessary, take corrective action. This might range from redefining sales territories to dismissing ineffective sales employees.

Sales Promotion

As we have seen, sales promotion is a set of special activities that seek to motivate target customers, company salespeople, and middlemen and their sales forces toward desired responses. It is helpful to distinguish between the use of sales promotion as targeted to consumers and its use for "trade purposes"—to support and stimulate middlemen and sales forces.

CONSUMER SALES PROMOTION

Sales promotion is often directed at consumers. When fear of terrorism dampened overseas travel, British Airways staged a huge "giveaway." On one special day, every seat on flights leaving from fifteen U.S. gateway cities for London—a total of 5,200 seats—was free. Sperry & Hutchinson (S&H), the Green Stamp company, has test marketed "electronic trading stamps." The S&H GiftSaver Card System—which involves a host of computer checkout terminals and personalized

A Coca-Cola robot attracts a lot of attention in a supermarket. In this advertising or a form of sales promotion?

consumer cards similar to credit cards—produced strong increases in sales at Frank's Supermarket in Glastonbury, Connecticut, a retailer that has offered the traditional green stamps to customers for years.[7]

Vision Cable, in Alexandria, Louisiana, sent subscribers entry forms for an American Airlines vacation sweepstakes along with discount coupons that were good at the local pharmacy, paint store, and pizza parlor. Consumer sweepstakes such as those used regularly by Reader's Digest and Publisher's Clearinghouse are another popular consumer sales promotion device.

Food products producers are major users of promotional "cents-off" coupons. Since the mid-1980s, packaged goods firms have spent about two-thirds of their advertising budgets on sales promotion. However, several of the largest users, such as Colgate-Palmolive, Campbell Soup Company, Kraft, and General Foods, are slowing down their spending. At Colgate, redemption rates for coupons fell more than 10 percent from 1984 to 1985. Some marketing experts feel that a saturation point has been reached in such promotions.[8]

Another important sales promotion activity is point-of-purchase (POP) advertising. The Point of Purchase Advertising Institute has reported the volume of POP advertising expenditures at more than $8 billion per year in recent years. An example of a successful point-of-purchase display is the L'eggs "boutique," which drew much attention to this brand of panty hose. Timex watches are often featured in a rotating countertop display case to draw the attention of passing customers. The "Pepsi Challenge" taste test is another successful example of a point-of-purchase display.

TRADE PROMOTION

Sales promotions can also be directed to a manufacturer's, wholesaler's, or retailer's sales force. To influence wholesalers and retail dealers, an incentive in the form of trade allowances is often used. Such price discounts allow the dealer to pass on special deals to consumers. Dealer contests and premiums can also be effective. For example, Miller Brewing Company has supplied taverns with lighting fixtures. Nestlé Corporation has offered an all-expenses-paid vacation for the top salesperson in each sales territory. Many firms give their dealer's salespeople "push money" (PMs)—cash payments—to gain their attention and support.

PUBLIC RELATIONS AND PUBLICITY

Public relations, as we have seen, includes any communication to correct erroneous impressions, to counter the impact of events that might harm the reputation of an organization, or to explain the organization's purposes. Its effect on sales is usually indirect and long-term, such as Dow Chemical's campaign to improve its image, which had been hurt by its association with napalm and Agent Orange in the Vietnam war.

Utility companies have used public relations programs to combat the effect of criticism of their use of nuclear reactors to generate electricity. To reduce this criticism and to give the public a chance to see the safety features built into such plants, some utility companies conduct guided tours. Your college probably has a public relations department that sends speakers to nearby high schools to point out the advantages of attending the college.

Publicity, as we have seen, is communication through the news media as a legitimate part of the news. It is often part of the public relations program of an organization, and it is usually inexpensive because its only cost is preparing the news story or press release. But only items considered "newsworthy" by the press are used. Very often, carefully prepared items are never printed or broadcast.

News stories often serve public relations goals by combatting bad news. Chrysler Corporation made sure that its side of the reports about employees tampering with odometers got into the newspapers. Chrysler publicly admitted the mistakes and offered extended warranties to the affected buyers.

Experts in publicity tend to agree that firms should cooperate with regulatory agencies and the news media when "bad news," such as auto recalls, occurs. Firms should provide relevant facts rather than attempt to cover them up. A firm that is ordered to recall a product should provide the media with information for consumers on how to get the product repaired or replaced.

Summary

Promotion is communication that gains attention, teaches, reminds, persuades, and reassures. Its major forms are advertising and personal selling. A model of the communication process helps in understanding promotion and some of the problems it encounters.

Advertising is nonpersonal communication paid for by an identified sponsor. Most of it is brand advertising. Institutions involved in advertising include ad departments of firms, advertising agencies—which do most of the ad planning and creating—and the media. The leading media are newspapers, TV, magazines, radio, and direct mail. The choice of media by an advertiser might hinge on the medium's ability to reach target audiences, its ability to deliver the message effectively, or its CPM.

A good print ad uses its headline, illustration, copy, and signature to get a message across. A good layout and good use of color and shapes help an ad guide a reader through the AIDA (attention, interest, desire, and action) process. Broadcast media ads also benefit from "AIDA thinking."

Personal selling is direct, two-way, personal promotion. It might also use the AIDA sequence as a guide in influencing a prospect. Need satisfaction selling is a high-quality form of selling that is oriented toward solving problems for customers. Good salespeople do some prospecting and/or qualifying. Next, they get to know their products, formulate sales strategies, answer customers' objections, close the sale, and then follow up.

The sales manager's responsibilities include building an effective sales force, directing and motivating the sales force, and monitoring the sales effort.

Sales promotion is a set of special activities that seek to motivate target customers, company salespeople, and middlemen and their sales forces. In so doing, a firm's advertising and personal selling activities are supplemented. Public relations, often with the help of publicity, also supports the promotion effort by protecting the firm's good name and generally furthering the growth of the firm or other organization.

Review Questions

1. What are the main components of the promotional mix?

2. Describe the parts of a communications model.

3. Name the important advertising media in the order of their volume in the United States.

4. Describe the functions of an advertising department, an ad agency, and the advertising media.

5. What is the AIDA process? Does it apply to personal selling?

6. What are the broad responsibilities of a sales manager?

7. Describe two forms of sales promotion.

Discussion Questions

1. Explain how advertising and personal selling complement each other. Illustrate this by an example of a firm that you are familiar with.

2. Write a brief piece of copy for a television commercial announcing a new chain of sandwich shops called Margy's to be introduced in your city next month. Critique the copy.

3. Write a paragraph giving advice to a salesperson for a hardware wholesaler going out on his or her route for the first time.

4. Describe a situation confronting a large corporation in which clever use of publicity and public relations is needed.

Key Terms

promotion
promotional mix
advertising
personal selling
sales promotion
public relations
publicity
communication process

brand advertising
primary demand advertising
institutional advertising
advertising agency
account executive
advertising media
AIDA process
need satisfaction selling

order taking
order getting
missionary selling
prospecting
qualifying
cooperative advertising

COMEBACK FOR CONTAC

Contac and two other SmithKline Beckman Corporation products marketed in capsule form were withdrawn in March 1986 after government investigators discovered rat poison in capsules from several packages. Six months later the company brought back the product in a clear, sealed capsule and introduced the product in caplet (solid tablet as opposed to the powder in a capsule). The recall and Contac's subsequent reintroduction cost the pharmaceutical and health products maker $50 million.

A subsequent survey, according to SmithKline, found that the reintroduction was worth the great expense—equal to almost a year's sales. SmithKline discovered that Contac had more than regained its market share of the cold medicine market. In the fall of 1986, Contac had a share of 11.8 percent—up from about 8.7 percent before it had withdrawn the brand. Contac sales had roughly equalled those of Actifed, the market leader, before the withdrawal of Contac.

Drug industry analysts were less enthusiastic about the strategy. One analyst felt that SmithKline was "buying sales" by giving a $1-off coupon for a $3.50 item. Other industry experts agreed that the overall promotional expense was too great for the benefits it brought.[9]

Questions
1. How would you describe the promotional objectives of SmithKline?
2. What promotional budgeting technique did SmithKline use? Compare it to those described in the chapter.
3. Do you agree or disagree with industry critics of the SmithKline reintroduction efforts and the methods employed? Why?

MIND OVER MINORS: PROMOTING ARTIFICIAL INTELLIGENCE

Human Edge Software first developed Mind Prober in 1985. Mind Prober was intended as a means of analyzing and gaining the upper hand in relations with other adults. It sold more than 150,000 units and was named by *Business Week* as "bestselling new product/educational software" in that year. The controversial advertising theme raised a lot of eyebrows, but *Info-World*, a weekly magazine of the computer industry, called it "perhaps the most shrewdly-marketed expert systems package to date." Human Edge plastered thousands of 1940s-style Hollywood posters in major cities, suggesting that the Mind Prober system was like George Orwell's "Big Brother" and that it "is so accurate it is frightening." *Playboy* was a major ad medium for the product.

Human Edge later introduced a second product, Mind Over Minors, which is directed toward computer-owning teachers and parents to help them learn to motivate and discipline children. As is the case with Mind Prober, Mind Over Minors requires that the user enter into the computer certain adjectives describing his or her own personality and that of the person to be influenced. The program then develops a customized communication program to influence the child.

The ad campaign for Mind Over Minors, like the one used for Mind Prober, consisted of initial placement of posters in major cities, followed by a series of ads in major computer and educational publications, plus an insertion in regional editions of *Parents* magazine. While not quite as sensational as the themes used for Mind Prober, the campaign followed a similar pattern.

An introductory ad featured the provocative headline "Boot The Kids." One poster features a devious-looking ten-year-old red-headed boy and is headlined "Just Released for Good Behavior."[10]

Questions
1. What media other than those identified could you suggest for Mind Over Minors? For Mind Prober?
2. Could computer disk recorded advertising be a useful medium in this case?
3. Would any of the sales promotion activities described in the chapter help in the marketing of Mind Over Minors?

LEARNING OBJECTIVES

After reading this chapter, you will be able to:

- Explain the relationship between distribution and the creation of utilities.

- Describe two common channels of distribution for industrial-organizational and consumer products.

- Explain the concept of a vertical marketing system and show how such a system may be achieved.

- Describe the functions performed by wholesalers and distinguish between merchant and agent wholesalers.

- Contrast the operations of supermarkets, department stores, and discount stores.

- Explain the total cost concept as it relates to transportation and warehousing choices for physical distribution.

We have seen how firms handle three parts of the marketing mix: promotion, product, and price. The fourth element of the marketing mix is distribution (sometimes called place). Distribution is necessary because most products are not used by the same firm or person that makes them. Nor are products usually used or consumed at the same time that they are made or in the same place. Before it is used or consumed, an automobile, a candy bar, or a printing press must be moved, stored, and exchanged. In Chapter 11 we learned of the concept of utility and its four components: form, time, place, and ownership utility. Distribution consists of marketing activities that contribute time, place, and ownership utility to products. Products are worth more to users because of distribution activities. We will examine the structure of distribution, including the groups of institutions that participate in distribution by buying and selling—the channel members—and those that help in a physical sense: transportation and storage firms.

We also describe the variety of wholesale and retail institutions that participate in distribution and see how the functions performed by wholesalers and retailers differ. This includes an explanation of how, over time, the pressures of competition have shaped these institutions.

The latter part of the chapter is centered on the activities of firms that specialize in physical movement and storage. We compare the modes of transportation and see how they compete for business. We explain how important it is to view the entire process of storage and transportation as a single physical distribution system.

Motivating store managers is a challenge every retailer faces. Finding qualified people to buy franchised outlets is a problem in the franchising industry. A Denver franchisor of tire stores, Big O

Tires, Inc., believes that it has a single solution for both difficulties.

For the most of its 25 years in business, Big O has allowed store managers to acquire equity in its franchised outlets in reward for making the stores profitable. Under incentive contracts, a share of the store's profit is set aside to pay for the manager's stake. "It's a great growth vehicle to build on the stores already out there," says company president Steven P. Cloward. "And it's a great way to develop good, strong managers."

"For a young guy with no money and a lot of energy, there's nothing that beats it," says Bob Jones, a Big O store owner in northern California.

Mr. Jones started as a Big O "tire buster"—changing and refurbishing used tires—in 1966. A few years later, he bought his first Big O tire store in Martinez, California, through an incentive contract. He and his brother Ron now own seven stores in whole or part

and are opening three more. They have sold, or plan to sell, equity in eight of the stores to their managers.

One of those managers is Jeffrey Wandel, 27, who will soon own 50 percent of a Big O store in Sonoma. His stake will cost $143,000, which covers inventory, equipment, and a profit for the Jones brothers. But none of that amount will come out of Mr. Wandel's pocket. Instead, as an incentive to make the store as profitable as possible, the Jones brothers have allocated to Mr. Wandel a portion of the store's earnings, which he will use to make a down payment on his stake. He will then have 10 years to pay the balance, drawing on his 50 percent share of the store's profits.

Bob Jones says that he and his brother don't mind giving up some profit in order to have a more dedicated manager in each store. "You want him to have an incentive to do as good a job as you would do yourself," he says.[1]

Franchising, as we will see in this chapter, is one way in which distribution activities are controlled by producers. The incentives offered to Big O managers illustrate the importance of having retail outlets—a distribution system's direct contact with consumers—strongly identified with the producer of what is sold. We will take a good look at the ways in which products are distributed and the methods used to make the distribution system serve customers efficiently.

Channels of Distribution

distribution
channel of distribution

Distribution consists of all marketing activities that contribute time, place, and ownership utility to products. The **channel of distribution** is the firm or set of firms that are actively engaged in buying and selling products as they go from producer to user. Channels perform many of the essential marketing functions we studied in Chapter 11. These include storing, transporting, and risk taking as well as the obvious func-

middlemen

wholesalers

retailers

tions of buying and selling. As we will see, the number and variety of functions performed by each member of the channel may be quite different in each specific channel.

Middlemen are the firms that participate in the buying and selling of a product as it moves from producer to user. The two major categories of middlemen are wholesalers and retailers. **Wholesalers** are middlemen that sell primarily to retailers, other wholesalers, or manufacturers. **Retailers** are middlemen that sell to households and individuals. They sell a wide variety of consumer goods, usually in small individual amounts.

Any channel that uses middlemen reduces the number of contacts and transactions between channel members as products flow in the process of distribution. Figure 14-1 shows how the use of wholesalers reduces the number of transactions that would be needed if producers had to sell directly to retailers. The dozens of manufacturers who produce the goods sold in an independent drug store or hardware store, for example, need to deal with only one or two wholesalers in a geographic region. In turn, the wholesalers need to call on and serve only the retailers in their region. Walker's Pharmacy can order much of what it needs from one or two wholesalers in the area and can count on speedy delivery. Just think how complicated and expensive marketing would be if all consumer goods makers had to deal directly with all households. Without either wholesale or retail middlemen the costs of distribution would be staggering.

Channels also correct for the difference between the product mix of a given producer and the product mix desired by a user at the time that the user makes a purchase. Since these two mixes rarely match, other firms are often needed to complete the marketing process. General Foods and General Mills produce many consumer products. But when a shopper enters a supermarket, the shopper generally wants to buy the products of firms such as Procter & Gamble, Campbell, and Heinz as well as those of General Foods and General Mills. Wholesalers bring all of these products together and make them available to supermarkets and other retailers. This gives the grocery shopper the convenience of buying a broad assortment of products in one place.

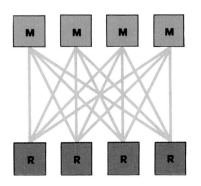 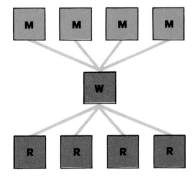

FIGURE 14-1 / Direct versus indirect sale. Without the wholesaler, each retailer would have to deal with all four manufacturers. Each manufacturer would also have to deal with all four retailers. With the wholesaler, each retailer and each manufacturer need deal only with one intermediary.

M = Manufacturer   W = Wholesaler   R = Retailer

TYPICAL CHANNELS OF DISTRIBUTION

Figure 14-2 illustrates several things about typical channels of distribution. It shows, for example, that more firms tend to be involved in channels for selling consumer products than in channels for selling industrial-organizational products. The channel can be direct (from producer to user as shown in channels numbered 1 and 5) for both product types. Direct sale, however, is much more common in the case of industrial products than consumer products. Avon Products and Electrolux Vacuums are consumer products that are sold directly, but they are the exception to the rule. Most consumer products are sold through longer, more complex channels, such as those numbered 2, 3, and 4 in Figure 14-2. Many food products, for example, are sold by their producers through large supermarket chains like Winn-Dixie and Safeway. Many other food and other convenience products are sold by their producers through wholesalers to smaller retailers. Sometimes, the services of an agent or broker might also be required, as illustrated in channel 4.

Industrial-organizational markets are often reached by direct channels. Firms like Pratt & Whitney (producers of aircraft engines) deal directly with their customers. However, many firms serving wider industrial markets, such as those for medical equipment, might choose to deal through a single middleman (intermediary), such as an industrial distributor or an agent (channels 6 and 7 in Figure 14-2). Makers of industrial-organizational products like Canon copiers and Hammerhill Bond stationery, with especially large numbers of users or widely scattered markets, might choose channel 8, which employs agents as well as industrial distributors, thus broadening their capacity to reach scattered or remote users.

CHANNEL DIMENSIONS

We can describe a channel of distribution in terms of its vertical dimension (length) and its horizontal dimension (breadth). The length depends on the number of times the product changes hands from the time it leaves the producer until it reaches the user. This dimension is also measured by the number of levels of middlemen directly involved with the sale of the product.

The breadth of a channel—that is, how many firms handle a product at a single level, such as at retail—depends mostly upon the product class: industrial-organizational, convenience, or shopping. Convenience goods are generally sold through many retail outlets of many different types. Nonprescription drugs like Tylenol and Pepto-Bismol are good examples of this. By contrast, the channel for many industrial-organizational products is likely to be as narrow as it is short.

SELECTING CHANNELS

Typical manufacturers of industrial-organizational products sell to a much smaller number of customers than typical consumer products manufacturers. Thus Xerox can afford to send salespeople directly to

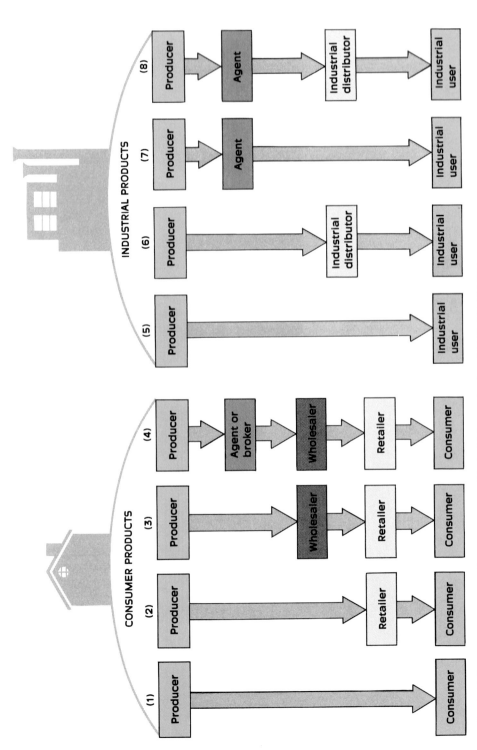

FIGURE 14-2 / Typical channels for consumer and industrial-organizational products. (*Source:* William F. Schoell and Joseph P. Guiltinan, *Marketing: Contemporary Concepts and Practices,* 3rd edition, Allyn and Bacon, Boston, 1988, p. 364.)

A seaside taffy maker that produces and sells taffy at the same location has a direct channel of distribution.

many of its customers. This would be too costly for Procter & Gamble or Pillsbury because their final customers number in the millions. In deciding how to get products to customers, marketers compromise between reducing cost and providing the best service and convenience. The final structure of a channel depends on:

- The number and size of customers
- The functions that the channel is expected to perform
- The costs of operating the channel
- The need to control the way the channel operates

A producer of lathes selling to a handful of industrial firms might sell directly to customers. A producer of toothbrushes selling to millions of customers, by contrast, will need a long (several levels of middlemen) channel. If customers expect credit and lots of attention from a retailer, the channel must end with some kind of full-service retailer who will provide these services. New car dealers, for example, are very service-oriented.

A firm like Tandy Corporation can operate its own Radio Shack retail stores because it can spread the store's overhead cost over a large number of products, many of which have large profit margins. A manufacturer of blankets could never afford to do this. The need to control a channel often determines whether or not a producer tries to operate its own channel intermediaries. The merger craze of the 1980s has made channel planning and control difficult for many manufacturers and middlemen, as you can see in the What Do You Think? box. Such

WHAT DO YOU THINK?

What Will the Wave of Mergers Do to Distribution Channels?

There have been so many mergers, acquisitions, and divestitures in various industries that it is difficult to keep track of the players without a scorecard. In 1985 alone, more than 3,000 deals involved nearly $180 billion in assets. In 1986, mergers, takeovers, and buyouts ran 21 percent ahead of the previous year. This creates great uncertainty for manufacturers and distribution channels about the future of their relationships.

When manufacturers undergo organizational change, their distributors, dealers, and retailers feel the impact. For example, Whirlpool Corporation acquired KitchenAid, Inc., another appliance maker, and within five months dismissed all of KitchenAid's former distributors.

When the mergers involve middlemen themselves, there are serious effects on the manufacturers who supply them. For instance, McKesson Corporation, the largest American pharmaceutical wholesaler, acquired Mass Merchandisers, Inc., a $326 million distributor of housewares, hardware, and health and beauty aids sold primarily through food stores. Manufacturers who previously supplied Mass Merchandisers and reached only the food trade now sell through a wholesaler with a large window on the drug store trade—a genuine bonanza for them.

Then again, a merger sometimes creates a smaller window on the market or closes a window entirely. Pepsico, Inc., which already owned the Taco Bell and Pizza Hut chains, recently acquired Kentucky Fried Chicken Corporation. Angered competitor Wendy's International, Inc. banished Pepsi-Cola products from its hamburger outlets and substituted Coca-Cola. Takeovers can affect competitors as well as the marketing channel participants.

Ideally, corporate reorganizations and related channel realignments would be predictable; manufacturers and distributors could plan for the change. But many mergers and acquisitions occur without warning. Even after the fact, firms seldom give detailed information about a reorganization to their partners in the marketing channel.

The evidence is conclusive that mergers are upsetting many long-standing and efficient channels. Middlemen in the age of mergers will have to be careful in writing contracts with manufacturers. Manufacturers, too, will need to have contingency plans for channel changes in anticipation of mergers. Will channels of the future be different because of the specter of mergers? What do you think?

Source: Allan J. Magrath and Kenneth G. Hardy, "When Mergers Rock Distribution Channels," *Business Marketing,* June 1987, p. 68.

uncertainty can play havoc with efforts to create some vertical marketing systems.

VERTICAL MARKETING SYSTEMS

The degree of coordination of effort of channel members may range all the way from zero to 100 percent. The members of a channel can be quite independent of each other, settling any differences or conflicts as they arise. The chances for good communication and speedy action in

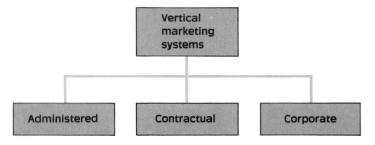

FIGURE 14-3 / Three major forms of vertical marketing systems. (*Source:* Adapted from William F. Schoell and Joseph P. Guiltinan, *Marketing: Contemporary Concepts and Practices,* 3rd edition, Allyn and Bacon, Boston, 1988, p. 384.)

vertical marketing system (VMS)

this kind of channel are not very great. On the other hand, **a vertical marketing system (VMS)** is a channel arrangement that provides complete or nearly complete coordination of effort within the channel. This coordination may be provided by three different forms of control. (See Figure 14-3.) An *administered VMS* achieves this coordination by virtue of the leadership of a channel leader, usually the producer, who sets goals and defines strategies for the marketing of the product. The channel leader also uses some form of market power (public brand acceptance, financial strength, or sheer size) to get other channel participants to cooperate.

A second, more tangible source of channel coordination is the *contractual VMS.* By means of a franchise or other legal contract the producer (or sometimes a middleman) requires other channel members to follow a specially designed marketing plan. The franchise agreement, as in the case of Pizza Hut, might specify design of retail facilities, minimum investment for retail outlets, training requirements for personnel, as well as prices, margins, minimum order sizes, and other aspects of channel operation.

The third way to achieve a true VMS is to *own a channel* in large part or completely. This is known as the corporate form of VMS. When a manufacturer sells through its own sales branches at the wholesale level, it is using the corporate VMS approach. The financial investment that the channel leader must make in such a system, however, is very large in comparison to the first two types of VMS.

Marketers are always trying to develop new and better channel systems to reach their customers. Xerox, for example, began producing and marketing copiers for small-volume users to compete with copiers by Savin and other rival firms. After experimenting with its own retail stores, Xerox decided to sell through independent retailers.

Service firms and nonprofit organizations also face problems of distribution, since they too must reach out for the people they serve. Banks are opening more branches and convenient electronic tellers. The Salvation Army and Goodwill Industries, by placing their collection boxes in shopping centers, make it easy for people to donate their used clothing and other items.

DEGREE OF MARKET COVERAGE

One aspect of channel design relates to the number of middlemen chosen to deal directly with users in a given market. There are three options. One is to practice *intensive distribution*. This refers to the use of a great many outlets in a market, such as a Coca-Cola bottler might use. This maximizes the consumers' opportunity to buy. The entire category of convenience goods—razor blades, cigarettes, foods, and so on—tends to be sold intensively.

For shopping and specialty consumer goods and for industrial goods, either selective or exclusive distribution is used. *Selective distribution* means picking a few of the best middlemen available in a market, such as in selecting apparel stores to sell Hart, Schafner & Marx clothing. When product image and service are important, selective distribution is likely to be used. Franchising may be used to achieve selective distribution and sometimes to achieve exclusive distribution.

Exclusive distribution is the extreme form of selectivity, when only one outlet is used in the market. Honda might, for example, select only one Acura dealership in a medium-sized city. Such a practice helps develop loyalty and motivation among the chosen middlemen. It also tends to give the producer more control over the way that the product is sold.

Wholesaling and Its Institutions

The broadest definition of wholesaling is all selling and related activity except that which deals directly with ultimate consumers. It consists mainly of sales to manufacturers, retailers, and other middlemen. Wholesalers stay in business by performing functions for firms that supply them and functions for firms that they sell to. These functions include buying, selling, transportation, storage, providing market information, financing, and risk reduction—all of the marketing functions.

The three principal categories of wholesalers are merchant wholesalers, merchandise agents and brokers, and manufacturers' own wholesaling units. The three are quite different. Merchant wholesalers are the most important. (See Figure 14-4).

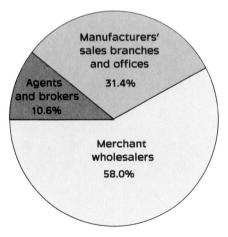

FIGURE 14-4 / Relative shares of total wholesale trade by major types of wholesalers. (*Source:* 1982 Census of Wholesale Trade.)

MERCHANT WHOLESALERS

merchant wholesaler

The **merchant wholesaler** is an independent middleman that takes title to goods and resells them to retailers or industrial-organizational buyers. The operation of the merchant wholesaler provides for an efficient flow of products through the channel of distribution. This middleman:

- Buys in large quantities and sells in small quantities
- Makes it possible for the retailer to simplify its buying process
- Often takes credit risks that manufacturers might not accept
- Guarantees delivery on short notice so that retailers need not keep large stocks

Merchant wholesalers are either full-service wholesalers or limited-service wholesalers. Among the full-service wholesalers are general-line wholesalers (such as grocery, drug, or hardware wholesalers), specialty wholesalers (such as frozen food wholesalers), and rack jobbers. Rack jobbers stock displays of special merchandise (not in the retailer's principal line), such as paperback books in food stores, and relieve the retailer of inventory expense and market risk on the items they handle.

MERCHANDISE AGENTS AND BROKERS

merchandise agents and brokers

Merchandise agents and brokers include several kinds of wholesaling middlemen that do not take title to the products they sell and that sell on behalf of a principal for a commission. Three important types of middlemen in this category are manufacturers' agents, brokers, and selling agents. A **manufacturers' agent** is an agent that represents several noncompetitive manufacturers in a limited geographic territory for a stated period of time. Without taking possession of products, such representatives aggressively seek to establish these products in the designated territory. A manufacturers' agent might, for example, help a maker of industrial cleansers to introduce the line in California. The agent would be paid a commission only for the actual sales made. This represents a more cost-efficient way of distributing in a new territory than dealing directly through wholesale industrial suppliers (merchant middlemen).

manufacturers' agent

selling agent

A **selling agent,** like a manufacturers' agent, represents a principal for a commission, except that it might handle competing lines and has nationwide representation rights. Selling agents act like the marketing department of the firms they represent.

merchandise brokers

Merchandise brokers are agents that merely bring buyers and sellers into contact with each other and do not have continuous relationships with the firms they represent. Their main "product" is market information. Because they perform few marketing functions, their commission is lower than that paid to agents.

Other common forms of agent middlemen are commission merchants, which often represent farmers by bringing their products to the central market and selling them on commission, and auction companies, which sell on behalf of their principal to the highest bidder in such diverse product areas as livestock, antiques, used cars, and citrus fruit.

MANUFACTURER WHOLESALING UNITS

Many manufacturers operate their own wholesaling units at locations apart from the factories themselves. Some of these facilities are sales branches, and others are known as sales offices. Sales branches, such as those run by Westinghouse Electric Supply Company, carry extensive inventories of the firm's products and serve as the shipping point for the orders received from customers in the region in which it is located. Sales offices also receive orders on behalf of the firm, but they relay the orders to the factory, from which they are then shipped. Sales offices serve as the base from which the firm's salespeople operate.

Retailing and Its Institutions

Retailing is the distribution activity that ordinary people know the most about. This is because we have so much contact with the corner convenience store, neighborhood shopping center, or supermarket. Retailing is part of everyday life in the United States.

Retailing includes all activities involved in selling or renting consumer products and services directly to ultimate consumers for their personal or household use. Retailers, such as Macy's or Food Lion, add utility to the products they make available to their customers by the services they offer, their reputations for courtesy and fair dealing, their helpful personnel, and their carefully planned store locations.

THE IMPACT OF RETAILING

The economic importance of retailing is made apparent by the huge sales figures for 1987 in Table 14-1 (on p. 414). The top twenty retailers alone sold about $250 billion worth of products to U.S. households, about $2700 to $2800 per capita. The share of retail business held by the top twenty retailers continues to rise.

TYPES OF RETAIL INSTITUTIONS

Retailers come in all types and sizes, from small shoe stores to giant discount stores. Some offer service, some do not. Some offer wide lines of merchandise, and some offer narrow ones. Some are parts of huge chains, and others are small, family-owned proprietorships.

Lucky Stores, Kroger Company, and Safeway Stores, Inc. are among the largest supermarket chains in the United States. Many other supermarkets are small independents. Still others are regional chains, such as Ralph's in California and Delchamp's on the Gulf Coast. **Supermarkets** are large, departmentalized, self-service retail stores that sell meat, produce, canned goods, dairy products, frozen foods, and many non-food items such as toys, magazines, and toiletry items. Supermarkets

supermarkets

TABLE 14-1 / The 20 largest retailing companies in 1987 ranked by sales

Rank	Company	Sales ($ millions)	Profits ($ millions)
1	Sears Roebuck	48,439.6	1,649.4
2	K mart	25,626.6	692.2
3	Safeway Stores	18,301.3	(495.4)
4	Kroger	17,659.7	246.6
5	Wal-Mart Stores	15,959.3	627.6
6	J.C. Penney	15,332.0	608.0
7	American Stores	14,272.4	154.3
8	Federated Department Stores	11,117.8	313.0
9	Dayton Hudson	10,677.3	228.4
10	May Department Stores	10,314.0	444.0
11	Winn-Dixie Stores	8,803.9	112.3
12	Southland	8,076.5	(66.4)
13	Great Atlantic & Pacific Tea	7,834.9	95.0
14	F.W. Woolworth	7,134.0	251.0
15	Lucky Stores	6,924.8	151.7
16	Marriott	6,522.2	223.0
17	Zayre	6,186.5	143.3
18	Melville	5,930.3	285.4
19	Albertson's	5,869.4	125.4
20	R.H. Macy	5,210.4	(13.8)

Source: "The 50 Largest Retailing Companies," *Fortune*, June 6, 1988. FORTUNE, © 1988 by Time Inc. All rights reserved.

are high-volume, low-margin stores. This means that they depend on rapid turnover of inventories for profit. Their profit margin on each sale is much lower than that of some other retail store types.

department stores

Department stores are stores that typically carry wide and deep merchandise lines including clothing, furniture, housewares, toys, and cosmetics. Large department stores like Macy's, Wanamaker's, Marshall Field, and Nieman-Marcus are known throughout the country. Many others operate independently or are owned by large department store groups, such as Federated Department Stores, Inc. They usually have several clothing departments and one of most of the other product lines. Many department stores lease some of their departments. Restaurants, beauty salons, confectionary departments, and a variety of service departments such as optical sales and repair and travel services are often leased to small entrepreneurs.

discount stores

Discount stores are stores that sell a wide variety of merchandise at discount prices, stressing high turnover and self-service. They might sell appliances, groceries, drug items, and clothing at discount prices. Wal-Mart and Kmart are examples of large nationwide discount chains. Regional discount chains include Murphy Mart, which operates in the east and midwest, and Family Dollar Stores, which operate in the southeast. They are growing rapidly in importance. Notice that several discount stores appear among the top twenty retailers shown in Table 14-1.

Among the newest and most successful retailing institutions is the *warehouse club.* These are huge, membership-only, combination retail-wholesale operations that sell all kinds of branded merchandise. They carry groceries, appliances, tires, clothing, liquor, and countless other items at very low prices. Sam's Wholesale Club (owned by Wal-Mart Stores, Inc.) and Costco Wholesale Club are among the most successful examples. Hypermarkets are large institutions with broad merchandise offerings, but they may have somewhat higher prices than wholesale clubs. Hypermarkets may also include service departments such as cafeterias and beauty salons. Meijer's Thrifty Acres, located near Detroit, is a hypermarket.

Recent years have seen a phenomenal growth in nonstore retailing. In various ways, nonstore retailers reach consumers with many kinds of products without the need for retail store locations. Some of the major forms of nonstore retailing include in-home retailing, telephone retailing, catalog retailing, direct-response retailing (including cable TV home shopping), and automatic vending.

Department stores increase their variety of goods and services by leasing out some departments such as beauty salons.

In-home retailing involves selling in private homes. This permits product demonstration in a realistic setting under relaxed, informal conditions. Often, as in the case of Amway, Avon, and Mary Kay Cosmetics, Inc., this is done through huge national staffs of salespeople who rely heavily on personal and family contacts. Some, such as Tupperware, rely heavily on party plan selling in which salespeople recruit hosts or hostesses to hold parties at their homes and invite friends and acquaintances.

Telephone retailing may be done by home improvement firms, real estate firms, and traditional department store organizations like Sears. They might employ lists of previous customers or purchased contact lists to solicit purchases. Sometimes they use automated telephoning equipment to reach large numbers of prospects at low cost.

Catalog retailing often complements traditional department store retailing.

Order Out.

Now you can satisfy your craving for Bloomingdale's without leaving home. Order up a full year of Bloomingdale's By Mail catalogues. Then, let yourself be tempted by our sizzling fashions—all presented with that luscious Bloomie's style. And delivered right to your door.

Start with our delectable spring preview issue.
Just mail this coupon with $3. You'll receive a full year of fashion catalogues plus a $3 gift certificate.

Name _____
                                              400
Address _____
City _____ State _____ Zip _____

Mail to: Bloomingdale's By Mail Ltd., Dept. 400,
P.O. Box 4160, Huntington Station, NY 11746

Please allow 4-6 weeks for shipment.   © 1988 Bloomingdale's By Mail Ltd.

THE ELECTRONIC AGE

How Is Electronic Shopping Changing the Way You Buy?

Electronic shopping has come to the college campus as it grows more important in the retailing of every kind of product. L.G. Balfour Company, manufacturer of class rings, is installing Infoport electronic shopping terminals in campus stores. The system presents product lines, features, and benefits. Students touch a video screen to see the presentations. This gives students a more effective retail-ordering system. It gives them year-round service instead of having sales reps on campus for just a few days, as has been the practice.

Noxell Corporation, maker of Noxema and of the Clarion line of cosmetics, has successfully introduced the computer for customer selection of cosmetics. Noxell's in-store computer helps women select the best shade of makeup. You can tell the computer your hair and eye color and the type of color of your skin. In a moment, you receive advice on the best combination of facial cosmetics for you.

Students and the general public are also using cable TV home shopping—those all-day marathons of flashy salesmanship selling everything from gold chains to toys to small appliances and home furnishings.

The early signs of cable TV retailing success have been impressive. Annual sales were growing fast in the late 1980s. The fact that the giant retailer Sears, Roebuck & Co. participated in this new marketing institution made other conventional retailers sit up and take notice. Sears signed with QVC Network, Inc. to sell its huge variety of merchandise. QVC became a kind of electronic middleman for Sears and other sellers.

The way that students like yourself respond to these new retailing systems will have a lot to do with the future of U.S. marketing and the role that electronics plays in it.

Sources: "Jewelry Stores, College Campuses Get ByVideo Terminals," *Marketing News,* Feb. 27, 1987, p. 20; Mark Ivey, Mary J. Pitzer, Kenneth Dreyfack, and Mark N. Vamos, "Home Shopping: Is It a Revolution in Retailing—Or Just a Fad?" *Business Week,* Dec. 15, 1986, pp. 62–69; Faye Rice, "Making Millions on Women Over 30," *Fortune,* May 25, 1987, pp. 75ff.

Catalog retailing has been around for many years, often as an adjunct to traditional retailer operations, such as Spiegel and Sears. Specialized versions, such as the Book-of-the-Month Club and Columbia Record Club are also familiar names. Growth in catalog retailing is attributed to the rise in two-earner households and to increasing crime- and traffic-related problems of metropolitan area living. However, in recent years, many successful catalog retailers have added in-store retailing to their operations. Firms such as Land's End, L.L. Bean, and Esprit have benefitted hugely from this trend.

Direct-response retailing also benefits from the lifstyle trends noted above. It depends largely upon television and radio advertising and the use of toll-free telephoning. Recordings, health insurance, and kitchen gadgets have been sold this way for years. More recently, cable TV home shopping such as is offered by Home Shopping Network, Inc. has extended this concept to a wide variety of products.

Automatic vending continues to perform a special kind of retail function. It is evolving in its own way. The familiar candy, beverage, and cigarette vending machines provide office and factory workers with easy access at any time of the day. This same general principle has become firmly entrenched in self-service banking, photocopy services, postage stamps in post offices, and even the sale of movie video-cassettes. The growth of automatic vending is restricted, however, by the high cost of paper money change makers and the rising cost of vandalism.

Physical Distribution

physical distribution process

The **physical distribution process** is the physical flow, including transportation, warehousing, handling, and related activities, that occurs between the production and the consumption of products. The growth in volume and variety of products sold and new transport technology have turned marketers' attention toward the problem of physical distribution, or logistics. Physical distribution includes the physical movement of raw materials and semimanufactured products into and through the plant and the movement of finished products out of the plant to middlemen and on to the ultimate consumers or industrial-organizational users.

facilitating middleman

A **facilitating middleman** is a specialist in physical distribution functions, such as a trucking company or a warehousing company. Facilitating middlemen differ from the other middlemen we have discussed in that they are rarely directly involved in the buying and selling functions.

COMPONENTS OF A PHYSICAL DISTRIBUTION SYSTEM

A physical distribution system for a given product consists of a series of components or subsystems that together bring the product to its ultimate user. Ideally, these subsystems are integrated so that the operations of the firms that participate in them are coordinated. The main subsystems are the transportation subsystem, the warehousing subsystem, and the inventory control, materials-handling, and order-processing subsystems. Manufacturers, wholesalers, and retailers, as well as facilitating middlemen share in the work of these subsystems.

THE TRANSPORTATION SUBSYSTEM

The transportation subsystem dominates physical distribution. Raw materials must be moved to factories and finished products, to wholesalers or retailers or household users. The subsystem includes several major modes of transportation.

MODES OF TRANSPORTATION

Firms choose among railroads, motor trucks, air freight, and, in some cases, ships and barges or pipelines to move their products. The decision is in the hands of the traffic manager who tracks the flow of materials, delivery dates, and storage space. The goal is to coordinate all aspects of physical distribution, thereby ensuring customer satisfaction at the lowest cost. As can be seen in Figure 14-5, there have been some dramatic shifts in the relative importance of the various modes of transportation.

RAILROADS The railroad's major advantage has always been low-cost, long-haul transportation for heavy and bulky products that have a low value in relation to weight. Steel, heavy equipment, lumber, and grain are examples of products hauled by railroads. The railroad provides reliable service because weather conditions do not often affect it. Railroads also offer economies of scale. One diesel engine can pull one or many loaded cars. This enables the railroad to spread the cost of fuel over a large number of shipments.

Railroads cannot offer speedy handling of small shipments nor reach into many points within large cities. It takes some time to assemble many shipments and load rail cars. Also, large cities restrict rail lines to protect the quality of life of their citizens.

TRUCKING The major advantage of motor truck transport is flexibility. Trucks can go anywhere there is a road. The shipper can reach many more customers by truck than by any other mode. There are many different specialized types of trucks. Because the required investment is small, many shippers own and operate their own trucks. With trucks, service is speedy and available door-to-door. Service providers such as cable television depend on the trucking industry as much as factories do.

WATERWAYS Water transport is important in both domestic and foreign commerce. The major advantage is low-cost transport for low-value, bulky products. As bulk goes up and value goes down, the advantage of water transport increases. On the other hand, as delivery time becomes

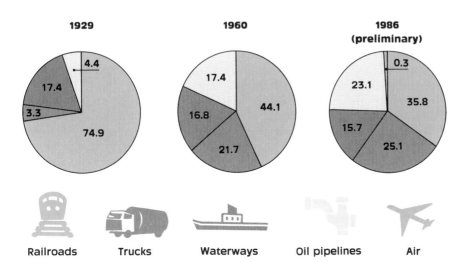

FIGURE 14-5 / Percent distribution of ton-miles of domestic intercity freight traffic by mode of transportation for selected years. (*Source:* 1986 preliminary data from the Association of American Railroads, *Railroad Facts*, 1987, p. 32.)

PHYSICAL DISTRIBUTION

An oil pipeline is a speedy and specialized mode of transportation in which the cost of shipment per ton is quite low after the initial investment has been made.

more important, using ships and barges becomes less attractive. Furthermore, some places are not accessible by water. Barge shipment is usually very reliable. During the severe drought in the summer of 1988, however, most river barge systems—including the Mississippi—were interrupted by low water levels for an extended period.

PIPELINES   Pipelines are the least visible of the modes, although they move many millions of tons of goods over many miles. Thousands of miles of pipelines move crude and refined petroleum, chemicals, and natural gas from major production points and ports of entry to cities all over the nation. A process called batch processing permits several different products to be moved at the same time. Black Mesa Pipeline transports a coal-water slurry mixture from the Black Mesa mines in Arizona across 273 miles of desert to a power plant in southern Nevada.

Pipelines are almost completely unaffected by weather. Once they are installed, the cost of operation is very low. Very little labor is involved in operating them.

AIRLINES   At one time, airplanes were considered basically people carriers. At best, they could move only very high-value, low-bulk cargo. But jumbo jets, more airports, and modern materials-handling techniques changed all that. Air transport is speedy and safe and helps shippers to reduce other distribution costs. Many airlines appeal to the shipper by saying that if it is willing to spend a little more money on transportation, its other distribution costs can be reduced.

A major area of growth in air freight has been in overnight traffic in small packages. Firms like Emery Air Freight, DHL Airways, and UPS have developed this type of freight successfully with the help of large advertising budgets. The UPS ad stresses the benefits of its overnight shipping service.

OWNERSHIP OF TRANSPORTATION

There is a legal relationship between a firm that wants to move freight (the shipper) and the transportation firm (the carrier) that will handle

The amazing growth of overnight package delivery services like UPS has been based on the fast, efficient service they provide.

the actual transport. Carriers (railroads, truckers, shipping companies, etc.) can be

- Common carriers
- Contract carriers
- Private carriers

common carrier

A **common carrier** is a transportation firm that offers its services to the general public at uniform, published rates. These carriers' rates and services are supervised by public agencies. Railroad rates, for example, are regulated by the Interstate Commerce Commission (ICC). Recent years have seen a good deal of deregulation in the transportation industry. It started with the airlines and has spread to the railroad and trucking industries. Our transportation system is more competitive now, and price competition is much more common. This is important to physical distribution managers who search for ways to reduce costs.

contract carrier

When a firm needs to move freight but cannot or does not choose to use a common carrier, it might call on a contract carrier. A **contract**

It takes a lot of distribution and a lot of deliveries to keep thousands of Burger King restaurants running smoothly. In this country, much of that distribution is handled by Distron, a subsidiary of Burger King Corporation.

Distron is headquartered in Miami and has a network of warehouses around the country. They distribute supplies to Burger King company-owned restaurants as well as to many of the Burger King franchisees, according to a Distron executive. (Franchisees always have the option of buying their supplies from another source, as long as those supplies meet Burger King standards.) But as the distribution arm for Burger King, Distron does more than just "distribute" supplies. They are also in charge of purchasing and have a network of managers in charge of getting the best products at the best price for Burger King restaurants.

Here is how the actual distribution of products from Distron warehouses to Burger King restaurants takes place. Those big 40-foot-long tractor trailers that you occasionally see making deliveries to a Burger King are actually divided into three separate sections for frozen goods (burger patties, etc.), refrigerated goods (vegetables), and dry goods (cups and plates, etc.). The front of the truck is a freezer compartment kept at 0–10° Fahrenheit; the middle section is refrigerated at 42–50° Fahrenheit, and the back is not refrigerated at all. Starting in the early afternoon and going on through the night, the truck is loaded at a regional Distron warehouse. The idea is to get the truck to leave around midnight to get to the area where the deliveries must be made as early as possible. Some of the truck drivers are given the keys to the restaurants in their area so that they can deliver the products before the restaurants open. The main thing, though, is to make their deliveries as quickly as possible. This is usually accomplished early in the morning where there are no distractions and little traffic. (As you might imagine, they must avoid the 11:30 A.M. to 1:00 P.M. peak time completely.)

The delivery itself usually takes just under an hour, and the drivers carry the supplies from the truck to the restaurant, where the supplies are stacked up inside the back.

Like many large distribution companies, Distron is experimenting with ways of letting their customers report what supplies they need. In many stores, assistant managers or restaurant managers fill out order forms and then phone their orders in to order takers at Distron. Many of the restaurants are experimenting with a computerized system, in which the order is simply punched in at the restaurant. In general, the entire ordering process is gradually becoming more high-tech. In some restaurants, computer printouts show managers how much of which product they should buy on the basis of the sales the restaurant should have that day. This in turn is based on the restaurant's historical sales for that day and week. At Burger King and elsewhere, distribution is thus becoming an increasingly sophisticated business, one that can mean the difference between success and failure for the corporation.

Questions

1. Does Burger King Corporation have a vertical marketing system? If so, which type of system is it?

2. Do you think Distron uses public warehouses?

3. Which is probably the best type of carrier for Burger King Corporation—common carrier, contract carrier, or private carrier?

carrier is a transportation firm, such as a trucking company, that negotiates private agreements with shippers to handle their freight. This is a contract between the shipper and the carrier. The shipper might want customized service and a guarantee of availability without investing in its own truck or barge fleet.

private carrier

For many firms a private carrier makes good sense. A **private carrier** is a transportation service owned and operated by the shipper itself. If a manufacturer or middleman, for example, owns and operates its own transportation, it is a private carrier. This kind of operation is justified when a large, predictable volume exists and common or contract carriers are not as economical or cannot do exactly what the shipper needs. Many oil companies, for example, own fleets of ships to transport their oil.

THE WAREHOUSING SUBSYSTEM

Warehousing regulates the flow of products through a marketing channel. It focuses on having the right quantity of each type of product in the right place at the right time. Good warehousing provides enough of the product to users when needed but does not produce excessive storage and other inventory carrying costs.

public warehouse

A warehousing plan determines the number, size, and location of warehouses as well as their ownership. Warehouses, of course, can be built, owned, and operated by the firm that needs them. Warehouses can also be leased by the user from a private owner, usually for an extended period. There is a third important option in the form of public warehousing. A **public warehouse** is an independently owned warehousing business that offers services to the general public, much as a common carrier offers transportation. The user pays only for the space and the period of time that space is occupied. The public warehouse might also offer its customers a variety of services related to its distribution activities in a geographic area, as listed in Table 14-2 (on p. 424). This could be an ideal choice for a firm with a need for temporary distribution or an uncertain volume of distribution in a new area.

Like other goods, Nike athletic shoes must be warehoused between production and final purchase, either at the plant or at an off-site warehouse.

TABLE 14-2 / Services offered by public warehouses

Storage	The seller can stockpile products until needed for delivery to customers.
Break bulk and reshipping	The seller ships in carload or truckload lots to the warehouse. The warehouse breaks bulk and delivers to the seller's local customer.
Stock spotting	The seller locates inventories of finished products near large customers rather than at the plant. The warehouse provides local delivery upon receipt of orders from those customers.
Management and labor expertise	Public warehouses are specialists in performing physical distribution activities.
Financing	Public warehouses issue warehouse receipts that can be used by customers as collateral for bank loans.

Source: William F. Schoell and Joseph P. Guiltinan, *Marketing: Contemporary Concepts and Practices*, 3rd ed., Allyn and Bacon, Boston, 1988, p. 455.

OTHER PHYSICAL DISTRIBUTION SUBSYSTEMS

Inventory control subsystems are methods of controlling the level of inventories at various points of the physical distribution system. Such a system considers when orders should be placed and how large the orders should be. The cost of carrying inventory, including such things as storage, insurance, damage, taxes, interest, and obsolescence, as well as the order-processing cost are computed so as to estimate the economic order quantity. The **economic order quantity (EOQ)** is the amount that a firm should order for inventory replenishment if it wants to minimize the sum of its carrying costs and order-processing costs.

economic order quantity (EOQ)

The order-processing subsystem consists of activities such as order receipt, credit approval, invoice preparation, and collection of accounts. Computers have revolutionized the speed and accuracy of this accounting-related subsystem. Related information appears in Chapter 20.

The materials-handling subsystem is intimately connected to the transportation and warehousing subsystems. It involves the activities of physically moving products into and out of plants, warehouses, and transportation terminals such as ports and railyards. New technology has greatly improved the efficiency of materials handling. Such simple devices as the pallet and forklift have greatly reduced materials-handling costs. Even greater has been the more recent development of containerization. **Containerization** is the practice in modern transportation of using standard large containers, preloaded by the shipper, sealed and delivered as a unit to the destination without breaking the seal.

containerization

Modern containers move every type of freight. Containers are loaded at the shipper's plant, sealed, and moved to the receiver's plant. Instead of many separate boxes or single units, one large standard container is handled quickly and efficiently. Containers move easily from truck to train (piggyback), from train to ship (fishyback), or from truck to plane (birdyback). These are all forms of intermodal transportation. The savings in distribution cost can be great because of reduced theft and damage as well as lower transport rates on intermodal movements.

The Total Cost Concept

total cost concept

At one time, physical distribution management was mainly concerned with minimizing the cost of transportation. This is a narrow view because the transportation cost is often less than half the total cost of physical distribution. Modern firms apply the total cost concept. The **total cost concept** demands that when a given method of transportation is under consideration, all costs related to it be weighed and their sum minimized. All of this must be done without sacrificing the desired level of customer service. Related costs include those of storage and handling as well as losses and costs related to running out of stock. Concentrating only on transportation costs can lead to unprofitable distribution decisions.

Many firms have developed distribution systems that depend on computers to schedule the flow of products from a manufacturer to a consumer or an industrial user. They select the best location for intermediate storage points and the best means of transportation. These computer-based systems take into account the costs of transporting and storing as well as the cost of running out of merchandise. Such accurate cost systems are common when the channel is under the control of a retailer or manufacturer. The objective of modern physical distribution management is to achieve a balance between costs and service.

Summary

Marketers create channels of distribution to reach their customers. In some cases, manufacturers sell directly to consumers and industrial-organizational users. In other cases they use middlemen such as retailers, wholesalers, and agent middlemen. The selection of channels depends on the number and size of customers, the functions that need to be performed, the cost of performing them, and the need to control the way they are performed.

Retailing institutions (supermarkets, department stores, and others) vary greatly in the breadth of lines they carry, in the services they offer, and in their organizational structure. Wholesale functions are performed either by merchant wholesalers, by merchandise agents and brokers, or by manufacturer wholesaling units, such as sales branches. These institutions sell consumer goods in large quantities to retailers and industrial goods to business firms and institutions.

Facilitating middlemen such as railroads and warehousing companies also participate in the process. Choices must be made between investment in private transportation and warehousing, the leasing of such facilities, and the use of public facilities such as common carriers or public warehouses. Choices among the various modes of transportation are also necessary. In some cases a true physical distribution system is built. This applies the total cost concept and provides the level of service that customers want at the lowest achievable cost.

Review Questions

1. What effect might the addition of a middleman to a channel of distribution have on the number of transactions and contacts?

2. Describe two typical channels of distribution for consumer products and two typical channels for industrial products.

3. On what factors does the final structure of a channel of distribution depend?

4. Describe three ways to achieve a vertical marketing system.

5. What functions are performed by the merchant wholesaler?

6. Describe the operations of three types of merchandise agents and brokers.

7. What are the major subsystems of the physical distribution system?

8. Contrast the features of common, contract, and private carriers.

Discussion Questions

1. A friend tells you that he can save you a lot of money buying dining room furniture. He says that he can get it from a dealer who "eliminates the middleman." Analyze this statement. Is this possible? Why or why not?

2. What is the chance that non-store retailing will take over one-third or more of the retail business in the United States? Give arguments supporting this possibility and arguments opposing it.

3. Show how the total cost concept might apply to distributing expensive flowers from nurseries in California to florists in the New York City area.

Key Terms

distribution
channel of distribution
middlemen
wholesalers
retailers
vertical marketing system (VMS)
merchant wholesaler
merchandise agents and brokers

manufacturers' agent
selling agent
merchandise brokers
supermarkets
department stores
discount stores
physical distribution process
facilitating middleman
common carrier

contract carrier
private carrier
public warehouse
economic order quantity (EOQ)
containerization
total cost concept

LOSING THE CHAIN IMAGE

A Chi-Chi's Mexican restaurant in Peoria, Illinois, was having difficulty attracting customers. The problem was not the competition. It arose from several other factors, according to Don Paisley, the restaurant's general manager.

One problem was the depressed local economy. Another was a community perception that the chain restaurant was taking local money out of town, while putting smaller, family-owned restaurants out of business. Consultant Alan Zuckerman of Indianapolis had a plan to correct the perception problem. Zuckerman calls it "community networking." It involves getting the client firm into public relations activities such as facility tours for Brownie troops.

The local chain outlet developed a marketing team of employees who knew the local town or neighborhood. This team then brought in representatives of leading charities, community groups, and local media. These were community people who advised the team about the town's favorite charities and current popular local events. They also gave the Chi-Chi's restaurant some feedback about how the local community perceived it.

The next step in the community networking strategy was a planning session for the year, using the extensive file of community-based data that had been collected.

Some of the programs used to gain local favor include promotions with the local baseball team and contributions to the St. Jude's Children's Fund.

The Chi-Chi's manager and employees are personally involved in most fundraisers. Strong personal commitment on the part of management and workers is essential for the community networking program to accomplish its goal: the recognition of a chain outlet as a true part of the local community instead of as an outsider.[2]

Questions

1. What advantages do franchise outlets like Chi-Chi's have over local restaurants?
2. What are the natural advantages of locally owned independent restaurants?
3. What did the community networking strategy do to overcome the local restaurant advantages?
4. What strategies can the locally owned restaurants pursue that might strengthen their competitive position relative to Chi-Chi's?

A NEW WAY TO SELL COMPUTER PROGRAMS

ComputerLand, one of the nation's largest computer products retailers, is trying out a new way to sell computer programs. The "Hands On" system fits in a 30-square-foot kiosk similar to a 1950s record store listening booth. Using a computer monitor, a shopper can sample hundreds of programs through video tutorials and demo disks. The user first calls up a list of software classifications, such as spreadsheet programs. From there he or she can see 6- to 10-minute videos explaining each program.

There are some questions about whether this system can really replace the more conventional retail clerk. For one thing, the system cannot provide the customer with a complete instruction manual for each program. Others argue that the system really is not needed at all because there are so few software packages that sell in large volume.[3]

Questions

1. If you were manager of a small independent computer store, would you consider using such a system? Why or why not?
2. If you were the marketing director for a large software producer such as IBM or Apple, would you want your products included in this system? Why or why not?
3. What is there about the nature of the product that might favor such a state-of-the-art retailing system?

Reginald F. Lewis has been featured prominently in the world's financial journals ever since he masterminded the largest leveraged buyout of a non-U.S. firm in history, the $985 million takeover of the international food behemoth Beatrice Company, a deal he describes as "something like the gnat swallowing the elephant."

This coup, in which Lewis competed against groups lead by such giants as Nestlé, Wesray, Citicorp, and Shearson Lehman Brothers, came on the heels of his stunning turnaround of the McCall's company, a faltering sewing pattern concern. Lewis and his investors bought the company for $1 million in equity and $28 million in debt. As is his style, he brought top management of McCalls into the deal, listened to their ideas, and diversified. The two most successful years of the 113-year-old company's history followed and his TLC group sold the company to the John Crowther Group of Britain for $63 million in cash. The buyer also absorbed $32 million in McCall's debt.

An economics graduate of Virginia State University, Lewis wrote

SECTION FIVE

Financial Management

his third-year thesis at Harvard Law School on takeovers. After graduation, he joined a prestigious Manhattan law firm which he left to form his own firm, specializing in venture capital. In 1983, he formed TLC Group.

Lewis said he was attracted to Beatrice because the food business is stable, and the company includes processing and distribution units. Beatrice International includes 64 operating companies in 31 countries serving more than 1.7 billion consumers, and had sales in 1986 of more than $2.5 billion. He also liked its European base. "With the budget deficit, I believed the dollar would continue to be under pressure. Therefore, Europe was not a bad place to be with respect to having your earnings in currencies other than U.S. dollars."

The Europeans like him, too. Don Pedro Ballve, head of the Spanish meat processing company Compofrio, said, "He understands that money is not everything. He knows that the history and culture of the company and the other assets, not just market share, are all connected to the business."

TLC originally offered $950 million for Beatrice. For help in reaching that figure, Lewis turned to a friend who headed the "junk bond" department at the investment banking firm Drexel Burnham Lambert. Drexel and TLC put some thirty people—accountants, bankers, and lawyers—on the deal. (A leveraged buyout means the new company is bought primarily with borrowed funds that the dealmaker hopes to repay with funds generated by the acquired company's assets or through sales of that company's assets.)

Lewis, a hard worker who energizes others, describes himself as "committed." Even though this deal was of a far greater magnitude than anything he had ever attempted before, Lewis was undaunted: "Size in today's marketplace isn't the key factor," he said. "The question is the quality of the assets and the underlying earnings power of those assets. When you have a good handle on that, then you know what you're capable of financing."

LEARNING OBJECTIVES

After reading this chapter, you will be able to:

- Distinguish between financial and managerial accounting processes.

- Prepare a chart showing the major information flows of accounting.

- Complete the principal accounting equations.

- Explain the functions of the balance sheet and income statement.

- Explain the relationships among transactions, accounts, and double-entry bookkeeping.

- Explain how an investor might use the financial statements of a firm that he or she might wish to invest in.

- Show how the return on net worth and current financial ratios are used.

- Explain the function of cost accounting.

In this chapter you will find out what accounting is all about and who uses the information it provides. We will introduce and explain two major financial accounting statements and their use as well as various managerial accounting tools.

By the time you complete the chapter you will understand better the role of the accountant, especially that of the certified public accountant. We will pay special attention to financial accounting and the concept of the basic accounting equation. This will include a detailed treatment of the balance sheet and of the accounts—assets, liabilities, and owners' equity—that comprise it. This is followed by an examination of the income statement and its major accounts: sales revenues and expenses. The relationships between all of these major accounts are explored by introducing double-entry bookkeeping and its use in recording financial transactions.

You will also learn how financial accounting is used by investors, lenders, and prospective lenders to study a firm's financial condition. This will tie into the computation and use of basic financial ratios.

The chapter closes with an overview of the important role of managerial accounting. Special attention is given to budgeting and cost accounting.

"Homer, if you don't get those invoices and check stubs to the office in Baton Rouge this week, you can just hang it up."
Ed Simpson, the owner of a Baton Rouge, Louisiana, construction company, was

talking to his construction superintendent, Homer Huntley. Mr.
Simpson had come to the construction site after repeated
phone calls and notes had failed
to get Mr. Huntley to submit the
documents needed to record expenditures and progress on the
job he was supervising.

By the time Mr. Simpson left the
small construction shack, Homer
was furious. He muttered under
his breath, "Bookkeepers! Don't
they have anything better to do
than ruin my day?" He started
yanking invoices, check stubs,
handwritten notes, and other papers off the nails he had driven
into the shack's walls as a
haphazard system for job records.

Homer stuffed the papers into a
brown grocery bag he had been
using as a trash container, folded
the bag's top and fastened it with
a nail pulled from the wall.
Scratching about in the top
drawer for a writing instrument,
he found a felt-tip pen and wrote
Simpson Construction Company's
address on the bag. On his way
home that night, Homer stuffed
the bag into a mailbox outside
the local post office.

For years after that the bag hung
on the wall in the accounting office at Simpson Construction
Company. It was a constant re-
minder of the sloppiness and dis-
dain of many field personnel for
ordinary accounting procedures
and practice.[1]

The way accounting is done changes over time, depending on the prevailing thinking of professional accountants and changes in tax law. It
has been a very long time, however, since Homer's casual view of
accounting has been acceptable. Changes in the way accounting is done
can materially affect how much is really known about a firm's financial
results. However, many of the traditional accounting principles tend to
remain the same for long periods of time. They provide a uniform basis
for businesspeople's evaluation and comparisons of the performances
of their own and other firms.

What Is Accounting?

Business firms all own things like cash, merchandise, and buildings.
They also buy and sell such things in the search for profit. As all this
happens, the story of the financial success or failure of the firms un-
folds. But it can be told accurately only if businesses assign appropriate
values to and keep good records of all the things they own, buy, or sell.
This is why business firms maintain a system of accounting and why
Simmons Construction Company tacked Homer Huntley's brown bag
on the wall. **Accounting** is a process of measuring, recording, interpreting, and reporting data that reflect the financial condition of the firm.

Accounting processes are of two general types: financial accounting and managerial accounting. **Financial accounting** is a "scorekeeping process" that is meant to keep several interested groups (inside and
outside the firm) informed of the financial condition of the firm. When

accounting

financial accounting

a bank is thinking of loaning money to a business, it must have a reliable picture of the firm's condition. The owners of a firm must have some means of measuring its progress or decline. Often they must evaluate management or decide whether to expand operations. People who are thinking of investing in a business need good financial information, too. And the government is always interested in how a firm is doing. It usually has tax collection in mind. The financial accounting system is designed to provide this kind of information to these parties, as shown in Figure 15-1.

To report this information correctly, the financial accounting system must make an accurate evaluation of what the firm owns, owes, buys, and sells. This process is guided by generally accepted accounting principles. **Generally accepted accounting principles** are a body of theory and procedure developed by the Financial Accounting Standards Board (FASB), a group recognized as representing the accounting profession. Accountants look upon FASB rules as standard guides to their practice. Homer Huntley, the construction supervisor in our introductory example, probably still does not know or care about FASB, so it is up to accountants to learn the standards and to uphold them.

The second major accounting process is known as **managerial accounting.** It serves the firm's managers by calling attention to problems and aiding them in planning, decision making, and controlling the

generally accepted accounting principles

managerial accounting

FIGURE 15-1 / Accounting information flows.

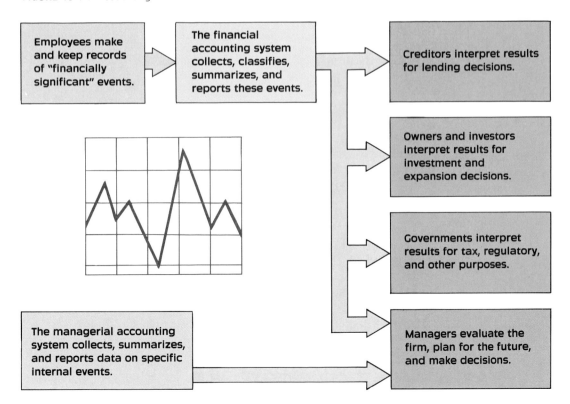

firm's operations. A production manager, for example, might want to know how much it costs to run a new piece of equipment for a day. The sales manager, as we saw in Chapter 13, wants to keep tabs on the selling expenses per dollar of sales made by each salesperson. The controller wants to limit unnecessary telephone calls. All of these internal processes help managers do a better job, but they are not reported by the ordinary financial accounting system. The latter presents "scorekeeping" information for owners and others on matters such as "What are this company's assets at the end of the year 1990?" and "How much profit did the company make?" The management accounting system instead answers questions like "Is each salesperson meeting his/her quota?" and "Which offices are running up large phone bills?" (See Figure 15-1.)

Accounting, then, is a valuable tool for keeping people informed. To do this well, it must do two things. A system of accounting must first identify the data that is relevant to the firm's operation. It must then process that data as quickly and cheaply as possible. Today, computers are quite helpful in doing all of this. But it is the accountants who tell the computers what to do.

WHAT IS AN ACCOUNTANT?

An accountant does much more than keep books. Accountants know basic procedures for recording financial events (transactions) quickly, accurately, and with maximum security. They know enough about the law to build a system of accounts that reflects those laws, especially tax laws. They know where to find specialized information about laws and the answers to other tough questions as they relate to the firm they serve. For example, an accountant for the International Paper Company might keep a library relating to land valuation and the use of natural resources. An accountant must also be aware of the history and policies of the firm in order to meet its financial and managerial accounting needs.

certified public accountant (CPA)

A **certified public accountant (CPA)** is an accountant who has fulfilled the legal requirements of his or her state for knowledge in accounting theory, practice, auditing, and law and who is licensed to sign legally required financial reports. Often CPAs' knowledge must be quite broad because they deal with the accounting processes of many different firms. Their duty to report the financial position of a firm extends to the general public as well as to the firm that hires them. Auditing (checking the accuracy of records) makes up much of the independent CPA's work. An independent CPA certifies that financial statements of a firm were prepared in accordance with generally accepted accounting principles. Decision makers (investors, lenders, and managers) expect the CPA's opinion to be a truly independent one so that they can rely on the firm's financial statements. The Arthur Young ad (on p. 436) suggests the kinds of involvement necessary to do high-quality work for the clients of a large accounting firm.

Some accountants perform the accounting function for one firm only. They supervise accounting clerks, bookkeepers, and computers that do the everyday recordkeeping. They prepare statements and keep top management informed. Some private accountants are responsible

WHAT DO YOU THINK?

Should CPA Firms Regulate Themselves?

In recent years there have been a substantial number of "audit failures." This means that a firm suffers serious business problems soon after receiving from its independent CPA auditor firm a "clean" opinion on its financial statements. This, in turn, has led to passage of a new American Institute of CPAs (AICPA) regulatory program that depends on peer review. The peer review process involves one firm of CPAs evaluating the quality control of the audit procedures of another.

Arguments that have been raised against peer review include those advanced by the American Bar Association. The ABA considered peer review for legal firms a few years ago but dropped the proposal because of two possible problems. Peer review brings up problems of confidentiality of client records. It also might involve conflicts of interest—a client of the reviewing accounting firm may be a competitor of the client of the reviewed accounting firm.

Many CPA firms, especially smaller ones, have opposed any mandatory form of peer review because of the cost of doing reviews (estimated by an officer of AICPA to be from $4,000 for a small firm to as much as $1 million for the largest CPAs). They also claim that there is no evidence that peer reviews reduce the audit failure rate.

On the favorable side, the Securities Exchange Commission (SEC), overseer of the accounting of firms whose stocks are publicly traded, has proposed mandatory peer review. Such review, the SEC says, will require companies to reveal more negative news in their annual reports, reducing the likelihood of audit failures. Many accountants felt that, if the peer review system had not been worked out, more oppressive government regulation of auditing practice would have followed. One U.S. Representative had threatened to reintroduce legislation to force auditors to develop stricter standards.

The AICPA has also been working on tougher standards that require the auditing firm to provide "reasonable assurance" that financial statements are not "materially misstated because of fraud or error." This language puts a larger burden on auditors than the traditional statement that the financial position of the firm is "fairly presented in conformity with generally accepted accounting principles on a consistent basis." This kind of standard, while separate from the question of peer review, stems from the argument that the business community and the general public have the right to expect more from auditors than they have been getting. Is self-regulation the answer? What do you think?

Sources: Lee Berton, "Self-Regulation By Accountants Divides Industry," *The Wall Street Journal* June 20, 1986, p. 1; Lee Berton, "Rewriting the Rules: Jerry Sullivan Leads Effort to Increase Auditors' Responsibility," *The Wall Street Journal*, Dec. 17, 1986, p. 25; Lee Berton, "SEC to Rule Soon on Peer Review for Accountants," *The Wall Street Journal*, Jan. 8, 1987, p. 2; and Lee Berton, "CPA Group Sued over Bid to Require Membership in a Self-Regulatory Unit," *The Wall Street Journal*, March 31, 1987, p. 12.

for internal auditing. They make sure that accounting is being done as it should be. Some accountants who do auditing work have the title of certified internal auditor. This is a professional certification granted by the Institute of Internal Auditors on the basis of an exam somewhat like that given to CPAs.

Accounting firms like Arthur Young do much more than just prepare tax returns for their clients.

certified management accountant (CMA)

Another important certification received by private accountants is that of certified management accountant. A **certified management accountant (CMA)** is an accountant who has met the educational and experience requirements set by the Institute of Certified Management Accountants (an arm of the National Association of Accountants) and passed a five-part examination.

Financial Accounting

Every business—whether it is a corporation, partnership, or sole proprietorship—has an owner or a group of owners. Whoever owns a firm

Inventory of raw materials like aluminum is an asset that appears on the balance sheet of many manufacturers.

is likely to want to know how much the firm is worth and how it is doing. Accounting helps owners find these things out.

One way to figure what a firm is worth is to take all the things a firm owns, put a value on each one, and then add them all up. This could include cash, equipment, buildings, land, and anything else a firm owns. An **asset** is whatever a firm, organization, or individual owns that has a dollar value. It is recorded on the firm's books at its historical cost—what it originally cost the firm to acquire.

asset

But the real value of a firm to the owners is usually something less than the total value of its assets. This is because most firms borrow money in one way or another to conduct the business. When the firm buys merchandise on credit or when it gets a loan from the bank, it receives assets (inventory or cash), but it also incurs a debt or liability. A **liability** is a claim held by outsiders against the firm's assets.

liability

If the firm goes out of business, it is obliged to repay outsiders' claims (liabilities) before the owners can claim any of the remaining assets. The **owners' equity,** or claims of owners against a firm's assets, is equal to the amount of the firm's assets minus the amount of the liabilities. Owners' equity is also called a firm's *capital*.

owners' equity (capital)

THE BASIC ACCOUNTING EQUATION

basic accounting equation

The **basic accounting equation** is a mathematical statement of the balance between what a firm owns, what it owes, and what the owners' share is worth. It is written as follows:

$$\text{ASSETS} = \text{LIABILITIES} + \text{OWNERS' EQUITY (CAPITAL)}$$
or
$$\text{ASSETS} - \text{LIABILITIES} = \text{OWNERS' EQUITY (CAPITAL)}$$

FINANCIAL ACCOUNTING

"Scorekeeper and internal financial consultant" is how the senior vice-president and controller of Burger King Corporation describes his job. However, being chief financial officer for a company that size actually involves some enormous responsibilities.

The "scorekeeper" role is a major job in itself. As chief scorekeeper for Burger King Corporation, the controller and his department must keep track of the company's financial performance—what are sales, why they are up (or down), what profits are, and so on. He is also in charge of an audit group, which keeps track of the company's performance for Pillsbury. As a company with many subsidiaries, Pillsbury's top management naturally needs some way of keeping close track of how each of the subsidiaries is doing. Pillsbury has thus established a network of semi-independent audit groups like the one at Burger King Corporation. Each is located in its subsidiary's headquarters and is responsible to the head of its subsidiary. But controllers like the one at Burger King Corporation also report to the controller's office at Pillsbury. In that way, Pillsbury (and most other large firms) can keep track of how its far-flung subsidiaries are doing.

The controller's group also acts in four main ways as internal financial consultants to Burger King. First, they are part of the company's investment decision-making team. As such, they help do the financial investment analysis work that helps let managers know whether or not a proposed store location is a good one. Second, they are part of the company's sales and profit analysis group. They analyze specific marketing plans to determine things like breakeven points. That way, they help management decide whether or not the marketing plan for a product such as Burger King's Whopper® sandwich is a sound one.

However, they do not just consult on the plans for existing products. The group also plays a big role in new product planning, as part of the company's new product development team. They help the new product team to quantify sales estimates and determine what the product's profits will be on the basis of "pro forma" or projected sales and expense figures.

Finally, the group acts as consultants to Burger King Corporation's senior management in developing the firm's strategic plans. At Pillsbury, strategic planning is a three-stage process. In the summer a nonfinancial plan is presented by each subsidiary. For Burger King the plan covers things like the company's plans for growth, adding new menu items, and streamlining its operations. In the fall and winter these plans are then presented in more detail. Finally, for the third-stage spring presentation, the controller's group gets heavily involved. They help develop a budget for the year and a specific "micro plan." This shows specific tactics that Burger King Corporation plans to use next year in terms of advertising campaigns and new store openings, for instance. The controller's group develops financial figures for this plan so that the company and Pillsbury can predict sales, expenses, and profits.

Questions

1. Burger King Corporation's controller describes his job as a combination "scorekeeper and internal financial consultant." What does that suggest to you?

2. How important is the controller's role in strategic planning?

3. The controller's audit group is semi-independent. Does this mean that Burger King Corporation does not receive accounting services from external, independent CPAs?

To review what the equation means in the context of a firm, let's examine the facts relating to Dan's Records, Inc. This small retailer of record albums, tapes, compact disks, and related merchandise has assets totaling $64,000. (See Figure 15-2.) The firm also owes $28,000 to various lenders. This means that the owners' equity is equal to $36,000.

$$\text{ASSETS} = \text{LIABILITIES} + \text{OWNERS' EQUITY (CAPITAL)}$$
$$\$64,000 = \$28,000 + \$36,000$$

The equation is in balance. It must be in balance because the sum of the claims on the right-hand side by definition equals the sum of the assets on the left. This equation is the basis of the balance sheet.

FIGURE 15-2 / Dan's Records, Inc. balance sheet, December 31, 1990.

Assets			Liabilities and Stockholders' Equity		
CURRENT ASSETS:			**CURRENT LIABILITIES:**		
Cash	$4,000		Accounts payable	$5,000	
Accounts receivable	18,000		Accrued wages	1,000	
Merchandise inventories	10,000		Estimated tax liability	7,000	
Prepaid expenses	2,000		Total current liabilities		$13,000
Total current assets		$34,000	**LONG-TERM LIABILITIES:**		
PROPERTY, PLANT, & EQUIPMENT:			Bonds payable		$15,000
Land		4,000	Total liabilities		$28,000
Building	$20,000		**STOCKHOLDERS' EQUITY:**		
Less accumulated depreciation	4,000	16,000	Capital stock	$25,000	
INTANGIBLE ASSETS			Retained earnings	11,000	
Goodwill		10,000	Total stockholders' equity		36,000
TOTAL ASSETS		$64,000	**TOTAL LIABILITIES AND OWNERS' EQUITY**		$64,000

THE BALANCE SHEET

The **balance sheet** is a financial statement that shows what a firm owns, what it owes, and what the owners' interest is worth at a given point in time. This is sometimes called a *statement of financial position*. Since a new balance sheet is computed by a firm's accountants at least yearly, a set of balance sheets can be used to trace financial changes in one firm over time. Investors might use such a set of balance sheets as a physician would use a set of X-rays taken at different times to measure the process of healing or growth. Balance sheets make up an important part of a firm's annual report to stockholders. An investor might also compare the balance sheets of two firms at the same point in time (usually at the end of a year). This comparison could help the investor decide which firm is the better investment.

Figure 15-2 is an example of a simple balance sheet for Dan's Records, Inc. as of December 31, 1990. It is an expanded, more detailed version of the basic accounting equation. It shows the kinds of assets and liabilities and the amount of each as well as the components of

The stock of books in your college bookstore is a current asset, called merchandise inventory, on the store's balance sheet.

owners' (in this case, stockholders') equity. The three major classes of assets are current assets; property, plant, and equipment; and intangible assets.

current asset

A **current asset** is an asset that the firm normally expects to hold no longer than a year. Examples are cash (currency and checking account), accounts receivable, merchandise inventories, and prepaid expenses. Accounts receivable are amounts owed to the firm by customers buying on credit. Merchandise inventory consists of all goods purchased by the firm for resale but which have not yet been sold. Prepaid expenses might include prepaid insurance premiums that have not yet been used up (see Figure 15-2) or legal fees paid in advance. The **accrual** principle in accounting means that a firm charges off expenses only in the accounting period (usually the calendar year) in which the firm's operations benefit from the expense and not necessarily in the period in which the actual cash payment was made.

accrual

Some small firms, especially service firms, keep accounting records on a cash basis instead of an accrual basis. This means that they charge off purchases of supplies, insurance policies, and so on entirely during the accounting period in which they buy them. This avoids such asset accounts as prepaid expenses and such liability accounts as accrued expenses (benefitted from but not paid for).

Property, plant, and equipment last longer than current assets. Printing presses, big computers, and nuclear reactors are examples of such fixed assets. In the case of Dan's Records, Inc. there are two items listed—land and building. **Depreciation** is a process of writing off the cost value of long-lived assets during the period that they contribute to the earnings of the firm. Accounting practice required that depreciation be reflected in the balance sheet. The amount of depreciation is deducted from the asset value on the balance sheet. (See Figure 15-2.)

depreciation

A final class of assets is also shown in Figure 15-2. *Intangible assets* have no physical form or clearly defined value. Goodwill is an intangible asset—the extra value of a firm because of the firm's good reputation. According to accepted accounting principles, goodwill can be shown on the books only if the firm has been purchased at a price greater than the tangible capital value (the difference between tangible assets and liabilities) of the firm at the time of purchase. In Figure 15-2 we can see that Dan's Records, Inc., a corporation, bought the previous proprietorship, Phil's Record Shop, and paid $10,000 more than the tangible capital value of the business. Accepted accounting principles require that this asset be amortized (written off gradually). However, for simplicity's sake we do not show this amortization in the financial statements of Dan's Records, Inc.

As we move over to the right-hand side of the balance sheet in Figure 15-2, we also move to the right-hand side of the basic accounting equation. We encounter two main types of liabilities: current liabilities and long-term liabilities. A **current liability** is a debt that will be paid off within a year from the balance sheet date. This category can include accounts payable or accrued wages (wages earned but unpaid) as found in Figure 15-3 (on p. 442).

current liability

A long-term liability will not be paid off within a year. It is, of course, owed to an outsider. In this case, bonds payable in the amount of $15,000 are the only long-term liability of Dan's Records (Figure

Net sales			$267,000	(100.0%)
Less cost of goods sold			152,000	(56.9%)
Gross profit			$115,000	(43.1%)
Less operating expenses:				
Wages and salaries	$68,200	(25.5%)		
General and administrative expenses	38,000	(14.2%)		
Interest expense	1,500	(0.6%)	107,700	(40.4%)
Income (earnings) before taxes			$7,300	(2.7%)
Less income tax expense (paid and accrued)			2,000	(0.7%)
Net income (earnings)			$5,300	(2.0%)
Earnings per share of common stock*			$53	
*Assumes 100 shares of common stock outstanding				

FIGURE 15-3 / Dan's Records, Inc. income statement, year ending December 31, 1990.

15-2). Bondholders, as we will see in Chapter 18, are long-term lenders; they are *not* owners of corporations, as stockholders are.

Stockholders' equity is the same owners' equity we saw in our basic accounting equation. Since Dan's is a corporation, the owners are stockholders. The stockholders' equity is divided into two parts: capital stock and retained earnings. Capital stock in the amount of $25,000 is the original investment of the stockholder-owners. **Retained earnings** represent what the firm has plowed back into the corporation from profits over the years but has not paid out in dividends.

retained earnings

USING THE BALANCE SHEET

Dan's management now has a "snapshot" of the financial position of the firm as of the close of business for 1990. Dan can use it to help plan for future borrowing needs. The local bank can use it to decide how much to lend the firm. Prospective investors might use it to decide whether to buy some of the corporation's stock or how much to pay for it.

Later in this chapter we will discuss how financial ratios (relating two or more items from financial statements) can make the balance sheet information even more useful. Meanwhile, let's examine the income statement and the information it provides to managers and outsiders.

THE INCOME STATEMENT

revenue

expense

In the course of its operations a firm receives payments for goods or services it provides to others. It also makes payments to employees, suppliers, and others who have contributed to its operation during the period. **Revenue** is the term accountants apply to the amount of cash or accounts receivable a firm receives in payment from others over a period of time. It is mostly a flow of income from sales by the firm. **Expense** is the using up of resources by a firm in the pursuit of revenue. Wages, rent, and utilities are commonly-incurred business expenses.

The firm needs to calculate its success or failure every year (or quarter or month). It does so by matching revenues and expenses over the period. If we subtract expenses from the corresponding revenues, we get the net income (net earnings) for the period. This is another name for net profit. This calculation can also be expressed as an equation:

REVENUES − EXPENSES = NET INCOME (or NET EARNINGS)

income statement

Like the basic accounting equation we presented earlier, this equation summarizes a financial statement. The financial statement in this case is called the income statement. The **income statement** summarizes revenues and expenses and shows the flows that occurred over a period of time. Net income increases the owners' equity, and net loss (when expenses exceed revenues) reduces it. The income statement for Dan's Records for the year ending December 31, 1990, is presented in Figure 15-3.

Dan's sold $267,000 worth of records, compact disks, and tapes during the year. The selling price of the products sold is used in the valuation of revenues rather than the original cost. Sales are designated as "net sales" because any discounts or returns and allowances granted to customers have already been subtracted from the original (gross) sales.

The actual cost of goods sold is deducted from net sales. The cost of goods sold is calculated as follows. First, a physical count (inventory) of goods in stock at the end of the year is taken. The cost of these goods is then subtracted from the sum of the cost values of (a) the inventory a year earlier and (b) purchases made during the year. Dan's had $22,000 in inventory at the beginning of the year, bought $140,000 more during the year, and had $10,000 remaining when the closing inventory was taken ($22,000 + $140,000 − $10,000 = $152,000). Manufacturers, whose operations and uses of inventories are quite different from those of a retailer, ordinarily would need a more complex treatment of this deduction from net sales.

THE ELECTRONIC AGE
Computers and Auditing—Dollar Unit Sampling

One of the techniques used by auditors when they are faced with the task of verifying huge numbers of accounts or transactions is probability sampling. This amounts to picking out accounts or transactions from the whole set of accounts or transactions on a random basis. The theory is that if a large enough sample is examined this way, the auditor (and all those who rely on the auditor's verification) can be confident that sample data truly represents the complete set of accounts or transactions from which the sample was taken.

Dollar unit sampling (DUS) is a widely used substitute for traditional probability sampling, and it can be done on a personal computer. Instead of directly picking accounts to audit, it picks every "nth" dollar unit and audits the account in which that dollar unit is found. Suppose there were 2,000 accounts receivable to be verified in an audit of Blessey's Department Store and the total asset value is $1.8 million. The firm first decides on how far off they can permit their estimate to be. According to the rules of sampling, this determines the number of dollar units that will need to be selected (the sample size). Then this number is divided into the total number of asset dollars to get the *sampling interval*. If the sample size were 1,800, then the interval would be 1,000. ($1,800,000/1,800 = 1,000). The computer program does the rest. It zeroes in on every 1,000th dollar and picks the accounts in which those dollars fall to be audited. The larger the account is, the greater its chances of being picked for audit.

All of this sounds complicated. But for the firm with its accounts already in a personal computer system the DUS program can really simplify the work of the auditor. Furthermore, it is thought to provide a more accurate sample than more traditional methods.

Source: Gordon B. Harwood, George J. Davis, and Paul Borowoski, "Save Time with Computerized Dollar-unit Sampling," *The Internal Auditor,* April 1987, pp. 41–46.

gross profit

The difference between net sales and cost of goods sold is **gross profit.** Figure 15-3 shows a few expense accounts—wages and salaries, general and administrative expenses, and interest expense. The difference between gross profit and operating expenses is $7,300—income (or net profit) before taxes. From this amount, taxes (paid as well as accrued) are deducted in the amount of $2,000. Notice that the taxes that apply to this year's operations—whether paid or not—are rightfully deducted from this year's revenue. This is another example of the principle of accrual. Net income is $5,300 or 2 percent of sales. Of this the board of directors can allocate a part (or all) to dividends. Any remainder goes to owners' equity as retained earnings.

USING THE INCOME STATEMENT

The income statement, even without the financial ratios we will discuss later in this chapter, is a very useful tool. It is one way of looking at how the firm operated during the year. Anyone can tell at a glance what the firm earned, what its main expenses were, and how earnings and expenses compare to sales. Comparing different items on the statement to net sales is easy if you use the percentages of net sales to the right of the dollar amounts. Dan can tell, for example, whether general and administrative expenses, as a percent of sales, are rising from year to year. Dan can also easily compare these percentages to the corresponding percentages calculated for certain competitors and to industry averages. He can measure relative efficiency and profitability. If the average firm of this type shows operating expenses, as a percent of sales, to be much lower than 40.4 percent, Dan or the firm's banker has reason to ask some hard questions about operations.

THE STATEMENT OF CASH FLOWS

Accountants are beginning to use the new *statement of cash flows*. It replaces the "statement of changes in financial position" in financial reporting as directed by the FASB. The new statement is restricted to

Cash flows from operating activities:		
Cash received from customers	$10,000	
Dividends received	700	
Cash provided by operating activities		10,700
Cash paid to suppliers and employees	6,000	
Interest and taxes paid	1,750	
Cash disbursed for operating activities		7,750
Net cash flow from operating activities		2,950
Cash flows from investing activities:		
Purchases of property, plant, equipment	(4,000)	
Proceeds from disposals of property, plant, equipment	2,500	
Acquisition of Company ABC	(900)	
Purchases of investment securities	(4,700)	
Proceeds from sales of investment securities	5,000	
Loans made	(7,500)	
Collections on loans	5,800	
Net cash used by investing activities		(3,800)
Cash flows from financing activities:		
Net increase in customer deposits	1,100	
Proceeds of short-term debt	75	
Payments to settle short-term debt	(300)	
Proceeds of long-term debt	1,250	
Payments on capital lease obligations	(125)	
Proceeds from issuing common stock	500	
Dividends paid	(450)	
Net cash provided by financing activities		2,050
Effect of exchange rate changes on cash		100
Net increase (decrease) in cash		$1,300

FIGURE 15-4 / The Sample Corporation statement of cash flows, 1990. (*Source:* Financial Accounting Standards Board exposure draft, 1987. Copyright by Financial Accounting Standards Board, High Ridge Park, Stamford, Connecticut, 06905, U.S.A. Reprinted with permission. Copies of the complete document are available from the FASB.)

receipts and disbursals of cash during the year. (See Figure 15-4 on p. 445.) It divides cash flows into three groups: (1) cash flows from operating activities, (2) cash flows from investing activities (such as purchases of plant and equipment or collections on loans), and (3) cash flows from financing activities (such as proceeds from issuing common stock or payments to settle short-term debt). The statement requires that the total amounts of cash and cash equivalents at the beginning and end of the reporting periods be shown, using the same titles as used in the balance sheet for cash. This new statement provides a good measure of a corporation's liquidity. Noncash transactions are reported separately.

We turn now to the method of recordkeeping that leads to financial statements like the balance sheet, income statement, and statement of cash flows. It is known as the *double-entry* system.

TRANSACTIONS AND DOUBLE-ENTRY BOOKKEEPING

transactions
accounts

The process leading to the construction of the financial statements we have described requires a day-to-day data recording and accumulation system. The effects of certain events, such as when firms buy and sell or borrow money, are entered as transactions into various accounts. **Transactions** are financially significant events that raise or lower the balances (net dollar amounts) in accounts. The **accounts** are individual records for specific assets, liabilities, owners' equity, revenues, and expenses. The system of accounts and transactions in the framework of the accounting equations is known as **double-entry bookkeeping** because every transaction changes the balances in at least two accounts at the same time. The set of entries arising from a transaction must balance out in the firm's set of books.

double-entry bookkeeping

To be more specific, double-entry transactions are entered in a book called a journal when the accounting staff receives the information. At a later time the accumulated journal entries are posted (transferred) to another book called the ledger. As the Dac Software ad indicates, many firms keep their ledgers in their computers instead of in simple book form. At the end of an accounting period the final balances in the ledger accounts are used to prepare the financial statements.

FINANCIAL ACCOUNTING—USERS AND USES

How does financial accounting help people like investors, lenders, and borrowers? We will start with the case of Dr. Geraldine Franklin, who invested in Dan's Records, Inc.

Geraldine Franklin is a retired doctor. She has just invested a small part of her savings in the common stock of Dan's Records, Inc. She owns 100 common shares, which represent 20 percent of Dan's 500 common shares outstanding at the end of 1990. Dr. Franklin wants a reasonable return on her investment in the form of dividends.

Dr. Franklin wants financial information, so she turns to a copy of Dan's Records, Inc.'s annual report, which she received in the mail. It contains the balance sheet and the income statement that we saw in

Accounting software can help a firm with both financial accounting and managerial accounting.

Figures 15-2 and 15-3. She can learn a lot about the quality of her investment from these financial statements.

Let's review how these statements came to be. Dr. Franklin could not make a wise decision about her investment if someone (Dan's accountant or controller) had not set up an accounting system that did the following things:

- Retained facts about financially significant events (transactions) on a variety of source documents
- Classified these transactions into accounts
- Summarized accounts in financial statements
- Distributed statements to stockholders

Now that Dr. Franklin has her financial statements, she can start to evaluate her investment and compare it to similar statements for other firms, which she can get from her stockbroker. One thing she will look at is *earnings per share*. This is equal to total profit for the year divided by the total number of shares of stock issued by Dan's Records, Inc. In this case it amounts to $5,300/$500 or $10.60 for the year 1990.

Financial accounting also helps credit givers to make decisions. Suppose University Consultants wants to sign a long-term $20,000 contract with Dan's to provide a variety of consulting services. It is important for University Consultants to feel comfortable about Dan's financial condition. This contract would require a commitment of much of University Consultants' resources to solution of Dan's business problems. Failure to receive prompt payment for these services could be financially disastrous for the consultant.

University Consultants will use a number of sources of information for this purpose and will depend a lot on the facts found in Dan's financial statements. It will look especially hard at financial data that might bear on Dan's ability to pay its current bills. The information found in the annual report, together with credit information from Dun & Bradstreet, will be satisfactory.

Dan's accounting system should be able to provide a summary of its past payment behavior if the firm wishes to give this information to University Consultants. In practice, this kind of data is often made available by independent credit-reporting services, such as Dun & Bradstreet.

FINANCIAL RATIOS

The numbers on the financial statements take on more meaning when they are related to each other. For instance, the net profit of a firm is more meaningful when it is calculated in terms of the firm's sales or its owners' equity. Such relationships are usually expressed as financial ratios.

financial ratio

A **financial ratio** is a value obtained by dividing one value on a financial statement by another value. A particular firm's financial condition can be judged by comparing several important ratios of items found in its financial statements to the typical ratios of similar types of firms. Dun & Bradstreet is a pioneer in the development and analysis of such ratios. For years it has published "industry average" ratios for many kinds of firms. These provide benchmarks by which the financial condition of similar firms may be evaluated.

Let's look at several of the ratios as derived from Dan's Records, Inc.'s financial statements. (See Figure 15-5 for a summary of the ratios discussed in this chapter.) Perhaps the most important ratio for measuring a firm's profitability or overall performance is called return on net worth or return on stockholders' equity. **Return on net worth** is equal to net income divided by the firm's most recent net worth or stockholders' equity. (Note that this is not the same thing as the "earnings per share" calculated earlier.) If Dan's most recent stockholders' equity is $36,000, then the value of this ratio is $5,300/$36,000 = 0.1472 or 14.72 percent. What does this percent say about Dan's overall performance? The firm made $14.72 per hundred dollars of net worth. Is this good or bad? Creditors, banks, and Dan's management will judge this by comparing it to past years' return on stockholders' equity and to returns of similar firms. In fact, this is a rather good return—Dan's stockholders are getting more earnings on a dollar of investment than stockholders of similar retail corporations are getting. Prospective creditors and banks or other lenders are likely to feel confident about doing business with Dan's because of such a profit ratio. However, there are other ratios to consider in judging Dan's creditworthiness.

return on net worth

TO MEASURE PROFITABILITY

FIGURE 15-5 / Financial ratios.

> **Return on net worth**
>
> Net Income / Net worth = Return on net worth
> $5,300 / $36,000 = 0.1472 or 14.72 percent

TO MEASURE EFFICIENCY

> **Inventory turnover ratio**
>
> Cost of goods sold / Average inventory value = Inventory turnover
> $152,000 / ($22,000 + $10,000)/2 = 9.5

TO MEASURE LIQUIDITY

> **(1) Current ratio**
>
> Current assets / Current liabilities = Current ratio
> $34,000 / $13,000 = 2.62
>
> **(2) Quick ratio**
>
> Current "cashable" assets / Current liabilities = Quick ratio
> $22,000 / $13,000 = 1.69

current ratio

A credit ratio that is widely used to measure a firm's liquidity (ability to pay current debt) is known as the current ratio. The **current ratio** is a measure of a firm's liquidity. It is computed by dividing current assets by current liabilities. The result indicates how easily current debt could be paid off with current assets. On December 31, 1990, Dan's current ratio was $34,000/$13,000 or 2.62. This current ratio is quite good. Even a current ratio of 2 to 1 is generally considered good, so Dan's is clearly liquid. The retailer could easily pay off its current debts. Even if we apply the tougher standard of liquidity—the

quick ratio

quick ratio—to Dan's balance sheet, the firm looks good. The **quick ratio** is a very strict measure of a firm's liquidity. It is computed by dividing current liabilities into immediately "cashable" current assets. These include cash, accounts receivable, notes receivable, and marketable securities but does not include inventories. For Dan's the quick ratio is $22,000/$13,000 = 1.69. A quick ratio even as low as 1 would be considered acceptable by many credit analysts.

inventory turnover ratio

While the return on net worth ratio measures overall performance and the current and quick ratios measure liquidity, still another ratio measures efficient use of assets. The **inventory turnover ratio** is an important measure of efficiency that is computed by dividing average inventory value into cost of goods sold. For Dan's this is equal to $152,000/($22,000 + $10,000/2) = 9.5. (The previous year's balance sheet showed merchandise inventory of $22,000.) This turnover ratio is higher than most similar firms have, so it suggests efficient use of inventories and good judgment in merchandise selection. The expected turnover ratio would be much higher for grocery stores, which tend to sell food quickly, and much lower for jewelry stores, whose inventories move more slowly.

Modern accounting also includes internal management tools. Although financial accounting helps, a good manager needs certain managerial accounting tools as well.

Managerial Accounting

Managerial accounting provides information for a manager's own use. It helps management to plan. Managers can measure and control performance, set prices, and analyze situations. The biggest difference between managerial and financial accounting is that managerial accounting lacks traditional rules and principles. Management is free to make up its own systems.

Managerial accounting practices are less rigid than those of financial accounting. Different systems are found in different firms. The idea is to keep any of a great variety of records or summaries of costs and revenues that managers need to plan or control. They might want to evaluate other managers or to judge the success of new products or a new piece of equipment. The common thread in such practices is the comparison of performance to a standard. Managerial accounting allows the accountant to be more inventive and flexible than financial accounting does.

The use of managerial accounting, especially with the help of computers, allows managers to make better-informed decisions.

Such special accounting is needed to measure the performance of departments, products, or managers within the firm as a whole. The Account-A-Call Corporation ad (on p. 452) promises, for example, to help a firm analyze its phone costs; allocate them by division, cost center, and individual; and eliminate abuse of phones by employees. Regular financial accounts that focus on overall firm profit are not enough to do this kind of thing.

If the Steelcase Corporation, for example, wishes to evaluate the performance of its sales force, it must maintain adequate records of the sales force's activities. Suppose those records show that the average travel expenditure per salesperson has been 20.2 cents per month per square mile of sales territory. After analysis the sales manager might decide to adopt this average amount as a standard. Any salesperson whose expenses exceed this standard will be checked out, and this cost is controlled.

Managerial accounting can be used in many ways. It can set minimum order sizes, decide whether to shut down a production line, help a manager allocate funds for growth among territories, or set standards for entertaining customers. Such managerial accounting activities usually fall under one of two headings: budgeting and cost accounting.

Managerial accounting systems help the firm to compare past and present performance, control costs, and plan for the future.

BUDGETING

By tradition, financial accounting is not expected to predict a firm's condition. Predicting is a risky business, but it must be done. Managers use special managerial accounting tools to help them make predictions. One such device is the budget.

budget

A **budget** is a formal dollars-and-cents statement of expected performance. Budgets enable managers (1) to *plan* carefully for the future, (2) to *examine* present and past performance critically, and (3) to *coordinate* the plans made by different parts of the firm. A budget might be very specialized, or it might be general. It might be a short-term (one year or less) or a long-term budget.

The marketing manager, for example, is expected to prepare an advertising budget for the coming year. In consultation with the advertising agency and the controller, the marketing manager will specify how to spend the money allocated to meet advertising objectives. This includes the amount designated for each product to be marketed, the amounts earmarked for each advertising medium, and a month-by-month schedule for the year's spending.

sales forecast

The **sales forecast** predicts what sales will be over a certain period of time. It is the starting point for a general (master) budget. This forecast depends on what effect the marketing manager thinks the planned changes in the marketing mix will have on sales. Sometimes the sales forecast is tied to a projection of Gross National Product or to industry sales forecasts. Large firms often employ a staff of economists and have computer facilities to construct models to predict sales. A small firm might simply assume a 5 percent increase over the current year. Either way, the sales forecast is a keystone for planning.

COST ACCOUNTING

Cost accounting includes responsibility accounting and product cost accounting. **Responsibility accounting** is a system for classifying costs incurred according to certain responsibility centers so as to evaluate the performance of such centers and their managers. The costs of operating the shipping department, for example, might be collected in a shipping department responsibility center so that the efficiency of the department can be monitored regularly. Figure 15-6 shows how responsibility accounting works.

responsibility accounting

Suppose that a plant has set up responsibility centers to control its costs and one such center is the plant loading dock. The dock superintendent buys an insect fogger to reduce the problem of mosquitoes on the dock. The accounting system assigns this cost to the loading dock responsibility center. Company accounting policy classifies such an expenditure as controllable and further classifies it as a "miscellaneous operating expense." During the month the loading dock incurs thirty-seven other cost items. Six of these were required by general company policy and so were determined to be uncontrollable by this responsibility center. The other items, including purchase of paint for the dock floor and parts for the dock scale, are classified by type. The paint is classified as a "maintenance expense" and the scale parts as a "mechanical repair cost." At the end of the month, all controllable expenses are totaled by type and reported to the plant manager. The manager now has a monthly measure of the controllable costs incurred by this responsibility center. This helps the manager to evaluate the dock's efficiency for the month.

product cost accounting

Product cost accounting is a system that uses cost centers to allocate all costs to the various products made by a firm. This gives a firm a better idea of which products are profitable and which are not. Some firms use standard product cost accounting systems. *Standard costs* assigned in such a system are those that should have been incurred, not those actually incurred. Differences between actual and standard costs are called *variances* and are charged to variance accounts.

There are other applications of management accounting besides

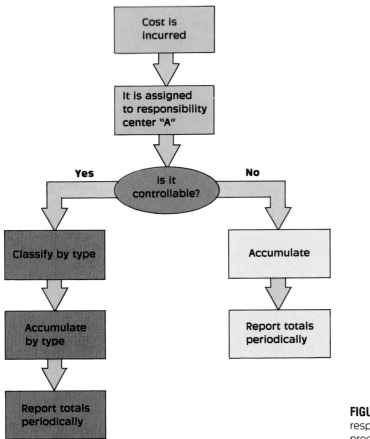

FIGURE 15-6 / The responsibility accounting process.

budgeting and cost accounting. These include breakeven analysis (see Chapter 12), forecasting techniques, and many others. You will learn more about these topics if you take courses in accounting.

Summary

Financial accounting is a "scorekeeping process" that is meant to keep several interested groups (inside and outside the firm) informed as to the financial condition of the firm. It is done by public accountants, including CPAs, who have a major responsibility for accounting standards, and private accountants, who do financial and managerial accounting for their own (nonaccountant) firms. Managerial accounting serves managers by calling attention to problems and aiding them in planning, decision making, and controlling the firm's operations.

The major accounting equation is written as follows: ASSETS = LIABILITIES + OWNERS' EQUITY (CAPITAL). The income equation is REVE-

NUES − EXPENSES = NET INCOME. These equations summarize the following financial accounting statements: (1) the balance sheet, which presents the amounts of assets, liabilities, and net worth of a firm at one point in time, and (2) the income statement, which summarizes revenues, expenses, and net earnings of the firm.

The system of accounts and transactions in the framework of the accounting equations is known as double-entry bookkeeping because every transaction changes the balances in at least two accounts at the same time.

People use the financial statements and the financial ratios derived from them to judge whether a firm is (1) a good investment, (2) a good credit customer, or (3) able to repay a loan on time. Earnings per share is a good measure of the overall performance of a firm. The current ratio (current assets divided by current liabilities) is a good measure of the firm's liquidity—its ability to meet its current debt obligations.

Managerial accounting includes budgeting and cost accounting. A budget is a formal dollars-and-cents statement of expected performance. Budgets enable managers (1) to plan carefully for the future, (2) to examine present and past performance critically, and (3) to coordinate the plans made by different parts of the firm.

Cost accounting is a broad component of managerial accounting. It usually takes the form of responsibility accounting or product cost accounting. In either case, costs must be identified and assigned to improve internal managerial control of operations.

Review Questions

1. What kinds of data does accounting provide? Give two examples.

2. Who uses the data provided by the accounting process?

3. Must all accountants be CPAs? Explain.

4. What is the basic accounting equation? Show how a change in one side must result in a change in the other?

5. What are the three major classes of accounts on a balance sheet?

6. What is meant by the principle of accrual? Explain by giving an example involving wages.

7. Explain the process of double-entry bookkeeping.

8. Show how a current ratio is computed and used.

9. In what way could an accounting system help to control an expense such as salespeople's entertainment expenses? Explain.

Discussion Questions

1. What do we mean when we say that financial accounting is relevant?

2. Is it possible for a transaction to occur without affecting the balance of any account?

3. How is depreciation related to the balance sheet?

4. What is the relationship between managerial accounting and the management function of controlling, as discussed in Chapter 5?

Key Terms

accounting

financial accounting

generally accepted accounting principles

managerial accounting

certified public accountant (CPA)

certified management accountant (CMA)

asset

liability

owners' equity (capital)

basic accounting equation

balance sheet

current asset

accrual

depreciation

current liability

retained earnings

revenue

expense

income statement

gross profit

transactions

accounts

double-entry bookkeeping

financial ratio

return on net worth

current ratio

quick ratio

inventory turnover ratio

budget

sales forecast

responsibility accounting

product cost accounting

Cases

ACCOUNTING STANDARDS AND THE PINEAPPLE INDUSTRY

The pineapple and sugarcane industries of Hawaii are very big business. Their profitability depends in part on how costs associated with the growing of these major Hawaiian crops are handled by accountants for these industries and the Internal Revenue Service. For many years, the IRS had allowed growing costs to be treated as an expense rather than included in the value of the inventory of the crop held by the growing firm.

In the mid-1970s, Congress made changes in the tax code that would have required corporate farmers to add such growing costs to inventory value (the "deferred crop" method). The IRS worked out a special exemption from this rule for Hawaiian farmers, provided that the industry-favored expensing was viewed as compatible with "generally accepted accounting principles." After much debate on the issue, the American Institute of CPAs (AICPA) agreed in the mid-1980s to allow the industry-supported accounting practice. The impact of this decision was judged by economists to have saved these industries more than $170 million in cash outflow. Some observers felt that the entire pineapple and sugarcane industries might otherwise have failed, dealing a heavy blow to the economy of the state of Hawaii.[2]

Questions

1. If you were the accountant for a Hawaiian corporation with pineapple farming operations at the time of the favorable ruling by the AICPA, what effects would the ruling have had on your balance sheet?

2. What effect would it have had on your income statement?

3. Which accounting equations as applied to these industries were affected by the favorable ruling and how were they affected?

4. Is the accounting theory discussed in the case relevant to financial accounting or to managerial accounting or to both?

ERNST & WHINNEY— A CASE OF ACCOUNTING ETHICS?

The Federal Deposit Insurance Corporation sued Ernst & Whinney, the third biggest U.S. accounting firm, seeking $250 million for its allegedly faulty audit of four collapsed Tennessee banks owned by the Butcher brothers in Tennessee.

In the case of one of the banks, which collapsed in 1983—United American Bank in Knoxville—Ernst & Whinney issued a clean audit opinion on its financial statement in January of that year. Twenty days later the bank was closed by federal regulators, and it has since been merged with another bank. Jake Butcher and C. H. Butcher are serving jail terms on fraud charges.

The suit charges that Ernst & Whinney violated auditing standards by relying on internal audit staffs of the banks for confirmations of commercial loans. It also alleges that the accounting firm discovered that the banks forgot to mail confirmations covering $16 million of such loans.

The suit also alleges that Ernst & Whinney's partner in charge of Butcher bank audits, Walter Boruff, borrowed $53,000 from Butcher banks during the years the accounting firm performed the audits, and at other times.

Ray Groves, chairman of Cleveland-based Ernst & Whinney, said that the firm would "vigorously defend itself against these allegations." The suit, he added, is "another example of the FDIC attempting to push off to an auditor its own regulatory obligations."[3]

Questions

1. Review the text explanation of the role of the CPA and evaluate the behavior of Mr. Boruff.
2. To whom does a CPA firm have obligations in pursuing its auditing function?
3. Examine the What Do You Think? box on page 435 and reevaluate the Ernst & Whinney suit in the light of the new peer review plan of the AICPA.

Money, Banking, and Other Financial Institutions

After reading this chapter, you will be able to:

- Explain the evolution, functions, and characteristics of money.

- Identify the various types of depository institutions.

- Distinguish between M1 and M2 and their components.

- Explain the functions of the commercial banking system.

- Outline the structure and functions of the Federal Reserve System.

- Distinguish among and give examples of contractual savings institutions, investment companies, and finance companies.

WHAT'S AHEAD

In this chapter we will focus mainly on the financial institutions that are important to business in the United States. Many of them will be familiar to you because you do business with such institutions as commercial banks and savings and loan associations.

Although you might not do business directly with the Federal Reserve System, you certainly have read or heard news about its activities. The "Fed" touches your life in many ways. For example, if you borrow money to buy a new car, the interest rate you pay is influenced by the Fed.

On the other hand, we will look at some financial institutions that will probably be less familiar to you. These include commercial finance companies and factoring companies.

The chapter begins with a look at the functions and characteristics of money. Money in our economic system means much more than coins and paper currency.

Next we will discuss the operation and regulation of the commercial banking system. The commercial bank plays a major role in our banking system.

Another major topic is the organization and operations of the Federal Reserve System. The "Fed" is the central bank of the United States.

The chapter ends with a look at some of the other nondepository financial institutions. These are the contractual saving institutions, investment companies, and finance companies. We will also look at deregulation and the emergence of the financial services company.

The day the bank called his loan, Bob Hofmiller thought it was some sort of a joke. He couldn't believe that any lender would choose that particular moment to end its relationship with his

company. After all, bridge decay was a hot issue in the summer of 1984, thanks to the collapse of a bridge on the Connecticut Turnpike the previous year—and Mr. Hofmiller's company, D.F.M. Enterprises Inc., just happened to be in the bridge inspection equipment business. After years of scraping by, D.F.M. had suddenly found itself flooded with requests for information from around the country. In a matter of days, the State of New York was due to sign a contract for more than $1 million of D.F.M.'s bridge inspection devices, and other big orders were in the offing. "And once we had an order in hand," says Hofmiller, D.F.M.'s vice-president, "there was practically no risk."

But the bank did not see it that way. "Our local bank had just been acquired by Connecticut National Bank, and the new guys told us to pay off our loans. They wanted nothing to do with us."

For the next few weeks, Mr. Hofmiller and his brother Richard, president and founder of D.F.M., scrambled to find another source of capital. With the company's future hanging in the balance, they finally convinced a local savings bank to lend them $50,000. Today, D.F.M. Enterprises is a $2.2 million business sporting a $500,000 line of credit.

Several years after D.F.M.'s loan was called by Connecticut National Bank in 1984, two young lending officers from the bank called on Mr. Hofmiller. Unaware of any previous experience, the pair inquired about D.F.M.'s credit needs. As Mr. Hofmiller recalls, "I could see their eyes light up when I told them about our $500,000 credit line from another bank." They launched into their sales pitch, explaining all the wonderful things their bank could do for a company like D.F.M. Mr. Hofmiller let them go on at length. When they were finished, he said the bank sounded great, but he thought they might want to hear a little story about something that had happened a few years earlier—when their bank had not wanted to do business with D.F.M.[1]

Bob Hofmiller's business, like all others, needs money to carry out management's plans. Money, whether provided by the firm's owners or borrowed from lenders, is needed to conduct business operations. Had Mr. Hofmiller been unable to find another source of capital, the company could easily have folded—just when business was about to really boom. Let's begin the chapter with a look at something that is important to Mr. Hofmiller and every other businessperson: money.

What Is Money?

money

Money is anything that people generally accept as payment for goods and services. In ancient societies, people used objects like goats, cattle, shells, wool, beads, and spices as money. A goat, for example, had inherent utility as a source of milk and meat. But it could also be used

How do U.S. dollars differ from
the earliest forms of money?

as money. Its owner could barter (exchange) the goat directly for other
goods and services.

Over time, people began to accept certain agreed-upon objects in
exchange for any good or service. These objects could be animal skins,
fishhooks, rings, pots, or whatever else the members of a particular
society agreed were valued objects. Each of the objects served as a
medium of exchange. If fishhooks were the medium, the value of other
goods and services could be expressed in terms of fishhooks.

As early as the 1100s B.C., the Chinese started using tool-shaped
metal money that represented the objects they commonly exchanged.
For example, there were miniature bronze spades and knives. Coins
were probably first minted by governments (or other authorities) during
the 600s B.C. The maker stamped a value on the coins—in effect, guaranteeing their value. All coins that contained the same amount of a
valued metal such as gold or silver were equal in value. This greatly
enhanced the efficiency of exchange.

The introduction of paper money, probably during the 1200s A.D.
in China, was another major advance. Unlike goats, which gave milk,
and coins, which were made of valued metals, paper money had no

value of its own. It was valuable, however, because it could be exchanged for valued metals.

In fact, it is people's willingness to accept objects that enables the objects to serve as a medium of exchange. In the United States, for example, coins issued by the Bureau of the Mint and paper money issued by the Bureau of Engraving and Printing (two bureaus of the Department of the Treasury) are money. Although the coins and paper money are not all backed up 100 percent by valued metals, we accept them as money because they are backed by the "full faith and credit" of the U.S. government. Checks are also money. Though often called "plastic money," credit cards like Visa and MasterCard are not really money. They are credit arrangements that involve the cardholder, the company that issued the credit card, and the merchant who accepts the card.

THE FUNCTIONS OF MONEY

As indicated in Figure 16-1, money serves three primary functions. It is a medium of exchange, a store of value, and a unit of account.

As a *medium of exchange*, money is generally accepted as payment for goods and services. It enables people to exchange without having to barter. Instead of farmers trading goats directly for fertilizer and other goods and services, they can sell their goats and use the proceeds (money) to buy other goods and services. Money facilitates economic progress by simplifying the exchange process.

As a *store of value*, money provides a convenient way of holding wealth in a ready, easy-to-use form until it is needed. Of course, wealth can also be held in other forms like real estate, art, and stocks and bonds. However, money is more liquid. It can be converted into goods and services much more quickly than other wealth can. But as we have seen elsewhere in our book, inflation undermines money's function as a store of value.

As a *unit of account*, money is a common measuring stick for all goods and services. Their value can be measured and expressed in money terms. A car might be worth $18,000, a wisdom tooth extraction

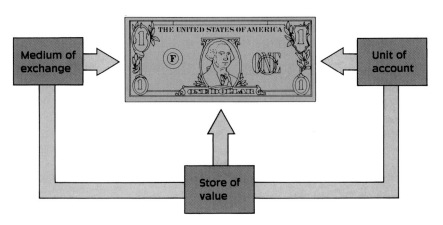

FIGURE 16-1 / The primary functions of money.

might be worth $275, and a pizza might be worth $12. Clearly, money is a standard of value.

IDEAL CHARACTERISTICS OF MONEY

Many objects have served as money throughout history. But some are better forms of money than others. As Figure 16-2 indicates, in order to perform its three major functions, money should be (1) durable, (2) portable, (3) divisible, (4) stable, (5) scarce, and (6) liquid.

Money should be *durable* and last for a reasonable period of time. Coins, for example, circulate longer than paper money. A U.S. one dollar bill lasts about 18 months. Larger bills last longer because they are handled less in circulation. Worn-out money is regularly withdrawn from circulation through our banking system.

Money should be *portable* so that it can easily serve as a medium of exchange. Coins and paper money are far superior to stones in this regard.

Divisibility is another desirable feature. The U.S. dollar, our standard monetary unit, can be broken down into fractional money—half-dollars, quarter-dollars, dimes, nickels, and pennies. Each is worth a certain portion of the dollar.

Money should be *stable* in value. Inflation reduces both the value of money and the willingness of people to hold it as a store of value. People prefer to hold other assets like land, art, and precious jewels during periods of high inflation.

Money should also be *scarce*. This is one of the reasons why it is

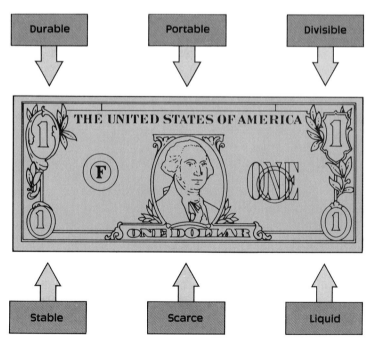

FIGURE 16-2 / Ideal characteristics of money.

valuable. Governments go to great lengths to prevent counterfeit money from getting into circulation.

Finally, money must possess *liquidity*. It must be convertible more quickly and more easily than other forms of wealth into other goods and services.

THE ROLE OF DEPOSITORY INSTITUTIONS IN CREATING MONEY

The purpose of financial institutions is to provide for the creation, use, and flow of money. Some are private, some are governmental, and some (like the Federal Reserve System) are a mixture.

Some financial institutions are referred to as financial intermediaries. A **financial intermediary** is an institution that performs a middleman function by accepting funds from savers and lending those funds to borrowers.

financial intermediary

Financial institutions serve consumers, businesses, and nonbusiness organizations. As these customers' needs and the laws that regulate financial institutions change, new types of institutions appear, and some old types might disappear. The same, of course, is true of the types of services they offer.

As Figure 16-3 shows, there are four classes of financial institutions: (1) depository institutions, (2) contractual saving institutions, (3) investment companies, and (4) finance companies. We discuss depository institutions in this section. The other three classes are covered later in this chapter.

depository institution

Commercial banks, savings banks, savings and loan associations, and credit unions are depository institutions. A **depository institution** is a financial institution that is authorized to accept deposits that are withdrawable by check and that can obtain federal deposit insurance for up to $100,000 for each account. These institutions have one thing in common: they create liabilities, such as checking accounts, that are considered money. Savings banks and savings and loan associations are often called *thrift institutions*, or *thrifts*.

commercial bank

The commercial bank is the major provider of banking services to business firms. A **commercial bank** is a privately owned, profit-seeking depository institution that serves its business and nonbusiness customers by accepting deposits that can be withdrawn on demand, by accepting savings deposits, and by making loans. Commercial banks are the main source of short-term loans for business firms.

Federal Deposit Insurance Corporation (FDIC)

The **Federal Deposit Insurance Corporation (FDIC),** created by Congress in 1933, is an independent government agency that insures each account in member banks up to $100,000. Banks that are insured by the FDIC and get into trouble because of problems like bad loans and investments are bailed out. The FDIC is named receiver of insured banks that are declared insolvent.

In a typical case, FDIC liquidators are sent to a bank that the agency declares to be insolvent. They enter the bank shortly before closing time and post notices on walls, change door locks, and dismantle automated teller machines. FDIC officials affix blue seals to cash drawers while armed guards are stationed in the lobby. Meanwhile, employees

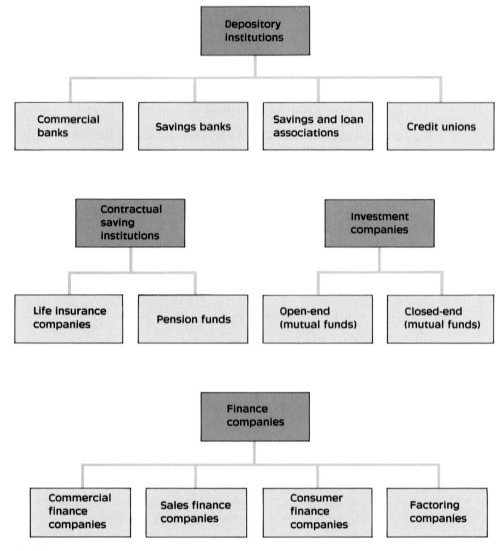

FIGURE 16-3 / The four classes of financial institutions.

are told that they are now on the FDIC's payroll. The FDIC then begins accepting bids for the failed bank from other banks that are interested in acquiring it.

A **savings and loan association (S&L)** is a financial institution that accepts deposits from the general public and lends funds mainly for mortgages on homes and other real estate. In recent years, S&Ls have become more active in lending money to a wider variety of commercial and consumer borrowers. An S&L can be a mutual company (owned by depositors) or a stock company (owned by stockholders). The Federal Savings and Loan Insurance Corporation (FSLIC) insures each account in member S&Ls up to $100,000.

savings and loan association (S&L)

savings bank

credit union

A **savings bank** is a financial institution that accepts deposits from small savers, pays them interest, and invests the funds mainly in real estate mortgages and government securities. However, savings banks also make loans to businesses. Most are mutual savings banks, which means that they are owned by the depositors. Stockholder-owned savings banks also operate in various parts of the country, but most of these have become commercial banks. The FDIC insures accounts at member savings banks.

A **credit union** is a cooperative savings association formed by the employees of a company or nonbusiness organization. The members own and operate the credit union. They can add to their accounts by payroll deduction or by making direct deposits. They can also borrow from the credit union at a cost that is usually lower than what outside lenders charge. The National Credit Union Administration (NCUA) insures each account in member credit unions up to $100,000.

THE MONEY SUPPLY

As Figure 16-4 indicates, we can distinguish between M1 and M2 when discussing the money supply in the United States. M1 is a narrower perspective of what constitutes money than M2.

M1

currency

M1 **M1** is a measure of the money supply in the United States that includes only currency and demand deposits. All M1 money can be used as a medium of exchange.

Currency is coins and paper money that make up the cash money in a society. About one-fourth of the M1 money supply in the United

End of June 1988 = $776.2 billion

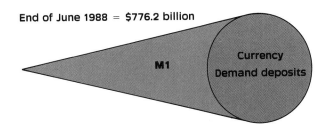

FIGURE 16-4 / Two perspectives on the money supply. (*Source: Barron's,* July 25, 1988, p. 140.)

End of June 1988 = $3.0 trillion

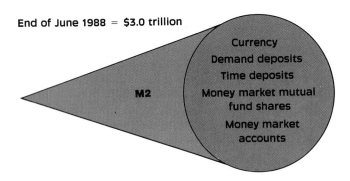

States is accounted for by currency (including cashier's checks, money orders, and traveler's checks).

demand deposit

A **demand deposit** is a checking account that enables the depositor to withdraw funds from the account immediately and without advance notice. Financial institutions that offer checking accounts must honor their depositors' checks immediately on demand. Demand deposits are our most important type of money, accounting for roughly three-fourths of the M1 money supply in the United States.

The traditional demand deposit is a non-interest-bearing checking account at a commercial bank. Newer types are a negotiable order of withdrawal account and a share draft account.

negotiable order of withdrawal (NOW) account

share draft account

A **negotiable order of withdrawal (NOW) account** is an interest-bearing checking account offered by commercial banks, savings banks, and savings and loan associations. NOW accounts usually require a minimum balance, with penalties for going below that amount. A **share draft account** is an interest-bearing checking account offered by credit unions.

M2

M2 **M2** is a measure of the money supply in the United States that includes all of the components of M1 (currency and demand deposits) plus time deposits, money market mutual fund shares, and money market accounts at commercial banks and other types of financial institutions.

time deposit

A **time deposit** is money placed in a financial institution that remains there (on deposit) for a period of time and that earns interest during this period. The financial institution uses this money to make loans to its customers. For example, a commercial bank pays interest to its time deposit holders and charges interest to its borrowers.

The two basic types of time deposits are regular passbook accounts and certificates of deposit (CDs). Passbook accounts, intended mainly for small savers and nonprofit organizations, generally have no enforced time requirement. Although a financial institution *can* require thirty days' notice before withdrawals can be made, they seldom do. A

certificate of deposit (CD)

certificate of deposit (CD) is a time deposit in a financial institution that is made for a certain period of time at a fixed rate of interest. The time period can range from several days to several years. CDs are available to all and are insured up to $100,000. The interest rate paid is higher than that paid on regular passbook savings, but early withdrawal results in a penalty.

Depository institutions also offer a money market CD. The interest rate on newly issued money market CDs may change each week, but the rate that is in effect on a particular CD at the time of its issue remains in effect until its maturity. The interest rate that the institution pays is tied to the interest rate paid on six-month U.S. Treasury bills.

money market mutual fund

The costs involved in early withdrawal from a CD stimulated development of the money market mutual fund and the money market account. A **money market mutual fund** is a pool of funds invested in U.S. Treasury bills, commercial paper (corporate debt instruments), and "jumbo" ($100,000 or more) CDs. The interest rate paid to investors varies with the return received from the fund's various investments. Because there are many investors in a money market mutual fund, it is possible to enter or withdraw at any time. In addition, inves-

money market account

near-money

tors can add to their accounts or withdraw a part of their investment without penalty. Some of the funds permit limited check writing against the balance. A **money market account** is an account at a bank or other financial institution that pays interest rates comparable to those paid by money market mutual funds and permits the depositor to write a limited number of checks against the account.

Time deposits, money market mutual fund shares, and money market accounts are often referred to as near-money. **Near-money** is assets that are almost as liquid as currency and unrestricted demand deposits but that cannot be used directly as a medium of exchange.

The Commercial Banking System

The commercial bank is the heart of our banking system. Figure 16-5 shows some of the many services that commercial banks offer to their customers.

COMMERCIAL BANK DEPOSITS AND LOANS

Before the 1980s, only commercial banks could accept both time and demand deposits throughout the United States. Banks paid interest on time deposits (savings accounts) but not on demand deposits (checking accounts). The other depository institutions were not allowed to accept demand deposits. However, the introduction of NOW accounts (interest-bearing checking accounts) has blurred the distinction between demand deposits and time deposits. All types of depository institutions now offer checking accounts.

NOW accounts usually require a minimum balance, with penalties for going below that balance. NOW depositors receive monthly or quar-

FIGURE 16-5 / Examples of services provided by many commercial banks.

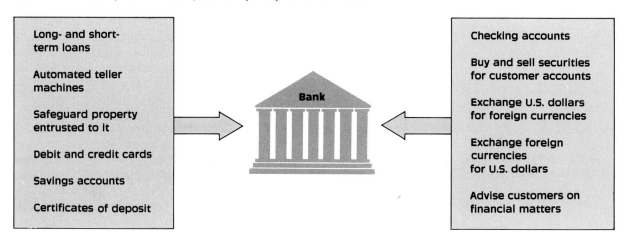

terly computer-prepared statements summarizing the account's activity during the period. There is no need for a passbook.

Commercial banks are the major source of short-term (one year or less) loans for businesses. Although they make long-term loans to some firms, commercial banks prefer to specialize in providing short-term funds.

prime rate of interest

Borrowers pay interest on their loans. Large firms with excellent credit records tend to pay the prime rate of interest. The **prime rate of interest** is the lowest rate charged to major business customers by a specific large bank. The prime rate often differs from one bank to another and from one region to another. It is a general indicator of the availability of loanable funds. A high rate, for example, shows that money is scarce.

Commercial banks offer both secured and unsecured loans. A *secured loan* is backed by collateral such as a firm's accounts receivable. If the borrower cannot repay the loan, the bank sells the collateral. An *unsecured loan* is backed only by the borrower's promise to repay it. Only the most creditworthy borrowers can get unsecured loans.

DEPOSIT EXPANSION

Suppose you have $100, take it to a commercial bank, and open a checking account. Because it is unlikely that you will write checks against the entire amount, some of that money will remain in your account. Your bank can earn interest by lending some of it to borrowers. Banks that are subject to federal regulation must keep some portion of their demand deposits as cash in their vault or as deposits with a Federal Reserve Bank. These are *legal reserves.*

Let's assume that the reserve requirement is 10 percent. Your bank, then, must keep $10 of your $100 deposit in legal reserves. It has $90 to lend. Now suppose Angela Smith borrows that $90 from your bank. Angela has $90 added to her checking account. Assume that she writes a check for $90 payable to Wal-Mart. Wal-Mart's bank ends up with a $90 deposit. But Wal-Mart's bank has to keep only 10 percent of $90 ($9.00) in legal reserves. Wal-Mart's bank can therefore lend out $81.00.

This is the process of *deposit expansion.* It can continue as shown in Figure 16-6 (on p. 470). The commercial banking system creates money in the form of demand deposits. Of course, the process of deposit expansion is much more complex in practice. General economic conditions, for example, influence the willingness of bankers to make loans and the willingness of borrowers to borrow.

As Figure 16-6 shows, your original deposit of $100 could result in an increase of $1,000 in new deposits for *all* banks in the commercial banking system. Remember, we are assuming a reserve requirement of 10 percent. Thus your original deposit of $100 could expand by ten times (the reciprocal of the reserve requirement, 100/10). If the reserve requirement were 20 percent, your original deposit could expand by only five times (100/20) or to $500. Our example in Figure 16-6 assumes that no borrower takes part of his or her loan in cash and that the

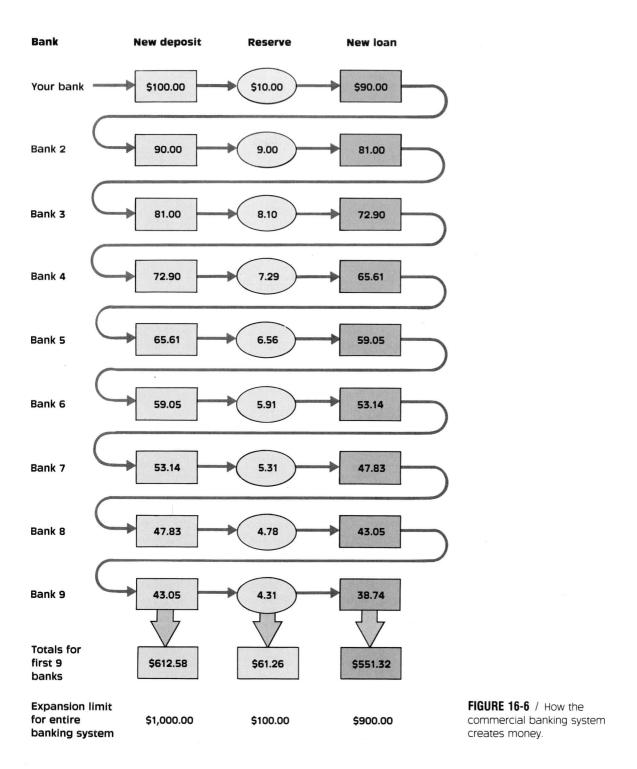

Bank	New deposit	Reserve	New loan
Your bank	$100.00	$10.00	$90.00
Bank 2	90.00	9.00	81.00
Bank 3	81.00	8.10	72.90
Bank 4	72.90	7.29	65.61
Bank 5	65.61	6.56	59.05
Bank 6	59.05	5.91	53.14
Bank 7	53.14	5.31	47.83
Bank 8	47.83	4.78	43.05
Bank 9	43.05	4.31	38.74
Totals for first 9 banks	$612.58	$61.26	$551.32
Expansion limit for entire banking system	$1,000.00	$100.00	$900.00

FIGURE 16-6 / How the commercial banking system creates money.

banks want to lend as much as they legally can. Otherwise, the increase would be less than $1,000.

ELECTRONIC FUNDS TRANSFER

electronic funds transfer (EFT)

Commercial banks and some other financial institutions now use electronic funds tranfer (EFT) to provide many of their basic financial services. **Electronic funds transfer** combines computer and communication technology to transfer funds or information into, from, within, and among financial institutions. Examples include the following:

- Automated teller machines (ATMs), or 24-hour tellers, are electronic terminals that let you bank at almost any time of day or night. Generally, you insert a special card and enter your own secret identification number to withdraw cash, make deposits, or transfer funds between accounts.
- Pay-by-phone systems let you telephone your financial institution and instruct it to pay certain bills or to transfer funds between accounts by merely pushing the proper buttons on your phone.
- Direct deposits or withdrawals allow you to authorize in advance specific deposits and withdrawals on a regular basis. You can arrange to have paychecks and Social Security checks automatically deposited and recurring expenses, such as insurance premiums and utility bills, automatically paid.

debit card

- Point-of-sale transfers let you pay for retail purchases with your debit card. A **debit card** is a type of plastic money that, when used, immediately reduces the balance in the user's bank account. The money for the purchase is immediately transferred

Automated teller machines have become a familiar means of electronic funds transfer.

IT'S YOUR BUSINESS
Payment Methods in the United States

According to a recent survey by the Payment Systems Education Association (PSEA), cash and personal checks are still the most widely used payment methods in the United States. The study of payment choices was divided into three sections: (1) purchase amount, (2) place of purchase, and (3) type of item purchased. The following paragraphs highlight some of the findings.

In terms of payment choices by *purchase amount*, 70 percent of the respondents said they would use cash for items costing less than $50 but would write checks for items priced higher. About one-third of the respondents reported using credit cards for purchases of more than $100. Only 5 percent said they use credit cards for purchases of less than $50. Debit cards and electronic transfer are barely used, less than 1 percent of those surveyed reporting that they would be likely to use them for purchases in any price range.

Place of purchase seems to affect the payment methods just as much as price. For example, 90 percent of the respondents said they would probably use cash in a convenience store, 76 percent said they would probably use cash at a gas station, and 66 percent would pay cash at a pharmacy; 55 percent said they would use cash at a department store. Fewer than 2 percent said they would use debit cards or electronic transfer in any of the stores mentioned in the study.

The *type of item purchased* also seems to affect the payment methods. Thus 81 percent use cash to pay for restaurant dinners, and 64 percent use cash for groceries; 75 percent use personal checks for insurance payments, and 69 percent use personal checks when they pay their mortgages or rent. Fewer than 1 percent use debit cards or electronic transfer to pay for groceries, mortgage or rent payments, restaurant dinners, mail-order items, or insurance bills.

In summary, the survey clearly shows that cash and personal checks remain the most popular way for Americans to pay. As the president of PSEA says, "We were a little surprised at the lack of debit card use, particularly in light of recent promotional efforts by gas stations and grocery stores." Apparently, Americans do not yet consider debit cards and electronic transfer to be significant payment options.

Source: "What Cashless Society? Consumers Still Like to Pay with Legal Tender," *Marketing News*, Dec. 4, 1987, p. 3. Reprinted from *Marketing News*, published by the American Marketing Association.

from your bank account to the store's account. You can do this while on vacation far from your home bank, as long as your bank's and the local bank's computers are tied into the same network. As indicated in the It's Your Business box, however, most Americans do not yet use debit cards and electronic transfers.

REGULATION OF THE COMMERCIAL BANKING SYSTEM

Commercial banks chartered by the federal government are national banks. Those chartered by state governments are state banks. National banks are audited by the Comptroller of the Currency. State banks are audited by state banking authorities. Lending, investment, and branching policies are regulated by the Federal Reserve, which we discuss later in this chapter. Figure 16-7 show the overlapping jurisdictions of the four banking industry regulators.

Perhaps you have read about "banking panics" or "runs on banks." The last series of major panics occurred during the Great Depression, when depositors everywhere lost faith in the economy and wanted to withdraw their funds. A typical bank, however, could not possibly pay off all its depositors. Banks keep only a small percentage of their customers' deposits in cash. Many banks failed because they simply could not call in all their outstanding loans fast enough.

All national banks must carry deposit insurance with the FDIC, and most state banks voluntarily do so. Each insured bank pays a fee (based on its total deposits) for this insurance. The FDIC uses these funds to pay off depositors (up to $100,000 per account) who have accounts in banks that fail. The FDIC has the authority to examine all insured banks and to assist in the merger of troubled banks with other healthy financial institutions.

In recent years we have had some failures and runs on banks and savings and loan associations. In 1987, 184 banks failed, a 54-year record. Between 1979 and 1987, 631 federally insured banks with state or national charters closed their doors. Managerial incompetence was the primary cause.[2]

FIGURE 16-7 / Regulation of the commercial banking system.

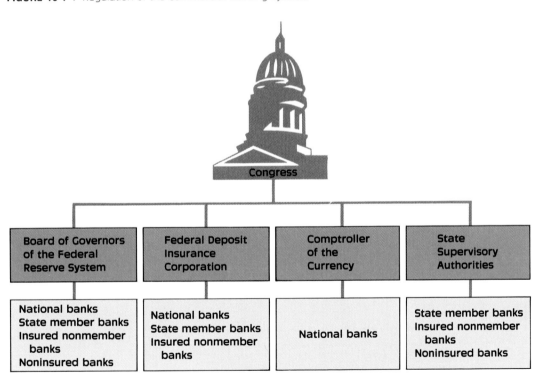

Bank fraud is also receiving more attention. There were 2,900 major bank fraud investigations under way at the end of 1986—twice as many as in 1983. The FDIC now requires banks or examiners to call in criminal prosecutors as soon as foul play is suspected. In 1987, for example, federal prosecutors announced indictments against the former chief executive officer of the failed Empire Savings & Loan Association and six associates on conspiracy, racketeering, and fraud charges.[3]

The Depository Institutions Deregulation and Monetary Control Act of 1980 (DIDMCA) brought tremendous changes to the financial industry. Figure 16-8 highlights the major provisions of the act. Deregulation has made financial institutions more competitive.

Some people believe that some reregulation is needed. For example, one controversial area has been the "float"—the interest banks earn because of check-clearing delays. Some banks did not give depositors of checks access to the money until the checks cleared. If a bank set a holding period of ten days and your check actually cleared in three days, the bank earned interest on your money for seven days.

The Expedited Funds Availability Act takes effect in two stages. Effective September 1, 1988, funds deposited in the form of cashier's checks, certified checks, and government checks must be available to depositors the next business day. Local checks must be available within three business days. Banks, thrifts, and credit unions are permitted to hold funds written on out-of-town institutions for as many as seven business days after deposit. In 1990 the maximum hold periods were scheduled to shrink to two days for local checks and to five days for out-of-town checks.[4]

The What Do You Think? box touches on another important aspect

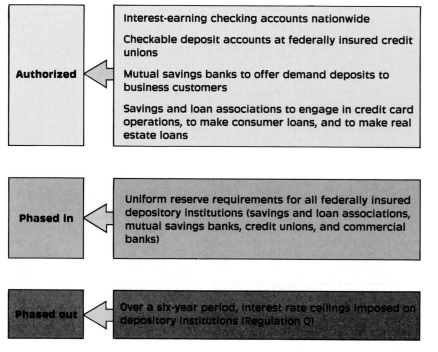

FIGURE 16-8 / Major provisions of the Depository Institutions Deregulation and Monetary Control Act of 1980.

Authorized

Interest-earning checking accounts nationwide

Checkable deposit accounts at federally insured credit unions

Mutual savings banks to offer demand deposits to business customers

Savings and loan associations to engage in credit card operations, to make consumer loans, and to make real estate loans

Phased in

Uniform reserve requirements for all federally insured depository institutions (savings and loan associations, mutual savings banks, credit unions, and commercial banks)

Phased out

Over a six-year period, interest rate ceilings imposed on depository institutions (Regulation Q)

of the regulation of commercial banks: interstate banking. It also makes a distinction between money center banks and regional banks.

The Federal Reserve System

Federal Reserve System (the Fed)

The heart of the commercial banking system in the United States is the Federal Reserve System. The **Federal Reserve System (the Fed),** the central bank of the United States, was created by the Federal Reserve Act of 1913 to control the nation's money supply.

WHAT DO YOU THINK?
Will Superregional Banks Gobble up Smaller Regional Banks?

Big-league commercial banking in the United States used to be confined to the money center banks—the huge banks in New York, Chicago, and San Francisco. Examples include J.P. Morgan, Citicorp, Bankers Trust, Chase Manhattan, and Security Pacific. Now, however, big-league banking is spreading rapidly across the country.

Based in economically strong regions and growing in size and profitability, superregionals have become banking's financial stars. Over the next few years, many bankers and analysts predict, some superregionals will join the ranks of the nation's largest banks and compete nationally with money center institutions for consumer and midsized business accounts.

Under existing law, to operate in any state other than its home state, a bank must receive the new state's permission. This is why the United States does not have nationwide banking organizations like those that exist in other countries. The superregionals' surge has been sparked by recent state laws permitting banks within certain multistate areas to operate across state lines. That privilege—denied to money center banks—has triggered a wave of regional mergers. A 1985 U.S. Supreme Court decision upheld regional banking compacts.

Four major banking regions are taking shape, with fewer than half a dozen superregional banks or thrifts moving to dominate the market in each of them.

- **New England:** Providence-based Fleet Financial Group Inc.; Boston-based Bank of New England Corporation and Bank of Boston Corporation.
- **Southeast:** Atlanta-based Sun-Trust Banks; Charlotte-based First Union Corporation, NCNB, Inc., and First Wachovia Corporation.
- **West Coast:** San Francisco–based Wells Fargo Company and First Nationwide Savings; Los Angeles–based First Interstate Bancorp and Great Western Financial Corporation.
- **Middle Atlantic states to the Midwest:** Columbus, Ohio–based Banc One Corporation; Detroit-based NBD Bancorp; Pittsburgh-based PNC Financial Corporation.

Will superregional banks gobble up smaller regional banks? What do you think?

Source: Robert Guenther, "Financial Stars: Some Regional Banks Grow Rapidly, Reach Major-League Status," *The Wall Street Journal,* Oct. 1, 1987, pp. 1, 12. Reprinted by permission of *The Wall Street Journal.* © Dow Jones & Company, Inc., 1987. All Rights Reserved.

ORGANIZATION OF THE FED

The Federal Reserve System encompasses twelve districts and is supervised by a board of governors.

THE BOARD OF GOVERNORS   The board of governors of the Federal Reserve System is composed of seven members who are appointed by the President of the United States with the advice and consent of the Senate. Each member is appointed to a fourteen-year term. The board provides general direction to the twelve Federal Reserve Banks. It can audit their books, and it coordinates their operations in the public interest.

FEDERAL RESERVE DISTRICTS AND BANKS   The United States is divided into twelve districts, each of which has a Federal Reserve Bank (FRB) that is owned by member commercial banks in the district. (See Figure 16-9). Each FRB has nine directors, three of whom are appointed by the board of governors to represent the general public. The other six—three to represent bankers, three to represent business—are elected by member commercial banks. Within each district there are several zones, each containing a branch of the district FRB.

THE FEDERAL ADVISORY COUNCIL   The Federal Advisory Council is composed of twelve members, one from each FRB. The council advises the board of governors.

FIGURE 16-9 / Federal Reserve districts.

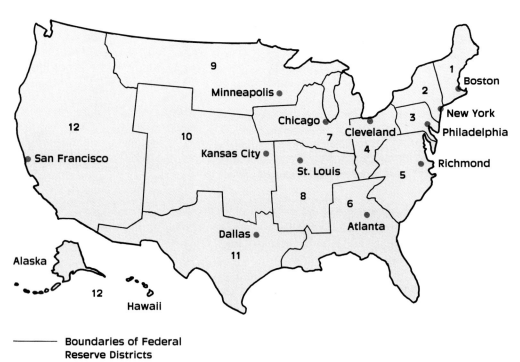

Boundaries of Federal
Reserve Districts

THE FEDERAL OPEN MARKET COMMITTEE (FOMC)   The Federal Open Market Committee (FOMC) consists of the seven members of the board of governors plus five FRB representatives. It sets the Fed's open market policy by directing the FRBs to buy or sell government securities. These open market operations are discussed later in this chapter.

MEMBER BANKS   Of the roughly 15,000 commercial banks in the United States, only about 5,500 are members of the Federal Reserve System. This includes all of our major commercial banks. All national banks must be members. State-chartered banks may join if they meet the Fed's requirements.

OPERATIONS OF THE FEDERAL RESERVE

As the central bank of the United States, the Fed is responsible for fulfilling a number of functions. As indicated in Figure 16-10, the Fed's three major functions are managing the money supply, supervising banks, and performing service functions.

MANAGING THE MONEY SUPPLY   The most important Federal Reserve function is managing the growth (or reduction) of the money supply. The Fed seeks to accomplish this through its monetary policy. The goal is to make enough money and credit available to stimulate economic growth, which creates jobs and makes more goods and services available. But the Fed has to exercise great care to avoid introducing too much money and credit into the economy because that tends to result in inflation. The Fed must also consider the effects of its monetary policy on the value of the dollar in relation to other countries' currencies.

Ideally, the Fed's monetary policy and the President's and Congress's fiscal policy (government spending and taxation) will work in harmony to promote steady economic growth. The Fed's three major

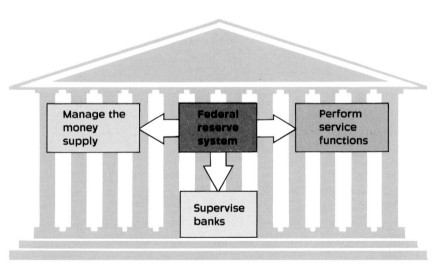

FIGURE 16-10 / The Federal Reserve System's three major functions.

tools for conducting monetary policy are open market operations, discount rate changes, and reserve requirement changes.

Open market operations. Savings bonds, Treasury notes, and Treasury bills are financial obligations of the federal government. The Federal Reserve Banks engage in open market operations with respect to these securities. **Open market operations** involve purchases and sales of U.S. government securities by Federal Reserve Banks as instructed by the Federal Open Market Committee in order to implement the Fed's monetary policy.

If the FOMC wants to *increase* the money suppy, it directs FRBs to *buy* government securities from their member banks. The FRBs pay for these securities by crediting the reserve accounts of their member banks. This increases member banks' lending ability because cash (not government securities) counts as part of their reserve requirements.

If the FOMC wants to *decrease* the money supply, it directs FRBs to *sell* government securities to their member banks. This reduces member banks' reserve accounts at the FRBs and therefore reduces their lending ability.

Open market policy is the Fed's main tool for regulating the money supply. The Fed transacts its open market operations on a daily basis.

Discount rate changes. The **discount rate** is the interest rate charged to depository institutions for borrowing at the Fed. Each FRB sets its own discount rate, subject to approval by the board of governors. Raising the discount rate makes member banks less willing to borrow. It also causes them to raise the interest rate they charge their borrowers, which reduces the money supply. Lowering the discount rate has the opposite effect. Changes in the discount rate are considered important as "announcements" of the Fed's monetary policy.

Reserve requirement changes. The **reserve requirement** is the percentage of deposits that depository institutions must keep in vault cash or as deposits with the Federal Reserve Banks. The board of governors sets the reserve requirement for all depository institutions. Lowering the reserve requirement increases the money supply. Raising it decreases the money supply. Commercial banks' deposits can expand, as we have seen, by a factor equal to the reciprocal of the reserve requirement percentage. Thus if the reserve requirement is 20 percent (⅕), an initial cash deposit can lead to an expansion of deposits five times as large. (Figure 16-6 illustrated the process of deposit expansion.) The Fed does not change reserve requirements very often because such changes have a major impact on bank reserves. Figure 16-11 summarizes the Fed's three money supply controls.

SUPERVISING BANKS The Fed is responsible for regulating commercial banks. Its responsibilities here include (1) approving requests to open a branch or to merge with another bank, (2) enforcing regulations, and (3) admitting banks to membership in the System. Each of the twelve FRBs supervises and examines the member banks in its district.

(margin terms) open market operations

discount rate

reserve requirement

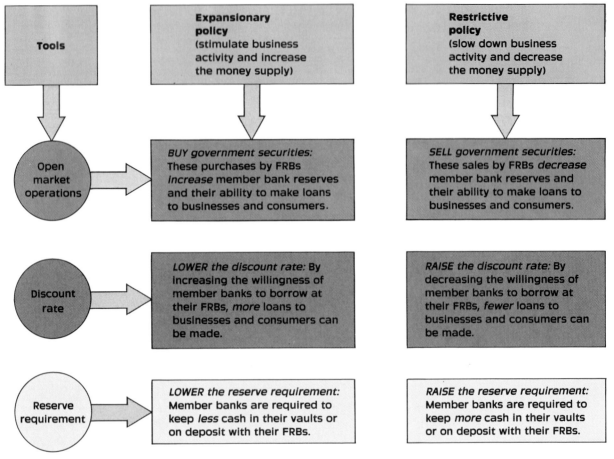

Tools	Expansionary policy (stimulate business activity and increase the money supply)	Restrictive policy (slow down business activity and decrease the money supply)
Open market operations	*BUY government securities:* These purchases by FRBs *increase* member bank reserves and their ability to make loans to businesses and consumers.	*SELL government securities:* These sales by FRBs *decrease* member bank reserves and their ability to make loans to businesses and consumers.
Discount rate	*LOWER the discount rate:* By increasing the willingness of member banks to borrow at their FRBs, *more* loans to businesses and consumers can be made.	*RAISE the discount rate:* By decreasing the willingness of member banks to borrow at their FRBs, *fewer* loans to businesses and consumers can be made.
Reserve requirement	*LOWER the reserve requirement:* Member banks are required to keep *less* cash in their vaults or on deposit with their FRBs.	*RAISE the reserve requirement:* Member banks are required to keep *more* cash in their vaults or on deposit with their FRBs.

FIGURE 16-11 / Federal Reserve System monetary policy actions.

PERFORMING SERVICE FUNCTIONS   The Fed also provides a number of important services to the U.S. Treasury and to the public.

- To help maintain an efficient payments system in the United States, the Fed provides a nationwide automated clearinghouse for checks and drafts and a communications center at Culpeper, Virginia, for the transfer of funds by wire, known as "fedwire."
- The Fed's District Reserve Banks and their branches physically house much of the coins and paper money in circulation. Member banks that need paper money and coins can get it at the local branch. They can also make deposits of paper money and coins at the local branch. The District Reserve Banks therefore provide for the movement of paper money and coins throughout the nation. They also remove worn and damaged coins and paper money from circulation.
- As the bank for the U.S. Treasury, the Fed takes care of the paperwork involved when the government sells securities such as

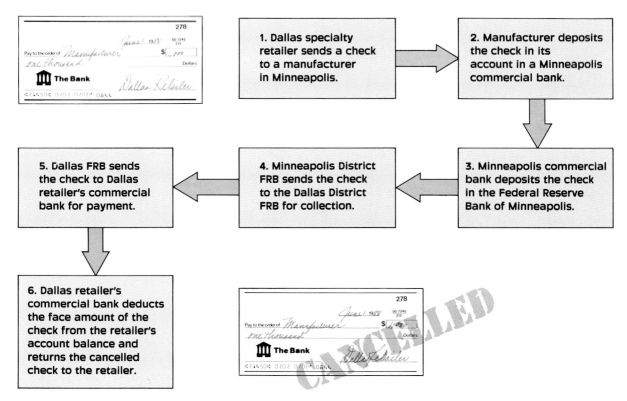

FIGURE 16-12 / How a check is cleared through the Federal Reserve System.

savings bonds, Treasury bills, and other types of government securities to investors, either directly through the Fed or through various types of securities brokers.

- The Fed holds the legally required reserve accounts of member banks and acts generally as a bank for banks.
- The Fed makes sure that state member banks comply with consumer protection regulations, such as Truth in Lending and Equal Credit Opportunity.

Figure 16-12 illustrates the various stages a check goes through as it is being cleared through the Federal Reserve System. Not all checks, however, are cleared through the Fed. Many small banks in rural areas pay larger banks to provide this service for them. In addition, commercial banks have their own systems for clearing checks written and deposited within the same city. But when checks are drawn on banks in various Federal Reserve Districts, they are cleared through the Fed.

Other Financial Institutions

Financial institutions, as we saw earlier, generally fall into one of the following four categories: depository institutions, contractual saving

In the process of being cleared, each check you write must go through a sorting system, at either the Federal Reserve clearinghouse or a commercial bank.

institutions, investment companies, and finance companies. Because of deregulation, however, the services they offer have become increasingly similar.

In 1970, Congress defined a bank as an institution that (1) accepts deposits that may be withdrawn on demand and (2) makes loans to businesses. A **nonbank bank** (also called a limited service bank) is a financial institution that makes loans to businesses or offers checking accounts, but not both. Nonbanks are not under the Fed's control.

nonbank bank

FINANCIAL SERVICES COMPANIES

Some firms simply call themselves financial services companies or "financial supermarkets." A **financial services company** is a financial institution that offers under one roof the full variety of services that once could be had only by going to many different types of financial institutions. These services may include stock brokerage, insurance, real estate sales and financing, banking, and credit.

financial services company

The idea of financial supermarkets took root in 1981 when American Express, Sears, and Prudential Insurance Company all bought major securities firms. American Express bought Shearson, Sears bought Dean Witter, and Prudential bought Bache. American Express has continued to acquire firms in the securities business. Shearson, for example, bought Lehman Brothers Kuhn Loeb in 1984 and E.F. Hutton in 1987. Many banks now offer discount brokerage services. Many also rent space to firms that sell real estate and insurance.

Nonfinancial businesses are also intruding into the world of finance. Sears, the giant retail chain, owns Dean Witter, a securities firm that offers checking accounts. It also owns a savings bank and Coldwell Banker, a real estate brokerage firm. Sears is also in the insurance business. Ford Motor Company has also diversified into financial services during recent years. It owns First Nationwide Bank, the seventh-largest savings institution in the United States.

The wave of acquisitions and mergers among financial institutions during recent years is an attempt on their part to dominate the financial services industry. Expansion outside of their traditional line of business has led to marketing problems for some, however. Banks, brokerage firms, and insurers are not used to selling one another's products. To what extent the financial services companies will replace or absorb existing institutions remains to be seen.

Many U.S. banks operate abroad—and many foreign banks do business in the United States. Other financial institutions are also becoming more involved in global operations. Consider that Japanese-based Nomura and Daiwa Securities are primary dealers in U.S. government securities. Nippon Life Insurance owns a 13 percent stake in Shearson Lehman Brothers. Sanwa Bank owns a Chicago-based leasing company and a California bank. The future will undoubtedly see the further development of huge global banks and other financial institutions.

In the discussions that follow we take a closer look at nondepository financial institutions. These are contractual savings institutions, investment companies, and finance companies.

CONTRACTUAL SAVING INSTITUTIONS

Life insurance companies and pension funds are contractual saving institutions. They create assets that form a contractual relationship with buyers.

life insurance company

A **life insurance company** is a company that shares risk with its policyholders for payment of a premium. Some of the money from premiums is then loaned out to individuals, firms, and nonbusiness organizations or is invested.

pension fund

A **pension fund** is money put aside under a pension plan set up by employers or labor unions to provide for the systematic payment of benefits to retired employees. Pension fund managers invest the funds in corporate stocks and bonds, government securities, and commercial property mortgages. They also make loans to businesses. Because their cash outflows are long-term and highly predictable, the fund managers can invest for the long term. Contributions from employers and employees and disbursements to retired employees are contractual obligations.

INVESTMENT COMPANIES

investment company

An **investment company** (or mutual fund) is a financial institution that pools funds obtained from individual investors to purchase a portfolio of assets that may include stocks, bonds, or money market securities.

Such companies offer investment expertise and allow the investor to diversify investments.

Closed-end investment companies have a fixed number of shares that are publicly traded among investors. In effect, they are traded like the shares of stock of companies like IBM and General Motors. Their value is determined by supply and demand.

Open-end investment companies do not have a fixed number of shares. They stand ready to sell an unlimited number of shares to investors. They also stand ready to buy back shares from investors who want to sell some or all of their shares. The value of a fund's shares depends on the value of the securities held by the fund.

One type of investment offered by open-end investment companies is the money market mutual fund. As we saw earlier, this is an alternative way for people and organizations to earn interest outside of depository institutions. The fund invests the money it receives from investors and pays them an interest rate that varies with the rate the fund earns on its various investments. There are many investors in a money market mutual fund, so—unlike a money market CD—investors can invest and withdraw at any time without penalty. Some of the funds permit check writing.

FINANCE COMPANIES

Finance companies are a major source of credit to both firms and consumers. Many finance companies are active in various types of lending.

commercial finance company

A **commercial finance company** is a financial institution that makes loans to firms using accounts receivable, inventories, or equipment as security (collateral). Sometimes firms use commercial finance companies in addition to banks. In other cases, firms use them when their credit positions are too weak to satisfy a bank. CIT is an example of a commercial finance company.

sales finance company

A **sales finance company** is a financial institution that specializes in financing installment purchases made by consumers and firms. When a consumer buys a durable good from a retailer who is on an installment plan with a sales finance company, the loan is made directly to the consumer. The item bought serves as security for the loan. Westinghouse Credit Corporation is a sales finance company. As explained in the Burger King capsule (on p. 484), Westinghouse Credit has also expanded into other types of services. The business credit division offers innovative ways to finance the growth of business firms.

consumer finance company

A **consumer finance company,** or a personal finance company, is a financial institution that makes personal loans to consumers. These companies do not make loans to businesses. Small loans may be made on a "signature basis," without security. Larger loans may require collateral such as a car or furniture. Beneficial Finance is an example of a consumer finance company.

factoring company

A **factoring company** (or factor) is a financial institution that seeks to make a profit by buying accounts receivable at less than face value from a firm and collecting the face value of the accounts from the firm's customers. The factor buys, pays for, and owns the accounts receivable outright. Merchant Factors Corporation is an example of a factor. Some

APPLICATION: BURGER KING

Franchise Financing

Buying a Burger King franchise is an expensive proposition. The average non–real estate cost runs about $341,000. This includes such costs as the franchise fee, equipment, decor, and landscaping.

The cost of the land and the building can run from just under half a million dollars to close to a million dollars. The total investment required to become a Burger King franchisee can be very substantial.

However, a Burger King franchisee is usually required to come up with only about $150,000 in cash—still a very big amount. Banks and other types of financial institutions might help to finance the rest.

Ramon Moral (whom we profiled in Chapter 4) says that "when you open a Burger King® restaurant you don't want to get into the real estate business because this will limit your borrowing power. So instead of trying to buy the land and build the building entirely with your own money, companies like Westinghouse Credit Corporation might build to suit you." The ongoing cost will be about 12 percent of sales. Burger King Corporation might be willing to lease real estate to a franchisee.

Of course, once you own and operate five or six restaurants, you will gradually be able to go to the bank yourself and borrow all the money you need for subsequent stores. This is because banks look at things like your earning power and

your assets when deciding whether to lend you money. Banks want to know that you can make your payments and that, if you do not, they can at least recoup their investment. If you have several healthy Burger King® restaurants, the banks will have a good deal of confidence in your ability to repay the loan.

Questions

1. What advice would you offer to Burger King Corporation regarding the use of credit cards and debit cards by its customers?

2. Why is Burger King Corporation willing to lease land to some of its franchisees?

3. Which of the financial institutions discussed in this chapter are likely to be useful to a Burger King franchisee?

commercial banks, like Manufacturers Hanover, have opened factoring divisions in recent years.

Summary

A broad view of money is that it is anything that people generally accept as payment for goods and services. The three primary functions of money are to serve as a medium of exchange, a store of value, and a unit of account. In order to perform these functions, money should be durable, portable, divisible, stable, scarce, and liquid. In our economic system, financial institutions can actually create money. A checking account, for example, is money according to both the M1 and M2 definitions of the money supply.

The four classes of financial institutions are depository institutions, contractual savings institutions, investment companies, and finance companies. Depository institutions include commercial banks, savings banks, savings and loan associations, and credit unions.

The commercial bank is the major provider of banking services to business firms. The commercial banking system creates money in the form of demand deposits. The Depository Institutions Deregulation and Monetary Control Act of 1980 deregulated many parts of the financial services industry. It is becoming harder to distinguish among the various types of financial institutions.

The heart of the commercial banking system is the Federal Reserve System. The Fed is the central bank of the United States. Its three main functions are managing the money supply, supervising banks, and performing service functions. Its three tools for conducting monetary policy are open market operations, discount rate changes, and reserve requirement changes.

The financial services company is a rather recent development. This is an institution that offers under one roof the full variety of services that once could be had only by going to many different types of financial institutions. Some of these institutions have been more successful than others in diversifying into new areas.

Contractual saving institutions create assets that form a contractual relationship with buyers. Examples are life insurance companies and pension funds.

Investment companies pool funds obtained from investors in order to purchase a portfolio of assets that may include stocks, bonds, or money market securities. Two types of investment companies are the closed-end and open-end types.

Finance companies are active in various types of lending. Examples of such companies include commercial finance companies, sales finance companies, consumer finance companies, and factoring companies.

Review Questions

1. What are the functions of money?

2. What are the ideal characteristics of money?

3. What are the four broad classes of financial institutions?

4. What are the four basic types of depository institutions?

5. How does the commercial banking system create money?

6. What are the three major functions of the Federal Reserve System?

7. What is a financial services company?

8. Why are life insurance companies and pension funds called contractual savings institutions?

Discussion Questions

1. Do we really need four different types of depository institutions? Could we eliminate all but the commercial bank and still manage to conduct our financial affairs?

2. Do you think the debit card will become as popular as the credit card? Explain.

3. Shopping malls were founded on the idea that people like one-stop shopping. Some of the financial services companies are based on the same concept. Is shopping for clothing, home furnishings, and the other products typically found in shopping malls really much different from shopping for a home, a mortgage, insurance, a checking account, and a certificate of deposit?

4. Should the concept of social responsibility affect how investment managers for giant insurance companies and pension funds invest their billions of dollars?

Key Terms

money

financial intermediary

depository institution

commercial bank

Federal Deposit Insurance Corporation (FDIC)

savings and loan association (S&L)

savings bank

credit union

M1

currency

demand deposit

negotiable order of withdrawal (NOW) account

share draft account

M2

time deposit

certificate of deposit (CD)

money market mutual fund

money market account

near-money

prime rate of interest

electronic funds transfer (EFT)

debit card

Federal Reserve System (the Fed)

open market operations

discount rate

reserve requirement

nonbank bank

financial services company

life insurance company

pension fund

investment company

commercial finance company

sales finance company

consumer finance company

factoring company

Cases

THE FEDERAL RESERVE SYSTEM REACTS TO A CRISIS

The stock market's collapse on Monday, October 19, 1987, created a dilemma for the Fed. Beginning the previous September, the Fed had begun to tighten credit in response to fears in the financial markets that inflation was rising in response to an overheated economy. A tighter credit policy is intended to boost interest rates, slow down economic growth, and reduce inflationary pressures. Stock traders and analysts favored this tight credit policy in order to fight inflation.

Immediately after the collapse, those same people were asking the Fed to ease credit—to push down interest rates—in order to avoid a recession. The big drop in stock prices refocused the financial markets' attention from inflation to recession. The market crash reduced consumer wealth by at least a half-trillion dollars. One expected result was a big drop in consumer spending. Concern about an overheating economy disappeared. In its place there was fear that the economy would come to a screeching halt.

On Tuesday, October 20, Alan Greenspan, chairman of the Federal Reserve Board, tried to calm the financial markets with a one-sentence statement that was intended to reflect the Fed's switch from an anti-inflation policy to an antirecession policy. "The Federal Reserve, consistent with its responsibilities as the nation's central bank, affirmed today its readiness to serve as a source of liquidity to support the economic and financial system." As a result, interest rates began to tumble.

Questions

1. If the Fed wants to pursue a tighter credit policy, should it buy or sell government securities? Should it raise or lower the discount rate? Should it raise or lower the reserve requirement?
2. In the "flight to quality" after the stock market "meltdown," investors who were taking billions of dollars out of the stock market started buying U.S. Treasury securities. Would that help or hinder the Fed's antirecession policy?
3. How do big federal budget deficits affect the Fed's ability to ease credit?

AMALGAMATED BANK OF NEW YORK

Amalgamated Bank of New York is a union bank that was founded in 1923 by the Amalgamated Clothing Workers. It is still owned by the 284,000 members of its successor, the Amalgamated Clothing and Textile Workers. Heralded as the wave of the future by labor leaders earlier in the century, labor banking was a flop. Out of some thirty-six labor banks founded in the 1920s, only Amalgamated in New York and Brotherhood Bank & Trust in Kansas City, Kansas, remained at the end of 1987.

Amalgamated survived largely because its union owner insisted on conservative banking and professional management. In contrast, the Brotherhood of Locomotive Engineers set up banks across the country during the 1920s and quickly branched into securities and even Florida land development. Losses piled up, and the union was out of the banking business by 1931.

In 1987, Amalgamated teamed up with Metropolitan Life Insurance Company in a proposal to of-fer a comprehensive money management program to the AFL-CIO's 14.5 million members. Amalgamated is also helping three New York locals of the Bridge, Structural and Ornamental Iron Workers union use some of their pension money to finance low-cost home mortgages for their members. The bank is considering expanding the service to other unions, many of which have retirement trust funds under Amalgamated's care. Unions account for up to two-thirds of Amalgamated's $1.1 billion in deposits, and its trust department holds an additional $3.2 billion in pension and health-and-welfare funds.[5]

Questions

1. What similarities, if any, do you see between today's financial services companies and the banks that the Brotherhood of Locomotive Engineers set up in the 1920s?
2. Does Amalgamated's teaming up with Metropolitan Life Insurance Company make Amalgamated a financial services company?
3. In the light of the growing volume of funds in pension funds, do you think that more unions will seek to set up their own banks?

SEVENTEEN

Financial Strategies

After reading this chapter, you
will be able to:

- Describe a financial manager's main duties.

- Outline the general sources
  of funds and the criteria for
  evaluating them.

- Define working capital and
  explain why managing it is
  so important to the firm.

- Illustrate the use of two major sources of short-term
  credit: trade credit and commercial bank loans.

- Distinguish among promissory notes, drafts, and commercial paper.

- Explain the main uses of
  long-term capital and how
  the capital budget fits into
  long-range planning.

- Show the relationships
  among mergers, acquisi-
  tions, asset redeployment,
  restructuring, raiders, and
  greenmail.

The financial manager's ability to raise funds and allocate them to the most profitable investments has always been critical to the operation of a business. Today, the pressures of difficult financial times have forced managers to be even more effective in meeting their firms' financial needs. This is true for meeting long-term capital needs, as well as for finding sources of short-term funds. In this chapter we examine the demands for short-term funds and the sources of such funds for business firms. We also review the sources and the uses of intermediate and long-term funds, as well as the alternative of leasing and special financing methods such as mergers and acquisitions. We will look at the alternatives of debt and equity financing and the criteria by which a choice between them may be made.

It finally happened—Bruce Springsteen and Michael Jackson are moving to Japan. They are not moving literally, of course. Don't expect the Boss to be popping into geisha houses instead of bars on his evening motorcycle trips through town, and forget about Jackson putting his pet chimpanzee on a diet of sushi. But the firm that produces all the Springsteen and Jackson hits— CBS Records—was sold to Sony in 1987, so their record production is moving, even though the singers are not.

The sale was a direct result of some high-powered corporate finance. Several years before, an investor team headed by billionaire Lawrence Tisch made a bid for CBS Corporation and won. The team took over not only the CBS television network, but also various radio and TV stations that CBS owned. CBS also owned book publishers and several businesses, including the very successful CBS Records.

Investors know that taking over firms as big as CBS often involves incurring debts of hundreds of millions of dollars. This is because major investors often borrow the funds they need for the takeover. In other words, they buy the firms with borrowed funds. Sooner or later these debts must be paid off. In takeovers like these, that usually means sooner rather than later.

The interest on such debts can be staggering, so they are usually paid off quickly before the payments bleed the firm dry. The easiest way to pay off these huge debts is usually to sell off big chunks of the firm itself.

That is just what Lawrence Tisch did with CBS. CBS Records had a great year in 1987. Big hits included Michael Jackson's *Bad* album and Bruce Springsteen's *Tunnel of Love.* The time was ripe for getting the best price possible for CBS Records. Tisch sold CBS Records to Sony for $2 billion.

The deal seems to be good for almost everyone involved. CBS and Tisch can pay off some debts and still have cash with which to buy new TV stations. Sony can diversify into a business other than consumer electronics, their mainstay. What will the sale mean for stars like Springsteen and Jackson? That is a little harder to tell. As you can imagine, the record industry relies heavily on creative talent, including producers and executives, not just singing stars. If Sony intends to replace CBS Records' creative staff with its own people, some changes could be in store for Michael and Bruce.[1]

As in the case of CBS Records, the concepts of "takeover," "corporate raider," and "restructuring" have become very common. As a result, financial management has taken on increased importance in most firms. Raising funds, managing cash, and making major investments have always been vital, of course. But now, with the prevalence of raiders, takeovers, and international competition, good financial management can determine more than ever whether or not a firm will survive.

The Financial Manager and Financial Planning

Financial decisions are made by the financial manager (who may be called the controller, chief financial officer, treasurer, or vice-president for finance). This executive forecasts the firm's long- and short-term financial needs. He or she then meets these needs with the help of banks and other financial institutions. As the guardian of the owners' equity, the financial manager must get the best return on the owners' investment without taking needless risks.

Company presidents may include social or other noneconomic objectives in their decision making, such as contributing to the local United Way campaign. However, financial managers must think of dollars and profits. They specialize in funds and their allocation. They provide the president with a purely economic, profit-maximizing point of view.

A financial manager's responsibilities are:

- To evaluate and select from alternative sources of funds.
- To identify and satisfy the firm's short-term capital and long-term capital needs in the face of risk.
- To manage risk while maximizing the firm's return on assets and the value of the firm itself (as measured by the price of its stock if it is a corporation).
- To develop a financial plan that describes how the firm's projected financial needs will be met.

GENERAL SOURCES OF FUNDS

Where do business funds come from? For some firms there is little choice. For example, the owner of a small new retail store might have no option but to supply all her firm's startup funds herself or to get her family to help her. Sometimes even giant corporations find themselves with few options, though. After the stock market crash of October 1987, Australian financier Robert Holmes à Court saw the value of his Bell Resources Ltd. plummet by over $700 million almost overnight. As a result, organizations like Merrill Lynch Capital Markets and various banks were reluctant to invest in or lend money to Mr. Holmes à Court. His only option was to sell all or part of his firm. Most firms, however, have some choice in their sources of funds. The basic choice is between debt financing and equity financing.

The owner of a small retail store might have to supply all her firm's startup funds herself or obtain a bank loan based on her personal creditworthiness.

debt financing

equity financing

Debt financing is the use of borrowed funds. This could mean a major corporation issuing bonds or a barber shop borrowing $1,000 for sixty days from a local bank.

Equity financing is the provision of funds by the owners themselves. This could involve selling more stock to new or existing owners. It could also involve using money that the business itself produced, such as retained earnings or funds available through depreciation (deducted from revenue but not actually spent). Managers and shareholders are often at odds over the use of retained earnings as a source of long-term capital. Shareholders often prefer to have the profits paid out as dividends rather than having them retained. Since the mid-1970s, U.S. nonfinancial corporations have used equity less than debt in their financing plans.

CRITERIA FOR EVALUATION OF SOURCES

maturity

Several important considerations help a firm to decide between the use of debt and equity. These are shown in Figure 17-1. **Maturity** refers to the amount of time until a debt must be paid. If funds are internal (equity), they need not be repaid at all. If they are borrowed, the date of maturity (due date) is fixed by the lender in consultation with the borrower.

Debt financing	Equity financing

When must it be repaid?

Fixed deadline	No limit

Will it make claims on income?

Yes, regular and fixed	Only residual claim

Will it have claims on assets?

In liquidation, creditors come first	In liquidation, shareholders must wait until creditors are paid and preferred equity precedes common equity

Will it affect management power?

No, doesn't affect	May cause challenge of corporation control

How are taxes affected?

Bond interest is deductible	Dividends are not deductible

Will it affect management flexibility?

Yes, many constraints	No—few constraints

FIGURE 17-1 / Comparing debt and equity financing.

Equity and debt financing also differ in how they affect claims on assets and income. Issuing bonds means that the new bondholders will get the designated interest payment before stockholders get any dividends. They have a prior claim on income. Bondholders also come before stockholders if the firm goes out of business. They are paid off out of the proceeds of the sale of the firm's assets before stockholders receive anything.

Still another factor in deciding between debt and equity relates to control of the corporation. If a firm issues more common stock and this stock is bought by newcomers to the firm, the original common stockholders could lose control over the election of the firm's board of directors. A bond sale would not cause such a risk for the controlling shareholders.

Other things must be considered as well. Interest payments to bondholders are deductible as an expense by the company. This can mean a tax advantage for bonds over stock. Being in debt can also reduce one's flexibility. For example, the lender may be able to dictate what products must be sold, what purchases can be made, and perhaps who the officers of the firm should be. Being in debt always means giving some control to the lender.

Financial markets also play a role when a firm seeks new sources of capital. Sometimes there is a lot of money available to lend, and sometimes there is not. The final selection is often a compromise between what management would like most and what suppliers of capital are willing to give.

leverage

Of course, the main reason businesses borrow in the first place is that they believe they can earn a higher return on borrowed dollars than the cost of the interest they must pay to their lenders. **Leverage** is using borrowed funds to earn more money than the amount that must be paid in interest on the funds.

We should not leave the subject of long-term financing without emphasizing one last potential drawback of debt. Whether for a corporation or an individual's personal needs, debt can reduce independence and flexibility. In favorable economic times—when sales are rising and income is rolling in as planned—debt payments are manageable, and the debt gets paid off. The problem with debts arises when things do not go as planned and the debt cannot be paid. Then the debtor might have no choice but to sell off assets and/or go out of business. The prudent financial manager avoids too much debt and does not forget about equity. (The same applies to individuals and personal debt.)

Short-Term Financing

Firms have three kinds of financial needs. These are needs for short-term, intermediate-term, and long-term capital. The time frame for short-term funds is generally a year or less. We look first at the uses and then at the sources of short-term funds.

USES OF SHORT-TERM FUNDS

The firm uses its short-term funds to invest in short-term (current) assets such as:

- Cash and checking accounts
- Accounts receivable
- Inventories

It also uses its short-term funds to pay two current liabilities (or debts):

working capital

net working capital

- Accounts payable (trade credit, such as money owed to suppliers)
- Notes payable (usually payable to a commercial bank)

Working capital is a firm's investment in current assets such as cash and inventories. It is important that a firm be able to pay its current liabilities or debts when they come due. **Net working capital** equals current assets minus current liabilities and so reflects a firm's ability to pay its current debts.

Figure 17-2 (on p. 496) illustrates the flow of working capital. The transactions that cause increases and decreases in current asset accounts are as follows.

Cash and checking accounts are *increased* by

1. Borrowing from the bank (thus creating notes payable),
2. Cash sales of items from finished goods inventory, and
3. Payments by customers on their accounts.

Cash and checking accounts are *decreased* by

4. Payments to creditors (accounts payable),
5. Cash purchase of finished goods, and
6. Payments of notes payable to the bank.

Accounts receivable are *increased* by

7. Credit sales (selling items on credit)

and *decreased* by

3. Payments by customers on their accounts.

Finished goods inventory is *increased* by

5. Cash purchase of finished goods and
8. Purchase of finished goods on credit (if this were a manufacturing firm, finished goods inventory would also increase from internal production of finished goods)

and *decreased* by

2. Cash sales and
7. Credit sales.

The transactions that cause increases and decreases in current liability accounts are as follows:

Accounts payable are *increased* by

8. Purchase of finished goods on credit

and *decreased* by

4. Payments to creditors.

Short-term notes payable are *increased* by

1. Borrowing from the bank

and *decreased* by

6. Payments of notes to the bank.

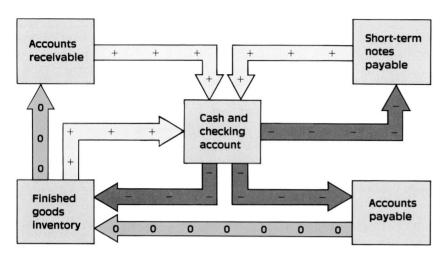

Working capital flows may:

Increase cash account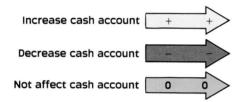

Decrease cash account

Not affect cash account

FIGURE 17-2 / Flows of working capital.

This is a simplified version of the flow of working capital. (There are also other inventories besides finished goods, especially when manufacturing processes are involved. Some work is always in process, for example.) Let us now look at the main uses of short-term funds.

CASH AND CHECKING ACCOUNTS The financial manager must first handle working capital carefully so as not to interrupt or slow the firm's regular operations. The firm needs to have enough cash coming in to meet bills, wages, and other current payments. **Liquidity** is the firm's ability to make payments that are due. If the Mangham Feed Store has a payroll of $800 due next Monday and a repair bill of $500 due on the same day, the manager must examine Mangham's liquidity. Suppose the firm has only $200 in its checking account and expects no significant cash inflow before Monday. Some borrowing might be in order, maybe from the bank.

The financial manager seeks to balance liquidity with profit. The goal is to minimize idle cash balances by keeping "near-cash" on hand. "Near-cash" is earning assets that pay interest to the firm but that are also easy to cash in when needed. Examples are certificates of deposit (CDs) in banks or short-term government securities such as Treasury bills. Tying up cash in long-term investments, such as bonds of another firm, does *not* meet the goal of balancing liquidity with profit. This is because these bonds might not be quickly convertible into cash. They could also involve some loss because of changes in their market value.

liquidity

ACCOUNTS RECEIVABLE Credit sales represent another use of short-term funds. A firm that sells on credit is basically using its funds to finance its customers' operations. (After all, if the customer had to pay cash, the money would be in the seller's bank account instead of in the buyer's.) The financial manager and the sales manager often disagree on credit policies. The sales manager sees credit as a means of boosting sales. The financial manager might see it as a waste of working capital and perhaps as a source of loss if credit customers fail to pay debts.

Notice that credit sales represent a *use* of short-term funds. To the customers who buy on credit, however, credit is a *source* of short-term funds. When interest rates are high, many firms are slow to pay their bills. In effect, they are using their suppliers as a source of working capital. By stretching out payments to their suppliers, the buying firms conserve their working capital. They might also avoid the need to borrow money at high interest rates to pay their bills. In periods of high interest rates, many suppliers tighten up on their credit policies in an attempt to get their customers to pay their bills on time.

The financial manager is responsible for achieving a balance between risk-taking and return on assets. If an increase in receivables results from purchases by paying customers, profits will increase. If products are sold to people who do not pay their bills, profits could decrease. The financial manager uses Dun & Bradstreet or other credit reporting services to evaluate credit customers. Figure 17-3 (on p. 498) is an example of a credit report. A credit report provides financial facts to help measure the risk of selling on credit to the firm being reported on.

INVENTORIES Another current asset is the inventory of finished goods. Raw materials are changed into finished goods through the production process. Between these two stages they are called "goods in process." The financial manager seeks to reduce excess inventories at all three stages. There could be a conflict with the production manager, who wants large inventories to keep the production line running smoothly.

How much inventory should be kept on hand? As explained in Chapter 10, the answer depends on several things. However, a brief example can help illustrate how complex the financial manager's job is.

Suppose the sales manager at Monsanto forecasts a 10 percent increase in sales of plastic during the coming year. The production manager bases estimates of raw materials needs—ethylene, propylene, benzene, and so on—on this sales forecast. Suppose that Monsanto's purchasing agent can receive a big discount if the regular order of these raw materials is increased by 20 percent. Should Monsanto's financial manager approve this use of funds to earn the additional discount? The correct answer depends in part on whether Monsanto could use these additional funds in some other, more profitable way, such as by allowing Monsanto customers longer credit terms, thus attracting more customers. It is also possible that the bigger order of materials would require costly storage space—enough to offset the price advantage. Perhaps Monsanto's financial manager also knows that producers of ethylene, propylene, and benzene have huge inventories on hand. If such large oversupplies are expected to continue for some time, there is a good chance that prices will actually fall. This would tend to discourage the larger order at this time.

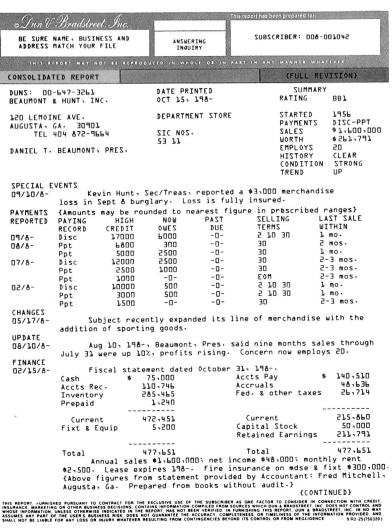

Reporting dates for section are shown in the
left margin of the Report. Other dates identifying
specific occurrences are contained within their sections.

FIGURE 17-3 / A credit report.

PREPAID EXPENSES   Still another use of working capital involves the current asset "prepaid expenses." A firm could buy a three-year fire insurance policy, for example. Paying the three-year premium in one lump sum amounts to *prepaying* the insurance coverage.

A financial manager carefully evaluates the option to pay insurance premiums in advance. The choice depends on the other uses that could be made of those funds. Prepaying expenses is wise when the savings exceed the opportunity costs. **Opportunity costs** are the benefits lost by not using funds in another way. Suppose a small furniture manufacturer can reduce its fire insurance premium by $50 if it pays for two years' coverage in advance. Instead of $1,000 for two years, the firm would pay $950. The firm would save $50 but would have tied up a lot of money in insurance. On the other hand, the firm might pay for only one year's coverage ($500) and invest the remaining funds ($450) in another asset. If the return on the alternative investment—that is, the opportunity cost—exceeds the $50 savings, then the insurance should not be prepaid. For example, suppose that by investing the $450 in a certificate of deposit at its bank, the firm can earn 13 percent per year. Within one year it would earn $58.50 on that $450. It makes sense for the firm not to lay out the $450 for the extra year's insurance at this point. The opportunity cost is too great.

The current (and expected) interest rate is obviously a major factor in making all such financial decisions. This is because it helps to determine what idle dollars could earn.

A financial manager should have an overview of the flow of working capital such as we saw in Figure 17-2. He or she must understand this flow and its timing from one use to another. If the firm has a good sales forecast and a good collection policy, it can achieve the goal of providing *enough* working capital but *not too much*.

MANAGING EXCESS CASH   Firms often find themselves with excess cash—in other words, with more cash than they need to fund expenses and operations. As a rule, excess funds should be invested in marketable securities.

As mentioned previously, not just any type of marketable security will do. Obviously, financial managers will not want to tie up funds they might need next month by investing in a long-term bond that will not mature for ten years. The short-term marketable securities they invest in must therefore be very secure (in other words, as good or almost as good as cash). And they must be decidedly short-term, with a maturity of no more than a year or so.

Obligations of the U.S. Treasury are as safe as cash (since government-printed cash would not be much good if the United States could not pay its obligations). *Treasury bills* are auctioned weekly by the Treasury and have maturities of 91 days and 182 days. One-year bills are auctioned periodically. *Treasury notes* have original maturities of one to seven years, while *Treasury bonds* have original maturities over seven years. Bills, notes, and bonds all pay interest. Actually, they are usually sold at a discount from face value. A $10,000 Treasury bill might sell for $9,000, so that when it is redeemed at the end of the year, the effective interest rate was about $1,000/9,000 = 11.1 percent. A financial manager who wanted to tie up his or her firm's funds for, say, ten months could buy a Treasury bill. Or the manager could buy a Treasury note or bond from someone else who has already held it for a while, so that it now matures in only ten more months.

Other federal agencies like the Federal National Mortgage Association (nicknamed Fannie Mae based on the first letters of its name) also sell securities, which they guarantee. These are a bit harder to market than Treasury obligations and so pay a slightly higher interest rate.

Commercial paper consists of short-term unsecured promissory notes issued by finance companies and certain corporations. Although unsecured (not backed by specific collateral such as machinery or buildings), commercial paper is usually sold only by the strongest firms, like Ford or Kodak. It is therefore a safe use for a financial manager's excess short-term funds.

A *repurchase agreement* or "repo" is the sale of short-term securities (like government notes) by a securities dealer to an investor (like a firm with excess short-term cash). The twist in this case is that the dealer agrees to repurchase the securities at a specified future time. For example, suppose a financial manager wants to hold a U.S. Treasury bond for only ten months. She could agree to purchase a bond with a maturity of twelve years from a dealer, with the understanding that the dealer will repurchase the bond after ten months at a specific price. The dealer should make a profit, the financial manager's company should have earned interest on its excess short-term cash, and all should gain.

However, it does not always work out that way. In what became known as the "ESM scandal" a dealer named ESM Securities agreed to sell to and repurchase from many investors such as banks, companies, and municipalities government securities. Many of these investors left the securities with ESM instead of taking possession of them. ESM then sold the same securities to other investors. When ESM had to pay up and buy back the securities, it had no money. Because the securities had all been sold several times, the investors could not sell them to get their money back. Almost all the buyers of ESM's "repos" lost millions of dollars.

Finally, as we explained in Chapter 16, *certificates of deposit* (CDs) are short-term deposits that a firm puts in a bank for a specified interest rate and amount of time, say six months. If the firm leaves the CD for the full six months, it earns all the agreed-to interest. If the firm takes the CD out early, there is a penalty, so it earns substantially less.

SOURCES OF SHORT-TERM FUNDS

Some of a firm's short-term (current) financial needs represent a predictable minimum amount—what the firm *knows* it will always need. Much of this fixed part of current asset needs can actually be supplied from the same long-term sources that fund fixed asset needs. We will discuss these in the next section.

However, most short-term cash needs are not fixed. Variable short-term (current) asset needs are partly seasonal and partly just plain unpredictable. All of these variable short-term needs and some of the fixed current assets can be met from three principal sources:

- Trade credit
- Commercial bank loans
- Commercial paper

Trade credit, or "open book account," is credit extended by sellers to buyers. It differs from other types of short-term credit because no financial institution is directly involved. To the seller, trade credit means accounts receivable. To the buyer, it means accounts payable. When one firm (manufacturer, wholesaler, retailer) buys materials or merchandise from another, the transaction is handled in open book accounts with no complex credit papers. The buyer records a new account payable. The seller makes an entry showing a new account receivable. Nearly 90 percent of sales are handled in this way.

In effect, the seller "lends" the buyer money for the period between receipt of the goods and payment for them. Without this type of credit, many firms could not survive. Some retailers, for instance, cannot afford to pay for merchandise until they have sold most of it to their own customers. The same type of credit exists between the consumer and the retailer. When you charge the purchase of a TV to your account at a department store, for example, the store is really lending you money for a while. Instead of calling this an open book account, most people call it a charge account.

Most trade credit involves cash discounts for early payments. Some firms borrow to take advantage of these discounts. The bank lending rate is generally below the effective rate on trade credit, which can be more than 36 percent per year.

Commercial banks accept deposits and lend a part of these funds to business firms for their short-term financial needs. Commercial banks are the most popular credit source among small business borrowers.

The demand for and supply of commercial credit affects how bankers make loans. When money is short, bankers are likely to become more careful about those to whom they lend money. In any case, a bank always checks a new borrower's past credit record and ability to manage. The bank also screens loan applications on the basis of the firm's current ratio and other financial ratios. The bank loan officer might obtain a credit report such as the one presented in Figure 17-3.

A bank expects the loan to be repaid normally out of sales and seasonal declines in the borrower's inventories and accounts receivable. The bank and borrower must agree on four principal terms of a commercial loan:

- The general nature of the arrangement
- The interest rate
- The quantity and type of security (if any)
- The repayment date

unsecured loans

Unsecured loans are loans offered for short-term uses with no security or pledge of assets as guarantee of repayment. A bank will offer unsecured loans to favored customers or customers with exceptionally good prospects for repayment. Such loans often take the form of a line of credit or revolving credit.

line of credit

A **line of credit** is an informal agreement by a bank to extend credit up to a certain amount to a customer for a short period of time. The customer must usually agree to maintain its creditworthiness. It must also agree to "clean up" the loan—pay it off and be free of bank debt for at least thirty days—before taking out the loan again. The bank is not legally bound to extend a loan under the terms of a line of credit. However, most banks feel bound to honor such lines of credit.

Many big commercial banks have added a new twist to the old business of lending money to firms. These commercial banks have a dilemma. The loan-making market is so competitive that they cannot make a profit on the loans they make to some of their best and biggest customers. They therefore sell the loan to some other (usually smaller) bank that has less overhead or that can raise money more cheaply. The company thus gets the big bank's advice and a loan. The big bank gets an administration fee for arranging the loan. The smaller bank gets the interest on the loan.

The problem is that some firms do not like to have their loans resold to other parties. If anything goes wrong and the firm cannot make its payments on time, it wants to know that it can go back and talk the problem over with the bank that is familiar with the firm's operations and problems. The firm cannot very well do that if its loan has been sold to other parties.

Soon there might be a market in these loans. Then the loans could be parceled out and sold to thousands of investors. If that happened and the firm that took out the loan ran into a problem, it would have nowhere to turn. But there are some pluses for the borrower in this kind of arrangement. The borrower does get the big bank's advice, and the big bank has to do the work of finding the smaller banks or investors to buy the loans.

If you were a financial manager, would you want to deal with a bank that gave good advice but sold your loans? What do you think?

Sources: "Securitizing the American Dream," *The Economist,* June 14, 1986, pp. 70–71; Holly Liss, "Loan Sales: Are they Sales or Financings?," *The Magazine of Bank Administration,* Nov. 1987, p. 35.

---

revolving credit agreement

A **revolving credit agreement** is a formal commitment by a bank to lend up to a certain amount to a customer over a specified period of time. Most revolving credit arrangements are for more than one year. The bank is legally bound to have funds available for the revolving loan. Customers usually pay a fee for this, whether or not they take out the loan.

secured loan

Many commercial loans to smaller firms and to firms with lower credit ratings are "secured" loans. A **secured loan** is a loan in which the lender is protected by a pledge of the borrower's assets, or *collateral.* Secured loans may also be arranged by firms that have reasonably good credit records and wish to borrow unusually large sums or want favorable interest rates. Items pledged as security for loans might include accounts receivable, inventories, equipment, stocks, or the cash value of life insurance policies.

floor financing

A special kind of secured financing is called floor financing. **Floor financing** is a type of financing in which the borrower holds the inventory and the proceeds from the sale of that inventory in trust for the lender. Auto dealers often use floor financing. The bank pays the auto maker for the cars shipped to the dealer. The dealer signs a trust receipt security agreement. This specifies what cars the loan covers and what can be done with them. When the cars are sold, the proceeds must go to the bank to pay off the loan.

Commercial banks are also the major institutions involved in the use of the other credit instruments described below: promissory notes, drafts, and acceptances. Other lending institutions, as described in Chapter 16, are also used by firms for short-term financing. These include finance companies as well as the new diversified financial services companies.

promissory note

A **promissory note** is a written pledge by a customer (borrower or "maker") to pay a certain sum of money (principal and interest) to a supplier (payee) at a specified future date. (See Figure 17-4.) Promissory notes are used in some industries in place of open book accounts. However, they are used most often in credit sales to customers who have poor credit ratings or who are slow in making payments on open book accounts. The seller feels more secure in selling to such a buyer when the seller has a note signed by the buyer acknowledging the debt.

If a promissory note is negotiable, the supplier can sell it to another party. Suppose Supplier A sells merchandise to Buyer B. Supplier A takes Buyer B's promissory note for $1,000 to be paid in 180 days at 15 percent interest per year. If Supplier A wanted to get the money sooner, Supplier A could sell the note to a bank. Supplier A would get $1,000 (the face value of the note) minus a fee for this service. Buyer B would pay $1,000 plus interest to the bank on the due date. If Supplier A sells the note *with recourse*, the bank can collect from Supplier A if Buyer B fails to make good on the note.

There is a big difference between a promissory note and a draft. A promissory note is a *promise to pay* that is made by the maker, the

FIGURE 17-4 / A promissory note.

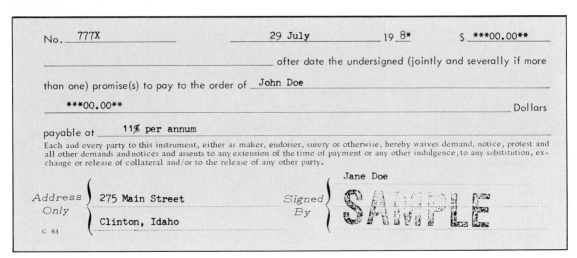

person who promises to make the payment. A draft is an *order to pay* that is made by the drawer, the person who is to receive the payment.

When Supplier A (drawer) ships merchandise to Buyer B, Supplier A sends two documents. One is the bill of lading. This is a written document from the carrier (transportation company) acknowledging receipt of the merchandise for delivery and setting out the terms of the shipping contract. The other document is a trade draft. A **trade draft** is an order to pay prepared by the supplier, ordering the buyer to pay a certain amount of money for the merchandise. A **trade acceptance** is an order to pay from a seller that has been signed (accepted) by the buyer in order to get the merchandise from the carrier. The trade acceptance is returned to the supplier (see Figure 17-5). There are two types of trade drafts: sight drafts and time drafts.

trade draft

trade acceptance

If it is a *sight* draft, Supplier A (drawer) has the bank present it for immediate payment by Buyer B (drawee). If it is a *time* draft, Supplier A can hold it until the date specified on the trade acceptance and then send it to Supplier A's bank, which will present it to Buyer B for payment. If Supplier A wants the money earlier, it can sell the trade acceptance to Supplier A's bank.

Suppose Supplier A does not want to use a trade draft but is unwilling to accept a check drawn on Buyer B's account. Supplier A can require Buyer B to pay with certified checks or cashier's checks. A certified check is certified to be cashable. The bank immediately deducts the amount of the check from Buyer B's account and stamps the check "certified." This ensures that the check will not bounce. The bank charges a small fee for this service (see Figure 17-6).

A cashier's check is a check written by the bank's cashier. The check is drawn on the bank itself (not on Buyer B's account), and the payee is specified on the check. The bank collects the amount of the

FIGURE 17-5 / A trade acceptance.

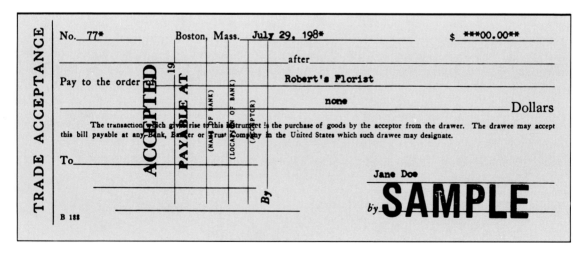

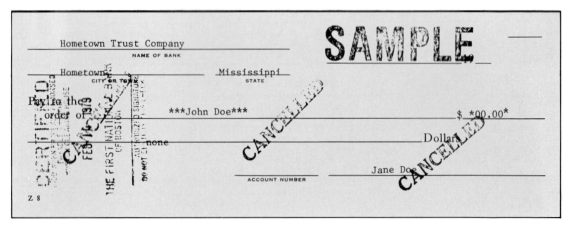

FIGURE 17-6 / A certified check.

check from Buyer B plus a small fee, or it charges Buyer B's account (see Figure 17-7).

Commercial paper houses also serve the short-term financial needs of business firms. The instruments they deal in—commercial paper—allow a firm to borrow money without collateral or security in the form of asset pledges. As mentioned earlier, these unsecured loans depend on the good faith of the issuing firm. They usually bear an interest rate below that available through commercial banks for unsecured loans.

Commercial paper can be both a source and a use of a firm's short-term funds. Big firms can raise money by selling commercial paper, so for them it is a source of funds. Other firms buy or invest in these big

FIGURE 17-7 / A cashier's check.

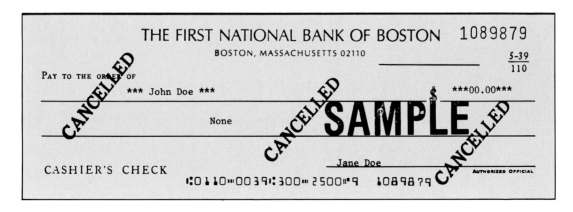

firms' commercial paper, so for them commercial paper is a use of their excess short-term funds.

Commercial paper houses act as middlemen, bringing lenders and borrowers together. They operate on a relatively small profit margin. Insurance companies frequently offer such loans (by buying the commercial paper). The amounts are usually large—several hundred thousand dollars. Small or poorly financed firms would not ordinarily be able to get such funds. When interest rates for long-term loans and bonds are high, some large firms borrow using commercial paper to avoid long-term financial commitments at high rates.

Long-Term Financing

Long-term financing means raising funds that are to be used to finance assets such as plant and equipment that have a life of ten years or more.

The basic choice in financing, as we saw in Figure 17-2, is between debt and equity financing. Much of the firm's short-term (working) capital needs are borrowed from banks or advanced from suppliers in the form of trade credit. To meet longer-term financing needs, firms use a combination of debt and equity sources. The securities market, the subject of Chapter 18, provides many of these sources.

Clearly, the quality of production and marketing management is important to a firm's success—that is, to its sales and profitability. However, from the owners' perspective the final test of success depends equally on the skills of the financial manager. That final test is the return that owners get on their investment—their profit as a percentage of their equity. The financial manager plans for and determines the firm's long-term capital needs and minimizes the cost of such capital. The financial manager thus helps to maximize the owners' rate of return.

USES OF LONG-TERM CAPITAL

Long-term capital is funds invested in land, buildings, machinery and equipment, and other fixed assets that determine the firm's future direction. Selecting investments that will produce long-term sales and profits involves some difficult decisions.

Financial managers make these long-term decisions with the help of some of the accounting devices we saw in Chapter 15. One of these is the capital budget. This is based on expected sales growth and technology changes. It projects capital needs for from five to twenty years. **Capital budgeting** is the process of planning expenditures on assets whose returns are expected to extend beyond one year (usually for five or more). The three major categories of capital spending by business as a whole in the United States are for equipment (from wrenches to robots), business construction (buildings, etc.), and business purchases of cars and trucks.

Long-range planning obviously requires some careful forecasting. In capital budgeting, decisions about the wisdom of an investment

capital budgeting

depend on several things, including the cost of the assets, expected profits from the assets, and the timing of the expenditures and revenues. But projecting these things over five years or more can be tricky. Financial managers use every scrap of information about the firm's long-range plans and expectations. They must take the environment into account, too. This includes changes in consumer needs and tastes that might require changes in plant machinery and equipment. For example, big manufacturing companies like General Motors needed billions of dollars of long-term capital for modernizing and automating their factories. Financial managers in these firms not only help project these needs, but also help secure the capital.

SOURCES OF LONG-TERM CAPITAL

Corporations have access to more types of long-term funds than do partnerships and sole proprietors. But all three forms of ownership can

High-yield bonds can be used to raise long-term capital.

choose between equity and debt financing. Let's look at financing for corporations first.

SOURCES FOR CORPORATIONS   Corporate long-term capital (at least for larger firms) is available in the public securities market through stock issues

APPLICATION: BURGER KING
Turning Assets Into Cash

Suppose you were president of a company that owned over 1,000 of its own restaurants around the world. The parent company needed a cash infusion to balance out an expected decline in pretax net income for the year. You would not want to simply sell off assets, for instance by selling 100 or so restaurants to private owners. That is because you would want to maintain control over those restaurants and continue to get some of the advantages of their sales. What would you do?

If you were at Burger King Corporation, you might set up a Master Limited Partnership, the way Pillsbury Corporation did in 1987. The basic idea of a Master Limited Partnership is to turn long-term assets into ready cash. Pillsbury formed the "Burger King Investor's Master Limited Partnership" and in February 1987 sold 98 percent of its equity to the public at $20 a unit, or a total of almost $93 million.

What do investors in the partnership get? For one thing, they get the deeds and leases to 128 Burger King® restaurants throughout the United States. They also get a slice of the rental income paid by the independent franchisees who are operating restaurants on the partnership's properties. Since rent is tied to a restaurant's sales, any increase in sales could prove a bonanza to the partnership. Of course, if the properties go up in value, the value of the partnership's shares could increase as well.

What is in it for Burger King Corporation and Pillsbury Corporation? Several things. After paying the expenses of selling the stock to the public, Pillsbury Corporation ended up with a cash infusion of over $86 million. That is one big benefit.

Beyond that, Pillsbury Corporation and Burger King Corporation wrote the partnership agreement in such a way that they still control important aspects of all 128 restaurants. For example, Burger King Corporation can require that any of the partnership's restaurants remodel or expand with the partnership paying 70 percent of the expenses. And if any of the restaurants see their sales go down for any reason, Burger King Corporation can temporarily forgo rent payments. That could be very helpful to the franchisee in getting through a rough period, but the partnership could end up absorbing 70 percent of the share of the loss.

In any case, the shares of the partnership were gobbled up by investors on Wall Street, who seemed happy to have the opportunity to participate directly in the fast food franchise business.

Questions
1. What role do you think Burger King Corporation's chief financial officer played in the decision to set up the Master Limited Partnership?

2. Is this an example of equity or debt financing? Explain the pros and cons to Burger King Corporation of this approach to financing in this particular case.

3. Why do you think investors were so eager to buy shares in the Master Limited Partnership?

and bond issues. Issuing preferred stock is a source of growth funds for corporations with stable earnings. Common stock is more likely to be issued when good growth is expected, but earnings are considered to be unpredictable. We will discuss this in Chapter 18.

A corporation that needs additional financing for the long run may also issue bonds. A major decision in any bond issue is selecting a method to pay off bondholders. One very attractive way for a strong, growing firm is by debt replacement—relying on the firm's ability to exchange maturing bonds for new bonds or stock. In this way, profits can be plowed back in for additional growth. In other cases, firms set up a sinking fund to retire maturing bonds. A **sinking fund** is money put aside each year from profits to pay off bonds when they mature. This is more likely to be done in a firm that is not expanding or that might find this investor protection feature the only way to attract bond investors. Also, using a sinking fund will lower the interest rate required on a bond because repayment of bondholders is protected and their risk is lowered.

sinking fund

A profitable firm also has the option of using profits to pay dividends or plowing them back into operations. Plowing profits back permits fixed asset (plant and equipment) growth without the use of borrowed funds. Often referred to as "retained earnings," this is a form of equity financing.

Common shareholders may or may not favor such financing, depending on their investment goals. Investors who view their shares as growth stock expect it to appreciate over the long run. They do not demand immediate dividends. Others invest for immediate income. They prefer to receive regular (and large) dividend checks rather than have profits stay in the business.

Conflict over the "dividend versus retained earnings" policy can also occur between managers and shareholders, unless the managers are also major shareholders. The availability of large amounts of invested capital is usually more attractive to managers than to shareholders.

If profits provide for enough retained earnings to cover all capital spending, then the firm does not have to raise funds through additional borrowing or sales of stock. Generally, though, firms do spend more on capital investments than they retain from earnings each year.

Another outside source of long-term funds is insurance companies, which have huge reserves to invest. They make these funds available, especially to large corporations, for long-term investment at rates similar to or somewhat lower than those demanded by bondholders.

VENTURE CAPITAL   When Steve Jobs and Steve Wozniak needed funds to get their Apple Computer Company out of their garage and into a real production facility, they went to a venture capital firm. As we explained in Chapter 3, a venture capital firm specializes in providing financing for small firms that have high growth potential.

Most small firms do not have the options that major corporations do when it comes to raising funds. Most entrepreneurs rely first on their own savings and on those of their families and friends. Commercial banks may also supply some loans. However, these usually must be backed by assets like machinery and by the entrepreneur's personal

Like many new electronics firms, Apple Computer started up with the help of venture capital.

promise to pay. Going to the capital markets to raise money via stocks and bonds is usually not an option. Tapping this source is generally too expensive. Furthermore, few investors want to take a chance on an untested firm with no track record.

That is where several types of venture capital firms come in. The Small Business Investment Company Act of 1958 empowered the Small Business Administration (SBA) to license and regulate small business investment companies. These private firms derive part of their funds from the SBA and are in business to help small firms get the funds they need to grow. Other venture capital firms represent individuals or partnerships that want to invest in high-risk, high-potential new firms. Many of the electronics firms in "Silicon Valley" got their start from venture capitalists.

Of course, venture capitalists can often exact a high price for their services (which is why some critics call them "vulture capitalists"). The applicant first gets a thorough examination. The firm must have a well-thought-out and detailed business plan and a financial prospectus. In addition, the venture capitalist generally gets substantial equity ownership in the new venture. Many write the financial agreement in such a way that if certain conditions are not met, the venture capitalist can actually take over the firm.

In any case, venture capital firms serve a very useful function. For many new ventures they are really the only source for long- or short-term funds.

SOURCES FOR NONCORPORATE FIRMS   Sole proprietorships depend primarily on the personal funding of the owner-manager for its financing. Partnerships have the same limitation, except that there are two or more partners to contribute fixed capital. Of course, if they succeed, noncorporate firms can also generate new funds internally by retained earnings. In addition, the amount charged for depreciation is not an actual cash outlay. It is therefore available for current or long-term financing.

lease

One way to avoid the need for long- or intermediate-term financing for land, buildings, or equipment is to lease them. A **lease** is an agreement to grant use of an asset for a period of time in return for stated regular payments. Leasing assets can have several advantages over borrowing funds to purchase them:

- It reduces the debt that appears on a firm's balance sheet, since a lease is not considered a debt for accounting purposes.
- Leased equipment may be replaced with more modern equipment without the loss incurred in replacing owned equipment.
- It is often a tax advantage to lease because the entire lease payment is tax deductible.
- A lease is usually a known, predictable cost factor and, in a sense, is an aid in financial planning.

Many leasing arrangements also provide the flexibility of a purchase option, should changing circumstances favor purchase at a later date.

Syntex Corporation, a multinational drug manufacturer, leases computers as a means of keeping up with changing computer technology. Syntex uses a lot of computers, and a lease arrangement lets the firm trade in old computers for new ones without the problem of disposing of the old ones. Even many smaller firms favor leasing. Jansson, Inc., a fast-growing printing firm, leases all of its equipment so that it can add new equipment at the exact time it needs to expand.

Intermediate-Term Financing

Between the short-term borrowing period (one year or less) and the long-term period (usually ten years or more) there is intermediate-term financing. To fill this kind of need, firms are turning to a variety of sources. One traditional source is the term loan from a commercial bank or an insurance company. A **term loan** is a loan made by a financial institution to a borrower for a specific period of time, such as five years. It is usually accompanied by a promissory note and secured by collateral to protect lenders in case of default.

term loan

equipment trust certificates

Some firms use equipment trust certificates to raise intermediate-term funds. **Equipment trust certificates** are backed by the equipment that is purchased with revenues from the sale of the certificates. Such intermediate-term obligations are a popular means of avoiding long-term bond issues at high fixed interest rates.

Another source of funds is the issuance of notes to investors. For example, one airline offered to the public $40 million of seven-year notes. (Notes involve shorter maturities than do bonds—usually three to five years.) The airline announced that it was borrowing the money to pay short-term bank debt and to expand operations. Securitizing assets like accounts receivables is often another option. We will discuss securitization shortly.

rolling over

Other firms avoid long-term commitments when interest rates are high by turning to the short-term market. They are borrowing by means of short-term commercial paper and rolling over. **Rolling over** is successive renewals of short-term notes as a substitute for longer-term financial commitments. This kind of invasion of the short-term money market by the long-term market stems from many firms' unwillingness to obligate themselves to high fixed interest payments when they believe that rates might be coming down.

The Changing Nature of Financial Management

During the last ten years or so, dramatic changes have occurred in the way in which firms raise money. For one thing, as we will see, firms have been borrowing much less money from banks. Instead, they often raise the money they need themselves, perhaps by selling bonds directly to investors. Three important things triggered these changes: deregulation, securitization, and internationalization.

deregulation

Anyone who has used a phone or bought an airline ticket has experienced deregulation. **Deregulation** is the relaxation or elimination of laws governing how an industry does business. For example, AT&T is no longer the only phone company you can use to make long-distance calls or from whom you can buy phones. And the prices that airlines charge for tickets and the routes they fly are no longer closely regulated by the government.

Deregulation has also occurred in banking and in the financial markets. For example, in 1981, deregulation removed the restrictions on the rate of interest that banks can pay to their depositors. To compete, banks therefore now pay more. What effect do you think this had on the interest rate banks charge their corporate customers for loans? If banks have to pay depositors more interest to get them to deposit their money, banks will probably also have to charge their customers more for loans. This has had the effect of making bank loans less attractive to companies as a source of funds.

Furthermore, deregulation has allowed other types of institutions to do things that only commercial banks used to be able to do. For example, savings and loan associations, which used to specialize in loans for housing, can now make industrial loans. Even some firms like General Electric are beginning to operate a bit like banks themselves, sometimes even making loans to each other.

Deregulation is taking place in other countries as well. In England the deregulation of financial markets culminated to what became known as "Big Bang." On that day, commercial banks could also start operating as stockbrokers, helping customers to buy and sell securities such as stocks and bonds.

All in all, deregulation has had a big effect on how firms raise funds. Probably the greatest consequence has been that companies now get less of their funds from bank loans. They get more by raising it through selling bonds or sometimes stock.

securitization

Securitization was the second big change in the 1980s. **Securitization** means selling securities backed by assets like accounts receivable or mortgages to investors. For example, suppose Mighty Big, Inc. wants to raise money but does not want to get a bank loan. It might arrange to have publicly tradable securities issued that are backed by the firm's substantial accounts receivable. (The securities might be in the form of "notes." Notes are a type of debt security that usually have a maturity of three to five years and pay investors a set interest rate.) Securitization is thus a second way in which financial markets are changing the way firms raise funds.

Internationalization is a third important change. Internationalization refers to the fact that the financial markets of different countries are increasingly intertwined. For example, do you remember what happened on October 19, 1987, when the New York Stock Market crashed? That night, stock markets in Japan, Australia, Hong Kong, Paris, and London were also thrown into disarray. This is because markets today are internationalized. Investors in Japan do not just buy Japanese stocks, but also stocks in New York, California, and London. So when the value of Japanese (or British) investors' holdings on the New York Stock Exchange fall, they might have to quickly sell what they own in their own countries to cover their losses.

Similarly, financial managers' freedom to hunt for investors overseas has increased in recent years. For example, the world's biggest exporter of capital is Japan. Japanese investors now buy much of the stocks and bonds issued by corporate America. The *Eurodollar* and *Eurobond* markets are two more examples of this internationalization of financial markets. *Eurodollars* are U.S. dollars on deposit in foreign banks (usually a European bank). *Eurobonds* are bonds sold in a country other than one in whose currency the bond is denominated. For example, if General Motors sells $20 million of bonds in France rather than in the United States, the bonds would be called Eurobonds. Why might GM do this? Perhaps because it believed that by tapping the more abundant money available in the foreign market, it could sell its bonds more cheaply than it could in the United States.

Extraordinary Financing Arrangements

Financial managers are often called upon to assist in handling extraordinary financing arrangements. Consider, for example, the big job the finance people at Chrysler faced when the firm's top management decided it wanted to buy American Motors from Renault. Carrying out the financing of such a venture goes beyond the ordinary conduct of the firm's operations. Such needs are extraordinary and call for specialized financing arrangements. We will look at three kinds of extraordinary financing arrangements:

- Mergers
- Acquisitions
- Asset redeployment

MERGERS AND ACQUISITIONS

As we saw in Chapter 3, some firms seek to grow by combining with other firms. These firms may or may not be in the same line of business. The combination can take the form of a merger or an acquisition. Although the terms are used almost interchangeably, there are still some technical differences between them.

Mergers are not a new device for growth. The Clayton Act of 1914 (to be explained in detail in Chapter 21) was passed in part to deal with the antitrust problem that some mergers raise. A merger takes place when two firms join together to form a new firm. The new firm is usually created under friendly terms, and the stockholders of each merger partner usually get newly issued stock of the new firm. One of the largest mergers in recent years was the $2.3 billion merger of two transportation companies, Santa Fe Industries and Southern Pacific.

An *acquisition* is the purchase by one firm of a controlling interest in another. To accomplish this, one firm bids for part or all of another firm's stock. The bid may involve a cash offer for 100 percent of the target firm's stock. Or it may involve a cash offer for part of the target firm's stock followed by an offer to exchange stock in the acquiring firm for the balance of the share it wants. If an attempt at aquisition succeeds, the acquiring firm owns all or part of the acquired firm.

The acquired firm may be in the same industry as the acquiring firm, or it may be in an unrelated industry. Recent examples of acquisitions within the same lines of business include Chrysler's acquiring American Motors in the auto industry and Phillips Petroleum's acquiring General American Oil Company of Texas. There have also been some well-known acquisitions across industry lines, such as the General Motors purchase of Electronic Data Systems and Xerox's acquisition of the insurance firm of Crum and Forster. In the 1980s the Coca-Cola Company decided to diversify. It therefore acquired Columbia Pictures Corporation. However, after the spectacular flop of the movie "Ishtar," Coca-Cola decided to reduce its ownership of Columbia to just under 50 percent.

We discussed hostile takeovers in Chapter 3. In a hostile takeover attempt, the target firm's board of directors opposes the acquisition. In such a case the firm that wants to acquire the target firm can bypass the target's board and try to convince individual stockholders to sell their shares to the would-be acquirer. The target firm's board may then respond by trying to convince stockholders not to sell their shares or by looking for a "white knight" to save it from the raider.

A popular method of acquisition is the leveraged buyout, which you might remember from Chapter 3. A leveraged buyout (LBO) is the

BUSINESS IN THE NEWS
Raiders, Restructuring, and Greenmail

Recently, financier Carl Icahn tried to take over the giant USX (formerly United States Steel) Corporation, while Anglo-French financier Sir James Goldsmith came within a whisker of gobbling up Goodyear Tire and Rubber Company. Meanwhile, T. Boone Pickens, the head of a small Texas oil firm, was trying again to capture a far bigger prize, the huge Phillips Petroleum Company.

What's going on? The raiders are at work. "Raiders" is the name given to a group of shrewd financial experts. They use their knowledge of finance and ability to raise money through loans and junk bonds to try to buy huge concerns like USX. They have the know-how and the friends, and they have the knack for raising the funds they need to make the offers.

What do giant firms do when attacked by raiders? Sometimes they have no choice but to cave in. That is what Revlon finally did with Pantry Pride. Caving in is often easier when the raider promises a firm's top managers handsome "golden parachutes" in the form of huge bonuses if they leave after the firm is acquired. Other firms try to redeploy assets, while still others restructure. Restructuring is a catch-all phrase that includes tactics like stock buybacks—buying the firm's stock back from other stockholders to raise its price. Westinghouse Electric recently raised its stock price by $23 per share that way. Spinoffs (sales to existing stockholders) and divestitures (sales to other firms) are examples of asset redeployment. Subsidiaries are sold off to generate cash and raise the value of the firm's stock price. (Raising the stock price makes it harder for raiders to buy it.) Cutting out layers of management and other employees to make the firm "lean and mean" is another restructuring tactic. Because excess expenses are cut out, profits go up, and so—it is hoped—do stock prices.

Other victims of raiders try paying greenmail to get out of raiders' clutches. Greenmail is a lot like blackmail. Greenmail represents a (usually) huge payment that a raider's victim pays to the raider to get the raider to sell back its stock in the firm and stop trying to take the firm over. The stock is often bought back at a price that is much higher than its worth on the open market. In 1987, British media magnate Robert Maxwell bought a huge stake in publisher Harcourt Brace Jovanovich (HBJ). HBJ borrowed hundreds of millions of dollars to buy Mr. Maxwell's stock. That left HBJ with a huge debt, which it had to pay down by selling some profitable subsidiaries. Mr. Maxwell, meanwhile, made a huge profit on his raid.

Sources: Bruce Nussbaum, "Deal Mania," *Business Week*, Nov. 24, 1986, pp. 74–76; Bill Powell, "The Raiders: A Quick Fall from Grace, but 'Greenmail' Is Alive," *Newsweek*, Dec. 8, 1986, p. 88; Nicholas Gilbert, "Thank You Ivan," *Financial World*, Dec. 23, 1986, p. 180.

acquisition of a company by a buyer that is financed mostly with borrowed funds secured by the firm's assets, its cash flow, or both. While the term "leveraged buyout" is new, the concept has been around for a half century or more.

The modern LBO first appeared in the early 1970s. Owners of a privately held firm wanted to take their money out of the firm, so they sold out to a group that included some of the firm's managers. The managers raised borrowed funds from banks and other investors to

'bal·əns

Balance:
• *To bring into harmony. To achieve a state of controlled equilibrium. A dynamic stability.*

Balance at Rockwell International is based on our leadership position in serving the needs of customers in four important business segments: aerospace, electronics, automotive and general industries.

We have established this balance through careful acquisition and divestiture and through capital investment of nearly $3 billion over the last five years.

This balance, enhanced by a favorable ratio between commercial and defense programs, gives Rockwell the dynamic stability to perform and grow consistently through varying economic conditions.

Since 1976 Rockwell has grown in sales from $4.7 billion to $12.3 billion. And we have achieved 11 consecutive years of increased earnings.

To learn more about the company that is balanced to achieve consistent performance, write: Rockwell International, Department 815F-101, P.O. Box 17510, Pittsburgh, PA 15235.

Rockwell International

...where science gets down to business

Aerospace / Electronics / Automotive
General Industries / A-B Industrial Automation

Acquisition and divestiture have helped Rockwell International to achieve a dynamic stability.

finance the purchase. For example, Denny's, Inc. agreed to be acquired by an investor group in a leveraged buyout. The investor group included most of the firm's top management, which borrowed most of the money for the purchase.

ASSET REDEPLOYMENT

As we explained in Chapter 3, conglomerate mergers and acquisitions were quite popular during the 1960s. A *conglomerate* results when a firm merges with (or, more commonly, acquires part or all of the stock of) firms in very different lines of business.

Many conglomerates have been selling off some of the firms (subsidiaries) they had previously acquired. **Asset redeployment** is the selling of company divisions. It is also called asset divestment, dediversification, or deconglomeration. Whatever the process is called, there are several reasons for it. Competitive pressure to boost profits is one big reason. High interest rates and economic slowdowns (which reduce sales and profits) have an effect. Also, top managers want to focus more specifically on the existing divisions that they can manage well and that offer high profit potential. They might also acquire other firms that offer more profit potential than some of their existing divi-

asset redeployment

sions. Return on investment is the bottom line. Firms are no longer content with a rate of return that may be below the prime rate of interest. Financial managers play a key role in identifying which divisions or operations should be sold and potential candidates for acquisitions.

The bottom line—return on investment—was why Warner Communication, Inc. sold its Atari, Inc. unit. After Warner purchased Atari, the video game unit's sales reached $2 billion in just ten years. However, sales later dropped sharply. The fad had peaked. So management decided that Warner would be a better firm without Atari.

Summary

The financial manager's job is complex and requires a variety of talents. He or she must be aware of the firm's present and future needs for working capital. The financial manager must also evaluate and select sources of funds. In deciding between alternative sources of funds, the manager considers many factors: when must it be repaid? Will it make claims on income? Will it have claims on assets? Will it affect management power? How are taxes affected? Will it affect management flexibility?

For short-term funds the major sources are trade credit, commercial banks, and commercial paper. The firm uses its short-term funds to invest in short-term assets such as checks and cash, accounts receivable, and inventories. Financial instruments such as promissory notes, drafts, and trade acceptances are used to manage the flow of short-term funds.

The basic choice in financing is between debt and equity, and this applies to long-term financial decisions as well as short-term ones. Long-term capital is capital invested in land, buildings, machinery and equipment, and other fixed assets. While the uses to which long-term capital is put tend to be the same for many types of firms, the sources of long-term capital depend on several things including the size of the business and whether or not it is incorporated. For example, corporations can issue common and preferred stock as well as bonds to raise long-term capital. Small firms and those not incorporated generally must rely on family and friends for infusions of the required cash or on small business investment companies. Venture capital firms (including small business investment companies) also provide long-term capital. Venture capital firms are in the business of providing capital to promising startup companies.

From the firm's point of view, long-term financing decisions are as crucial to success as production and marketing decisions. They require a commitment of funds for ten years or more. Capital budgets help the financial manager to plan for capital needs. The securities market, to be discussed in the next chapter, provides the major source of such funds. Increasing use is also being made of intermediate-term financing (one to ten years). Leasing as an alternative to intermediate- or long-term borrowing is common, especially for equipment needs.

Situations that require extraordinary financing include mergers, acquisitions, and asset redeployment. During the last ten years or so, dramatic changes have also occurred in the way in which firms raise money. Three important things have triggered these changes—deregulation, securitization, and internationalization.

Review Questions

1. Briefly explain why it is important to distinguish short-term financing from long-term financing.

2. What specific uses are made of working capital?

3. How can short-term notes payable be increased and how can they be decreased?

4. How do debt and equity financing differ in terms of their maturity? In terms of their claims on income?

5. Distinguish between a promissory note and a trade acceptance.

6. Name and explain two sources of intermediate-term financing.

7. What capital need is served by an "open book account" or trade credit? Compare this source to the commercial bank.

8. Give several examples of uses of long-term financing.

9. How are repurchase agreements used?

10. What are the pros and cons of using venture capital firms to help raise funds?

Discussion Questions

1. What role do you think a firm's financial manager plays in making decisions about potential candidates for a takeover?

2. What are the relative advantages of leasing versus purchasing?

3. What factors should the financial manager consider in evaluating the use of short-term, intermediate-term, or long-term debt?

4. What conditions might lead a firm to undertake asset redeployment?

Key Terms

debt financing
equity financing
maturity
leverage
working capital
net working capital
liquidity
opportunity costs
commercial paper

trade credit
unsecured loans
line of credit
revolving credit agreement
secured loan
floor financing
promissory note
trade draft
trade acceptance

capital budgeting
sinking fund
lease
term loan
equipment trust certificates
rolling over
deregulation
securitization
asset redeployment

A LEVERAGED BUYOUT AT GAF

Christmas 1987 came early for GAF chairman Samuel Heyman—on October 19, to be exact. On that day the stock market plunged, saving Mr. Heyman and his partners millions of dollars as they launched a leveraged buyout of GAF.

In a leveraged buyout (LBO) a group, usually including some of the firm's present managers, borrows money to buy out the firm. Before the stock market crash on October 19, Mr. Heyman and his group announced an LBO bid at $66.50 a share. But the market crashed, and the price of GAF common stock fell to a low of $31.

GAF immediately began buying back shares on the open market, eventually picking up six million shares at an average price of $38 a share. This saved Mr. Heyman $171 million on his bid, since there were six million shares that he and his group did not have to buy ($66.50 − $38 × 6 million shares = $171 million). Mr. Heyman then offered $48.50 a share instead of $66.50. If the deal were to go through, Mr. Heyman himself would be able to take home about $135 million for his fancy financial footwork.

But it could get better. If the deal were to go through, the firm would have equity of $50 million and debt of from $1.5 billion to $2 billion. If Mr. Heyman were to hold onto GAF, pay down the debt, make a few acquisitions, and sell part of the firm back to the public, the value of GAF could rise. Mr.

Heyman, say some experts, could end up with a share worth $655 million within three or four years.[2]

Questions

1. How could management use asset redeployment and restructuring to improve the new (post-LBO) performance of GAF?
2. Do you think LBOs are always this successful? What do you think would have happened if Mr. Heyman and his group had made their offer six months earlier and actually bought all the shares of stock at $66.50 a share before the stock market crash?
3. What are some of the drawbacks to GAF if its management group assumes that enormous $2 billion debt? What do you think the group should do to reduce it?

CASH IN THAT DEBT FOR EQUITY

According to *The Wall Street Journal*, the byword is "equitize." Michael Milken and other officials at investment banker/stockbroker Drexel Burnham Lambert are telling many corporate clients to replace debt and bonds with equity or with "convertible" bonds, which eventually could be converted by bondholders into stock.

From a corporate financial manager's perspective, replacing

debt with equity can give a company more financial flexibility by reducing interest charges. When equities were trading at new highs (as they were on May 5, 1987), trading bonds in for equity seemed to make a lot of sense. That is why many companies including Occidental Petroleum and Fruit of the Loom sold hundreds of millions of dollars worth of stock to buy back debt and reduce interest payments. Prime prospects for paying down debt are companies like Union Carbide. Union Carbide took on over $2.5 billion in debt in 1986 to defeat a takeover attempt by another firm. Companies like Union Carbide drove their debt through the roof, so to speak, to make their companies less attractive to raiders.[3]

Questions

1. What are some of the disadvantages to a firm's stockholders of trading in debt for equity?
2. Why would firms like Union Carbide drive up their debt to make their firms look less attractive? In other words, in what way does debt make a firm like Union Carbide look less attractive to a raider?
3. In light of the fact that the stock market crashed about five months after Drexel Burnham Lambert gave its advice, what do you think of the timing and quality of the advice?

EIGHTEEN

The Securities Market

LEARNING OBJECTIVES

After reading this chapter, you will be able to:

- Outline the activities of the public securities market.

- Explain what is meant by stock value and how this relates to stock dividends and stock splits.

- Explain the use of bonds in corporate financing.

- Describe the characteristics of organized securities exchanges and the over-the-counter market.

- Explain the role of the Securities and Exchange Commission in the securities market.

- Translate a quote for a stock or bond, as reported in *The Wall Street Journal,* into dollars-and-cents terms.

- Compare speculating and investing.

Most firms (especially larger ones) depend on the securities market for raising external funds. In this chapter we explain the securities market in detail, including the types of securities available (such as bonds and preferred stock) and basic aspects of securities like dividends and credit risk. We also explain the role of investment banks and brokerage houses, which help companies raise money and sell their stocks and bonds.

When most people think of the securities market, they usually think of stock exchanges like the New York Stock Exchange. The workings of such exchanges is covered next in this chapter. We also explain in some detail the mechanics of opening a stock market account and buying and selling stocks. To do that, we explain how to read a stock quotation and a few of the factors that affect stock and bond prices. We will describe how the market is regulated and the ways in which buyers and sellers deal with risk. If you are not already a stock investor, this chapter could start you on the road to riches. But before you jump in blindly, consider what happened on Black Monday—October 19, 1987.

After climbing steadily for five years, the New York Stock Exchange plummeted on October 19, 1987, dashing the hopes of millions of investors. In New York they called it Black Monday,

the day the stock market dropped more than 500 points, wiping out over half a trillion dollars in wealth in just a few hours.

Big and small investors were hit. Everywhere, crowds of small investors poured into brokers' offices to try to sell stocks and find out what was happening. One distraught customer, faced with mounting losses, shot his broker. The big investors were also hit hard. On October 18, Michael Eisner, the President of Walt Disney Company, owned stock valued at over $139 million. Within weeks of Black Monday, its value was halved—Mr. Eisner had lost almost $70 million. TransWorld Airlines chairman and takeover artist Carl Icahn saw the value of his personal holding company drop by an incredible $700 million during roughly the same period.

The stocks of even the biggest, most solid firms nosedived. IBM's stock finished Black Monday at 104, down $72 from its high just two months earlier. If you had bought fifty shares of IBM at $176 per share in August, your $8,800 investment would have melted down to $5,200 by the night of October 19—a loss to you of $3,600. And IBM is a big, "blue chip" stock—one of the most solid. Smaller firms were hit even harder, and many were wiped out. Panic reigned as traders on the floor of the New York Stock Exchange tried, often in vain, to find buyers for the millions of shares that their customers wanted to sell.

The panic quickly spread to other markets around the world. The Tokyo exchange fell 15 percent in a day, and the London exchange fell 22 percent in two days. The New Zealand and Hong Kong stock markets (to the dismay of investors wanting to dump their stocks) refused to open for business for a full week, after which they opened to dramatic drops.[1]

Almost everyone is aware of the stock market crash of 1987, and many people were directly touched by it. Of course, not just individual investors were caught in the crash. As we will discuss in this chapter, business firms use the securities markets to raise much of the funds they need to run their businesses. They also depend on middlemen such as investment bankers and stockbrokers to help them raise these funds.

The Securities Market

public securities market

With very few exceptions, most large and medium-sized corporations use the public securities market as a source of long-term funds. The **public securities market** is the millions of people who buy stocks and bonds, the business and nonbusiness organizations that also buy (invest in) corporate securities, and the various securities middlemen who bring together buyers and sellers of securities.

TYPES OF SECURITIES

There are basically three types of securities traded in the public markets: common stocks, preferred stocks, and bonds. As we saw in Chapter 3, only corporations issue stock. Firms all over the world raise funds by issuing common stock, or preferred stock.

While a firm need not be a corporation to issue bonds, it usually must be well-financed and sound if it is to attract any buyers for its bonds. You might want to review the discussion of common stock and preferred stock in Chapter 3. Table 18-1 outlines several types of preferred stock.

COMMON STOCK

book value

market value

par value

There are three basic ways to value or "price" common stock. **Book value** is the difference between the dollar values of what a company owns (its assets) and what it owes (its debts, or liabilities) divided by the number of shares of common stock. **Market value** is the price the shares of stock are selling for on the market. This changes daily in response to supply and demand. **Par value** is the value the corporation that originally issued the stock certificate printed on it. This is called par value stock. If no value is placed on the stock certificate, it is called no-par stock.

Except for certain highly technical matters the par value of a stock is not important. There is usually no relationship between the par value of a stock and its book value or market value. In most cases the book value, market value, and par value of a corporation's stock are three different amounts.

Consider the giant corporate takeovers of recent years. We discussed several examples in earlier chapters. A firm becomes an attractive target for a takeover when the market value of its stock is low. Sometimes a firm's market value falls below its book value. When this

TABLE 18-1 / Types and characteristics of preferred stock

Type	Characteristics
1. Cumulative preferred	1. Dividends not paid in one year or more accumulate and must be paid before common stockholders receive dividends.
2. Noncumulative preferred	2. Dividends not paid in one year or more need not be paid in future years but, in a given year, must be paid before common stockholders receive any dividends.
3. Fully participating preferred	3. Once the dividend stated on the stock certificate is paid and the common stockholders receive the same sum, preferred shareholders share in any remaining dividends.
4. Nonparticipating preferred	4. Shareholders are entitled only to the dividend stated on the stock certificate.
5. Convertible preferred	5. Preferred shareholders can convert their preferred stock to common stock at their option.
6. Redeemable preferred	6. Preferred stock issued with a call price at which price the issuing corporation can legally require the holder to sell his or her shares back to the corporation.

occurs, an acquiring firm can in effect buy the firm below its book value. Obtaining plant and equipment in this way is often cheaper than starting from scratch.

Three other stock terms are also important. These are the stock split, cash dividend, and stock dividend. A **stock split** gives stockholders a greater number of shares but does not change the individual's proportionate ownership in the corporation. Sue Adams, for example, owns 100 shares of IBM common, which is selling at $100 per share. The market value of her shares is $10,000. If the directors vote for a 4-for-1 stock split, Sue will have 400 shares valued at $25 per share. The total market value of her shares right after the split is still $10,000. The purpose of the split is to reduce the selling price per share. This may eventually make the stock attractive to more buyers, increase the demand for it, and raise its selling price.

A **cash dividend** is a payment of cash to stockholders. It rewards stockholders for their investment in the corporation.

If a corporation wants to keep its cash, it might declare a stock dividend. A **stock dividend** is a payment to stockholders of additional shares of stock rather than payment of cash. A 20 percent stock dividend means that each stockholder gets two new shares for each ten he or she already owns. A stock dividend is a way to reward stockholders when a firm wants to reinvest its earnings in the business. It conserves cash. Like a stock split, a stock dividend does not increase the stockholder's proportionate share of ownership in a corporation.

BONDS

Although all corporations issue common stock, not all issue bonds. Stockholders provide equity (ownership) capital, while bondholders are lenders (although they are also considered "investors" as far as the securities market is concerned). Stock certificates represent ownership, while bond certificates represent indebtedness.

A **bond** is a written promise that the borrower will pay the lender, at some stated future date, a sum of money (the principal) and a stated rate of interest. Bondholders have a claim on a corporation's assets and earnings, which comes before the claims of common and preferred stockholders. Federal, state, and city governments as well as nonprofit corporations also issue bonds.

Most bond issues are sold to insurance companies and pension funds. The agreement under which bonds are issued (the *indenture*) names a trustee to represent the bondholders' interests. This trustee is usually a large bank or trust company. Table 18-2 describes several important types of bonds.

A main factor in determining a bond's quality and attractiveness is its *credit risk*—the likelihood that bondholders will not get their investment back. When you buy a bond (from a company, a city, or the United States), you are basically buying two things. First, you get the firm's promise that it will pay you a fixed amount of *interest* on specified dates. You also get a promise that at a specified time the firm will repay the *principal* on the bond. For example, if you bought a $1,000 bond, then the firm might agree to repay you your $1,000 in ten

stock split

cash dividend

stock dividend

bond

TABLE 18-2 / Types and characteristics of bonds

Types	Characteristics
1. Secured bonds	1. Backed by security pledged by the issuing corporation. This can be sold by the trustee and the proceeds used to pay off the bondholders if the corporation fails to pay principal and/or interest.
(a) Real estate mortgage bonds	(a) Secured by real property.
(b) Chattel mortgage bonds	(b) Secured by movable property.
(c) Collateral trust bonds	(c) Secured by stock and bonds in other corporations which are owned by the issuing corporation.
2. Debenture bonds	2. Not secured or backed by specific assets but by the general credit strength of the issuing corporation.
3. Registered bonds	3. Owner's name is registered with the issuing corporation and is printed on the certificate. Interest is mailed to him or her by the corporation or its trustee.
4. Coupon bonds	4. Owner's name is not registered and does not appear on the certificate. Owner must clip coupons from the bond and present them to the corporation's bank.
5. Convertible bonds	5. Can be converted to common stock at the bondholder's option.
6. Serial bonds	6. The issuing corporation issues a large block of bonds which mature at different dates.
7. Sinking fund bonds	7. The issuing corporation makes annual deposits with the trustee so that those deposits will be available to redeem the bonds upon maturity.
8. Callable bonds	8. Can be redeemed by the issuer prior to maturity.
9. Municipal bonds	9. Issued by cities or municipalities. The interest income is not subject to federal income tax. (Note that in 1988 the U.S. Supreme Court ruled that in certain cases the interest income from municipal bonds can be subject to federal income tax.)
10. Junk bonds	10. Bonds that are rated below investment grade (AAA or AA) by bond-rating services Moody's and Standard and Poor's.

years and also to pay you $100 per year in interest every year until that time. Credit risk represents the likelihood that the firm will not be able to keep its promise to pay interest and buy back the bond.

Credit risk depends on many things, including the firm's profits, how much plant and equipment it owns, and how much other debt it owes. Most investors in bonds cannot afford to analyze the credit risk of a bond themselves. They rely on two ratings services, Moody's and Standard and Poor's. Both rate the most credit-worthy bonds as "Triple A" (AAA). (See Figure 18-1.) These are bonds judged to have negligible risk of default and thus the highest quality. "Double A" bonds are almost, but not quite, as high in quality. They are not as free of default risk as are Triple A bonds. However, both Triple A and Double A bonds are considered "investment-quality" bonds. Bonds rated less than investment grade (A, Baa, Ba, and lower) are considered risky. There is a significant chance that the firm issuing such bonds will not be able to pay the interest or repay the principle as promised. The Business in the News box discusses these lower-grade bonds, known as junk bonds, which have become very important in financing takeovers.

INVESTMENT BANKS AND BROKERAGE HOUSES

Two important middlemen in the U.S. securities markets are investment banks and brokerage houses. Each has a special role in the purchase and sale of stocks and bonds. Many firms like Merrill Lynch, Shearson-Lehman-Hutton, and Citicorp act as both an investment bank and a brokerage house.

investment bank

primary market transaction

An **investment bank** (or underwriting house) is a financial institution that does not accept deposits from the general public but helps corporations to sell new issues of stocks and bonds. A **primary market transaction** takes place when a stock or bond issue is sold for the first time by a firm. The only time the issuing firm receives cash for the securities sold is in the primary market.

Suppose a major brewery decides to expand one of its plants and wants to sell $25 million of bonds. It might contact an investment bank to assist in the sale. If the bank's study of the brewery's financial condition reports favorably on the issue, the bank might offer to buy the bonds. If the brewery accepted the offer, it would receive the proceeds, and the investment banker would offer the bonds for sale to investors, hoping to make a profit.

The investment bank earns a profit by charging a commission for its services and by selling the securities at a higher price than it paid for them. If the risk of selling a large issue of stocks or bonds is too great for one investment bank, several might combine in a syndicate to underwrite the issue. Each investment bank in this underwriting syndicate agrees to take a portion of the securities offered for sale.

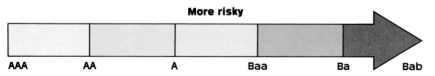

More risky

AAA   AA   A   Baa   Ba   Bab

FIGURE 18-1 / Grades of bonds.

BUSINESS IN THE NEWS
Junk Bonds

When Ted Turner, President of Turner Broadcasting System, Inc., decided to buy MGM/UA Entertainment Company, he relied on junk bonds for the money. So did Ronald Perlman, when his Pantry Pride, Inc. gobbled up Revlon for $1.8 billion. In the past few years, takeover artists have increasingly relied on "junk" to finance their purchases.

Because these low-grade bonds are risky, investors used to shun them, but this has changed. Brokers like Drexel Burnham Lambert, Inc. have issued billions of dollars of junk bonds (bonds of less than AAA or AA rating) for companies. The special twist today is that junk bond experts like Drexel's Michael Milken have been able to create a powerful network of individuals and institutions that are willing to buy these risky bonds. (Mr. Milken contends that they are really not so risky, especially when you invest in the junk bonds of several firms at once.) In 1987, about $35 billion were raised via junk bonds, and Drexel handled about 40 percent of these junk issues. (Mr. Milken earned about $40 million in 1986.)

Junk bonds are a powerful new force in the securities market. Firms use junk bonds to raise billions of dollars that they might otherwise have gone to banks to borrow. Furthermore, many of the well-publicized corporate takeovers of the past few years—such as Texas Air Corporation's taking over Eastern Airlines and Carl Icahn's taking over TWA—were financed in whole or part with junk bonds sold by firms like Drexel. Junk bonds have made it possible for takeover specialists to borrow huge sums of money to take over giant firms. They have changed the whole face of U.S. industry by triggering a series of mergers and consolidations.

Source: Anthony Bianco and Chris Farrell, "Power on Wall Street," Business Week, July 7, 1986, pp. 56–62; "Junk Comes Out of the Cellar," The Economist, Sept. 2, 1987, pp. 83–84; Chris Farrell, "Junk Bonds Finally Face the Acid Test," Business Week, Nov. 16, 1987, p. 64.

In addition to helping firms raise funds by selling securities in the primary market, investment banks perform another important function. In Chapter 17 we discussed the use of mergers and acquisitions as a financing arrangement. Investment banks like Salomon Brothers and Morgan Stanley help firms to acquire other firms or to be acquired. They assist in negotiating prices but represent only one of the two firms involved.

A **brokerage house** is a firm that buys and sells securities on behalf of its investor-clients. Securities are traded among investors in what is called the secondary market. The **secondary market** includes the organized exchanges like the New York Stock Exchange as well as the over-the-counter market (to be discussed below).

Large brokerage houses perform many functions for corporations and investors:

- They engage in investment banking when they help corporations to sell new securities issues.

brokerage house

secondary market

The stockbroker is the communications link between the investor and the securities exchanges.

- They perform a brokerage function when they buy and sell previously issued securities on behalf of their investor-clients.
- They perform a credit function when they finance purchases made on credit by securities buyers (margin purchases).
- They perform a research function when they compile information about firms.
- They perform an advisory function when they use their research to advise their corporate clients on issuing new securities and their investor-clients on buying and selling securities.

It is common to distinguish between full-cost and discount brokerage houses. Discount brokerage houses like Charles Schwab and Quick and Reilly charge lower commissions to their clients than full-cost brokerage houses. They are able to charge less because they do not provide some of the functions listed above, such as the advisory function. Investors who know which stocks and bonds they want to buy or sell can save on commissions by using such discounters.

Another development in the securities industry is the acquisition of investment banks and brokerages by both financial and nonfinancial firms like Citicorp and Sears. These firms try to increase their market share by offering a wide variety of financial services.

BANKING, INVESTMENT BANKING, AND THE GLASS-STEAGALL ACT

The Glass-Steagall Act was passed in 1931 largely in reaction to unsavory practices by many bankers in the decade preceding the Great Depression. The act itself is actually a few paragraphs in a banking bill. It basically sought to separate commercial banking activities and the securities underwriting activities of banks. One of its main aims was to make sure that ordinary commercial banking activities (in particular, insured deposits from businesses and depositors) did not find their way into risky investment banking activities like underwriting a firm's sales of stock.

In 1988 a banking reform bill submitted by Senator William Proxmire of Wisconsin and Senator Jake Garn of Utah sought to eliminate this barrier between commercial banking activities and underwriting. Commercial banks can now legally become involved in certain underwriting activities.

There were several reasons for this change. For one thing the Proxmire-Garn bill only recognizes what was increasingly the case anyway. "Nonbank banks" like Sears and American Express were setting up institutions that could accept deposits while they also involved themselves in underwriting. Deregulation had allowed these nonbank banks to compete with regular commercial banks. The commercial banks therefore found themselves at a disadvantage because they (but not the nonbank banks) were restrained by the Glass-Steagall Act.

ORGANIZED SECURITIES EXCHANGES

securities exchange

A **securities exchange** is an institution set up by brokerage houses to reduce the cost and increase the efficiency of buying and selling financial securities. Buyers and sellers of securities can deal with each other through members of the exchange. Members buy "seats" on the exchange. Membership enables them to trade securities on the exchange "floor." The New York Stock Exchange (NYSE) is the most important U.S. securities exchange. Along with the London and Tokyo exchanges it is one of the three largest in the world. Table 18-3 (on p. 530) shows highlights of the NYSE's history.

The NYSE is made up of roughly 1,400 individual members who hold memberships called "seats" on the exchange. The securities of most major corporations are listed on the NYSE. Only securities that have been traded for some time on other exchanges and are widely held can be listed on the NYSE. The company must pay a fee before its security can be listed.

The American Stock Exchange is a national exchange like the NYSE, only smaller. The AMEX has 650 regular members who hold seats on the exchange. Members of the exchange come from all fifty states and from more than twenty foreign countries. The listing requirements are lower on the AMEX than on the NYSE. It is thus easier for newer, smaller companies to get their stocks listed on the AMEX.

listed securities

Listed securities are securities traded on organized stock exchanges such as the New York Stock Exchange and the American Stock Exchange.

A corporation does not receive money from the sale of its securities on stock exchanges. Suppose an investor buys 100 shares of Abbot Laboratories' common stock on an exchange (in the secondary market). The money goes to the previous owner of the shares, not to Abbot Laboratories. Only when the stock was originally issued through an

TABLE 18-3 / Historical dates of the New York Stock Exchange

March 8, 1817	Constitution and the name "New York Stock & Exchange Board" adopted.
March 16, 1830	Dullest day in history of Exchange (31 shares traded).
January 29, 1863	Name changed to "New York Stock Exchange."
November 15, 1867	Stock tickers first introduced.
November 13, 1878	First telephones introduced in Exchange.
December 15, 1886	First million share day (1,200,000 shares).
July 31, 1914	Exchange closed through Dec. 11, 1914—World War I.
October 29, 1929	Stock market crash—16,410,000 shares traded.
June 6, 1934	Enactment of Securities Exchange Act of 1934.
December 1, 1964	New ticker—900 characters a minute—put into service.
July 14, 1966	New NYSE Stock Price Index first quoted.
December 20, 1967	Transmission of trade and quote data from floor fully automated.
December 30, 1970	Securities Investor Protection Act signed.
April 30, 1975	Fixed commission system abolished.
May 24, 1976	Specialists began handling odd lots in their stocks.
February 3, 1977	Foreign broker/dealers permitted to obtain membership.
April 17, 1978	First 60 million share day in history (63,493,000 shares).
August 7, 1980	New York Futures Exchange started trading.
January 7, 1981	First 90 million share day in history (92,881,000 shares).
August 3, 1984	First 200 million share day in history.
December 11, 1985	Dow Jones Industrial Average closed for the first time over 1500, at 1511.70.
September 11, 1986	Dow Jones Industrial Average fell a record 86.61 points to close at 1792.89.
October 19, 1987	"Black Monday." Dow Jones average crashed more than 36 percent, to 1738.74.
October 20, 1987	"Terrible Tuesday," the day after the crash. New York Stock Exchange apparently came close to closing around midday.
January 8, 1988	Presidential task force on market mechanisms report on the October 1987 crash presented. It concluded that "The financial system approached breakdown" on October 20 and called for radical changes in the markets.

Source: New York Stock Exchange, "You and the Investment World."

investment banker and distributed through a brokerage house (in the primary market) did Abbot Laboratories receive money. The stock exchange was not involved.

The securities exchanges, the brokerage houses, and the over-the-counter market (to be examined later in this chapter) all play roles in the secondary market. The secondary market for securities includes all reselling of securities by investors after the securities have first been issued by corporations.

BUYING A LISTED SECURITY

Suppose you want to buy a listed security. Figure 18-2 shows the steps you would take in the process of buying a listed security.

If you have no experience in the market, your first step is to go to a branch office of a brokerage house and open an account. A corporation has only a certain number of outstanding shares (issued by the corporation and owned by investors). If you want to buy some of those shares, you must deal with the people who own them. The brokerage house brings you (the buyer) and the shares' owner (the seller) together.

When you go to the brokerage house, you will be introduced to an account executive. This person is often called a stockbroker because he or she works for a brokerage house. If you are serious about investing, take the time to get to know your account executive.

Suppose that after talking with your account executive, Ms. Per-

FIGURE 18-2 / Buying a listed security.

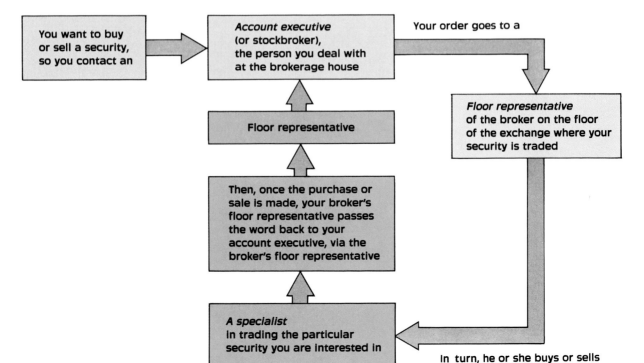

kins, you decide to buy some General Motors common stock. You ask Ms. Perkins what the selling price is. She uses an electronic device such as Quotron, which is linked to the stock exchange. It tells her the last price at which the stock sold. Now you must make a decision. If you tell Ms. Perkins to buy "at market," she will buy the number of shares you want at the lowest price offered. If that price is $42 per share, you will pay $4,200, plus commission for 100 shares. But suppose you want to pay no more than $40 per share. You can place a "limit order" with Ms. Perkins. Your order will not be filled unless she can find someone willing to sell for $40 or less per share.

round lot
odd lot

Most stock purchases are made in round lots. A **round lot** is the established 100-share unit of stock trading. An **odd lot** is a purchase of stock that is not in round hundreds and so involves additional transactions fees.

If you place an "at market" order, Ms. Perkins contacts her firm's New York office. That office contacts its representative on the New York Stock Exchange floor, who goes to the post where GM stock is traded. The floor person buys the shares at the offering price. No delay is involved because someone is always willing to sell if a buyer is willing to pay the seller's asking price.

Almost instantly, Ms. Perkins will get an electronic message direct

On the floor of the New York Stock Exchange, your stockbroker's representative might deal with a specialist to buy or sell stocks for you.

EIGHTEEN / THE SECURITIES MARKET

from the exchange floor telling her that the transaction is complete. Meanwhile, the seller's account executive sends his or her client's stock certificate to GM's stock transfer agent, who cancels it and issues a new certificate in your name. This may be held by your account executive for safe keeping or sent to you.

On the floor of the stock exchange, your broker's representative might deal with a *specialist* in order to buy you the shares of General Motors. A specialist is a member of the New York Stock Exchange who specializes in "making a market" for one or more stocks.

Suppose you said you wanted to pay no more than $40 per share for GM stock. Also suppose that the lowest price a seller is willing to take for the stock is $42 per share. The specialist in GM stock is supposed to "make a market" in GM stock. In other words, he or she is supposed to make sure (as far as is practical) that buyers can buy GM and sellers can sell GM shares that they want to sell. The specialist might offer to sell your broker's representative some of the specialist's own shares of GM at $40, just to keep the market in GM shares flowing. He might offer to buy (for his own account) shares at $42.

It is obvious that a specialist who keeps buying at $42 and selling at $40 will not be in business very long. The specialist is supposed to subordinate his or her own best interests to the exchange's need to keep the sale of stocks flowing smoothly. However, over time, specialists do manage to buy shares for less than they sell them. They are thus able to make a profit and stay in business.

THE OVER-THE-COUNTER MARKET

over-the-counter (OTC) market

Most securities are unlisted. Unlisted securities are not listed on any of the organized securities exchanges. They are traded in the over-the-counter market. The **over-the-counter (OTC) market** is a network of securities dealers who are in constant touch with each other, trading stocks and bonds of medium-sized firms as well as some national corporations. Generally, new issues of stocks and bonds are sold for the first time on the OTC market before they become listed on an organized exchange. Most government bonds and the stocks of most banks, mutual funds, and insurance companies are traded on the OTC market.

Securities dealers in the OTC market often buy securities in their own name. They expect to sell them at a higher price to their clients. These dealers also buy shares at the request of their clients. Dealers receive a commission for this. Dealers selling to one another charge a wholesale price and sell to their customers at a retail price.

The National Association of Securities Dealers, Inc. (NASD) is the self-regulatory organization for the OTC securities market. In 1971 it created a computerized communications system that collects, stores, and reports price quotations to brokers and dealers. This system is called NASD Automated Quotations (NASDAQ). Brokers and dealers are connected by this system, which enables them to get up-to-the-second price quotations. A broker can get a price quote on a security that is quoted by NASDAQ merely by pushing a button. This enables efficient trading of securities in the OTC market.

THE GLOBAL MARKET

The October 1987 stock market crash may have started in New York, but it certainly did not stop there. Within two days, markets in Australia, London, and Paris had also crashed. Several, like those in Hong Kong and New Zealand, closed entirely. This chain reaction underscores the fact that securities markets today are truly global. What happens in Tokyo, London, or New York will affect all the other markets, too.

There are three reasons why the markets are increasingly globalized and interdependent. First, more big investors (such as insurance companies) have moved a portion of the funds they invest in securities portfolios overseas. Second, many firms' securities are now traded on more than one country's exchange. If Sony falls on the New York Stock Exchange, it will probably fall later that day in Tokyo, too (which is why stock markets are now called "24-hour markets"). Third, stockbrokers and investment bankers, sensing this globalization, have—thanks to deregulation—taken to setting up shop in other countries. In December 1986, for example, the Federal Reserve Bank of New York gave permission for the first time to two foreign firms to be "primary dealers" to sell U.S. Treasury bonds to the public. In 1984–1986, London opened its stock market to all comers, allowing firms like Merrill Lynch, Bache, and Salomon Brothers to set up offices there to sell stocks. Even Japan, which has traditionally been conservative in these matters, now lets foreign firms buy seats on its exchange.

As a result, securities markets have truly gone global. And in the wee hours of October 20, 1987, after the New York crash, investors throughout the United States stayed up late to see how the markets in Asia and Europe would react. They hoped to get some signal of what to expect when the New York Stock Exchange opened later that day.[2]

SECURITIES REGULATION

Both the issuance of new securities and trading in previously issued securities are regulated by state and federal laws. At the state level, blue-sky laws apply mainly to the sale of new securities. Their purpose is to prevent corporations from issuing worthless securities to unsuspecting investors. Issuing corporations must back up securities with something more than just "the blue sky." These laws also generally require stockbrokers to be licensed and securities to be registered before they can be sold.

At the federal level the Securities Act of 1933 protects the public from interstate sales of fraudulent securities. It is a "truth in securities" law. Issuers of new securities must file a detailed registration statement with the Securities and Exchange Commission (SEC) before the securities are offered for sale to the public. The registration statement must disclose all information about the firm that might affect the value of its securities. Such information would include earnings, financial condition, and officers' salaries. In addition, every prospective buyer of the securities must be given a prospectus. A **prospectus** is a summary of the registration statement filed with the Securities and Exchange Commission that contains information about the firm, its operations, its

prospectus

management, the purpose of the proposed issue, and anything else that would be helpful to a potential buyer of the securities.

Although the SEC has broad regulatory powers, it does not judge the relative merits of individual securities. This fact is reflected in the statement below, which appears in the prospectus accompanying most security issues:

> These securities have not been approved or disapproved by the Securities and Exchange Commission nor has the commission passed upon the accuracy or adequacy of this prospectus. Any representation to the contrary is a criminal offense.

WHAT DO YOU THINK?

Is Insider Trading a Bad Thing?

The SEC licenses brokerage houses and establishes codes of conduct for them. A person who owns more than 10 percent of a firm's stock must register as an "insider" with the SEC. Such a person must file a report with the SEC if he or she does any trading in that firm's stock. The purpose is to prevent insider manipulation of the stock's selling price.

The whole matter of inside information blew up in 1985–1986. In April–May of 1985, Nabisco Brands hired investment banker Shearson Lehman. Nabisco wanted advice on its merger talks with R.J. Reynolds. A banker at Shearson then told Dennis Levine, who worked at Drexel Burnham Lambert, about the proposed merger. Mr. Levine in turn relayed information about the merger to financier Ivan Boesky. Mr. Boesky then bought over 300,000 shares of Nabisco, betting—on the basis of his inside informa-

tion—that the stock price would rise. Mr. Boesky also agreed to pay Mr. Levine 5 percent of his profits on Nabisco. In May–June 1986, after watching Mr. Levine for some time, the SEC closed the net on him. It charged him with earning over $12 million in illegal profits through insider trading over six years.

The trail then led to Ivan Boesky. In the biggest insider trading case ever uncovered, Mr. Boesky agreed to give up $50 million in illegal profits and pay $50 million in additional penalties. He also received a three-year prison sentence. While cooperating with the SEC, Mr. Boesky agreed to tape phone conversations, thus implicating others who were trading on illegal "inside" information.

Many people believe that Mr. Boesky got a raw deal. Some believe that insider information like this just means that some

people work harder than others to do their homework. Others say that inside traders actually perform a valuable function by pushing the price of the stock closer to its new value through their buying and selling. "How can you keep things like mergers and acquisitions a secret?" say others. Is insider trading a bad thing? What do you think?

Source: William Glaberson, Jeffrey Lederman, Christopher Power, and Vicky Cahan, "Who'll Be the Next to Fall?" *Business Week*, Dec. 1, 1986, pp. 28–30; Anthony Bianco and Christopher Farrell, "How the Boesky Bombshell Is Rocking Wall Street," *Business Week*, Dec. 1, 1986, pp. 31–32; James Stewart, "Boesky Disclosed 'Rampant' Criminality in Securities Industry," *Wall Street Journal*, Dec. 15, 1987, p. 7.

Again, the SEC is not required to judge the value or riskiness of individual securities. However, the registration statement and prospectus are supposed to make sure that investors have all the facts, pro and con.

The SEC was established by the Securities Exchange Act of 1934. The SEC is a five-member commission appointed by the President with the consent of the Senate. The Securities Exchange Act requires all corporations whose securities are listed on national securities exchanges to file registration statements with the SEC. They must also file annual reports with the SEC to update their registration statements.

The Securities Exchange Act was amended in 1938 by the Maloney Act. This act created a private trade organization, the National Association of Securities Dealers, Inc. (NASD), to regulate the OTC market, as was mentioned above. The SEC, however, retains final authority over the OTC market.

The Investment Company Act of 1940 brought the operations of mutual funds under the SEC's jurisdiction. (Recall that a mutual fund is in the business of investing in groups of stocks. Investors then buy shares in the mutual fund, in the hopes that the fund's manager will succeed in choosing good stocks to invest in.) The Securities Investor Protection Act of 1970 established the Securities Investor Protection Insurance Corporation. It provides insurance protection (against fraud or a broker going out of business while still owing clients money) to investors who leave their securities with their brokerage houses for safe keeping. It also provides insurance protection to investors who leave cash with their brokerage houses.

Stock and Bond Prices

Stocks and bonds that are traded on the exchanges and the OTC market are listed and reported in the financial section of many daily newspapers. *The Wall Street Journal* gives especially detailed coverage.

STOCK PRICES

Figure 18-3 explains the meaning of the various columns relating to the stock prices as reported in *The Wall Street Journal*. The corporation's name (in abbreviated form) is shown along with the number of shares sold (expressed in round lots of 100 shares). Prices are quoted in dollars, and fractions of a dollar ranging from ⅛ to ⅞. A quote of 50⅝ means that the price per share is $50.625. Follow the steps for the highlighted line in Figure 18-3 to understand each column.

BOND PRICES

Like stock prices, bond prices change from day to day. These changes reflect the cost of borrowing funds, since firms issue bonds to borrow money.

Prices of domestic corporation bonds, U.S. government bonds, and

1. High Low

32¼ 23⅝

During the last 52 weeks the highest price was $32.25 and the lowest, $23.625.

2. Stock

AbtLb

Abbreviated company name —Abbot Laboratories.

3. Div

$.84

Annual dividend based on last quarterly or semiannual declaration.

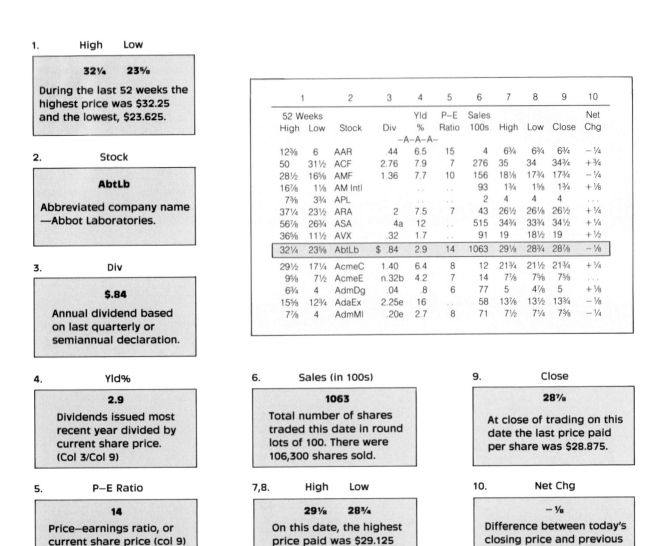

1		2	3	4	5	6	7	8	9	10
52 Weeks High	Low	Stock	Div	Yld %	P–E Ratio	Sales 100s	High	Low	Close	Net Chg
			–A–A–A–							
12⅜	6	AAR	.44	6.5	15	4	6¾	6¾	6¾	– ¼
50	31½	ACF	2.76	7.9	7	276	35	34	34¾	+ ¾
28½	16⅝	AMF	1.36	7.7	10	156	18⅛	17¾	17¾	– ¼
16⅞	1⅛	AM Intl		. .	. .	93	1¾	1⅝	1¾	+ ⅛
7⅜	3¾	APL		. .	. .	2	4	4	4	. . .
37¼	23½	ARA	2	7.5	7	43	26½	26⅛	26½	+ ¼
56⅞	26¾	ASA	4a	12	. .	515	34¾	33¾	34½	+ ¼
36⅝	11½	AVX	.32	1.7	. .	91	19	18½	19	+ ½
32¼	23⅝	AbtLb	$ .84	2.9	14	1063	29⅛	28¾	28⅞	– ⅛
29½	17¼	AcmeC	1.40	6.4	8	12	21¾	21½	21¾	+ ¼
9⅝	7½	AcmeE	n.32b	4.2	7	14	7⅞	7⅝	7⅝	. . .
6¾	4	AdmDg	.04	.8	6	77	5	4⅞	5	+ ⅛
15⅝	12¾	AdaEx	2.25e	16	. .	58	13⅞	13½	13¾	– ⅛
7⅞	4	AdmMl	.20e	2.7	8	71	7½	7¼	7⅜	– ¼

4. Yld%

2.9

Dividends issued most recent year divided by current share price. (Col 3/Col 9)

5. P–E Ratio

14

Price–earnings ratio, or current share price (col 9) divided by earnings per share in most recent year.

6. Sales (in 100s)

1063

Total number of shares traded this date in round lots of 100. There were 106,300 shares sold.

7,8. High Low

29⅛ 28¾

On this date, the highest price paid was $29.125 and the lowest, $28.75 per share.

9. Close

28⅞

At close of trading on this date the last price paid per share was $28.875.

10. Net Chg

– ⅛

Difference between today's closing price and previous day's closing price. Price decreased by $0.125.

FIGURE 18-3 / How to read a stock quotation.

foreign bonds are reported separately. Bond prices are expressed in terms of 100, even though most have a par value of $1,000. A quote of 85 means that the bond's price is 85 percent of par, or $850.

A corporation bond selling at 155¼ would cost a buyer $1,552.50 ($1,000 par value times 1.5525) plus commission. U.S. government bonds are quoted in 1/32 points. A $1,000 par bond quoted at 101 8/32 would cost $1,012.50 ($1,000 times 1.0125) plus commission. In the financial pages the selling price would be shown as 101.8 rather than 101 8/32. The interest rate on bonds is also quoted as a percentage of par. Thus "6½s" pay 6.5 percent of par value per year. A "6½s" $1,000 par bond would pay $65 interest per year.

The market value (selling price) of a bond at any given time depends on (1) its stated interest rate, (2) the going rate of interest on other bonds in the market with a similar amount of risk, and (3) its redemption or maturity date (the day the firm is supposed to buy back the bond).

If a bond carries a higher stated interest rate than the going rate on similar quality bonds, it will probably sell at a premium above its face value. In other words, its selling price will be above its redemption price. If a bond carries a lower stated interest rate than the going rate on similar quality bonds, it will probably sell at a discount. In other words, its selling price will be below its redemption price. That is how the market adjusts the interest rate you get when you buy the bond.

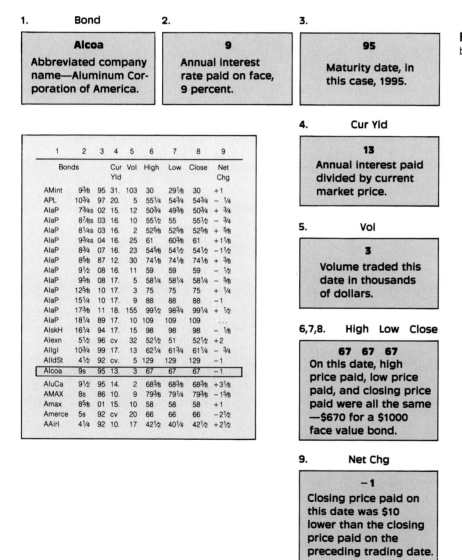

1. Bond

Alcoa
Abbreviated company name—Aluminum Corporation of America.

2.

9
Annual interest rate paid on face, 9 percent.

3.

95
Maturity date, in this case, 1995.

1	2	3	4	5	6	7	8	9
Bonds			Cur Yld	Vol	High	Low	Close	Net Chg
AMint	9⅜	95	31.	103	30	29⅛	30	+1
APL	10¾	97	20.	5	55¼	54¾	54¾	− ¼
AlaP	7¾s	02	15.	12	50¾	49⅜	50¾	+ ¾
AlaP	8⅞s	03	16.	10	55½	55	55½	− ¾
AlaP	8¼s	03	16.	2	52⅝	52⅝	52⅝	+ ⅝
AlaP	9¾s	04	16.	25	61	60⅜	61	+1⅛
AlaP	8¾	07	16.	23	54⅝	54½	54½	−1½
AlaP	8⅝	87	12.	30	74⅛	74⅛	74⅛	+ ⅜
AlaP	9½	08	16.	11	59	59	59	− ½
AlaP	9⅝	08	17.	5	58¼	58¼	58¼	− ⅝
AlaP	12⅝	10	17.	3	75	75	75	+ ¼
AlaP	15¼	10	17.	9	88	88	88	−1
AlaP	17⅜	11	18.	155	99½	98¾	99¼	+ ½
AlaP	18¼	89	17.	10	109	109	109	...
AlskH	16¼	94	17.	15	98	98	98	− ⅛
Alexn	5½	96	cv	32	52½	51	52½	+2
Allgl	10¾	99	17.	13	62¼	61¾	61¼	− ¾
AlldSt	4½	92	cv.	5	129	129	129	−1
Alcoa	9s	95	13.	3	67	67	67	−1
AluCa	9½	95	14.	2	68⅜	68⅜	68⅜	+3⅛
AMAX	8s	86	10.	9	79⅜	79¼	79⅜	−1⅝
Amax	8⅝	01	15.	10	58	58	58	+1
Amerce	5s	92	cv	20	66	66	66	−2½
AAirl	4¼	92	10.	17	42½	40¼	42½	+2½

4. Cur Yld

13
Annual interest paid divided by current market price.

5. Vol

3
Volume traded this date in thousands of dollars.

6,7,8. High Low Close

67 67 67
On this date, high price paid, low price paid, and closing price paid were all the same —$670 for a $1000 face value bond.

9. Net Chg

−1
Closing price paid on this date was $10 lower than the closing price paid on the preceding trading date.

FIGURE 18-4 / How to read a bond quotation.

Suppose you bought a $1,000 par value bond in 1980 for $650. Its stated interest rate is 6 percent, and its maturity or redemption date is 2000. You paid $650 for the bond, and its rate is 6 percent per year of par value ($1000). You get $60 per year in interest. Based on your actual investment of $650, your yield is 9.2 percent (60/650 = 0.092). If you hold it to maturity, you get $1,000 for a bond that originally cost you only $650. This "extra" $350, of course, increases your true, or effective, yield. The amount of the premium or discount depends largely on how far in the future the maturity date is. The maturity date is indicated after the interest rate. Figure 18-4 explains the various columns in a bond quotation.

STOCK AND BOND PRICE AVERAGES

To give investors an overall idea of the behavior of security prices, several stock and bond averages are reported. The various Dow Jones averages include (1) the average of thirty selected industrial stocks (Dow Jones Industrials Average, or DJIA), (2) the average of twenty selected transportation stocks, (3) the average of fifteen selected public utility stocks, and (4) a composite average of the preceding sixty-five stocks. The movement of the DJIA since 1960 is shown in Figure 18-5.

The Standard & Poor's Index covers 500 selected stocks. Because the Standard & Poor's Index includes a much larger sample of stocks than the Dow Jones averages, it could be a better measure of overall market behavior.

All common stocks on the NYSE are averaged via the NYSE index. With this an investor can tell in dollars and cents how much an average share changed in price on a given day. The Dow Jones bond averages

FIGURE 18-5 / For the period 1982–1987 the stock market, as measured by the Dow Jones Industrial Average, resembled bull more than bear.

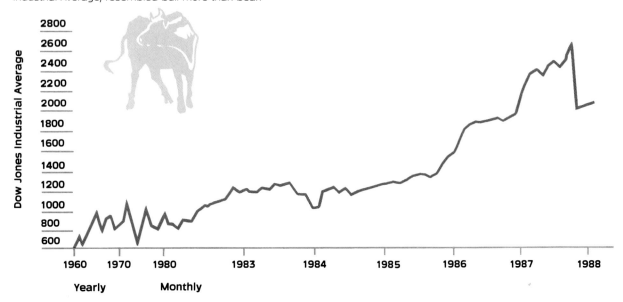

and several others provide information about the behavior of the bond market.

HOW TO BUILD A DOW JONES INDEX

The Dow Jones index of thirty industrials was established in 1928. Since then, many firms have come and gone. What happens when one of the firms that used to comprise the index goes out of business or simply needs to be replaced?

The evening before the change in components takes place, the DJIA is first calculated in the same way as it was on the preceding day. Then *The Wall Street Journal* makes a theoretical calculation. The Dow Jones index's stock prices are added up, but the stock to be deleted is excluded and the new one is included, as if the change had already happened. The total is then divided by the average from the preceding day. The result is a new divisor. This new divisor is then used to calculate the average until the next adjustment is needed. That way the Dow Jones average does not suddenly bump up or down when a stock is added or dropped.

The current roster of thirty industrials is as follows:

Allied—Signal	International Paper
Aluminum Company of America	McDonald's
American Express	Merck
American T&T	Minnesota M&M
Bethlehem Steel	Navistar
Boeing	Philip Morris
Chevron	Primerica
Coca-Cola	Procter & Gamble
DuPont	Sears Roebuck
Eastman Kodak	Texaco
Exxon	Union Carbide
General Electric	United Technologies
General Motors	USX Corp
Goodyear	Westinghouse Electric
IBM	Woolworth

Speculating and Investing

In the discussions that follow, we contrast speculating and investing. The differences are significant.

SPECULATING

speculative trading

Some people think that buying stocks and bonds is a way to get rich quickly. They often buy on the basis of hot tips. **Speculative trading** is the buying or selling of securities in the hope of profiting from near-term future changes in their selling prices. As the CompuServe ad suggests, people who "try to tame the market" need timely information.

Sometimes speculators do strike it rich, but the losers far outnum-

Do Not Attempt Without CompuServe.

Get all the facts as fast as the experts do before you try to tame the market.

Without accurate, up-to-the-minute data you can easily get taken for a ride on Wall Street. That's why it's important to get your hands on CompuServe. The fastest, most reliable source of comprehensive financial data available.

Now, just like Wall Street's most prestigious firms, you can check out a tip or find a hot, money-making lead in a matter of seconds. Investigate any area of interest. Or scan CompuServe's financial news highlights to find new areas to investigate. Including…

Continuously updated quotes on over 10,000 issues.

MicroQuote II—12 years of daily historical prices, along with dividends, splits, distributions and interest payments on more than 90,000 stocks, bonds, mutual funds, options, foreign exchange rates and hundreds of market indexes.

Graph trends quickly online. Review your portfolio performance, investigate returns in bull and bear markets. Screen for stocks to buy, or transfer prices and dividends to your microcomputer for detailed analysis.

Standard & Poor's descriptive information on over 3,000 companies.

Value Line Data Base II—extensive, fundamental data for analyzing the performances of over 1,800 major corporations.

Disclosure II—descriptive and financial information from the SEC filings and annual reports of over 8,500 companies.

Institutional Broker's Estimate System (I/B/E/S)—earnings projections from top research analysts on over 3,000 widely followed companies.

You can also research technical market trends, review economic projections and high-powered market analyses. Get expert advice on retirement, financial planning, managed accounts, taxes and insurance. Evaluate your own portfolio, even connect to a variety of at-home banking and brokerage services.

And all this comes with CompuServe's base of news, weather, telecommunications, special interest and entertainment services.

Compare CompuServe's rates to the cost of expensive floppy-based sources. Compare our up-to-the-minute delivery to time-consuming publication research. Compare the depth and breadth of our virtually infinite databases to any other source of investment information.

Then see your nearest computer dealer for a CompuServe Subscription Kit. Suggested retail price is only $39.95 and includes $25 of online time.

For more information or to order direct, call or write:

CompuServe

Information Services
P.O. Box 20212
5000 Arlington Centre Blvd.
Columbus, OH 43220
800-848-8199
In Ohio, call 614-457-0802

An H&R Block Company

In buying securities, there is no substitute for up-to-the-minute data.

ber the winners. Speculating is most popular during a bull market. A **bull market** is one in which stock prices as a whole are rising and there is a great deal of optimism among speculators. Speculating is less popular in a bear market. A **bear market** is one in which stock prices as a whole are falling and there is a great deal of pessimism among speculators.

MARGIN TRADING *Margin* is the percentage of the purchase price of stock that must be paid in cash. A speculator will use whatever margin or credit he or she can get when buying stock.

    Margin trading is buying more shares than a given amount of money would ordinarily buy because the shares are bought partly on credit. Stockbrokers put up the shares bought "on margin," as collateral for the loans used to finance their clients' margin purchases. As long as the price of a stock bought on margin rises, there is no problem. The collateral increases in value. But if the price falls, the broker will want more cash from the investor or will sell the shares.

    In the 1920s, many speculators were buying on 10 percent margin. In other words, they had to put up only $100 to buy $1,000 worth of stocks. When stock prices began falling, brokers and their bankers started selling, in large volume, the stocks they held as collateral. This helped to bring on the eventual collapse of the stock market. To protect against such a collapse, the Federal Reserve System now sets the margin requirement at a much higher level—today, it is 50 percent.

SHORT SELLING Speculators may also profit from selling stocks when prices are falling. Martha Todd, an established client of Broker B, believes that the selling price of IBM common stock will fall in the next few weeks. It is now selling at 117. Martha does not own any IBM stock but "borrows" some shares from her broker. (Remember that many investors do not take possession of the stock certificates they own but let their brokers hold them. Thus brokers can "lend" some of this stock to their other clients.)

    Martha tells her broker to sell 500 of these borrowed shares at 117. If the price subsequently falls, Martha buys the shares to "cover"—pay back—her earlier sale. She buys, say, at 107. She thus makes a $10 profit (less commission) on each of the 500 shares. But if the price went up instead of down, Martha would incur a loss. This practice is called short selling. **Short selling** is the sale of a security that the speculator does not own but has borrowed from his or her broker. At some time in the future the broker will tell the speculator to "cover" the short sale and repay it to the broker. Under SEC regulations, insiders are not allowed to sell their firm's stock short.

INVESTING

Unlike a speculator, an investor buys securities for the long haul. (By the way, before you consider either investment or speculation, you should have a cushion of cash reserves and adequate life and health insurance. You should be able to choose when you want to sell your shares and not be forced to sell them because you need cash.)

bull market

bear market

margin trading

short selling

Your investment goals should guide your buying and selling decisions. Goals vary among investors, but each investor should have definite goals. One important goal for some investors is to protect their invested dollars. You could do this by putting your money in a safe deposit box. But this earns nothing, and the buying power of those dollars declines because of inflation. You would be wiser to place your funds in an insured savings account at a bank or S&L or in a NOW account. You might also buy U.S. Savings Bonds. These are safe and can easily be converted to cash. You could also earn more with a certifi-

APPLICATION: BURGER KING
Burger King and Pillsbury

On Friday, February 26, 1988, Pillsbury Corporation's stock closed at $36.25, up over almost 10 percent ($3.12) on the New York Stock Exchange. Volume was very heavy at 1.39 million shares. What makes a stock like Pillsbury jump almost 10 percent in less than a day?

In this case, the cause was rumors that Pillsbury Corporation was going to sell its Burger King® restaurant chain. Three days later, the board of Pillsbury was due to convene in Naples, Florida, amid speculation that it would take major action that would affect Burger King Corporation, its Miami-based subsidiary.

The jump in stock prices helped to show how sensitive Pillsbury's own fortunes had become to the performance of its big Burger King Corporation subsidiary. A short time before, newspaper headlines were announcing, "Burger King Revenues Keeping Pillsbury Doughboy Fat," a reference to the fact

that the subsidiary's income was helping to boost Pillsbury's performance. In 1986, for example, pretax earnings of Pillsbury's restaurants group (primarily Burger King) totaled $220 million, or 53 percent of Pillsbury's total pretax earnings.

But by 1987 the picture changed. The headline in *Nation's Restaurant News* for March 9, 1987, read "Pillsbury's Restaurant Sales Depressed Corporate Profits." It was becoming apparent that the restaurant chain would have to be restructured to revive its lagging performance.

Late in 1987, Pillsbury announced its restructuring plan. It would sell or close fifteen Burger King® restaurants and upgrade 145 more. It would sell three small restaurant chains (including the Chinese-style take-out "Quick Wok"). It would also slim down its Godfather's Pizza unit.

But some stock market investors felt that Pillsbury

needed to trim more. That is why Pillsbury stock jumped by almost 10 percent when rumors began circulating that Pillsbury's board planned to sell off or cut costs at Burger King Corporation.

Questions
1. The closing price of Pillsbury's stock on February 26, 1988, was $36.25. Was that par value, market value, or book value? Explain.

2. Was the almost 10 percent increase in the price of Pillsbury's stock on February 26, 1988, the result of actions taken by investors or speculators? Explain.

3. Explain how asset redeployment (discussed in Chapter 17) was involved in the restructuring plan that Pillsbury announced in late 1987.

cate of deposit. A money market mutual fund, as we saw in Chapter 16, offers both good return and easy withdrawal. If you wish even higher returns, you must take a greater risk. For other investors (especially younger ones), growth is an important goal. They want to see their investment grow as fast as possible, subject to a reasonable amount of risk.

Of course, different investment strategies involve different degrees of risk. Investing in preferred stocks of established and profitable corporations is less risky than investing in common stocks of new ventures. In terms of return, however, the new venture might prove to be the better investment. In other words, risk and return tend to be directly related: as risk goes up, so does the potential for a good return.

There is no one answer to the question of how much risk an investor should take. When you invest, you must consider things like your financial situation, age, investment goals, patience, and self-discipline. To put it simply, if your goal is to get rich quickly, you will have to take a lot more risk than someone whose goal is to get rich more slowly and surely. Many savings and loan association and bank ads feature tables that illustrate this point. Suppose you start an account at age 23 and deposit $2,500 each year. If you receive 8 percent interest compounded annually, you will be a millionaire by age 63. You will have $1,106,475 in your account.

The typical investor wants a safe investment that will generate regular earnings and have a lot of potential for future growth. But it is hard to satisfy all three of these objectives.

Investing in securities involves keeping up with developments in the economy and in the industries and firms in which you invest. If you do not have the time or know-how to do this, you might invest in a mutual fund. Buying a share in a mutual fund makes you part-owner of all the securities owned by the fund. Owning one or more shares in a mutual fund lets you spread your risk over a broad range of securities. Mutual funds are professionally managed. Before they were created, only people with large sums to invest could afford to hire professional managers to oversee their portfolios (the stocks and bonds that they own).

OPTIONS AND FUTURES

As you can see, the securities market can be very exciting. Fortunes can be made (and lost) in hours. Sophisticated speculators and investors use certain special techniques to boost the odds in their favor.

put option

call option

OPTIONS   In the securities market an option gives you the right to buy (or sell) a security at a specific price and time. A **put option** entitles a trader to sell stock to the endorser who made the contract available. A **call option** gives a trader the right to buy a specific stock at a specific price and at a specific time in the future (usually 30, 60, 90, or 180 days). With a put option in hand you are guaranteed that you can sell the stock at a specific price. And with a call option you are guaranteed to be able to buy it at a specific price. (See Figure 18-6.)

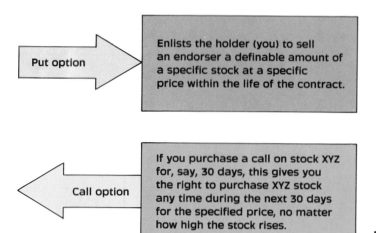

Put option → Enlists the holder (you) to sell an endorser a definable amount of a specific stock at a specific price within the life of the contract.

Call option ← If you purchase a call on stock XYZ for, say, 30 days, this gives you the right to purchase XYZ stock any time during the next 30 days for the specified price, no matter how high the stock rises.

FIGURE 18-6 / Puts and calls.

Why buy an option? For one thing, it can be a cheap way to speculate in the stock market. For example, suppose you think the price of XYZ, Inc. will rise from $40 per share to about $60 per share in the next 90 days. To buy 100 shares now would cost you $4,000. But you could buy a call option for this particular stock for, say, $300. This would give you an option to buy the stock during the next 90 days at today's price, $40. If the stock goes up, you will still be able buy it for $40 per share. You can buy it for $40 (thanks to your option) and sell it (if it has gone up) at, say, $48 per share. You would thus make $800, minus the $300 you spent to buy the option. This would make a net profit of $500 on your $300 investment.

Of course, if the stock did not rise in price, you would simply not exercise your option to purchase the stock at $40. You would lose the $300 you spent for the option. Options are traded on many exchanges, the largest being the Chicago Board Options Exchange.

futures contract

FUTURES CONTRACTS A **futures contract** is a contract for the delivery of an asset at a specific price and future time. The term "futures contracts" developed out of the world of commodities trading. At the Chicago Mercantile Exchange, businesspeople and others agree to buy or sell commodities like coffee beans, silver, and pork bellies (from which bacon is made). Most of the trading is for future deliveries, so the sales involve futures contracts.

Today, the term "futures contract" applies not just to commodities but to certain financial securities as well. Futures contracts are traded for U.S. Treasury bonds, for instance. Another very popular financial futures contract is for stock market indexes, particularly the Standard & Poor's Index of 500 selected stocks on the New York Stock Exchange.

Suppose that the Standard & Poor's 500 index one day was 250 and you believed that the market (and the index) was heading up. If you were to add up the per share values of all the 500 stocks in the index on that day, you would find that they were worth around $120,000. Now, instead of laying out $120,000, you could buy an S&P 500 Index Futures Contract, putting down only about $7,500—a tiny part of what those stocks are worth. If the index did rise, the value of your futures contract would also rise. This is a little like owning a package of 500 stocks worth $120,000 without actually having to lay out the money to buy the stocks themselves.

You might have noticed that futures contracts sound a little like stock options, and they are. As with options, futures contracts give you the right to buy or sell specific securities at a specific price during a specific time. But with an options contract, it is up to you whether you "exercise your option" and actually buy or sell the security. If you do not exercise, you just lose the money you paid for the option.

Futures contracts can be much riskier. If you buy a futures contract, you are obligated to buy or sell the asset, as the case may be. Suppose you took a futures contract to buy, say, 10,000 pork bellies in June at a price of $10 per belly. You thought pork bellies were going to go up to $15 each. So you thought you would be able to buy 10,000 bellies at $10 each and sell them in June for $15 each for a big profit. But disaster struck, and bellies dropped in price to $9 each. With a futures contract you are obligated to buy the bellies at $10 each, for a loss of $1 per belly if you sell them right away. Chances are that you will not actually take delivery of 10,000 pork bellies. (You will sell them to a food wholesaler long before they are to be delivered to you.) But you must pay the person with whom you made the contract the difference in price between the $10 per belly you owe and the price that day for bellies ($9 each). A futures contract (unlike an option) obligates you to either (1) buy or sell the asset or (2) pay for the loss. They can therefore be quite risky.

Summary

The public securities market is made up of the millions of people who invest in corporate securities and the middlemen who bring them together to buy and sell. These middlemen include brokers and investment bankers.

There are many different types of securities. Examples include the various types of stocks and bonds.

An investment bank does not accept deposits from the general public. It helps corporations to sell new issues of stocks and bonds. A brokerage house is a firm that buys and sells securities on behalf of its investor-clients. The secondary market includes the organized exchanges like the New York Stock Exchange as well as the over-the-counter markets. Today, the markets for stocks and bonds are truly global. Activity on the exchanges of one country tend to be reflected quickly on exchanges around the world.

Investing in securities can be exciting and rewarding. To help protect investors, the Securities Act of 1933 requires firms to publish a great deal of information about themselves and the risks that might be involved with owning their securities.

Stock and bond prices and volume of sales are reported for every business day in *The Wall Street Journal* and other newspapers. Figure 18-3 explains how to read a stock quotation and to identify such things as yearly highs and lows, dividends, and P-E ratios. Figure 18-4 explains how to read a bond quotation.

A speculator looks mainly for short-term profits from buying and selling securities—in some cases by selling something he or she does not own (short-selling). Speculating is very popular during bull markets and much less popular in bear markets. Margin trading—buying stock with credit supplied by the stockbroker—and trading in options are two techniques that speculators often use. An investor generally takes a longer view. Investors do not emphasize frequent short-term stock purchases and sales as speculators often do.

Review Questions

1. List and define three different concepts of "value" for common stock.

2. What is the purpose of (a) a stock split, (b) a stock dividend, and (c) a cash dividend?

3. What is a brokerage house?

4. What is the purpose of a stock exchange?

5. How do listed securities differ from unlisted securities?

6. What is a stockbroker?

7. Is speculation more likely during a bear market or a bull market? Explain.

8. Explain margin trading and short selling.

9. What balancing of objectives is required in a good investment plan?

Discussion Questions

1. Why might a bond's market value (selling price) be more than its face value (redemption price)?

2. How important are investment banking houses in helping business to raise the funds needed to meet capital budgeting expenditures?

3. Why are stock price averages, such as the Dow Jones Industrial Average and the Standard & Poor's Index, watched so closely by investors and reported daily by the news media?

4. Is the use of financial futures by business speculating or investing?

Key Terms

public securities market	par value	stock dividend
book value	stock split	bond
market value	cash dividend	investment bank

primary market transaction
brokerage house
secondary market
securities exchange
listed securities
round lot

odd lot
over-the-counter (OTC) market
prospectus
speculative trading
bull market
bear market

margin trading
short selling
put option
call option
futures contract

Cases

DOING THEIR JOB TOO WELL?

By February 1988, some stock market analysts were beginning to wonder whether the managers at Warner-Lambert might not have been doing their job too well. Although the drug manufacturer's stock was selling only in the mid-70s, experts were estimating that the stock was really worth more like $100 a share.

It seems that Warner-Lambert had very conservative accounting practices. It therefore understated the firm's book value at under $15 a share, although Warner-Lambert and its famous brand names were probably worth many times more than that. Warner-Lambert's big-name brands included Hall's Cough Drops, Trident, Chiclets, Listerine, and Dentyne. In addition to over-the-counter health care products, the firm also owned a lot of high-powered prescription drugs, including Lopid, a new cholesterol-reducing agent. It was estimated that these products could drive up Warner-Lambert sales by perhaps 20 percent per year.

Some experts suspected that Warner-Lambert's management had done its job too well in keeping debt to a minimum and understating its book value. As a result, the firm was a possible takeover target.

This would be less likely to happen if the firm had high debt or if its book value was already reported as high.

Questions

1. What, if anything, do you think is the relationship between a firm's book value and its common stock price?
2. Do you think that management did its job too well by keeping debt down and book value conservatively stated? Why or why not?
3. Check your newspaper today and find out what Warner-Lambert's financial data looks like. What is its stock price? What is its P-E ratio? How do you explain the change?

HOW EXPERT ARE THE EXPERTS?

Jane Winsoune wanted to become a stock market analyst but was bothered by one very big fact: fund managers—those experts who manage billions of dollars of other people's funds because the fund managers are supposedly expert at analyzing stocks and trends—usually underperform the broad Standard & Poor's stock market in-

dex. In other words, they do not do as well as someone who simply invested money in a broad range of stocks. For example, 70 percent of the active fund managers in one study came up with stock market selections that ended up performing more poorly than if they had simply invested all their money in the stock market averages and not done any analyzing at all. A recent article in The Economist points out that "only a handful of notable exceptions have consistently outperformed the average. Most money managers would have done better by choosing a portfolio (of stocks) out of a hat."

Why is this the case? Jane knew that studies showed that top stock market analysts are simply very bad at forecasting firms' future earnings. Yet it is, of course, projections of those earnings that most analysts use to determine their stock market picks. The depressing conclusion seems to be that someone could probably do just about as well picking stocks at random over the long run as she would analyzing the company's financial records and prospects.[3]

Questions

1. Do you believe that it does not pay to analyze a firm,

since predicting a firm's earnings is difficult (or impossible)? Why? What other factors might influence the value of a firm's stock?

2. Assuming that it is almost impossible to accurately forecast a firm's stock price and earnings, who should do better in the long run in the stock market—speculators or investors? Why?

3. Do you think you are better off using a full-service stockbroker who can provide investment advice or a discount broker who will just execute your buy and sell orders? Why?

4. Does the poor track record of stock managers suggest that Jane should find another occupation? Why?

NINETEEN

After reading this chapter, you will be able to:

- Distinguish between pure and speculative risk.

- Outline the steps necessary in risk management.

- Explain the four principal strategies for dealing with risk.

- Explain the major public insurance programs that affect business.

- List the questions that must be answered by insurers before they decide to accept a risk.

- Explain the two principal purposes for which a firm might purchase insurance.

- Outline the main classes of insurance that business firms purchase.

- Advise a risk manager about selecting an insurer and an insurance agent.

Risk Management Strategies

WHAT'S AHEAD

Business risk is unavoidable. To manage it requires a special kind of skill, as we will see in this chapter. We begin by cataloging the types of risk that might be faced by a business firm, distinguishing between pure risk and speculative risk. This leads to discussion of a recommended procedure for managers to follow in managing risk. The procedure requires (1) identifying the risks likely to be faced, (2) estimating the relative importance and frequency of these risks, and (3) deciding on the best way to deal with each.

Next, we outline and evaluate four different strategies that are available for dealing with risk: assuming risk, minimizing it, avoiding it, and shifting it.

We then describe the private insurance industry and the public sources of insurance, such as Social Security and workers' compensation, that affect business planning. This is followed by a look at the standards by which insurers determine what they will and will not insure.

We continue with a description of the major classes of insurance that firms are likely to buy. These are divided into types of insurance to protect the firm's resources (property damage, liability, loss of earning power, criminal loss, and others) and those that provide the employees with important fringe benefits (such as health and life insurance). The chapter closes with a description of some of the newer forms of life insurance and some guidelines for selecting insurance companies and agents.

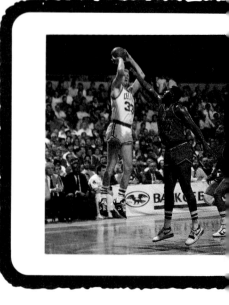

Ted Dipple, the founder and president of American Sports Underwriters, Inc. (ASU), has insured Pete Rose, Meadowlark Lemon, Hank Aaron, Reggie Jackson, John Havlicek, and many of the Boston Celtics.

ASU now has much of the U.S. sports insurance market in its home court. "Ask any sports fan on the street who the dozen best athletes in the country are. Chances are we insure them," says Mr. Dipple. ASU underwrites for pros who need coverage and also provides catastrophic sports injury insurance for NCAA colleges. The latter type of insurance provides lifetime medical, rehabilitation, and income benefits to students in athletic programs, their coaches, and cheerleaders who are injured while practicing, playing, or traveling for the sport.

For professional players, ASU writes permanent disability policies that pay when a career ends unexpectedly. One of the most famous cases involved former Washington Redskins quarterback Joe Theisman, whose leg was broken in a game in 1985, ending his career. He had a $1.4 million policy from ASU's competitor, Lloyd's of London.

One day in Atlanta, the riskiness of Mr. Dipple's business was really brought home to him. He had signed a major player to a comprehensive policy in the morning and was driving to the airport in the afternoon. Over the radio he heard a news report that his newest client had been in a car accident. If this kind of thing occurred frequently, he would be out of the risk-bearing business. To avoid such losses, Mr. Dipple investigates ever player who seeks insurance. He checks the athletes' record of injuries, looking at their frequency and severity by sport, by position, and by age of the athlete. He studies how much time an athlete will play on artificial turf and in night games. He also considers the player's character, alcohol or drug use (if any), and other risk-related factors. This helps ASU set premiums so that they can cover losses and make a profit. It also helps the firm to screen out prospective policyholders for whom the risks are too great or not measurable.

ASU took a serious step when it stopped selling insurance to players in professional football. This withdrawal from a major pro sport occurred because of the growing number of serious injuries in the sport that were traceable in part to the use of artificial turf and steroids. The risks had grown too great.[1]

Just as sports performers and the people who insure them need to find a way to manage risk, so does the business manager or owner. To protect a business firm's resources, a manager may try to reduce risk or to avoid it, or he or she may purchase insurance.

Kinds of Risk

As we saw in Chapter 1, risk is the chance of loss. It is part of the complex process of business management and cannot be avoided entirely. All the firm's resources are subject to risk. Protecting them is a major task of the risk manager. In many firms an employee has the title "risk manager." Sometimes the risk management function is performed by the owner, general manager, or financial officer. Sometimes the job is shared by several employees. In any case, someone in the firm must manage risk. Table 19-1 lists many areas in which businesses risk losses.

Everything involves risks, though the degree of risk can vary greatly. In lending money, for example, we risk the possibility that the money will not be paid back. In buying things we risk the possibility of defective merchandise. In running a factory we risk liability for accidents to employees or visitors. In owning buildings and cars we run risks of fire, vandalism, and theft. Businesses risk the chance that secret processes or designs will be stolen, and they risk the death of corporate officers. All of these threaten the firm's resources and must be dealt with if the firm is to survive and prosper.

pure risk

speculative risk

There are two general types of risk: pure risks and speculative risks. A **pure risk** is one that offers a chance of loss only. There is no chance of gain. Examples of pure risk are risk of fire and risk of death. A **speculative risk** is a "gamble," in which there is a possible gain as well as a possible loss. Buying securities, as we saw in Chapter 18, is an example of taking a speculative risk. When an investor buys a stock or a bond, the price could increase or decrease. Even the very decision whether or not to go into business involves speculative risk. The firm can succeed or it can fail.

The distinction between pure and speculative risks is important. As we have seen at several points in this book, firms do face speculative risks. Such chances of gain or loss are the "meat and potatoes" of doing business in a competitive economy. The manager's own skills, the quality of the firm's resources, and many other factors are the best "insurance" available. In this chapter, however, the focus is on pure risk management—dealing with situations that could cause losses to

---

TABLE 19-1 / Business risk checklist

Recognizing natural disasters and other areas of potential loss is critical if a business is to develop a thoughtful risk management plan. Below are some of the ways in which a business may be exposed to loss.

Boiler and machinery accidents	Maritime workers' injuries
Burglary	Motor vehicle accidents
Business interruption	Political factors
Cargo loss	Pollution liability
Contractual obligations	Product liability
Directors' and officers' liability	Product recall
Earthquake	Professional liability
Employee dishonesty	Robbery
Fire	Vacant/unoccupied building(s)
Flood	Vandalism
Glass breakage	Workers' accidents and injuries

the firm without chance for gain. Whether and how a manager elects to use insurance in such cases is also a test of his or her skill.

risk management

Risk Management

Risk management is the process of identifying the risks to which a firm is likely to be exposed, estimating the frequency and size of losses from such risks, and determining the best way to deal with each of them. Figure 19-1 shows the three steps in risk management.

IDENTIFYING RISKS

To identify the pure risks that a firm is likely to encounter, the risk manager must take a careful look at all of the firm's operations. Starting perhaps with Table 19-1, the risk manager must communicate with each operational manager to see which risks exist.

ESTIMATING THE SIZE AND FREQUENCY OF POTENTIAL LOSSES

The second step in dealing with risks is to estimate their significance. This includes anticipating the size of the possible losses and how often they are likely to happen. This helps to set a priority for dealing with risk. The most serious risks must be dealt with first.

For larger and older firms, making such estimates is simplified by looking at records of past experience with losses. The plant records will indicate, for example, how many work-related accidents happened on the premises each year for the last ten years. The same procedure can provide estimates of theft, fire, or other losses.

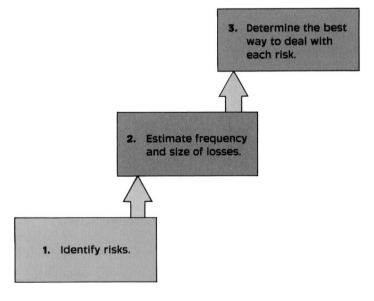

FIGURE 19-1 / Steps in risk management.

3. Determine the best way to deal with each risk.

2. Estimate frequency and size of losses.

1. Identify risks.

Small or new firms must depend on historical records of similar firms, to the extent that such information is available in public records or through trade associations. These firms' loss prediction might therefore be somewhat unreliable.

Certain kinds of losses are especially hard to estimate because of recent and rapid growth in their incidence. These include product and professional liability losses. The variety of types of liability as well as the wide range of size of court-awarded judgments make it especially hard to predict losses.

DETERMINING THE BEST WAY TO DEAL WITH EACH RISK

A firm has four strategies that it may use to deal with risk. They can sometimes be used in combination. The strategies are:

- Assume the risk
- Minimize the risk
- Avoid the risk
- Shift the risk

self-insurance

ASSUMING THE RISK   To assume the risk means to practice some form of self-insurance. **Self-insurance** means preparing ahead of time to deal with a possible loss by setting aside funds to cover the loss or—in the case of a very large firm—treating loss as an inevitable expense of doing business. If, for example, a large chain of shoe stores regularly sets aside a certain amount to cover the possibility of fire in one of its outlets, it is practicing self-insurance. The idea is that in a very large operation, some fire damage is bound to happen. Instead of paying premiums to insurance firms, the self-insurer "pays itself" in advance, anticipating later loss. Some firms, professionals, and local governments have formed "risk retention groups" to pool similar risks.

MINIMIZING THE RISK   Risk minimization is a very common strategy. It often accompanies risk assumption or risk shifting. It consists of finding ways of doing things that reduce the risk of loss without abandoning the firm's normal activities. For example, a firm can install sprinklers, inspect heating systems, and discourage smoking in warehouses or retail stores.

Mechanized cash control systems, for example, help protect against theft, as do basic cash audit procedures. Most firms set up standard procedures for writing checks and making cash purchases. Banks protect themselves from major credit card counterfeiting losses by adding to the card a laser image, which is hard to duplicate.

Security procedures also help firms minimize losses from theft of new ideas and processes. Personnel working in sensitive areas are carefully screened, and the movement of critical documents is monitored. Computer systems often employ special coding of sensitive records, especially in communicating within or between computer systems.

Careful patent protection is still another way to protect a firm from losses. A patent protects product and process ideas by legally discouraging their imitation by rivals. Copyrights do the same for literary and artistic works.

APPLICATION: BURGER KING
Making the Restaurants Safe

The director of safety and risk management at Burger King Corporation, Don Herbstman, is both a numbers-oriented executive and a voice of conscience. He gauges his department's success by the money it saves the corporation and—of greater import—by the resolution of issues that affect employees' and customers' safety. Some recent examples include:

• Nonslip crew shoes that have reduced the number of falls by more than half.

• Fire sprinklers that do the impossible: use water to cool and smother a grease fire.

More important, the director's zeal for challenging tradition and the resulting benefits have converted people throughout the system to the wisdom of safety.

"We exist to protect crew members and customers. If we do our job right, risk is reduced, people don't get hurt, and property doesn't get damaged.

"We're using new mats in the freezer, the cooler, at the self-service drink station, and in the customer entry area. They're time-consuming to clean, but they provide substantial savings by reducing slips and falls.

Without mats, a fall that results in a serious injury, like a broken hip, can cost upwards of $50,000. You would have to sell a lot of Whopper® sandwiches to make up for that. And who can afford the image of being a place where people get hurt?

"I will do whatever I can to reduce the frequency of accidents and the cost of loss. Anything to that end is fair game. That approach gives me tremendous latitude for creativity. The only limitations are those you place on yourself.

"The last few years, management has become more concerned with and supportive of our loss-control efforts. The cost factors are so compelling—for insurance, loss due to property damage and personal injury, litigation and disruption of business. Loss is really waste; it's negative profits and must be controlled.

"Burger King's ultimate cost of losses for fiscal '87 was projected at about $21 million. That's almost 10 percent of our planned profits. It has become a mandatory goal to reduce those losses. We'll beat the projection for '87 by more than $3 million.

"We're part of Pillsbury's effort to rethink the company's approach to settling claims. We want to avoid litigation because it can multiply your cost by a factor of ten. Under the program we developed, if someone falls, you give them your attention, make sure they're comfortable, and then promptly call to see how they're doing.

"In a pilot claims-management program in the Florida region, we've had 27 claims during the past four months, and only one has gone to litigation. If you're treated fairly, chances are you won't sue. Casualty costs for our restaurants are $8 million to $9 million a year, but I think we can ultimately reduce them by 30 percent.

"I think we're ahead of everybody in the business. But I don't have to compare this department to somebody else's to feel good. After all, safety is an area of performance, not competition.

"But I can see how far we've come in the last three or four years. I have a terrific staff. And the more success we have, the more confidence and the more credibility we have. We haven't peaked yet. I know there's always so much more that can be done."

Questions

1. Develop a business risk checklist, similar to the one in Table 19-1, for Burger King Corporation. Be as specific as possible.

2. How do Mr. Herbstman's efforts fit into Burger King Corporation's risk strategies?

3. Of the types of insurance discussed in Table 19-4, which are the most important to a Burger King franchisee?

Most major credit cards now carry laser images, which are difficult to duplicate and so minimize the risk of counterfeiting.

There is always a danger that changes in market conditions will hurt a firm. For example, a retailer who is afraid that certain goods will be hard to sell can minimize losses by buying on consignment instead of outright (see Chapter 14). A retailer or manufacturer might also protect itself against sudden cost rises by stocking large quantities of supplies, raw materials, or finished goods when prices are low.

AVOIDING THE RISK   A third strategy is risk avoidance. This is very long-range strategy. It dictates whether or not the firm will participate in major ventures, such as opening a sales office in a new region or investing $10 million in research and development. This strategy obviously works only for operations or ventures that are still only being considered. If an activity is already taking place, the nearest thing to risk avoidance is risk minimization on a grand scale. Exxon cut its losses by getting rid of its office automation business. Some doctors have even quit medicine to avoid the mounting risk of malpractice suits and/or the accompanying rise in malpractice insurance premium rates.

SHIFTING THE RISK   Still another strategy for dealing with nearly all pure risks is to shift them. Many retailers and wholesalers, for example, shift

insurance policy

some of the risks of carrying inventories by stocking only the bare essentials, allowing the firm's supplier to assume such risks as obsolescence, pilferage, and fire.

A more important way of shifting risk is through insurance. Insurance companies assume all kinds of risks for firms (or individuals) for a price. In other words, a firm exchanges the risk of uncertain losses for the known cost of insurance (the premium). It does this by paying a premium for a policy that pays the firm if it sustains certain types of losses. An **insurance policy** is a contract between the insurer and the insured person or firm that specifies (1) the types of risks that are covered, (2) the amount of coverage, (3) the name of the person or corporation covered, and (4) the premium to be paid. (See Figure 19-2.) The Travelers ad describes some of the kinds of policies available through insurance companies.

COMBINATIONS OF RISK STRATEGIES

In most businesses, risk strategies are used in various combinations. Insurance firms will lower premiums for customers that take certain risk-reducing precautions. Buildings that are equipped with good

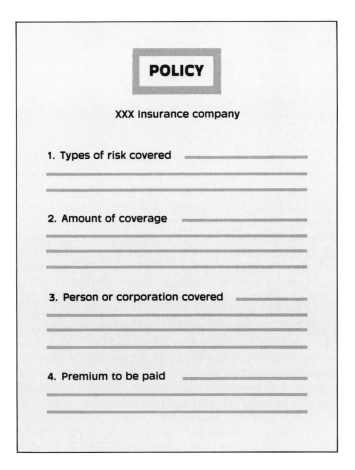

FIGURE 19-2 / What an insurance policy specifies.

Insurance companies provide many ways to shift risk.

sprinkler and alarm systems cost less to insure. Banks that install fire-proof files and restaurants that prohibit smoking might also get premium reductions as a result. When firms practice self-insurance, they usually become very conscious of reducing risk. They are likely to train employees how to react in the case of fire or other perils, for example. They are also likely to give new products extra-careful testing for safety to reduce the likelihood of product liability claims.

Businesses that operate nationwide often use different strategies for dealing with the same kind of risk in different parts of the country. If crime is less prevalent in one of the firm's rural offices, the firm might choose to self-insure at that site and buy crime insurance (shift the risk) for its urban locations.

Insurance

Insurance is available from private as well as public sources. Each source is important to business in special ways.

PRIVATE INSURANCE COMPANIES

stock insurance companies

mutual insurance companies

Private insurance firms are primarily of two forms. **Stock insurance companies** are ordinary, profit-seeking corporations, the stockholders of which are not necessarily their customers (policyholders). They make their profits from selling policies and from investing premium income. **Mutual insurance companies** are corporations owned by the policyholders, to whom any profits are returned as dividends or lowered insurance premiums. Both forms of insurance companies assume the risks of business firms.

Huge private insurance companies like Prudential of America,

TABLE 19-2 / **The ten largest U.S. life insurance companies (ranked by assets), 1987**

Rank	Company	Assets ($ millions)	Premium and Annuity Income ($ millions)
1	Prudential of America	108,815.2	14,049.4
2	Metropolitan Life	88,140.1	13,963.8
3	Equitable Life Assurance	49,288.2	5,501.8
4	Aetna Life	45,684.6	7,964.1
5	Teachers Insurance & Annuity	33,210.4	3,059.7
6	New York Life	31,843.7	5,596.0
7	Travelers	28,595.5	3,826.6
8	John Hancock Mutual Life	27,354.9	4,403.1
9	Connecticut General Life	26,785.5	2,761.0
10	Northwestern Mutual Life	22,602.9	3,626.3

Source: Adapted from "The 50 Largest Life Insurance Companies," Fortune, June 6, 1988, p. D25. © 1988 Time Inc. All rights reserved.

TABLE 19-3 / **The ten largest U.S. diversified insurance companies (ranked by assets), 1987**

Rank	Company	Assets ($ millions)	Revenues ($ millions)
1	Aetna Life & Casualty	72,754.3	22,114.1
2	CIGNA	53,495.2	16,909.3
3	Travelers Corp.	50,164.7	17,459.1
4	American International Group	27,907.7	11,278.3
5	Transamerica	23,318.6	7,174.6
6	Lincoln National	18,003.9	6,960.1
7	Paine Webber Group	12,956.2	2,437.0
8	Continental	12,151.4	6,731.2
9	Kemper	10,741.5	3,668.6
10	USF&G	10,141.2	4,826.1

Source: Adapted from "The 50 Largest Diversified Financial Companies," *Fortune*, June 6, 1988, p. D19. © 1988 Time Inc. All rights reserved. Only firms primarily engaged in sale of insurance other than life insurance are included.

Aetna Life and Casualty, and Metropolitan Life meet the insurance needs of millions of individuals and business firms. Table 19-2 lists the top ten life insurance firms. Table 19-3 lists the top ten diversified insurance companies. These tables show how these firms rank in terms of size of assets and revenue. Prudential and Metropolitan are by far the largest life insurers. Aetna, CIGNA, and Travelers are dominant among diversified insurance firms. There are many hundreds of smaller insurance firms, too, which provide services to domestic business and firms operating in other parts of the world.

The private insurance industry is worldwide in scope. Most of the world's insurance centers are in the United States, Canada, Western Europe, Japan, and Hong Kong. The United States is the largest user of insurance, buying slightly less than half of the world's insurance. Japan, West Germany, and Great Britain follow in that order.

As you can tell from the AEGEN International, Inc. ad (on p. 562), some firms specialize in insuring multinationals. Firms like AEGEN have offices worldwide and can deliver insurance services to businesses wherever their international activities take them.

PUBLIC SOURCES OF INSURANCE

State and federal governments are also in the insurance business. State governments offer workers' compensation insurance and unemployment compensation programs. The bulk of the cost of both programs is paid by employers. These can be a major cost of doing business. Unem-

Special types of insurance are available to firms that have multinational operations.

ployment compensation costs during periods of recession and unemployment can be especially high.

The federal government operates the Social Security program, otherwise known as Old-Age, Survivors, Disability, and Health Insurance (OASDHI), which covers 90 percent of the U.S. work force. Since the Great Depression of the 1930s, OASDHI has been an important part of our economic life, a major means of protecting older, disabled, and poor citizens from economic hardship. The cost is shared by workers and their employers. Self-employed people pay a higher percentage than do people employed by others.

Medicare is a federal program of medical insurance for people 65 years of age or over. It is partly funded by the OASDHI contributions of workers and partly by payments made by users of Medicare. Many private firms write Medicare supplementary insurance to cover some of the costs of medical care for seniors that are not paid by Medicare. Many costs of such care outside of hospitals, such as nursing homes, are not covered by Medicare. Congress regularly considers changes in this government program.

As we saw in Chapter 16, the federal government sponsors, through the FDIC and FSLIC, programs to insure savings in various forms of financial institutions. Through the Federal Housing Administration (FHA) and the Veterans Administration (VA) the federal government aids in the financing of real estate. The FHA insures housing lenders like banks against default on loans. The VA guarantees such lenders under a special low-down-payment loan program for veterans who qualify.

Public programs also support special risks such as those of crop loss and flood. The Federal Crop Insurance Corporation provides insurance against serious crop losses to farmers. The National Flood Insurance Association provides compensation to homeowners and businesses for the effects of disastrous flooding.

In addition, there is the Federal Pension Benefit Guaranty program established in 1974 by the Employee Retirement Income Security Act (ERISA). ERISA strengthens and stabilizes the nation's private pension programs. For firms that have such programs, ERISA's Federal Pension Plan Termination Insurance Corporation guarantees payment of pension benefits in the event of bankruptcy.

The Logic and Language of Insurance

The insurance company is a professional risk taker, but it takes only certain types of risk. Insurance is available to business firms only to cope with *pure* risks. We will examine the question of which pure risks may be assumed by insurers and which may not.

HOW INSURANCE FIRMS EVALUATE RISKS

An **insurable risk** is one that an insurance firm has judged acceptable for coverage. When an insurance firm is making this judgment, it asks the following questions about the risks and the circumstances surrounding them. If the answers are favorable, the risk is insurable.

- Is the loss truly accidental?
- Does it conform to the law of large numbers?
- Is it personal rather than catastrophic?
- Are the losses suffered often small?
- Are the losses measurable in dollars?
- Are there special circumstances that multiply the risk?

ACCIDENTAL VERSUS INTENTIONAL LOSS   Should the loss be under the control of the insured, rather than accidental, the insurer would not want to insure against such a loss. Whenever there is evidence that the insured firm or individual caused the loss (often by arson or intentional damage), the insurance firm refuses to pay a claim or delays payment until there is a thorough investigation.

THE LAW OF LARGE NUMBERS   Insurance firms study the losses suffered by firms or individuals over time, and their rate-making specialists make predictions of future losses. Such predictions depend on the law of large numbers. The **law of large numbers** is a mathematical concept that lets insurers estimate losses during a given future period, using evidence from the past. In other words, if the insurance firm has a large number of policyholders, it can predict from knowledge of past losses how many losses are likely to be suffered in the future. In the case of life insurance the incidence of past deaths is monitored. (See Figure 19-3.)

law of large numbers

Past experience and the law of large numbers give insurance firms a fair idea of how much they will have to pay out in claims. They set their premiums at levels that allow them to cover expected claims and operating costs, plus a reasonable profit for stock companies.

actuaries

Actuaries are the loss-predicting experts of insurance companies. They might know from historical records that in a year, on the average, 100 of the 5,000 buildings that they insure will actually suffer a fire

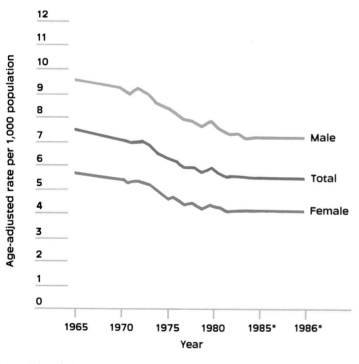

FIGURE 19-3 / Age-adjusted death rate in the United States (rate per 1,000 population). (*Source: Life Insurance Fact Book*, 1987.)

* Provisional data

loss. They also know that recent evidence shows that the average loss per fire is $40,000. Excluding an adjustment for inflation, the average premium must be $800 per year plus something extra to cover operating costs and profit ($800 × 5,000 = $40,000 × 100). If total operating costs (plus profit in the case of stock companies) are $1,000,000 and the inflationary effect on payments of claims is expected to be 5 percent, then the average premium will be $1,040 per building for the year ($5,200,000/5,000 = $1,040). Inflation has added $40, and operating costs and profit have added $200 to the basic amount of $800.

PERSONAL VERSUS CATASTROPHIC LOSSES   An insurer tries to avoid writing insurance for a group if the risk would damage all members in the group at the same time. For example, a fire insurance firm would not concentrate all its coverage in one section of a city. A catastrophic fire there could affect too many policyholders and ruin the insurance firm. Private insurers avoid writing flood policies for low-lying coastal regions for the same reason.

THE SIZE OF TYPICAL CLAIMS   Insurers do not want to get involved with "nickel and dime" claims. They can avoid small claims by setting
deductible
deductibles, specified by the insurance policy. The **deductible** is the portion of any loss that the insured firm or individual agrees to pay. The insurance company pays the rest, up to the limits of the policy. Small claims that are expensive to handle, such as those for minor thefts or auto scrapes, are eliminated.

MEASURABILITY OF LOSS IN DOLLARS   Insurance firms avoid insuring against losses to which it is difficult to assign a dollar value. Sometimes the

Insurers must be able to assign dollar values to losses in order to make fair settlements on claims such as automobile damages.

The 1987 collapse of the Institute for Immunological Disorders in Houston, the first exclusively AIDS-oriented hospital in the country, symbolized a major struggle in the medical insurance industry. The IID was reported losing $600,000–800,000 per year and had fewer than twenty patients in its beds despite the presence of more than 1,200 AIDS patients in the Houston area. The hospital was clearly underfunded.

After comparing the costs (estimated at $30,000–40,000 per year per patient) of providing medical care for AIDS sufferers and the availability of funds from medical insurance and other sources, the Houston hospital announced that it was closing. Its patients were transferred to general-purpose private and public hospitals and treatment centers.

The health insurance industry faces some similar hard choices with AIDS as the number of cases—and the cost of handling each case—rises. The disease, which is fatal, promises to bring huge claims that could bankrupt some insurance companies if the number of diagnosed cases reaches 270,000, as predicted for 1991 by the Centers for Disease Control. Other predictions are much higher. The Rand Corporation estimates that the cost of treatment in 1991 will reach $37 billion.

The insurance industry knows that homosexuals and intravenous drug users as a group have a higher probability of contracting the disease than others. It also has the medical technology to identify people who have been exposed to the virus and thus are most likely to develop AIDS. This means that the industry has the ability to refuse to issue insurance policies to many people who might later file huge AIDS-related claims.

The use of such risk classification, whether based on lifestyle or predictive tests for the presence of AIDS-related antibodies in the blood, has raised charges of discrimination and invasion of privacy. In some states, such screening has been prohibited by law. The managers of insurance firms are finding themselves caught between the conflicting demands of two groups. On one side are clients who are not in high-risk categories as well as shareholders, who expect insurance premiums to truly reflect predictable risks and to allow for a fair profit. On the other side are the high-risk groups, often supported by regulators, who defend these groups' rights to privacy and nondiscrimination.

One side argues that everybody is entitled to quality health care, but everybody is not entitled as a matter of right to health insurance from a private provider. This, they argue, is a matter of voluntary, private contract. People who buy insurance want to pool risks with others who have the same potential risks.

The other side says that the industry simply cannot ignore the societal costs of refusing insurance to people with a high risk of developing AIDS. As an article in the New York Times notes, "Either way, the public will end up picking up their health care tab, if not through higher insurance premiums, then through welfare programs and, ultimately, higher taxes."

Clearly, the combination of the AIDS epidemic and medical testing breakthroughs has turned the theoretical underpinnings of insurance inside out, probably irrevocably. Political and social considerations as well as traditional underwriting techniques begin to enter insurance rate-making decisions.

Does AIDS require changes in the risk-estimating processes of the insurance industry? What do you think?

Sources: David Tuller, "Trying to Avoid an Insurance Debacle," The New York Times, Feb. 22, 1987, Sec. 3, pp. 1, 8; Gordon Bock, "A Burden Too Heavy to Bear," Time, Aug. 31, 1987, p. 39; Dean Mayer, "Money Woes Afflict AIDS Hospitals," HealthWeek, July 27, 1987, pp. 6, 57.

value of an object to the insured is a matter of taste, nostalgia, or other personal attachment that does not mean much to others (except immediate family or friends). In such cases there is no objective way of arriving at a fair payment in the event of claim of loss. To avoid such problems, as in the case of life insurance, the policy is written for a specific dollar amount.

ADVERSE CIRCUMSTANCES Insurance firms may deny insurance or raise premiums in cases in which special loss potential exists. This is done to protect against the law of adverse selection. The **law of adverse selection** states that persons or firms facing high risks (dangerous operations or occupations or past records of ill health) are more likely to seek insurance than others are. As the What Do You Think? box indicates, this is a special problem in the case of insuring persons with a high risk of suffering from AIDS.

law of adverse selection

IMPLICATIONS FOR THE RISK MANAGER

The six criteria that influence insurance firms to accept or reject an opportunity to insure a firm can also guide the risk manager of, for example, a tool shop in evaluating the use of insurance. If small losses such as theft of hand tools occur frequently, it might be wise to absorb these losses and find ways to reduce theft rather than bother with getting theft insurance coverage. If losses are difficult to measure in dollars, the risk manager might make a similar decision.

For the firm with large, widespread operations involving huge numbers of buildings, the law of large numbers might lead the risk manager to practice self-insurance. This is particularly likely when the manager has good records of past property damage losses among these buildings. The logic of insurance works for the risk manager just as it does for the professional insurer.

OTHER INSURANCE CONCEPTS

insurable interest

An **insurable interest** in something is an interest such that the interest-holder can show that it would suffer a loss from the peril insured against. If the Ford Motor Company leases a building, it can buy insurance protection against losses from a fire in the building, even though Ford does not own the building. Ford has an insurable interest in the building because it could suffer a great financial loss from such a fire. Any corporation has a similar insurable interest in the life of its president, so it can insure the president's life.

principle of indemnity

The **principle of indemnity** means that an insured party cannot collect more than the actual cash value of the loss. If a firm has a $100,000 policy and suffers a $70,000 loss, it cannot collect more than the loss amount.

coinsurance

Another important concept is that of coinsurance. **Coinsurance** is the sharing of risk between the insured and the insurer. If a policy has a deductible feature, the insured assumes the risk up to the deductible amount. Beyond the deductible the insured may continue to share (coinsure) the loss with the insurance firm—perhaps 10 percent or 20 percent of the loss. Most fire, health, and accident policies employ the principle of coinsurance.

Types of Insurance for Business

Business firms buy insurance protection for two main reasons: to shift the risks they encounter in their operations and to provide benefits for their employees. Several different types of insurance are purchased for each of these reasons. To protect itself against risks, a firm usually buys several types of property damage insurance, liability insurance, insurance against loss of earning power, insurance against criminal loss, and special types of insurance protection relating to credit losses, nonperformance, and real property title flaws. The second role of insurance purchased by businesses, as we saw in Chapter 8, relates to the provision of employee fringe benefits. These insurance benefits usually include group health, disability, workers' compensation, unemployment, and life insurance. A summary of the major types of insurance bought by business firms from private insurers is given in Table 19-4.

PROPERTY DAMAGE INSURANCE

Because most firms own a wide range of assets that need protection, we will begin with property damage insurance. Virtually all firms carry fire and extended coverage insurance and automobile collision insurance.

Business firms, like individual homeowners, insure their buildings and contents against fire. Suppose a food broker's warehouse originally cost $200,000 and the current cost of rebuilding it is $400,000. The firm has a $500,000 fire insurance policy and suffers a total loss by fire. In this case it can collect $400,000. Under the principle of indemnity the insured food broker cannot collect more than the actual cash value of the loss.

Total destruction by fire is rare. Most business property is insured for less than its total replacement cost. As we have noted, the principle of coinsurance is widely used in property insurance. Insurance companies include a coinsurance clause in fire and extended coverage policies to induce firms to carry adequate coverage—usually 80 percent of the replacement value of the property. Suppose the food broker has a $200,000 fire insurance policy with an 80 percent coinsurance clause. The $200,000 is only 50 percent of the cost to rebuild the warehouse. If the broker suffers a $30,000 loss from fire, the insurer will pay only $18,750 of the loss. The insured gets paid a fraction of the loss equal to the amount of the policy divided by $320,000 (80 percent of the $400,000 replacement cost). In this case the fraction is 200,000/320,000 or 5/8. Five-eighths of $30,000 is $18,750. If the food broker had bought a $320,000 fire insurance policy, covering 80 percent of the cost to rebuild, the insurer would have paid the full $30,000 loss, or any amount of loss up to the face value of the policy ($320,000).

Fire insurance protects against losses caused by fire or lightning.

TABLE 19-4 / **Types of insurance purchased by business firms**

Type of Insurance	Purposes
Fire	Protects against fire damage, usually includes coinsurance provision. Building and contents usually covered, often accompanied by similar coverage against windstorms, earthquakes, and theft.
Auto	Firms purchase several coverages for company-owned vehicles, including property and bodily injury liability, collision (covering damage to own vehicle), and medical payments coverage relating to occupants of owned vehicle. Comprehensive coverage protects vehicles against fire, theft, windstorm, vandals, etc.
Criminal loss	Protects against loss from burglary, robbery, and other forms of theft. Protection against embezzlement is known as fidelity bonding.
Marine	Ocean marine protects ships, cargoes against collision and other perils at sea. Inland marine protects against inland transportation losses.
Health and accident	Variety of coverages to protect employees against losses stemming from accidents and poor health. Usually the firm shares the cost with employees and deducts employee shares from paychecks. Sometimes includes sick pay in the event of loss of salary during illness.
Liability	Public liability protects against legal claims by nonemployees for damages stemming from firm's products or operations on or off firm premises. Workers' compensation insurance protects against workers' claims. In most states this is mandatory. It includes work-related accident or illness.
Political	Protects against losses stemming from seizure of a plant by a foreign government, freezing of assets in a foreign bank, and other perils a business faces when operating in a foreign country.
Credit	Protects against losses stemming from nonpayment of accounts.
Title	Protects against losses due to defects in title to real property.
Surety	Protects against losses from nonperformance of contractual obligation.
Business interruption	Protects firms against loss of business during time that premises are closed during repairs after a catastrophe.
Life	Can serve to protect the firm in the case of death of a key person. Also serves as a common fringe benefit for employees. The employer buys a group policy. Trends in individually purchased life policies are toward universal life and variable life, which provide special savings and tax-deferral features as well as insurance.

Most firms buy extended coverage against perils such as windstorm, riot, and water damage. The contents are usually insured as well as the building. The principle of indemnity and the traditional coinsurance provision also apply to extended coverage.

Autos and trucks owned by business firms are often insured against damage from collision as well as from vandalism and other damages (comprehensive coverage). Automotive insurance policies also include (1) liability for damage to others, (2) liability for bodily injury, (3) medical payments for the insured, and (4) uninsured motorists coverage, which pays for bodily injury the insured would have been legally entitled to if the other party to the accident had been insured.

In some states there are "no-fault" insurance plans. Such plans require that claims be paid by the policyholder's insurance firm without regard to fault. These laws also limit the victim's right to sue, thereby reducing the legal costs related to insurance.

When a firm ships goods by public transportation, it usually protects these goods with some form of marine insurance. This type of insurance also protects the shipowner or other transportation firm. It includes *ocean* ("blue water") *marine* insurance, which covers perils connected with international shipments by sea, and *inland marine* insurance, which covers domestic shipments, whether by barge, coastal vessel, trucks, rail, or even air.

LIABILITY INSURANCE

Business firms rely heavily on various forms of insurance protection against legal liability arising from its operations or its products. You will recall from Chapter 15 that a liability is something that a firm owes. If a firm is judged liable for losses or injuries sustained by customers or visitors, some form of liability insurance policy might pay off or reduce the resulting debt.

comprehensive general liability insurance

Comprehensive general liability insurance provides basic protection against losses stemming from the firm's legal liability to others. Separate policies may also be obtained for specific forms of liability. These might include public liability insurance to protect against claims resulting from injuries to customers on store premises or other accidents arising from the firm's normal operations. (Public liability insurance is often included in homeowner's policies for private individuals.)

product liability insurance

Product liability insurance shifts risk related to claims by product users of injury or illness caused by such use. There has recently been a great rise in the number and size of legal claims by consumers against producers of various consumer products (see Chapter 22). The Johns Manville Corporation, for example, has had huge liability losses because of the asbestos-related injuries its products and operations are claimed to have caused. In May 1982, Eli Lilly and Company introduced a drug called Oraflex that eased arthritic pain. Three months later, Lilly was forced to withdraw the drug from the market because of reports of several deaths among the drug's users. Two years later, Lilly had settled one claim for $6 million but still faced over 100 lawsuits resulting from just this one of their many products.

Firms that hold the property of others in their possession, such as warehousing and transportation firms, often carry *bailee liability insurance*. This protects them against claims of damage to others' goods while in their possession.

Doctors, lawyers, and other professionals protect themselves with professional liability insurance, often called *malpractice insurance*.

INSURANCE AGAINST LOSS OF EARNING POWER

Many events can cause a firm to suffer losses of earning power. If a fire causes a supermarket to close its doors for several weeks, or a major

BUSINESS IN THE NEWS

Substitutes for Original Equipment Body Parts Create Insurance Controversy

Insurance agents are caught in the middle of a nationwide fight over parts used to repair auto bodies that have been damaged in accidents.

Auto makers—including GM, Volvo, Toyota, Ford, and Nissan—are telling customers to insist on parts made by the original auto body manufacturer when they have auto body repairs made. In one ad, GM says that auto insurance companies are reimbursing policyholders only enough to pay for inferior replacement parts. GM recommends that consumers complain about this to their insur-ance companies and insist on genuine GM parts. The auto makers say that inferior parts do not withstand corrosion and are not as crashworthy as parts made by the original manufac-turers (OEMs).

The non-OEM parts, how-ever, cost as much as 40 percent less than the auto makers' parts, according to the Aftermarket Body Parts Association (ABPA). The ABPA says that these parts are similar in all significant ways, although they might not withstand rust and corrosion as well as the auto makers' parts. The federal government has not set standards for such parts, most of which are made in Taiwan, Brazil, Mexico, Can-ada, Germany, and Italy.

Neither the National Asso-ciation of Professional Insur-ance Agents nor the Independent Insurance Agents of America has adopted a position on the controversy.

Source: "Trends . . . The Crash Parts Fight," *Insurance Review*, April 1987, p. 6.

---

executive or owner dies, or political upheaval forces closure of a for-eign-based operation, serious loss of profits can ensue. Insurance can offer a solution.

business interruption insurance

Business interruption insurance pays the insured firm for profits and overhead costs lost as a result of a specific peril, such as fire. A firm can also buy contingent business interruption insurance and extra ex-pense insurance. The former covers losses related to the interruption in delivery of supplies, and the latter covers the cost of renting temporary quarters when a specific peril strikes the firm.

key person life insurance

Key person life insurance insures the life of a major employee, such as the president of a firm. Obviously, such a loss cannot be wholly measured in dollars, but the insurance can compensate for the possible "loss of business momentum" resulting from the person's death. The proceeds can also help pay for recruitment or training expenses in-curred in this period. Similar policies are available to compensate the firm for the impact of a key person's disability. Life insurance may help to prepare for the death of a partner or a major stockholder in a closely held corporation. As we saw in Chapter 3, the articles of partnership often specify that if one partner dies, the surviving partners will have the option to purchase the deceased partner's interest from his or her

If a tornado strikes a store that has business interruption insurance, not only the physical damages are covered, but also estimated profits lost during the time the firm is rebuilding.

estate. Such a buy-and-sell agreement is often accompanied by the firm's purchase of insurance policies on the lives of major partners. The firm uses the proceeds of such policies to purchase the deceased's interest and allow the firm to continue operations with a minimum of delay. Closely held corporations can make similar use of life insurance in the event of a major stockholder's death.

political risk insurance

Political risk insurance protects firms against losses resulting from actions taken by foreign governments or even foreign terrorists against the firm's property. An insured firm can be reimbursed, for example, if a foreign government suddenly revokes its import license or will not pay for goods delivered by the insured.

CRIMINAL LOSS INSURANCE

Most firms carry protection against criminal loss. This covers losses from burglary, robbery, and other forms of theft. Burglary includes break-ins that have left visible marks of entry. Robbery is taking property by means of violence or threat of violence. These risks are covered by crime insurance. Sometimes there are separate policies for burglary, robbery, and other forms of theft. Insurance against embezzlement is known as *fidelity bonding*. It can be purchased for individual workers, for specific jobs, or for all employees. Special protection can also be bought for losses from forgery and other forms of dishonesty.

surety bonding

Surety bonding protects the firm from losses due to nonperformance of a contract. Should a contractor not complete construction of a shopping center at a specified date, for example, a surety bond would reimburse some of the center developer's losses. This bond is usually purchased by the contractor rather than the developer. Bonds perform the same kind of risk-shifting function as insurance policies. They differ only in that bonding involves three parties rather than two. Besides the protected party and the risk-assumer, there is the designated principal (an employee in the case of a fidelity bond and a contractor in the case of a surety bond).

CREDIT AND TITLE INSURANCE

Two other forms of insurance commonly used by business firms are credit insurance and title insurance. *Credit insurance* protects firms from losses from nonpayment of debts by customers who in fact cannot pay them. To protect against credit losses caused by the borrower's death, some firms also take out credit life insurance on the borrower's life. *Title insurance* protects a firm's purchase of real estate against defects in the title to the property. This insurance is especially important to firms such as shopping center developers that purchase real estate often.

GROUP HEALTH INSURANCE

With the rising cost of medical care the demand for various forms of health insurance has spread to most U.S. firms. Group health insurance plans are now standard parts of most firms' benefits programs. Sometimes the cost is shared with employees, and sometimes it is assumed entirely by the firm.

Health insurance programs may include the following forms of insurance coverage:

- Hospitalization insurance pays for most ordinary expenses related to hospital services. Limits may be set for the daily room rate and for standard medical services, tests, and procedures. Deductibles and coinsurance may also be featured. Blue Cross is the best-known plan.
- Surgical and medical payments insurance covers the fees of physicians, including surgeons, within limits set by the policy.
- Major medical or catastrophic illness insurance protects against a major part of the medical costs that exceed the limits of coverage of hospitalization and medical payments policies. Some provide coverage of $1,000,000 or more.
- Dental insurance usually provides for ordinary dental care expenses, excluding major orthodontic services and other expensive items such as bridgework.

In addition, some firms also provide limited coverage for mental health services, optical care, and other medical needs that are not provided by the forms of insurance described above. Employees of some firms are provided, in lieu of regular health insurance plans, with membership in a health maintenance organization (HMO), such as Kaiser Permanente, or insurance by a preferred provider organization (PPO).

health maintenance organization (HMO)

A **health maintenance organization (HMO)** is a comprehensive health care system with a fixed, prepaid cost per year to the member for all services received, regardless of type or quantity. It is administered by a group of medical service providers (clinic(s), hospital(s), doctors) tied together by contract. These providers must predict the demands upon them when setting the fee per member. Some employers absorb the entire fee, but employees usually pay part. Employees like the fact that the paperwork of many insurance plans is eliminated. Critics are concerned about the limited choices among providers that HMOs allow patients and about the effects of the plan administrators' need to keep within the budget provided by the contracted fees. A **preferred provider organization (PPO)** is a group of health care providers who offer to business firms a package of services for their employees at reduced rates. Unlike HMOs, the PPO charges for each individual service and procedure. The users usually have greater choice of providers than HMO members have.

preferred provider organization (PPO)

DISABILITY INSURANCE AND WORKERS' COMPENSATION

disability income insurance

Disability income insurance provides employees with income when they are unable to work because of an accident or sickness. Some employers provide disability insurance at their own expense. Under a sick leave plan, part of the worker's salary is paid when he or she cannot work because of sickness or accident. In the case of total disability an income protection plan pays a certain percentage of the employee's salary while he or she is disabled.

As we noted earlier, federal and state governments also provide for employee disability. The most widely held disability insurance is through Social Security. People who have been covered by Social Security for several years (it varies with the person's age) and suffer grave

By training employees in the proper handling of hazardous materials, a firm safeguards its workers and minimizes the amount of workers' compensation it must pay.

disability that is expected to last twelve months or to result eventually in death receive such disability benefits. Dependents are also eligible.

workers' compensation

Workers' compensation programs are also very common (covering about 85 percent of workers). All fifty states have such programs, though their provisions regarding level and duration of benefits vary greatly from state to state. Farm workers, self-employed people, and workers in very small firms and nonprofit organizations are excluded in many states. The employer pays the entire cost of the premium, and disbursements start earlier than under the Social Security program. The premiums that employers pay vary with the degree of hazard involved in the work. Rates for miners, for example, would be much higher than those for clerical personnel.

Workers' compensation insurance provides payments for medical costs and compensation for loss of income as well as rehabilitation costs, if any. If the employee dies as a result of the specific injury or illness, workers' compensation pays death benefits to survivors.

LIFE INSURANCE

life insurance

Life insurance pays a cash benefit to a surviving person or firm (the beneficiary) upon the death of the insured person. This provides a degree of financial security to the insured person's family or firm. Nearly all employers provide such protection to their employees as a major fringe benefit (the cost is sometimes shared with employees). Life insurance can be purchased by individuals and is available to firms as group life insurance.

Life insurance has grown rapidly in the last twenty years. Group life coverage has grown even faster. It is ordinarily written as a single master policy covering all employees as defined in the policy. This form of life insurance is cost-efficient and may be offered at lower cost than individual equivalent coverage. It may take several of the forms described below. Often, medical exams are not required for such policies. Within certain limits, life insurance benefits are tax deductible to the employer.

Among the most common forms of life insurance are term insurance and ordinary whole-life insurance. In recent years, partly because of tax law changes, interesting new varieties have been added.

Term life insurance policies are issued for definite time spans such as 5, 10, or 15 years. If the insured person dies, the policy's face value is paid to his or her beneficiary. If the insured person outlives the term of the policy, neither the insured person nor the beneficiary receives anything. Term insurance is pure protection.

Under *ordinary whole-life* insurance the insured person (or the employer) pays premiums until death, at which time the beneficiary receives the policy's face value. If the insured person cancels the policy during his or her life, that person is paid the cash surrender value, or savings value, of the policy, which increases during the life of the policy. This provides savings as well as protection. The insured person can also borrow money against the current cash value of the policy.

Universal life insurance, which first became available in 1981, has become very popular. It provides for savings and for "pure" insurance. Unlike ordinary whole-life, a universal life policy allows the policyholder to know how much of the premium pays for protection and how much is invested. The amount invested, or the cash value, earns a rate of return based on current market conditions, and such earnings are tax-deferred. The insured person can also borrow against such a policy.

Variable life insurance also provides the combination of insurance and investment and allows greater flexibility. The insured person can choose the type of investment he or she wants—stocks, bonds, money market funds. The cash value and the death benefit both fluctuate, depending on the success of the investments the insured person has selected. Single-premium variable life insurance provides the benefits of variable life, but it is purchased by a lump sum payment at the policy's inception. The insured person may borrow against earnings and principal without tax obligation. The single-premium feature is also available in whole-life policies and annuity plans now offered by many insurance companies. In mid-1988, however, Congress was reviewing the nontaxability of loans and withdrawals from single-premium policies.

SELECTING AN INSURER AND AN AGENT

Besides selecting the types of insurance needed, the risk manager must give a lot of thought to which insurance company to select for each type of coverage. Although the cost of specific insurance coverage is a factor in selecting an insurer, it might not be the most important.

The risk manager should take a long, hard look at the stability, reputation for economic soundness, and service of the insurers under consideration. The soundness of an insurance firm can be checked in *Best's Reports*. This guide to insurance companies is available in many public libraries. A rating of A or A+ in *Best's* indicates financial strength and soundness.

The manager should also investigate the quality and extent of services (especially claims service) of alternative insurers. This includes the insurer's claims settlement practices and its reputation for well-trained, knowledgeable service and claims personnel. It also includes the geographic outreach of the insurer. Does it have claims representatives in all the places in which you do business—including where your salespeople travel and your trucks make deliveries?

In the final analysis the quality of insurance agents may be as important as the quality of the insurance carrier itself. A good agent can play an important part in the development of a company's risk management program. A skilled and interested sales representative can, for instance, aid in decisions about the risks to be covered and the amounts of coverage needed. The agent can also provide tips on risk reduction that can lower the premiums. One indication of a qualified agent is the certification as a chartered life underwriter (CLU) or a certified property and casualty underwriter (CPCU). These certifications indicate that the agent has completed an extensive training program in a special field. Such an agent also has experience and a reputation of professionalism to uphold. It is a good idea, in any case, to interview several agents before choosing one. A good personal client-agent relationship greatly enhances the value of an insurance policy. In many cases the agent assumes an advisory relationship to the business manager that is not unlike that of a CPA or an attorney.

Summary

Pure risks offer a chance of loss but no chance of gain. Speculative risks offer possible gain as well as possible loss. Risk management in business is directed primarily toward pure risk.

Risk management in business firms consists of three steps: identifying likely risks, estimating the frequency and size of the losses involved, and choosing the best way to deal with each. The risk manager can assume the risk, minimize the risk, avoid the risk, or shift the risk. Some combination of these is also possible. Shifting risk is usually a matter of buying insurance.

Insurance is available from many private insurers as well as from federal and state governments. The federal government operates the Social Security program, which includes disability insurance and Medicare as well as the public retirement program. The federal government also sponsors financial, agricultural, disaster, and pension insurance programs.

When an insurance firm considers offering a specific coverage, it inquires about the accidental nature, the predictability, the possible catastrophic nature, the size of claim, the measurability, and the adverse selection of the risk to be insured. The answers to these questions also help the risk manager to decide how to deal with the firm's risks.

Business firms buy insurance protection for two main reasons: to shift the risks they encounter in their operations and to provide benefits for their employees. They may purchase property damage insurance including fire, marine, and automobile damage policies. They may need several forms of liability insurance, insurance against loss of earning power, crime insurance of several types, and credit or title insurance.

As benefits for their employees, firms may choose from a variety of group health plans, disability, and life insurance. Disability programs are supplemented by Social Security and workers' compensation.

In choosing an insurer a firm should examine the insurer's economic stability, strength, service reputation, and geographic coverage. One should consider the training of the insurance firm's and/or the insurance agent's employees and their record of timely claims disposition. The agent should be well-informed about the firm's needs and easy to communicate with.

Review Questions

1. What is the function of the risk manager? How does he or she go about estimating potential losses?

2. Define self-insurance. Is it more likely in small firms or in large, widespread operations?

3. To whom is a firm most likely to shift risk?

4. Describe some of the kinds of insurance available from public sources.

5. What are the characteristics of an insurable risk?

6. Describe three types of property damage insurance.

7. Distinguish between product liability insurance and bailee liability insurance.

8. Describe several types of criminal loss insurance.

9. Why should a firm buy life insurance for its key people?

Discussion Questions

1. Why can some firms use self-insurance while others cannot?

2. Explain how the law of large numbers enters into premium setting in the insurance industry.

3. Explain how a risk manager might employ a combination of risk strategies.

4. What is the difference between the benefit to a firm of purchasing fire insurance and the benefit that it receives from purchasing health insurance for its employees?

5. The Monarch Corporation, a U.S. producer of machine tools, has been operating in a small, underdeveloped nation for two years. It hears rumors of a revolution in the country that is likely to lead to a very "anticapitalist" government. What kind of insurance does Monarch need? Are the premiums likely to be high? Discuss.

Key Terms

pure risk
speculative risk
risk management
self-insurance
insurance policy
stock insurance companies
mutual insurance companies
Medicare
insurable risk
law of large numbers

actuaries
deductible
law of adverse selection
insurable interest
principle of indemnity
coinsurance
comprehensive general liability insurance
product liability insurance
business interruption insurance

key person life insurance
political risk insurance
surety bonding
health maintenance organization (HMO)
preferred provider organization (PPO)
disability income insurance
workers' compensation
life insurance

WHAT ABOUT THE SPEED LIMIT?

After years of debate and controversy over the 55 mph nationwide speed limit set in 1972, Congress modified the law to let states raise the limits on more than 75 percent of interstate highways. The Reagan Administration, the Secretary of Transportation, and the National Governors Association endorsed the change. Rural states have been the strongest advocates of change. Arguments for the change included the high cost of enforcement and the fact that the 55 mph law encouraged lawbreaking.

Several insurance industry groups opposed the change vigorously. The Insurance Institute for Highway Safety (IIHS) argued that a national telephone survey showed that 58 percent of respondents favored retaining the old limit. The IIHS says that the fatality rate per 100 million miles on interstate highways was 1.21 in 1984, a 32 percent decline since 1973, the first full year of the reduced speed limit.

The American Insurance Association also opposed the higher limit, claiming that since it was adopted, the speed limit has saved 2,000 to 4,000 lives and 35,000 to 62,000 injuries annually.[2]

Questions
1. What business reasons would the insurance industry have for opposing the higher speed limit? Discuss.
2. In states that returned to 65 mph on many interstates, what do you supposed happened to insurance rates? Why?
3. Which types of business firms would probably support the higher speed limit? Why would they?

ALBERMARLE VENTURES

Sally Brightson was named risk management director for Albermarle Ventures in 1984. One of her most difficult assignments involved Albermarle's purchase of Marker Waste Management, a fairly successful solid waste disposal firm in the Pittsburgh area. In March 1986 (the time of the acquisition), Marker operated six solid waste disposal facilities within a 200-mile radius of Pittsburgh.

Until the acquisition was made, Albermarle's primary activity was in labor-intensive service industries, primarily employment and training services and security for office buildings. The risks had been pretty much routine except for some aspects of the security services. Marker's waste disposal was quite a different matter. The firm was very vulnerable to liability suits related to radiation poisoning and other chemical poisoning. These liability risks extended to the water supplies of local communities as well as to Marker's own employees, whose health was at risk from exposure to toxic chemicals.

Ms. Brightson had managed risk mostly by purchasing insurance and setting up normal risk minimization policies. For example, liability insurance premiums for security guards in office buildings were reduced by careful screening and training of security personnel and heavy reliance on electronic surveillance and automatic alarm devices tied to police and fire stations.

Questions
1. How did the risk management responsibility of Sally Brightson change with the acquisition of Marker?
2. What are her main alternatives for dealing with the new risks?
3. If insurance policies are one answer to the new risk management problem, list the types of insurance that might play a part.
4. What are the possibilities of self-insurance for Albermarle? Are they greater or smaller after the acquisition? Why?

Audie Cashion calls himself "a black sheep" and says others often call him "crazy." But this 23-year-old has every intention of becoming a millionaire by the age of 25 and playing a role in achieving world peace and the commercialization of space in his lifetime.

Already, this top student in high school who failed two courses his freshman year in college has established a thriving export business, selling early American furniture, Indian jewelry, crafts, upholstery, pickles, and a "Snoopy Dream Machine" to Japanese customers.

How does an upstart undergraduate with no credentials go to a foreign country and start a business? In Cashion's case, a lot of research and many one-on-one contacts, for example, with Japanese students on exchange programs. He also credited the United States and North Carolina Departments of Commerce for their help in identifying products and markets.

How did an undergraduate acquire start-up money? He said it was a combination of a little venture capital from his partner, sam-

SECTION SIX
Special Topics

ples from the suppliers who also provided credit, and "some creative financing."

Cashion began his business, TradeEast Horizons, in May of 1987 with a classmate in a University of North Carolina Japanese language course. In mid-1988 the firm was reconstituted as Cashion Trading Co., Ltd., and moved to Princeton, N.J. He targets the younger, freer-spending generations he describes as taken with the West, ironic since his own interest in Japan grew from a fascination with its food, martial arts, and spiritual values.

"Shell-shocked" after flunking courses his freshman year, Cashion became impatient to develop "real world" skills. In the summer of 1985, he had an internship with the North Carolina Commerce Department and also made his first visit to Japan—a two-week trip with a nonprofit international group. Back home, he took the fall semester off. That break in his studies "really got me started in business," said Cashion, who returned to college and graduated with a degree in economics. In his extracurricular life Cashion hoped to join a fraternity, but was blackballed. That painful experience he sees now as "a big turning point," leading him to start an Entrepreneurs Club. It became affiliated with the International Association of Collegiate Entrepreneurs, which, in turn, provided important contacts for Cashion when he needed them in Japan.

On another trip to Japan in the summer of 1986, Cashion "saw the Japanese buying American products that weren't suited to the Japanese market," such as furniture that was too big for most Japanese homes. He knew he could do better. His strategy involves implementing his belief that, "We have to market to other countries on their terms, not on U.S. terms." He has already done business with Seibu Department Stores, which he said is "as widespread as KMart, but as upscale as Macy's." In five years, the young entrepreneur said, "I'd like to have a complete grasp of what the Japanese market is, to speak Japanese well enough to do business in that language, to expand to Korea, China, and even Russia .... One of my goals is world peace and I believe in detente through trade."

Managing Information with Computers

In this chapter we look at the computer's growing role in business. We start with a definition of a computer or data processing system.

This is followed by an examination of the main hardware components of a computer: the central processing unit and storage systems, supplementary storage, and input-output devices. We discuss the latest computer technology and the impact of the newest powerful personal computers and networking on the way businesses are using computers.

Computer software has taken on a greater role in the development of computer systems. We examine the development of system software as well as the variety of horizontal and vertical applications software packages. After a brief look at the major computer programming languages used in business and science, we examine the role of documentation in software development.

This leads to a description of three major ways in which business has applied the fantastic talents of the computer. We examine the application of management information systems to marketing, finance, and accounting problems; the use of computer-assisted design and related production process applications; and the revolution in word processing and office automation.

The chapter closes with a discussion of people's reactions to the use of computers and the problems of security and privacy in computer use.

At Nissenbaum's
auto junkyard
in Somerville,
Massachusetts,
someone is
on the phone
looking for a 1979
Buick engine.
Nissenbaum's,
which seems to
have one of
almost everything,

does not have one of those. So salesman David Butland turns to a nearby personal computer, types a brief message, and punches a button that dispatches his request by satellite to 600 other yards across the country.

Three minutes later, a dealer in Dallas offers an engine for $650. Mr. Butland waits. A California dealer offers the same price. He waits. Then someone in Maine who can see Mr. Butland's request but not the earlier replies offers the same engine for $550. Mr. Butland grabs it and sells it for $700.

"We've probably boosted our looking-for-parts business 75 percent since we got this," Mr. Butland says, patting a keyboard that is protected from grimy fingers by a sheet of plastic wrap. Another marketplace is being transformed by computers.

Computers are everywhere in business today. Although most firms use them for "number crunching" or word processing, a growing number of firms are buying and selling by computer. Industries are changing as a result.

By extending their in-house computer systems into the offices of their customers and suppliers, firms like Nissenbaum's are creating electronic marketplaces and demonstrating just how computers can change the way business is done.

"These systems in some cases dramatically change the balance of power in buyer-supplier relationships, provide entry and exit barriers, and shift the competitive position of industry rivals," says James Cash, a Harvard Business School professor who studies corporate computer use.

For companies that deal in "recycled auto parts," as Nissenbaum's prefers to call them, computers have widened what was once a strictly local market into a national one.[1]

Stories like that of Nissenbaum's auto junkyard are becoming familiar all over the United States. For years, small businesses of every type, as well as middle-sized and large businesses, have been profiting by applying the marvelous power of computers.

What Is a Computer?

computer

A **computer**—or more exactly a computer system—is a system that uses electronics to receive, store, retrieve, manipulate, and communicate large amounts of data very quickly and precisely. It is a marriage of machinery with a system of electronic "instructions" that set the machinery into motion. We will explore these two "partners in the computer system" (hardware and software) later in the chapter. Computer systems are sometimes called electronic data processing systems.

Computers come in a variety of sizes. A very large computer, called a mainframe, can handle much of the data needs of a large corporation, government agency, or university from a central location. Mainframes typically cost at least $1,000,000. A super-mainframe such as a Cray

THE ELECTRONIC AGE

How Today's Computer Evolved

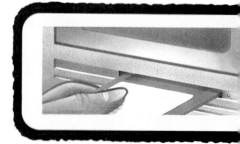

It is difficult to place the birth of the modern computer in time. Some would credit Charles Babbage's "analytical engine," invented in 1936. Others would point to IBM's early work with punched-card accounting systems. Perhaps most would agree that the University of Pennsylvania scientists who developed the vacuum tube, digital ENIAC in 1946 were really the inventors of computers as we have come to know them.

The development of computers is usually discussed within the framework of five "generations." The first generation included machines similar to ENIAC that used vacuum tubes and were capable of performing about 5,000 arithmetic operations per second. The invention of the transistor in 1947 led to the development of second-generation computers, which were much smaller, used less power, generated less heat, and were capable of performing 50,000 operations per second. The third generation of computers resulted from the development in 1960 of integrated circuits (ICs), the equivalent of many transistors "printed" on a silicon chip. The IC-based computers were still smaller, cooler-running, and much faster than their predecessors. The late 1960s saw the development of large-scale integration (LSI). This packing of even more components on one chip resulted in a fourth generation of computers. Manufacturers of fifth-generation computers use very large-scale integration (VLSI) to produce machines that are very small, very fast, and much less expensive than earlier types. The most sophisticated VLSI chip might contain the equivalent of one million transistors. The sixth-generation VHSIC (very high-speed integrated circuit) chips, now in development, could contain as many as 35 million components.

From the fourth generation (LSI) on, the term "microprocessor" has been used to refer to a more-or-less complete "computer on a chip." Microprocessors make both general-purpose and specialized computers smaller, lighter, and cheaper to build. They are now available for watches and clocks, to improve auto efficiency, to control a dishwasher or microwave oven, or to operate a video game. Thousands of new products and even industries have come about because of microchips. Sales of these new products are measured in the hundreds of billions of dollars.

computer might cost several million dollars. Minicomputers (sometimes divided into small and medium-sized computers) cost much less, from about $20,000 to a few hundred thousand dollars. Minicomputers can meet the needs of a division of a major corporation or a small business. Since 1982, personal computers (PCs), also called microcomputers or "micros," have vaulted into a dominant position.[2] These desktop machines can meet the needs of the individual office worker or, in some cases, entire offices. PCs costing between $500 and $10,000 are now more powerful than the $5,000,000 mainframes of the 1970s. The growth in the PC's power and popularity is having a great impact on how computers are used to serve business needs.

Computers have wide-ranging applications inside and outside of business. You are probably accustomed to computer-assembled term grade reports from your college and computer-made bills from the telephone company. Computers do thousands of repetitive operations such as billing quickly and accurately for big and small institutions. They also store masses of information and produce any part of it upon command.

They also do more specialized jobs. Pitney Bowes, Inc., long-time specialist in speeding up mailing activities, has developed the A300 Allocator (see the accompanying ad), which helps to allocate postal expenses and hooks up with Pitney Bowes' electronic mailing systems. Ford's EEC-IV on-board automotive computer can save fuel and help the engine run better. It can also provide better starts, keep records for the mechanic, and help the firm with quality control.

A 200-pound robot computer produced by Denning Mobile Robotics works as a prison guard. The machine can detect an unlocked door, travel to that door, and determine whether an escape has taken place. Vynet Corporation has developed a V300 line of voice-response systems that can "speak" in any language and make a pushbutton phone act like a computer terminal, delivering more than twenty-seven hours of voice messages simultaneously on thirty-six telephone lines. Such a system can answer questions from customers or present a "telemarketing" sales message.

Roger Nichols invented a computer system that he calls Wendel. Wendel is an electronic studio musician that stores and outputs sounds digitally (in computer code) and can produce almost any kind of drumbeat for recording purposes. Business applications might not always be as dramatic as Wendel, but they are becoming more and more creative as business firms get used to computers.

The Elements of a Computer

hardware

software

The two major parts of a computer system are its hardware and its software. **Hardware** consists of the machinery and electronic components of a computer system, such as the keyboard or printer. Hardware cannot work without the right software. **Software** is the set of instructions necessary to put the computer hardware into motion. This includes instructions giving operating instructions to the computer itself as well as directions for carrying out specific applications of the computer.

Computer Hardware

Hardware does the following tasks in logical order:

- Input
- Storage
- Manipulation
- Output

Pitney Bowes has used electronic technology in its mailing systems to meet more of its customers' needs.

Doing these tasks requires several kinds of hardware: input devices, the central processing unit (CPU), read-only memory, random-access memory, and output devices. As shown in Figure 20-1 (on p. 588), some systems also use supplementary data storage devices such as hard disks.

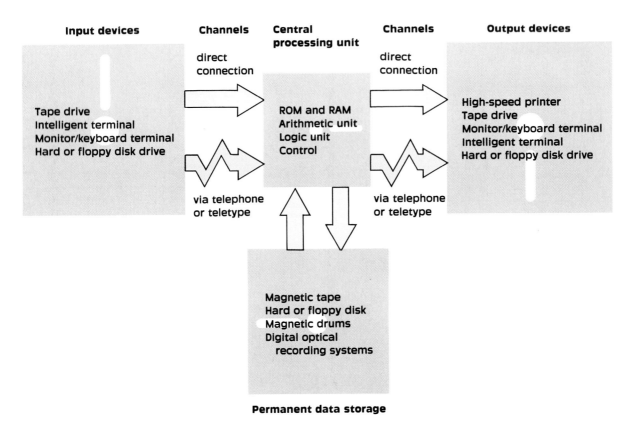

Input devices	Channels	Central processing unit	Channels	Output devices
	direct connection		direct connection	
Tape drive Intelligent terminal Monitor/keyboard terminal Hard or floppy disk drive		ROM and RAM Arithmetic unit Logic unit Control		High-speed printer Tape drive Monitor/keyboard terminal Intelligent terminal Hard or floppy disk drive
	via telephone or teletype		via telephone or teletype	

Magnetic tape
Hard or floppy disk
Magnetic drums
Digital optical
   recording systems

Permanent data storage

FIGURE 20-1 / Hardware components of a computer system.

THE CENTRAL PROCESSING UNIT AND STORAGE SYSTEMS

central processing unit (CPU)

The **central processing unit (CPU)** is the heart of a computer and includes an arithmetic unit for performing calculations, a logic unit for comparing values and helping the computer to "make decisions," and a control unit that "supervises" the computer's internal operations and sends instructions for controlling the whole system. Closely associated with the CPU are two types of electronic memory—read-only memory and random-access memory. **Read-only memory (ROM)** is permanent computer memory that contains and saves instructions for the control unit. When a computer is turned on, the control unit reads the instructions contained in ROM and "learns how to be a computer." **Random-access memory (RAM)** is volatile (temporary) computer memory that is active only while the computer is switched on. The computer uses RAM to store the application programs and data with which it is currently working.

read-only memory (ROM)

random-access memory (RAM)

SUPPLEMENTARY STORAGE

A computer's electronic memory can be added to by means of magnetic or optical storage systems quite apart from the system's ROM and RAM.

Magnetic storage media range from 5.25-inch floppy diskettes that can store 180,000 characters (numerical digits, letters, or other characters) to hard disks that have a capacity of storing 20 million, 40 million, 60 million, or even 200 million characters. Optical storage systems are now available that can store several hundred million characters. Table 20-1 describes several special-purpose input, output, and storage devices.

TABLE 20-1 / Special-purpose input, output, and storage devices

Device	Purpose
COM (computer output microfilm)	Displays data on a monitor from microfilm. *Example:* parts specifications at a large warehouse
OMR (optical mark recognition) reader	Reads data recorded in pencil on documents. *Example:* computer-graded test answer sheets
MICR (magnetic ink character recognition) reader	Reads characters written on documents with magnetic ink. *Example:* account number and amount on check
UPC (universal product code) reader	Reads the special product code identification bars on grocery items as they pass over the checkout counter at the supermarket
Voice digitizer	Translates voice input into digital form for processing in the computer
Mouse	Allows bypass of keyboard to monitor for inputs
Laser printer	Provides quiet, high-speed, combination type and graphics printing
Digital optical recording	Provides mass memory in compact form
Line printer	Prints one complete line of output at a time. Provides a very high rate of output and is usually used with mainframes.
Dot matrix printer	Uses pins impacting on inked ribbon to form characters that consist of groups of dots. Dot matrix printer speeds range from a low of 30 cps (characters per second) for high-quality output to 360 cps for draft-quality output
Optical scanner	Reads printed material and converts the characters to digital signals that can be recognized by the computer
Modem	Modulator-demodulator converts a digital signal (on-off pulses) into a modulated tone and vice versa so that computers may communicate with each other over telephone lines

INPUT AND OUTPUT DEVICES

input and output (I-O) devices

Input and output (I-O) devices are the hardware that is used to get information into or out of the computer. Such "user interfaces" put people into contact with computers. On personal computers the monitor, keyboard, disk drive, and printer—all directly wired to the CPU—are the chief I-O units. On mainframes the magnetic tape drive, hard magnetic disk drive, and high-speed printers (as well as the monitor-keyboard combination) are the most common I-O units. They are directly wired to the CPU or connected by modem to remote points. A

modem

modem modulates or converts a digital signal (on-off pulses) into a tone that can be transmitted over telephone lines and then reconverts to communicate with faraway personal computers, mainframes, or remote memory units. New ways to tie computers together, along with the growing power of personal computers, are revolutionizing business firms' use of computers.

Laser printers use laser technology to provide fast, excellent-quality print and graphics for a wide variety of computer output needs. These state-of-the-art printers can serve mainframe or personal computers. They work at high speeds and provide great flexibility in the variety and quality of type and graphics (charts and pictures) they can produce. Laser printing is often used in what is called "desktop publishing," the use of small computers to produce newsletters, advertisements, and other publications.

PERSONAL COMPUTERS, NETWORKS, AND DISTRIBUTED DATA PROCESSING

The personal computer (PC) was introduced in the late 1970s. Since then, the computer world and the business world have not been quite the same. This mighty midget of computers is so inexpensive and powerful that managers in large and small firms are rethinking their computer needs. Although many managers of small firms might still be skeptical about having their own system, the financial reasons for not doing so have disappeared. PCs can help smaller firms by providing word processing, spreadsheet analysis, database management, general accounting, inventory, payroll, and billing capabilities at low cost. Clerks, secretaries, floor salespeople, production workers, and many other operational-level employees can use PCs after a short training program.

In larger firms, PCs have had a similar huge impact. In the 1970s and early 1980s a growing workload and shortage of trained computer staff led many large firms to centralize management information and analysis in mainframes. This often caused conflict between users at various remote points and those controlling the central computer. But the newer, more powerful PCs together with new networking systems have changed all that.

distributed data processing (DDP)

Distributed data processing (DDP) is a decentralized approach to information handling that relies on tying powerful PCs together into networks and bringing computer power to many different points in the large firm. This approach depends on linkages of computers and related components that are called networks. **Local area networks**

local area networks (LANs)

As the cost of PCs decreases, more and more small business firms are finding them to be cost-effective tools for communication, planning, and data processing.

(LANs) are systems that connect computers—PCs, minicomputers, or mainframes—along with high-speed laser printers and/or disk storage components within a locality. These units are usually located close to each other, within distances of one mile or less, and are connected by ordinary telephone lines or coaxial cables. This makes it possible for firms to achieve complete office automation and communication in one operating network. True LANs require a specialized central system. These include StarLAN, 802.5 Token-Ring, and others, which are designed according to standards set by the Institute of Electrical and Electronic Engineers. Some computers and the appropriate network systems are sold prepackaged by Digital Equipment Corporation and IBM.

Communication between computers at greater distances (wide area networking) is usually done by means of telephone lines, using modems to convert computer signals to telephone signals and back again. Organizations using long-distance communication between computers may use commercial telephone service or even develop their own satellite links.

The Corporate Services Group of Chase Manhattan Bank has installed a network that connects IBM and Apple microcomputers to larger computers to link five buildings in the Wall Street area. This network permits the computers to work together by sharing data, storage capacity, and output devices. The network will eventually be expanded to facilities in upstate New York.

Computer Software

Software is a necessary companion to hardware. It is just as important as hardware and is the part of computer systems that is undergoing the most rapid change and growth. There are two main kinds of software: system software and application software. Software usually comes with documentation that explains how to use or modify it.

SYSTEM SOFTWARE

Perhaps the most important idea in software is the basic idea of a program. A **computer program** is a detailed set of instructions for a computer, written in a special computer language. *Programming* is the process of writing programs or instructions to computers.

computer program

System software consists of internal programs that tell the computer system how to manage the various tasks assigned to it. It becomes a more or less permanent part of the computer system. It might, for example, automatically allocate a certain part of the computer's memory to perform internal "housekeeping" tasks. It might specify the way that certain input-output devices may be used or manage the "traffic" between units in a LAN.

system software

An **online system** exists when those using the system are constantly in direct communication with the computer, either by telephone or directly wired in. An airline employee who gets a request for a reservation can call the central computer to see whether space on Flight 901, say, is available. The clerk can also reserve seats if the flight is not already fully booked.

online system

A **real-time system** is an online system that can respond instantly and make programmed responses. A real-time system can be used for constant energy management of a large building. The Citicorp Building in New York saves energy because its system monitors temperatures, office usage, and other factors that affect energy use. The computer reads information sent constantly by sensors at various points in the complex. It then sends instructions to the temperature and lighting systems.

real-time system

Some business computers still use batch processing. **Batch processing** occurs when data are entered into computers in batches from time to time rather than continuously. The system might be inoperative for long periods. Paperwork accumulates and then is entered into the computer. The rapid adoption of online terminal work stations in business is making batch processing obsolete.

batch processing

A crucial component of software is the language or code used to write programs. System software, then, includes languages that computers understand.

Machine language consists of binary code (0s and 1s only), and different versions of it relate to specific computers or sets of computers. It is used because the CPU understands only whether its tiny memory cells are on or off. A cell that is turned on is recognized as a 1, and a cell turned off is recognized as a 0. Figure 20-2 illustrates how binary code translates into the numbers we are used to using.

machine language

Assembly language is a language that is used to write system software. It is not entirely binary but lies between machine language and the higher-level (English-like) languages, such as BASIC. Assembly language is an intermediate-level language.

assembly language

American Standard Code for Information Interchange (ASCII)

The **American Standard Code for Information Interchange**

Decimal number			Binary number			
Place	Place		Place	Place	Place	Place
10	1		8	4	2	1
	0					0
	1					1
	2				1	0
	3				1	1
	4			1	0	0
	5			1	0	1
	6			1	1	0
	7			1	1	1
	8		1	0	0	0
	9		1	0	0	1
1	0		1	0	1	0

FIGURE 20-2 / Binary numbers and their decimal (standard) number equivalents.

(ASCII) is a standard computer code for numbers, letters, and special characters shared in the United States by many producers of word processing and other software. There are binary (two-digit), decimal (ten-digit), and hexidecimal (16-digit or letter-number combination) versions of ASCII code.

APPLICATION SOFTWARE AND PROGRAMMING

application software

Application software consists of programs that do practical jobs for the computer user. It includes special-purpose programs that compute payrolls or do general ledger accounting. It also includes more widely applicable programs like word processing or electronic spreadsheets. Such software is not a regular part of the computer's operating system. Application software is often written in one of the major computer languages. These include FORTRAN, BASIC, Pascal, C, and Lisp.

SOFTWARE PACKAGES

A variety of software packages are growing in importance in businesses that use personal computers. Electronic spreadsheets are especially useful. An **electronic spreadsheet** is a general-purpose program that allows the user to enter and manipulate numerical and alphabetic data in a computer screen format that is much like an accountant's lined pad. Lotus 1-2-3 is the most widely used single software package for PCs. Other spreadsheet packages are SuperCalc, Multiplan, and Silk. These packages present on the screen a ready-made blank spreadsheet or accounting pad. By using the great variety of commands that the package provides, the user can write headings and numbers in the blank spaces (cells) and create formulas that tie the numbers found in some of the designated spaces with other numbers in the spreadsheet. For example, the spreadsheet in Figure 20-3 shows sales for the Fortune Corporation by product type. Column B, row 10 is designated as the location (cell) for entering the sum of the numbers in column B, rows 2 through 9 (the sales of each of eight different products produced by Fortune Corporation). The Fortune employee who prepared this spreadsheet told the program to compute the sum of these cells (B2–B9) and place it in cell B10. This employee also entered the alphabetic headings and marginal titles.

Any kind of mathematical formula can be used to tie the cells together. Spreadsheets also contain special functions for financial and scientific computations and usually have the ability to generate graphs and charts out of numbers. This makes it easy to work with statistical tables, forecasts, ledger accounts, and the like.

Suppose Fortune Corporation wants to show projected sales of each product class for the next five years at a 10 percent annual growth rate. The spreadsheet user can do this easily by entering the formula for such growth and applying that formula to the sales amounts in Column B. This would result in additional entries (not shown in Figure 20-3) in columns C–G, lines 2–10. The computer would then answer the ques-

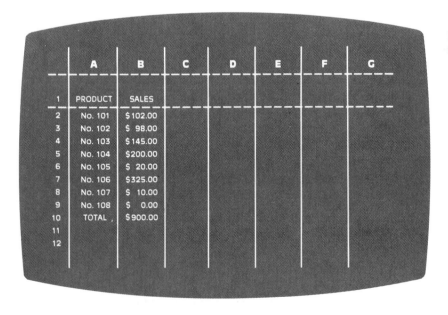

FIGURE 20-3 / An electronic spreadsheet.

	A	B	C	D	E	F	G
1	PRODUCT	SALES					
2	No. 101	$102.00					
3	No. 102	$ 98.00					
4	No. 103	$145.00					
5	No. 104	$200.00					
6	No. 105	$ 20.00					
7	No. 106	$325.00					
8	No. 107	$ 10.00					
9	No. 108	$ 0.00					
10	TOTAL	$900.00					
11							
12							

By using commercial software packages, many firms can incorporate computers into their operations without the time and expense of writing their own programs.

tion "What if sales grew for five years at 10 percent per year?" The user can just as easily see the results of a 5 percent growth rate or any rate at all. Spreadsheets are good at answering the question "What if?"

Word processing, spreadsheet, database management, and communication packages are called *horizontal packages*, as are graphic presentation packages, "desktop publishing," and various engineering and design-related packages. They are called "horizontal" because they can be used by a wide variety of firms for many different purposes.

Some packaged software is designed for special users. Quantel Frame software is made for retail management and is especially good for inventory analysis. MDS Quantel, Inc. also produces Hal, especially made for internal hotel-restaurant control systems. Such specialized packages are called *vertical packages*.

DOCUMENTATION

documentation

An important part of software is known as documentation. **Documentation** means an explanation either in English (or other spoken language) or in diagram form of what a computer program does, how it is used, and how it works.

Documentation is important to both those who write programs and those who use them. Programmers are interested in the documentation of the design, logic, function, and utility of the program. Users are interested in the purpose of the program, when to use it, and what preparations are necessary to run it. Documentation for the user is written in the language of the nation in which the program is to be used. It is given to the user in the form of operator instructions. When you buy a PC, it usually comes with plenty of user documentation for the operating system, such as DOS, and perhaps for BASIC programming.

The underlying structure of a program is traditionally documented with a flowchart. Flowcharts (or block diagrams) such as the one shown in Figure 20-4 give a picture of the logical steps in a program. This figure describes the steps taken to produce a weekly payroll for a sales

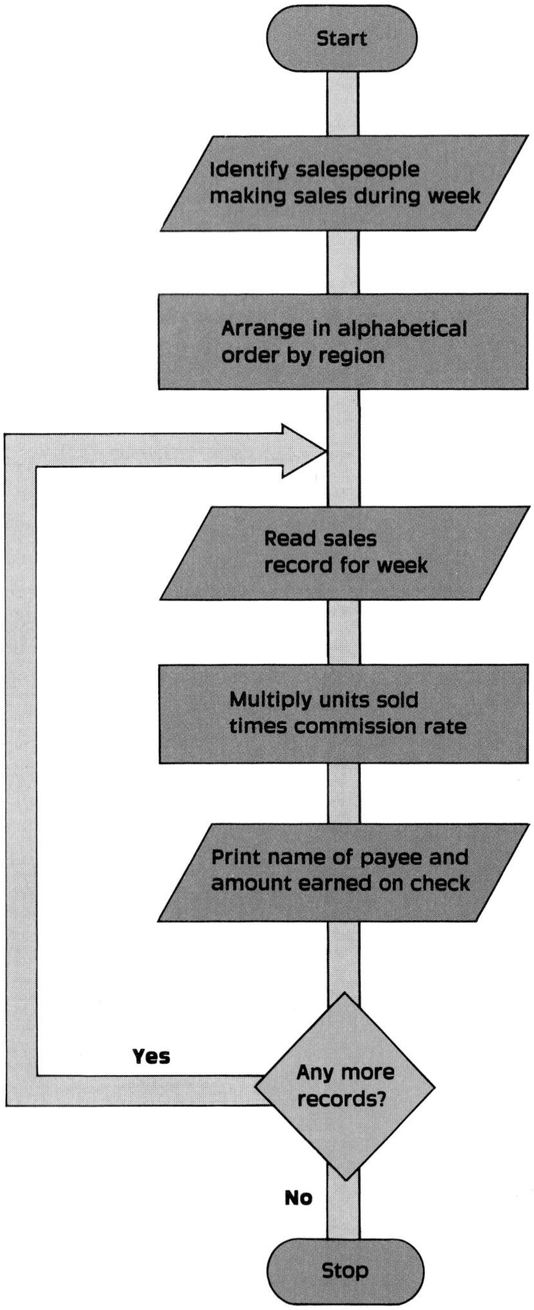

FIGURE 20-4 / A flowchart (block diagram) for a payroll.

force whose income depends on their commission on sales. It is a bit simpler than a real-life computation, which might include different commission rates on different products and various tax deductions.

Business Applications of Computers

From what we saw in the introductory example of Nissenbaum's junkyard as well as from our earlier chapters on production, marketing, and accounting, one thing is clear. Much of a firm's success or failure de-

APPLICATION: BURGER KING
On-Site PCs

Burger King Corporation is using personal computers to help its restaurant managers make decisions faster and better. Here's how they're doing it.

First, computerization of a firm like Burger King Corporation is aimed at accomplishing several goals. One is to give the restaurant managers more time to actually manage. Putting personal computers in restaurants will help Burger King managers to automate about 20 hours a week worth of reports that they must now do by hand. That alone is a big savings and will let the managers devote more time to running their restaurants more efficiently.

But there is a lot more that Burger King Corporation can do with such a system, according to a Burger King Corporation information systems executive. He points out that with the PCs tied into regional computers, corporate management can keep

better track of individual restaurant performance. Reports can be printed to answer questions like: What is this restaurant's sales compared to the same time last year? What is the ratio of the restaurant's investment in inventory to sales? Are they using too much labor for their current level of sales? Such reports can not only help keep corporate management informed, but will also help managers run their restaurants more efficiently.

The PCs will also help manage a restaurant's inventory and ordering process. Particularly when tied in with computerized point-of-sale cash registers that record every item sold, the system will keep track of how much of each item is used up so that the ordering process itself can then be automated.

Moving up to the level of the headquarters in Miami, the computerized individual restaurant data will also provide

new information on how each product is selling and what trends are taking place. That should help corporate management fine-tune things like advertising programs and new product development.

Questions
1. What do you think is the major benefit of computerization to a Burger King restaurant manager?

2. What do you think is the major benefit of computerization to Burger King Corporation headquarters in Miami?

3. To what extent should Burger King Corporation attempt to automate operations at Burger King restaurants?

pends on its ability to collect, process, organize, and retrieve information. Nissenbaum's salesman must find scarce parts quickly. The accounting department of every firm must collect data about transactions and produce financial statements. Manufacturers must record costs of production and set production schedules. Financial managers must measure cash flows and make capital budgets. They even turn to computers for scoring credit applicants. The computer applies a formula to the applicant's credit, asset, and income information and "decides" whether the firm will accept the new account.

A successful firm must be able to gather, store, combine, and use masses of data efficiently and quickly. If a computer is well designed and well used, it can do all of this for firms of any size.

MANAGEMENT INFORMATION SYSTEMS

management information systems (MIS)

Computers play a big role in top management decision making. **Management information systems (MIS)** consist of data collection, organization, and summary, which are integrated so that decisions can be made more quickly and often more accurately. A diagram of an MIS is presented in Figure 20-5. The figure illustrates the demand flow—what information is needed—and the supply flow—how it reaches the decision maker.

MARKETING APPLICATIONS MISs have many uses in marketing activities. Gulf South Beverages, Inc., a PepsiCo regional distributor, uses a special program to keep track of inventories of its many soft drink products and to forecast consumer demand. Market Facts, Inc. and many other marketing research firms use systems to store and manage incoming data from telephone surveys. Computer-based research activities to monitor advertising effectiveness and sales force operating expenses are also common.

FINANCE APPLICATIONS All kinds of financial problems and financial institutions have applications for MISs. Union Savings and Loan Association, like many S&Ls and banks, can get instant data on a customer's balance from such a system. It can also do an internal analysis of all of its mortgage accounts and develop estimates of future inflows of mortgage note payments. Any business can apply an electronic spreadsheet like Lotus 1-2-3 or SuperCalc to financial problems. Spreadsheets can answer "what if?" questions such as "What would happen to my return on investment if I bought this new bond issue?" or "What would happen to my cost of borrowing if interest rates rose from 9 percent to 10 percent?"

ACCOUNTING APPLICATIONS The examples above could also be classified as accounting applications, mostly managerial accounting. There are some extremely important financial accounting applications as well. Even the small business can use many forms of ready-made programs for accounts receivable, inventories, payroll, and other accounting jobs. These provide accurate and speedy data summaries for financial statements. The payroll program also computes and often prints paychecks,

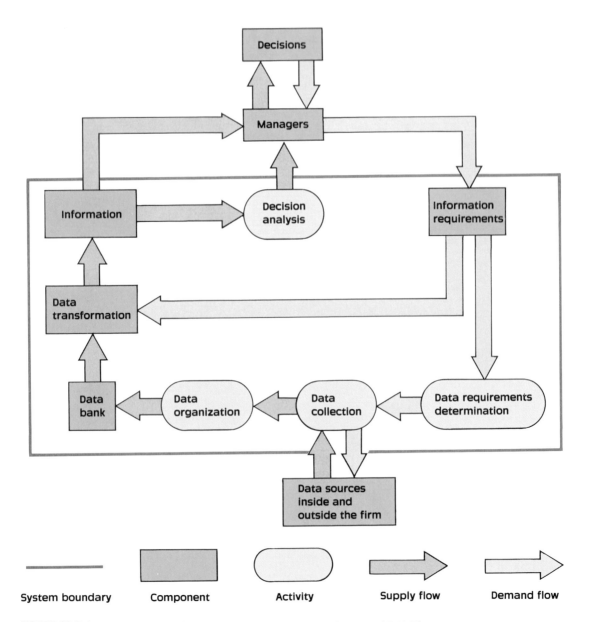

FIGURE 20-5 / A management information system. (*Source:* J. C. Carter and F. N. Silverman, "Establishing a MIS," *Journal of Systems Management,* 1980, p. 16.)

including deductions for Social Security and income taxes. It can also print W2 forms for employees at the close of the year.

DATABASE MANAGEMENT SYSTEMS   When large sets of data are maintained and are continuously altered, expanded, and used, many firms and nonprofit institutions employ a database management system. A **database management system (DBMS)** provides for easy, continuous updating of a set of data used by an organization, together with easy access to

database management system (DBMS)

summaries and analysis of the data. The U.S. Social Security Administration, for example, maintains an up-to-date database containing the earnings and Social Security contributions of more than a hundred million workers. It depends on regular reporting of new data by millions of employers. Several book publishers provide college bookstores with DBMS software for a microcomputer that will allow the bookstore to get current prices on most college textbooks and help them keep track of their textbook inventory. Ashton-Tate's dBase III is a popular software package for managing databases.

COMPUTER-ASSISTED DESIGN, ENGINEERING, AND MANUFACTURE

Huge growth is also found in technical applications of computers. We saw some of this in Chapter 10. CAD (computer-assisted design), CAM (computer-assisted manufacture), and CAE (computer-assisted engineering) are well established in business. General Motors has equipped its small car division with CAD equipment for chassis design, induction/emission, and transmission/axle work. Three-dimensional models of the chassis, motor, and associated parts are used to check how they fit together. CAD packages are now available for microcomputers, making it possible for individuals with limited budgets to use computers for design work. Special CAD software, called graphics packages, for mainframes, minicomputers, and microcomputers are useful for preparing bar charts, graphs, and similar visual aids for business reports.

COMPUTERS, AUTOMATION, AND ROBOTICS

A system or process is automated when it regulates itself. Some automated processes are fairly simple and do not require computers. An example is a household heating and air-conditioning system. The thermostat lets the system operate without much human interference.

A petroleum refinery is a more complex system that requires a computer for automation. At many points in the refining process, data must be constantly fed into a computer. The information relates to such things as the rate of flow and the temperature. The refinery's central computer has been programmed to use such data to control the refining process.

The computer makes certain computations and relay instructions to machinery in the factory. It does this according to the program fed into it at an earlier time. Valves are opened and closed, and temperatures are raised and lowered automatically.

Robotics, as we saw in Chapter 10, is computer-guided production technology. Machines do many factory jobs that used to be performed by humans, do them better, and never get tired. The Japanese, starting with ideas developed in the United States, have successfully applied robotics to industry. This is one reason for Japan's growing dominance in many areas of mass production. Ford and other U.S. auto makers have now introduced robotics in their plants. Robotics has improved the consistency and precision of many auto production processes, including the fit of doors and the uniformity of paint application.

A computer-controlled lathe takes much of the guesswork out of difficult tool production tasks.

BUSINESS USE OF EXPERT SYSTEMS

As computers get faster and more powerful, there is increasing optimism that computer scientists will be able to build a computer that imitates some of the brain's more complex functions. Although much of the brain's functioning is still not understood, the term "artificial intelligence" (AI) is being applied to some advanced computer systems and their software. AI includes computer applications to language processing, vision systems, and speech recognition and synthesis. Expert systems are only one part of AI, but they have had a widespread impact on some business decisions.

expert system

An **expert system** is a specialized computer program designed to process data relevant to a particular problem or decision to simplify or even conclude the decision-making process.

One expert system developed by Human Edge Software Corporation is designed to help salespeople develop sales strategies for specific customers. Like most expert systems, "The Sales Edge" is a computer program that asks its user some multiple-choice questions. The user reads the questions on the screen and types in replies. The questions in this case relate to the personality of the customer or prospect and the personality of the salesperson. "The Sales Edge" program, using a large set of rules about personalities, their relationships, and expected behavior (its knowledge base) helps the salesperson narrow down the choice of an appropriate sales approach.[3] Other expert systems have been developed to help set prices, to screen credit applicants, and to simplify many other operational decisions.

WORD PROCESSING AND OFFICE AUTOMATION

word processing system

In still another area of business—the office—the computer is making its mark. A **word processing system** is a text-editing computer program that manipulates letters, words, tables, and paragraphs. Some small, special-purpose computers are used only for word processing. However, the trend is to use general-purpose personal computers that can do many jobs besides word processing. WordPerfect and WordStar are two of the most popular word processing software systems. They can be used on most major microcomputers.

office automation (OA)

Office automation (OA) is a combination of word processing, electronic spreadsheets, DBMS, and new communications networks. The fastest-growing segment of OA is data communications. Data communications are often facilitated by local area network (LANs).

When Kramer & Frank, a St. Louis account collection firm, first decided to use computers, it used unconnected, stand-alone personal computers and Ashton-Tate's dBase II database software program. The firm soon outgrew this system, having to manage records of 10,000 accounts. The solution was a LAN that tied the PCs together, running Ashton-Tate's networked version of dBase III. This enabled the firm to keep using its old data files and avoid having to change to a totally new

system. The LAN helps track debtor account balances and deposits, computes the interest accrued on each account, remits money to clients, prints out statements and checks, automatically makes the appropriate number of copies, and even issues a summons if necessary.[4] Ashton-Tate also offers RapidFile, a specialized software product for filing tasks, as shown in the accompanying ad.

Associated Milk Producers, Inc. (AMPI), a 28,000-member collective of dairy farmers, is successfully using electronic interoffice communication. AMPI has more than forty offices in twenty-one states. Managers and employees in all offices can get direct access to each other instantly. They can send and receive "electronic mail" memos, as well as reports on legislation, prices, and financial information from central data files or small input stations. It is as simple as typing in the message on a personal computer and using certain commands to send it to distant members tied in with the computer system. Many other firms use one of several brands of facsimile, or "fax," devices to communicate. A fax device "reads" a printed page or illustration and sends it over a telephone line to a designated reception point, where another fax machine reproduces the material exactly.

How People React to Computers

Human reactions to the computer range from worship to outright fear. Most people who really know computers reject these extremes. Rather, they have learned that the computer is a marvelous tool. They have found that the different abilities of people and computers can be brought together and that their combined power can be used very effectively.

Fear of the computer takes different forms. Some people are afraid that society will become too dependent on complex control systems. A small human error in programming or data entry could produce chaos. Some feel that the computer can bring about mass job loss. Others fear the changes that new ways of doing things bring to the firm. Still others fear the computer for another reason. They know that the government and many private agencies store huge quantities of personal data about private citizens. They believe that this is a violation of their right to privacy.

Closely related to the question of privacy is the fear of loss through computer crime. Clever thieves and pranksters have found ways to abuse computer systems, often violating bank accounts or payroll systems for their personal gain. This is a growing problem that computer system designers are working on. Naturally, the techniques being used to combat such theft are not much publicized. Some computer criminals interfere just for the perverse fun of doing so. The Business in the News box (on p. 604) discusses a relatively new type of computer crime: computer viruses.

One measure that is being tested specifically to avoid the theft of private information is coding. This is not unlike the coding used in military and CIA communications. Such codes are developed by specialized computer consulting firms for use by all kinds of businesses.

BUSINESS IN THE NEWS
Spreading a Computer Virus

Shai Bushinsky, an Israeli computer expert, says, "It might do to computers what AIDS has done to sex." He is referring to a "computer virus" being spread by an unknown person at Hebrew University in Jerusalem.

A computer virus is a self-propagating set of computer commands that spreads from one computer memory to another and is introduced by a saboteur who wants to damage the system. At Hebrew University the virus threatened to wipe out research data, financial statements, lists of students, and other information vital to students, teachers, and administrators.

The computer infected all disk files that were exposed to it. They, in turn, contaminated "healthy" computers and disks. Instead of infecting each program or data file once, the malignant commands copied themselves over and over, consuming increasing amounts of memory. Unchecked, the sabotage could eventually have wiped out the entire system.

Local computer experts devised a two-phase program called "immune" and "unvirus" that tells users whether their disks have been infected and applies an antidote to those that have been. A senior programmer at the university reported that the person responsible had to know how to avoid some of the system's security devices to write directly into the CPU as he or she did.

Source: "Electronic 'Virus' Preys on University's Computer Files," (Associated Press) *Asheville Citizen*, Jan. 8, 1988. © 1988 The Associated Press.

All messages on SWIFT, a computer network linking 500 banks, are being sent in coded form.

Sometimes people (even managers) believe that a computer will magically solve all their problems. This can cause as many problems for a firm as fear of the computer. The truth is that managers must plan very carefully. They must get accurate data and a debugged program (one in which all the problems have been worked out) before they can count on using a computer's output. Someone invented the term GIGO ("garbage in—garbage out") to describe how much the computer depends on reliable human input. A chimpanzee is unlikely to be able to count its toes, even with a computer's help!

Summary

A computer is a system that uses electronics to receive, store, retrieve, manipulate, and communicate large amounts of data very quickly and precisely. It is a marriage of the machinery itself—hardware—with a system of electronic instructions—software—that set the hardware into motion. The major parts of the computer hardware are the central processing unit, input devices, output devices, and supplementary data storage devices.

Personal computers are growing so powerful that they are assuming much of the work in large and small businesses. Networking systems tie PCs together and tie them with larger computers. The result is a huge growth in distributed data processing. Great advances are also being made in computer speed, memory size, and printers and other input and output devices.

In the computer industry, software sales are growing even faster than hardware sales. Most of the growth is in application software, or programs that do practical jobs for the computer user. This includes special-purpose programs such as those that compute payrolls as well as more widely applicable programs like word processing and electronic spreadsheets.

System software consists of internal programs that tell the computer system how to manage the various tasks assigned to it. System software becomes a more or less permanent part of the computer system. Application software does practical jobs for the computer user such as payrolls, accounting, and word processing.

Computer languages are an integral part of software. Machine language is directly understandable by the computer's CPU. Higher-level languages are used to write applications software. Documentation, including flowcharting, helps people understand, edit, and employ application programs.

Computers serve business in many ways. They make it possible, for example, to create management information systems to collect, organize, and summarize data.

Businesses also use the graphics capabilities of computers in engineering applications like computer-assisted design (CAD), computer-assisted manufacture (CAM), and computer-assisted engineering (CAE). Business offices have benefitted greatly from office automation, which combines the use of word processing with computerized spreadsheets, DBMS, and new communications networks.

Human reactions to computers include fear of the change or job loss they might bring. There are also growing fears of the threat to privacy computers might encourage. Some firms expect too much from computers, not really understanding that computers are just very sophisticated tools. Many firms are concerned about various forms of computer crime that can occur.

Review Questions

1. Name the major hardware components of a computer. How are they interrelated?

2. Give the highlights of the history of the computer.

3. How have the new powerful PCs and networking affected the use of computers by business?

4. What is a binary number? How do binary numbers relate to digital computers?

5. What is a computer language?

6. What does a computer program do? Give a business example of the use of a program.

7. Explain what is meant by documentation and draw a simple flowchart.

8. Identify three major classes of business applications of computers.

9. How do people react to the use of computers?

Discussion Questions

1. What startling modern accomplishments do you think never could have happened without computers?

2. Review the experiences you had yesterday and try to determine which of them were influenced by the existence of computers.

3. Discuss possible uses you might have for an electronic spreadsheet.

4. Are people becoming less afraid of computers?

Key Terms

computer
hardware
software
central processing unit (CPU)
read-only memory (ROM)
random-access memory (RAM)
input and output (I-O) devices
modem
distributed data processing (DDP)
local area networks (LANs)

computer program
system software
online system
real-time system
batch processing
machine language
assembly language
American Standard Code for Information Interchange (ASCII)
application software

electronic spreadsheet
documentation
management information systems (MIS)
database management system (DBMS)
expert system
word processing system
office automation (OA)

LIMITS TO EXPERT SYSTEMS IN THE STOCK MARKET?

Morgan Stanley & Co., PaineWebber, Inc., Salomon Brothers, Kidder Peabody & Co., and Bear, Stearns & Co.—five of America's largest brokerage firms—announced in 1988 that they would voluntarily suspend their program trading activities for an indefinite period. Program trading is using a kind of expert system to decide when to buy and sell securities. The systems differ, but they contain rules relating to a combination of factors, such as current stock prices and indexes of future stock prices, that lead to large buy and sell orders.

The major stockbrokers stopped using such an automated system because they believed that such action was necessary to restore confidence in the marketplace and to bring many private investors back into the market.

When the stock market collapsed in October 1987, some analysts blamed the program trading systems. The theory was that once the market began to fall, program trading was a kind of automatic accelerator of the downward spiral of prices. Program trading probably at least contributed to the crash.

Questions

1. Does the action by the five brokerage firms indicate a lack of confidence in expert systems? In computers in general? Explain.
2. Should professionals in the securities market or in any other business activity allow expert computer systems to replace their own judgment?
3. Do computers give professionals in the stock market an unfair advantage over small individual investors? Explain.

THE INSTALLATION OF A LAN AT WATERMAN'S FREIGHT HOUSE, INC.

In September 1987, Jack Waterman, president of Waterman's Freight House, Inc., decided to install thirty Zenith personal computers for his 120-desk office staff, which was spread out over four floors of a skyscraper in Philadelphia. Mr. Waterman provided a training program for his employees so that they could perform many routine office tasks, including word processing, and so that they could "talk" to the mainframe and its hard disk–based data bank located at the top floor.

Among the uses that were being served were (1) inquiries as to the availability of space for customers on scheduled shipping runs, (2) ordering of packing materials through the purchasing office, and (3) preparation of all accounting records and transferral of such information to the accounting department located on the same floor as the mainframe.

Waterman employees, after much debate among themselves, decided to approach Mr. Waterman about the purchase and installation of a modern local area networking (LAN) system for the company's headquarters operations.

Questions

1. When the PCs were first bought, was Waterman's going to a system of distributed data processing? Discuss.
2. What types of hardware might have been employed in the overall system at Waterman's?
3. What major advantages for office operation could the employees have claimed in making their request for a LAN?
4. When the PCs were purchased, was it necessary to maintain the same mainframe as was used for two years before their purchase? Would the LAN make any difference in this regard? Discuss.

Government and Business

After reading this chapter, you will be able to:

- Illustrate government and business interaction.

- Show how antitrust laws maintain competition.

- List and describe the purpose of several federal administrative and regulatory agencies.

- Describe two major types of protection provided by regulation.

- Outline the major events in the trends toward regulation and toward deregulation of U.S. business.

- Give examples of at least three different roles played by government in the environment of business.

- Show how the major forms of taxation affect business.

WHAT'S AHEAD

Government and business interact constantly. Business provides government with much of its tax revenue. It also gets involved with the operation of government by engaging in lobbying and supporting political action committees. We will show that the most complex role that government plays with respect to business is that of regulator. It regulates in one way by maintaining competition through antitrust laws like the Sherman Act, the Clayton Act, and the Robinson-Patman Act.

We will also see how the federal government engages in regulation for protecting people. This includes the many ways in which government acts to protect the environment and consumers.

Also important to the conduct of business are the procedures for regulation and enforcement followed by regulatory agencies. We will show how the regulatory agencies, such as the Federal Trade Commission, and the courts interact in this process. We will see how waves of regulation and deregulation have done much to shape the environment of business.

We will also review the variety of other roles played by government, including those as competitor of business, stabilizer of the economic environment, supporter and customer of business, and housekeeper for the nation. We will close with a look at the impact of government's taxing authority on business decision makers. We will examine separately the effects of corporate and personal income tax, sales tax, property taxes, and excise taxes.

In late 1985 an automobile parts manufacturer in Columbus, Indiana, was threatened with a hostile takeover by a Canadian group. The Columbus firm employed 2,000 local workers and was heavily involved with the community. The company's founder had built two schools for the town, and the company had recently contributed money so that the local board of education could hire a top-notch superintendent.

The chairman of the board of Arvin Industries, Inc. did not want the Belzberg family of Canada to gain control of his company. He went to his friend Robert Garton, who was President Pro Tempore of the Indiana Senate, and asked for help. The state of Indiana was already in the process of revising and updating its entire set of laws relating to corporations. To expedite matters, Mr. Garton was able to get the section dealing with corporate takeovers treated separately by the Indiana Senate in time to save Arvin Industries. Although the law was challenged by other companies attempting takeovers in Indiana, the Supreme Court of the United States upheld it. As a result of this law, an investor who acquires 20 percent or more of an Indiana firm loses the voting rights of the shares unless the other shareholders decide to reinstate them.

The goal of this law and others like it in twenty-one states is to protect corporations from hostile takeover attempts. Company executives and local leaders both have stakes in keeping local businesses locally operated. They fear that an outside owner's only interest will be the bottom line and that the personality of the company and of the community may be at risk.[1]

Indiana's antitakeover law is an example of how government and business interact. This law illustrates government's roles as a supporter of business and an economic stabilizer. It also shows how a government acts as a regulator. In this chapter we review these and the other roles that federal, state, and local governments play in the business environment.

How Government and Business Interact

When we first looked at the challenges facing business in Chapter 2, we observed that a whole range of challenges are posed by the political-legal environment. This, of course, means government. Business influences the way in which government operates, and government influences the way in which business operates.

Business is the principal generator of revenue for government. It creates most of the jobs and personal income, sales, and corporate income on which taxes are levied. These taxes are the major source of government revenues, so when business slows down, government revenues slow down with it.

As we saw in Chapter 2, business plays a big role in the election process by lending moral support to employees' political action committees (PACs). Sometimes, this helps business groups get their favorite candidates elected. They also engage in lobbying to persuade

Professional associations such as NARD, which represents independent retail pharmacists, take an active interest in the passage and enforcement of laws that affect their business.

members of Congress or state or local lawmakers to pass certain laws. (See the NARD ad.) Many firms also lobby through trade associations, often with the help of professional lobbyists who have offices in Washington, D.C., and in state capitals.

Chambers of Commerce are formed in local areas and at the state and national levels to influence lawmaking and to improve the climate for business. Historically, they have supported laws that result in lower business taxes, tighter restrictions on unions, fewer regulations of their own activities, and limits on imported goods.

Sometimes, however, businesses do not agree on which laws to support or oppose because of conflicting interests. Large insurance companies, for example, are likely to favor tighter restrictions on smoking in restaurants, while local restaurant associations might oppose such laws.

Lobbying activity is especially strong among large defense contractors. Favorable legislation can mean millions of dollars in government contract revenues, cost savings from eased air pollution regulations, or tax exemptions for locating a new factory in a given state.

Sometimes, state and local governments actively pursue new industry and do not have to be lobbied to do so, as illustrated in the Alabama Development Office ad. They seek the economic advantages of new factories—jobs for the citizens and increased tax revenues for the state.

Sometimes, it is essential for business and government to cooperate. U.S. immigration laws regulate the hiring, wages, and work conditions for immigrant laborers on U.S. farms and in other businesses. Since 1987, when the Simpson-Rodino Act was passed, farmers and other businesses that employ immigrants must cooperate with the U.S. Immigration Service by providing proof that workers are in the United States legally. This means filling out a checklist for verifying each worker's immigration status. The new immigration law will not work without the serious participation of business.

Government has many ways of influencing the decisions and success of business firms. It can do so through the executive branch (the President), the legislative branch (the Senate and the House of Representatives), or the judicial branch (the court system) and at the federal, state, or local level. It can regulate or deregulate, raise taxes or cut taxes. It can encourage or discourage business investment, buy a firm's products, or buy those of the firm's competitor. Government plays many roles in the life of the business manager.

The Regulatory Role of Government

For many years it has been accepted that government regulation of business has its place. This role was exercised as far back as 1889, when the Interstate Commerce Commission was formed to regulate railroad rates. Ever since then, lawmakers have argued over the proper relationship between competition and regulation.

Competition itself tends to act as a kind of regulator. If competition works, products are sold at fair prices, and firms make fair profits. Firms that cannot compete by producing good products at competitive prices disappear from business life. If firms really struggle to win customers, such competition improves business performance. However, it does not always guarantee fair prices and good products. U.S. history shows that government action is sometimes necessary to ensure that firms compete. Two government agencies—the Antitrust Division of the Justice Department and the Federal Trade Commission—take such action.

ANTITRUST LAWS—MAINTAINING COMPETITION

Influenced by the economic theory of Adam Smith, our nation's policy toward business for more than a century was one of *laissez-faire* ("hands off"). Over time, it became clear that laws were needed to keep

antitrust laws

businesses competing. Otherwise, one or several large businesses could take over a given industry. **Antitrust laws** are a set of federal laws dating back as far as 1890 that are aimed at (1) increasing effective competition, especially among large firms, and (2) reducing the concentration of economic power. Unfortunately, there has never been a very clear agreement in Congress, in the courts, or even among businesses on how to define "effective" competition. Is an industry competitive only when new firms can enter the market? Is an industry competitive only if its prices truly reflect its costs of production plus a fair profit? Or is an industry competitive simply because there are many competitors in existence, none of which truly dominates the market?

The main foundations of antitrust law are the Sherman Antitrust Act of 1890, the Clayton Act of 1914, and the Federal Trade Commission Act of 1914. These laws set up the means for maintaining competition and eliminating monopoly abuses in the marketplace. Monopoly is a market condition in which a single firm produces a product for which there is no close substitute. The word "trust" was once used to mean a huge, monopolistic or nearly monopolistic firm. Such a seller can demand high prices because of the lack of competitors. Sometimes, oligopoly (several large sellers in a market) can have effects similar to those of a true monopoly (one seller). The antitrust laws helped to maintain competition by defining many of the terms involved in the formation of monopolies and the abuse of monopoly power.

The Sherman Act prohibits "contracts and conspiracies in restraint of trade" and sets out criminal penalties for violation. It is very general in its language but is aimed at prohibiting monopolistic activity. The Clayton Act spells out some specific anticompetitive practices. For example, it affects selling practices of business by outlawing tying contracts, which restrict competition. A **tying contract** requires a buyer to buy unwanted items from a seller in order to buy something else that the buyer wants. When such an action is found to injure competition, a manufacturer of machine tools, for example, could not legally require that a customer buy its line of solvents in order to buy the tools. An **exclusive dealing agreement** requires a buyer, as a condition of sale, to refrain from dealing in products that compete with those of the seller. If a retailer or an industrial distributor were carrying Brand X, an exclusive dealing agreement would prevent the retailer or industrial distributor from carrying competitive Brand Y. Exclusive dealing agreements are in many cases prohibited by the Clayton Act.

tying contract

exclusive dealing agreement

interlocking directorate

A third practice prohibited by the Clayton Act is the interlocking directorate. The **interlocking directorate** is the overlapping of membership of the boards of directors of firms competing in the same market.

The Federal Trade Commission Act set up the Federal Trade Commission (FTC) to administer (along with the Justice Department) various parts of the antitrust laws. The FTC Act also banned various unfair trade practices.

The Robinson-Patman Act of 1936 and the Wheeler-Lea Act of 1938 helped to further clarify and tighten the earlier laws on price discrimination and false or deceptive advertising. The Celler-Kefauver Act of 1950 gave the FTC power to review certain proposals for mergers so as to prevent excessive concentration of power in an industry.

In the 1970s, antitrust laws were again "fine-tuned." The Antitrust Procedures and Penalties Act (1974) raised the fines and the criminal penalties of the Sherman Act. The Antitrust Improvements Act (1976) called on firms to notify regulatory agencies in advance of a merger. This gives the FTC or the Justice Department time to look at the effects of such a merger on competition.

How well antitrust laws work is a tough question to answer. They present a real hardship to some firms, which seem to spend years in and out of court because of them. Antitrust laws also prevent some combinations of business operations that could lead to greater efficiency and lower final prices. Such combinations could strengthen U.S. firms' positions in international competition. However, many experts agree that, when administered fairly and vigorously, antitrust laws do help to slow down or prevent the growth of monopoly power. This means more effective domestic competition and better market prices for the buyer.

PROTECTING THE ENVIRONMENT

Many laws passed to regulate business are for the purpose of protecting people. As we saw in Chapters 8 and 9, many forms of protection have been established for workers. Minimum wage laws, occupational safety laws, civil rights laws, and antidiscrimination laws provide protection for people. In Chapters 16 and 18 we described some of the institutions and laws that protect people from the effects of bank failure and securities fraud. Besides these, there are federal and state laws designed to protect the people by protecting the environment.

Laws to protect certain parts of the environment have been around since the turn of the century. The Refuse Act of 1899 prohibited dumping into navigable waters without a permit. Further regulation appeared in the 1940s and 1950s to restrict the use of certain poisons and to strengthen the earlier efforts to control water pollution. However, environmental protection by law really got its start in the 1960s and 1970s.

The Clean Air Act of 1963 and subsequent amendments in the 1960s began to control air quality, in part, by setting standards for auto emissions. The Water Quality Act of 1965 permitted states to set water quality standards. The Solid Waste Disposal Act passed in the same year authorized research and help to state and local governments to control solid waste problems.

The first giant step in the direction of a cleaner environment came with the passage in 1969 of the National Environmental Policy Act. This law established the Environmental Protection Agency (EPA), which consolidated under one head several agencies that had been responsible for various aspects of environmental quality. It also put some real teeth into enforcement of environmental standards. It set up the Council on Environmental Quality to advise the President on the environment and to review environmental impact statements.

environmental impact statement

An **environmental impact statement** is a statement of effects on the environment that might result from a proposed government or government-contracted project. Such a statement must be filed by the agency or firm responsible for the project before a project can be started. Construction of an interstate highway in Mississippi, for example, was delayed for years in the 1970s because of threat to the habitat of the sandhill crane, an endangered species of waterfowl. Similar threats, as well as some much more directly harmful to human welfare, have been reported in environmental impact statements and have added substantially to industrial and federal project construction costs.

Figure 21-1 shows how business and government shared the overall cost of pollution abatement and control from 1975 to 1985. Business's share of pollution costs has risen from about one-third to about three-fourths of the total. Of the total of $67.3 billion spent in 1985, the two largest kinds of pollution-related expenditure were for operation of pollution-related capital equipment (24.3 percent) and for motor vehicle exhaust pollution devices (18 percent).

Monitoring, sampling, and recordkeeping are part of the EPA program. EPA regulations require businesses to control the levels of different chemicals their factories release into the air and water. Many businesses have had to change production methods or install expensive antipollution devices to meet clean air or clean water standards.

The Federal Water Pollution Act of 1972 set clean water standards on an industry-by-industry basis and specified fines and prison terms for violation. The law is meant to control thermal pollution and discharge of particulate and toxic wastes into rivers, lakes, and streams.

In 1980, Congress initiated what is now called the Superfund for hazardous waste cleanup purposes. It was enacted to authorize a federal response when a hazardous substance is released or might be released into the environment. Superfund responses include "removals" or short-term emergency actions related to fires or explosions and "remedial actions" taken at sites identified on the National Priorities List. As of 1986 the National Priorities List included 850 hazardous waste sites and about 13,000 other sites that had been assessed. A tax on the

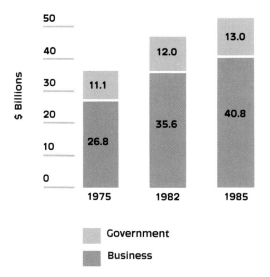

FIGURE 21-1 / Business and government spending on fighting pollution (adjusted for inflation to constant 1982 dollars). (*Source:* Kit D. Farber and Gary L. Rutledge, "Pollution Abatement and Control Expenditures, Revised Estimates for 1972–83," *Survey of Current Business*, July 1986, pp. 94–106; Kit D. Farber and Gary L. Rutledge, "Pollution Abatement and Control Expenditures, 1982–85," *Survey of Current Business*, May 1987, pp. 21–25.

manufacture of petroleum and forty-two chemicals has been used to create the fund, but other forms of taxation are under consideration.

PROTECTING THE CONSUMER

As we saw in Chapters 2 and 11, the consumer has benefited from government protection for many years. The Pure Food and Drug Act was passed in 1906, the Federal Trade Commission Act in 1914, and the Wheeler-Lea Act and the Food, Drug, and Cosmetic Act in 1938. All of these moved in the direction of better consumer protection, but the biggest burst of popular consumerist activity came in the 1960s and 1970s, led primarily by Ralph Nader. Nader and others made the public very conscious of consumer rights. In the early 1960s, President John F. Kennedy proclaimed the four basic consumer rights: the right to choose, the right to be informed, the right to be heard, and the right to safety, as detailed in Figure 21-2. With such strong support from the President and the public it was inevitable that Congress should pass new consumer legislation.

Some important consumer protection laws are the Fair Packaging and Labeling Act (1966), the Consumer Credit Protection Act (1968), the Consumer Product Safety Act (1972), and the Magnuson-Moss Warranty Act (1975). The Consumer Credit Protection Act makes it easier for people to understand and compare interest charges. Lenders must disclose the finance charge and the annual percentage rate (APR) of that charge. The Fair Packaging and Labeling Act regulates packaging and labeling for consumer goods. It also provides for voluntary adoption by firms of uniform industry standards. Depending on the type of

FIGURE 21-2 / The rights of consumers.

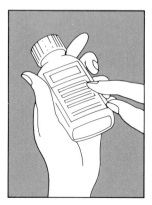

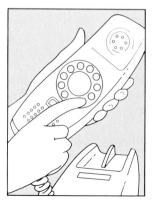

The right to choose from an adequate number of products and brands

The right to be informed of all the important facts about the good or service (price, durability, health and safety hazards, etc.)

The right to be heard by producers and government when treated unfairly or when a question or complaint arises

The right to safety in the use of all goods and services

BUSINESS IN THE NEWS
Champion and the Pigeon River

For two generations the people of Canton, North Carolina, and surrounding towns have depended on the Champion paper mill for employment. The local YMCA, the Canton city government, the churches, and most of Canton's local institutions need this huge mill, which employs 2,000 people. Indeed, they could hardly imagine life without Champion.

During much of the 1980s, Champion International Corporation and its Canton Mill management have been involved in a dispute with the U.S. Environmental Protection Agency and North Carolina and Tennessee environmental agencies over the use of the Pigeon River. The Pigeon runs by the mill and flows northward, along the borders of the Great Smoky Mountains National Park into Tennessee. For many years the Champion Mill has used the water of the Pigeon River as a major part of its paper-manufacturing process. The mill could not operate without the river.

The EPA and many of the citizens of Newport, Tennessee, and other towns along the Pigeon River, supported by an environmentalist group known as the Dead Pigeon River Council, want Champion to improve the quality of the water it discharges into the river. Part of their complaint has to do with the brownish color of the water when it leaves the mill. Still other complaints relate to the alleged release of dioxins (believed to cause cancer) and other polluting chemicals into the river. Authorities responsible for preserving natural resources in this beautiful part of the country have testified that fish and other water-dependent life have suffered, as has use of the river as a recreational resource.

In 1987 and 1988 the EPA held public hearings in Asheville, North Carolina, a few miles east of Canton, and in Knoxville, Tennessee, close to the affected area. The two meetings were very well attended. The meeting in Asheville was dominated by Champion employees, their families, and what seemed like the entire population of Canton. They recited the history of their dependence on the paper mill and outlined the serious eco-nomic consequences of closure of the mill. The hearing in Knoxville was attended by many of the same employees from North Carolina as well as by citizens and environmental groups (mostly from Tennessee) who feared the ecological as well as economic impact of not meeting the EPA's water quality standards.

After these meetings there was talk of compromise. A reduction in the water color standard would reduce the cost of a new water treatment system at the plant and perhaps allow it to operate profitably. Proposals that would keep the mill operating and save the economy of Canton, but that would restore reasonable water quality to the people along the river, were being attempted. The EPA decided to grant a three-year "variance" or permission for Champion to violate the standards for water color. The water will be much clearer—but not up to EPA standards—for the time being. Further testing is being done of the Pigeon River at various points in North Carolina and Tennessee to establish the source and level of alleged dioxin contamination.

consumer good, this act regulates the amount of nutritional or usage information required on the label. The label in Figure 21-3 shows that a serving of Ovaltine (with 8 ounces of milk) provides 20 to 30 percent of the U.S. recommended daily allowances of twenty important vitamins, minerals, and other nutrients.

The Consumer Product Safety Act of 1972 set up the Consumer Product Safety Commission, which collects and studies information related to product safety. The commission also develops and circulates safety standards and bans products that are deemed unsafe. Large fines can be levied for violation. The Magnuson-Moss Warranty Act gave the FTC power to set guidelines for product warranties offered by manufacturers. We will say more about warranties in Chapter 22.

HOW ADMINISTRATIVE REGULATION WORKS

Many government agencies other than the Justice Department and the FTC are involved in regulation of business. Table 21-1 (on p. 620) lists some regulatory areas assigned by law to various federal agencies.

Government policy says that businesses affected by such rules must be given a chance to express their views of proposed rules before the rules are finally adopted. Firms are notified of possible changes well in advance in the *Federal Register*, a government publication. The

FIGURE 21-3 / An informative label.

TABLE 21-1 / Some important administrative and regulatory agencies

Agency	Major Purpose
Interstate Commerce Commission (ICC), created in 1889	To regulate railroad rates, ICC jurisdiction extends to all forms of interstate public transportation with the exception of air carriers, pipelines for gas and water, and certain motor and water carriers operating in metropolitan areas.
Federal Trade Commission (FTC), created in 1914	To prevent unfair methods of competition and unfair or deceptive practices in interstate commerce, including false advertisements.
Food and Drug Administration (FDA), created in 1938	To prohibit adulteration and misbranding of foods, drugs, devices, and cosmetics.
Equal Employment Opportunity Commission (EEOC), created in 1965	To settle complaints of discrimination in employment because of alleged bias in hiring, upgrading, salaries, and other conditions of employment.
Environmental Protection Agency (EPA), created in 1970	To set standards for and to enforce standards of quality in air, water, and other environmental elements.
National Highway Traffic Safety Administration (NHTSA), created in 1970	To improve the safety performance of motor vehicles, drivers, and pedestrians. Also publishes mandatory fuel economy standards for automobiles since the 1978 model year.

idea is to invite criticism so that serious problems that might arise after the rules are implemented can instead be solved in advance.

The force of any agency is felt in several ways. Much can be done, for example, by encouraging a firm to comply voluntarily with regulations. **Voluntary compliance** means that a firm agrees to do what an administrative agency advises without having to hold a hearing. The FTC, for example, upon the request of a firm, will provide an advisory opinion on a certain new pricing policy. The opinion clarifies whether or not the new pricing plan is lawful. If it is not lawful, the firm may comply voluntarily by canceling the new pricing policy and avoiding costly legal proceedings.

Regulatory agencies such as the FTC and the Department of Transportation also issue trade practice rules and trade regulation rules.

voluntary compliance

trade practice rules

trade regulation rules

consent order

Trade practice rules are purely advisory rules developed by federal administrative bodies in conference with industry representatives to guide firms in avoiding future violation of the law. **Trade regulation rules** are binding rules published by government administrative bodies that are made available to all competitors and used to bring cases against alleged violators.

Federal agencies often settle a case informally if a firm agrees to discontinue actions the agency feels are in violation of federal rules. In 80 percent of the cases the firm signs a consent order. A **consent order** is an agreement by a firm that is presumed to be in violation of administrative law to "cease and desist" a practice. It generally avoids the need for further action by the federal agency. However, if the firm refuses to stop, the agency makes a formal complaint, and one of its examiners holds a hearing on the question. The examiner reviews the facts and makes a decision. The decision may then be reviewed by the full commission if necessary. Beyond this stage the firm may appeal through the court system, even to the U.S. Supreme Court.

In 1987 the Department of Transportation (DOT) found that Continental Airlines was violating consumer credit laws by delaying refunds on unused tickets. The department also found that the airline was not meeting other standards for airline customer service. The airline signed a consent order with the DOT. Continental agreed to refrain from violating federal regulations concerning airline service and promised to spend $69 million to upgrade its facilities.[2]

REGULATION AND DEREGULATION

Since 1900 the pendulum of regulation has swung back and forth. In this most crucial aspect of government-business relations, it is important for business managers to be aware of the history of government regulation.

THE GROWTH OF REGULATION   As we noted earlier, government regulation of business in the United States began with the Interstate Commerce Act of 1889 and the Sherman Antitrust Act of 1890. Regulations increased during the first two decades of this century in an attempt to control the excesses of huge monopolies like Standard Oil and U.S. Steel. The new antitrust laws showed the nation's resolve to maintain competition.

More laws were passed during the Great Depression—primarily to protect the basic rights of employees, retirees, consumers, and investors. The Wagner Act strengthened the unions; the Social Security Act helped to protect retired people; the Food, Drug, and Cosmetic Act protected consumers; the Securities and Exchange Commission Act helped protect investors; and the Robinson-Patman Act further tightened control of anticompetitive pricing. These new laws were passed mostly because public confidence in business was very low during the Depression.

During the Eisenhower years after World War II, public attitudes toward business improved, and government regulation eased up. For example, the Taft-Hartley Act improved business's position in dealing with unions.

During the 1960s and 1970s, many new laws affecting business behavior were enacted. Consumer protection was enhanced by the Consumer Product Safety Act. Minority and women's rights were strengthened by several laws, especially the Civil Rights Act of 1964, as we saw in Chapter 8. The Occupational Safety and Health Act aimed to improve safety in the workplace, and the National Environmental Policy Act aimed to clean up the environment. These laws and their generally strict enforcement by the courts and federal agencies produced a period of intense regulation. Regulation of competition was also further increased.

THE ERA OF DEREGULATION By the end of the 1970s, especially after the election of Ronald Reagan to the Presidency in 1980, an era of deregulation had begun. In 1977 and 1978 the Air Cargo Act and the Air Carrier Regulatory Reform Act deregulated air cargo and air passenger service, respectively. The Motor Carrier Act of 1980 and the Staggers Rail Act of the same year deregulated the trucking and railway industries. Thousands of new trucking firms and many new regularly scheduled airlines came into being. The Regulatory Flexibility Act (1981) greatly reduced the regulation of small businesses. Rules on auto safety and fuel economy that had been increasing expenses for the ailing automobile industry were eased or removed completely. Deregulation of financial institutions brought about huge changes in the functions performed by financial services firms such as Merrill Lynch and by commercial banks and savings and loan associations.

Enforcement of some of the consumer, environment, and antimerger laws weakened in the early 1980s, partly in response to the 1981–

As a result of deregulation in the airline industry, many new commuter airlines have started up to serve small markets.

1982 recession and partly because of the "hands off" philosophy of the Reagan administration. Less vigorous enforcement by the Antitrust Division of the Justice Department and the Federal Trade Commission contributed to a flood of mergers and acquisitions. The government's economic policy dictated that for the United States to compete in world markets it needed bigger, stronger companies. The result was dozens of mergers of large businesses that would not have been allowed in the 1970s.

The number of suits filed by the FTC dropped sharply from that of the two previous decades. In 1984 the Justice Department, jointly responsible with the FTC for enforcement, revised its guidelines for mergers in the following industries: industries facing foreign competition, declining industries, and industries in which merger would improve efficiency. The acquisition of Radio Corporation of America (RCA) by General Electric Company, for example, was approved.

In a separate action, Congress amended the Sherman Act to reduce liability for damages resulting from some joint ventures for research and development. This was done to encourage research by U.S. firms.

Daniel Oliver, chairman of the Federal Trade Commission, described the government's "temptation to overregulate" and interfere in the marketplace as the single greatest threat to consumers' welfare. His concept of consumer protection has angered many lawmakers, consumer groups, and antitrust attorneys, who contend that the agency has become ineffective, suffers from low morale, and seems too eager to protect business interests.[3]

In the near future we will see whether the deregulation trend continues or "reregulation" begins. Indiana's antitakeover law, as described in the chapter opening feature, might indicate a trend toward regulation of takeovers, for example. Calls for stronger regulation have ensued from evidence of slackened safety practices in some of the airlines and from the failure of savings and loans in several states, the "insider trading" scandals, and the stock market crash of October 1987.

The direction taken by the U.S. Supreme Court might make the largest difference in the regulation versus deregulation controversy. The retirement of Justice Lewis Powell and the failure of the Reagan administration to replace him with Robert H. Bork or Douglas H. Ginsburg, who were known to have "hands off" philosophies with respect to business, leaves the future of the high court's antitrust position in doubt. The effect on antitrust law of the naming of Justice Anthony M. Kennedy to Justice Powell's seat will unfold as we move into the 1990s.

Other Roles of Government

GOVERNMENT AS COMPETITOR

The two major political parties often differ on what government should do—how much it should regulate and how much it should compete with business. When a government takes over a service, it removes private business from that area of economic activity. The Tennessee Valley Authority (TVA), a major federal agency that produces electric

The U.S. Postal Service has improved its Express Mail service in response to competition from private delivery services like United Parcel Service and Emory Air Freight.

power, is a good example. The TVA was established during the Great Depression, when private industry was unwilling to risk the investment needed to provide electricity to some rural parts of the South.

For some years now the government-run National Railroad Passenger Corporation (known as Amtrak) has operated most of the railroad passenger service in the United States. Amtrak competes directly with Greyhound (which recently bought out its chief bus line rival, Trailways) and indirectly with the airlines. The U.S. Postal Service competes with United Parcel Service, Federal Express, and other delivery services. The U.S. Forestry Service competes with private tree nurseries. It raises 150 million trees at twelve nurseries around the country, and the private nurseries do not like it.

Many people feel that such competition is healthy. They say that the government competitors provide a benchmark by which private firms can be measured.

When the United States entered the space race, the federal government set up the National Aeronautics and Space Administration (NASA). The required investment was too great, and the potential payoff on the investment was too far off and intangible for private investors to assume the risk alone. Some people believe that the United States government should own and operate shipyards to compete with privately owned shipyards. The federal government is in the mail delivery and social security "businesses," and local governments are typically in the water, sewage, and garbage collection "businesses." These services are felt to be too important to the public welfare to be left to private firms. Philadelphia-based Consolidated Rail Corporation (Conrail) was created in 1976 from the Penn Central Railroad and five other bankrupt Northeastern railroads in order to maintain railroad freight service in 15 states throughout the Northeast and the Midwest.

As we saw in Chapter 1, the British government has returned many state-owned enterprises to private ownership in recent years. But what about the United States?

When President Reagan moved into the White House in 1981, he ordered his Secretary of Transportation, Drew Lewis, to start the process of returning Conrail to private ownership. This was in line with Mr. Reagan's 1980 campaign promise to support privatization. **Privatization** is the transfer of services from government to private ownership and control. The U.S. Immigration and Naturalization Service has five privately run detention centers in Denver, El Paso, Houston, Los Angeles, and Laredo, Texas. Sanitation and other public services are often privatized at the municipal level.

The What Do You Think? box presents two different perspectives of privatization with a special emphasis on whether or not privatization might be practical in developing nations.

privatization

WHAT DO YOU THINK?

Is Privatization a Good Idea?

Good arguments have been offered for privatization of public institutions, but there are also valid concerns about the application of privatization, especially in developing countries.

"Privatization is spreading and succeeding throughout the world—in developed and developing countries, in democracies and dictatorships and in capitalist, socialist and communist nations.

"Privatization means relying more on the private sector and less on government to satisfy people's needs. In the United States, its greatest inroads have been in state and local governments. For example, the average city now contracts out 27 percent of its municipal services in whole or in part to private firms, and the number is growing. Surveys of public officials reveal that they are privatizing their services on the pragmatic grounds that it cuts costs while maintaining or improving service quality; multinational studies, including my own [E. E. Savas] support these conclusions."

Counterarguments can be made as to the use of privatization in developing countries. "There are simply too many barriers and costs to privatization, limiting the number of companies a country can privatize. In many countries, political or ideological considerations stand in the way of privatization. Ministries or labor unions may be reluctant to give up control of an enterprise. . . . Formidable economic barriers to privatization may (also) exist. Potential buyers usually have alternative opportunities; realistically, there may not be buyers for any but the best-performing state enterprises, those offering low risk and high profit potential. . . .

"Finally, national governments have a multitude of potentially worthwhile (or politically necessary) economic and social programs on their agenda and they cannot fund all of them. They must carefully weigh the political, social, and economic costs and benefits of the choices they ultimately make. Because privatizing every state firm is an unrealistic goal, governments must select their candidates with great care."

Sources: E. E. Savas, "Private Enterprise Is Profitable Enterprise," *The New York Times,* Feb. 14, 1988, p. 2F; Lawrence H. Wortzel, " 'Privatizing' Does Not Always Work," *The New York Times,* Feb. 14, 1988, p. 2F. Copyright © 1988 by the New York Times Company. Reprinted by permission.

GOVERNMENT AS ECONOMIC STABILIZER

Whereas government's role as regulator is mostly to maintain competition in individual industries, its role as economic stabilizer is focused on macroeconomics—the big picture of our nation's stable economic growth and development. Starting with the Great Depression, our government assumed a large part of the responsibility for the nation's economic welfare and stability. President Franklin D. Roosevelt's program of legislation, the "New Deal," reflected this new role. It provided for banking and financial controls, which made it possible for the Federal Reserve System and the Treasury to adjust the nation's money supply. It included new laws for protection of worker's job security. It also included the Social Security program to ease the economic problems of retirement.

After World War II, more laws were passed to strengthen the economy. These were the Employment Act of 1946, the Humphrey-Hawkins Full Employment Act of 1978, and the Gramm-Rudman-Hollings Balanced Budget and Emergency Deficit Control Act of 1985.

The Employment Act declared federal responsibility to promote full employment, maximum economic growth, and price stability. It created the Council of Economic Advisers to help the President reach these goals. The council and the President must present an annual economic report to the nation, describing the state of the economy and current government programs to deal with it.

The Humphrey-Hawkins Act declared similar goals for employment, growth, and price stability. Added long-term goals included a balanced federal budget and an improved balance of trade. Experience proved that these objectives were not being met. Still another means of controlling spending was needed.

The Gramm-Rudman Act, as it is commonly known, makes specific national deficit reduction goals that the Congress must meet each year until 1991. In that year the federal budget should be balanced. Although the Gramm-Rudman Act is the source of much debate, its demand for a balanced federal budget has begun to have an impact. Responding to growing concerns abroad and at home about the huge U.S. trade and budget deficits, lawmakers are coming to believe that a balanced budget is important for economic stability. The stock market crash in 1987 was taken as a further sign of the need to balance the budget, to make our nation more productive and competitive in trade, and thus to improve the trade balance.

GOVERNMENT AS SUPPORTER

Government is not always the adversary of business. In fact, it is often its advocate. We saw this in the discussion of Indiana's antitakeover law at the beginning of this chapter and in the description of the Small Business Administration programs in Chapter 4.

The federal government has also supported commodity prices and has paid farmers to reduce production of wheat, corn, and other crops in order to keep prices high. Such support has kept many farming businesses, large and small, afloat through hard times such as the 1988 drought. Budget problems at the national level have put major pressure on Congress to reduce these supports in recent years.[4]

Manufacturers and banks, too, are sometimes aided by the government. Harley-Davidson, Inc., the motorcycle manufacturer, was aided by import restrictions on its foreign competitors. The restrictions improved Harley-Davidson's market share and profitability. Even huge corporations like Continental Illinois Bank, Chrysler Corporation, and Lockheed Aircraft have received large federal loans, loan guarantees, and other forms of support to help them through extremely hard times. These "bailouts" were thought necessary to protect regional economies and jobs and, in some cases, to secure the nation's defense. Lockheed and Chrysler are major defense contractors.

Another way in which government supports private enterprise is with information. Since 1980, federal legislation has been adopted requiring some 300 federally funded laboratories to encourage transfer of innovative technology to private firms and universities. The labs spend about $18 billion each year on research. Qualified firms need only pay a minimal licensing fee.[5]

The federal government also provides a wealth of statistical data that helps business. The U.S. Censuses—including the Census of Population, the Census of Housing, the Censuses of Retailing, Wholesaling and Selected Services, the Census of Manufactures, and others—are critical for business planning and marketing research.

GOVERNMENT AS CUSTOMER

The federal government is by far the single largest buyer of goods and services in the nation. The government spends billions of dollars each year for everything from rockets to rubber bands, from research on the Strategic Defense Initiative to advertising campaigns for the Army. Naturally, almost every business in the country wants a piece of this huge pie. As we saw in Chapter 11, government purchasing systems are quite formal and carefully specified by law. These systems control roughly one-fifth of all purchases in the United States. It is important that businesses be familiar with this huge market.

The federal government also often "buys" scientific research from business firms to serve the public interest. Federal appropriations for AIDS research, for example, has helped pharmaceutical firms to develop their research expertise. Huge contracts for the Strategic Defense Initiative or "Star Wars" program have done the same for many technical and defense-related contractors. Government-supported research often becomes the basis for commercial products, too. For example, the powdered drink mix Tang was first developed for the NASA space program.

Direct government purchases are often made by means of public bidding. A local government example is shown in Figure 21-4 (on p. 628). The ad invites bids from contractors. Public bidding is designed to eliminate favoritism or political influence in the award of contracts. It also provides for economical use of public funds. For such a system to work well, notice of the contract and bidding details must be given to as many prospective bidders as possible.

INVITATION FOR BIDS

The D.C. Public Schools, is soliciting bids on IFB NO. 096-AA-04-0-8-BB to furnish and install security alarm systems at various school buildings. All located within Washington, D.C. Bid Bond is required. Wage rates have been predetermined by the U.S. Department of Labor. The documents are available for pick up by calling (202) 724-4131/32. Bids will be publicly opened and read on March 25, 1988 at 2:30 P.M. in the Conference Room of the D.C. Public Schools, Procurement Branch, Room 807, Division of Logistical Support, 415 12th Street, N.W., Washington, D.C. 20004. COST RANGE: $250,000-$500,000.

FIGURE 21-4 / A classified ad by a public agency inviting bids on a public construction project. (*Source:* D.C. Public Schools.)

Many firms survive or fail depending on their success in getting government contracts. Some firms never even try for them. The government buys nearly every type of good and service, so many firms that do not currently have government contracts might succeed if they worked at getting them. Many of these firms would benefit from learning how to bid. Often, bidding systems provide "set-aside" funds to guarantee participation by minority and small business firms in large contracts.

GOVERNMENT AS "HOUSEKEEPER"

Just as the government serves the average citizen, it also serves the average business. Federal, state, and local governments provide a wide variety of services that make normal business operations possible. Cities and towns provide streets, lighting, sewers, and sanitation services. They provide security for firms such as grocery stores, insurance agencies, wholesalers, and factories. Cities or school districts provide educational opportunities for employees and their dependents. All of this helps to provide a "business climate" that can attract industry to a particular city or state.

Taxation

revenue taxes

restrictive taxes

Another part of the business climate is taxation. Taxes are imposed and collected by government at the federal, state, and local levels. **Revenue taxes** are taxes whose main purpose is to fund government services and programs. These represent the majority of taxes at all levels of government in the United States. Another class of taxes is called restrictive taxes. **Restrictive taxes** are levied to control certain activities that legislative bodies feel should be controlled.

REVENUE TAXES

income tax

Three main forms of revenue taxes are income taxes, property taxes, and sales taxes. **Income tax** is a tax paid by individuals and corporations on income received in a given tax year. Income taxes are the primary taxing devices at the federal level. All three types are used in different combinations at the state and local levels.

Figure 21-5 gives you some idea of how much the federal government relies on income taxes for revenues. During the period 1970–1976 the average percentage of total federal revenues from individual income tax was 45 percent, the average received from corporate income tax was 15 percent, and the average received from social insurance was 28 percent. In 1980 these percentages were 47, 12, and 31 percent, respectively. In the President's proposed budget for 1989, individual taxes represent 43 percent, corporate income taxes 12 percent, and social insurance 37 percent. The corporate income tax share is declining, but its contribution to Social Security is rising.

For tax years beginning after mid-1987, federal corporate tax rates start at 15 percent for income up to $50,000. This ranges up to 34 percent of income over $75,000. Individual income tax rates are as follows. Single taxpayers in 1988 paid 15 percent on taxable income up to $17,850 and 28 percent on income over $17,850. Married persons filing jointly paid 15 percent on taxable income up to $29,750 and 28 percent on income above $29,750.

FIGURE 21-5 / Federal receipts: 1970–1976 average, 1980, and 1989 (proposed), percentage by major source. (*Source:* U.S. Office of Management and Budget.)

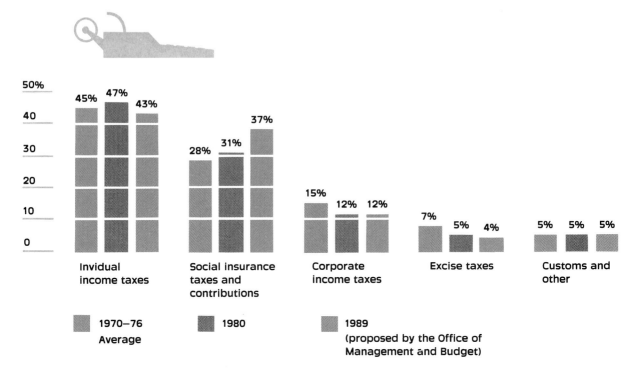

These tax rates are the result of Congress's overhaul of the U.S. Tax Code in the Tax Reform Act of 1986. Besides reducing the number of tax brackets and lowering rates, the bill removed many of the exemptions, deductions, and loopholes for individuals that existed in the old tax law. The result of the entire overhaul for individuals and businesses was intended to be "revenue neutral," that is, it was to keep the overall income tax "bite" at about the same level as it was before the Act. The picture is sure to change again in the tax years after 1988.

The 1986 tax law also included many changes for businesses. For instance, businesspeople could deduct only 80 percent of the cost of meals and entertainment and only when those meals were shown to be directly business-related. Another important change for businesses was the repeal of the investment tax credit—a deduction from tax obligation equal to 10 percent of the amount invested in many kinds of capital goods. This made it more expensive for a business to buy new equipment and buildings. The law also changed the rules for depreciation of property so that depreciation deductions from taxable revenue were reduced significantly for many businesses.

Sales taxes, which are collected by retailers, often make up an important part of state and local revenues.

progressive tax

Both federal and state income taxes are examples of progressive taxes. A **progressive tax** is one that is levied at a higher rate on higher-income taxpayers and at a lower rate on lower-income taxpayers.

Many individual states and some cities also levy individual and corporate income taxes. Some of these localities simplify computation of these taxes by basing them directly upon the amount paid by the business or individual in federal income tax.

FICA, the Social Security tax, is viewed by many people as a kind of income tax. Business firms and their employees each pay 7.51 percent of the employee's salary up to a maximum of $45,000. Businesses act both as a payee and a collector of FICA taxes. It represents 37 percent of federal revenues, as shown in Figure 21-5.

Sales taxes are levied by cities, states, and various local agencies such as school boards and fire districts. A sales tax is paid through retail stores, which act as collection agents when they sell their merchandise. The rate of sales tax varies greatly from state to state and from city to city. It also applies to different groups of products in different areas. Often, food and drug sales are exempted. A sales tax is an example of a regressive tax. A **regressive tax** is one by which poorer people pay a higher percentage of income than higher-income people pay. All pay the same percent of the selling price of what they buy at retail. But poorer people spend a much higher percent of their income in retail stores than middle-income and rich people do.

regressive tax

Property taxes include real estate taxes and personal property taxes on businesses and individuals. The property tax rates also vary from state to state and community to community. A property tax rate is generally a fixed percentage of the assessed value of the property in question. If a plant is assessed by the local assessment board to be worth a million dollars and the real property rate is 0.005 (one-half of 1 percent), the plant owner must pay $5,000 for a tax year. Sometimes, new businesses are granted exemptions from property taxes as an incentive for locating in a community or state.

Personal property taxes apply to such things as automobiles, trucks, equipment, inventories, and other non-real property owned by businesses or private individuals. They may or may not apply to financial assets. The rate is usually applied to personal assets held at the end of the calendar year.

value-added tax (VAT)

Still another form of revenue tax is being debated. The **value-added tax (VAT)** is a tax applied each time a good changes hands. It amounts to a percentage of the difference between the buying and the selling price and is paid by the seller. It would act as a type of national sales tax. The tax is already in use in Michigan and in many nations of Europe. It could replace the income tax completely if it could find enough support in Congress. VAT taxes are often criticized as being regressive.

RESTRICTIVE TAXES

Two major taxes are levied not just for their revenue. They are (1) federal and state excise taxes on jewelry, alcohol, tobacco, and gasoline and (2) import duties. Excise taxes serve both as a "deterrent of ex-

APPLICATION: BURGER KING
Legal Constraints on Restaurant Owners

When you own a business in the United States, the government is not just something "out there" that you read about in the newspapers. You must deal with the government—local, state, and federal—every day that you are in business.

The relationship can be a little frustrating at times, as one Burger King franchisee can attest. He opened his first Burger King® restaurant in 1969, at the age of 36. Good judgment and hard work paid off for him. He owns over 46 Burger King restaurants, including several in Rhode Island. His is one of the largest privately held chains of Burger King® restaurants in the country.

Government actions can be a two-edged sword for any business owner. Government provides essential services such as fire protection, police, and sewers and water in return for tax dollars. It also helps to educate potential employees and regulate business within a system of laws.

But government's efforts are not always so helpful, or at least they do not seem to be. For example, anyone opening a restaurant must comply with local building and zoning laws. A restaurant cannot be put in an area that is zoned (approved) only for houses, for instance. Each restaurant also has to comply with strict laws that specify approved building materials and construction to make sure the building is safe.

The problem is that getting building plans approved by the government and then dealing with the inspectors can sometimes be frustrating. To open his first restaurant, for example, he had to cope with a court order stopping construction. More recently, the Rhode Island Department of Environmental Management issued a stop-work order at his new headquarters in Cranston, Rhode Island. The order related to sediment that was collecting in a nearby stream.

Of course, while the construction and restaurant opening are being held up, the business owner is still running up expenses for land payments, labor, and various loans. Government-business interactions can often be quite tense. The frustrating thing, he says, is the way the problems sometimes just drag on. "It's okay to have a problem. It's okay to protect the environment. But you've got to act on it. You don't just sit there and let it drag and drag."

Questions

1. From an antitrust perspective, how would you define "effective" competition in the fast foods industry?

2. What do you think a franchisee would consider to be government's primary role as it interacts with business? Why?

3. Suppose that a local city government is considering whether or not to privatize the feeding of children in the public schools, inmates in the city's prison, and patients in the city-operated hospital. As a local Burger King franchisee, how would you react?

Source: "Burger King," *Ocean State Business*, May 13, 1985, pp. 9–11.

cesses"—to discourage what many regard as behavior that should be curtailed by government—and as a revenue source. Import duties were once a major revenue source as well as a kind of protection for home industries. The growth of free trade in the post–World War II era has resulted in a reduction in this revenue source. However, as long as the U.S. balance of trade remains unfavorable, there is always a chance that public sentiment in favor of import duties will reverse this trend.

Summary

Business and government interact in many ways. Business lobbies to influence government and involves itself in elections to public office. Government regulates many business activities and serves the business establishment in many other ways.

The Sherman, Clayton, and Robinson-Patman Acts are designed to maintain competition by prohibiting actions that tend to restrain trade. They are enforced by various administrative agencies, by the Justice Department, and by the court system.

The Environmental Protection Agency supervises the standards for air, water, and other forms of pollution mandated by the National Environmental Policy Act and other acts. These have resulted in significantly better environmental conditions in many parts of the United States but have raised the costs of production and waste disposal for many industrial firms. Many consumer protection laws, such as the truth in advertising and truth in packaging laws, have helped the average consumer.

The history of government regulatory activity began with the Interstate Commerce Act in 1889 and the Sherman Act in 1890. More laws were passed during the Great Depression to protect the basic rights of employees, retirees, consumers, and investors. The Robinson-Patman Act further tightened the regulation of monopolies. During the 1960s and 1970s, more laws controlling business were enacted. These included regulations for worker safety and several minority employment laws. By the end of the 1970s an era of deregulation had begun. As this era continued, regulating agencies permitted a flood of mergers and acquisitions. The government's economic policy dictated that for the nation to compete in world markets it needed bigger, stronger firms.

Besides being a regulator of business, government is also a competitor of business, an economic stabilizer, a supporter, a customer, and a "housekeeper" for business. It is a competitor when it expands postal service or builds a hydroelectric dam. It is an economic stabilizer when it helps to control the money supply. It is a supporter when it guarantees home loans or provides tax exemptions to attract industry to a region. It is a customer when it buys products such as bombers, typing paper, and consulting services. It is a housekeeper when it provides mail delivery, fire protection, and police services for business.

The levying of revenue taxes such as the corporate income tax has a great effect on the income of firms and thus on the funds available for expansion and for payment to owners. All firms collect income and FICA taxes from employees by payroll deductions. Retail firms also bear the burden of collection of sales taxes. Restrictive taxes like customs duties affect international trade. Excise taxes affect sellers of gasoline, tobacco, and luxury items by raising the prices of such merchandise and by requiring middlemen such as tobacco wholesalers to collect and forward proceeds to the government.

Review Questions

1. Describe some of the ways in which business influences government.

2. What is the main reason for antitrust laws?

3. Give two concrete examples of the deregulation of business.

4. Describe the way in which the FTC deals with an antitrust case.

5. Give examples of the roles of government as competitor and as economic stabilizer.

6. Distinguish between progressive and regressive taxes.

7. Describe the principal types of revenue taxes and how they affect business.

Discussion Questions

1. Why are "consumerism" issues not as popular in the 1980s as they were in the 1960s?

2. Does government act as supporter of small business as much as it acts as supporter of large business?

3. Which of the roles of government with respect to business is the most important from business's point of view? Which is most important from the consumer's point of view?

4. What effect could the loss of the investment tax credit have on a small business?

Key Terms

antitrust laws
tying contract
exclusive dealing agreement
interlocking directorate
environmental impact statement

voluntary compliance
trade practice rules
trade regulation rules
consent order
privatization
revenue taxes

restrictive taxes
income tax
progressive tax
regressive tax
value-added tax (VAT)

JUST HOW FIRE RESISTANT SHOULD COMMERCIAL PLANES BE?

Commercial airlines argue that air travel is one of the safest forms of transportation, but between 1974 and 1984 in the United States an average of 30 people per year who survived when a plane crashed died when the plane then caught fire. Largely because of two such tragedies—an Air Canada flight in 1983 in which 23 people died and a British Airways fire in 1985 in which 55 people were burned to death—the Federal Aviation Administration (FAA) enacted new guidelines for the construction of commercial airliners. By August 1990, materials used in the interiors of new airplanes and those being renovated must meet strict guidelines limiting the amount of heat they release in a fire.

Aircraft producers, including Boeing and McDonnell Douglas Corporation, are trying to develop safer materials, but they feel that the FAA's standards are too high. They developed what they consider to be much improved construction materials, but these did not meet the FAA tests. The agency and the aircraft firms do not agree on the cost of meeting the standards either. The industry cost estimate is more than 100 times as high as the FAA's estimate.[6]

Questions

1. Which of the government's roles is the FAA playing in this case?
2. If, for example, it were possible to guarantee no more air passenger deaths by fire by requiring the aircraft producers to spend $5 billion, would you recommend the expenditure? Would your answer be different if 20 percent higher airfares were a necessary result?

HOW SHOULD THE GOVERNMENT DEAL WITH THE TOBACCO INDUSTRY?

Beginning in 1965, health warning labels were placed on cigarette packages, but the controversy over smoking dates from 1865. Even back then, when packaged cigarettes had just been introduced, selling them to minors was prohibited. And by 1895, an active antismoking league had been formed. In fact, this group was so successful that cigarette smoking was banned in fourteen states by 1917. But during the two world wars and up until 1953, cigarette sales boomed, and antismoking groups faded from the scene. All prohibitions against smoking had been repealed by 1930.

After the mid-1950s, the number of reports linking smoking to health problems grew. Pressure was brought on Congress to warn the public. In 1965, warning labels were required. In 1970, television and radio ads for cigarettes were banned. More recently, the package warnings were made stronger. There has been a constant battle between the tobacco industry and health advocates. Some people would like to see the sale of cigarettes made illegal. The tobacco industry has had to fight to stay alive.[7]

Questions

1. Which of the government's roles come into play in this case?
2. What rights of the tobacco industry are in question here? What about the rights of smokers? What about the rights of nonsmokers?
3. Do you feel that the tobacco farmer has a right to farm subsidies? Why or why not?

Business Law and Ethics

n this chapter we will focus on two main topics: business law and ethics. The law touches many aspects of business activities and operations. Businesspeople must know which laws pertain to their activities and understand the letter and spirit of those laws. Just as in our personal lives, ignorance of the law is not a proper excuse for not complying with it.

The chapter begins with a look at the role of law in society. We will study the sources of law and distinguish between public and private law.

Next we will focus more specifically on business law—that body of law that has particular application to business activities. The specific areas of business law that we will look at include the Uniform Commercial Code and the laws of contracts, agency, bailment, property, warranty, negotiable instruments, torts, and bankruptcy.

Following our survey of business law, we will take an in-depth look at business ethics. We will show how business ethics and the law are related. Next comes an examination of ethical codes, in which we will also look at the need for training managers and workers to deal with ethical problems.

The latter part of the chapter poses a number of ethical dilemmas that might arise as businesspeople interact with stakeholders. We will look at ethics and customer relations, ethics and supplier relations, ethics and competitor relations, ethics and employee relations, and ethics and ecology.

The chapter ends with a brief look at another dimension of ethical behavior—whistleblowing.

The International Association for Financial Planning (IAFP), with 25,000 members, is the largest professional organization for people in the business of helping customers plan their financial futures.

Financial planners sell various investments to their clients. Planners make their money either from fees charged to the customers or from commissions paid by the companies offering investment opportunities.

At a recent meeting of the IAFP the center of attention was not a new service for planners to offer their customers. It was a new Porsche sports car. Oppenheimer Management Corporation was offering the car to help promote three new mutual funds. Whichever planner got the highest total sales of those funds—exceeding $5 million with a minimum of 10 sales—by the end of the year would win the choice of a Porsche 944 Turbo, a Jaguar XJ-S, or a Corvette.

While the contest intrigued some planners, it outraged others. They feared that financial planners, who present themselves as offering objective investment advice, would be compromised by contests tied to how much of a particular product they sell.

Although no planner would acknowledge that a contest has made him or her push the wrong product at the wrong time, some planners and sponsors of investment products say that it happens.

Most financial planners insist that abuses are rare. The needs of the client, they say, are uppermost in the minds of the large majority of planners. Others add that incentives are merely part of the free enterprise system, whether they are offered to computer salespeople, brokers, or financial planners.

Still, some groups of financial planners have become concerned enough that they have adopted ethics policies covering "noncash incentives." The policies state that planners who accept such prizes have a duty to disclose them to their clients. However, the policies are not clear on the crucial matter of when and how the incentives should be disclosed.[1]

Financial planners must abide by certain laws. For example, if they enter into a contract with a client, it must meet the requirements of a valid contract. In addition, the members must abide by the government's rules covering the sale of securities. They also have to abide by the rules of their professional association, the Institute of Certified Financial Planners. That association has a code of ethics that establishes standards of behavior for its members. Let's begin our examination of business law and ethics with a look at the role that law plays in society.

The Role of Law in Society

law

Law is the set of standards, principles, and rules a society establishes to govern the actions of its members. The law protects individuals and organizations from wrongdoers. It also spells out rules by which we must abide and the penalties for failure to do so.

SOURCES OF LAW

Law evolves and grows over time in response to changes in a society's norms and values. Laws arise from (1) customs and judicial precedents, (2) legislative action, and (3) administrative rulings. The three corresponding types of law are common law, statutory law, and administrative law.

common law

Common law is the body of unwritten law that has grown out of previous judicial decisions and accepted practices and customs. Common law was originated and developed in England, and the United States inherited that system. All states have English common law as their basis, except Louisiana, where the French Civil Code is used. Where there is no explicit written law, court decisions are based on *precedent*. This means that decisions made in earlier cases involving the same legal point will guide the court. Common law is often called *case law*.

statutory law

Statutory law is a system of laws that are written, or codified, by legislative bodies. City councils, state legislatures, and the Congress of the United States all enact statutory laws. The U.S. Constitution, which is the supreme law of the land, and the various state constitutions are the primary basis for statutory law.

administrative law

Administrative law is the set of rules and regulations developed by government agencies and commissions on the basis of their interpretations of the specific statutory laws that they administer. The Federal Trade Commission, for example, issues regulations that pertain to practices such as false and deceptive advertising.

PUBLIC AND PRIVATE LAW

Regardless of its source, law can also be classified as public or private. The classification depends on whether the law seeks to protect society as a whole or individual members of that society.

public law
private law

Public law is the branch of law that relates to society as a whole—for example, criminal law and administrative law. **Private law** (or civil law) is the branch of law that relates to relationships between individuals, groups of individuals, and corporations. Business law is a part of private law. Insider trading on Wall Street, false advertising, patent infringement, and price fixing are covered by public law. Jayne's Fashion Shoppe's failure to pay Orlando Creations for a shipment of dresses is covered by private law.

business law

Business Law

All law affects business in some way, directly or indirectly. **Business law** is the body of law that pertains particularly to business activities.

The discussions that follow focus on the most important concepts of business law that are identified in Figure 22-1.

THE UNIFORM COMMERCIAL CODE

Many laws pertaining to business are state laws. These all govern the same general kinds of business activity. However, since they were enacted by individual state legislatures, they vary from state to state. This creates problems for firms that do business in many of the states.

Efforts to bring some degree of uniformity to state laws relating to business began in the 1890s. By the 1950s, uniform laws pertaining to specific business matters such as sales, partnerships, negotiable instruments, and related subjects had been developed and adopted by nearly all of the states. These generally accepted acts included the Uniform Sales Act, the Uniform Partnership Act, and the Uniform Negotiable Instruments Act. The problem was that not all of the states adopted all of these acts.

Uniform Commercial Code (UCC)

A uniform and comprehensive code was needed that would include all of the various uniform acts. The result was the Uniform Commercial Code. The **Uniform Commercial Code (UCC)** is a statute that combines and coordinates several specific uniform acts regarding business into one overall commercial code. All states except Louisiana have adopted the UCC in its entirety. Louisiana has adopted only a portion of it.

The UCC does not cover all areas of commercial law. For example, the code provides that it shall be supplemented by the principles of common law that pertain to fraud and the capacity to contract. Also, the various states still rely on common law precedent in solving some commercial disputes.

CONTRACTS

People engage in a great many transactions and agreements in the business world. For example, firms contract with suppliers for materials, customers for purchases, and employees for jobs.

FIGURE 22-1 / Major concepts of business law.

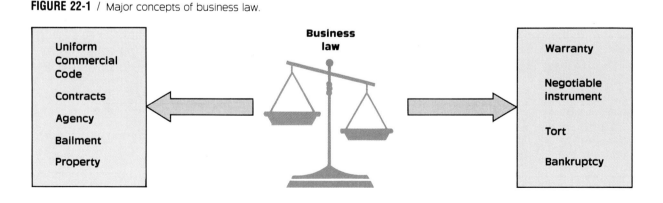

A **contract** is a mutual agreement between two or more people to perform or not perform certain acts. An oral contract is enforceable, but proving its specific details might be difficult, especially if there are no witnesses. To be valid, a contract must include the following elements:

- An *agreement*: An offer seriously and clearly made by one party to another party, who must accept it seriously and clearly and without reservation.
- *Consideration*: Something of value that each party gets or gives. With few exceptions it must be shown that both parties intended to bargain and have actually exchanged something for a contract to be enforceable by a court. Consideration can take the form of money, other property, or individual rights.
- *Competence*: The ability to incur liability (debt) or to gain legal rights. A person who is insane or below a certain age (it varies from state to state) might not be legally competent to make a contract.
- A *legal purpose*: A contract cannot be enforced unless the actions agreed upon are legal in the jurisdiction where the contract is made.

A court will enforce a contract if it meets the four requirements. Figure 22-2 (on p. 642) is an example of a contract that has all the necessary elements to be binding on both parties.

In most cases, contracts are honored, and both parties are satisfied. In other cases, both parties agree to cancel the agreement. Special circumstances may sometimes allow one party to be excused from fulfilling his or her part of a contract. A person who is bankrupt, for example, has a legal excuse for not living up to the terms of an installment credit agreement. This person is not in breach of contract. **Breach of contract** occurs when one party to a contract fails to live up to the contract's terms without having a legal excuse for doing so.

A person who has suffered breach of contract by another has three alternatives under the law: (1) discharge, (2) damages, or (3) specific performance. Suppose Wagner Pet Supply agrees to deliver 100 baby white rabbits to Sam's Flower Shop by April 1, in time for a major Easter promotion, for $300. But Wagner calls Sam on April 1 and says he cannot make delivery until after Easter. Under the law, Sam can do any of the following:

1. *Discharge.* Whenever one party to a contract fails to deliver or violates any of the terms of an agreement, the second party is free simply to ignore his or her obligation under the contract. In this case, Sam can choose not to pay the $300 to Wagner and may contact another pet supplier.
2. *Sue for damages.* One party to a contract has the right to sue for damages (legally demand payment for loss) because of the nonperformance of the other. Sam can go to court and sue Wagner for any loss sustained because of Wagner's failure to honor the contract. This could include any increase in Sam's cost for the pets paid to a second pet supply house plus all of Sam's court costs in bringing the suit itself.

AGREEMENT

This agreement, made this 5th day of March, 1989, between Sam's Flower Shop, hereinafter called "the buyer" and Wagner Pet Supply, hereinafter called "the seller."

WITNESSETH:

In consideration of their mutual promises contained herein, the parties hereto agree as follows:

The buyer agrees to purchase one hundred (100) live white rabbits.

The seller agrees to deliver said rabbits to buyer not later than April 1, 1989.

The buyer and the seller both agree to a selling price in the full amount of $300.00, the said amount to be paid not later than ten days from the date of delivery.

IN WITNESS THEREOF, the said parties have hereunto set their hands on this, the date first above written in this agreement.

Witness:

Shirley Cole

(for both parties)

Sam Carter
Bill Wagner

FIGURE 22-2 / A typical written agreement to buy and sell.

3. *Require specific performance.* A party can be required to live up to the original terms of the agreement if money damages are not adequate to compensate. In other words, if there were still time to meet the original delivery date and there were no other sources of supply, the court might insist that Wagner deliver the rabbits as promised.

✗ AGENCY

agency-principal relationship

Many business relationships are based on the law of agency. An **agency-principal relationship** is an arrangement in which one party (the agent) is authorized and consents to act on behalf of another party (the principal). An agent must always act for the benefit and under the control of the principal. The principal is liable for the agent's acts that come within the scope of the agent's authority.

As we saw at the beginning of this chapter, financial planners act as agents for the producers of investments. The investment companies are the principals and thus are bound by agreements made by the planners with customers. Financial planners are paid a commission on the investments they sell. Many agents are paid by principals on the commission basis.

NOT ON TEST

BAILMENT

Similar to the agency-principal relationships and also common to everyday business practice is the bailor-bailee relationship. The law of bailment covers the surrender of personal property by one party to another with the expectation that the property will be returned in the future. The person surrendering the property is the *bailor*. The person receiving the property is the *bailee*.

bailor-bailee relationship

A **bailor-bailee relationship** is an arrangement in which one party (the bailor) gives possession and control of his or her property to another party (the bailee) but retains ownership of that property. A public warehousing company (the bailee) might store a large shipment of goods for a manufacturer (the bailor). Transfer of these goods to the warehousing company is known as a *bailment*. The bailee accepts certain responsibilities for safekeeping of the goods.

PROPERTY

property

Property means ownership of a tangible or intangible thing that has value, including the right to possess, use, or dispose of it. The two main types are real property and personal property.

real property

Real property is land and its permanent attachments, such as houses, garages, trees, mineral rights, and office buildings. Real property is often referred to as real estate.

personal property

Personal property is all tangible and intangible property other than real property, such as furniture, clothing, cars, bank accounts, stock certificates, and government securities. Personal property is movable. We discussed *trademarks* and *patents* in Chapter 12. Both are personal

A firm's real property may include buildings and land; its personal property may include equipment, furniture, cash, and securities.

copyright

property. Copyrights are also personal property. A **copyright** grants creators of dramatic, musical, and other intellectual properties or their heirs exclusive rights to their published or unpublished works for as long as the creator lives, plus 50 years. The Copyright Office of the Library of Congress issues copyrights.

TRANSFERRING PROPERTY

deed

Deeds and leases are important in the transfer of rights to real property. A **deed** is a legal document by which an owner of real property transfers ownership to someone else. A *quitclaim deed* merely transfers the seller's interests with no guarantees about the deed's quality. With a *warranty deed* the seller can be held liable for any liens or other defects that are not noted in the deed.

A lease, as we discussed in Chapter 17, is an agreement to grant use of an asset for a period of time in return for regular stated payments. The property owner is the landlord or lessor. Leasing permits the lessee (or tenant in the case of real property leases) to avoid the need for long- or intermediate-term financing for the land, building, or equipment needed for the business. By leasing, the lessee avoids carrying extra debt on his or her balance sheet.

title

The transfer of rights to personal property is accomplished by a transfer of title. A **title** indicates legal possession of an item of personal property and the right to use it. When you sell your car, you must sign over the title to the new owner.

WARRANTY

warranty

A **warranty** is a representation, or a legal promise, made by the seller that assures the buyer that the product is as represented by the seller. There are two kinds of warranty: express and implied.

An *express warranty* is a specific representation made by the seller about the product. An example is a label on a shirt that says "50 percent cotton, 50 percent polyester."

An *implied warranty* is an unstated warranty legally imposed on the seller that suggests that all merchandise will perform properly for the purpose intended. Suppose you buy a food blender and the motor burns out after one week's normal use. You could return the blender or keep it and sue for damages, even though no express warranty was made. The warranty was implied.

The Federal Trade Commission requires sellers to specify the time period covered by a warranty and spell out the meaning of the warranty. For most products, sellers offer limited warranties. Some warrant their products against "defects of material or workmanship" for 30 or 90 days. Others go a lot farther. Sears, for example, offers a one-year replacement guarantee (not just repair) on some of its appliances and a lifetime warranty on its Craftsman hand tools.

NEGOTIABLE INSTRUMENTS

negotiable instrument

Negotiable instruments are an important part of business. A **negotiable instrument** is a piece of paper that is evidence of a contractual relationship and that can be transferred from one person or business to another. Examples include checks and certificates of deposit.

In addition to being written, the UCC says that a negotiable instrument must (1) be signed by the person who puts it into circulation (the maker or drawer), (2) contain an unconditional promise to pay a certain amount of money, (3) be payable on demand or at a specific future date, and (4) be payable to the order of a specific person or to the order of the bearer of the instrument.

endorsement

Negotiable instruments are transferred from one party to another by endorsement. **Endorsement** is the act of signing one's name to a negotiable instrument, having the effect of making it transferable to another party.

The UCC discusses four types of endorsements. When you sign only your name on the back of a check made out to you, you are making a *blank endorsement.* (See Figure 22-3.) A *special endorsement* specifies a particular person to whom the instrument is transferred. A *qualified endorsement* limits the endorser's liability in case the instrument is backed by insufficient funds. For example, suppose you have a check made out to you by J. S. Jones. You want to use the check to buy a new dress. By writing "without recourse" above your signature on the back of the check, you limit your liability in case Jones has insufficient funds to cover the amount of the check. A *restrictive endorsement* limits the negotiability of the instrument. If a check is made out to you

FIGURE 22-3 / The four types of endorsements.

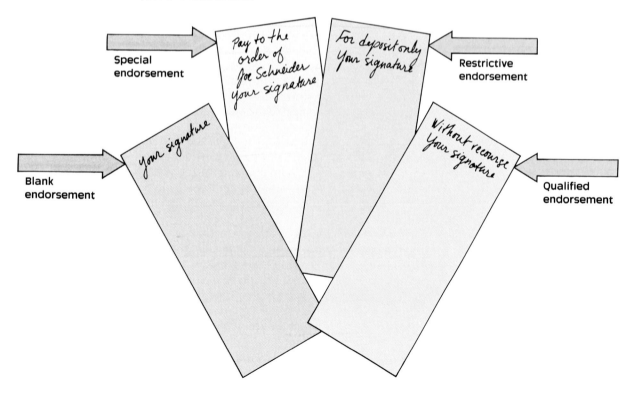

Special endorsement

Pay to the order of Joe Schneider your signature

For deposit only Your signature

Restrictive endorsement

Blank endorsement

your signature

Without recourse Your signature

Qualified endorsement

and you endorse it by writing "for deposit only" above your signature, it can only be deposited in your account.

TORTS

tort

A **tort** is a wrongful act, other than a breach of contract, that violates private law and results in injury to a person's body, property, or good name. Examples of torts are trespass, assault and battery, libel (defamatory words written about another person's character), slander (defamatory words spoken about another person's character), false imprisonment, fraud, and infringement of patent. Tort law is concerned with compensating people who are injured because of torts committed by others. The two major groups of torts are intentional tort and negligence.

intentional tort

Assault, slander, and libel are examples of intentional torts. An **intentional tort** is a wrongful act that is purposefully committed and results in injury to another person's body, property, or good name. A security guard in a department store who uses unreasonable force to detain a suspected shoplifter might be committing a tort. Under the law of agency the store itself could be held liable for any injury to the suspect.

Another business-related example of an intentional tort is patent infringement. For example, IBM has contended that some foreign computer manufacturers have infringed on its patents in producing IBM "clones."

negligence

As far as business is concerned, the most common type of tort activity is negligence. **Negligence** is a wrongful act that causes injury to another person's body, property, or good name as a result of careless, but not intentional, behavior.

Negligence exists when a person has failed to exercise reasonable care in his or her behavior. If such negligence causes injury to another person, the person who failed to exercise reasonable care is liable for the damage. For example, the manager of a discount store positioned buckets around the store because of a leaky roof. The roof had been leaking for seven weeks when a shopper slipped in water from an overturned bucket. Most people probably would find it unreasonable for the manager to wait so long to have the roof repaired. Thus the store was held to be negligent and liable for the customer's injuries.

In numerous cases in business, negligence is alleged to be the cause of customer and employee injury and death. In recent years, however, the area of negligence that has been in the news most is product liability.

product liability

Product liability is the concept that businesses are liable for injuries caused by negligence in the design, manufacture, sale, and use of products. Some states have extended the concept of product liability so that a person who takes a company to court need not demonstrate that injury was due to negligence or that the company was at fault. This tougher concept is called strict product liability. **Strict product liability** is a concept that businesses are liable for injuries caused by their products even if there is no proof of negligence or fault in the design, manufacture, sale, and use of products.

strict product liability

APPLICATION: BURGER KING

The Battle of the Burgers®

When your main competitor spends about $300 million per year more than you do on advertising, you have to do something dramatic to make yourself heard.

That was the situation facing Burger King Corporation executives in early 1982. While their earlier advertising themes like "Have it your way®" and "Aren't you hungry®" had been successful, it was still tough competing against a giant like McDonald's. So, in late 1982, Burger King Corporation launched "The Battle of the Burgers®" campaign. This ad campaign compared Burger King hamburgers directly to those of McDonald's and Wendy's. Burger King's ads said that its surveys showed that customers preferred Burger King burgers to those of McDonald's or Wendy's. The dramatic ads said that the Burger King Whopper® sandwich won nationwide tests over McDonald's and Wendy's. The ads also said that Burger King's burgers were bigger and were flame broiled, not fried like those of their competitors.

Wendy's and McDonald's sued Burger King Corporation. They claimed that the Burger King ads were inaccurate and that they did not show which burgers were really best. Without in any way agreeing that their competitors were right, Burger King Corporation agreed to phase out the ads. Wendy's and McDonald's dropped their suits. However, the ads must have had an effect. Burger King's sales shot up by 10 percent in 1982, almost twice McDonald's 5.8 percent increase.

The agreement by which Burger King dropped its ads and its competitors dropped their suits in no way required that Burger King Corporation desist from comparative ads again. In 1983 it launched another round of "Battle of the Burger®" ads featuring the theme that flame broiling is best.

In 1984 the Battle of the Burgers went international. In West Germany, the regulations on comparative advertising are strict. Ads cannot be dishonest or misleading, cannot degrade another product, and must serve a consumer need. Burger King ads in West Germany stressed the differences between flame broiling and frying.

Meanwhile, in the United States the battle of the burgers goes on. In 1988, Burger King Corporation launched a new campaign: "We do it like you'd do it.®" Among other things the ads ask "Why aren't there outdoor frying pans?" (Because, of course, most people broil their burgers, as does Burger King.) The new ads make their point without knocking the competitors by name.

Questions

1. Comparative advertising is advertising in which the marketer compares its brand to rival brands identified by brand name. What are the potential benefits and dangers of this type of advertising to Burger King Corporation?

2. Develop a code of ethics for Burger King Corporation.

3. Develop a hypothetical situation that poses one or more ethical dilemmas for a Burger King franchisee.

Critics of the strict product liability doctrine claim that it unfairly makes manufacturers liable for any injury related to their products whether the manufacturer could have foreseen or prevented it or not. They also say that it unfairly makes manufacturers liable even when the injury might reasonably have been avoided by the injured person.

market share liability

Market share liability is a concept that allocates liability for product injuries among manufacturers of a class of product on the basis of their share of the market. This doctrine was established by the California Supreme Court in a 1980 case. The plaintiff, Judith Sindell, filed a class action suit against six firms that manufactured DES between 1941 and 1971. DES is a drug that was authorized by the Food and Drug Administration (FDA) in 1947 on an experimental basis for use in preventing miscarriages. DES had been authorized by the FDA before 1947 for other uses. In 1971 the FDA ordered manufacturers to cease marketing DES as a miscarriage preventative.

Although roughly 200 manufacturers marketed DES at the time Ms. Sindell's mother took it, not all of them were included in the suit. When Ms. Sindell's precancerous growths were discovered years after her mother took the drug, it was impossible to determine which of those firms had produced the specific batch of DES that had caused Ms. Sindell's injury. Her lawyers asserted that (1) the manufacturers named in the suit produced 90 percent of the DES marketed and (2) they could be held liable in proportion to their market share even though Ms. Sindell could not identify which firm produced the drug that caused her injury. This doctrine removes the requirement, previously essential in any type of product liability action, that a plaintiff show that a specific product was the direct cause of the injury.

BANKRUPTCY

bankruptcy

Bankruptcy is a condition in which a firm or an individual cannot meet maturing financial obligations (insolvency) and has liabilities that exceed the value of its assets. Such a person or firm is said to be in bankruptcy. Federal legislation covers the bankruptcy procedure. The purpose is to relieve bankrupt people and firms of financial obligations so that they can start anew.

Bankruptcy can be voluntary or involuntary. Under *voluntary* bankruptcy a debtor (person or firm) files a petition in federal court claiming inability to pay debts because the debts exceed available assets. Under *involuntary* bankruptcy one or more creditors file a petition requesting that a person or firm be judged bankrupt.

Individuals have two options under the Federal Bankruptcy Act. Bankrupt individuals can set up a three-to-five-year debt repayment plan (Chapter 13 of the bankruptcy act) while retaining most of their assets. The other option (Chapter 7, which is also available to firms) is to set up a liquidation plan under which a person's or a firm's assets are divided among creditors. Most businesses that go bankrupt do so under Chapter 11 of the act. Once a firm files, it has court protection from creditors and can continue to operate instead of having to liquidate. Most of the firms that file for voluntary bankruptcy eventually emerge to survive and grow. The reorganization gives a firm time to seek new sources of funds and to make deals with creditors. Chapter 11 is intended to encourage reorganization rather than liquidation.

Several years ago Manville Corporation filed under Chapter 11 to at least temporarily suspend thousands of product liability lawsuits. The suits were filed by people who claimed to have contracted cancer and other diseases caused by asbestos, which Manville produced. Three years later, A.H. Robins took a similar step. Robins was facing thousands of product liability lawsuits from claimants who suffered from life-threatening infections, infertility, spontaneous abortions, and other injuries caused by its Dalkon Shield birth control device.

Many people criticized Manville and Robins for filing under Chapter 11. Some said that the companies were acting unethically if they filed to avoid having to pay as much in damages as the firms would have without the bankruptcy proceedings. Others defended the filings. They said that if the companies were to be liquidated, people whose injuries might not show up until years after the firms were gone would probably never be compensated.

Business Ethics

The behavior of business owners, managers, and employees is governed to a large extent by the laws we discussed in Chapter 21 and elsewhere in this book. Still, these laws provide only a minimum standard of behavior. Recent scandals, such as those involving insider trading in the stock market and the selling of national secrets by U.S. citizens, have focused attention on business and white-collar crime. More than in the past, people who commit white-collar crime are receiving jail terms. These include board members of major corporations, bankers, lawyers, journalists, and investment analysts.

business ethics

The recent scandals have also refocused attention on business ethics. **Business ethics** is a system of "oughts"—a collection of principles and rules of conduct based on beliefs about what is right and wrong business behavior. Behavior that conforms to these principles is considered to be ethical business behavior. Otherwise, it is unethical.

While the laws of a country and a system of ethics might seem to be separate, laws are really only products of a culture's ethics. For hundreds of years, philosophers have discussed ethics, laws, and how ethical decisions should be made.

Some philosophers say that behavior is ethical if it follows the will of God. This school of thought says that guidelines for moral and ethical behavior are to be found in religious writings. They believe that the Bible, the Koran, or another religious writing is the basis for determining whether an action is "good" or "bad."

Some other philosophers judge an action by its value to society. Utilitarianism asks the question, "What is the utility of this behavior or action for society as a whole?" It holds that the best action is that which does the most good for the most people. It says that to behave ethically, we should choose to maximize the benefits to society.

There are, of course, other schools of thought about what is ethical behavior. The important point is that ethics provides the framework for our system of laws.

The Meat Inspection Act of 1906 was a major accomplishment for advocates of consumer protection.

ETHICAL CODES

Individual business firms, industry associations, nonprofit organizations, and professional groups often establish their own ethical codes.

The U.S. government also has an ethics office—the Office of Government Ethics—as do many states and local governments. A **code of ethics** is a formal, published collection of values and rules that are used to upgrade and guide behavior. A firm's code of ethics sets standards for dealing ethically with all of its stakeholders. Such codes deal with issues like accepting business gifts, attempting to influence government regulatory officials, and using company property for personal use.

Company codes of ethics range from one-page general statements to lengthy booklets of detailed rules. The underlying belief is that ethical behavior is in the firm's best long-run interest. But to have any real meaning, the code must be communicated to employees, contain provisions for dealing with violations, have solid backing by top manage-

CORPORATE VALUES

Sound, responsible human relationships are the foundation of our way of doing business. Therefore, we place primary value upon the people who are our customers, our employees, and our agents, brokers and consultants.

- We are dedicated to serving customers and working with them to identify and respond to their needs. Our dealings with customers will be courteous, helpful and cooperative.

- Because all of our employees are important to our success, we will respect their individuality, recognize and reward their good performance, provide opportunities for their growth and advancement, and encourage their participation in decision-making.

- Our agents, brokers and consultants are vital to our success. We are committed to responsive and responsible relationships with them.

We consider respect, trust and integrity to be essential in all our dealings. We expect honest, ethical behavior from ourselves and we encourage it in others.

Because our associates live and work in the larger context of society, we value and encourage responsible individual and corporate citizenship. We recognize our obligation to be a positive influence in the communities in which we operate.

We are both progressive in our outlook and prudent in our management of our resources. We value high-quality work and superior results at the individual, unit and corporate levels.

Without apology, we are profit-oriented, for only profitable companies can adapt and survive to meet their long-term commitments to their customers, their employees and their stockholders.

FIGURE 22-4 / A statement of corporate values for the Provident Companies. (*Source:* Provident Companies, Chattanooga, TN.)

ment, and be consistent with the company's values and the corporate culture. A statement of corporate values for Provident Companies is reproduced in Figure 22-4.

Ethics training workshops are becoming more common as a way to train both managers and workers to deal with ethical problems. A typical workshop focuses on a hypothetical situation that poses several ethical dilemmas. Figure 22-5 is an example of an abbreviated case study from a recent workshop. McDonnell Douglas Corporation, General Dynamics, and Chemical Bank are among the growing number of companies that are using these workshops.

In the discussions that follow, we look briefly at several ethical dilemmas that can arise when businesspeople deal with customers, suppliers, competitors, and employees. (See Figure 22-6 on p. 652.) Ethical issues also often arise in connection with ecology.

Jack Smith, division vice-president of a major defense contractor, opens a bulky envelope marked "Confidential and Personal." In it he finds a set of figures that appear to be cost data worked up by his company's major competitor for a Navy fighter plane contract. An accompanying note from one of Jack's best marketing managers attests that the document is the real thing. Clearly, this could be a major advantage in preparing Jack's company's own bid.

Jack calls in two trusted aides to discuss the pros and cons of using the figures. His marketing vice-president sees no problem; everyone in the industry tries to get reliable intelligence on competitors' plans, and Jack himself had recently reminded his top managers how vital this was. But Jack's executive assistant warns of possible risks. The figures might have been bought or obtained with a promise of some quid pro quo; if so, it could blow up in the company's face if discovered.

What should Jack do?

FIGURE 22-5 / The secret envelope. (*Source:* Alan L. Otten, "Ethics on the Job: Companies Alert Employees to Potential Dilemmas," *The Wall Street Journal,* July 14, 1986, p. 17. Reprinted by permission of *The Wall Street Journal,* © Dow Jones & Company, Inc., 1986. All Rights Reserved.)

Business firm	Advertising practices Personal selling practices Product decisions Marketing research practices Pricing practices	Customers

Business firm	Order practices Delivery practices Gift giving practices Entertainment practices	Suppliers

Business firm	Corporate spying Corporate dirty tricks Takeover practices	Competitors

Business firm	Sexual harassment Health and safety practices Two-tier work force Drug and alcohol addiction	Employees

FIGURE 22-6 / Some sources of ethical issues that can arise as a firm interacts with stakeholders.

ETHICS AND CUSTOMER RELATIONS

Many interactions between firms and their customers are governed by laws. Price fixing and false advertising, for example, are illegal. But what happens when the law that pertains to a certain practice is unclear—or nonexistent?

In advertising there often is a very fine line between legal puffery (minor exaggeration in claims about a product) and illegal deception. Does a different set of ethical factors come into play for advertising aimed at children? Are special ethical guidelines needed for advertising sponsored by hospitals, physicians, attorneys, and accountants?

There are also possibilities for unethical behavior with customers in personal selling. A salesperson talking one-on-one to a prospect might be able to apply extra pressure and sell something that could

What ethical factors are involved in TV advertising targeted to children?

harm the customer. The financial planners we discussed at the beginning of this chapter were offered large sales incentives by the suppliers of various investments. Is it ethical, or fair to the customer, for the planner to push an investment in order to get the gift? Should the planner tell the customer of the gift?

Ethical issues often involve the product itself. For example, is it ethical for auto makers to force accessories on buyers by making them standard equipment rather than options? What about grouping many options into a package that a customer must take to get discounts—or else pay higher prices for the individual options? What about buying a competitor's product, tearing it apart to learn how it works, and copying it without violating the product's patent? Is it ethical to design products to wear out within a short time after purchase?

Other areas in which ethical questions arise in dealing with customers include marketing research and pricing. Have you ever been called on the phone or approached in a shopping mall to answer questions in a marketing research study—and felt that the interviewer was trying to sell you something? What about charging higher prices to less educated people who are less skillful in negotiating prices when buying durable goods like cars, furniture, and major appliances?

ETHICS AND SUPPLIER RELATIONS

Quite often a supplier or a producer will rely heavily on the other in doing business. The firm in the stronger position could treat the other unethically. For example, a strong supplier might threaten a producer with delivery delays to encourage bigger orders. Or a strong producer, dealing with a small supplier, might demand price cuts.

The giving and receiving of gifts between suppliers and customers can also raise ethical issues. Although a firm's ethical code may prohibit accepting gifts, the practice is often to "overlook" these gifts. When is a gift to a purchasing agent a token of appreciation? When is it a bribe?

ETHICS AND COMPETITOR RELATIONS

Unfair treatment of competitors is an area that is heavily regulated by law. As we saw in Chapter 21, antitrust law seeks to prevent larger firms from unfairly hurting smaller competitors. Still, ethical questions arise in dealings between competing firms—for example, corporate spying and corporate dirty tricks.

Corporate spying is most likely to occur in high-tech industries. The dividing line between competitive intelligence gathering and corporate spying can be very thin. Some firms have been known to pay janitors for supplying the contents of trash cans from research and development labs. The Business in the News box indicates that corporate espionage is not limited to high-tech firms, however.

Sometimes corporate dirty tricks take the form of rumors about a competitor's product. Even false rumors can severely damage the victim and its products. If the source of such a rumor can be located, legal action is possible. But in most cases it is almost impossible to pinpoint where a rumor began.

Another situation in which ethical questions arise is when one company tries to take over or buy out another. In 1986, Pennzoil sued Texaco for interfering with Pennzoil's plans to buy a third oil company, Getty Oil. A state court jury in Texas found that Texaco had induced Getty to break a legal agreement with Pennzoil. Texaco had used its larger size and position as a major buyer of Getty's oil to convince Getty to stop a merger agreement with Pennzoil. In April 1988, Texaco handed $3 billion over to Pennzoil to settle the $10.3 billion judgment Pennzoil had won months earlier in the Texas court.

ETHICS AND EMPLOYEE RELATIONS

Chapter 8 covered many of the issues that relate to ethical treatment of employees. Honesty in dealing with employees, fair methods of awarding raises and promotions, and the physical safety of employees while on the job should be high priorities for every business.

Instances of sexual harrassment on the job have made the news in recent years. Sexual harassment is a violation of federal civil rights law, and the offended worker can sue the employer. Still, many incidents go unreported because the harassed employees fear for their jobs. Employers have an ethical obligation to ensure that victims will not be mistreated if they pursue legal remedies.

Employers are ethically bound to inform workers of any job-related actual or potential threats to their health or safety. The Occupational Safety and Health Administration and other government agencies set guidelines for the exposure of employees to hazards at work. But these guidelines may be incomplete, or technology may change so fast that new dangers are created faster than they can be detected and controlled.

The trend toward a two-tier work force (insiders and outsiders) in many industries also raises ethical questions. Mergers, acquisitions, and foreign competition are causing many firms to let go many of their long-term employees (insiders) and replace them with temporaries and part-timers (outsiders). This can cut costs and perhaps make the firms more competitive. Employers have to pay fringe benefits to permanent employees but not to temporaries and part-timers. Many of these same firms are turning to small outside suppliers for the component parts needed to make their main products. We discussed just-in-time inventory management in Chapter 10. An analyst at the Bureau of Labor Statistics says of these companies, "Now they want a just-in-time work force."[2] Ethical issues include the employer's obligations with respect to severance arrangements, retraining for new jobs, and relocation assistance to laid-off workers. Employers may also have ethical responsibilities related to the "insiders'" concerns about job security.

One area of growing importance is company efforts to help employ-

BUSINESS IN THE NEWS
Corporate Spying in the Casket Industry

Marc C. Feith received a two-month jail term after pleading guilty to stealing his employer's documents and trying to sell corporate secrets to the firm's biggest competitor. His employer, Hillenbrand Industries, Inc., is a maker of caskets and hospital beds.

While on a general assignment to gather information on the competition, Mr. Feith ultimately adopted cat-burglar tactics. He changed from dark business suits into jeans and a ski mask for nighttime searches of competitors' trash, where he found information on such things as secret merger plans.

Emboldened by his employer's approval, he says, he combed through dumps in the dark and paid a trash hauler for access to his truck, where Mr. Feith risked being crushed in a compactor. A manager at Hillenbrand started to call him "director of covert activities." But Mr. Feith was not impeded until he turned on his employer and broke the law by raiding Hillenbrand's files and trying to sell the contents to Service Corporation International, Hillenbrand's major competitor.

Although Hillenbrand leads the casket industry, competitors in its stagnant market are consolidating into formidable opposition. The industry abounds in advances for metals coating and factory automation. And while Hillenbrand has a long written ethics policy, it does not mention how far an employee may go to find out what the competition is up to.

Source: Robert Johnson, "Inside Job: The Case of Marc Feith Shows Corporate Spies Aren't Just High-Tech," *The Wall Street Journal,* Jan. 9, 1987, pp. 1, 11. Reprinted by permission of *The Wall Street Journal,* © Dow Jones & Company, Inc., 1987. All Rights Reserved.

ees with drug and alcohol addiction. What is the best way to battle drugs on the job? The old barriers against firms taking action, such as the belief that "it is a societal problem and not a work-related problem" are falling. Many firms are setting up programs to combat drugs, providing psychiatric counseling for employees, and resorting to urinalysis to identify users. In a few cases, employers are installing video cameras or hiring undercover agents.[3] Many such actions are highly controversial.

We should also mention that rapid change in the work world is also raising new questions about the ethical relationship between employers and employees. The Electronic Age box focuses on some of the possible causes of employee dishonesty.

ETHICS AND ECOLOGY

As we saw in Chapter 2, ecology is the relationship between living things and their environment. Environmental protection yields tremendous social benefits. It also costs money.

There is currently a controversy over the use of nonbiodegradable plastic packaging. Landfills are running out of space, and items like plastic coffee cups and grocery bags take up room at disposal sites. Furthermore, such products can cause problems for marine life when they are dumped in our oceans. Nevertheless, the makers of paper bags and plastic bags are competing head to head. Suppose the plastic bag makers undercut the price of paper bags. What kinds of ethical dilemmas do buyers for the supermarkets face?

Environmental inspections are becoming more common before sale of industrial, and even some residential, properties. Some states require sellers to notify buyers if hazardous waste had been disposed of or stored on the land. Some other states go further and require an inspection and, if needed, a cleanup before title to the property can be transferred. In recent years there has been a big increase in the number of independent environmental consultants.[4] The ethics of sellers, buyers, consultants, inspectors, and cleanup companies come into play here. For example, what ethical responsibilities does a consultant have if he or she suspects that the owner is not being honest in answering the consultant's questions about the history of use of the property? What if the current owner has owned the property for only a short period of time and the prior owner is not available for questioning? What kinds of records should the consultant research, and in what depth, to fulfill his or her ethical obligation?

WHISTLEBLOWING

Whistleblowing is another dimension of ethical behavior that organizations are facing. Suppose an employee gets caught up in an ethical dilemma. Among the actions the employee might take are to keep quiet, to resign, or to "blow the whistle" on management.

whistleblowing

Whistleblowing is the action of publicly reporting what are perceived to be an organization's wrongdoings. A *whistleblower* is one who reports activities that he or she believes to be wrong or harmful to any of the organization's stakeholders. Whistleblowing ranges from

THE ELECTRONIC AGE

A Stimulus to Scams and Embezzlements?

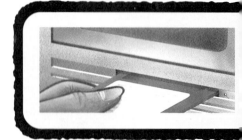

Bank fraud, which covers a range of ways to steal money from lending institutions, has increased greatly in recent years. Regulators, investigators, and prosecutors offer lots of theories on the fraud outbreak, but most agree that greed is the basic cause.

Other factors to consider include deregulation, crashes, easy pickings, and technology. If greed often provides the motive, financial deregulation has provided rich new opportunities—especially at thrifts. In 1982, savings and loans were allowed to move from their traditional area of lending for single-family housing into lending for condominiums, office towers, and other high-risk ventures. The result has been a frenzy of questionable loans to friends and insiders, phony asset appraisals, and other misdeeds.

Investigators say that the fraud outbreak might never have come to light without some disastrous crashes in the energy, agriculture, and real estate industries. Frauds are easy to hide when profits are good. Moreover, many normally honest bankers have resorted to fraud in efforts to save institutions battered by bad loans.

Traditionally, fraud has been easy pickings because it is one of the easiest crimes to get away with. To avoid bad publicity, banks often choose not to prosecute employees caught stealing.

But the electronic age is also playing a big role. "High tech and computers make it easier to move money, easier to hide it, easier to steal it," says the chief of the special activities section at the Federal Deposit Insurance Corporation.

For example, an up-and-coming branch manager at a Utah bank tried to cover up a bad $75,000 loan he had made to a gambler by loaning the gambler still more money. The gambler said he would go to Las Vegas and win enough betting on sports to repay the loans. The branch manager used the bank's computers to help set up phony accounts through which he eventually channeled some $4 million to the gambler. The scheme was uncovered only because the bank's president, unable to find a magazine to carry with him into the restroom, picked up a sheaf of computer records instead and discovered that a usually dormant account held some $800,000. The manager pleaded guilty to fraud in federal court in Salt Lake City shortly after the bank collapsed in 1986.

Source: Charles F. McCoy, "Financial Fraud: Theories Behind Nationwide Surge in Bank Swindles," *The Wall Street Journal*, Oct. 2, 1987, p. 15. Reprinted by permission of *The Wall Street Journal*, © Dow Jones & Company, Inc., 1987. All Rights Reserved.

telling the news media to informing and working with government regulatory agencies.

Whistleblowing can lead to reprisals such as firings and demotions. Slowly but steadily, however, some states are beginning to protect whistleblowers. Meanwhile, enlightened employers are realizing that they can benefit if they heed the health, safety, and other warnings of conscientious employees. They are using hotlines, confidential questionnaires, and other devices to encourage employees to speak up without fear of retaliation.

AN INTERNATIONAL PERSPECTIVE

In 1987, almost immediately after the disclosure that a Toshiba Corporation unit had sold militarily important technology to the Soviet Union, two top Toshiba executives resigned. Such resignations are a form of apology in Japan. Employees of Toshiba America, however, insisted that the firm make an equally public statement in the United States, which it did with full-page newspaper ads. Although both U.S. and Japanese managers are responsible for the bottom line, the Japanese corporate chief is expected to make symbolic gestures and, at times, personal sacrifices that most U.S. executives are not. It is part of the Japanese code of ethics.[5]

Ritual resignations by Japanese chief executives are "almost a feudal way of purging the community of dishonor," says George Lodge, a professor at the Harvard Business School. "This is far different from the Anglo-Saxon legalistic tradition," he says, in which an employee is bound by contract rather than as a member of a corporate community.[6]

The incident recalls the resignation in 1985 of the president of Kikkoman Corporation after a scandal over tainted wine. That same year the president of Japan Air Lines resigned after a jet crash that cost over 500 lives. He remained in office only long enough to see that arrangements had been made to bury the dead and assist the bereaved—a process that included personal calls on victims' families.[7]

Summary

Law is the set of standards, principles, and rules a society establishes to govern the actions of its members. It touches everyone's day-to-day life. It protects us from wrongdoers and spells out the rules by which we must abide.

Law evolves over time. Common law grows out of previous judicial decisions and is based on precedent. Statutory law is codified, or written, law. It is enacted by city councils, state legislatures, and the U.S. Congress. Administrative law is developed by government agencies and commissions.

Public law is the branch of law that relates to society as a whole. Private law is the branch of law that relates to relationships between individuals, groups of individuals, and corporations. Business law is that body of law that pertains particularly to business activities.

The Uniform Commercial Code combines and coordinates several specific uniform acts (such as the Uniform Sales Act and the Uniform Partnership Act) that pertain to business into one overall commercial code.

A contract is a mutual agreement between two or more people to perform or not perform certain acts. To be valid, a contract must include an agreement, consideration, competence of the parties to the contract, and a legal purpose. If there is a breach of contract, the remedies are discharge, damages, and specific performance.

Many business relationships are based on the law of agency and the law of bailment. The former focuses on the legal duties of two parties who engage in an agency-principal relationship. The latter is concerned with the surrender of personal property by one party to another with the expectation that the property will be returned in the future.

The law of property distinguishes between real property and personal property. In the sale of property the question of warranty often becomes important. The two kinds of warranty are express warranty and implied warranty.

A negotiable instrument is a piece of paper that is evidence of a contractual relationship and can be transferred from one person or business to another. Checks and certificates of deposit are examples.

Trespass, assault and battery, fraud, libel and infringement of patent are examples of torts—wrongful acts that injure a person's body, property, or good name. The most common type of tort in business is negligence. The concept of product liability is considerably broadened by the concepts of strict product liability and market share liability.

Bankruptcy results when a firm or a person cannot meet maturing financial obligations (insolvency) and has liabilities that exceed the value of assets. Bankruptcy can be voluntary or involuntary. Most firms that go bankrupt do so under the provisions of Chapter 11 of the Federal Bankruptcy Act.

Widely reported instances of white-collar crime in recent years have focused attention on the topic of business ethics. Business ethics is a collection of principles and rules of conduct based on beliefs about what is right and wrong business behavior. Ethics provide the framework for our system of laws.

A code of ethics is a formal, published collection of values and rules that are used to upgrade and guide behavior. Business firms, industry groups, nonprofit organizations, and professional groups often establish ethical codes.

Ethical dilemmas often arise in situations in which businesspeople interact with each other and the public. Ethical codes therefore often include specific provisions for dealing with customers, suppliers, competitors, and employees. Ethical issues also often arise in connection with ecology.

Whistleblowing is another dimension of ethical behavior. It is the action of publicly reporting what are perceived to be an organization's wrongdoings.

Review Questions

1. What is a valid contract?

2. What remedies are available to a firm that has suffered a breach of contract?

3. What is an agency-principal relationship?

4. How does negligence differ from an intentional tort?

5. How does the concept of strict product liability differ from the concept of negligence?

6. Why do most businesses that go bankrupt do so under the provisions of Chapter 11 of the Federal Bankruptcy Act?

7. What is a code of ethics?

8. How is whistleblowing related to the subject of ethics?

Discussion Questions

1. A manufacturer of small home appliances has just cut all its prices by 10 percent. It has also been advertising that its products will no longer carry any warranty. "You buy it, it's yours! At our prices, we can't afford to take back anything." What advice would you give this manufacturer about its warranty plans?

2. In your opinion, does the concept of strict product liability tend to discourage companies from investing in new product development?

3. Would you expect a lot of similarity or a lot of dissimilarity among different firms' codes of ethics?

4. Is there any relationship between ethical business behavior and the firm's profitability?

Key Terms

law
common law
statutory law
administrative law
public law
private law
business law
Uniform Commercial Code (UCC)
contract
breach of contract

agency-principal relationship
bailor-bailee relationship
property
real property
personal property
copyright
deed
title
warranty
negotiable instrument
endorsement

tort
intentional tort
negligence
product liability
strict product liability
market share liability
bankruptcy
business ethics
code of ethics
whistleblowing

THE FTC VERSUS THE AICPA

A. Marvin Strait took over as chairman of the 255,000-member American Institute of Certified Public Accountants (AICPA) in September 1987. Almost immediately, he and the former chairman, J. Michael Cook, got ready to battle with the Federal Trade Commission over FTC claims that the accounting profession is stifling competition within its own ranks and denying clients access to certain services.

Earlier in 1987, the FTC had asked the institute to drop its longstanding ban on contingent fees. Under the ban, accountants cannot charge fees contingent on the benefits or profits they get for clients, as can lawyers and other consultants. Instead, accountants charge a flat hourly fee. The FTC also wants accountants to be able to take commissions, incorporate their firms, and use names other than their personal names in a firm's title. The institute's ethics rules banned these practices.

Both Mr. Strait and Mr. Cook are adamant that such steps would erode an accountant's independence. Mr. Strait says, "Accountants can't be compared with architects, engineers, and doctors because we do audits for a third party—the public—and thus have to be purer." Mr. Cook adds, "When we audit a client company's books, independence is the keystone to our integrity. If our fees depend on what benefits we can obtain for our clients, we can hardly be the public's watchdog."

The FTC in a letter to state accounting regulators in June 1987 said that it wanted the ban dropped to "permit increased competition" and to "benefit consumers by permitting accountants to provide services that consumers want." The ban, the FTC said, "may harm consumers by restraining price competition among accountants."[8]

Questions

1. What source of law is present in the case?
2. Why would the AICPA's ethics rules ban the practices the FTC favors?
3. Suppose you are a new certified public accountant just starting your own practice. Would you side with the FTC or the AICPA?

A SMOKELESS CIGARETTE

After four years of trying, RJR Nabisco, Inc. announced a new cigarette that it said would produce little smoke, no tar, no ashes, and no smell. "The world's cleanest cigarette," boasted RJR's vice-chairman in 1987.

Other people had doubts and questions about the product. Can RJR sell this hybrid as a mainstream cigarette? Can it promote the apparent health benefits of the new product without undercutting its other cigarette brands? Is smoking too far gone as a socially acceptable practice to be revived by such a product?

Taste is just a part of what RJR must get right. The new cigarette must also have the right feel, take the right amount of time to light, and produce the right thickness of exhaled smoke. RJR says the cigarette will give off some smoke, but only immediately after being lighted. Exhaled smoke will resemble normal cigarette smoke but will dissipate more quickly and will not smell or contain many of the compounds some find so objectionable in regular cigarette smoke.

If the new cigarette is indeed somewhat safer (scientists say they do not yet know enough to judge its safety), RJR cannot say so without casting further doubt on all other cigarettes and courting potential liability trouble. "The marketing key really," says one industry executive, "is in the ability to communicate the benefits without running afoul of the law or putting the rest of the company out of business."[9]

Questions

1. What area of the law do you think RJR is most concerned about in connection with the possible marketing of this new product?
2. Would you recommend promoting any health benefits for the new cigarette?
3. On the basis of the information in the case, what would you advise RJR to do with the new cigarette?

TWENTY-THREE

LEARNING OBJECTIVES

International Business Strategies

After reading this chapter, you will be able to:

- Explain how international trade benefits trading countries.

- Identify and give examples of the various types of barriers to international trade.

- Distinguish between a country's balance of trade and its balance of payments.

- Explain why firms export and import products.

- Identify and explain the major tasks exporters face in exporting products from the United States.

- Explain how a firm might enter a foreign market other than by exporting.

- Demonstrate how environmental elements can affect a multinational company.

WHAT'S AHEAD

In this chapter we will look at an increasingly important topic to businesspeople: international business. As we will see, trade among countries broadens the market and permits greater exchange and specialization. It enables each country to use its limited resources to the best advantage.

Despite the advantages of trade, there are many trade barriers. Distance is a natural barrier. As we will see, there are also tariff and other barriers created by government. Examples of nontariff barriers are quotas, embargoes, government procurement policies, government standards, customs procedures, and subsidies and countervailing duties. As governments recognize the mutual benefits from trade, they want more trade and work to eliminate the tariff and nontariff barriers.

We will also look at the balance of trade and balance of payments. These two topics have been much in the news during recent years. Related to those topics and just as much in the news are foreign exchange rates—for example, the value of the U.S. dollar in relation to the Japanese yen, the West German mark, and so on.

Getting involved in exporting requires familiarity with licensing requirements, shipping documents, international financing, collection documents, and methods of payment. As we will see, various types of middlemen are available to help exporters.

In addition to exporting, firms can enter foreign markets through foreign licensing, foreign assembly, turnkey operations, management contracts, and overseas production subsidiaries. As we will see, multinational companies make the greatest commitment to international business.

The chapter ends with a look at the environment of international business. The surest way to fail in any type of overseas business dealings is to assume that countries and people are all alike. We will also see that some multinational companies are pursuing a globalization strategy. This, however, is a controversial approach to doing international business.

According to the U.S. Department of Commerce, the U.S. trade surplus in business services dropped from $10 billion in 1981 to less than $1 billion in 1987. Advances in computers and telecommunications have made it vastly easier for securities houses, banks, accounting and advertising firms, and others to expand their global operations.

Clearly, foreign firms are penetrating the U.S. market in an increasing range of business services. For example, the United Kingdom's Blue Arrow PLC became the world's largest employment-services concern when it acquired Milwaukee-based Manpower, Inc. in September 1987. Even businesses as mundane as janitorial services are going international. ISS AS of Denmark, for example, now scrubs office buildings in some fifteen countries. Its U.S. subsidiary ranks among the biggest operators of its kind in the U.S. market.

Challenges are coming from across the Pacific, as well. U.S. construction and engineering firms blame their shrinking international market share on increased competition from developing nations, a closing of the technology gap among industrial countries, and a generally tighter market. They also blame Japan for effectively shutting them out of the Japanese market, while Japanese construction firms in 1987 did $2.3 billion of U.S. work.

Furthermore, some foreign firms, particularly Japanese firms, pour money into developing new construction methods and patenting the machines and materials needed for them. Thus, for work on certain sections of the Washington, D.C., subway system, U.S. contractors used Austrian and Japanese technology and equipment. Such proprietary technologies help foreign firms gain a foothold in the U.S. market, though protectionist measures here could block some inroads. The Washington Metropolitan Transit Authority recently rejected a U.S.-Japanese joint bid for work on a new subway line, in the first invocation of a recently enacted law intended to force Japan to open its public works market.[1]

Our goods-producing industries have had to face up to increasingly intense competition during recent years. Now we are finding that our service industries are vulnerable, too. Just as we could not escape foreign competition in the industrial economy, we cannot escape it in the postindustrial services economy. Let's begin the chapter with a look at the nature of international trade.

International Trade

International trade is the exchange of products among countries. Taking a global view of the market leads to greater specialization and exchange. Let's examine some of the basic principles that explain why nations specialize in certain kinds of products.

absolute advantage

Absolute advantage is the position a country enjoys when it is the only country that can provide a certain product or when it can offer the product at a lower cost than any other country. If a product can be produced only in Switzerland, any country that wants it must trade with Switzerland. If a product can be produced at a lower cost in

France, other countries must trade with France or pay the higher cost of producing it themselves. If all nations followed this principle of absolute advantage, each would produce only the products in which it enjoyed an absolute advantage, importing all other products.

But suppose a country can produce everything its people consume more efficiently than all other countries. It can still benefit from trade by specializing in those products in which it is the most productive. **comparative advantage** **Comparative advantage** is the position a country enjoys when it produces the products in which it has the greatest advantage, or the least disadvantage, in relation to other countries. The country should concentrate on these and import the other products it needs.

Although there are few examples of absolute advantage in the real world, there are many examples of comparative advantage. But the products that a given country produces depend on many factors. These include presence of natural resources, cost of labor and capital, and nearness to markets. International trade lets each nation use its scarce resources more economically.

The United States has a comparative advantage in producing wheat because the production process requires a lot of land and expensive machinery (capital) but not much labor. We also have a comparative advantage in many of the service industries. But as we saw at the beginning of this chapter, our comparative advantage in business services is eroding. We are at a comparative disadvantage in producing goods like clothing and hand-made rugs. Countries with low-cost labor have the comparative advantage in these products.

EXPORTS AND IMPORTS

exports **Exports** from a country are products produced in that country and sold in another. Our exports account for about 11 percent of our GNP. Exports account for a much larger percentage of the GNP of many other countries such as West Germany, Japan, and the Netherlands. For example, exports account for about 24 percent of West Germany's GNP.

Since World War II, West Germany and Japan have become major exporting nations. More recently, the newly industrialized countries like South Korea, Brazil, and Taiwan have also become major exporters. As we saw in Chapter 2, our share of total world exports has been declining.

How important are exports to U.S. business? Some of our industries, such as chemicals, computers, and aerospace, depend heavily on exports for sales and profits. Table 23-1 (on p. 666) identifies the ten largest industrial exporters in the United States in 1987. Our biggest export category, however, is farm products, which account for about 18 percent of our total exports.

imports **Imports** into a country are products that are sold there but were produced in another country. The United States imports more than any other country. Whereas we export more services than we import, we import more goods than we export.

Twenty cents out of every dollar Americans now spend go for imports. We depend totally on imports for coffee because we cannot grow coffee beans here. We depend heavily on imports of petroleum to

**TABLE 23-1 / The ten largest U.S. exporters in 1987
(ranked by dollar volume of exports)**

Rank	Company	Exports ($ millions)	Exports as % of Sales	Ranked by Exports as % of Sales
1	General Motors	8,731.3	8.6	37
2	Ford Motor	7,614.0	10.6	30
3	Boeing	6,286.0	40.9	2
4	General Electric	4,825.0	12.3	23
5	International Business Machines	3,994.0	7.4	41
6	E.I. du Pont de Nemours	3,526.0	11.6	29
7	McDonnell Douglas	3,243.4	24.7	5
8	Chrysler	3,052.3	11.6	26
9	Eastman Kodak	2,255.0	17.0	12
10	Caterpillar	2,190.0	26.8	4

supplement domestic sources. While not nearly as critical, imports of many, many other products such as VCRs and cars add to our enjoyment of life.

Our exports create jobs for the people who produce them and get them to overseas markets—manufacturers, middlemen, transportation firms, banks, and insurance firms. Imports create jobs for people involved in importing products. They also place U.S. dollars in the hands of the foreign sellers who can use them to import U.S. products.

Despite its many benefits, there are many barriers to trade. One is a natural barrier—distance. Suppose a product can be produced more cheaply in country X than in country Y. The cost to X of shipping it to Y might wipe out X's production cost advantage. The big problem, however, is the created barriers: tariff and nontariff barriers.

TARIFF BARRIERS

tariffs

Tariffs are duties, or taxes, that a government puts on products that are imported into (or, on rare occasions, exported out of) the country. *Revenue tariffs* are set low because the purpose is to raise money, not to reduce imports. *Protective tariffs* are set high enough to discourage imports of foreign products that are priced lower than (and therefore reduce sales of) comparable domestic products.

As suggested in Figure 23-1, people try to justify protective tariffs on several grounds. The infant industry argument says that tariffs are needed to protect new domestic industries from established foreign rivals. The home industry argument contends that domestic markets belong to domestic firms. The cheap wage argument holds that imports

FIGURE 23-1 / Arguments for protective tariffs.

from low-wage countries will force domestic firms to reduce wages in order to compete. The defense argument says that certain industries are vital for defense and should be protected in case of war.

Opponents say that infant industries grow up protected and never learn to compete. Domestic consumers, they say, pay higher prices when lower-priced foreign-made products are not available. Furthermore, they contend, many industries that are only very remotely related to defense are protected.

NONTARIFF BARRIERS

quota

embargo

As Figure 23-2 (on p. 668) shows, there are many other created barriers to trade besides tariffs. A **quota** is the maximum amount of a product that can be imported or exported. Most quotas apply to imports. The United States has a quota on the amount of textiles that can be imported.

An **embargo** is a prohibition or suspension of foreign trade in general or of foreign trade of specific imports or exports. The United States has embargoed the importing of South African Krugerrands (gold coins).

A nation can give preference to domestic firms in government purchase contracts through its government procurement policies. Government standards, such as safety and health regulations concerning various products, can also be effective trade barriers. Until recently, when the European Court of Justice struck down the beer purity law, West Germany was able to tightly limit beer imports because of a Bavarian beer purity law dating back to 1516. The law required that beer sold in Germany be made only from barley, malt, hops, water, and yeast—allegedly to protect the health of Germans. The law kept out most foreign beers, which usually contain a variety of additives and may be brewed from other cereals such as rice or corn.[2]

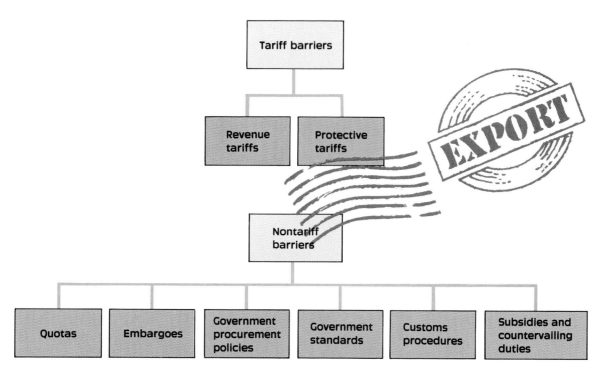

FIGURE 23-2 / Examples of created barriers to trade.

Each nation also has its own rules for inspecting and valuing imports. These customs procedures can be used as trade barriers. For example, custom officials could inspect each new foreign car entering the country, rather than a sample of them. Governments also sometimes use subsidies and countervailing duties. A government can use export subsidies to encourage exports by giving financial help to firms that produce these exports. Then the exported product can be sold in the foreign market at a price lower than that of comparable domestic products there. A country whose domestic industry is being harmed by subsidized foreign competition can impose a countervailing duty on the product to offset the foreign subsidy.

dumping

Subsidies and countervailing duties are often associated with dumping. **Dumping** is the practice of selling substantial quantities of a product in a foreign country at prices that are below either the home-market price of the same product or the full cost (including profit) of producing it. U.S. firms often complain about dumping here. Under the U.S. Antidumping Act they must show that the foreigners' prices are lower here than in the home countries and that U.S. firms are being directly harmed. Only then will the U.S. Department of Commerce investigate. If it finds that a foreign firm engaged in dumping, duties are assessed on the dumped products to wipe out the foreign firm's price advantage. Foreign-made steel, shoes, TVs, and computer chips have been dumped in the United States during recent years.

As we saw in Chapter 2, protectionism has become a major issue. Some people in the United States have been demanding stiffer tariffs, quotas, and embargoes against countries that they consider to be unfair trading partners.

REMOVING TRADE BARRIERS

International trade makes it possible for trading partners to raise their standard of living. Governments can promote trade by removing trade barriers.

General Agreement on Tariffs and Trade (GATT)

One of the most important international trade agreements is GATT. The **General Agreement on Tariffs and Trade (GATT)** is a multilateral treaty through which member countries act jointly to reduce trade barriers. In operation since January 1, 1948, GATT has reduced tariff and nontariff barriers to trade.

The U.S. government promotes international trade in many ways. For example, government agencies (1) make loans to American exporters who cannot get financing from a private source, (2) provide various types of insurance to U.S.-based firms that have operations abroad, and (3) make loans to foreign governments to use in buying U.S.-made products.

The U.S. Department of Commerce's Bureau of International Commerce organizes trade missions, operates permanent trade centers abroad, and sponsors district export expansion councils. The U.S. Department of State also helps U.S. firms to promote their products in foreign markets.

State and local governments and private groups also promote trade. State and city officials go overseas to lure foreign firms to their areas. The Chamber of Commerce of the United States, the National Foreign Trade Council, and world trade clubs are important sources of information.

The Balance of Trade and the Balance of Payments

balance of trade

A country's **balance of trade** is the difference in value between its total exports and its total imports. A country that exports more than it imports has a *favorable* balance of trade, or a surplus. When a country imports more than it exports, it has an *unfavorable* balance of trade, or a deficit. For the first time since 1888 the value of our imports exceeded the value of our exports in 1971. Our balance of trade has been unfavorable every year since, except for 1973 and 1975.

balance of payments

Even if a country has a favorable balance of trade, it can still have an unfavorable balance of payments. A country's **balance of payments** is the diference between money flowing into the country and money flowing out of that country as a result of trade and other transactions. An unfavorable balance means more money flowing out than flowing in. For the United States to have a favorable balance of payments for a given year our exports, foreign tourist spending in this country, foreign investments here, and earnings from overseas investments must be greater than our imports, U.S. tourist spending overseas, our foreign aid grants, our military spending abroad, the investments made by U.S. firms abroad, and earnings of foreigners from their investments in the United States. (See Figure 23-3.)

In almost every year since 1950 the United States balance of payments has been unfavorable. Our balance of trade was favorable during

FIGURE 23-3 / Requirements for the United States to have a favorable balance of payments. (The arrows indicate the direction of the flow.)

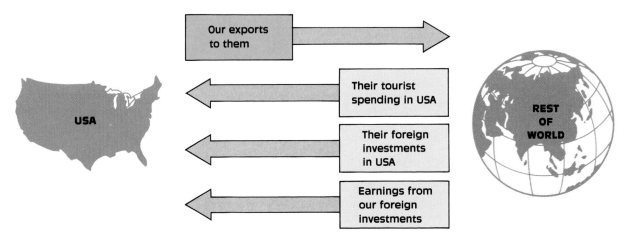

Total of above flows must be greater than:

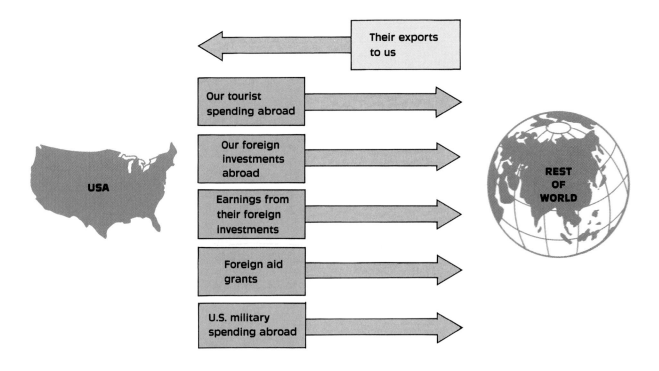

the 1950s and 1960s. But spending by U.S. firms and tourists abroad, foreign aid, and military spending abroad more than offset the favorable balance of trade.

A country's balance of trade and balance of payments are affected by the value of its currency in relation to other currencies. The **foreign exchange rate** is the ratio of one currency to another; it tells how much a unit of one currency is worth in terms of a unit of another. Figure 23-4 shows the New York foreign exchange selling rates for Monday, January 18, 1988, and Friday, January 22, 1988. Notice that one U.S. dollar was worth 5.6675 French francs on January 18 and 5.6230 francs on January 22. One French franc was worth 0.1764 U.S. dollars on January 18 and 0.1778 dollars on January 22. Thus the U.S. dollar declined slightly in value against the French franc during that week.

A currency's value on foreign exchange markets depends mainly on the supply of and demand for that currency. Its exchange rate with any other given currency will vary as supply and demand change. Fluctuating exchange rates add another element of risk to international business.

The stronger the dollar is in relation to the West German mark, for example, the greater the number of marks needed to buy a dollar. This

foreign exchange rate

FOREIGN EXCHANGE

Monday, January 25, 1988

The New York foreign exchange selling rates below apply to trading among banks in amounts of $1 million and more, as quoted at 3 p.m. Eastern time by Bankers Trust Co. Retail transactions provide fewer units of foreign currency per dollar.

Country	U.S. $ equiv. Mon.	U.S. $ equiv. Fri.	Currency per U.S. $ Mon.	Currency per U.S. $ Fri.
Argentina (Austral)	.2611	.2611	3.83	3.83
Australia (Dollar)	.7158	.7160	1.3970	1.3966
Austria (Schilling)	.08467	.08511	11.81	11.75
Belgium (Franc)				
Commercial rate	.02853	.02862	35.05	34.94
Financial rate	.02847	.02857	35.12	35.00
Brazil (Cruzado)	.01247	.01247	80.22	80.22
Britain (Pound)	1.7688	1.7880	.5654	.5593
30-Day Forward	1.7665	1.7858	.5661	.5600
90-Day Forward	1.7623	1.7809	.5674	.5615
180-Day Forward	1.7574	1.7733	.5690	.5639
Canada (Dollar)	.7825	.7813	1.2780	1.2800
30-Day Forward	.7814	.7802	1.2798	1.2817
90-Day Forward	.7796	.7785	1.2827	1.2845
180-Day Forward	.7770	.7759	1.2870	1.2888
Chile (Official rate)	.004092	.004092	244.40	244.40
China (Yuan)	.2687	.2687	3.7220	3.7220
Colombia (Peso)	.003776	.003776	264.80	264.80
Denmark (Krone)	.1552	.1557	6.4430	6.4220
Ecuador (Sucre)				
Official rate	.003968	.003968	252.00	252.00
Floating rate	.004454	.004454	224.50	224.50
Finland (Markka)	.2553	.2462	4.0770	4.0620
France (Franc)	.1764	.1778	5.6675	5.6230
30-Day Forward	.1764	.1777	5.6700	5.5260
90-Day Forward	.1760	.1774	5.6805	5.6385
180-Day Forward	.1754	.1767	5.7005	5.6580
Greece (Drachma)	.007468	.007493	133.90	133.45
Hong Kong (Dollar)	.1283	.1283	7.7995	7.7920
India (Rupee)	.07663	z	13.05	z
Indonesia (Rupiah)	.0006031	.0006031	1658.00	1658.00
Ireland (Punt)	1.5835	1.5900	.6315	.6289
Israel (Shekel)	.6402	.6402	1.5620	1.5620
Italy (Lira)	.0008097	.0008163	1235.00	1225.00
Japan (Yen)	.007822	.007868	127.85	127.10
30-Day Forward	.007843	.007888	127.51	126.77
90-Day Forward	.007880	.007926	126.91	126.17
180-Day Forward	.007942	.007991	125.92	125.14
Jordan (Dinar)	2.9762	2.9762	.336	.336
Kuwait (Dinar)	3.7106	3.7106	.2695	.2695
Lebanon (Pound)	.002178	.002178	459.00	459.00

FIGURE 23-4 / New York foreign exchange selling rates, Jan. 18 and Jan. 22, 1988. (z = not quoted.) (*Source: The Wall Street Journal*, Jan. 26, 1988, p. 47. Reprinted by permission of *The Wall Street Journal*, © Dow Jones & Company, Inc., 1988. All Rights Reserved.)

makes imports from West Germany and travel within West Germany cheaper for Americans. But it also makes our exports more costly to Germans.

The weaker the dollar is in relation to the West German mark, the fewer the number of marks needed to buy a dollar. This makes imports from West Germany and travel within West Germany more costly for Americans. But it also makes our exports less costly to Germans. The What Do You Think? box deals with the opportunities and challenges posed by the weaker dollar of recent years.

WHAT DO YOU THINK?

Will U.S. Managers Make Quality Job One Throughout Our Economy?

The weaker dollar of recent years has given U.S. manufacturers a golden opportunity to win back customers, rebuild buyer loyalty, and gain market share at home and abroad. But to make the most of this promising opening, U.S. companies must do more than exploit the price advantage that has grown as the dollar has fallen from its 1985 peak. Research and development, dealer responsiveness, and, perhaps most important, higher product quality are among the nonprice factors that will help determine whether U.S. companies can reclaim business lost to foreign competition when the dollar was high. U.S. companies are keenly aware that the high quality of Japanese products is helping Japan protect market share here despite the weak dollar.

"Despite the hoopla and rhetoric, quality isn't yet Job One across America," say C. Jackson Grayson and Carla O'Dell, authors of American Business: A Two-Minute Warning. Another expert stresses that successful quality control programs begin by defining quality from the customer's point of view. Then quality considerations are built into every stage of the production process from product design to shipping.

In a 1986 survey, people were asked, "What is responsible for the decline, if any, in the quality of U.S. products in recent decades?" Here is what they said:

Managers care more about profits	31%
Declining workmanship standards	16
Business and labor don't cooperate	13
Business doesn't enforce standards	10
Too much government regulation	7
Unmotivated, untrained workers	7
All of these	6
Don't know	4
Too little investment in R&D	3
Product quality hasn't declined	3

How important is quality? Will U.S. managers make quality "job one" throughout our economy? What do you think?

Source: Kenneth H. Bacon, "The Outlook: Higher Quality Helps Boost U.S. Products," The Wall Street Journal, Jan. 11, 1988, p. 1. Reprinted by permission of The Wall Street Journal, © Dow Jones & Company, Inc., 1988. All Rights Reserved.

Exporting and Importing

Exporting and importing are two major international business activities. As Figure 23-5 shows, firms engage in these types of operations for a variety of reasons.

WHY DO FIRMS ENGAGE IN EXPORTING?

Some mass production industries must produce in large volumes to get the cost-per-unit down to a low level. If the home market is too small to absorb this output, these firms look abroad for customers.

Another reason to export relates to the product life cycle concept, which we discussed in Chapter 12. Producers of products that are in the maturity stage in the domestic market may be able to export those products to markets where they are in the growth stage. For example, many home appliances are in the maturity stage in the United States. Sales of such products would be limited to new households and replacements in the U.S. market if there were no exporting.

Still another reason relates to the nature of competition in the foreign market and the cost of marketing in that environment. The U.S.

FIGURE 23-5 / Reasons why firms engage in exporting and importing.

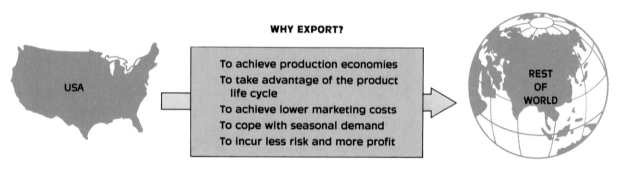

WHY EXPORT?

To achieve production economies
To take advantage of the product life cycle
To achieve lower marketing costs
To cope with seasonal demand
To incur less risk and more profit

USA → REST OF WORLD

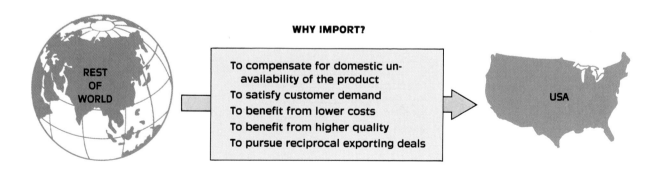

WHY IMPORT?

To compensate for domestic unavailability of the product
To satisfy customer demand
To benefit from lower costs
To benefit from higher quality
To pursue reciprocal exporting deals

REST OF WORLD → USA

market is highly competitive. If there is less competition in a foreign country, the exporter might enjoy lower marketing costs there.

The demand for many products is seasonal. Many U.S. firms shift their off-season production into foreign markets where the product is in season. This may lower production cost as a result of better production scheduling.

Finally, a firm might find it less risky and more profitable to sell its existing products in foreign countries than to develop new products for sale at home. Its skills may be put to best use this way.

WHY DO FIRMS ENGAGE IN IMPORTING?

Firms import products that are not otherwise available domestically, to supplement domestic sources, and to satisfy their customers' demands for imported products. Prices of foreign products, even after adding shipping and other costs of importing, are often lower than similar products made in the United States. In addition to the lower price, U.S. consumers might perceive the foreign-made product to be equal or higher in quality.

Some firms import in the hope that it will lead to reciprocal exporting of products to the foreign suppliers. It's the "I'll buy from you, you buy from me" idea carried out across national borders.

GETTING INVOLVED IN EXPORTING

Exporting may be intentional or unintentional, solicited or unsolicited. For example, a firm that supplies parts to Ford Motor Company might not know that some of Ford's products are exported. This is unintentional exporting as far as the supplier is concerned. Some firms engage in unsolicited exporting. A firm might receive and fill an unsolicited order from a foreign buyer. Although the firm knows that the buyer is abroad, it did not solicit the order. Our main concern is with exporters who intentionally solicit orders from foreign buyers.

Suppose you have found a profitable export opportunity and you are ready to start exporting. The It's Your Business box gives some useful information to help you get started. You must also familiarize yourself with (1) licensing requirements, (2) shipping documents, (3) collection documents, (4) methods of payment, and (5) export middlemen.

LICENSING REQUIREMENTS You will need a license from the U.S. Department of Commerce to engage in exporting. Your product and its destination determine the type of license you need.

You must apply for a validated export license to export products that are in short supply at home or have potential military use. You also need such a license to export products to countries deemed unfriendly to the United States. Each application is considered individually, and if a license is granted, it will set forth the conditions under which the products may be exported. Our government publishes a list of products and countries for which validated licenses are needed.

You need only a general export license to export to a friendly country products that have no potential military use and are not in short

IT'S YOUR BUSINESS

Getting Started in the Exporting Business

Experts say that 250,000 U.S. manufacturers have products with export potential. But just 250 firms account for 80 percent of U.S. exports. Nearly half of the total overseas sales of those 250 firms are made by the top 50 firms. What if you want to get involved in exporting? Where can you get some help?

The U.S. Department of Commerce is the federal agency most responsible for promoting and facilitating exports. The department has 1,200 trade advisors in sixty-seven offices in the United States and 127 offices in sixty-six other countries. But before meeting with one of the trade advisers, consider spending $19.50 on two books put out by the department.

A Basic Guide to Exporting ($8.50) is a beginner's bible, containing all you need to know to get into exporting. It contains addresses and phone numbers for the department's offices and for 521 other groups, public and private, in the United States and abroad. All offer information for U.S. exporters. The guide also takes the first-time exporter through the steps from making the first export sales contract to collecting the cash for the goods or services. It introduces all the intermediaries along the way and explains what they do. The book even has information on 140 other books and periodicals covering specific areas of interest to U.S. exporters.

The other book is *Partners in Export Trade* ($11), a state-by-state directory with information on 4,500 companies, including banks that finance exporters; companies, manufacturers, and service organizations that are exporters; and management firms, research firms, and others that assist exporters.

The books are available from the Superintendent of Documents, U.S. Government Print-ing Office, Washington, D.C. 20402.

Another helpful source is the *Exporter's Guide to Federal Resources for Small Business*. The 111-page paperback explains the role of each federal department and agency and provides the names, addresses, and phone numbers of numerous government contacts for export assistance. It too is available from the Superintendent of Documents or from regional offices of the Small Business Administration.

Source: Steven Golob, "Export Expertise," *Nation's Business*, Jan. 1988, pp. 26–30. Reprinted by permission, *Nation's Business*, January, 1988. Copyright 1988, U.S. Chamber of Commerce.

---

supply at home. The U.S. government classifies such products as acceptable for export without the need to consider individual applications to export them.

SHIPPING DOCUMENTS A shipper's export declaration is required for all products exported from the United States. This document declares the quantity and dollar value of the products and must be filed with the collector of customs at the port of exportation. Other important shipping documents include dock receipts, bills of lading, packing lists, and insurance certificates.

A dock receipt shows that the products have been received in good condition by the carrier and in the stipulated quantity. A bill of lading is (1) a document of title, (2) a contract between the shipper and the transportation company, and (3) a receipt for the products the shipper has placed on the carrier. A packing list is a complete, itemized description of the products—weight, size, type of packing, and so on. An insurance certificate is a form certifying that freight insurance was obtained, the value insured, and the type of insurance coverage.

COLLECTION DOCUMENTS   To receive payment for your exported products, you must complete several types of documents. These include commercial invoices, certificates of origin, and inspection certificates.

A commercial invoice is a bill for the products from you to the buyer. It shows all the facts associated with the sale—descriptions, costs, and insurance carrier, delivery date, payment terms, and so on. A certificate of origin certifies that the products were made in the United States. An inspection certificate states that the products were inspected by a third party to ensure that they are as described by the exporter to the importer.

METHODS OF PAYMENT   The most common methods of handling payment are cash in advance, open account, letter of credit, and drafts.

Cash in advance eliminates the risk that the buyer will not pay. With an open account arrangement the seller ships the products to the buyer, and the seller's commercial invoice indicates the buyer's liability to pay. A letter of credit is a document from the buyer's bank guaranteeing that it will pay you for the products if you meet the conditions set out in the letter. A draft, or bill of exchange, is a written demand for payment. You could, for example, draw a draft instructing the buyer to

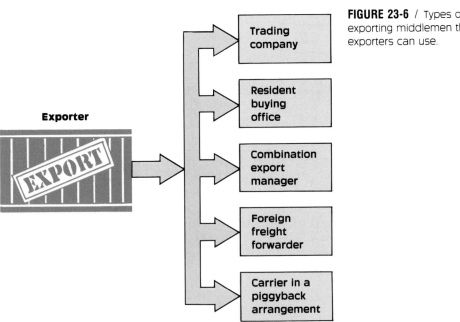

Exporter

Trading company

Resident buying office

Combination export manager

Foreign freight forwarder

Carrier in a piggyback arrangement

FIGURE 23-6 / Types of exporting middlemen that exporters can use.

pay the invoice to the buyer's bank. Your bank would send the draft to the buyer's bank for collection.

Although most exporters prefer to be paid in their currency, they may permit buyers to pay in their own currency. Your banker can give you information about foreign exchange rates and help you protect yourself from extreme fluctuations.

USING EXPORT MIDDLEMEN   What we have described are only some of the major tasks you would face as an exporter. You may need some help from one or more of the export middlemen identified in Figure 23-6.

trading company

One way of getting involved in exporting with a minimum of effort is through a trading company. A **trading company** is a business that buys and sells products in many countries, either in its own name or as an agent for its buyer-seller clients. It offers many services to its clients—importing, exporting, providing service on their products, storing, and transporting. The best known trading companies in the world are based in Japan, such as C. Itoh & Co. Ltd., Sumitomo Corporation, and Mitsubishi Corporation. The C. Itoh ad discusses some of the company's diverse activities.

Trading companies engage in a wide variety of activities.

resident buying office

Another approach to exporting is to sell to a resident buying office. A **resident buying office** is a government-owned or business-owned facility that is set up in a foreign country to buy products that are made there. Many foreign governments and firms have such offices here that buy U.S.-made products. Sales to them are similar to sales to domestic customers because they handle all the details of exporting.

combination export manager

If you want to sell to buyers in several countries, you could use a combination export manager. A **combination export manager** is a domestic agent middleman that serves as the export department for several noncompeting manufacturers on a commission basis. This middleman has a long-term relationship with clients.

foreign freight forwarder

Foreign freight forwarders can also help. A **foreign freight forwarder** is a domestic agent middleman that consolidates small export shipments into large ones, arranges for transportation and insurance, and handles both export and import documentation for clients. This middleman often picks up the client's freight, moves it to the port, arranges for overseas shipment, and even arranges to have the products moved from the foreign port to the buyer.

piggyback exporting

You might also decide to be a rider in a piggyback exporting arrangement. **Piggyback exporting** is the use by one firm (the carrier) of its overseas distribution network to sell noncompetitive products made by other firms (riders). The carrier might buy your products outright or sell them for you on commission.

Other Methods of Entering Foreign Markets

As Figure 23-7 shows, there are other ways to enter foreign markets besides exporting.

foreign licensing

Foreign licensing is an agreement in which a licensor gives a licensee in another country the right to use the licensor's patent, trademark, copyright, technology, processes, and/or products in return for a stated percentage of the licensee's sales revenues or profits resulting from such use. The licensor exports manufacturing and marketing know-how and property rights instead of physical products. The licensee

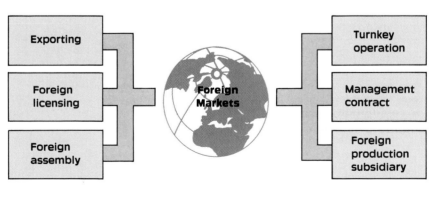

FIGURE 23-7 / Methods of entering foreign markets.

Why do you think these factory workers in Quanzhou, China, are producing shoes for Nike?

handles production and/or marketing in its market. Anheuser-Busch entered the Canadian market by licensing John Labatt to brew Budweiser in Canada. Burger King and many other fast food franchisors have entered foreign markets through licensing.

foreign assembly

Foreign assembly is an arrangement in which a firm exports component parts to a subsidiary or licensee in a foreign country for local assembly into the finished product. One benefit is that tariffs are lower on unassembled products than on assembled products. Increasingly, U.S., Japanese, German, French, and Italian auto makers are entering foreign markets by shipping auto parts to those countries for local assembly. Governments in many countries now require this in order to create jobs and tax revenues.

turnkey operation

A **turnkey operation** is an arrangement in which a supplier designs, builds, and trains the staff of an operating facility for a foreign buyer who runs the facility. The facility, such as an electricity-generating plant, is staffed by local nationals. In effect, all the buyer has to do is "turn the key" to make the facility operational.

management contract

A **management contract** is a pact in which one firm sells management services to operate a facility owned by someone else. For example, Marriott Corporation receives management fees for operating hotels that are owned by others throughout the world. Management contracts are often involved in turnkey operations. The contractor-builder agrees to manage the facility until local managers are prepared to take over.

foreign production subsidiary

Many firms that do business abroad set up their own production subsidiaries to produce their products in the foreign markets. A **foreign production subsidiary** is a subordinate company established in another country by a parent company for the purpose of production. For example, Lever Brothers Company is the U.S. subsidiary of Unilever Group, which is the Anglo-Dutch parent. Firms like Unilever are called multinational companies.

It's a job most people would love to have. From his home base in South Florida, the president of Burger King International travels the globe, overseeing the company's international operations. With managing directors for sectors like the United Kingdom and France reporting to him, this executive is always on the go, managing the chain's current restaurants and future expansion.

A big part of what you learn in international operations, he says, is that you have to be sensitive to and adapt to cultural differences if you want to be successful. In France, for instance, even your subordinates might bristle at having to pick you up at the airport, while in the United States that would be considered common courtesy. It's not that the French are unfriendly. This is just one of the numerous differences in cultural traits to which a person in international business must be sensitive.

For this reason, international executives place a high premium on cross-cultural experience when they are hiring new employees. "We might get fifty applicants for a lawyer's job, for instance, but the one who gets the job will most likely have had some solid experience in working or studying abroad." That is one way of being sure that a potential international manager really knows how to work successfully with people from other cultures.

Another big part of the company's success in opening up overseas restaurants is in maintaining the same high standards that apply to its domestic restaurants. Whether you are in Spain, England, Germany, or Hong Kong, you will see the same familiar Burger King logo. You will also see very much the same menu, and you will notice that the burgers and fries and drinks taste like they do back home.

One of the company's busiest restaurants opened just a few years ago at London's bustling Gatwick airport. The Gatwick facility was the fourteenth Burger King® restaurant in England. It seats 240 customers, employs 100 crew members, and is open 24 hours a day. "Every new restaurant is special but it's especially so here at Gatwick," says the managing director for the United Kingdom. "We won the contract in the face of the fiercest competition from our major competitors, which indicates quality positioning and everything that's good at Burger King."

Questions

1. Does globalization make sense for Burger King Corporation? Why?

2. Can a multinational company train its personnel who are involved in international operations to be sensitive to and adapt to cultural differences? Explain.

3. How would you describe Burger King Corporation's method of entering foreign markets?

---

multinational company (MNC)

Multinational Companies

A **multinational company (MNC)** is a firm that is based in one country (the parent country) and has production and marketing activities spread in one or more foreign (host) countries. MNCs often do more business outside their home countries than they do at home. Unilever and Royal Dutch/Shell Group, for example, do more than 80 percent of their business in host countries.

Most foreign subsidiaries of U.S.-based MNCs are wholly owned. Outright ownership means that there are no local part-owners and the parent can more easily coordinate subsidiary operations with its own.

joint venture

However, there is a strong worldwide trend toward requiring joint ventures. In international business a **joint venture** is a partnership of two or more parties, based in different countries, who share ownership and control of the venture's operations and property rights. For example, New United Motor Manufacturing, Inc., a joint venture between General Motors and Toyota, builds the Chevrolet Nova in Fremont, California.

FOREIGN MANUFACTURING OPERATIONS

Why do MNCs set up plants overseas? One reason is the growth in buying power in some countries. This creates enough demand for some products that it pays the MNC to manufacture in these countries rather than export finished products to them.

Another factor is the growing spirit of nationalism, especially in the less developed countries (LDCs) that export raw materials. Instead of exporting the raw materials to the developed countries, the LDCs want MNCs to set up plants in their countries to use the raw materials there. This creates local jobs, gives the government some control over the MNC's operations, and increases the tax base.

Still another factor is the lower cost of producing in some countries. This can be due to lower labor costs, lower interest rates, lower taxes, government subsidies, or greater supplies of raw materials.

regional trading bloc

Finally, the formation of regional trading blocs in some areas of the world might favor foreign manufacturing operations for some firms. A **regional trading bloc** is a group of countries that agree to eliminate barriers to trade among member nations. In 1958, for example, Belgium, France, Italy, Luxembourg, the Netherlands, and West Germany formed the European Community (EC), or the European Common Market. Since then, Denmark, Ireland, the United Kingdom, Greece, Spain, and Portugal have joined. Plans call for the free movement of goods, capital, and people among the twelve EC countries by the end of 1992. This will be a major step toward a "United States of Europe," the ultimate goal that the founders of the EC had in mind in the 1950s.

There are no tariffs on exports and imports among member countries of the European Community. But all members apply a common tariff on products entering from nonmember countries. Thus a U.S. exporter is at a disadvantage in competing with a French firm to export products to other Common Market countries. Many U.S. firms have set up subsidiaries in member countries to get behind this tariff wall. For example, Procter & Gamble makes its Heads & Shoulders dandruff shampoo in a single plant within the European Community for all of Europe and sells it in a "Euro-bottle" labeled in eight languages.

FOREIGN OPERATIONS IN THE UNITED STATES

Since the end of World War II, U.S.-based MNCs have made direct investments in many foreign countries. More recently, foreign-based

MNCs and individuals have been making direct investments in the United States. Our highly stable political system attracts investment from countries where terrorists are active or where government officials are antibusiness.

Foreign investment in the United States takes many forms. Some foreign firms build plants here. Others buy and modernize existing plants. Some foreign investors buy U.S. government securities, securities of U.S. corporations, and real estate. Unilever, for example, recently paid $3.1 billion for Chesebrough-Ponds, Inc., the U.S. company whose brands include Vaseline, Vaseline Intensive Care, and Q-tips.

The Multinational Business Environment

We discussed the importance of environmental monitoring in Chapter 2. When a firm does business in more than one country, it must monitor the environment in each.

THE ECONOMIC ENVIRONMENT

As a country becomes more economically developed, it undergoes many changes. These include declining employment in agriculture and basic manufacturing, increasing urbanization, and a rising literacy rate. Although all nations want fuller economic development, LDCs that are rich in natural resources attract more interest as potential markets and bases for setting up plants.

In addition to different levels of economic development among countries, there are often different levels within a country. The major cities in an LDC might be highly industrialized while other areas are primitive by comparison. In such a dual economy, people who work in the industrialized sector earn much higher incomes.

Other important elements of the economic environment include the tax structure, inflation rates, employment levels, per capita GNP, and stability of the economic system. These too must be monitored.

THE COMPETITIVE ENVIRONMENT

cartel

The competitive environment can be very unlike that in the United States. For example, cartels are popular in some parts of the world, including Europe. A **cartel** is a group of firms in different countries (or a group of countries, such as the Organization of Petroleum Exporting Countries, or OPEC) that agree to operate as a monopoly by regulating production and prices. Instead of competing, cartel members agree to limit output, share markets, and fix prices. Although cartels are illegal in the United States, it may be legal for U.S.-based firms to join in such agreements in foreign markets if participation does not affect the U.S. market.

In some countries, MNCs compete in many industries with government-owned enterprises. Often, even privately owned companies are heavily subsidized by the government. Acceptable competitive practices can also vary greatly. It might be hard to distinguish between "fair" and "cutthroat" competition.

More and more, global competition involves countertrading. **Countertrades** are transactions in which purchases are paid for with something other than money and credit as the medium of exchange. The most basic type of countertrade is simple barter. Buyer and seller exchange products directly rather than deal in currency or credit. Among the more complex types is the buyback. For example, the supplier might build a plant for the buyer. Under a separate agreement the supplier agrees to buy some of the plant's output. In other words, the buyer pays for the plant through the sale of part of its output to the supplier.

countertrades

THE TECHNOLOGICAL ENVIRONMENT

The cost to an MNC of producing a particular product can vary among countries depending on the level of technology present. Modern transportation, communication, and data processing facilities cannot be taken for granted. Besides economic dualism, technological dualism exists in many LDCs. Industries based on modern technology exist in the larger cities, while industries based on centuries-old technology exist in the less urban areas.

MNCs tend to derive their competitive advantage in foreign markets by introducing something new—new products, new production methods, new marketing techniques, and so on. Thus MNCs are engaged in the transfer of technology, which we discussed in Chapter 2.

Industries based on ancient technology still thrive in some LDCs, as in this batik factory in Java.

THE SOCIAL AND CULTURAL ENVIRONMENT

MNCs must understand cultural differences within and among the countries in which they do business. There may be major and minor differences in the elements of the social and cultural environment that are shown in Figure 23-8.

Language differences complicate business activity. Unilever's Timotei shampoo is a big hit in Europe but failed its market test in the United States. One reason was that Americans had trouble pronouncing the name.

Aesthetics pertains to a culture's concepts of beauty and good taste as expressed in its music, dance, folklore, drama, and art. MNCs must be sensitive to the aesthetic preferences of different cultures. They must also understand religion's role in the culture. In most Western societies, religion is not a total way of life as it is in the Islamic world.

MNCs must also understand the cultural values and attitudes of the people with whom they do business. Unilever, Procter & Gamble, and Colgate-Palmolive come up against tremendous cultural differences with respect to the use of products like toothpaste, deodorant, shampoo, and toilet soap in different markets. Values and attitudes about work, risk taking, change, the family, and material well-being vary greatly among cultures. So do social classes, customs, and taboos. In some cultures, for example, it is unacceptable for women to work outside the home. Concepts of time also vary. U.S. salespeople who insist on setting definite times for sales calls tend to spend a lot of time

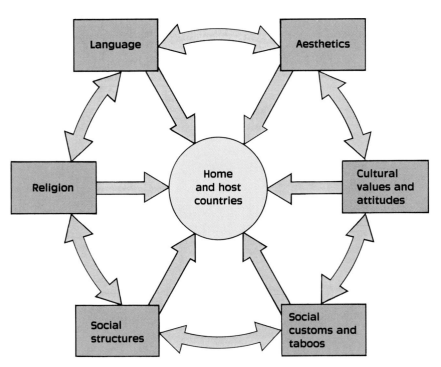

FIGURE 23-8 / Elements of the social and cultural environment. (*Source:* William F. Schoell and Joseph P. Guiltinan, *Marketing: Contemporary Concepts and Practices*, 3rd Edition, Allyn and Bacon, Boston, 1988, p. 710.)

waiting for Arab and Latin American prospects, who are less time-bound than we are.

THE POLITICAL-LEGAL AND ETHICAL ENVIRONMENT

Each country adopts its own internal system of government and laws, determines how it will relate to other countries, and decides how it will deal with foreign-owned firms within its borders. These laws affect the proportion of ownership an MNC can have in its subsidiary, the subsidiary's objectives, and its hiring and purchasing policies. Local content laws, for example, require MNCs that make products like cars to buy a set percentage of the parts locally.

As shown in Figure 23-9, confiscation, expropriation, nationalization, and domestication are among the major political risks MNCs face. Confiscation occurs when a host country takes over an MNC's property without paying for it. Expropriation occurs when a host country forces an MNC to sell its property and gives the MNC partial payment. The government may turn ownership of confiscated or expropriated property over to local nationals by selling or giving it to them. If the government retains ownership, the plants are said to be nationalized.

domestication

Domestication is an effort by a host government to shift decision-making power from the MNC to local nationals. In Mexico, for example, domestication involves local content laws, majority ownership of foreign subsidiaries in Mexico by Mexicans, import substitution programs, and so on. To stimulate its domestic auto industry, Mexico has banned auto imports since 1962.

exchange control

Exchange control is another political risk. **Exchange control** is a situation in which a government limits access to its country's currency by foreigners. A U.S. firm with a profitable subsidiary overseas wants those profits to go to its U.S. owners. If the subsidiary is in West Germany and West Germans buy its products, they pay with marks. But the U.S. owners want dollars. If West Germany is short on dollars, it might stop the subsidiary from sending the profit to the United States by limiting the amount of marks that can be converted to dollars.

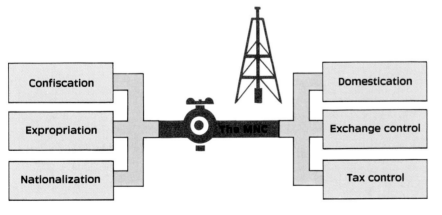

FIGURE 23-9 / Major political risks confronting multinational firms.

tax control

Tax control is another political risk. **Tax control** is the imposition of discriminatory taxes on foreign investments by a government for the purpose of exercising power over those investments.

A firm operating in different countries is also subject to different legal systems. What is legal in one may be illegal in another. Sometimes the same situation exists in the field of business ethics. The firm is often caught in the middle, but it must be careful not to violate the laws and ethical standards in any country in which it operates.

GLOBALIZATION

globalization

In the What Do You Think? box in Chapter 13, we took a brief look at the practicality of global promotional programs. During recent years, the pros and cons of globalization have been debated. **Globalization** is a worldwide marketing strategy whereby a firm uses the same or very similar marketing mixes in all its markets. Instead of focusing on the differences among people in different countries, this strategy advocates looking first for similarities.

Which brands can you recognize on these signs in Chiang Mai, Thailand? The underlying strategy is globalization.

The globalization strategy is based on the belief that mass communication and high technology are creating similar patterns of consumption in otherwise diverse cultures. Proponents say that this allows firms to standardize manufacturing and distribution of products as diverse as Revlon cosmetics and Sony TVs. Opponents argue that the diversity of cultures and level of economic development among countries make globalization a very risky strategy.

Summary

International trade enables a country to specialize in producing the products in which it is the most productive. Each country should produce the products in which it has the greatest comparative advantage, or the least comparative disadvantage, in relation to other countries. It should import the other products it needs.

Despite its many benefits, there are many barriers to trade. Distance is a natural barrier. The big problems are the created tariff and nontariff barriers. Most tariffs are designed to discourage imports rather than raise revenue for the government. Nontariff barriers include quotas, embargoes, government procurement policies, government standards, customs procedures, and subsidies and countervailing duties.

Governments can promote trade by removing trade barriers. The General Agreement on Tariffs and Trade (GATT) is a multination effort to reduce trade barriers. U.S. government agencies make loans to U.S. exporters, provide various types of insurance to U.S.-based firms with overseas operations, and make loans to foreign governments to use in buying U.S. products. The Bureau of International Commerce, state and local governments, and private groups also promote trade.

A country's balance of trade is the difference in value between its total exports and its total imports. Its balance of payments is the difference between money flowing into the country and money flowing out of that country as a result of trade and other transactions. The United States has had balance of trade and balance of payments deficits for some time.

A currency's value on foreign exchange markets depends mainly on the supply of and demand for that currency. The foreign exchange rate tells how much a unit of one currency is worth in terms of a unit of another. Fluctuating exchange rates add to the risk of international business.

Firms export products for a variety of reasons. These range from selling excess inventories to seeking less intense competition and lower marketing costs. Firms also import products for a variety of reasons. The products might be unavailable or in short supply at home, or customers might think the imported versions are of higher quality.

Exporting may be intentional or unintentional, solicited or unsolicited. Exporters must secure either a validated or a general export license and execute several types of shipping documents and collection documents. The exporter must also arrange for international financing and complete several types of collection documents. The exporter may decide to use the services of an export middleman, such as a trading company or a combination export manager.

Nonexport options for entering foreign markets include foreign licensing, foreign assembly, turnkey operation, management contract, and establishing a foreign production subsidiary.

A multinational company is a firm that is based in one country (the parent country) and has production and marketing activities spread in one or more foreign (host) countries. A foreign operation can be a wholly owned subsidiary of the parent firm or a joint venture with a local firm. Growth in buying power, nationalism, and lower cost of production in host countries are among the reasons that MNCs set up operations overseas.

People who conduct business internationally must monitor developments in the economic, competitive, technological, social and cultural, political-legal, and ethical environments of the various countries in which they do, or hope to do, business. Instead of focusing on the differences among people in different countries, the globalization strategy advocates looking first for similarities. Proponents want MNCs to standardize as much as possible their manufacturing and distribution strategies. Opponents say that the diversity of cultures makes this a very risky strategy.

Review Questions

1. Why do governments impose tariffs on imports?

2. Why do governments create nontariff barriers to trade?

3. Why do business firms engage in exporting? What about importing?

4. What shipping documents are required to export goods from the United States?

5. What are the various methods of entering foreign markets?

6. Why do multinational companies set up plants overseas?

7. What are the major political risks multinational companies face?

8. Why would a firm pursue a strategy of globalization?

Discussion Questions

1. Why would a business firm engage in dumping? Is the practice good for consumers in the country in which the products are being dumped?

2. Which is better for the average American consumer, a weak dollar or a strong dollar?

3. What does "social responsibil-ity" mean to a multinational corporation?

4. Why has the U.S. balance of trade been unfavorable in recent years?

Key Terms

absolute advantage

comparative advantage

exports

imports

tariffs

quota

embargo

dumping

General Agreement on Tariffs and Trade (GATT)

balance of trade

balance of payments

foreign exchange rate

trading company

resident buying office

combination export manager

foreign freight forwarder

piggyback exporting

foreign licensing

foreign assembly

turnkey operation

management contract

foreign production subsidiary

multinational company (MNC)

joint venture

regional trading bloc

cartel

countertrades

domestication

exchange control

tax control

globalization

Cases

MARKETING KELLOGG'S CORNFLAKES TO PARISIANS

The instructions on the box say: *Pour into a bowl. Add milk, preferably cold, and sugar to taste. Eat.* This step-by-step recipe for preparing a bowl of cornflakes is a key weapon in Kellogg Company's increasingly successful campaign to get the croissant-munching French to try an American-style breakfast.

Kellogg has certainly been patient. Its cornflakes have been on sale in France since 1935, seriously on sale since a French subsidiary was established in 1968, and very seriously on sale since TV advertising for them was started in 1978. But only since Kellogg and such competitors as Quaker Oats Company and Nestlé S.A. of Switzerland began TV commercials have the French warmed to cold cereal.

As with any foreign product, Kellogg has had to overcome ingrained habits. More than 30 percent of adults in Paris skip breakfast entirely. Others have a cup of *café au lait* and a slice of bread and chocolate spread, or they grab a croissant and coffee while standing at a coffee bar on their way to work. Of those who eat cereal for breakfast, a staggering 40 percent pour on warm milk, market research shows.

So in addition to the instructions on the box, Kellogg's French TV commercials always show milk being poured from a transparent glass pitcher, traditionally used for cold milk, instead of an opaque porcelain jug, reserved for the hot milk usually added to the morning's coffee.

The hot milk problem is not nearly as crucial to Kellogg as the general no-breakfast problem and the residual anticorn bias. Corn came to French farms only after World War II, and more than 80 percent of what is grown in France is fed to pigs and chickens. "People don't even think about eating corn or things made from corn at a meal," says the editor of a French food magazine. "Wheat definitely, corn no." Packages of corn on the cob, found in the exotic vegetable section of some supermarkets, also include instructions for boiling and eating.[3]

Questions
1. Which of the environmental elements we discussed is the most relevant to Kellogg in this case?
2. Why do you think Kellogg established its French subsidiary in 1968?
3. What, if anything, should Kellogg do to deal with the no-breakfast problem and the anticorn bias in France?

BIOLAB COMPANY— THE UNASHAMED COPYCAT

Biolab Company is a five-year-old, family-owned firm in Thailand that makes a wide range of pharmaceutical products. Some of its best-sellers are generic versions of foreign-patented drugs.

According to Biolab's managing director, the firm's Cimulcer is just like Tagamet, while its Ranidine is just like Zantac. Tagamet and Zantac, the world's two best-selling drugs, are ulcer medicines produced by Smith-Kline Beckman Corp. and Glaxo Holdings, respectively. Biolab's managing director says, "Thailand's pharmaceutical industry isn't yet mature enough for patents. We haven't had time to copy enough."

Biolab's pirating activities, like other Thai operations that copy foreign-patented drugs, do not violate any Thai laws. The 1979 Patent Law excludes pharmaceutical products from patent protection.

A spokesperson for the Ministry of Commerce's patent and trademark division says, "Pharmaceuticals were excluded from our patent law to safeguard the public from certain abuses that might arise" if firms were allowed monopolies on specific drugs.

International drug firms, however, say they need patent protection to help recover the cost of research, clinical testing, and marketing of new medicines. Without it, firms are deterred from developing drugs, they contend. The multinationals also claim that Thailand is missing out on foreign investment in pharmaceuticals because of its lack of patent coverage.[4]

Questions

1. "Pharmaceuticals were excluded from our patent law to safeguard the public from certain abuses that might arise." What abuses do you think this spokesperson for Thailand's Ministry of Commerce had in mind?
2. Should an agency be established within the United Nations for the purpose of granting patents on products that are to be traded internationally?
3. Although perfectly legal, is it ethical for companies like Biolab to make copies of foreign-patented drugs?

A P P E N D I X   A ■

Career Planning and Job Hunting

career planning

career planning/
placement office

career counselors

What Is Career Planning?

Career planning is the process of choosing a career and going after a satisfying job in an organized, thoughtful way. Now that you have taken your first college class in business, you have a much better idea of what types of careers and jobs are available in the business world. You have taken a big first step in career planning.

It is not too early to begin familiarizing yourself with the resources that are available to you to help you in career planning. One resource that you will find on practically every campus is the career planning/placement office. A **career planning/placement office** is a campus office whose mission is to help students make satisfying career choices and find the right jobs. On your campus it might be called a placement office, a career planning office, or a career development center. We will refer to it here simply as a career planning office. Regardless of the name, it is your most valuable resource in the career planning process.

A typical career planning office includes a career library or resource center, brochures, personal counseling, personality and aptitude testing, workshops and seminars, and on-campus recruiting and interviewing. **Career counselors** are people in career planning/placement offices who advise and assist students in relating their interests, skills, and values to career and job choices.

Unfortunately, too many students postpone taking an active role in planning their careers. Some believe that a career decision will simply come to them eventually or that they will "fall into" something after graduation. Or they might think that an employment agency will find them the job they want. None of these fantasies is likely to come true. Figure A-1 (on p. 692) discusses some popular myths many college students have about career planning. Do you believe any of those myths?

Remember, getting that first job depends mainly on your own creativity, work, and energy. Most job hunters look for work in a very haphazard way, not realizing how much more effective and efficient their search would be if it were planned.

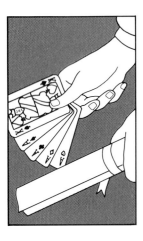

#1 Career counselors will tell me what careers are best for me.

Counselors in career planning/placement offices can help you discover for yourself what careers are best for you. But do not expect them to make your decisions for you. A good counselor will use testing and other educational methods to help you determine your strengths and to weigh the alternatives. You can benefit from a counselor's advice and knowledge, but ultimately, your future is in your own hands.

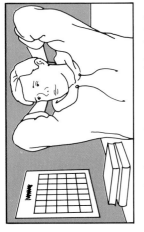

#2 Graduation year is soon enough to start planning my career.

Decisions about career and education are complicated, and implementing those decisions can consume years. Begin your career planning early so that you can achieve some of your short-term goals without a sense of panic. If you establish your direction during the first two years of school, you can arrange your curriculum to contribute to your goals. Take the appropriate courses, get summer internships, participate in a co-op program, or do relevant volunteer work. Then you can spend graduation year narrowing down the job hunt.

#3 Getting a job after graduation is mostly a matter of luck or of whom you know.

Although luck and contacts are important, the energy you devote to job hunting is the real key to success. By taking time to plan your career goals, develop a résumé, and identify employers, you will add to your list of helpful contacts and essentially create your own luck. Success goes to energetic people who put something of themselves into the job hunt.

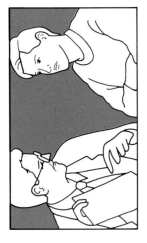

#4 Researching careers is a waste of time.

Research into careers is critical to career planning. The most common reason students are undecided about their future is that they have not explored the careers available to them. There are numerous ways to explore careers:

- Read career information available in your career planning/placement office.
- Take part in a career exploration group or enroll in a career planning course.
- Obtain a summer job that is consistent with your interests and abilities.
- Secure an internship in a career field of interest through your college.
- Attend school-sponsored Career Days.
- Interview employers as part of an independent study or special course project.
- Participate in field trips to potential employers that are sponsored by campus organizations or your career planning/placement office.

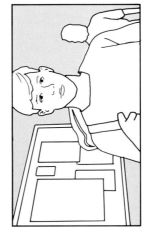

#5 You can never get too much information when making an educational or career decision.

Although gathering and evaluating information is crucial to effective decision making, it can become a never-ending process, especially if you feel insecure about finally making a choice. Somewhere along the line you will reach a point at which you have enough information. You will have read the literature. You will have talked to people. You will have observed and experienced some job situations. Don't use the information-gathering process as an excuse to put off making a decision.

FIGURE A-1 / Some common myths about career planning.

The Job Market Iceberg

hidden job market

The job market, like an iceberg, is mostly under the surface. The part you see in classified ads, campus recruitment activities, and employment agencies is only the tip. The **hidden job market** is that portion of available jobs that is never publicized. Between 80 and 90 percent of all job openings are not advertised.

passive job hunting

We can distinguish between passive and active job hunting. **Passive job hunting** is an approach to securing employment in which the individual simply reacts to job vacancies as they become known through friends, contacts, or classified ads. If you are a passive job hunter, you simply mail a letter of application and a résumé to the employer and wait to be offered an interview. You probably have given little thought to career goals and even less to matching your skills to the challenges of the job in question. You have not researched the job market, know little about careers in general and jobs in particular, and do not know how to determine the relationship between your talents and an employer's needs. In other words, you place the situation entirely in the employer's hands.

active job hunting

Active job hunting is an approach to securing employment in which the individual takes control of the job search, determining career goals, identifying interesting jobs, and going after opportunities. This approach takes a lot more thought, energy, and courage than passive job hunting. But it pays off. In the process of research and interviewing, as an active job hunter you will learn a great deal about careers. You will come in contact with a variety of employers in the hidden job market as well as the more obvious ones. You can make a good impression by asking thoughtful questions and expressing concern for meeting employers' needs.

Steps to Job Search Success

You stand a better chance of succeeding if you organize your career planning and job search activities. Figure A-2 shows the steps in an effective job search.

STEP 1: ASSESS YOURSELF

career self-assessment

Career self-assessment is the process of discovering one's interests, skills, and values and relating them to career possibilities. Your interests, skills, and values are the categories of personal traits about which potential employers are most concerned. Depending on how well you know yourself or how much you know about the world of work, the self-assessment process might reveal some surprises. It might also be more difficult than you expected. But you need not go about the task alone.

One way to assess yourself is to make your own lists of traits that relate to interests, skills, and values. You might, for example, make a list of your hobbies, all your past jobs and what you liked about them,

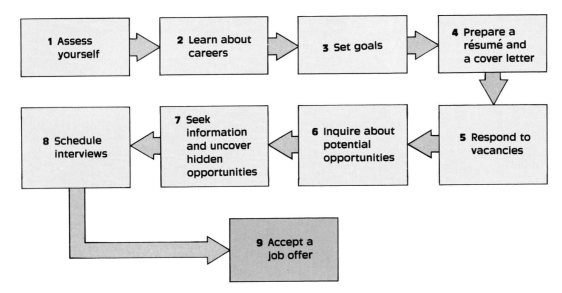

FIGURE A-2 / The job search process. (*Source:* Thomas Bachhuber, University of Maryland *Placement Manual*, University Communications, Rahway, N.J., 1984.)

your favorite school courses, and personal characteristics that you are proud of.

Besides making your own lists, you can assess yourself with the aid of standardized tests such as the Strong-Campbell Inventory, which assesses your interests, and the Myers-Briggs personality test, which reveals how you interact with others. These inventories and tests can be obtained through your career center. A career counselor can help you apply the results to develop an appropriate career plan. Figure A-3 shows a typical set of lists on interests, skills, and values. You can check off the ones that apply to you, or rank them, or use them as ideas to develop your own lists.

STEP 2: LEARN ABOUT CAREERS

Your efforts to learn about careers will be more focused after self-assessment. You might discover an aptitude for a career field you never considered or a lack of aptitude for one you always thought was for you. You will know which career fields truly fit your interests, skills, and values, so you can concentrate your research in the proper areas.

But how do you learn about careers? A very straightforward way is to go to your school's career library or to the career section of the school or public library. There the librarian can direct you to professional journals, directories, and publications that contain general occupation descriptions. For example, the *Dictionary of Occupational Titles* contains thumbnail sketches of many occupations. The *Occupational Outlook Quarterly* contains articles that describe occupations and the employment prospects for each of them. The career library might also have videotapes on specific careers or on the job market.

Your present interests

☐ Like to work with mechanical objects.
☐ Like to work outdoors.
☐ Like to work with scientific concepts.
☐ Like to solve theoretical problems.
☐ Like to use my imagination and creativity.
☐ Like to work in free and independent surroundings.
☐ Like to help people solve problems.
☐ Like to listen to and talk with others.
☐ Like to speak in front of groups.
☐ Like to work with computations and numbers.
☐ Like to work in an organized and supervised environment.

Your present values

☐ Value being well-liked by others.
☐ Value having financial security or independence.
☐ Value having a satisfying philosophy of life.
☐ Value getting to the top in my career.
☐ Value having a close-knit family relationship.
☐ Value being free to do what I want.
☐ Value completing my education to a high level.
☐ Value my health, both physical and psychological.
☐ Value a satisfying and fulfilling relationship or marriage.
☐ Value time for leisure, recreational and cultural pursuits.

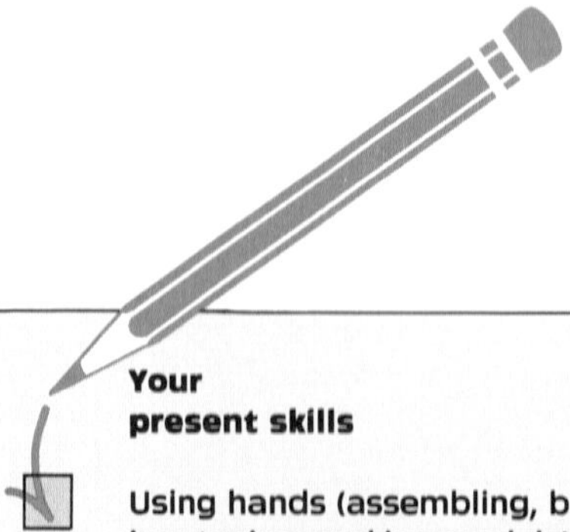

Your present skills

☐ Using hands (assembling, building, typing, making models).
☐ Using whole body (sports, camping, traveling).
☐ Using mind (problem-solving, researching, evaluating, remembering).
☐ Using creativity (designing, imagining, being an "idea" person).
☐ Using intuition (showing foresight, planning, balancing factors).
☐ Using artistic abilities (paints, crafts, working with colors).
☐ Using words (writing, talking, debating, editing, teaching).
☐ Using helping skills (understanding, counseling, interviewing).
☐ Using performing skills (lecturing, acting, playing music).
☐ Using leadership skills (directing others, initiating, managing).
☐ Using eyes (observing, filing, showing attention to detail).
☐ Using number skills (calculating, computing, accounting).
☐ Using responding skills (following through on what others have developed, applying others' ideas).

FIGURE A-3 / Interest, skill, and value inventory. (*Source:* John Holland, *The Self-Directed Search,* Consulting Psychologists Press, Palo Alto, Calif., 1972.)

Talk to people who have chosen a career that interests you. Some colleges offer a career alumni network or a mentor program in which a graduate allows a student to accompany him or her for a day on the job in addition to providing job leads and networking contacts. Of course, you can learn about careers through first-hand experience by taking a part-time or temporary job in a field you are considering.

Take career planning courses. Some colleges offer credit and non-credit courses. Course work might include an opportunity to research the career areas that interest you.

STEP 3: SET GOALS

Setting career goals might come naturally to you as you study careers, meet people, and generally experience life. If you are not so lucky, goal-setting can seem like an overwhelming task. It will become easier as you go through the career-planning process, one step at a time. Through self-assessment and career research you will have learned what careers are suited to you and what careers most interest you. As the results of these two steps become clearer to you, so will your goals.

You might start out with the idea of accomplishing something that will take many years—perhaps you don't yet know how many years. But with some thought you can decide what steps are necessary to achieve your long-term goal. These steps—taking certain courses, working at certain jobs—will be your short-term goals. Once you have estimated the time it will take to achieve your short-term goals, you will have an idea how far off your long-term goal achievement is.

Keep in mind that most people change careers three to five times during their lives. They switch jobs even more often. Although your first job will influence your career, it will not control it. So, even if that job does not quite fit into your long-term goals, it could be the most realistic opportunity you have at this time in your life.

Goal setting is easier for the career planner who has gone through self-assessment and discovered his or her interests, skills, and values. But there are other factors to consider. Salary needs and geographical preference might be important enough to swing your career or job decision one way or the other. Figure A-4 shows how one college student filled out a goal-setting worksheet, taking salary needs and geographical preference into account. Use it as a model and perhaps you can come up with some helpful insights of your own.

STEP 4: PREPARE A RÉSUMÉ AND A COVER LETTER

résumé

Two major pieces of paperwork can make all the difference in your job search—your résumé and cover letter. A **résumé** is a biographical summary of a job applicant's education, work experience, activities, interests, career goals, and other personal information that is given to potential employers in the job application process. Your résumé could determine whether or not you will even obtain an interview because it is the potential employer's first impression of you.

A good résumé will not get you a job. But it will interest prospective employers enough that they will want to talk with you. A poor

A. *Values*
   1. Opportunity to travel
   2. Creativity
   3. Leisure time
   4. Seeing work through from beginning to end

B. *Work Activities*
   1. Activities involving the communication of ideas and information
   2. Activities involving creative thinking
   3. Activities involving business contact

C. *Career Areas*
   1. Visual Arts
   2. General Sales
   3. Customer Services
   4. Business Administration

D. *Job Titles*
   1. Artist
   2. Art Director
   3. Manager, Display
   4. Display Designer
   5. Salesperson, Art Objects
   6. Manager, Merchandise

E. *Kinds of Organizations*
   1. Private industry, small
   2. Eventually own business

F. *Geographic Preference*
   1. Flexible
   2. Considering Atlanta or Boston

G. *Salary Needs*
   $18,000–21,000, preferably top of range

Possible Goal Statement A

I wish to work in the general field of retail management, preferably in a small company. I would like to work independently on tasks, seeing them through from beginning to end. I would like to work in an organization that specializes in art, art supplies, or interior decorating products in the Boston or Atlanta area. The career areas I am interested in include visual arts, general sales, customer sales, and business administration—the kind of work that involves creative thinking and the communication of ideas and information through customer contact. Specific job titles for me to explore further include painter, artist, art director, display designer, display manager, merchandise manager, retail manager, art objects salesperson, and interior designer. My targeted salary is the top of the $18,000–21,000 range. I would like the kind of job in which I would have time in my off hours to possibly begin a master's degree program in Art Administration as well as get some extra financial resources together to start my own studio.

Possible Goal Statement B

I really love art and would like to work as an artist and be able to sell my art work. My long-range goal is to own an art studio in the Boston area. This would allow me the creativity I value and the opportunity to live close to Cape Cod, which I love.

What I like about owning my business is that I would have the flexibility to create my own hours and maybe travel to art shows. I probably would not have much leisure time at first, but if I am successful, I will eventually have more time to relax and travel. By owning my own studio I could combine visual arts, customer sales, and business administration.

Perhaps for now, I will try to locate an art studio owner who might be looking for someone to do sales. That way I could gain sales experience, build on my business skills, and get a first-hand look at owning a business.

Possible Goal Statement C

When I look at this worksheet, what really hits me is the job title "Display Designer." From what I know of this job, I would be able to combine my interests in the visual arts and business administration career areas, both of which involve creative thinking and the communication of ideas. I would like to work in a small company where I could be involved in different phases of design and see projects through from beginning to end. Maybe I could eventually do some consulting as a way of testing out my feelings about being my own boss.

When I look at all the important information about me on this worksheet, the one thing that is hidden is my desire to "make it as an artist." I believe in myself—my abilities in art fall into a lot of categories, and I think my ideas and my work will sell. I want to test that out. My goal is to test my art against the market—in Atlanta (because I believe the market is less competitive and I can live with my brother). First, I will get a labor or clerical job in Atlanta to support myself and then begin making contacts in the freelance art and design community. If I have not made substantial progress toward my goal after two years, I will look into more traditional art careers.

FIGURE A-4 / A goal-setting worksheet.

résumé will almost certainly eliminate you from further consideration. A résumé should be complete, yet concise. It should include all the important information about you without being wordy. Employers want to know about all your work experience, including work that does not directly relate to the job for which you are applying. For example, if you majored in economics, you might decide not to list your work experience in a cafeteria, on the swing shift in a factory, or as a dishwasher. You might think those jobs are too unrelated to your major. But a potential employer will think they say a lot about your motivation, attitude, and willingness to finance your education.

Tell about such jobs on your résumé in a way that best shows what you can do for a prospective employer. Do not misrepresent your experience, but do point out important accomplishments that will interest the employer. If you mowed lawns during summer vacations, don't just say "mowed lawns." Instead, say, "operated a lawn care business, solicited new accounts, and provided garden services for three summers." Use some key action verbs: *took responsibility for, supervised, directed, constructed, taught, managed, and took care of.* Figure A-5

First draft

FIGURE A-5 / The development of a résumé. (*Source:* Albert C. Van Roden and Thomas D. Bachhuber, *You're Hired,* Liberty Press, Berkeley, Calif., 1981.)

Name: John Jones
College Graduate: Kingsport University
Liberal Arts
Sociology Major: C+ average
Member tennis team
SAE fraternity

Central High School 700 Seventh Ave.
Hartford, CT 06150

References:

_____

_____

Job Experience:
    Factory worker (summer job)
    Sandwich maker (at college)
    House Painter (after college)

Hobbies:
    Fishing, hunting, tennis,
    and swimming

This résumé says YOU DON'T WANT ME, DO YOU?

It presents the applicant in the weakest possible light. It de-emphasizes work achievements indicating, instead that he likes to play.

It also shows without explanation that he had a manual job after graduating from college.

This résumé fails to give an employer a strong reason to want to talk to the applicant.

The message here is "file me."

shows an ineffective way of presenting one's background and how that draft can be changed to present the most positive image possible.

Design your résumé so that it is easy to read. It should not be longer than two pages. Potential employers do not have the time or interest to read unnecessary and irrelevant material. Highlight headings or set them to one side so that readers can easily locate items of special interest.

Arrange your résumé chronologically if your work history has been steady and relevant to your present job target. List the most recent

Second draft (after refining)

John Jones   April 1, 1989
42 Crane Lane
Easton, PA 17502
Phone: (555) 247-7777

Objective:	Sales trainee, established sporting goods manufacturer, leading to territory representative. Desire a position where I can immediately demonstrate my selling ability.	This résumé communicates: Initiative. Sales ability. Self-confidence. Risk-taking ability.
Education:	Kingsport University Binghampton, NY Liberal Arts Degree Central High School 700 Seventh Avenue Hartford, CT 06150	
Work Experience:	Self-employed painting contractor. Started business with partner. Sold and fulfilled 6/15/88 to present. Sold to four homeowners on one street, two by referrals from pleased customers.	Industrious. Organizational abilities. Effective interpersonal relations.
	Operated a very successful sandwich business at college. Made and sold sandwiches on campus at night for two years.	Responsible. Persistent. Continuity and dependability. Energy. Knowledge of plant operations.
	H.K. Smith, Inc. Held various factory jobs at two plants over three summers. Supervisor said I was one of the hardest working members of the summer crew.	
Other:	Tennis teams: #4 position in college #1 position in high school American Legion Award Hobbies: Sports, reading, making own fishing rods.	Competitiveness. Leadership. Diversity of interests.

experience first. If you have had a "checkered" career, your experience might look better presented functionally. Highlight your experience according to functions performed, as did the applicant whose résumé appears in Figure A-6. In either case, reproduce your résumé either by offset printing or by a high-quality photocopier. Use white or light-colored, high-quality paper.

cover letter

Never send a résumé without a cover letter. A **cover letter** is a document that accompanies a résumé and informs the employer of the writer's purposes in sending a résumé. Types of cover letters include the letter of application, in which the writer applies for a specific vacancy; an informal interview letter, in which the writer requests an interview to obtain information or do research; and a letter of inquiry, in which the writer asks whether openings exist. An example of a letter of application appears in Figure A-7 (on p. 702).

STEP 5: RESPOND TO VACANCIES

Although published job vacancies will be few, responding to them is an important part of your job search. They can be found almost anywhere—career centers, state employment services, private employment agencies, professional and trade association newsletters and journals, newspaper want ads, and notices on bulletin boards in various agencies, offices, and organizations. Respond to them with a letter of application and a copy of your résumé. Published job vacancies can also be indirectly helpful. For instance, even if a specific job is not for you, the ad can offer useful information. You can tell what business a company is in and what types of jobs must exist to support the advertised one. Ads can also trigger ideas, leading you to possibilities you had not considered.

STEP 6: INQUIRE ABOUT POTENTIAL OPPORTUNITIES

Although it is usually a long shot and requires a fair amount of work, writing personal letters to inquire about potential opportunities (include a copy of your résumé) might prove successful. Names and addresses of employers can be found in various directories in your library or career planning office. Friends, relatives, work supervisors, and faculty can also provide you with contacts. The key to success here is being in the right place at the right time. You might stumble across a vacancy that was just about to be written up. Your letter and résumé should be written to create enough interest that the employer with a vacancy will want to talk with you.

STEP 7: SEEK INFORMATION AND UNCOVER HIDDEN OPPORTUNITIES

Passive job hunters rely on want ads or mass résumé and letter mailings in their job search. As we said earlier, it is better to use the active approach.

One way to research a particular firm is to look in your career library for annual reports, pamphlets, and other information about the firm. Develop the habit of scanning business periodicals like *Business*

```
                Sherri Goldberg                                      March 1, 1989
                5 Esty Farm Rd.
                Newton Centre, MA 02159
                (617) 969-3997


     CAREER     To obtain a position of responsibility and challenge within the general field of busi-
  OBJECTIVE     ness management.

  EDUCATION     University of Massachusetts, Amherst. BA in Psychology - May 1989 3.63 G.P.A.

                Pertinent course work included Management, Marketing, Economics, Statistics; col-
                lege education included a wide variety of courses in Communications, Social Sci-
                ences, Health Sciences, Humanities.

    SUMMARY     INTERVIEWING and COMMUNICATIONS
         OF       Work experience at Local High School (1989) Functioned as a para-guidance
CAPABILITIES      counselor; counseled students on academic, drug and alcohol issues, social
                  difficulties, family problems; worked with administration on deciding optimum
                  solutions to crisis situations.

                  Committee to Select Residence Heads and Residence Assistants (1988-1989)
                  Screened, interviewed and selected individuals to act as residence heads (ad-
                  ministrators) and residence assistants (dorm counselors).

                  Student Advisory Board (1988-1989) Heard cases of student misconduct and de-
                  cided upon course of action, form of court hearings, made recommendations to
                  administration, interpreted laws and regulations.

                  Counselor (summers 1985-1988) Employed as children's counselor; respon-
                  sibilities included supervising activities, instructing in recreation, athletics,
                  aquatics; facilitated group living and cooperation, counseled personal, social,
                  and family problems.

                ADMINISTRATION
                  Work experience at Printing/Publishing Co. (1989) Responsibilities included data
                  entry for computer, planned promotional literature in subscription department.

                  Publicity Director for Theatre Arts Department (1986) Responsible for retaining
                  artist, printer, and distributors; directed all financial and scheduling matters.

                  Business Coordinator for Music Department (1986) Scheduled and arranged mu-
                  sical concerts, helped construct and interpret departmental policies, managed
                  finances.

                GROUP LEADERSHIP
                  Officer of National Sorority (1988-1989) Secretary for Sigma Delta Tau Sorority;
                  duties included organizing, coordinating, recording minutes at meetings.

                  Elected Member of Student Senate (1987-1989) Allocated activity funds, planned
                  and scheduled university activities, instituted and enforced regulations and laws
                  governing student body.

  REFERENCES    Will be furnished upon request by the Career Development Center, University of Mas-
                sachusetts, Amherst, MA 01003
```

FIGURE A-6 / A final resume.

2379 Third Avenue
Brookline, MA 02194
April 1, 1989

Mr. John M. Smith
Vice President of Marketing
New England Bank
P.O. Box 1000
Boston, MA 02159

Dear Mr. Smith:

This opening would be appropriate if a personal contact provided the initial information about the job.

I wish to be considered for the position of assistant to the director of marketing research in your marketing department. Dr. Parker, my faculty advisor, has advised me of the opening and suggested that I apply.

OR

This opening would be appropriate for a response to a published job vacancy.

I am writing in regard to a recently announced vacancy for an assistant to the director of marketing research that appeared in the *Boston Globe* of March 28, 1989. I feel that my qualifications and ambitions are consistent with those necessary for success in this field and would sincerely appreciate being considered as an applicant.

As you can see on the enclosed résumé, I will be graduating with a B.S. degree in marketing from the University of Lowell and will be available for employment after June 1, 1989. For the past two years I have been a part-time student worker in the marketing department at Lowell. I have gained valuable practical experience in conducting personal interviews, analyzing statistical data, and developing sampling plans. My most recent project was an analysis of our students' use of bank credit cards.

I would appreciate the opportunity to meet with you, at your convenience, to explore the possibility of securing the position of research assistant at New England Bank. My phone number is (617) 555-1354. I am looking forward to hearing from you. Thank you for your consideration.

Sincerely,

Joan Mann

Joan Mann

FIGURE A-7 / A letter of application.

Week, Fortune, and *The Wall Street Journal.* You might also try calling prospective employers for additional information regarding career opportunities.

STEP 8: SCHEDULE INTERVIEWS

Employers' representatives often come directly to campus to interview graduates or students in their final year. In most cases they represent those areas of the job market that are most in need—typically technical, computer science, engineering, and a number of business management functions such as accounting. Take advantage of this kind of opportunity.

Job interviews are the most important part of your job search. Yet few applicants spend enough time and effort preparing for interviews. They are either too anxious or too overconfident to realize that you can prepare for an interview. There are many typical situations and frequently asked questions that need not take you by surprise. When you know what to expect, you can plan your responses and handle the interview more effectively.

Your career library should have books and videotapes on interview preparation, and your career planning office might offer seminars or workshops on the subject. Once you understand interview protocol, you can practice in front of a mirror or with a cassette recorder and role-play with a friend or career counselor. The following are a few important interviewing tips:

- Know the interviewer's and the employer's names and their proper pronunciation.
- Arrive 15 to 20 minutes early for interviews. This might give you more time with the interviewer, or you might hear important information that you can use during your interview.
- Maintain effective eye contact with the interviewer.
- Be sure your personal appearance and your clothes make a favorable impression. Conservative clothing is most effective.
- Prepare for their questions. Most career planning offices have long lists of the types of questions typically asked by interviewers. But do not try to memorize answers. You will not make a favorable impression on the interviewer.
- Be prepared to ask questions about the company and the job.
- Remember that the first five minutes are critical. Research shows that the decision to hire or reject is usually made within the first five minutes of an interview. First impressions count!
- Write a short thank you note. Interviewers appreciate the thought and will be impressed by your courtesy.

STEP 9: ACCEPT A JOB OFFER

Preparing and practicing for interviews will give you a decided edge in the job market. And successful interviewing will lead to job offers. If you have talked yourself into several job offers, you could be faced with the "problem" of choosing which one to take.

You can make your choice easier by weighing the advantages of each job against your personal scale of priorities and then comparing each job to the other. A job with a very high salary might seem to be the obvious choice over a lower-paying one—but look again. Ask the employer what a typical workday would entail. The answer will be much more enlightening than a job description. Then compare the typical workday to your list of interests, skills, and values and ask yourself whether you could really do the work well and enjoy it.

Final Ingredients for Success

Planning a successful career and landing a satisfying first job require a number of qualities including organization and commitment. The beginning career planner must also develop personal traits such as initiative, assertiveness, courage, communication skills, and career knowledge.

Many people struggle through career decisions and transitions without the structure of a career planning program like the one we have discussed. But there is no need to make such important life changes in a haphazard way. Assistance is near in the form of career planning offices, career counselors, and career libraries.

Even the most organized career planners will experience frustration early on because the right job does not come easily. Research shows that most college graduates do not find rewarding jobs until 6 to 12 months after graduation. But after 12 months, more than 90 percent of all college graduates are in satisfying positions.

With such information in mind a beginning career planner should be prepared for early disappointments and view them not as signs of failure, but as learning experiences. Each attempt to find the right job is a chance to gain more information on what to do and what not to do the next time around. Embrace the task of planning your future as an adventure, welcome the support of counselors, friends, and loved ones, and discover how you can gain from all your experiences. Through your positive attitude and practical efforts, you will find your career direction and land a satisfying first job. And who could ask for a better start to life after college?

A P P E N D I X B

Statistics in Business

In the newspapers, in textbooks (including this one), in government reports, and on the TV news, we are surrounded by statistics. The average business manager needs to keep up with the competition, the economic environment, and what goes on inside the firm. To do this, the manager must be able to read, analyze, and interpret data. **Statistics** is a general term for numerical data and their collection, classification, analysis, interpretation, and presentation. The term is also applied to specific sets of numbers, such as "the statistics on last year's sales."

statistics

A business manager is especially interested in the use of statistics for decision making. He or she will need statistics to analyze data, interpret it, and make decisions of all kinds. The manager might need to decide, for example, how much of each type of goods to produce next month or how many salespeople are needed for the newly created sales district.

Analyzing Data

Let's examine a sales staffing problem and how statistics could be used to help solve it. We will look at the case of the Marsdon School Supply Corporation. This small midwestern school supply company is considering opening a new West Coast territory. Ann Gault, the sales director of the firm, started by examining the sales of the existing sales staff in the past year. This is shown in Table B-1 (on p. 706). She wanted each new salesperson to have the same average sales as the existing staff and needed to compute the average sales.

MEAN, MEDIAN, AND MODE

arithmetic mean

How do we determine the average sales per salesperson for last year? The most common type of average is the arithmetic mean. The **arithmetic mean** is the total of all numbers in a series divided by the *number*

Salesperson	Dollar Sales
Glover, J. A.	$ 98,000
Pond, M. R.	77,000
Gerritano, L.	75,000
Rush, G. G.	65,000
Perkins, M. G.	60,000
Blount, R. M.	53,000
Smith, M. L.	48,000
Bragg, S. F.	38,000
Mallen, E. W.	38,000
Wisner, E. W.	33,000
Archer, W. W.	20,000
Total Sales	$605,000

of numbers. In the case of the Marsdon Corporation, the arithmetic mean of sales per salesperson is $605,000 divided by 11, or $55,000.

median

A second kind of average is called the median. The **median** is the middle number of an array (an arrangement of numbers in ascending or descending order). The sales figures in Table B-1 are arranged in an array, so the median amount of sales by a salesperson is $53,000. R. M. Blount's $53,000 in sales is the median amount because exactly the same number of people sold more than Blount as sold less than Blount.

mode

Still another "average" or "measure of central tendency" is called the mode. The **mode** is the number that appears most often in a series of numbers. In this case the amount is $38,000 because this is the only amount appearing more than once. In this example the mean and median are fairly close to each other, and the mode is a much smaller number. It is quite likely that either the mean or the median is the best "average" for Ann Gault to use in making the decision. In this case, let's assume that she used the arithmetic mean, $55,000, to represent the "typical" sales volume for a salesperson.

CORRELATION

variable

It is said that daily sales of ice cream are *correlated* with the temperature outdoors. Some people feel that taller people are more successful in selling than shorter people—that height is *correlated* with sales success. We use the term **"variable"** to mean something that varies or changes. In the simple examples cited above—ice cream sales, temperature, height, and sales success—are all examples of variables. The idea

correlation

of correlation is important in statistical analysis for business. **Correlation** between two variables means that there is a relationship between them so that variation in one is associated with variation in the other.

To continue with the Marsdon Corporation example, let's assume that past experience suggests that the annual sales of school supplies in the various states are correlated with the student populations of those states. Sales and number of students are the two variables in this case. Ann Gault went to the computer and produced Table B-2. It shows, for the twelve midwestern states in which Marsdon has been selling, the information needed for Ann to see whether these variables are really correlated. With the data from Table B-2, Ann created Figure B-1 (on p. 708). Figure B-1 is a linear graph or "plot" of the relationship (correlation) between Marsdon sales and school enrollment in the twelve states. In Figure B-1, each dot represents two variables for each of the twelve states: (1) school enrollment and (2) Marsdon sales. School enrollment is measured on the vertical scale of the graph (on its left edge), and sales on the horizontal scale (at the bottom). School enrollment in Ohio was 2,312 thousand, so the "Ohio dot" is directly across from the 2,312 thousand point on the vertical scale. Likewise, Marsdon sales in Ohio were $98 thousand, so the "Ohio dot" is directly above the $98 thousand point on the horizontal scale.

The dashed line moving upward and to the right in Figure B-1 is an approximation of the correlation between the two variables. Notice that the dots are clustered close to the line. This means that the two variables are *highly* correlated. The fact that the line slopes upward to the right means that the relationship between enrollment and sales is positive. **positive correlation** **Positive correlation** between two variables like this means that, in

TABLE B-2 / **School enrollment and Marsdon School Supply Corporation sales, 1989 in midwestern states**

State	School Enrollment (000)	Marsdon Sales ($000)
Ohio	2,312	98
Indiana	1,181	45
Illinois	2,404	109
Michigan	2,089	89
Wisconsin	1,014	50
Minnesota	867	48
Iowa	605	40
Missouri	998	55
North Dakota	134	20
South Dakota	143	10
Nebraska	323	28
Kansas	457	13
Total	12,527	605

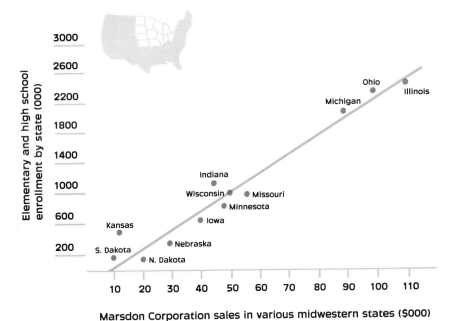

FIGURE B-1 / School enrollment and Marsdon School Supply Corporation sales by state.

general, as one increases, the other also increases, and likewise, if one decreases, the other decreases. **Negative correlation** is when one variable increases and the other decreases. When a line slopes downward to the right and the dots are clustered around it, this indicates that the correlation is negative. If the dots were widely scattered so that no clear pattern appeared, there would be no correlation.

The *Statistical Abstract of the United States* is a good source of statistics of all kinds. It shows that the group of states in the new West Coast territory have half as many students as the states already covered by Marsdon salespeople. Because of the evidence that there is strong correlation, it makes sense for Ann Gault to conclude that the West Coast district has the potential to produce about $300,000 in sales. She has reason to recommend that five new salespeople be hired. ($300,000/$55,000 = 5.45.)

It is wise to remember that statistical analysis like this gives us only a crude basis for predicting what will really happen.

FREQUENCY DISTRIBUTIONS

"Averages" like the mean, median, and mode are one way of summarizing sets of data like those in Table B-1. These single numbers tell us very little about the whole array of sales figures they represent. A more informative summary is known as a frequency distribution. A **frequency distribution** is a table showing the number of observations (individual sales records, for example) that fall in each of several categories. Table B-3 is a frequency distribution of the data in Table B-1.

The basic frequency distribution is shown in the column headed "Number." It shows that two salespeople sold more than $75,000, four

TABLE B-3 / **Frequency distribution of Marsdon Corporation salespersons' sales, 1989**

Dollar Sales	Salespersons	
	Number	Percent
More than $75,000	2	18.2
$50,001–75,000	4	36.4
$25,001–50,000	4	36.4
$25,000 or less	1	9.1
Total	11	100.1*

*The sum of percentages is off by one-tenth of one percent because of rounding. Traditionally, numbers are rounded to the nearest decimal, some up and some down. In this case the rounding (e.g., 2/11 = 18.18% which rounds to 18.2%) results in a slight exaggeration of the true total of percentages.

salespeople sold between $50,001 and $75,000, and so forth. At the right of this is a *percentage distribution* in the same $25,000-interval categories. These percentages may be calculated by dividing each of the "raw" frequencies by the total. Two divided by 11 equals .1818 or 18.2 percent. The numbers are rounded to the nearest tenth of one percent. Rounding is explained in the footnote to Table B-3.

From a frequency table like Table B-3, Ann Gault and other managers can get a quick idea of the range of sales volumes made by the individual salespeople and a feel for what the "typical" salesperson sells in a year. It tells more than an "average" like the arithmetic mean and somewhat less than the whole array in Table B-1. It is a lot quicker to digest than the whole array, however, so it is a convenient tool for analysis. This is especially true when very large numbers of sales records or other data sets are being examined. Ann Gault can tell immediately that one salesperson is performing well below the average or that two are performing well above it. For even more informative and dramatic representations of statistical facts, a wide variety of graphics have been developed. We will examine several such graphic presentations in Figure B-2 (on p. 710).

How to Present Data

Figure B-2 shows four types of graphics presentations used widely in business. These are the bar chart, pictograph, pie chart, and line graph. In the upper left position is the *bar chart*. This example compares starting salaries of graduates with several different majors for the years 1974 and 1984. In a business the bar chart could be used in many ways to show growth over time or to compare the size or volume of two different things at the same time.

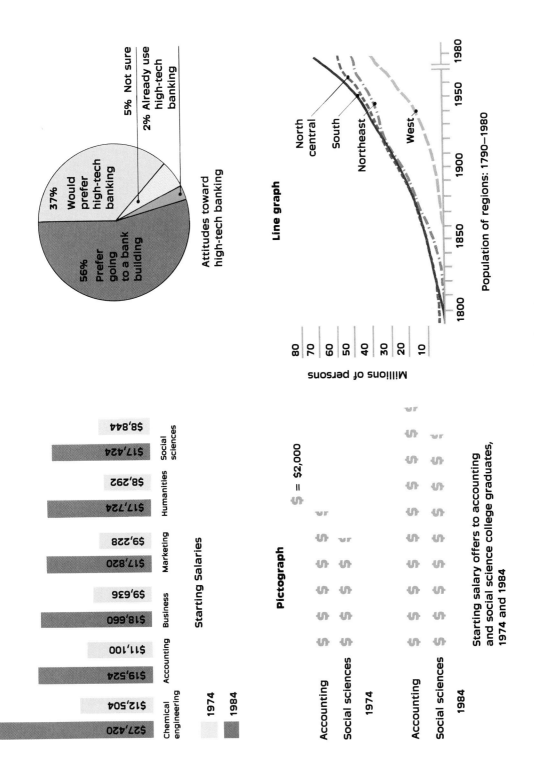

FIGURE B-2 / Common types of graphic presentation. Bar chart, pictograph, and pie chart reprinted by permission of *The Wall Street Journal*, © Dow Jones & Company, Inc., 1985. All Rights Reserved. Line graph from U.S. Department of Commerce, Bureau of the Census.

Pie chart

37% Would prefer high-tech banking

56% Prefer going to a bank building

5% Not sure

2% Already use high-tech banking

Attitudes toward high-tech banking

Line graph

North central

South

Northeast

West

Population of regions: 1790–1980

Millions of persons

80
70
60
50
40
30
20
10

1800 1850 1900 1950 1980

Bar chart

Starting Salaries

1974
1984

Chemical engineering $12,504 / $27,420
Accounting $11,100 / $19,524
Business $9,636 / $18,660
Marketing $9,228 / $17,820
Humanities $8,292 / $17,724
Social sciences $8,844 / $17,424

Pictograph

$ = $2,000

Accounting
Social sciences
1974

Accounting
Social sciences
1984

Starting salary offers to accounting and social science college graduates, 1974 and 1984

The *pictograph* shown at the lower left does much the same thing as the bar chart except that it helps dramatize the quantity being compared. The dollar signs in Figure B-2 dramatize the relative sizes of salaries offered to Accounting and Social Science graduates in two years.

In the upper right position is a *pie chart*, which is especially effective in showing percentages of a total. This example shows the percentages of responses to a survey regarding attitudes toward high-tech banking.

The lower right illustration is a *line graph*. It shows change in one or more items of data over time. It is similar to Figure B-1 except that time is on the horizontal scale. Notice also that it differs from Figure B-1 in that, in Figure B-2, the "dots" are connected. This makes sense in Figure B-2 because the dots follow from left to right in time sequence. This emphasizes change (growth) over time in a dramatic way. Here we can compare the population growth over time of four regions of the country.

Charts like these are easy to create with the help of personal computers. Many PCs have graphics capability. With the use of a good printer, a student or employee can turn computer-based tabular data into printed graphics in a matter of minutes.

G L O S S A R Y

absolute advantage The position a country enjoys when it is the only country that can provide a certain product or when it can offer the product at a lower cost than any other country. **(p. 664)**

accountability The act of holding subordinates liable. **(p. 199)**

account executive The person who is in charge of the entire relationship between the advertising agency and a particular client (account) and coordinates the work of the group of professionals involved in the client's ad program, including copywriters, artists, TV directors, and media buyers. **(p. 383)**

accounting The process of measuring, recording, interpreting, and reporting data that reflect the financial condition of the firm. **(p. 432)**

accounts Individual records for specific assets, liabilities, owners' equity, revenues, and expenses. **(p. 446)**

accrual The principle in accounting that means that a firm charges off expenses only in the accounting period (usually the calendar year) in which the firm's operations benefit from the expense and not necessarily in the period in which the actual cash payment was made. **(p. 441)**

acquisition One firm purchases another firm or a controlling interest in another firm. **(p. 90)**

active job hunting An approach to securing employment in which the individual takes control of the job search, determining career goals, identifying interesting jobs, and going after opportunities. **(p. 693)**

actuaries Loss-predicting experts of insurance companies. **(p. 564)**

adhocracy An approach to organizing in which there is a deliberate attempt to avoid pigeonholing employees into specialized jobs and to forbid blind adherence to the chain of command. **(p. 209)**

administrative law The set of rules and regulations developed by government agencies and commissions on the basis of their interpretations of the specific statutory laws that they administer. **(p. 639)**

advertising Any nonpersonal promotional activity for which a fee is paid by an identified sponsor. **(p. 378)**

advertising agency A firm that specializes in planning, producing, and placing advertisements in the media for clients. **(p. 382)**

advertising media Newspapers, magazines, television, radio, billboards, and other media that carry the messages designed by firms and their agencies to many receivers (customers or potential customers). **(p. 383)**

affirmative action plan A firm's detailed statement describing how it will actively recruit minorities and women and upgrade the jobs they currently hold. **(p. 55 and p. 229)**

agency-principal relationship An arrangement in which one party (the agent) is authorized and consents to act on behalf of another party (the principal). **(p. 642)**

agency shop A type of union security in which all employees for whom the union bargains must pay dues, but they need not join the union. **(p. 266)**

AIDA process A way of analyzing an ad in terms of bringing the reader or listener through stages of attention, interest, desire, and action. **(p. 387)**

American Standard Code for Information Interchange (ASCII) A standard computer code for numbers, letters, and special characters shared in the United States by many producers of word processing and other software. **(p. 592)**

antitrust laws A set of federal laws dating back as far as 1890 that are aimed at (1) increasing effective competition, especially among large firms and (2) reducing the concentration of economic power. **(p. 614)**

application software Consists of programs that do practical jobs for the computer user. **(p. 593)**

arbitration A process in which a neutral third party (an arbitrator) has the task of developing a solution to a problem that has labor-management negotiations bogged down. **(p. 272)**

arithmetic mean The total of all numbers in a series divided by the number of numbers. **(p. 705)**

assembly language A language that is used to write system software. **(p. 592)**

assembly line Consists of a fixed sequence of specialized machines and work stations for producing a product. **(p. 295)**

asset Whatever a firm, organization, or individual owns that has a dollar value. **(p. 437)**

asset redeployment The selling of company divisions. **(p. 516)**

authority The right to take action, the right to make decisions, the right to direct the work of others, and the right to give orders. **(p. 199)**

automation A system, process, or machine that operates automatically, a self-regulating system in which mechanical or electronic devices replace much of the monitoring and adjusting performed by workers. **(p. 304)**

background investigation A check of a job applicant's history by contacting former employers (if any), neighbors, teachers, and others who might be familiar with his or her past. **(p. 234)**

bailor-bailee relationship An arrangement in which one party (the bailor) gives possession and control of his or her property to another party (the bailee) but retains ownership of that property. **(p. 643)**

balance of payments The difference between money flowing into the country and money flowing out of that country as a result of trade and other transactions. **(p. 669)**

balance of trade The difference in value between a country's total exports and its total imports. **(p. 669)**

balance sheet A financial statement that shows what a firm owns, what it owes, and what the owners' interest is worth at a given point in time. **(p. 440)**

bankruptcy A condition in which a firm or an individual cannot meet maturing financial obligations (insolvency) and has liabilities that exceed the value of assets. **(p. 648)**

bargainable issues Matters that employer and union are permitted by law to discuss. **(p. 271)**

bargaining in good faith A process in which proposals are matched with counterproposals and labor and management make every reasonable effort to arrive at an agreement. **(p. 271)**

basic accounting equation A mathematical statement of the balance between what a firm owns, what it owes, and what the owner's share is worth. Assets = Liabilities + Owners' Equity (Capital) or Assets − Liabilities = Owners' Equity (Capital) **(p. 437)**

batch processing Occurs when data is entered into computers in batches from time to time rather than continuously. **(p. 592)**

batch production An intermittent production system that involves producing products in small batches—two or three items at a time or twenty gallons at a time. **(p. 294)**

bear market A market situation in which stock prices as a whole are falling and there is a great deal of pessimism among speculators. **(p. 542)**

behavior modification Involves changing (modifying) behavior through the use of rewards or punishment. **(p. 183)**

blacklists Contained the names of workers who were known to favor unions and were circulated among employers who then refused employment to the listed workers. **(p. 257)**

board of directors A group elected by the stockholders to govern a corporation's affairs and to develop general corporate policy. **(p. 85)**

bona fide occupational qualification (BFOQ) A selection requirement based on sex, age, religion, or national origin that is justified and legal as a basis for selecting job applicants. **(p. 228)**

bond A written promise that a borrower will pay the lender, at some stated future date, a sum of money (the principal) and a stated rate of interest. **(p. 524)**

book value The difference between the dollar values of what a company owns (its assets) and what it owes (its debts, or liabilities) divided by the number of shares of common stock. **(p. 523)**

boycott A concentrated effort by which a union tries to get the public to refuse to deal with the boycotted firm. **(p. 275)**

brand As defined by the American Marketing Association, "A name, term, symbol, or design, or combination of them which is intended to identify the goods or services of one seller or group of sellers and to differentiate them from those of competitors." **(p. 362)**

brand advertising Advertising to promote the particular brand of product sold by the advertiser. **(p. 382)**

breach of contract Occurs when one party to a contract fails to live up to the contract's terms without having a legal excuse for doing so. **(p. 641)**

breakeven analysis The computation of a price-quantity combination at which a firm covers its fixed and variable costs. **(p. 364)**

brokerage house A firm that buys and sells securities on behalf of its investor-clients. **(p. 527)**

budget A formal dollars-and-cents statement of expected performance. **(p. 452)**

bull market A market situation in which stock prices as a whole are rising and there is a great deal of optimism among speculators. **(p. 542)**

bureaucracy An approach to organizing that is characterized by a well-defined chain of command, a division of work between departments, a system of rules covering the rights and duties of all employees, a system of procedures for dealing with routine decisions, a selection process for employment and promotion based on technical competence, and an impersonality of relationships in which everyone is rewarded and punished on the basis of the same set of rules. **(p. 209)**

burnout The total depletion of one's physical and mental resources caused by excessive striving and stress to reach some unrealistic work-related goal. **(p. 247)**

business All profit-seeking activities that are organized and directed to provide goods and services to customers. **(p. 5)**

business cycle Fluctuations in the level of economic activity that an economy goes through over time. **(p. 40)**

business ethics A collection of principles and rules of conduct based on beliefs about what is right and wrong business behavior. **(p. 59 and p. 649)**

business incubator A facility that is operated by a government unit, a university, or a private investment group to provide low rent, shared office services, and management advice to new business ventures. **(p. 103)**

business interruption insurance Pays the insured firm for profits and overhead costs lost as a result of a specific peril, such as fire. **(p. 571)**

business law The body of law that pertains particularly to business activities. **(p. 639)**

business plan A document that spells out in detail the firm's mission, its objectives, and the actions (strategies and tactics) needed to achieve the firm's objectives **(p. 115)**

cafeteria benefit plans Flexible benefit plans that enable employees to pick and choose from available options and develop individualized benefit plans. **(p. 245)**

call option Gives a trader the right to buy a specific stock at a specific price and at a specific time in the future (usually 30, 60, 90, or 180 days). **(p. 544)**

capital A factor of production—the funds provided by investors, lenders, and retained earnings to finance a firm's activities. **(p. 12)**

capital budgeting The process of planning expenditures on assets whose returns are expected to extend beyond one year (usually for five or more). **(p. 506)**

capital formation The process of adding to an economy's productive capacity. **(p. 26)**

capital-intensive processes Production processes that depend more on machines than on people. **(p. 291)**

capitalism An economic system in which the decisions of private individuals and privately owned business firms determine which goods and services will be produced and how they will be distributed among the people. **(p. 17)**

career counselors People in career planning/placement offices who advise and assist students in relating their interests, skills, and values to career and job choices. **(p. 691)**

career management Giving employees the assistance and job opportunities that will enable them to form realistic career goals and realize them. **(p. 247)**

career planning The process of choosing a career and going after a satisfying job in an organized, thoughtful way. **(p. 691)**

career planning/placement office A campus office whose mission is to help students make satisfying career choices and find the right jobs. **(p. 691)**

career self-assessment The process of discovering one's interests, skills, and values and relating them to career possibilities. **(p. 693)**

cartel A group of firms in different countries (or a group of countries, such as the Organization of Petroleum Exporting Countries, or OPEC) that agree to operate as a monopoly by regulating production and prices. **(p. 682)**

cash discount A reduction in price as a reward for prompt payment in full. **(p. 368)**

cash dividend A payment of cash to stockholders. **(p. 524)**

centralization Decision-making authority is concentrated in the hands of a few people at the top of a firm. **(p. 200)**

central planning The practice by which a government drafts a master plan and directly manages the economy to achieve the plan's goals. **(p. 18)**

central processing unit (CPU) The heart of a computer—includes an arithmetic unit for performing calculations, a logic unit for comparing values and helping the computer to "make decisions," and a control unit that "supervises" the computer's internal operations and sends instructions for controlling the whole system. **(p. 588)**

certificate of deposit (CD) a time deposit in a financial institution that is made for a certain period of time at a fixed rate of interest. **(p. 467)**

Certified Management Accountant (CMA) An accountant who has met the educational and experience requirements set by the Institute of Certified Management Accountants (an arm of the National Association of Accountants) and has passed a five-part examination. **(p. 436)**

Certified Public Accountant (CPA) An accountant who has fulfilled the legal requirements of his or her state for knowledge in accounting theory, practice, auditing, and law and who is licensed to sign legally required financial reports. **(p. 434)**

channel of distribution The firm or set of firms that are actively engaged in buying and selling products as they go from producer to user. **(p. 404)**

closed shop A type of union security in which an employer can hire only union members. **(p. 266)**

code of ethics A formal, published collection of values and rules that are used to upgrade and guide behavior. **(p. 650)**

coinsurance The sharing of risk between the insured and insurer. **(p. 567)**

collective bargaining The process of negotiating a labor agreement between union and employer representatives and the process of administering an existing agreement. **(p. 259)**

collective bargaining agreement A document that sets forth the terms and conditions under which union members will offer their services to an employer. **(p. 259)**

combination export manager A domestic agent middleman that serves as the export department for several noncompeting manufacturers on a commission basis. **(p. 678)**

commercial bank A privately owned, profit-seeking depository institution that serves its business and nonbusiness customers by accepting deposits that can be withdrawn on demand, by accepting savings deposits, and by making loans. **(p. 464)**

commercial finance company A financial institution that makes loans to firms using accounts receivable, inventories, or equipment as security (collateral). **(p. 483)**

commercial paper Short-term unsecured promissory notes issued by finance companies and certain corporations. **(p. 500)**

common carrier A transportation firm that offers its services to the general public at uniform published rates. **(p. 421)**

common law The body of unwritten laws that has grown out of previous judicial decisions and accepted practices and customs. **(p. 639)**

common stock Shares of ownership in a corporation that confer voting rights and rights to residual earnings to common stockholders. **(p. 84)**

communication Transfer of information from a sender to a receiver. **(p. 211)**

communication process The process by which information (including facts and feelings) is transmitted from one person or group to another. **(p. 381)**

communism An economic system in which the citizens collectively own all of the country's productive capacity. **(p. 18)**

company culture The system of shared values and beliefs employees have about the standards and criteria used in the firm to judge achievement, individual contributions, and expertise. **(p. 213)**

comparable worth A legal concept that aims at paying equal wages for jobs that are of comparable value to the employer. **(p. 243)**

comparative advantage The position a country enjoys when it produces the products in which it has the greatest advantage, or the least disadvantage, in relation to other countries. **(p. 665)**

competition A rivalry among firms to attract customers in the hope of making a profit. **(p. 48)**

comprehensive general liability insurance Provides basic protection against losses stemming from the firm's legal liability to others. **(p. 570)**

computer (or *computer system*) A system that uses electronics to receive, store, retrieve, manipulate, and communicate large amounts of data very quickly and precisely. **(p. 584)**

computer-aided design (CAD) A process that enables designers of machinery parts and other items to sketch their design on a computer screen with an electronic pencil. (p. 306)

computer-aided manufacturing (CAM) A process that guides via computer the steps involved in producing a product. (p. 306)

computer program A detailed set of instructions for a computer, written in a special computer language. (p. 592)

conciliation A process in which a neutral third party (a conciliator) seeks to prevent labor-management negotiations from breaking down. (p. 272)

consent order An agreement by a firm that is presumed to be in violation of administrative law "to cease and desist" a practice. (p. 621)

consumer finance company (or *personal finance company*) A financial institution that makes personal loans to consumers. (p. 483)

consumerism Term used to describe organized efforts of consumers to demand honest and fair business practices. (p. 57)

consumer market The market for all goods and services that will be bought and used for their own sake (not to produce other goods and services). (p. 327)

consumer purchase decision models Representations of the processes by which consumers arrive at a purchase. (p. 334)

containerization The practice in modern transportation of using standard large containers, preloaded by the shipper, and delivered as a unit to the destination without breaking the seal. (p. 424)

contingency leadership theory A theory that holds that the style of leadership that is best for a situation depends on (is contingent on) the needs of the situation. (p. 175)

continuous production A production process that operates more or less continuously. (p. 296)

contract A mutual agreement between two or more people to perform or not perform certain acts. (p. 641)

contract carrier A transportation firm, such as a trucking company, that negotiates private agreements with shippers to handle their freight. (p. 421)

control chart A device on which upper and lower limits are drawn and some measurable aspect of the product (length, weight, etc.) is measured after inspection of the product. (p. 308)

controlling The task of ensuring that activities are providing the planned results. (p. 155)

convenience goods Items bought frequently, demanded on short notice, and often purchased by habit. (p. 350)

cooperative advertising Advertising for which the cost is shared by the manufacturer and retailer. (p. 396)

cooperative association (co-op) An incorporated organization whose user-members (owners) get back any revenue left after expenses are paid. (p. 94)

copyright Grants creators of dramatic, musical, and other intellectual properties or their heirs exclusive rights to their published or unpublished works for as long as the creator lives, plus 50 years. (p. 644)

corporate campaign Involves picketing to inform the employer's customers and others that the firm is nonunionized, a boycott to induce the employer's workers and customers to stop buying the firm's products, and a broader strategy aimed at the outside directors on the target firm's board of directors. (p. 276)

corporate charter A contract between the incorporators and the state that authorizes the formation of the corporation. (p. 81)

corporation A legally chartered organization that is a separate and legal entity apart from its owners. (p. 76)

corporation bylaws Rules by which a corporation will operate. (p. 86)

correlation Relationship between two variables so that variation in one is associated with variation in the other. (p. 706)

countertrades Transactions in which purchases are paid for with something other than money and credit as the medium of exchange. (p. 683)

cover letter A document that accompanies a résumé and informs the employer of the writer's purposes in sending a résumé. (p. 700)

craft unions Labor unions that are organized by crafts or trades such as plumbers, printers, and airline pilots. (p. 264)

credit union A cooperative savings association formed by the employees of a company or non-business organization. (p. 466)

cultural values Society's enduring beliefs that are shared by most of its people. (p. 55)

culture A society's sum total of knowledge, beliefs, values, customs, and artifacts that people use in adapting to their environment and hand down to succeeding generations. (p. 53)

currency Coins and paper money that make up the cash money in a society. (p. 466)

current asset An asset that a firm normally expects to hold no longer than a year. (p. 441)

current liability A debt that will be paid off within a year from the balance sheet date. (p. 441)

current ratio A measure of a firm's liquidity that is computed by dividing current assets by current liabilities. (p. 450)

database management system (DBMS) Provides for easy, continuous updating of a set of data used by an organization, together with easy access to summaries and analysis of the data. (p. 599)

debit card A type of plastic money that, when used, immediately reduces the balance in the user's bank account. (p. 471)

debt financing The use of borrowed funds. (p. 492)

decentralization Delegating authority to subordinates for most decisions while maintaining control over companywide matters (p. 199)

decertification The process by which employees legally terminate their union's right to represent them. (p. 277)

decision-making process The process of (1) recognizing a problem or opportunity, (2) gathering information, (3) developing alternatives, (4) analyzing the alternatives, (5) choosing the best alternative, (6) implementing the decision, and (7) evaluating the decision. (p. 161)

deductible The portion of any loss that the insured firm or individual agrees to pay. **(p. 565)**

deed A legal document by which an owner of real property transfers ownership to someone else. **(p. 644)**

deferred compensation Benefits that are received from an employer after retirement rather than while the recipient is working for that employer. **(p. 250)**

delegation The process of assigning responsibility, granting authority, and establishing accountability. **(p. 199)**

demand deposit A checking account that enables the depositor to withdraw funds from the account immediately and without advance notice. **(p. 467)**

departmentalization The process through which a firm's activities are grouped together and assigned to managers. **(p. 204)**

department stores Retail stores that typically carry wide and deep merchandise lines including clothing, furniture, housewares, toys, and cosmetics. **(p. 414)**

depository institution A financial institution that is authorized to accept deposits that are withdrawable by check and that can obtain federal deposit insurance for up to $100,000 for each account. **(p. 464)**

depreciation A process of writing off the cost value of long-lived assets during the period that they contribute to the earnings of the firm. **(p. 441)**

deregulation Relaxation or elimination of laws governing how an industry does business. **(p. 512)**

directing The process of providing the motivation and leadership that is necessary for ensuring that the firm's employees do their jobs and accomplish their goals. **(p. 154)**

disability income insurance Insurance that provides employees with income when they are unable to work because of an accident or sickness. **(p. 574)**

discharge The permanent dismissal of an employee against his or her will. **(p. 249)**

discount rate The interest rate charged to depository institutions for borrowing at the Federal Reserve System. **(p. 478)**

discount stores Retail stores that sell a wide variety of merchandise at discount prices, stressing high turnover and self-service. **(p. 415)**

dismissal An involuntary temporary or permanent separation of the employee from the firm. **(p. 249)**

distributed data processing (DDP) A decentralized approach to information handling that relies on tying powerful PCs together into networks and bringing computer power to many different points in the large firm. **(p. 590)**

distribution All marketing activities that contribute time, place, and ownership utility to products. **(p. 404)**

distributor brands (or *private brands*) Brands that are developed by middlemen. **(p. 362)**

divestiture When a firm sells off one or more of its divisions or units. **(p. 92)**

documentation An explanation either in English (or other spoken language) or in diagram form of what a computer program does, how it is used, and how it works. **(p. 595)**

domestication An effort by a host government to shift decision-making power from the multinational company to local nationals. **(p. 685)**

doublebreasted firm A unionized employer that sets up a nonunion subsidiary to do some of its work. **(p. 267)**

double-entry bookkeeping The system of accounts and transactions in the framework of the accounting equation. **(p. 446)**

dumping The practice of selling substantial quantities of a product in a foreign country at prices that are below either the home market price of the same product or the full cost (including profit) of producing it. **(p. 668)**

ecology The relationship between living things and their environment. **(p. 58)**

economic order quantity (EOQ) The amount that a firm should order for inventory replenishment if it wants to minimize the sum of its carrying costs and order-processing costs. **(p. 424)**

economic system A framework of arrangements for carrying out the specialization and exchange process. **(p. 9)**

electronic funds transfer (EFT) Combines computer and communication technology to transfer funds or information in, into, from, within, and among financial institutions. **(p. 471)**

electronic spreadsheet A general-purpose computer program that allows the user to enter and manipulate numerical and alphabetic data in a computer screen format that is much like an accountant's lined pad. **(p. 594)**

embargo A prohibition or suspension of foreign trade in general or of foreign trade of specific imports or exports. **(p. 667)**

employee compensation All forms of pay or rewards going to employees and arising from their employment. **(p. 241)**

employee orientation The process of providing new employees with basic information about the firm. **(p. 235)**

endorsement The act of signing one's name to a negotiable instrument, having the effect of making it transferable to another party. **(p. 645)**

entrepreneur A risk taker who starts and operates a business in hope of making a profit. **(p. 13)**

entrepreneurial networking A person's concerted effort to meet and share problems and experiences with other people in similar businesses including those who have just started out in business for themselves. **(p. 113)**

entrepreneurship A factor of production. The process of bringing land, labor, and capital together and taking the risk involved in producing a good or service in the hope of profit. **(p. 13)**

environmental impact statement A statement of effects on the environment that might result from a proposed government or government-contracted project. **(p. 615)**

equipment trust certificates Intermediate-term obligation that is backed by the equipment that is purchased with revenues from the sale of the certificates. **(p. 511)**

equity financing The provision of funds by the owners of the firm themselves. **(p. 492)**

equity theory of pay   States that a worker compares his or her inputs (or effort) and his or her outputs with those of other workers doing the same or similar jobs and a person tries to maintain a balance between what he or she puts into a job and what he or she gets out of it. **(p. 242)**

exchange   Trade, or giving up one thing to get another thing. **(p. 8)**

exchange control   A situation in which a government limits access to its country's currency by foreigners. **(p. 685)**

exclusive dealing agreement   Requires a buyer, as a condition of sale, to refrain from dealing in products that compete with those of the seller. **(p. 614)**

exit interview   A meeting between a manager and an employee who is leaving the firm for the purpose of determining why the employee is leaving. **(p. 249)**

expense   The using up of resources by a firm in the pursuit of revenue. **(p. 443)**

expert system   A specialized computer program designed to process data relevant to a particular problem or decision to simplify or even conclude the decision-making process. **(p. 601)**

exports   Exports from a country are products produced in that country and sold in another. **(p. 665)**

facilitating middleman   A specialist in physical distribution functions, such as a trucking company or a warehousing company. **(p. 418)**

factoring company   (or *factor*) A financial institution that seeks to make a profit by buying accounts receivable at less than face value from a firm and collecting the face value of the accounts from the firm's customers. **(p. 483)**

factors of production   The basic inputs of the productive system—land, labor, capital, and entrepreneurship. **(p. 11)**

factory of the future   A production facility that is composed of five basic elements: automation, robotics, just-in-time inventory, a flexible manufacturing system, and computer-aided design and manufacturing. **(p. 302)**

fashion obsolescence   Occurs when a firm designs something that people feel is prettier or "more stylish" than an existing product. **(p. 353)**

featherbedding   An activity by which unions require employers to pay employees for services they neither perform nor offer to perform. **(p. 260)**

Federal Deposit Insurance Corporation (FDIC)   An independent government agency created by Congress in 1933 that insures each account in member banks up to $100,000. **(p. 464)**

Federal Reserve System (the Fed)   The central bank of the United States that was created by the Federal Reserve Act of 1913 to control the nation's money supply. **(p. 475)**

financial accounting   A "scorekeeping process" that is meant to keep several interested groups (inside and outside the firm) informed of the financial condition of the firm. **(p. 432)**

financial intermediary   An institution that performs a middleman function by accepting funds from savers and lending those funds to borrowers. **(p. 464)**

financial ratio   A value obtained by dividing one value on a financial statement by another value. **(p. 448)**

financial services company   A financial institution that offers under one roof the full variety of services that once could be had only by going to many different types of financial institutions. **(p. 481)**

fiscal policy   The government's use of tax and spending programs to cope with macroeconomic problems. **(p. 38)**

fishbone diagram   An illustration that summarizes the four main possible sources of a quality problem—materials, manpower, methods, and machines. **(p. 307)**

fixed layout   A type of plant arrangement in which the product stays in one place and the machines, materials, and labor are brought to that one location. **(p. 296)**

flexiplace   A concept that allows or encourages employees to work at home or in satellite offices closer to home. **(p. 187)**

flextime   A plan whereby employees' flexible work day is built around a core of midday hours such as 11:00 A.M. to 2:00 P.M. and workers determine their own starting and stopping hours. **(p. 186)**

floor financing   Type of financing in which the borrower holds the inventory and the proceeds from the sale of that inventory in trust for the lender. **(p. 502)**

focus group interviews   An unstructured exploratory discussion on a given topic by eight to twelve people led by a moderator. **(p. 331)**

foreign assembly   An arrangement in which a firm exports component parts to a subsidiary or licensee in a foreign country for local assembly into the finished product. **(p. 679)**

foreign exchange rate   The ratio of one currency to another; it tells how much a unit of one currency is worth in terms of a unit of another. **(p. 671)**

foreign freight forwarder   A domestic agent middleman that consolidates small export shipments into large ones, arranges for transportation and insurance, and handles both export and import documentation for clients. **(p. 678)**

foreign licensing   An agreement in which a licensor gives a licensee in another country the right to use the licensor's patent, trademark, copyright, technology, processes, and/or products in return for a stated percentage of the licensee's sales revenues or profits resulting from such use. **(p. 678)**

foreign production subsidiary   A subordinate company established in another country by a parent company for the purpose of production. **(p. 679)**

form utility   Usefulness of a product that results from a change of form. **(p. 321)**

franchisee   The firm that is licensed to use the franchisor's products or services in a specified territory. **(p. 120)**

franchising agreement   A contract between a franchisor and a franchisee that spells out the rights and obligations of each party. **(p. 120)**

franchisor   A firm that licenses other firms to use its business idea and procedures and to sell its goods or services in return for royalty and other types of payments. **(p. 120)**

free enterprise (or *private enterprise*) An economic philosophy that advocates letting privately owned business firms operate with minimal government control. **(p. 16)**

frequency distribution A table showing the number of observations (individual sales records, for example) that fall in each of several categories. **(p. 708)**

functional authority A staff manager can exercise authority over line people in a specific, narrow area. **(p. 201)**

functional discount Discount granted to a customer in return for services rendered. **(p. 369)**

futures contract A contract for the delivery of an asset at a specific price and future time. **(p. 545)**

General Agreement on Tariffs and Trade (GATT) A multilateral treaty through which member countries act jointly to reduce trade barriers. **(p. 669)**

generally accepted accounting principles A body of theory and procedure developed by the Financial Accounting Standards Board (FASB), a group recognized as representing the accounting profession. **(p. 433)**

globalization A worldwide marketing strategy whereby a firm uses the same or very similar marketing mixes in all its markets. **(p. 686)**

golden parachute A package of benefits that is offered to inside directors and other top-level managers who lose their jobs as a result of merger or acquisition. **(p. 91)**

grapevine The entire network of informal contacts in a firm. **(p. 212)**

greenmail Occurs when (1) a raider buys a large portion of a cash-rich corporation's stock, (2) the raider informs its board of the takeover attempt, and (3) the board buys back the greenmailer's stock at a premium price in return for the greenmailer's promise not to go after the corporation for a stated period of time. **(p. 92)**

grievance A complaint that is filed against a condition thought to be unjust or wrong. **(p. 273)**

grievance procedures Provide an orderly system whereby the employer and the union determine whether or not the labor contract has been violated. **(p. 273)**

Gross National Product (GNP) An overall measure of a nation's economic output, measured as the sum of the market values of all the final goods and services that are produced during a year. **(p. 10)**

gross profit The difference between net sales and cost of good sold. **(p. 444)**

hardware Consists of the machinery and electronic components of a computer system, such as the keyboard or printer. **(p. 586)**

Hawthorne effect What happens when the researchers' interest in the people they are studying, not the experimental variables, causes the workers to be more productive. **(p. 170)**

health maintenance organization (HMO) A comprehensive health care system with a fixed, prepaid cost per year to the member for all services received, regardless of type or quantity. **(p. 573)**

hidden job market That portion of available jobs that is never publicized. **(p. 693)**

hostile takeover The target firm's board of directors opposes the acquisition, but the acquiring firm buys enough shares in the corporation to take control. **(p. 91)**

human relations An approach to managing that emphasizes the importance of the human or "people" element at work. **(p. 169)**

human resource A firm's employees, including both workers and managers. **(p. 222)**

human resource management (or *personnel management*) Consists of activities like recruiting, selecting, training, appraising, and compensating employees. **(p. 222)**

hygienes Incentives that satisfy lower-level needs. **(p. 181)**

imports Imports into a country are products that are sold there but that were produced in another country. **(p. 665)**

incentive pay Pay that a worker receives for producing above the normal output or quota. **(p. 241)**

income statement A financial statement that summarizes revenues and expenses and shows the flows that occurred over a period of time. **(p. 443)**

income tax A tax paid by individuals and corporations on income received in a given tax year. **(p. 629)**

industrial/organizational markets Markets for goods or services that will be used to produce other goods or services. **(p. 325)**

industrial unions Labor unions that are organized according to industries such as steelmaking, automaking, and clothing manufacturing. **(p. 264)**

inflation An increase in the prices of goods and services over a period of time that has the effect of reducing the purchasing power of a nation's currency. **(p. 10)**

informal organization The informal contacts, communications, and ways of doing things that employees always develop. **(p. 210)**

injunction A court order that prohibits a specified activity. **(p. 276)**

input and output (I-O) devices The hardware that is used to get information into or out of the computer. **(p. 590)**

institutional advertising Promotion of the firm's good name rather than any of its products. **(p. 382)**

insurable interest An interest in something such that the interest-holder can show that it would suffer a loss from the peril insured against. **(p. 567)**

insurable risk A risk that an insurance company has judged acceptable for coverage. **(p. 563)**

insurance policy A contract between the insurer and the insured person or firm that specifies (1) the types of risks that are covered, (2) the amount of coverage, (3) the name of the person or corporation covered, and (4) the premium to be paid. **(p. 558)**

intentional tort A wrongful act that is purposefully committed and results in injury to another person's body, property, or good name. **(p. 646)**

interlocking directorate The overlapping of membership of the boards of directors of firms competing in the same market. **(p. 614)**

intermittent production A production process that

starts and stops and starts again, maybe several times per hour. (p. 294)

inventory turnover rate The cost of goods sold in a period divided by average inventory value. (p. 371)

inventory turnover ratio An important measure of efficiency that is computed by dividing average inventory value into cost of goods sold. (p. 450)

investment bank (or *underwriting house*) A financial institution that does not accept deposits from the general public but helps corporations to sell new issues of stocks and bonds. (p. 526)

investment company (or *mutual fund*) A financial institution that pools funds obtained from individual investors to purchase a portfolio of assets that may include stocks, bonds, or money market securities. (p. 482)

job analysis A procedure through which a firm determines the duties and nature of the jobs to be filled and the skills and experience needed by the people who are to fill them. (p. 224)

job application form A document that collects job-related information on matters like name, address, previous employers, and education. (p. 231)

job description A written statement of what the jobholder actually does, the specific duties involved, and any tools, machinery, and supplies needed. (p. 225)

job enrichment Involves building motivators like opportunities for achievement into the job by making it more interesting and challenging. (p. 181)

job sharing A concept that allows two or more people to share a single full-time job. (p. 187)

job specification Takes the job description and states the qualifications needed for that job in terms of things like education, skills, and experience. (p. 225)

joint venture A special type of partnership set up by individuals or firms to accomplish a specific task or project. (p. 94) In international business, a partnership of two or more parties, based in different countries, who share ownership and control of the venture's operations and property rights. (p. 681)

just-in-time (JIT) inventory management An inventory control system that is designed to tie inventory level more closely to short-run production needs in order to reduce inventory requirements at production facilities. (p. 310)

key person life insurance Insures the life of a major employee, such as a president of a firm. (p. 571)

labor A factor of production. The human resource—the mental and physical effort available to produce goods and services. (p. 12)

labor-intensive processes Production processes that depend more on people than on machines. (p. 290)

labor union An organization of employees that is formed to deal collectively with the employer so as to advance the employees' interests. (p. 258)

laissez faire "Leave us alone": let businesspeople compete without government regulation or control. (p. 16)

land A factor of production. All natural resources. (p. 12)

law The set of standards, principles, and rules a society establishes to govern the actions of its members. (p. 638)

law of adverse selection The idea that persons or firms facing high risks (dangerous operations or occupations or past records of ill health) are more likely to seek insurance than others are. (p. 567)

law of demand The idea that as the price of a good or service goes up, the quantity demanded goes down. (p. 39)

law of large numbers A mathematical concept that lets insurers estimate losses during a given future period, using evidence from the past. (p. 564)

law of supply The idea that as the price of a good or service goes up, suppliers will tend to increase the quantity available. (p. 38)

leadership Occurs whenever one person influences another to work toward some predetermined goal. (p. 172)

leadership style Pattern of behavior that a person exhibits over time in leadership situations (situations in which he or she must influence other people). (p. 172)

lease An agreement to grant use of an asset for a period of time in return for stated regular payments. (p. 511)

leverage Using borrowed funds to earn more money than the amount that must be paid in interest on the funds. (p. 494)

leveraged buyout (LBO) The acquisition of a company by a group of investors that is financed largely with borrowed funds secured by the firm's own assets. (p. 84)

liability A claim held by outsiders against the firm's assets. (p. 437)

life insurance Pays a cash benefit to a surviving person or firm (the beneficiary) upon the death of the insured person. (p. 575)

life insurance company A company that shares risk with its policyholders for payment of a premium. (p. 482)

limited partnership A business in which one or more, but not all, of the partners are liable for the firm's debts only to the extent of their financial investment in the firm. (p. 93)

line authority The authority to issue orders to subordinates down the chain of command. (p. 201)

line of credit An informal agreement by a bank to extend credit up to a certain amount to a customer for a short period of time. (p. 501)

line organization An organizational structure in which each manager is directly responsible for an activity required to accomplish the organization's goals. (p. 202)

line-staff organization An organizational structure that has both line and staff departments. (p. 203)

liquidity A firm's ability to make payments that are due. (p. 496)

listed securities Securities traded on organized stock exchanges such as the New York Stock Exchange and the American Stock Exchange. (p. 529)

lobbying Efforts by a group of people who have the same special interest to influence the passage, administration, or enforcement of laws. (p. 61)

local area networks (LANs) Systems that connect computers—PCs, minicomputers, or mainframes—along with high-speed laser printers and/or disk storage components within a locality. **(p. 590)**

local union (or "*local*") The basic unit of union organization, made up of members in a single, relatively small geographical area. **(p. 264)**

lockout Employees are denied access to the plant until they accept the employer's terms of employment. **(p. 276)**

M1 A measure of the money supply in the United States that includes only currency and demand deposits. **(p. 466)**

M2 A measure of the money supply in the United States that includes all of the components of M1 (currency and demand deposits) plus time deposits, money market mutual fund shares, and money market accounts at commercial banks and other types of financial institutions. **(p. 467)**

machine language Consists of binary code (0s and 1s only), and different versions of it relate to specific computers or sets of computers. **(p. 592)**

maintenance of membership arrangement A type of union security that does not require workers to join the union, but union members who are employed by the firm must "maintain membership" by paying dues to the union while the labor contract between the union and employer is in effect. **(p. 267)**

management The process of achieving the organization's aims through the activities of planning, organizing, staffing, directing, and controlling. **(p. 139)**

management by exception A principle that holds that only significant deviations or exceptions from standards should be brought to the manager's attention. **(p. 156)**

management by objectives (MBO) A technique in which a superior and subordinates jointly set the subordinates' goals and periodically assess progress toward these goals. **(p. 153)**

management contract A pact in which one firm sells management services to operate a facility owned by someone else. **(p. 679)**

management development programs Training programs that prepare employees for management positions and improve the managerial skills of present managers. **(p. 238)**

management information systems (MIS) Consist of data collection, organization, and summary, which are integrated so that decisions can be made more quickly and often more accurately. **(p. 598)**

management process The basic functions of planning, organizing, staffing, directing, and controlling. **(p. 146)**

management pyramid Illustrates the levels of management in an organization (upper, middle, and lower) and reflects the fact that there are fewer managers at each successively higher level in an organization. **(p. 141)**

managerial accounting Serves the firm's managers by calling attention to problems and aiding them in planning, decision making, and controlling the firm's operations. **(p. 433)**

managerial grid A graph that depicts various leadership styles and shows how leaders can balance their concerns for the task and their employees. **(p. 173)**

managerial skills Conceptual, interpersonal, technical, emotional, and analytical skills plus the motivation to manage. **(p. 157)**

manufacturer brands (or *national brands*) Brands that are owned by manufacturers. **(p. 362)**

manufacturers' agent A wholesaling middleman that represents several noncompetitive manufacturers in a limited geographic territory for a stated period of time. **(p. 412)**

margin trading Buying more shares than a given amount of money would ordinarily buy because the shares are bought partly on credit. **(p. 542)**

market economy An economic system in which prices determine how the factors of production will be used and how the resulting goods and services will be distributed. **(p. 38)**

marketing The process of planning and executing the conception, pricing, promotion, and distribution of ideas, goods, and services to create exchanges. **(p. 320)**

marketing concept The belief that a whole firm must be coordinated to serve the needs of its present and potential customers and to do so at a profit. **(p. 323)**

marketing functions Activities needed to bring products from producer to user—(1) buying, (2) selling, (3) storing and transporting, (4) standardization and grading, (5) gathering marketing information, (6) risk taking, and (7) financing. **(p. 321)**

marketing mix The set of marketing strategies (promotion strategies, product strategies, price strategies, and distribution, or place, strategies) selected to reach and influence a certain market. **(p. 323)**

marketing research The application of the scientific method (fact finding, analysis, and experiments) to marketing problems and opportunities. **(p. 329)**

market penetration pricing Featuring a low price when introducing a new product. **(p. 370)**

market potential The maximum possible sales of a given type of product in a specific market over a stated period of time for all sellers of that product. **(p. 114)**

market segmentation The strategy of breaking down the market into parts and applying a special marketing mix to each part that the firm wishes to serve. **(p. 337)**

market share liability A concept that allocates liability for product injuries among manufacturers of a class of product on the basis of their share of the market. **(p. 648)**

market skimming pricing Featuring a high price when introducing a new product. **(p. 371)**

market value The price shares of stock are selling for on the market. **(p. 523)**

markup An addition or add-on to cost to reach a selling price. **(p. 364)**

mass market strategy Defines the target market as all potential buyers of brands in a product category. **(p. 337)**

mass production An intermittent production system that involves producing a large number of standardized items (like cars, ready-to-wear pants, toys, or hamburgers) in a standardized manner. **(p. 294)**

maturity The amount of time until a debt must be paid. **(p. 492)**

median The middle number of an array (an arrangement of numbers in ascending or descending order). **(p. 706)**

mediation A process in which a neutral third party (a mediator) suggests a compromise that will get the labor-management negotiations moving ahead and persuades the parties to accept this compromise. **(p. 272)**

Medicare A federal program of medical insurance for people 65 years of age or older. **(p. 563)**

merchandise agents and brokers Wholesaling middlemen that do not take title to the products they sell and that sell on behalf of a principal for a commission. **(p. 412)**

merchandise brokers Wholesaling middlemen that merely bring buyers and sellers into contact with each other and do not have continuous relationships with the firms they represent. **(p. 412)**

merchant wholesaler An independent middleman that takes title to goods and resells them to retailers or industrial-organizational buyers. **(p. 412)**

merger Two firms' combining to create a new firm. **(p. 90)**

middlemen Firms that participate in the buying and selling of a product as it moves from producer to user. **(p. 405)**

missionary selling A specialized selling effort aimed at making the jobs of the manufacturer's regular sales force and those of retailers and wholesalers easier without actually writing orders for the product. **(p. 395)**

mission statement A document in which top management establishes the specific nature and scope of its market and operations by answering the questions "What business are we in?" and "What do we want the business to become?". **(p. 115)**

mixed economy A blend of varying degrees of private enterprise, government ownership, and government planning. **(p. 24)**

mode The number that appears most often in a series of numbers. **(p. 706)**

modem A device that modulates or converts a digital signal (on-off pulses) into a tone that can be transmitted over telephone lines and then reconverts to communicate with faraway personal computers, mainframes, or remote memory units. **(p. 590)**

monetary policy The use of various tools and actions by the nation's monetary authority to regulate the growth rate of the nation's money supply. **(p. 38)**

money Anything that people generally accept as payment for goods and services. **(p. 460)**

money market account An account at a bank or other financial institution that pays interest rates comparable to those paid by money market mutual funds and permits the depositor to write a limited number of checks against the account. **(p. 468)**

money market mutual fund A pool of funds invested in U.S. Treasury bills, commercial paper (corporate debt instruments), and "jumbo" ($100,000 or more) CDs. **(p. 467)**

monopolistic competition A market situation in which there are many sellers and many buyers, but each seller's product is somewhat different from the others. **(p. 49)**

monopoly The opposite of pure competition—one firm produces a product that has no close substitute. **(p. 51)**

motivation A person's desire to satisfy an unfulfilled need. **(p. 178)**

motivators Incentives that satisfy higher-level needs. **(p. 181)**

multinational company (MNC) A firm that is based in one country (the parent country) and has production and marketing activities spread in one or more foreign (host) countries. **(p. 680)**

mutual company A corporation that issues no stock and is owned by its policyholders or depositors and whose surplus revenue, if any, is distributed among the owners in the form of dividends. **(p. 95)**

mutual insurance companies Corporations owned by the policyholders, to whom any profits are returned as dividends or lowered insurance premiums. **(p. 560)**

National Labor Relations Board (NLRB) The federal agency created by the Wagner Act to supervise union elections and prohibit unfair labor practices committed by employers and unions. **(p. 269)**

national union An organization set up to bring all the member local unions together for bargaining purposes. **(p. 264)**

near-money Assets that are almost as liquid as currency and unrestricted demand deposits but that cannot be used directly as a medium of exchange. **(p. 468)**

need satisfaction selling Personal selling that helps prospects identify and solve problems. **(p. 393)**

negative correlation A relationship between two variables such that as one increases, the other decreases in value; graphically portrayed, the relation is shown as a downward sloping line. **(p. 708)**

negligence A wrongful act that causes injury to another person's body, property, or good name as a result of careless, but not intentional, behavior. **(p. 646)**

negotiable instrument A piece of paper that is evidence of a contractual relationship that can be transferred from one person or business to another. **(p. 644)**

negotiable order of withdrawal (NOW) account An interest-bearing checking account offered by commercial banks, savings banks, and savings and loan associations. **(p. 467)**

net working capital Current assets minus current liabilities; reflects a firm's ability to pay its current debts. **(p. 495)**

nonbank bank (or *limited service bank*) A financial institution that makes loans to businesses or offers checking accounts, but not both. **(p. 481)**

nonprice competition A competitive situation in which rivals deemphasize the importance of price as a competitive tool. **(p. 51)**

nonroutine decision A decision that is nonrecurring and so cannot be completely planned for in advance. **(p. 160)**

objective A specific achievement to be attained at some future date. **(p. 152)**

Occupational Safety and Health Administration (OSHA) A federal agency that sets safety and health standards for U.S. workers. **(p. 246)**

odd lot A purchase of stock that is not in round hundreds and so involves additional transaction fees. **(p. 532)**

office automation (OA) A combination of word processing, electronic spreadsheets, DBMS, and new communications networks. **(p. 602)**

oligopoly A market situation in which a few large firms account for the bulk of an industry's sales. **(p. 51)**

online system Exists when those using the system are constantly in direct communication with the computer, either by telephone or directly wired in. **(p. 592)**

on-the-job training Having a person learn a job by actually performing it on the job. **(p. 236)**

open door policy The boss has "an open door" and employees can feel free to drop by and talk to him or her. **(p. 211)**

open market operations Involve purchases and sales of U.S. government securities by Federal Reserve Banks as instructed by the Federal Open Market Committee in order to implement the Fed's monetary policy. **(p. 478)**

open shop A type of union security in which an employer may hire union and/or nonunion labor. **(p. 266)**

operational planning The process of formulating shorter-term plans for implementing the firm's overall strategic plan. **(p. 150)**

opportunity costs The benefits lost by not using funds in another way. **(p. 499)**

order getting Active, aggressive pursuit and conversion of prospects to customers. **(p. 395)**

order taking Receiving and filling requests from customers—often repeat business. **(p. 395)**

organization chart Shows the title of each manager's position and, by means of connecting lines, shows who is accountable to whom and who is in charge of what department. **(p. 194)**

organization development Process for improving the company as a whole by letting the employees themselves analyze problems and suggest the solutions. **(p. 239)**

organization theory Concerned with understanding, explaining, and predicting how best to structure an organization to fulfill its goals. **(p. 208)**

organizing The process of arranging the resources of the firm in such a way that its activities systematically contribute to the firm's goals. **(p. 154 and p. 194)**

over-the-counter (OTC) market A network of securities dealers who are in constant touch with each other, trading stocks and bonds of medium-sized firms as well as some national corporations. **(p. 533)**

owners' equity (capital) The amount of the firm's assets minus the amount of the liabilities. **(p. 437)**

ownership utility The usefulness of a product that comes about through the passage of legal title to the final user. **(p. 323)**

participative leadership Leaders present problems or tentative solutions to their employees and let the employees take part in deciding how to solve the problem. **(p. 174)**

partnership As defined by the Uniform Partnership Act, "An association of two or more persons to carry on as co-owners of a business for profit." **(p. 73)**

partnership agreement An oral or written contract between the owners of a partnership that identifies the business and states the partners' respective rights and obligations. **(p. 73)**

par value The value of the corporation that originally issued the stock certificate printed on it. **(p. 523)**

passive job hunting An approach to securing employment in which the individual simply reacts to job vacancies as they become known through friends, contacts, or classified ads. **(p. 693)**

patent A document issued by the U.S. Patent Office to protect from imitation an invention, a chemical formula, or a new way of doing something. **(p. 363)**

pension fund Money put aside under a pension plan set up by employers or labor unions to provide for the systematic payment of benefits to retired employees. **(p. 482)**

performance appraisal The process of evaluating an employee's actual performance in relation to the standard or desired performance. **(p. 240)**

personal property All tangible and intangible property other than real property, such as furniture, clothing, cars, bank accounts, stock certificates, and government securities. **(p. 643)**

personal selling Any direct personal communication for the purpose of increasing a firm's sales. **(p. 378)**

personnel replacement chart Shows the current performance and ability of each employee who could be a potential replacement for the firm's important positions. **(p. 223)**

physical distribution process The physical flow, including transportation, warehousing, handling, and related activities, that occurs between the production and the consumption of products. **(p. 418)**

picketing Employees form a picket line and walk around a plant or office building carrying placards (signs) that inform other workers and the public that the employer is considered (by the union) to be unfair to labor. **(p. 275)**

piece rate A certain amount of pay a worker receives for each acceptable unit of output he or she produces. **(p. 241)**

piggyback exporting The use by one firm (the carrier) of its overseas distribution network to sell noncompetitive products made by other firms (riders). **(p. 678)**

place utility Usefulness of a product that results from a favorable change in its location. **(p. 322)**

planned obsolescence Occurs when a firm produces something new that replaces its own existing product, making it obsolete. **(p. 353)**

planning The process of setting goals and deciding on the methods of achieving them. **(p. 147)**

poison pill A defense that management adopts to make the firm less attractive to a current or potential hostile suitor in a takeover attempt. **(p. 92)**

political action committee (PAC) A group of people or organizations that is formed to raise campaign contributions for candidates for public office. **(p. 61)**

political risk insurance Protects firms against losses resulting from actions taken by foreign governments or even foreign terrorists against the firm's property. **(p. 572)**

pollution   The contamination of the natural environment by the introduction of harmful substances that endanger our health and even our lives. **(p. 58)**

positive correlation   A relationship between two variables such that as one increases, the other increases; or as one decreases, the other decreases; graphically portrayed, the relation is shown as an upward sloping line. **(p. 707)**

Preferred Provider Organization (PPO)   A group of health care providers who offer to business firms a package of services for their employees at reduced rates. **(p. 574)**

preferred stock   Shares of ownership in a corporation that usually do not confer voting rights but do give preference with respect to dividends and assets. **(p. 85)**

price   The element in the marketing mix that means the dollar cost per unit that buyers must pay, as well as the terms or conditions of sale that accompany price. **(p. 363)**

price competition   A competitive situation in which rivals compete mainly on the basis of price. **(p. 51)**

price lining   Grouping products with many different unit costs from many manufacturers at three or four price levels. **(p. 372)**

pricing model   A mathematical equation or set of equations that takes into account all of the important factors in a pricing situation to help decide on the "best possible" price. **(p. 368)**

primary data   Data originated and collected to solve a particular problem or to evaluate the effects of new marketing strategies. **(p. 329)**

primary demand advertising   Occurs when a firm or the members of a trade association advertise a general class of product without mentioning brands. **(p. 382)**

primary market transaction   Takes place when a stock or bond issue is sold for the first time by a firm. **(p. 526)**

prime rate of interest   The lowest rate charged to major business customers by a specific large bank. **(p. 469)**

principle of indemnity   An insured party cannot collect more than the actual cash value of the loss. **(p. 567)**

private carrier   A transportation service owned and operated by the shipper itself. **(p. 423)**

private enterprise   (or *free enterprise*) An economic philosophy that advocates letting privately owned business firms operate with minimal government control. **(p. 16)**

private law   (or *civil law*) The branch of law that relates to relationships between individuals, groups of individuals, and corporations. **(p. 639)**

privatization   The transfer of services from government to private ownership and control. **(p. 625)**

probability sampling   The selection of items from a large group so that each member of the group has a known (and often an equal) chance to be selected. **(p. 334)**

process layout   A type of plant arrangement in which the machinery, materials, and labor are laid out on the basis of the functions they perform. **(p. 296)**

product   The component of the marketing mix that is viewed as a "bundle of satisfactions," which might include a variety of things such as the warranty, the brand, the package, and the services that go with it. **(p. 346)**

product cost accounting   A system that uses cost centers to allocate all costs to the various products made by a firm. **(p. 453)**

production management   The set of activities aimed at planning, designing, staffing, and controlling a firm's production system. **(p. 287)**

production system   A method for converting inputs (such as raw materials, labor, or capital) into outputs (goods or services). **(p. 287)**

productivity   The relationship between the input of resources (the factors of production) and the output of goods and services. **(p. 48)**

product layout   A type of plant arrangement in which the machines, material, and labor needed to produce one particular product are laid out in an established sequence. **(p. 296)**

product liability   The concept that businesses are liable for injuries caused by negligence in the design, manufacture, sale, and use of products. **(p. 646)**

product liability insurance   Shifting of risk related to claims by product users of injury or illness caused by such use. **(p. 570)**

product life cycle   The four phases in the life history of a product—introduction, growth, maturity, and decline. **(p. 351)**

product mix   The array of products a manufacturer produces or a retailer sells. **(p. 355)**

professional managers   Employees whose career is management and who manage firms in which they are not major owners. **(p. 88)**

profit   The money that remains after a firm deducts its expenses of producing and marketing goods or services (expenditures) from its revenues (receipts). **(p. 6)**

progressive tax   A tax that is levied at a higher rate on higher-income taxpayers and at a lower rate on lower-income taxpayers. **(p. 631)**

promissory note   A written pledge by a customer (borrower or "maker") to pay a certain sum of money (principal and interest) to a supplier (payee) at a specified future date. **(p. 503)**

promotion   Any communication used for the purpose of increasing sales directly or indirectly. **(p. 378)**   Moving up to a higher position in the firm, usually one that provides more and more challenge. **(p. 247)**

promotional mix   A particular combination of advertising, personal selling, sales promotion, public relations, and publicity used by a firm. **(p. 378)**

property   Ownership of a tangible or intangible thing that has value, including the right to possess, use or dispose of it. **(p. 643)**

prospecting   Getting sales leads. **(p. 395)**

prospectus   A summary of the registration statement filed with the Securities Exchange Commission that contains information about the firm, its operations, its management, the purpose of the proposed issue, and anything else that would be helpful to a potential buyer of the securities. **(p. 534)**

proxy   A person who is appointed to represent another person and to vote as directed at a stockholder's meeting. **(p. 85)**

proxy fight A contest between a corporation's management and one or more outsiders to solicit enough votes to keep or take away control of a corporation's board of directors. **(p. 85)**

publicity Communication that is transmitted through the news media as a legitimate part of the news. **(p. 379)**

public law The branch of law that relates to society as a whole—for example, criminal law and administrative law. **(p. 639)**

public-private partnerships Programs that involve business and government working together to solve social problems. **(p. 61)**

public relations Any communication to correct erroneous impressions, to counter the impact of events that might harm the firm's reputation, or to explain the firm's purposes. **(p. 378)**

public securities market The millions of people who buy stocks and bonds, the business and nonbusiness organizations that also buy (invest in) corporate securities, and the various securities middlemen who bring together buyers and sellers of securities **(p. 522)**

public warehouse An independently owned warehousing business that offers services to the general public, much as a common carrier offers transportation. **(p. 423)**

pure competition A type of market structure in which there are many small sellers, many small buyers, a homogeneous product, easy entry into and exit from the industry by competitors, the same conditions for activity of all buyers and sellers, and perfect information in the hands of buyers and sellers. **(p. 49)**

pure risk A type of risk that offers a chance of loss only. **(p. 553)**

put option Entitles a trader to sell stock to the endorser who made the contract available. **(p. 544)**

qualifying Screening sales leads for likelihood of purchase and profitability as customers. **(p. 395)**

quality circle A group of five to ten specially trained employees who meet for an hour once a week to spot and solve problems in their work area. **(p. 185)**

quality control system A production system that sets a standard for an input or output and makes comparisons against this standard to prevent nonstandard items from going into or coming out of the production process. **(p. 307)**

quantity discount Granting lower prices to those who buy larger quantities. **(p. 369)**

quick ratio A very strict measure of a firm's liquidity that is computed by dividing current liabilities into immediately "cashable" current assets. **(p. 450)**

quota The maximum amount of a product that can be imported or exported. **(p. 667)**

random-access memory (RAM) Volatile (temporary) computer memory that is active only while the computer is switched on. **(p. 588)**

read-only memory (ROM) Permanent computer memory that contains and saves instructions for the control unit. **(p. 588)**

real property Land and its permanent attachments, such as houses, garages, trees, mineral rights, and office buildings. **(p. 643)**

real-time system An on-line system that can respond instantly and make programmed responses. **(p. 592)**

reciprocity A purchasing policy under which a customer buys from a supplier if that supplier also buys from its customer—"You buy from me and I'll buy from you." **(p. 312)**

recruiting The process of attracting job applicants (potential employees) with the use of such tools as advertisements, employment agencies, and word of mouth. **(p. 226)**

recycling The reprocessing of used materials for reuse. **(p. 59)**

regional trading bloc A group of countries that agree to eliminate barriers to trade among member nations. **(p. 681)**

regressive tax A tax by which poorer people pay a higher percentage of income than higher-income people pay. **(p. 631)**

reseach design The overall plan for conducting marketing research and obtaining data. **(p. 331)**

reserve requirement The percentage of deposits that depository institutions must keep in vault cash or as deposits with the Federal Reserve Banks. **(p. 478)**

resident buying office A government-owned or business-owned facility that is set up in a foreign country to buy products that are made there. **(p. 678)**

resignation Occurs when an employee voluntarily leaves the employer's service. **(p. 249)**

responsibility The obligation of a subordinate to perform an assigned task. **(p. 199)**

responsibility accounting A system for classifying costs incurred according to certain responsibility centers so as to evaluate the performance of such centers and their managers. **(p. 453)**

restrictive taxes Levied to control certain activities that legislative bodies feel should be controlled. **(p. 628)**

résumé A biographical summary of a job applicant's education, work experience, activities, interests, career goals, and other personal information that is given to potential employers in the job application process. **(p. 696)**

retailers Middlemen that sell to households and individuals. **(p. 405)**

retained earnings Represent what the firm has plowed back into the corporation from profits over the years but has not paid out in dividends. **(p. 442)**

return on net worth Net income divided by the firm's most recent net worth or stockholders' equity. **(p. 449)**

revenue The amount of cash or accounts receivable a firm receives in payment from others over a period of time. **(p. 443)**

revenue taxes Taxes whose main purpose is to fund government services and programs. **(p. 628)**

revolving credit agreement Formal commitment by a bank to lend up to a certain amount to a customer over a specified period of time. **(p. 502)**

right-to-work laws State laws that outlaw the union shop. **(p. 267)**

risk   The chance of loss. **(p. 6)**

risk management   The process of identifying the risks to which a firm is likely to be exposed, estimating the frequency and size of losses from such risks, and determining the best way to deal with each of them. **(p. 554)**

rolling over   Successive renewals of short-term notes as a substitute for longer-term financial commitments. **(p. 512)**

round lot   The established 100-share unit of stock trading. **(p. 532)**

routine decision   A decision that must be faced over and over. **(p. 160)**

salary   An employee compensation that is fixed on a weekly, biweekly, monthly, or annual basis. **(p. 241)**

sales finance company   A financial institution that specializes in financing installment purchases made by consumers and firms. **(p. 483)**

sales forecast   Predicts what sales will be over a certain period of time. **(p. 453)**

sales potential   The share of market potential that a firm might realize if it makes a maximal commitment of its resources to the effort. **(p. 114)**

sales promotion   A special set of activities that seek to induce or motivate desired responses in target customers, company salespeople, and middlemen and their salespeople. **(p. 378)**

savings and loan association (S&L)   A financial institution that accepts deposits from the general public and lends funds mainly for mortgages on homes and other real estate. **(p. 465)**

savings bank   A financial institution that accepts deposits from small savers, pays them interest, and invests the funds mainly in real estate mortgages and government securities. **(p. 466)**

scalar principle   States that there should be a clear chain of command from the highest to the lowest position in an organization. **(p. 195)**

S corporation   A corporation with no more than 35 stockholders that has the option of being taxed somewhat like a partnership. **(p. 79)**

secondary data   Data previously collected either by the user or by someone else for some purpose other than dealing with the current problem or decision. **(p. 330)**

secondary market   Includes the organized exchanges like the New York Stock Exchange as well as the over-the-counter market. **(p. 527)**

secured loan   A loan in which the lender is protected by a pledge of the borrower's assets, or collateral. **(p. 502)**

securities exchange   An institution set up by brokerage houses to reduce the cost and increase the efficiency of buying and selling financial securities. **(p. 529)**

securitization   Selling securities backed by assets like accounts receivable or mortgages to investors. **(p. 513)**

selection test   A set of questions, problems, or exercises for determining a person's knowledge, abilities, aptitudes, or qualifications for a job. **(p. 231)**

self-insurance   Preparing ahead of time to deal with a

possible loss by setting aside funds to cover the loss or—in the case of a very large firm—treating loss as an inevitable expense of doing business. **(p. 555)**

selling agent   A wholesaling middleman that represents a principal for a commission, except that it might handle competing lines and has nationwide representation rights. **(p. 412)**

sexual harassment   Defined by the Equal Employment Opportunity Commission as "unwelcomed sexual advances, requests for sexual favors, and other verbal or physical conduct of a sexual nature that takes place under any of the following conditions: (1) submission is made a condition of the person's employment, (2) submission to or rejection of such conduct is used as a basis for employment decisions affecting the person, or (3) it unreasonably interferes with the person's work performance or creates an intimidating, hostile, or offensive work environment." **(p. 230)**

share draft account   An interest-bearing checking account offered by credit unions. **(p. 467)**

shopping goods   Items that are taken seriously enough to require comparison and study before buying. **(p. 350)**

short selling   The sale of a security that the speculator does not own but has borrowed from his or her broker. **(p. 542)**

sinking fund   Money put aside each year from profits to pay off bonds when they mature. **(p. 509)**

small business   A firm that meets two or more of the following criteria: (1) the owners manage the business, (2) one person or a small group of people provides the financing, (3) the owners and employees live near the firm, and (4) the firm is small in comparison to others in the same industry (size may be measured in assets, number of employees, or sales revenues). **(p. 101)**

Small Business Administration (SBA)   An independent agency of the U.S. government that was created in 1953 to promote and protect the interests of small business firms. **(p. 127)**

Small Business Development Center (SBDC)   An SBA-sponsored operation in which faculty members from collegiate business schools and experienced businesspeople conduct research and provide consulting services to small business owners on a fee basis. **(p. 129)**

Small Business Institute (SBI)   An SBA-sponsored program in which faculty members from collegiate business schools with whom the SBA has contracts supervise senior and graduate students who serve as consultants to small business owners free of charge. **(p. 129)**

Small Business Investment Company (SBIC)   A privately owned, privately operated, SBA-licensed venture capital company that helps finance small firms that want to expand and modernize. **(p. 128)**

small business set-asides   Government contracts that are restricted to competition among small firms. **(p. 129)**

social audit   A thorough examination and assessment of all the activities a firm undertakes to develop social goals and implement social programs. **(p. 57)**

socialism   An economic system in which the government practices economic planning, owns the nation's major economic resources and many of its basic industries, and imposes heavy taxes to finance a welfare state. **(p. 19)**

social responsibility The concept that business is part of the larger society in which it exists and is accountable to society for its performance. **(p. 6)**

software The set of instructions necessary to put the computer hardware into motion. **(p. 586)**

sole proprietorship A business owned by one person. **(p. 70)**

span of control (or *span of management*) The number of subordinates reporting directly to a manager. **(p. 196)**

specialization (or *division of labor*) The division of work into component tasks so that each worker can concentrate on performing a particular task instead of performing many tasks. **(p. 8)**

specialty goods Products for which strong conviction as to brand, style, or type already exists in the buyer's mind and that the buyer will make a great effort to locate and purchase. **(p. 350)**

speculative risk A "gamble" in which there is a possible gain as well as a possible loss. **(p. 553)**

speculative trading The buying or selling of securities in the hope of profiting from near-term future changes in their selling price. **(p. 540)**

staff authority The authority only to assist and advise line managers. **(p. 201)**

staffing The process of recruiting, selecting, training, appraising, and developing employees. **(p. 154)**

stakeholders Owners, customers, and all the various groups of people who are affected by a firm's actions. **(p. 7)**

standard of living A measure of a society's economic well-being. **(p. 10)**

statistics A general term for numerical data and their collection, classification, analysis, interpretation, and presentation. **(p. 705)**

statutory law A system of laws that are written, or codified, by legislative bodies. **(p. 639)**

stock dividend A payment to stockholders of additional shares of stock rather than payment of cash. **(p. 524)**

stockholders (or *shareholders*) The owners of a corporation. **(p. 71)**

stock insurance companies Profit-seeking corporations, the stockholders of which are not necessarily their customers (policyholders). **(p. 560)**

stock split Gives stockholders a greater number of shares but does not change the individual's proportionate ownership in the corporation. **(p. 524)**

strategic planning The process of developing a broad plan for how a business is going to compete in its industry, what its goals should be, and what policies will be needed to achieve these goals. **(p. 150)**

strict product liability A concept that businesses are liable for injuries caused by their products even if there is no proof of negligence or fault in the design, manufacture, sale, and use of products. **(p. 646)**

strike A temporary withdrawal of all or some employees from the company's service. **(p. 275)**

strikebreakers Nonunion employees hired to take the place of the striking employees. **(p. 276)**

supermarkets Large, departmentalized, self-service retail stores that sell meat, produce, canned goods, dairy products, frozen foods, and many nonfood items such as toys, magazines, and toiletry items. **(p. 413)**

surety bonding Protects the firm from losses due to nonperformance of a contract. **(p. 572)**

system software Consists of internal programs that tell the computer system how to manage the various tasks assigned to it. **(p. 592)**

target market The group of present and potential customers that a firm aims to satisfy with its goods and services. **(p. 325)**

tariffs Duties, or taxes, that a government puts on products that are imported into (or, on rare occasions, exported from) the country. **(p. 666)**

tax control The imposition of discriminatory taxes on foreign investments by a government for the purpose of exercising power over those investments. **(p. 686)**

technological obsolescence What happens when someone invents something that works better than the existing product. **(p. 353)**

technology Application of science that enables people to do entirely new things or perform established tasks in new and better ways. **(p. 62)**

technology forecasting Process of gathering and interpreting evidence of scientific advances in a field and forecasting the direction of technological change and its impact on the firm. **(p. 63)**

tender offer An offer by one party (a raider) to buy all or a portion of another firm's stock at a higher price than its current market price. **(p. 92)**

term loan A loan made by a financial institution to a borrower for a specific period of time, such as five years. **(p. 511)**

Theory X An approach to management that assumes that most people dislike work and responsibility and prefer to be directed; are motivated not by the desire to do a good job, but by financial incentives; and must be closely supervised, controlled, and coerced into achieving organizational objectives. **(p. 170)**

Theory Y An approach to management that assumes that (1) people can enjoy work and will exercise substantial control over their own performance if given the chance, (2) workers are motivated by the desire to do a good job and by the chance to associate with their peers, not just by financial rewards, and (3) people might actually do better work if control is kept to a minimum and they are not threatened with punishment. **(p. 171)**

time deposit Money placed in a financial institution that remains there (on deposit) for a period of time and that earns interest during this period. **(p. 467)**

time utility Usefulness of a product that results from having it available when the consumer wants it. **(p. 322)**

title A document that indicates legal possession of an item of personal property and the right to use it. **(p. 644)**

tort A wrongful act, other than a breach of contract, that violates private law and results in injury to a person's body, property, or good name. **(p. 646)**

total cost concept Demands that when a given

method of transportation is under consideration, all costs related to it be weighed and their sum minimized. **(p. 425)**

trade acceptance An order to pay from a seller that has been signed (accepted) by the buyer in order to get the merchandise from the carrier. **(p. 504)**

trade credit (or *"open book account"*) Credit extended by sellers to buyers. **(p. 500)**

trade draft An order to pay prepared by the supplier, ordering the buyer to pay a certain amount of money for the merchandise. **(p. 504)**

trademark A characteristic symbol or a style of lettering of a brand name that is registered with the U.S. Patent Office. **(p. 363)**

trade position discount Allows special pricing for customers based on their position in the channel of distribution. **(p. 368)**

trade practice rules Purely advisory rules developed by federal administrative bodies in conference with industry representatives to guide firms in avoiding future violations of the law. **(p. 621)**

trade regulation rules Binding rules published by government administrative bodies that are made available to all competitors and used to bring cases against alleged violators. **(p. 621)**

trade war A situation in which one country imposes trade barriers against its trading partners and they retaliate with trade barriers of their own. **(p. 44)**

trading company A business that buys and sells products in many countries, either in its own name or as an agent for its buyer-seller clients. **(p. 677)**

transactions Financially significant events that raise or lower the balances (net dollar amounts) in accounts. **(p. 446)**

turnkey operation An arrangement in which a supplier designs, builds, and trains the staff of an operating facility for a foreign buyer who runs the facility. **(p. 679)**

tying contract Requires a buyer to buy unwanted items from a seller in order to buy something else that the buyer wants. **(p. 614)**

unfair lists Contained the names of employers whom unions considered unfair to workers because these employers would not hire union members. **(p. 258)**

Uniform Commercial Code (UCC) A statute that combines and coordinates several specific uniform acts regarding business into one overall commercial code. **(p. 640)**

union federation An organization that represents the unions that comprise it in presenting labor's views on political and social issues. **(p. 264)**

union security The right the union has to represent a firm's workers. **(p. 265)**

union shop A type of union security in which an employer may hire nonunion workers even if the employer's present employees are unionized. **(p. 266)**

unit production An intermittent production system that basically produces small quantities of product, often one at a time; often called "job shop" or "jobbing." **(p. 294)**

unity of command principle States that each person in an organization should report to only one supervisor. **(p. 196)**

unlimited liability The business owner is responsible for claims against the firm that go beyond the value of the owner's ownership in the firm. **(p. 72)**

unsecured loans Loans offered for short-term uses with no security or pledge of assets as guarantee of repayment. **(p. 501)**

value-added tax (VAT) A tax applied each time a good changes hands. **(p. 631)**

value analysis A process of reviewing existing product specifications as set by user departments (those units for which purchasing is done) and identifying and eliminating nonessential requirements. **(p. 312)**

variable A value that varies, or changes. **(p. 706)**

vendor analysis A process of evaluating and rating the technical, financial, and managerial abilities of potential suppliers in terms of their past performance. **(p. 312)**

venture capitalists Individuals and businesses that are willing to provide equity capital to entrepreneurs who have new products or new product ideas that are as yet unproven on the market but have a good chance of becoming successful. **(p. 118)**

vertical marketing system (VMS) A channel arrangement that provides complete or nearly complete coordination of effort within the channel. **(p. 410)**

voluntary compliance A firm agrees to do what an administrative agency advises without having to hold a hearing. **(p. 620)**

wage An employee compensation that is based on the number of hours the employee has worked. **(p. 241)**

warehousing Selection and use of buildings or facilities to store finished goods. **(p. 312)**

warranty A representation, or a legal promise, made by the seller that assures the buyer that the product is as represented by the seller. **(p. 644)**

whistleblowing The action of publicly reporting what are perceived to be an organization's wrongdoings. **(p. 656)**

white knight A firm that takes over another firm but allows the acquired firm to retain its existing board and corporate officers. **(p. 92)**

wholesalers Middlemen that sell primarily to retailers, other wholesalers, or manufacturers. **(p. 405)**

word processing system A text-editing computer program that manipulates letters, words, tables, and paragraphs. **(p. 601)**

worker-friendly programs Programs that make it easier for employees to adapt their work lives to the needs of their home lives and careers. **(p. 185)**

workers' compensation Provides payments for medical costs and compensation for loss of income as well as rehabilitation costs, if any. **(p. 575)**

working capital A firm's investment in current assets such as cash and inventories. **(p. 494)**

work sharing A temporary reduction in work hours by a group of employees during economic hard times in order to avoid layoffs. **(p. 187)**

yellow-dog contract Required an employee to agree, as a condition of employment, not to join a union. **(p. 258)**

PHOTO CREDITS

Title page— © George Herben/Woodfin Camp, Inc.; © Paula Lerner MCMLXXXVIII; © Michael Carpenter. *Section One:* p. xxiv—Brian Smale, Sharpshooter Studios. *Chapter 1:* p. 3—Picture Group/Picture Group photo; p. 10—© John Blaustein/Woodfin Camp, Inc.; p. 23, p. 28—© Paula Lerner MCMLXXXVIII. *Chapter 2:* p. 35—courtesy of Boston Beer Company; p. 40—© Campbell and Boulanger/Woodfin Camp, Inc.; p. 55—© David Dempster; p. 62—Photri. *Chapter 3:* p. 69—courtesy of Boston Beer Company; p. 71, p. 76, p. 90—© David Dempster. *Chapter 4:* p. 99, p. 111, p. 128—© David Dempster; p. 125—© Paula Lerner MCMLXXXVIII. *Section Two:* p. 134—courtesy of Robert Loughhead. *Chapter 5:* p. 137—courtesy of Brunswick Corporation; p. 140—Photri; p. 152—© Dick Luria/Folio, Inc.; p. 160—© David Dempster. *Chapter 6:* p. 167—Nik Kleinberg/Picture Group photo; p. 171—Photri; p. 182—© Earl Roberge/Photo Researchers, Inc.; p. 187—© Jan Halaska/Photo Researchers, Inc. *Chapter 7:* p. 193—courtesy of International Business Machines Corporation; p. 197, p. 201—© David Dempster; p. 211—© Gerard Fritz/Photri. *Section Three:* p. 218—courtesy of Cam Starrett. *Chapter 8:* p. 221—courtesy of International Business Machines Corporation; p. 223, p. 234—© David Dempster; p. 238—© R.S. Uzzell III/Woodfin Camp, Inc.; p. 246—© Michael Carpenter. *Chapter 9:* p. 255—© Steve Starr/Picture Group photo; p. 258—The Archives of Labor and Urban Affairs, Wayne State University; p. 265—© Kenneth Garrett/Woodfin Camp, Inc.; p. 275—© Lawrence Migdale/Photo Researchers, Inc. *Chapter 10:* p. 285—courtesy of Ford Motor Company; p. 290—© Angel Franco/Woodfin Camp, Inc.; p. 306—Photri; p. 309—© Chuck O'Rear, Woodfin Camp, Inc. *Section Four:* p. 316—courtesy of Randy Miller. *Chapter 11:* p. 319—courtesy of P Sainsbury PLC; p. 322, p. 326, p. 337—Photri. *Chapter 12:* p. 345—© David Dempster; p. 347—© R. Rathe/Folio, Inc.; p. 355—© Breton Littlehales/Folio, Inc.; p. 360—courtesy of Richardson-Vicks Ltd.; p. 369—© Will McIntyre/Photo Researchers, Inc. *Chapter 13:* p. 377—courtesy of Schlott Realtors; p. 384—© Sepp Seitz/Woodfin Camp, Inc.; p. 395—© David Dempster; p. 398—© Chuck O'Rear/Woodfin Camp, Inc. *Chapter 14:* p. 403—courtesy of Big O Tires, Inc.; p. 408—© Nick Sebastian/Photri; p. 415—© David Dempster; p. 420—© George Herben/Woodfin Camp, Inc.; p. 423—© Paula Lerner MCMLXXXVIII. *Section Five:* p. 428—Jeffrey Scales. *Chapter 15:* p. 431—© David Dempster; p. 437—© Kenneth Garrett/Woodfin Camp, Inc.; p. 440—© Jeff Zaruba/Folio, Inc.; p. 451—Photri. *Chapter 16:* p. 459—Yvonne Hemsey/Gamma-Liaison; p. 461—© Eric Poggenpohl/Woodfin Camp, Inc.; p. 471—© Robert Shafer/Folio, Inc.; p. 481—© Jeff Zaruba/Folio, Inc. *Chapter 17:* p. 489—Michael A. Patrick/Picture Group photo; p. 492—© Steve Chenn/Woodfin Camp, Inc.; p. 510—© John Blaustein/Woodfin Camp, Inc. *Chapter 18:* p. 521—Andrew Popper/Picture Group photo; p. 528—Cary Wolinsky/Stock, Boston; p. 532—© Bernard Gotfryd/Woodfin Camp, Inc. *Chapter 19:* p. 551—courtesy of the Boston Celtics, color by Dick Raphael Associates; p. 557—© Chuck O'Rear/Woodfin Camp, Inc.; p. 565—© John Blaustein/Woodfin Camp, Inc.; p. 572—Photri; p. 574—© Kenneth Garrett/Woodfin Camp, Inc. *Section Six:* p. 580—Duane Hall/VIS-TEC. *Chapter 20:* p. 583—© David Dempster; p. 591—Photri; p. 595—copyright Kindra Clineff 1988; p. 601—Richard Nowitz/Photri. *Chapter 21:* p. 609—courtesy of Robert D. Garton Associates; p. 622—© James Douglass/Woodfin Camp, Inc.; p. 624—© Angel Franco/Woodfin Camp, Inc.; p. 630—© Breton Littlehales/Folio, Inc. *Chapter 22:* p. 637—courtesy of Chevrolet Motor Division; p. 643—Peter Menzel/Stock, Boston; p. 649—© Culver Pictures; p. 653—© Ray Ellis/Photo Researchers, Inc. *Chapter 23:* p. 679, p. 683, p. 686—© Paula Lerner MCMLXXXVIII.

AD CREDITS

p. 9—courtesy of NCR Corporation; p. 17—Union Bank of Switzerland Marketing Service; p. 123—© 1988 Sylvan Learning Corporation; p. 200—American International Group, Inc.; p. 227—Management Recruiters Intl., Inc.; p. 305—courtesy of The Foxboro Company; p. 349—courtesy of Steelcase Inc.; p. 367—reprinted with permission from N W Ayer; p. 388—Johnson & Johnson; p. 389—© The Procter & Gamble Company. © McCormick & Co., Inc. Reproduced with Permission; p. 391—courtesy of Kraft, Inc.; p. 416—Bloomingdale's By Mail Ltd. (1985); p. 436—courtesy of Arthur Young & Company ©; p. 452—Alan Herman & Associates,

Agency, Alan Herman, art director and designer; p. 507—copyright Drexel Burnham Lambert Incorporated; p. 516—Rockwell International; p. 541—courtesy of CompuServe Incorporated; p. 559—William Esty Company, Agency; p. 587—courtesy of Pitney Bowes; p. 602—copyright © 1987 Ashton-Tate Corporation.

NOTES

Chapter 1

[1] "Special Report: Gorbachev's Russia," *Business Week,* Nov. 11, 1985, pp. 82–98; "Soviet Union: Inching Down the Capitalist Road," *Time,* May 4, 1987, p. 42; "Can He Bring It Off?" *Time,* July 27, 1987, pp. 30–39; Richard I. Kirkland, Jr., "Russia: Where Gorbanomics Is Leading," *Fortune,* Sept. 28, 1987, pp. 83–88; "Reforming the Soviet Economy," *Business Week,* Dec. 7, 1987, pp. 76–88.
[2] "America vs. Japan: A No-Win Game," *Business Week,* May 4, 1987, p. 33.
[3] "Laying the Foundation for the Great Mall of China," *Business Week,* Jan. 25, 1988, pp. 68–69.
[4] "Reforming the Soviet Economy," *Business Week,* Dec. 7, 1987, pp. 76–88.
[5] Richard I. Kirkland, Jr., "Russia: Where Gorbanomics Is Leading," *Fortune,* Sept. 28, 1987, p. 88.
[6] "Can He Bring It Off?" *Time,* July 22, 1987, p. 32.
[7] "Reforming the Soviet Economy," *Business Week,* Dec. 7, 1987, p. 78.
[8] "Why Tokyo Is Tinkering with the Treadmill," *Business Week,* Sept. 28, 1987, pp. 45, 48.
[9] "Japan's Latest Triumph: Hurdling the High Yen," *Business Week,* Jan. 18, 1988, p. 37.
[10] "Soviet Union: Inching Down the Capitalist Road," *Time,* May 4, 1987, p. 42.
[11] "Can He Bring It Off?" *Time,* July 22, 1987, p. 32.
[12] "A New Age of Capitalism," *Time,* July 28, 1986, p. 33.
[13] Adi Ignatius and Mark D'Anastasio, "Toying with Capitalism Themselves, Communists Soft-Pedal Market's Woes," *The Wall Street Journal,* Oct. 28, 1987, p. 53.
[14] "Capitalism in China," *Business Week,* Jan. 14, 1985, p. 55.
[15] "Soviet Union: Inching Down the Capitalist Road," *Time,* May 4, 1987, p. 42.
[16] Philip Revzin, "Competitive Surge: Free-Market Policies Gain Across Europe, Even in Socialist Lands," *The Wall Street Journal,* June 10, 1986, pp. 1, 14.
[17] "Hungary: Building Freedoms Out of Defeat," *Time,* Aug. 11, 1986, pp. 28–29.
[18] Barry Newman, "Hungary Plunges into State Capitalism," *The Wall Street Journal,* Dec. 23, 1987, p. 10.
[19] "Cuba Is Living on Borrowed Time," *Business Week,* Dec. 14, 1987, pp. 52, 54.
[20] "Soviet Union: At the Point of No Return," *Time,* Jan. 25, 1988, p. 46.
[21] "Reforming the Soviet Economy," *Business Week,* Dec. 7, 1987, p. 78.
[22] "Soviet Union: Inching Down the Capitalist Road," *Time,* May 14, 1987, p. 42.
[23] "Soviet Union: At the Point of No Return," *Time,* Jan. 25, 1988, p. 46.
[24] "Soviet Union: Inching Down the Capitalist Road," *Time,* May 14, 1987, p. 42.
[25] "Capitalism in China," *Business Week,* Jan. 14, 1985, pp. 53–59.
[26] "Soviet Union: Inching Down the Capitalist Road," *Time,* May 14, 1987, p. 42.
[27] Adi Ignatius, "Discontent, Anger Brewing Anew on China's Campuses," *The Wall Street Journal,* Dec. 17, 1987, p. 22.
[28] James P. Sterba, "China's Change: Peking's Streets Teem with Merchants Again as State Loosens Reins," *The Wall Street Journal,* June 16, 1986, pp. 1, 8. Reprinted by permission of *The Wall Street Journal,* © Dow Jones & Company, Inc., 1986. All Rights Reserved.
[29] Roger Cohen, "Struggling Back: After a Long Decline, Argentina Is Striving to Revive Economy," *The Wall Street Journal,* Nov. 12, 1986, pp. 1, 22. Reprinted by permission of *The Wall Street Journal,* © Dow Jones & Company, Inc., 1986. All Rights Reserved.

Chapter 2

[1] "For Sale: America," *Time,* Sept. 14, 1987, p. 54.

[2]Walter S. Mossberg, "The Outlook: Cost of Paying the Foreign Piper," *The Wall Street Journal*, Jan. 18, 1988, p. 1.

[3]"Let Us Shake Hands," *Time*, Oct. 19, 1987, p. 49.

[4]"For Sale: America," *Time*, Sept. 14, 1987, p. 52.

[5]"For Sale: America," *Time*, Sept. 14, 1987, p. 54.

[6]Richard Alm, "Made in the U.S.A. May Be (Gasp!) Cheaper," *The Times-Picayune*, Nov. 22, 1987, p. H-1.

[7]"Your Money Matters: Sticker Shock: U.S. Travelers Face Trauma of Sharply Devalued Dollar," *The Wall Street Journal*, Dec. 4, 1987, p. 37.

[8]"Singing the Shutdown Blues," *Time*, June 23, 1986, p. 58.

[9]"Singing the Shutdown Blues," *Time*, June 23, 1986, p. 59.

[10]"Singing the Shutdown Blues," *Time*, June 23, 1986, p. 59.

[11]"Why Image Counts: A Tale of Two Industries," *Business Week*, June 8, 1987, p. 139.

[12]"America's Leanest and Meanest," *Business Week*, Oct. 5, 1987, p. 79.

[13]"America's Leanest and Meanest," *Business Week*, Oct. 5, 1987, p. 78.

[14]"What's for Breakfast? Juice Wars," *Business Week*, Oct. 5, 1987, p. 110.

[15]Frank E. James, "Searle to Offer Full Guarantee for Its Drugs," *The Wall Street Journal*, Sept. 15, 1987, p. 4.

[16]"Taking on the World," *Time*, Oct. 19, 1987, p. 46.

[17]"America's Leanest and Meanest," *Business Week*, Oct. 5, 1987, p. 80.

[18]Lindley H. Clark, Jr., "Productivity's Cost: Manufacturers Grow Much More Efficient, but Employment Lags," *The Wall Street Journal*, Dec. 4, 1986, pp. 1, 23.

[19]Alan Murray, "The Outlook: The Service Sector's Productivity Problem," *The Wall Street Journal*, Feb. 10, 1987, p. 1.

[20]"America's Leanest and Meanest," *Business Week*, Oct. 5, 1987, p. 82.

[21]"Basking in Europhoria," *Time*, Oct. 19, 1987, p. 48.

[22]"The Push for Quality," *Business Week*, June 8, 1987, p. 136.

[23]"Basking in Europhoria," *Time*, Oct. 19, 1987, p. 46.

[24]"America's Leanest and Meanest," *Business Week*, Oct. 5, 1987, p. 82.

[25]"Basking in Europhoria," *Time*, Oct. 19, 1987, p. 47.

[26]"The Push for Quality," *Business Week*, June 8, 1987, pp. 139–140.

[27]"Singing the Shutdown Blues," *Time*, June 23, 1986, p. 60.

[28]"One Child in Four Lives with One Parent," *The Times-Picayune*, Feb. 4, 1988, p. E-3.

[29]"Aging: Can It Be Slowed?" *Business Week*, Feb. 8, 1988, p. 58.

[30]"Fuller Brush Is Going to the Malls," *The Times-Picayune*, Aug. 28, 1987, p. C-1.

[31]Timothy K. Smith, "Changing Tastes: By End of This Year, Poultry Will Surpass Beef in the U.S. Diet," *The Wall Street Journal*, Sept. 17, 1987, p. 1.

[32]"Critical Condition," *Business Week*, Feb. 1, 1988, p. 42.

[33]"The Heat Is On," *Time*, Oct. 19, 1987, p. 58.

[34]Eduardo Lachica, "Saving the Earth: U.S. Asks World Bank to Make Safeguarding Environment a Priority," *The Wall Street Journal*, July 3, 1987, p. 1.

[35]Selwyn Feinstein, "Labor Letter," *The Wall Street Journal*, Dec. 29, 1987, p. 1.

[36]"Is Deregulation Working?" *Business Week*, Dec. 22, 1986, p. 50.

[37]"R&D Scoreboard," *Business Week*, June 20, 1988, pp. 139, 151, 154.

[38]"The Technobandits," *Time*, Nov. 30, 1987, p. 42.

[39]"The Technobandits," *Time*, Nov. 30, 1987, p. 43.

[40]Jeffrey A. Tannenbaum, "Sony to Begin Selling VCRs in VHS Format," *The Wall Street Journal*, Jan. 12, 1988, p. 27. Reprinted by permission of *The Wall Street Journal*, © Dow Jones & Company, Inc., 1988. All Rights Reserved.

[41]Alan Murray, "New Book Rates Consumer Firms on Social Issues," *The Wall Street Journal*, Jan. 16, 1987, p. 25. Reprinted by permission of *The Wall Street Journal*, © Dow Jones & Company, Inc., 1987. All Rights Reserved.

Chapter 3

[1]Cynthia Crossen, "Companies Ask Holders to Limit Board's Liability," *The Wall Street Journal*, Oct. 7, 1986, p. 35.

[2]"News/Trends: Move to Delaware," *Fortune*, Dec. 22, 1986, p. 9.

[3]"Win or Lose, the Dodgers Are Power Hitters at the Gate," *Business Week*, Oct. 20, 1986, p. 66.

[4]"The Popular Game of Going Private," *Time*, Nov. 4, 1985, p. 55.

[5]Sonja Steptoe, "Suit Against Magazine Highlights Debate on Valuing Employee-Owned Companies," *The Wall Street Journal*, Sept. 16, 1986, p. 29.

[6]"The Job Nobody Wants," *Business Week*, Sept. 8, 1986, p. 56.

[7]Daniel Hertzberg, "Delaware Court Upholds the Use of 'Poison Pills,'" *The Wall Street Journal*, Nov. 20, 1985, p. 8.

[8]"A Flurry of Greenmail Has Stockholders Cursing," *Business Week*, Dec. 8, 1986, p. 33.

[9]Jolie Solomon, "Cincinnati Reds' Marge Schott Faces Problems Other Than Baseball Scores," *The Wall Street Journal*, June 6, 1986, p. 25.

[10]Joan C. Szabo, "Small-Business Update: Keeping It in the Family," *Nation's Business*, March 1988, pp. 14, 16. Reprinted by permission, *Nation's Business*, March, 1988. Copyright 1988, U.S. Chamber of Commerce.

[11]"News/Trends: From the Backboards to the Big Board," *Fortune*, Dec. 22, 1986, p. 8; Hal Lancaster, "Timeout: Despite Success of Celtics Sale, Doubts Remain About Sports Offerings," *The Wall Street Journal*, May 8, 1987, p. 17.

Chapter 4

[1]Udayan Gupta, "Small Business: For Some, Recipe for Success Could Be a Successful Recipe," *The Wall Street Journal*, March 30, 1987, p. 19. Reprinted by permission of *The Wall Street Journal*, © Dow Jones & Company, Inc., 1987. All Rights Reserved.

[2]Skip Wollenberg, "Women-Owned Businesses Growing Force in U.S.," *The Times-Picayune/The States-Item*, Sept. 5, 1985, p. B-3.

[3]Steven P. Galante, "Small Business: Business Incubators Adopting Niche Strategies to Stand Out," *The Wall Street Journal*, April 13, 1987, p. 25.

[4]Skip Wollenberg, "Women-Owned Businesses Growing Force in U.S.," *The Times-Picayune/The States-Item*, Sept. 5, 1985, p. B-3.

[5]Kevin T. Higgins, "Entrepreneurship Is a Quest for Independence," *Collegiate Edition Marketing News*, Feb. 1986, p. 6.

[6]Janet Wallfisch, "Women Plunge into Business," *The Times-Picayune*, Jan. 31, 1986, p. D-3.

[7]"Economy & Business: Venture!" *Time*, June 16, 1986, p. 59.

[8]"Economy & Business: Venture!" *Time*, June 16, 1986, p. 56.

[9]Thomas Petzinger, Jr., "Small Business Opportunities: So You Want to Get Rich?" *A Special Report: Small Business, The Wall Street Journal*, May 15, 1987, Sec. 4, p. 15D.

[10]Nancy L. Croft, "Taking the Franchise Route," *Nation's Business*, Oct. 1987, p. 33.

[11]Andrew Sherman, "Financing the Franchise," *Nation's Business*, Oct. 1987, p. 42.

[12]Bill Richards, "Starting Up: Blue-Collar Laborers, Laid off in Rust Belt, Try to Run Own Firms," *The Wall Street Journal*, Sept. 8, 1986, pp. 1, 12. Reprinted by permission of *The Wall Street Journal*, © Dow Jones & Company, Inc., 1986. All Rights Reserved.

[13]Sharon Nelton, "Managing Your Business: Polishing Women Entrepreneurs," *Nation's Business*, July 1987, pp. 61–63. Reprinted by permission, *Nation's Business*, July, 1987. Copyright 1987, U.S. Chamber of Commerce.

Chapter 5

[1]"A Slimmed-down Brunswick is Proving Wall Street Wrong," *Business Week*, May 25, 1984; Neil Martin, "A Conversation with the CEO: The Story of Brunswick Corporation" *Fortune*, Fall 1987; personal communication, April 19, 1988, Brunswick Corporation, One Brunswick Plaza, Skokie, Ill. 60077.

[2]Adapted from Gary Dessler, *Management Fundamentals: Modern Principles and Practices*, Reston Publishing Company, Reston, Va., 1985, pp. 2–20.

[3]Leonard R. Sayles, *Managerial Behavior*, McGraw-Hill, New York, 1964, p. 162.

[4]See, for example, John Campbell et al., *Managerial Behavior, Performance, and Effectiveness*, McGraw-Hill, New York, 1970, p. 75.

[5]"Who Made the Most—and Why," *Business Week*, May 2, 1988, p. 51.

[6]"Executive Pay: Who Got What in 1986," *Business Week*, May 4, 1987, p. 53.

[7]Henry Mintzberg, "The Manager's Job: Folklore and Fact," *Harvard Business Review,* July–August 1975, pp. 49–61.

[8]"You're fired!" *U.S. News & World Report,* March 23, 1987, p. 50.

[9]For a discussion, see, for example, "The Old Foreman is on the Way Out, and the New One Will Be More Important," *Business Week,* April 25, 1983, pp. 74–75.

[10]See Michael Porter, *Competitive Strategy,* The Free Press, New York, 1980, p. xvi.

[11]See, for example, Michael Porter, "From Competitive Advantage to Corporate Strategy," *Harvard Business Review,* May–June 1987, pp. 43–59.

[12]Steven Carrol and Henry Tosi, *Management by Objectives,* Macmillan, New York, 1973.

[13]Conceptual, interpersonal, and technical skills are based on Robert L. Katz, "Skills of an Effective Administrator," *Harvard Business Review,* September–October, 1974, pp. 90–102. Emotional and Analytical Skills are based on Edgar Schein, *Career Dynamics: Matching Individual and Organizational Needs,* Addison-Wesley, Reading, Mass., 1978, p. 19. Motivation to manage based on John B. Miner and Norman R. Smith, "Decline and Stabilization of Managerial Motivation over a 20-year Period," *Journal of Applied Psychology,* Vol. 67, No. 3, 1982, pp. 297–305.

[14]"Collapse of Fighting Capabilities Doom Stark, Navy Concludes," *The Miami Herald,* Oct. 2, 1987.

[15]David Stigg, "Ames Shares Fall on Posting of Lower Profits: Source Says Theft Is Part of Inventory Troubles Plaguing the Company," *Wall Street Journal,* Sept. 10, 1987; "Gremlins Are Eating up the Profits at Ames," *Business Week,* Oct. 19, 1987; Peter Hisey, "Shrinkage, Deep Markdowns Cause Ames Earnings Slump," *Discount Store News,* Sept. 28, 1987.

Chapter 6

[1]Arthur Thompson, Jr., "People Express Airlines, Inc.," in Arthur A. Thompson, Jr., and A. J. Strickland III, *Strategic Management,* Business Publications, Plano, Texas, 1987, pp. 307–342; "DOT Approves Takeover, Texas Air People Express Deal On," *Travel Weekly,* Nov. 3, 1986, p. 3; "Texas Air Wants to Cut Price in Deal for People," *Travel Weekly,* Nov. 10, 1986.

[2]F. L. Roethlisberger and William Dickson, *Management on the Worker,* Harvard University Graduate School of Business, Boston, 1947, p. 21.

[3]Edwin E. Ghiselli, *Exploration in Managerial Talent,* Goodyear, Pacific Palisades, Calif., 1971, pp. 39–93.

[4]Gary Latham and J. James Baldes, "The Practical Significance of Locke's Theory of Goal Setting," *Journal of Applied Psychology,* Vol. 60, No. 1, 1975, p. 123.

[5]Gary Latham and J. James Baldes, "The Practical Significance of Locke's Theory of Goal Setting," *Journal of Applied Psychology,* Vol. 60, No. 1, 1975, p. 124.

[6]See, for example, Donald J. Campbell, "The Effects of Goal-Contingent Payment on the Performance of a Complex Task," *Personnel Psychology,* Vol. 37, No. 1, Spring 1984, pp. 23–40.

[7]*1987 AMS Flexible Work Survey,* Administrative Management Society, Willow Grove, Penn., 1987.

[8]Jolie Solomon, "Heirs Apparent to Chief Executives Often Trip over the Prospect of Power," *The Wall Street Journal,* March 24, 1987, p. 29. Reprinted by permission of *The Wall Street Journal,* © Dow Jones & Company, Inc., 1987. All Rights Reserved.

[9]Carey W. English, Adapted from "Sweatshops Are Back—And They're Thriving," *U.S. News & World Report,* Jan. 16, 1984, pp. 68–69.

Chapter 7

[1]Geoff Lewis, "Can Bill Lowe Put IBM's PC Unit into Pinstripes? For the Fast Growth the Company Wants, Its Maverick Outfit Must Fit In," *Business Week,* Jan. 20, 1986, p. 83; Beth Freedman and Matt Karmer, "IBM Corporate Tightens Grip on PC Division," *PC Week,* June 18, 1985; Richard Diffy, "IBM Names New PC Product Line Chief: New ESO Head Will Confront Major Hotspots," *PC Week,* March 19, 1985.

[2]Some material in this chapter is based in part on Gary Dessler, *Management Fundamentals,* Reston Publishing Co., Reston, Va.: 1985, pp. 116–191.

[3]For a discussion, see, for example, Gary Dessler, *Organization The-ory: Integrating Structure and Behavior,* Prentice-Hall, Englewood Clifs, N.J., 1986, pp. 210–252.

[4]Eugene Walton, "How Efficient Is the Grape Vine?" *Personnel,* March–April 1961, pp. 45–49.

[5]E. Rogers and R. Agarwala Rogers, *Communication in Organizations,* The Free Press, New York, 1976, p. 82.

[6]Keith Davis, "Cut Those Rumors Down to Size," *Supervisory Management,* June 1975, p. 206.

[7]For a discussion, see Gary Dessler, *Applied Human Relations,* Reston Publishing Company, Reston, Va., 1983, pp. 178–194; Tom Burns and G. M. Stalker, *The Management of Innovation,* Tavistock, London, 1961, p. 119.

[8]John Frank, "The Loose-Reins Approach Pays Off for Kemper," *Business Week,* Sept. 8, 1986, p. 78; Steven Lesnick, "Management Style: On the Attack," *Insurance Review,* June 1986, p. 40.

Chapter 8

[1]Marilyn Harris, "A Lifetime at IBM Gets a Little Shorter for Some," *Business Week,* Sept. 29, 1986, p. 40; "10,000 Retiring Early Under IBM Program," *Electronic News,* Dec. 22, 1986, p. 13; Louella Miles, "Hitches in IBM Staff Cuts Jeopardize Growth," *Marketing,* Oct. 15, 1987, p. 4.

[2]Sara Rynes and John Bondreau, "College Recruiting in Large Organizations: Practice, Evaluation, and Research Implications," *Personnel Psychology,* Vol. 39 (Winter 1986), pp. 729–757.

[3]Gary Dessler, *Personnel Management,* Prentice-Hall, Englewood Cliffs, N.J., 1988, pp. 34–36.

[4]Lawrence Bridwell and Alvin Marcus, "Back to School—A High-Tech Company Sent Its Managers to Business School—To Learn 'People Skills'," *Personnel Administrator,* Vol. 32 (March 1987), pp. 86–91.

[5]Walter Fogel, "Intentional Sex-Based Discrimination: Can It Be Proven?" *Labor Law Journal,* Vol. 27 (May 1986), pp. 291–299.

[6]Richard Hellan, "Employee Assistance: An EAP update—A Perspective for the 80's," *Personnel Journal,* Vol. 65 (June 1985), p. 51.

[7]Herbert Freudenberger, *Burnout,* Bantam, Toronto, 1980, p. 17.

[8]Reprinted by permission from "Salomon Brothers: Just Gutfreunds?" *The Economist,* July 18, 1987, p. 74.

[9]Adapted from "Done by Prescription." Used by permission from *Bulletin to Management,* vol. 38, no. 27, p. 211 (7/2/87). Copyright 1987 by the Bureau of National Affairs, Inc.

Chapter 9

[1]"Bitter Negotiations Mark Final Session Between Line, Union," *Travel Weekly,* March 3, 1986, p. 1; Paul Engel, "Battle of Wills Spells Doom for Eastern," *Industry Week,* March 17, 1986; Ernest Blum, "Borman, Leaving Post, Regrets Stormy Labor Ties," *Travel Weekly,* June 8, 1986, p. 1.

[2]Arthur A. Sloan and Fred Witney, *Labor Relations,* 3rd edition, Prentice-Hall, Englewood Cliffs, N.J., 1977, p. 137.

[3]John Fossum, *Labor Relations,* Business Publications, Inc., Dallas, 1982, p. 4.

[4]Roger Jacobs and Cora Koch, "Greater Obstacles to Unions in Double Breasting," *Labor Law Journal,* Vol. 38 (July 1987), pp. 422–426.

[5]"Big Labor Tries the Soft Sell," *Business Week,* Oct. 13, 1986.

[6]Shane Permeaux, R. Wayne Moody, and Art Bethke, "Decertification: Fulfilling Unions Destiny?" *Personnel Journal,* Vol. 66 (June 1987), pp. 144–148.

[7]*Perspectives on Employment,* Research Bulletin #194, The Conference Board, 845 Third Ave., N.Y., N.Y., 10020, 1986.

[8]"AFL-CIO Launching New Strategy to Win Over Non-Union Workers," *Compensation and Benefits Review,* Vol. 18 (Sept.–Oct. 1986), p. 8.

[9]"The Battle for Corporate Control," *Business Week,* May 18, 1987, p. 107.

[10]Paulette Thomas, "Eastern Airlines May Face Strike by Machinists," *Wall Street Journal,* Dec. 3, 1987, p. 20; Thomas Retzinger, Jr., "Texas Air to Face New Set of Attacks by Eastern Unions," *Wall Street Journal,* Feb. 18, 1988, p. 11; Peter Engardio and Chuck Hawkins, "It's That Time at Eastern," *Business Week,* Feb. 2, 1987, p. 33.

[11]Pete Actheims, "Sorry Surrender in the NFL: Using Scabs, Team Owners Rout the Players," *Newsweek,* Oct. 26, 1987, p. 68; Alex Koflowitz, "Broken Play: Labor Experts Fault Football Players'

Strike Strategy,'' *Wall Street Journal*, Oct. 14, 1987, pp. 35, 37; Hal Lancaster, ''NFL Owners Reject Terms in Unions' Plan,'' *Wall Street Journal*, Oct. 14, 1987, pp. 36, 38.

Chapter 10
[1]Reprinted by permission from the Ford Motor Company, *Second Quarter Report to Stockholders*, Summer 1985.
[2]Kae H. Chung, *Management: Critical Success Factors*, Allyn and Bacon, Boston, 1987, Chapter 1.
[3]Kae H. Chung, *Management: Critical Success Factors*, Allyn and Bacon, Boston, 1987, p. 503.
[4]Lee Krajewski and Larry P. Ritzman, *Operations Management: Strategy and Analysis*, Addison-Wesley, Reading, Mass., 1987, p. 294.
[5]This discussion is based largely on Kae Chung, *Management: Critical Success Factors*, Allyn and Bacon, Boston, 1987, pp. 512–518.
[6]Lee Krajewski and Larry P. Ritzman, *Operations Management: Strategy and Analysis*, Addison-Wesley, Reading, Mass., 1987, p. 197.
[7]Based on Lee Krajewski and Larry P. Ritzman, *Operations Management: Strategy and Analysis*, © 1987, Addison-Wesley Publishing Co., Inc., Reading, Massachusetts. Case on page 451. Reprinted with permission.

Chapter 11
[1]John Marcom, Jr., ''Costly Neglect: British Industry Suffer from Failure to Heed Basics of Marketing,'' *The Wall Street Journal*, Jan. 14, 1987, pp. 1, 16. Reprinted by permission of *The Wall Street Journal*, © Dow Jones & Company, Inc., 1987. All Rights Reserved.
[2]Adapted from the American Marketing Association's definition in *Marketing News*, March 1, 1985.
[3]Laura Landro, ''Pay Cable-TV Networks Plot Ways to Revive Interest Among Viewers,'' *The Wall Street Journal*, March 31, 1987, p. 39. Reprinted by permission of *The Wall Street Journal*, © Dow Jones & Company, Inc., 1987. All Rights Reserved.

Chapter 12
[1]Linda M. Watkins, ''A Look at Hasbro's 'Moondreamer' Dolls Shows Creating a Toy Isn't Child's Play,'' *The Wall Street Journal*, Dec. 29, 1986, p. 21. Reprinted by permission of *The Wall Street Journal*, © Dow Jones & Company, Inc., 1986. All Rights Reserved.
[2]Sonja Steptoe, ''SmithKline to Push Marketing Efforts for Its Other Drugs,'' *The Wall Street Journal*, Jan. 10, 1986, p. 30.
[3]Ronald Alsop, ''Old Chewing Gum Favorites Find There's Life After Death,'' *The Wall Street Journal*, Sept. 11, 1986, p. 37.
[4]Cynthia F. Mitchell, ''Compaq Unveils Faster Versions of Deskpro 286,'' *The Wall Street Journal*, March 10, 1987, p. 9.
[5]Ronald Alsop, ''Companies Get on Fast Track to Roll Out Hot New Brands,'' *The Wall Street Journal*, July 10, 1986, p. 25.
[6]Peter Waldman, ''Search for Methods to Prolong Produce Freshness Bears Fruit,'' *The Wall Street Journal*, June 19, 1987, p. 2.
[7]''Displayable Shippers Aid Merchants,'' *Marketing News*, Sept. 26, 1986, p. 10.
[8]American Marketing Association Committee on Definitions, Ralph L. Alexander, chairperson, *A Glossary of Marketing Terms*, American Marketing Association, Chicago, 1960, p. 8.
[9]William Power, ''R You Thinking of a New Name for Your Firm? If So, B Careful,'' *The Wall Street Journal*, Dec. 2, 1986, p. 39.
[10]Patricia Bellew Gray, ''Law Firms Big Fee Hikes Reflect Higher Pay and Booming Business,'' *The Wall Street Journal*, March 19, 1987, p. 37.
[11]Ronald Alsop, ''Companies Pitch Elite Brands to Less Elite Target Audience,'' *The Wall Street Journal*, Nov. 6, 1986, p. 35. Reprinted by permission of *The Wall Street Journal*, © Dow Jones & Company, Inc., 1986. All Rights Reserved.
[12]Peter Waldman, ''Hewlett Sets 28% Price Cut for Model 840,'' *The Wall Street Journal* Jan. 27, 1987, p. 7. Reprinted by permission of *The Wall Street Journal*, © Dow Jones & Company, Inc., 1987. All Rights Reserved.

Chapter 13
[1]''Homes Get Major-Market Exposure,'' *Marketing News*, Jan. 30, 1987, p. 11.
[2]Robert J. Coen, ''Coen Sees Strong Ad Spending,'' *Advertising Age*, May 23, 1988, p. 6.

[3]Kevin T. Higgins, ''There's Gold in Silver Screen Product Plugs,'' *Marketing News* Oct. 11, 1985, p. 6.
[4]Adapted from William F. Schoell and Joseph P. Guiltinan, *Marketing*, 3rd edition, Allyn and Bacon, Boston, 1988, p. 523.
[5]Lynn G. Coleman, ''Auto Showrooms Brought to 'Where the Customers Are'—The Shopping Malls,'' *Marketing News*, June 5, 1987, p. 2.
[6]Kevin T. Higgins, ''Motivating the Sales Force,'' *Marketing News*, July 4, 1986, p. 6.
[7]Lynn G. Coleman, ''Electronic Trading Stamps Successful in Test Market,'' *Marketing News*, June 19, 1987, p. 2.
[8]Joanne Lipman, ''Firms Bid to Cut Sales Coupons, Other Incentives,'' *The Wall Street Journal*, Feb. 3, 1987, p. 37.
[9]Sonja Steptoe, ''SmithKline Says Contac Recouped Its Market Share,'' *The Wall Street Journal*, Feb. 3, 1987, p. 37. Reprinted by permission of *The Wall Street Journal*, © Dow Jones & Company, Inc., 1987. All Rights Reserved.
[10]''Provocative Promotion Is Planned for Artificial Intelligence Program,'' *Marketing News*, Nov. 21, 1986, p. 22.

Chapter 14
[1]Steven P. Galante, ''Tire Franchiser Offers Equity to Rev up Store Managers,'' *The Wall Street Journal*, Oct. 19, 1987, p. 35. Reprinted by permission of *The Wall Street Journal*, © Dow Jones & Company, Inc., 1987. All Rights Reserved.
[2]Joe Agnew, ''Local Involvement Helps Franchisees 'Dechain the Chain','' *Marketing News* Nov. 21, 1986, pp. 1, 30.
[3]Hank Gilman, ''Software Machines May Change the Way Programs Are Sold,'' *The Wall Street Journal*, Feb. 6, 1987, p. 23. Reprinted by permission of *The Wall Street Journal*, © Dow Jones & Company, Inc., 1987. All Rights Reserved.

Chapter 15
[1]Arthur Sharplin, ''Practitioners Forum—Brown Bag Bookkeeping,'' *Journal of Accountancy*, July 1986, pp. 123ff. Reprinted with permission from the *Journal of Accountancy*, Copyright © 1986 by American Institute of Certified Public Accountants.
[2]Steven L. Slepian, ''How a Proposed Accounting Change Threatened an Industry,'' *Management Accounting*, Nov. 1985, pp. 47–51. Copyright © 1985 by National Association of Accountants, Montvale, N.J. All rights reserved.
[3]Lee Berton, ''FDIC Sues Ernst & Whinney over Audit of 4 Butcher Banks, Seeks $250 Million,'' *The Wall Street Journal*, May 21, 1987, p. 6. Reprinted by permission of *The Wall Street Journal*, © Dow Jones & Company, Inc., 1987. All Rights Reserved.

Chapter 16
[1]Bruce G. Posner, ''Managing Money: Laughing All the Way from the Bank,'' *Inc.*, Dec. 1987, pp. 56–60. Reprinted with permission, *Inc.* magazine, December 1987. Copyright © 1987 by *Inc.* Publishing Company, 38 Commercial Wharf, Boston, MA 02110.
[2]''Study: Management Most to Blame for 1979–1987 Banking Failures,'' *The Times-Picayune*, Jan. 21, 1988, p. C-5.
[3]Andy Pasztor and Leonard M. Apcar, ''U.S. Spotlights Suspected Bank Fraud in Texas, but Skeptics Ask If Broad Effort Is Fated to Fail,'' *The Wall Street Journal*, Oct. 27, 1987, p. 68.
[4]''The Months Ahead,'' *Changing Times*, March 1988, p. 9; Robert Guenther, ''Banks Are Waging Last-Ditch Bid to Ease New Rules That Speed Up Check Clearing,'' *The Wall Street Journal*, April 7, 1988, p. 27.
[5]Robert L. Rose, ''Labor Lending: How a Union Survives in Banking by Pushing Services over Profits,'' *The Wall Street Journal*, Dec. 14, 1987, pp. 1, 12. Reprinted by permission of *The Wall Street Journal*, © Dow Jones & Company, Inc., 1987. All Rights Reserved.

Chapter 17
[1]Fred Goodman, ''CBS Records Sold to Sony,'' *Rolling Stone*, Jan. 14., 1988, p. 17; Tani Maher, ''What Will CBS Do with $1.4 Billion?'' *Financial World*, Jan. 12, 1988, p. 8; ''Sony Receives Clearances to Buy CBS Records Unit,'' *The Wall Street Journal*, Dec. 24, 1987, pp. 6, 10.
[2]Based on ''Look Who's Getting Rich on GAF,'' *Financial World* magazine, Jan. 12, 1988, p. 11.
[3]Ellyn Spragins, ''The Feast of Funding That Awaits Corporate Borrowers,'' *Business Week*, Nov. 3, 1986, pp. 91–96; ''Securitising the

American Dream,'' *The Economist*, June 14, 1986, pp. 70–71; Ann Monroe, ''Industrial Firms Are Using Receivables to Back Commercial Paper, Preferred,'' *The Wall Street Journal*, Oct. 7, 1987, p. 41.

Chapter 18

[1] Randall Smith, Steve Swartz, and George Anders, ''Black Monday: What Really Ignited the Market's Collapse After Its Long Climb,'' *The Wall Street Journal*, Dec. 18, 1987, p. 1; Floyd Norris, ''Crash Source: What Happened on Oct. 18 and What It Means,'' *Barron's*, Jan. 4, 1988, p. 12; ''London's System Did Well in Crash, Central Bank Says,'' *The Wall Street Journal*, Feb. 12, 1988, p. 22.

[2] ''The Roaring 'Eighties,'' *The Economist*, Oct. 24, 1987, pp. 84–85; ''The Trials and Tribulations of Triangular Trading,'' *The Economist*, Feb. 14, 1987, p. 69; ''Getting to Know the Bear,'' *The Economist*, Oct 31, 1987, pp. 67–68.

[3] Partly based on ''How to Value a Share,'' *The Economist*, Jan. 30, 1988, p. 66. Reprinted by permission from *The Economist*.

Chapter 19

[1] Gauri Bhatia, ''Insurer of Champions,'' *Insurance Review*, March 1987, pp. 28–32.

[2] ''Update . . . Fights Brew over 55,'' *Insurance Review*, April 1987, p. 10.

Chapter 20

[1] David Wessel, ''Marketing Tool,'' *The Wall Street Journal*, March 18, 1987, p. 1. Reprinted by permission of *The Wall Street Journal*, © Dow Jones & Company, Inc., 1987. All Rights Reserved.

[2] ''Computers: The New Look,'' *Business Week*, Nov. 30, 1987, pp. 114ff.

[3] Diane Lynn Kastiel, ''Psyching Out Buyers With AI,'' *Business Marketing*, March 1987, p. 60.

[4] ''Office Systems—What's Available Now,'' *1987 Inc. Office Guide*, pp. 10–12.

Chapter 21

[1] Michael W. Miller, ''How Indiana Shielded a Firm and Changed the Takeover Business,'' *The Wall Street Journal*, July 1, 1987, pp. 1, 14. Reprinted by permission of *The Wall Street Journal*, © Dow Jones & Company, Inc., 1987. All Rights Reserved. Also from Senator Robert Garton, personal communication.

[2] Paulette Thomas and Laurie McGinley, ''Continental Air to Pay $250,000 to Settle Charges over Consumer Protection Law,'' *The Wall Street Journal* June 15, 1987, p. 6.

[3] Andy Pasztor and Jeanne Saddler, ''FTC Chairman's Hands-Off View of Marketplace Prompts Scrutiny of Agency by Critics on the Hill,'' *The Wall Street Journal*, Feb. 4, 1987, p. 64. Reprinted by permission of *The Wall Street Journal*, © Dow Jones & Company, Inc., 1987. All Rights Reserved.

[4] Wendy L. Wall and Thomas F. O'Boyle, ''Rural Clouds: End of Crop Subsidies Sought in Trade Talks, Imperils Many Farms,'' *The Wall Street Journal* July 7, 1987, pp. 1, 23; Lee Smith, ''How to Cut Farm Spending,'' *Fortune* Nov. 10, 1986, pp. 97–103.

[5] Stanley Scott, Gary McCain, and Douglas Lincoln, ''Federal Labs Share Their Technology with Business,'' *Marketing News*, Feb. 27, 1987, p. 30. Reprinted from *Marketing News*, published by the American Marketing Association.

[6] Laurie McGinley, ''Flash Point: Airline Officials Clash With FAA on Fire Safety Proposal,'' *The Wall Street Journal*, July 3, 1987, p. 15.

[7] Ronald J. Troyer and Gerald E. Markle, *Cigarettes: The Battle over Smoking*, Rutgers University Press, New Brunswick, N.J., 1983, pp. 123–124. Copyright © 1983 by Rutgers, the State University. Reprinted by permission of Rutgers University Press.

Chapter 22

[1] Robert L. Rose, ''Incentives vs. Clients: Which Ones Most Concern Financial Planners?'' *The Wall Street Journal*, Nov. 24, 1986, p. 25. Reprinted by permission of *The Wall Street Journal*, © Dow Jones & Company, Inc., 1986. All Rights Reserved.

[2] Amanda Bennett, ''Growing Small: As Big Firms Continue to Trim Their Staffs, 2-Tier Setup Emerges,'' *The Wall Street Journal*, April 4, 1987, pp. 1, 16.

[3] ''Economy & Business: Battling the Enemy Within,'' *Time*, March 17, 1986, pp. 52, 55.

[4] Bill Paul, ''Looking for Environmental Hazards Become Common,'' *The Wall Street Journal*, Oct. 13, 1987, p. 6.

[5] Clare Ansberry, ''Forgive or Forget: Firms Face Decision Whether to Apologize for Their Mistakes,'' *The Wall Street Journal*, Nov. 24, 1987, p. 29.

[6] Christopher J. Chipello, ''Matter of Honor: Japanese Top Managers Quick to Resign When Trouble Hits Firm,'' *The Wall Street Journal*, July 10, 1987, p. 19.

[7] Christopher J. Chipello, ''Matter of Honor: Japanese Top Managers Quick to Resign When Trouble Hits Firm,'' *The Wall Street Journal*, July 10, 1987, p. 19.

[8] Lee Berton, ''A Battle Cry for America's Accountants,'' *The Wall Street Journal*, Sept. 23, 1987, p. 36. Reprinted by permission of *The Wall Street Journal*, © Dow Jones & Company, Inc., 1987. All Rights Reserved.

[9] Betsy Morris and Alix Freeman, '' 'Smokeless' Cigarette Is Expected to Pose Big Marketing Challenge,'' *The Wall Street Journal*, Sept. 18, 1987, p. 33. Reprinted by permission of *The Wall Street Journal*, © Dow Jones & Company, Inc., 1987. All Rights Reserved.

Chapter 23

[1] Christopher J. Chipello, ''Losing Ground: Foreign Rivals Imperil U.S. Firms' Leadership in the Service Sector,'' *The Wall Street Journal*, March 21, 1988, pp. 1, 8. Reprinted by permission of *The Wall Street Journal*, © Dow Jones & Company, Inc., 1988. All Rights Reserved.

[2] Scot J. Paltrow, ''EC Claims Victory as Court Overturns Germany's Age-Old Ban on Beer Imports,'' *The Wall Street Journal*, March 13, 1987, p. 22.

[3] Philip Revzin, ''While Americans Take to Croissants, Kellogg Pushes Cornflakes on France,'' *The Wall Street Journal*, Nov. 11, 1986, p. 36. Reprinted by permission of *The Wall Street Journal*, © Dow Jones & Company, Inc., 1986. All Rights Reserved.

[4] Helen E. White, ''Thailand's Drug-Copying Companies Keep Prices Down, Upset Foreign Firms,'' *The Wall Street Journal*, Dec. 1, 1986, p. 23. Reprinted by permission of *The Wall Street Journal*, © Dow Jones & Company, Inc., 1986. All Rights Reserved.

S U B J E C T I N D E X